Special Edition
Using
UNIX

Third Edition

Special Edition Using UNIX

Third Edition

Peter Kuo

Special Edition Using UNIX, Third Edition

Copyright © 1998 by *Que*

International Standard Book Number: 0-897-1747-6

Library of Congress Catalog Card Number: 98-85655

Printed in the United States of America

First Printing: *November, 1998*

00 99 98   4   3   2   1

Composed in *Century Old Style* and *ITC Franklin Gothic* by Que Corporation.

Trademarks

Warning and Disclaimer

Executive Editor
Jeff Koch

Acquisitions Editor
Jane Brownlow

Development Editors
Mark Cierzniak
Tom Dinse

Managing Editor
Brice Gosnell

Project Editor
Sara Bosin

Copy Editor
Geneil Breeze

Indexer
Bruce Clingaman

Proofreader
Benjamin Berg

Technical Editors
Eric Richardson
Matt Coffey

Layout Technicians
Tim Osborn
Staci Somers

Contents at a Glance

V Appendixes

Table of Contents

20 IP Routing 507

21 Advanced Networking 539

IV Network Services

Dedication

I'd like to dedicate this SE Using UNIX book to my fellow CNI classmates who were at the "UNIXWare from Hades" week in Chicago in 1992. Yes, that means you, "Margarita," and "TTYman!"

About the Lead Author

Peter Kuo, Ph.D. (Nuclear Physics, University of Toronto; MSc., Physics, Trent University), is president of DreamLAN Network Consulting Ltd., a Toronto-based consulting firm. Peter has worked with UNIX since the mid-1980s when he designed, developed, and implemented a real-time, UNIX-based, data-acquisition, analysis, and display system while working as a Post Graduate Fellow at the Saskatchewan Accelerator Laboratory (SAL). Since then, his interest expanded to also include networking. Peter is the first Canadian Enterprise CNE, one of the world's first Master CNEs and Master CNIs, and is the first Novell Certified Internet Professional (CIP) in the world. Furthermore, he is a Certified Network Expert (CNX Ethernet and Token Ring). In addition to presenting seminars at conferences, such as NetWorld+InterOp and NetWare Users International (NUI), Peter has authored, co-authored, and contributed to many computer books from Macmillan Publishing. When not working on books and articles, Peter is a volunteer Novell Support Connection SysOp on Novell's NSC Web Forum, assisting Novell in providing support to a world-wide audience on many advanced subject areas, such as connectivity, network management, NetWare 4, NetWare 5, and Novell Directory Services. You can reach him at peter@dreamlan.com.

About the Contributing Authors

Nalneesh Gaur works for TimeBridge Technologies as a systems engineer. His current work involves UNIX/Windows NT integration, Web design, and Internet/intranet security.

Gordon Marler is the UNIX System Architect for the Wireless Local Technologies Group of AT&T Wireless Services in Redmond, Washington. He has a B.S. in Computer Science Engineering from the University of Texas at Arlington. He's been working with UNIX since 1987, and received his first taste of a large UNIX environment at the Superconducting Super Collider particle accelerator lab as a member of the group of six system administrators responsible for approximately 750 workstations and the servers to support them. He programs in Perl, C, and Java, and especially likes to design large disk storage solutions for UNIX systems that must be highly available. He can be reached at gordon.marler@attws.com.

Chris Negus For the past 15 years, Chris Negus has written or contributed to dozens of books on the UNIX system, computer networking, and the Internet. As a consultant, Chris worked at AT&T Bell Laboratories and UNIX System Laboratories on UNIX System V development teams. Later he worked with Novell's UNIXWare system development. Most recently, Chris wrote *Internet Explorer 4 Bible* and *Netscape Plug-ins for Dummies* for IDG Books Worldwide. He was a contributing author for previous editions of *Using UNIX, UNIX Unleashed*, and *Microsoft Office Administrator's Desk Reference* for Macmillan Computer Publishing. Chris lives in Salt Lake City, UT with Sheree, Caleb, and Seth.

Terry W. Ogletree is a consultant and author based in Atlanta, Georgia. He has worked with networked computer systems since 1980, starting out on Digital Equipment PDP computers and OpenVMS based VAX systems. He has worked on UNIX-based systems and TCP/IP since

1985 and has been involved with Windows NT since it first appeared. He is the author of *Windows NT Server 4.0 Networking*, which is volume 4 of Sams' *Windows NT Server 4 Resource Library* and has contributed many chapters to other books published by Sams, including *Windows NT Server Unleashed* (and the Professional Edition) and *Peter Norton's Windows NT Server 4.0 Troubleshooting and Configuration*. He can be reached at ogletree@bellsouth.net.

Sriranga Veeraraghavan has been working at Cisco Systems, Inc. in the area of Network Management since 1996. He enjoys developing software in C/C++, Java, Perl, and Shell on Linux and Solaris. He has contributed to several UNIX and Linux books. He takes pleasure in listening to classical music, reading classical literature, mountain biking and playing Marathon on the home network with his brother, Srivathsa. Sriranga earned a bachelor's degree in Engineering from the University of California at Berkeley in 1997 and is currently working toward a master's degree at Stanford University. He can be reached at ranga@soda.berkeley.edu.

Daniel J. Wilson is a Senior Principal Consultant with Oracle Corporation and works out of the Indianapolis, Indiana practice. His background includes UNIX Systems Administration and Oracle Database Administration in both SMP and Clustered environments. He has extensive experience in UNIX systems and Oracle database performance tuning and troubleshooting. He has programmed in C, C++, COBOL, and SQL. He graduated from Ball State University, Muncie, Indiana in 1984. He currently resides just outside of Indianapolis with his wife Angela and their two children, Timothy and Emily. Many thanks to Linda Billingsley at PRC and to Ron James at Hewlett-Packard for providing the best support ever!

William D. Wood works at Software Artistry, Inc. as a support specialist on UNIX systems. He supports the Expert Advisor software it runs on SUN OS, HP/UX, and IBM AIX. He has specialized in multi-systems and remote systems support since 1985, when he started work at the Pentagon. He has solely supported infrastructures that span the world and just the U.S. He has also supported up to 80 UNIX machines at one time.

About the Technical Editors

Eric C Richardson (eric@rconsult.com) is a professional Webmaster with 9 years Internet experience and over two decades of work with computers under his belt. He has worked as college instructor, writer, consultant, and author in the Internet field. He currently oversees the Web sites and related extranet for Nabisco Incorporated. He is a member of the World Organization of Webmasters and is a member of their national accreditation board. He enjoys spending time with his wife Stacie and their daughter, Katie. He has written or co-authored eight books on the Internet, and has worked as editor on nearly a dozen.

Matt Coffey performs UNIX systems administration on SUN OS, Solaris, IBM AIX, and HP systems. He has been responsible for a SUN Parallel Database Server that supported users nationwide. Currently, he is supporting SUN Legacy systems and an IBM SP2 Frame comprised of over 30 individual nodes.

Acknowledgments

Writing a "generic" *SE Using UNIX* book is not an easy task. As you read through this book, you'll find that there are many subtle differences between different flavors of UNIX implementation. Trying to cover all the possible bases is next to impossible. However, as a result of the diligence of Mark Cierzniak and Tom Dinse, Development Editors of the book, the Technical Editors, Eric Richardson and Matt Coffey, and the hard work of all the contributing authors, you'll find this book to be an excellent reference material suitable for just about any flavor of UNIX you'll encounter.

A special thanks goes to my Acquisition Editor, Jane Brownlow, and Executive Editor, Jeff Koch, for offering me the opportunity to work on this edition of the book as the Lead Author. A big thank you also goes out to Tracy Williams, our team coordinator, for isolating us from all the administrative headaches.

I extend my appreciation and thanks to all Novell Support Connection volunteer SysOps and Novell folks for putting up the extra effort to cover my absence in order to complete this book. In particular, I thank Jim Henderson, Dave Parkes, Suzanne Miles, and Sandra Harrell for allowing me to disappear from the forums for days on end. I also thank Kim Groneman, the Novell SysOp Program Manager, for putting up with me for the past number of years and for not putting me in a leaky hotel room for NetWorld '98 in Atlanta.

Last, but not least, my sincere gratitude to my parents for feeding me periodically during the marathon writing sessions.

Tell Us What You Think!

As the reader of this book, *you* are our most important critic and commentator. We value your opinion and want to know what we're doing right, what we could do better, what areas you'd like to see us publish in, and any other words of wisdom you're willing to pass our way.

As the Executive Editor for the Operating Systems team at Macmillan Computer Publishing, I welcome your comments. You can fax, email, or write me directly to let me know what you did or didn't like about this book—as well as what we can do to make our books stronger.

Please note that I cannot help you with technical problems related to the topic of this book, and that due to the high volume of mail I receive, I might not be able to reply to every message.

When you write, please be sure to include this book's title and author as well as your name and phone or fax number. I will carefully review your comments and share them with the author and editors who worked on the book.

Fax: 317-817-7070

E-mail: opsys@mcp.com

Mail: Jeff Koch
Operating Systems
Macmillan Computer Publishing
201 West 103rd Street
Indianapolis, IN 46290 USA

Introduction

Who Should Use This Book?

The 1990s has been the fastest growth period for computer hardware development, and as a result, computer science has grown in leaps and bounds. The development and enhancement of operating systems is always a part of the advancement in computer science, and the UNIX operating system stands unmistakably above all other operating systems.

All operating systems have express limitations in one area or another—many operating systems are constrained by limitations in many areas—but UNIX has risen above the rest to provide the novice and the expert alike with an operating platform second to none. No one has *ever* argued that UNIX is *not* a full-featured operating system. The worst claim that could be made against UNIX is that it is an unforgiving, unfriendly operating system, filled with cryptic commands and difficult to master. Until now.

For more than twenty years, UNIX has been used by hundreds of thousands of people throughout the world and there have been many improvements made in the past decade in the area of user interface. The UNIX of today has revolutionized the workstation and personal computer industry. UNIX has evolved from a minicomputer operating system to one that crosses all hardware configurations, ranging from supercomputers (such as the Cray) down to the PCs (such as Intel 80386 machines).

Does UNIX sound too good to be true? The fact that you're reading this suggests that you're curious and interested in learning more about the operating system. This book is for you! Regardless if you have never heard of UNIX before, have worked with UNIX in the past and wondering what is the state of affairs with UNIX today, or are currently using UNIX, Que's *Using UNIX, Special Edition*, will provide you with invaluable information and serve as an excellent reference asset in your library.

N O T E Although this book is not intended to provide merely a cursory examination of UNIX capabilities, the beginning UNIX users will find information presented in this book complete, concise, and accurate without being overwhelming. However, if you want to start exploring UNIX on an even more basic level, take a look at Que's *Introduction to UNIX*. ▓

From the basics and introduction of the UNIX operating system to its treatment of advanced manipulation, *Special Edition Using UNIX* is for everyone, novices and experts alike, interested in knowing UNIX better. You'll learn about the developmental history of the operating system and find new and exciting applications of control provided through the graphical user interfaces. Utilities, network environments, system administration, and communication concepts are revealed simply and effectively. In short, *this book has it all, and this book does it all*.

What Do You Need To Know To Read This Book?

To keep the chapters uncluttered with trivial information, the following assumptions about what you know and what you don't know were made:

- It is assumed that you have knowledge of rudimentary computer concepts, such as CPU, disk drives, files, and directories.
- It is assumed that you are familiar with some basic computer skills such as mouse maneuvering, pull-down menu jockeying, keyboard navigation, and so on.
- Although not necessary, it would be an asset to have used a computer before, regardless of its operating system.
- It is *not* essential that you have used UNIX before.

N O T E   It is *not* necessary, but it would be helpful, that you have access to a UNIX system to try out the commands discussed in this book as it will better enforce the concept and material you have read. *There isn't a better learning tool than hands-on experience.* ▓

What Will You Learn While Reading This Book?

Other than the comprehensive and detailed treatment of each important topic in UNIX systems, you will find a lot of notes, tips, cautions, and other tidbits strewn throughout the book. The authors of this book are UNIX experts. The tidbits in this book are based on countless years of valuable hands-on experiences, or battle scars as some people call them, and expert advise from the authors of this book that you cannot easily obtain elsewhere, without it costing you a (sizable) down-payment for someone's mansion.

This book is also unique in that it is not for a specific version or flavor of UNIX like some of its competitors. It is applicable for *all* UNIX systems. But because there are differences between the different UNIX implementations, these variations are noted where applicable. Therefore, this book doesn't just teach you about a specific version of UNIX, but UNIX as a whole!

The generic, but detailed, treatment of UNIX features (along with specific notes, tips, and cautions) are what set this book, *Using UNIX, Special Edition*, apart from the other UNIX books available on the market today.

How Is This Book Organized?

The information in this book progresses from simple to complex as you move through the chapters. The information is separated into five parts, including appendices. Each part has its own particular emphasis and is self-contained. You can, therefore, choose to read only those areas that appeal to your immediate needs. However, don't let your immediate needs deter you from eventually giving your undivided attention to the rest of the book. You'll find a wealth of information in them all!

The following is a brief look at the contents of each chapter in *Using UNIX, Special Edition*:

Part I, "Getting Started," gets you familiar with the fundamentals and basics of UNIX.

- Chapter 1, "UNIX Environment Overview," gives you insight into the background of UNIX, its history, and a brief discussion of its capabilities and characteristics. It also introduces some of the different flavors of UNIX.
- Chapter 2, "Logging In," provides you with a "quick start" on the login and logout procedures of the UNIX operating system and a brief discussion about the importance of password security.
- Chapter 3, "UNIX Shells and System Commands," shows you why some people think UNIX is cryptic. You will discover the magical power of the UNIX shells and how to use them to command UNIX to do your bidding.
- Chapter 4, "vi Editor," instructs you on how to use the most commonly available screen-based editor in UNIX to edit text files.
- Chapter 5, "Files, Directories, and Permissions," details the UNIX file system structure and organization, file-naming convention, and directory hierarchy.
- Chapter 6, "UNIX Processes," explores UNIX's multiuser and multitasking capability.
- Chapter 7, "Essential Shell Scripting," introduces you to the capabilities of the UNIX shells through the use of shell scripting.
- Chapter 8, "Advanced Shell Scripting," gives you an more in-depth look at the powerful scripting capabilities available in UNIX shells.
- Chapter 9, "UNIX Windowing Systems," takes you on a tour of the CDE environment and the many tools that are offered within the desktop.

Part 2, "System Administration," provides you with information on how to administrate a UNIX system.

- Chapter 10, "Administrating Users Accounts and Groups," helps you develop your UNIX administrative skills in a multiuser environment.
- Chapter 11, "Startup and Shutdown," walks you through the necessary steps in the proper UNIX startup and shutdown procedures so that data integrity is ensured.
- Chapter 12, "Device Management," addresses the proper methods of adding new system devices and offers troubleshooting techniques and tips.
- Chapter 13, "File Systems," discusses common file systems used in the UNIX environment and how to maintain and monitor the file systems.
- Chapter 14, "Printing," covers all the bases from issuing print commands, checking printer status, canceling print jobs, and dealing with common printing problems.

■ Chapter 15, "Backup and Recovery," helps you develop a backup and recovery plan, select an appropriate backup device, and choose backup tools to automate your system backup.

■ Chapter 16, "Automating Tasks," introduces you to the cron facility and other UNIX commands to allow the automatic execution of any tasks, including the all important backup process.

Part 3, "TCP/IP Network Administration," introduces you to the ins-and-outs of TCP/IP networking.

■ Chapter 17, "Networking Essentials," offers an overview of networking in the UNIX environment, and introduces you to the files and tools that are essential for managing and connecting to machines in your network.

■ Chapter 18, "Internetworking," gives you an in-depth look into the networking components and networking technologies, such as TCP, UDP, SSL, Ethernet, FDDI, router and bridges, and so on.

■ Chapter 19, "Configuring TCP/IP," teaches you how to set up and configure TCP/IP on your UNIX host.

■ Chapter 20, "IP Routing," discusses the most common routing protocols in use in today's TCP/IP environment.

■ Chapter 21, "Advanced Networking," provides an overview to many advanced networking components and some future technologies including IPv6, firewalls, network address translation, and the multicast backbone.

Part 4, "Network Services," provides you with information on configuring and using some of the more popular and important UNIX networking services.

■ Chapter 22, "NFS," shows you Network File System design, sample uses, and setup and configuration of NFS clients and servers.

■ Chapter 23, "DNS," teaches you about the workings of Domain Name Services and the setting up and configuring of DNS primary, secondary, and cache-only nameservers.

■ Chapter 24, "Apache Web Server," uses the Apache Web Server as an example in explaining how Web servers, the http protocol, and CGI work, and to show you how to set up and maintain an effective Web site.

■ Chapter 25, "Sendmail and POP," presents everything you need to know about configuring and administrating Sendmail and POP.

■ Chapter 26, "Security," contains information about UNIX security and security tools that can help you detect potential weaknesses in your UNIX environment.

■ Chapter 27, "Performance Tuning," describes performance monitoring techniques, areas of performance tuning, and the many adjustments that you can make to a UNIX system to bring better overall performance.

Conventions Used In This Book

This book uses several special conventions. These conventions are listed here for your convenience.

UNIX is a case-sensitive operating system; that means when this book instructs you to type something at a command or shell prompt, you must type exactly what appears in the book *exactly as it is capitalized*. This book uses a `special typeface` for UNIX commands and filenames to set them off from standard text. If you are instructed to type something, what you are to type appears in **`bold in the special typeface`**. For example, if the book instructs you to type `cat` and press Return, you must press the letters c, a, and t and then press Return.

At times, you are instructed to press a key such as Return, Tab, or space. Keys sometimes are pressed in combination; when this is the case, the keys are represented in this way: Ctrl-h. This example implies you must press *and* hold the Ctrl key, press the letter h, and then release both keys.

N O T E This book uses a convention for key names that may differ from what you are accustomed to. To avoid confusion in the case-sensitive UNIX environment, this book uses lowercase letters to refer to keys when uppercase may be the norm. For example, this book uses the form Ctrl-h instead of Ctrl-H (the latter form may make some of you wonder whether you should press Ctrl *and* Shift *and* h).

Some examples show a listing with a portion of the screen after you type a specific command. Unless otherwise noted in the text, such listings show the command or shell prompt (usually a dollar sign, $), followed by what you type in bold. Do *not* type the dollar sign when you follow the example on your own system. Consider this example:

```
$ ls -l report.* > listing & <Return>
 3146
$
```

You should type only what appears on the first line (that is, type **`ls -l report.* > listing &`** and then press Return). The remainder of the listing shows UNIX's response to the command.

N O T E Often times, the need for Return following a command is implied and understood, so it may not be shown in the listing.

When discussing the syntax of a UNIX command, this book uses some special formatting to distinguish the required portions and the variable portions. Consider the following example:

```
ls filename
```

In this syntax, the *filename* portion of the command is variable; that is, it changes depending on what file you want the `ls` command to work with. The `ls` is required; it is the actual command name. Variable information is presented in *italics*; information that must be typed exactly as it appears is presented in nonitalic type.

In some cases, command information may be optional; that is, it is not required for the command to work. Following the convention used by most programs, square brackets ([]) surround those parts of the command syntax that are optional. In the following example, notice that the *filename* parameter is variable *and* optional (it is in italics as well as surrounded by square brackets); however, to use the optional -l parameter, you must type it exactly as it appears (it is not in italics; it is a *literal* option):

```
ls [-l] [filename]
```

Throughout the book, you will find the following boxes to draw your attention to important or interesting information:

N O T E The Note boxes contain asides that give you more information about the current topic. They provide insights that give you a better understanding of the task at hand or further clarification of a concept.

 T I P The Tip boxes tell you about UNIX commands or methods that are easier, faster, or more efficient than the traditional methods.

CAUTION

The Caution boxes contain warnings about things that you should not do, or do with care, or else potential accidents or disasters may ensue. *To err is human, and to really mess things up is a computer.* These boxes help you avoid at least some of the pitfalls.

 TROUBLESHOOTING

Troubleshooting boxes point out common UNIX problems and ways in which to solve them.

Getting Started

UNIX Environment Overview

by Peter Kuo

In this chapter

The Origin of UNIX

UNIX is the name of a *family* of computer operating systems. The UNIX system is one of the major advances in the progression of computer science. It has demonstrated that a powerful operating system can be largely machine-independent, and it has shown that powerful software tools can be used effectively by people in the course of using a computer to solve problems.

The original goal of UNIX was simply to provide a computing environment for computer science research and development. UNIX has since achieved—and far surpassed—its original design goal. You can easily find UNIX systems being used in all types of businesses today, ranging from accounting applications to architectural design to medical imaging to Internet Web sites to computer graphics for movies.

To sum UNIX up briefly—UNIX is both versatile and powerful, although it can be somewhat cryptic in its command syntax. To better understand and appreciate the uniqueness of UNIX systems, you need to know a little of the history behind its development and evolution.

History

It all started back in late 1960s in the AT&T Bell Laboratories with an operating system called Multics. Multics was a multiuser interactive system using a GE mainframe computer. In 1969, Bell Labs withdrew from the Multics project but had laid the foundation for what eventually became UNIX.

> **N O T E**   As is often the case in the computer field when it comes to naming, UNIX is a play on the word Multics—"uni" versus "multi." ▪

At about the same time as Bell Labs' withdrawal from Multics, Ken Thompson, the "grandfather of UNIX" working at Bell Labs, started playing with a reject Digital Equipment Corporation (DEC, now Compaq) PDP-7 minicomputer. Thompson wanted an operating system that could support the coordinated efforts of a team of programmers in a research and development environment. And to appease management, Thompson proposed that further UNIX systems development be supported by Bell Labs to provide a document preparation tool for the Bell Labs patent organization. An early version of UNIX using a PDP-11/20 was actually delivered to the Bell Labs patent organization in 1971.

> **N O T E**   Digital Equipment Corporation produced the PDP (Programmable Data Processor), the VAX (Virtual Address Extension), and Alpha series of mini- and mainframe computers; DEC also produced the RT-11, RSX-11, and VMS series of operating systems that ran on these machines. DEC equipment is widely used in education (such as universities) and research environments. In late 1997, DEC was purchased by Compaq Computer Corporation. ▪

From the beginning, two seemingly incompatible disciplines, programming (which is notorious for "non-documenting") and document preparation, have been the cornerstones of the UNIX system. However, in practice, the UNIX system has shown that text management tools (not just editors) are central to many disciplines, including programming. Without a powerful editor and a suite of file management tools, it would be next to impossible to accomplish a large software project where millions of lines of code and thousands of files need to be dealt with.

Thompson's initial efforts resulted in the creation of an operating system, a PDP-7 assembler, and several assembler language utility programs. In 1973, Dennis Ritchie at Bell Labs rewrote the UNIX system in his new creation, the C programming language. Ritchie specifically developed C, a general-purpose programming language, to further work on the UNIX system. C has proved to be adaptable to many different types of computer architecture, and it is now a commonly available programming language on all types of computers, ranging from the Cray supercomputer all the way down to personal computers. If UNIX had not been rewritten in a portable programming language, such as C, it would have been chained to the machine (the outdated PDP-7 in this case) on which it was developed. As a result of using C, it was possible to "port" (move) the entire operating system from one environment to another with a minimal effort.

N O T E   An *assembler* is a program that translates text instructions into machine language. It is much like a compiler, but a compiler works with "high-level" programming languages such as FORTRAN or C (which are much more readily understandable by humans) that are portable (at the source code level) between different operating systems. An assembler works with "low-level" commands that are difficult to understand (because they use mnemonics) and are specific to a given operating system.

N O T E   Portability is the capability to (easily) transport a program (such as a utility or even a whole operating system) from one platform to another so that it still performs the way it should.

The first port of UNIX was done by Ritchie and Stephen Johnson in 1976 to the Interdata 8/32. Since then, UNIX has been ported to virtually every popular (and some not so popular) computer architecture, ranging from Zilog Z80 and Z-8000 to Motorola MC68000/68010/68020, to Intel 8086/8088/80x86, to mini- and mainframe computers, to even the Cray supercomputer.

As UNIX gained acceptance within the Bell Labs, it began to proliferate throughout the rest of the Bell System companies (of which AT&T is the parent company). At the same time, much interest was generated at several prestigious academic institutions, such as the University of California at Berkeley (UC Berkeley) and Massachusetts Institute of Technology. In 1975, Western Electric Company (AT&T's manufacturing subsidiary), started to handle the task of licensing the UNIX system *source code* to outside interested parties. The fee for academic institutions was nominal (you could get UNIX for essentially the cost of a 9-track magnetic tape plus shipping and handling) to encourage them to use and further develop the UNIX system.

Perhaps because UNIX was so favored by the academic community ("bunch of hippies and nerds"), the business community never took UNIX seriously until the late 1970s and early 1980s. However, if it wasn't for the foresight of Thompson and Ritchie back in 1973, we might not know of the Internet, which so many of us depend on today!

N O T E Today's Internet utilizes the TCP/IP protocol, which is the core networking protocol in all versions of the UNIX operating system. And a major portion of the Internet itself would not exist if it were not for AT&T's telecommunications network, the electronic gateway that connects you to the rest of the world. ▨

▶ **See** "Examining the DoD Model," **p. 454**

Unlike most other operating systems, which were developed by computer manufacturers to sell computers, the development of UNIX did not have that in mind, at least not initially. AT&T was not in the business of computer hardware during the first decade of the UNIX system's development, and the UNIX system was not originally envisioned as a commercial product. UNIX has only become a commercial venture in response to the enormous demand that it itself has generated.

Versions of UNIX

Some of the confusion or difficulty surrounding the various "flavors" of UNIX systems available today is mainly a fault of AT&T's management. AT&T was reluctant to devote many significant resources to properly "parent" UNIX because it was mainly developed for and used as an in-house application by AT&T and its subsidiaries. AT&T management did not have any commercial design on it. However, because of the interest in UNIX generated outside AT&T, a number of would-be UNIX "guardians" (such as UC Berkeley) stepped in to help "raise the child," as it were. Unlike an ordinary commercial operating system, which is completely controlled by its manufacturer, the features in the UNIX systems available today are driven by perhaps six or seven major forces (such as Sun Microsystems, Hewlett Packard, IBM, and the Santa Cruz Operation), and about 100 lesser players.

N O T E Microsoft Corporation was an important player in the Intel-based UNIX arena in the early 1980s with its XENIX product. However, Microsoft has long since dropped its interest in UNIX in favor of the Windows platform. ▨

The lack of standardization between the various flavors of UNIX systems is caused by a number of reasons, mostly attributable to AT&T:

- No central authority to direct the development of UNIX systems. This problem is now addressed by the formation of The Open Group in 1996 (see the "Open Systems Standards" section later in the chapter).
- The way UNIX was licensed by AT&T. UNIX was sold as a source code product rather than a binary product. This means that those companies that resold UNIX with their own hardware could and would repackage it and make enough changes (to add "enhancements," for example) to introduce (usage) incompatibilities with other UNIX systems.
- AT&T left the development of key usability features (such as how to make UNIX easier to use by people who are not programmers) and hardware support unfinished. Therefore, when vendors received the UNIX source code, changes were made (to, for

example, disk drivers) to support the vendor's particular hardware. This made porting UNIX difficult.

■ Involvement from different competing companies—politics becomes an issue.

Fortunately, all major UNIX flavors available today can trace their development histories to one of two major UNIX "roots":

■ AT&T System V

■ BSD (Berkeley Software Distribution) v4

AT&T/USL System V   The first major public exposure of UNIX was made in July 1974 by Thompson and Ritchie in their classic paper "The UNIX Time-Sharing System" in the *Communications of the ACM* (Association for Computing Machinery). This paper was based on the (AT&T) Version 5 system. In 1976, Version 6 was made available throughout the Bell System and was distributed to universities around the world. Version 6 served as the basis for development of several variants of the UNIX system, including the MERT real-time UNIX derivative, the PWB (programmer's workbench) UNIX systems, and the early work on UNIX at UC Berkeley. Version 6 was the first UNIX system to be copied by Whitesmiths, Inc., to produce the first commercial work-alike UNIX called Idris.

In 1978, Bell Labs released Version 7 of the UNIX system. This version is considered to be the "blueprint" for modern-day UNIX systems. It featured the first release of the Bourne shell, the first shell (command interpreter) to combine a powerful interpretive programming language with powerful features for interactive command entry. Version 7 heavily influenced the PWB systems and was the basis for the UNIX 32V system for DEC VAX computers.

Bell System developed the PWB UNIX system, and it became Release 3.0, then 4.0, and finally in 1982 it evolved to Release 5.0. AT&T changed the name from Release 5.0 to System V, included a few additional documents, and proclaimed AT&T System V to be the UNIX standard. The original System V contained only the ed line editor, but later releases included the vi editor adopted from UC Berkeley.

In the late 1980s, AT&T spun off a company called USL (UNIX Systems Laboratories), which produced the source code for all UNIX System V derivatives in the industry. Interestingly enough, USL itself did not sell a shrink-wrapped product until the early 1990s. The last USL release of UNIX was UNIX System V Release 4.2 (more commonly known as SVR4.2) in 1990. In this version, a graphical user interface (GUI) called UNIX Desktop was added. UNIX Desktop provided the user with the familiar windowed environment seen on a majority of computers today. Also included in SVR4.2 was PC hardware support such as drivers for popular hard drives, CD-ROM drives, video cards, SCSI devices, and support for multiple processors.

As a joint venture between USL and Novell, Inc., in 1991, USL produced a shrink-wrapped version of SVR4.2 called UnixWare for the Intel hardware platform. It is available in two configurations: Personal Edition (PE) version and Application Server (AS); the Personal Edition is a single-user, networked platform for running applications, whereas the Application Server is a multiuser system and can offer services to other systems.

In 1993, Novell purchased USL and the UNIX System V product from AT&T, made USL part of Novell's UNIX Systems Group, and further developed UnixWare. In early 1997, Novell added Novell Directory Services (NDS), Novell's global directory service, support to UnixWare v2 to provide a single sign-on capability to both UNIX and NetWare (Novell's LAN operating system). In 1996, SCO bought the UNIX Systems business from Novell, and UNIX system source code and technology are now developed by SCO; however, SCO did not receive the rights to the UNIX trademark.

N O T E   With the purchase of USL and gaining ownership of the UNIX name by Novell from AT&T, Novell had an opportunity to solidify the UNIX industry plagued by too many UNIX variants. Alas, Novell never took up that challenge and later sold UnixWare off to one of their UNIX competitors, Santa Cruz Operation. ▧

BSD v4   During the late 1970s and early 1980s, when AT&T paid little attention to the growth of UNIX, Computer Science graduate students and professors at the University of California at Berkeley supported and improved UNIX. Being a university where there was much DEC equipment, the UNIX 32V system (which was based on AT&T's Version 7 code) was used as the starting point for development, and BSD 3 and BSD 4 for VAX computers were the results.

In 1991, leading computer scientists of the Computer Systems Research Group at UC Berkeley spun off a separate company, Berkeley Software Design, Inc., to commercially distribute BSD UNIX and its associated networking and Internet technologies. The BSDI Internet Server product is widely used by Internet service providers to provide Internet connectivity and to serve Web contents.

The BSD UNIX added some major features, such as the C shell, the vi editor, the Franz Lisp programming language, the Pascal programming language, networking support, improved interprocess communication via sockets and pseudo-ttys, virtual memory support, and many significant performance enhancements. The most significant contribution of the BSD project is probably the utilities developed to make UNIX more user-friendly, which the initial AT&T UNIX versions failed to provide.

▶ **See** "Introducing vi," **p. 84**

▶ **See** "Process," **p. 132**

▶ **See** "Device Files," **p. 296**

▶ **See** "Examining the DoD Model," **p. 454**

Linux   You probably have heard of the Linux operating system from different sources. But you might not know that Linux is *not* UNIX but is a UNIX *work-alike*. Linux is a product that mimics the form and function of a UNIX system but is *not* derived from any licensed UNIX source code. The foundation for Linux was developed by a Finnish man called Linus Torvalds back in the early 1990s while he was still an undergraduate student.

Many people considered Linux to be a product of the Internet: Torvalds made his source code available to others at *no charge* over the Internet. Since its initial availability, many programmers around the world have extended his code, adding functionality matching, but not ported from, that found in both BSD and System V UNIX systems and adding new functionality as well. You are always free to distribute Linux as you want, but whether you give it away or sell it, you must provide the source code together with the operating system binaries. As a result, there are many freely available utilities and specialty drivers available for Linux on the Internet. Linux support is also available for free on the Internet, via various Linux-related news groups.

> **CAUTION**
>
> Although Linux is available for free, you will find some companies selling Linux. What they are selling is not the Linux system itself but the additional support and add-ons the vendors offer.

Linux is not just for Intel-based platforms. It has been ported to and runs on the PowerPC— including Apples, the DEC Alpha-based machines, MIPS-based machines, and Motorola 68000-based machines. Starting with version 2.0, Linux also runs on machines with multiple processors (SMPs).

N O T E There are a number of "flavors" of Linux, such as the RedHat, Slackware, and Caldera Linux implementations. Most people consider the RedHat version to be the most complete of all Linux implementations.

Although Linux is not UNIX, if you are familiar with UNIX, you will be at home with Linux. If you are just starting out to learn UNIX, Linux is a cost-effective option because the price is right (*it's free!*), it supports a wide range of standard PC hardware peripherals, and the demand on hardware is low (you can easily get RedHat running on an Intel 80486/33 machine with only 100MB of hard disk space and as little as 8MB of RAM and still get good performance).

Major Commercial UNIX Versions Without going into any detail, it is, however, worth noting by name some of the major commercial UNIX systems available on the market today:

- SunOS and Solaris from Sun Microsystems   The two operating systems derived their roots from BSD.

ON THE WEB

http://www.sun.com   Sun Microsystems' home page

- HP/UX from Hewlett-Packard   The HP/UX operating system is based on UNIX System V Release 2, with important features from BSD 4.2. In essence, HP/UX is essentially a System V-type of UNIX with numerous extensions.

ON THE WEB

http://www.hp.com/esy   Hewlett-Packard's UNIX Enterprise Software home page

- Digital UNIX (formerly Ultrix) from Digital Equipment Corporation   Ultrix is derived from BSD 4.2.

ON THE WEB

http://www.unix.digital.com Digital Equipment Corporation's Digital UNIX home page

■ AIX from IBM Runs on the RS/6000 series of computers and PowerPCs. AIX (Advanced Interactive Executive) is based on UNIX System V and BSD 4.3 but is more of a hybrid of these two types of UNIX than HP-UX. AIX also contains several IBM-proprietary features, such as the Object Data Manager (ODM) and System Resource Controller (SRC). Its windowing system, AIXwindows Environment/6000 is based on the X Window System with OSF/Motif and is an optional product.

ON THE WEB

http://www.austin.ibm.com/software/aix_os.html IBM AIX's home page

■ Irix from Silicon Graphics Inc. (SGI) SGI is well-known for its UNIX-based graphics workstations.

ON THE WEB

http://www.sgi.com Silicon Graphics Inc.'s home page

■ SINUX and Reliant UNIX from Siemens Nixdorf Informations systeme AG (Siemens SNI) Reliant UNIX runs on SNI's own RM200, RM400, and RM600 systems, whereas SINUX runs on PCs.

ON THE WEB

http://www.siemensnixdorf.com/servers/softw_us/relia_us.htm Siemens SNI's Reliant UNIX home page

■ OpenServer and UnixWare from SCO At the time of this writing, SCO is shipping OpenServer 5.0 and UnixWare 2.12. But UnixWare 7.0, formerly code-named Gemini, will combine the best of both UnixWare 2.12 and OpenServer 5.0 into a single platform.

ON THE WEB

http://www.sco.com Santa Cruz Operation Inc.'s home page

Who Owns What?

After the preceding long winding history lesson and all the company spin-offs, mergers, and buyouts, have you been able to keep track of who owns what today in terms of UNIX? Table 1.1 will help you to keep that straight.

Table 1.1   Companies and Their Relationship to UNIX

Company	What It Owns
The Open Group	Trademark. Whoever wants to use the UNIX name on a product must contact The Open Group.
Santa Cruz Operation	Source code to UNIX.
The Open Group	The specification(s) that define what a UNIX system is.

The UNIX Operating System

An *operating system* is a program that manages the resources of a computer. One major function of the UNIX operating system, or any other operating system, is to isolate the users from the building blocks of the computer (such as disk drives and tape units). You don't need to understand internal combustion engines to drive a car, and you shouldn't have to understand computer architecture to use a computer. However, knowing some of the basics makes it easier and helps you from being overwhelmed by the jargon.

The UNIX operating system, and many other operating systems as well, is implemented in a layered manner, as illustrated in Figure 1.1. Each higher layer masks the complexity of the low-level functions by providing a slightly simpler and easier-to-use interface. Therefore, the users at the top "layer" do not need to know how to address a SCSI disk at the bit-and-byte level to retrieve a file from it; the user simply needs to call a utility (a high-level interface) to perform the task.

FIGURE 1.1
A layered view of the
UNIX operating system.

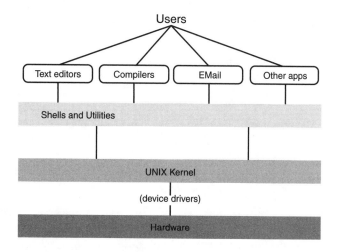

As one of the first steps to understanding the UNIX system, you should have a general understanding of the building blocks that underlie a computer. The following sections present some of these fundamentals. Because the UNIX kernel is the heart and brain of the UNIX operating system, we'll start with it first.

The UNIX Kernel

Certain operating system functions are used almost continuously. For example, the portion of the operating system that is involved in switching from one program to another (time sharing) is needed many times a second. In the UNIX system, all functions that are needed constantly and immediately are kept in memory for fast access. This memory-resident portion, which is also the heart of the UNIX operating system, is called the *kernel*. The UNIX kernel is responsible for controlling the computer's resources and scheduling user jobs so that each job gets its fair share of system resources, including access to the CPU as well as peripheral devices such as disks, printers, and tape drives.

Other less frequently used operating system functions, such as moving files from one place to another, are not provided by the kernel. Instead, these functions are performed through *utilities*, standard standalone programs that are invoked on demand by the user. In the UNIX system, it is easy and common for people to add to the stock of utilities by simply writing a new and useful program.

N O T E   As a comparison for those who are familiar with DOS: the UNIX kernel can be compared to the COMMAND.COM in DOS, which is the memory-resident portion of DOS. COMMAND.COM provides access to your hard drives and printers. When you issue a DIR command to obtain a directory listing, COMMAND.COM that does the work. Other DOS commands, such as FIND, are implemented as utilities (or external DOS commands, in DOS's parlance) in the form of FIND.EXE and the like, which are standalone programs separate from COMMAND.COM. ▦

Because the kernel communicates with the hardware, it is responsible for providing the following functions:

- ▦ Hardware management, through device drivers
- ▦ Multiuser support
- ▦ Multitasking scheduling

Hardware Management   Three categories of hardware management are provided by the UNIX kernel. The first is to manage access to different hardware devices, such as hard disks and printers. The second is to resolve conflicts due to concurrent access to the same device, such as three users saving files to the same hard disk. The third, and last, category of hardware management is device independence.

The first two management tasks can be handled easily by implementing naming standards for different devices and applying some type of scheduling mechanism to resolve access conflicts, such as a first come first serve system. The task of attaining device independence is a little tricky, and UNIX handles this uniquely.

Traditionally, computer systems could generally support peripherals such as printers, disk drives, modems, and terminals. However, the technology explosion in the past few years has added to this list other devices, such as CD-ROM and JAZ drives, that are too numerous to list. For an operating system to address a peripheral, the software must be able to communicate with the hardware. In the past, such device support was built directly into the operating system. As a result, you get faster access to the device because the necessary software code is an integral part of the operating system and is, therefore, tuned and optimized. The downside, however, is that only a limited set of hardware is supported because the kernel's developer cannot foresee all possible hardware combinations nor it is feasible to include all possible device support because new hardware is introduced constantly.

UNIX sidesteps the problem of adding new devices by viewing each peripheral as a separate file. As new devices are required, the system administrator adds the required link to the kernel and creates a new kernel. When the system is restarted with the new kernel running, you have access to the newly added device. This link or file is known as the *device driver*. The purpose of the device driver is to ensure that the kernel and the peripheral merge in the same fashion each time the device is accessed.

> **CAUTION**
>
> Device drivers are generally written by and supplied by the vendor of the hardware. Therefore, before you add a new peripheral to your UNIX system, make sure that a device driver is available first.

The key to device independence lies in the adaptability of the kernel. Some operating systems allow only a certain number of devices due to the amount of space they allocate in the kernel for device drivers. Because UNIX views device drivers as files, and because there is no limit on how many files UNIX can support, UNIX can accommodate any number of devices as long as the host's hardware architecture can support them.

Understanding Multiuser   Depending on the hardware being used and the work being performed, a single UNIX host can support anywhere from a single user to more than a thousand simultaneous users, each concurrently running a different set of programs. The multiuser concept should not be confused with multiple users updating the same file simultaneously, as the term multiuser often is used with database applications. Multiuser, in UNIX terms, is the capability of the kernel to allocate CPU time to many applications at once, thus serving many users at once when each is running one or more applications.

Multiuser is made possible using the *time sharing* concept. The goal of time sharing is to give each user her own unique working environment and the illusion of exclusive use of the machine. In an interactive computer system, the computer is always waiting for you to tell it to do something. Most of the time when you are pondering what to do next, the computer services requests from your fellow users without you realizing it.

> **N O T E**   Time sharing works by dividing each unit of time into a number of "slices." Each executing program receives a slice of time. When more programs are executing, each program receives a smaller slice than when only a few programs are running. Therefore, time sharing is also known as *time slicing* or *multitasking*. (Multitasking is discussed further in the "Understanding Multitasking" section later in this chapter.) ▪

In the multiuser mode, the kernel switches rapidly from one job to another, creating the appearance that the computer is performing many tasks simultaneously. In fact, the computer is making progress on one task and then switching to the next, and the next, and so on.

There will come a time that a single CPU becomes overloaded, either because of too many users or because too many tasks are being run, such that the kernel spends most of its time switching between programs and very little time actually running them. In such a situation, you need to either lower the CPU load by reducing the number of users or tasks being run, or install additional CPUs into the host (if supported) so that the kernel can shift some processing onto the extra processors.

Understanding Multitasking Multitasking, sometimes also referred to as *multiprocessing*, is the kernel's capability to run more than one job or process at a time, and each process is protected (separated) from one another (just like the kernel is protected from all other processes). Each process can communicate with each other through either a shared memory area or "pipes" between processes. (You will read more about pipes in Chapter 3, "Pipes, I/O Redirection, and Filters.") Offhand, it seems multitasking is the same as time sharing or time slicing. However, there is a subtle difference between the two.

In a traditional time sharing implementation, the CPU's attention is divided between the users; each user is given a process (or an environment), and within this process the user can only execute one task (program) at a time. UNIX, however, creates a separate process for each command issued by the user. Therefore, a UNIX user can have multiple processes active (running) at the same time, instead of having to run them sequentially. As a result, a UNIX user can achieve better productivity than a typical time sharing user because the UNIX user can complete more tasks within the same amount of time when compared to a sharing-sharing user.

Let's use a real-world example to better illustrate this point. Suppose that you are preparing your year-end expense report. You begin by starting your word processor to prepare your report. You then realize that you need data extracted from your accounts payable database. In a traditional time sharing (or any nonmultitasking) system, you need to exit your word processor, start up the database application, extract the data, exit the database application, and then restart the word processor. However, in a multitasking environment such as UNIX you can simply switch to a new window (if you are using a GUI)—without having to exit your word processor—start the database extraction there, switch back to your word processor window, and continue to work. You can check the progress of the database extraction from time to time by simply switching to that window, while still working on the report—you do not have to wait.

You can clearly see the benefits of having a true multitasking operating system such as UNIX. Besides reducing idle time (time in which you can't continue working on an application because a process has not yet finished), the flexibility of not having to close down an application before opening and working in others is infinitely more convenient. (Remember the frustration you had with DOS until Windows came along?)

N O T E Although UNIX has had multitasking capability since the late 1960s, other operating systems did not catch on for quite some time. For example, on the PC platform it was not until the late 1990s (with Windows 95 and Windows NT) that true multitasking was available.

UNIX Hardware

Two trends in the computer industry set the stage for the popularity of UNIX. First, advances in hardware technology created the need for an operating system that could take advantage of available hardware power. In the mid- and late-1970s and the early 1980s, minicomputers and RISC-based (Reduced Instruction-Set Computing) workstations began challenging the large mainframes in terms of flexibility and performance in specific application areas, such as graphics. Today, newer workstations, PCs, and Macs, especially those with the Alpha chipset and the new 64-bit processors, have challenged the minis in much the same way. The availability of powerful CPUs, fast yet inexpensive memory, and low-cost storage devices has allowed manufacturers to produce servers that can support multiuser operating systems such as UNIX.

Second, with the cost-performance ratio of hardware continuing to drop and with the success of IBM PCs, hardware manufacturers can no longer afford to develop and support *proprietary* operating systems for their particular hardware. They need a *generic* operating system that can be easily adapted to their machines. Additionally, software vendors that produce applications, such as accounting software, also need a generic operating system. It is simply too costly and time-consuming to develop and maintain different versions of the same software for different proprietary operating systems.

> **N O T E** A *proprietary operating system* is usually developed for, and supported by, the manufacturer of a specific type of hardware and will generally not run on other hardware platforms. An example is Digital Equipment Corporation's VMS operating system, which only runs on DEC VAX and DEC Alpha series of computers.

> **N O T E** A *generic operating system* is usually developed independent of a particular hardware platform and is generally not owned (but perhaps licensed) by the hardware manufacturers. The modern UNIX operating system is a prime example of a generic operating system because it is not tied to a particular hardware platform.

UNIX is one of the few generic operating systems around that fit the needs mentioned previously. Regardless of your hardware choice, you can find a flavor of UNIX for it. Do, however, be aware that certain flavors of UNIX, such as HP/UX, AIX, and SunOS/Solaris, have been custom-tailored to take advantage of the respective vendors' hardware; therefore, these UNIX implementations border on the proprietary operating system and generic operating system line. Table 1.2 shows a list of selected UNIX flavors and the hardware platform on which they run.

Common Features of UNIX

Despite the different flavors of UNIX available, because they all share the common root of being derived from either BSD or System V, all UNIX systems share certain common features and elements. This is what made UNIX skills so transportable between platforms.

Table 1.2   Common UNIX Flavors and the Hardware Platforms

Type of UNIX	Hardware Platform
AIX	IBM RS/6000 series computers
HP/UX	HP 700 series computers, HP9000 series computers, HP VISUALIZE B/C/J-Class workstations
Linux	Intel chipset, 80386 and higher
OFS/1	DEC VAX computers
SCO UnixWare	Intel chipset, 80386 and higher
SCO OpenServer	Intel chipset, 80386 and higher
Sun Solaris	Sun SPARC and UltraSPARC workstations, Sun Enterprise series computers
Ultrix	DEC VAX computers

N O T E   Although all UNIX systems have certain system utility programs, command-line options can differ from flavor to flavor. Therefore, by observing the command-line options used or the commands being used, you can get an idea of whether a user's background stems from BSD or System V or Linux. For example, someone with a System V background will use ps -ef to obtain a full listing of every process running on the system, whereas a person with a BSD background will try to use ps -aux instead. ▦

The following features can be found in every UNIX implementation, but the actual implementation may vary from flavor to flavor:

- ▦ Text editors   There are two common types of editors, *line* editors and *visual* (or screen) editors. Visual editors are best for interactive use, whereas line editors are usually better at executing predefined editing scripts.

- ▦ Text manipulation system utilities   Often, you may need to extract a portion of a file, sort it, and then import it into another file. UNIX provides utilities such as head, tail, cut, paste, and sort to provide such services. Also available are programmable languages, such as sed and awk, for text file manipulations.

- ▦ Software development tools   One of the strengths of UNIX is its rich software development environment, because that was what UNIX was originally designed to do. You can find compilers and interpreters for many computer programming languages, such as Ada, C, C++, FORTRAN, LISP, Pascal, PERL, and many others. Also available are many tools, such as make, SCCS (Source Code Control System), yacc, and lex.

- ▦ Command shells   The shell is a *command interpreter* that allows you to control your working environment as well as execute commands for you. For example, through the shell, you can call up your favorite editor, print a file, and copy a file from disk to tape. Several different shells are available, but each UNIX version at least supports the Bourne shell (sh) and the C shell (csh).

N O T E In many operating systems, the command interpreter is a part of the kernel. However, in UNIX, the shell is just an ordinary program, similar to the `cut` and `paste` programs or any other system utilities. The only thing special about a shell is that it is central to most of your interactions with the UNIX kernel. Because the shell is a separate entity from the UNIX kernel, you can choose to work with whichever shell you like best. ▨

■ **Hierarchical file system with built-in security** Files are named collections of information stored on a mass storage device such as a hard drive or tape. A *file system* is the organizational framework for the files. Older operating systems were "organized" by lumping files all together into one big heap. As long as there are only a few dozen files, a heap works fine. Unfortunately, such a simple file system is inappropriate for a multiuser system such as UNIX where there can be several hundred thousand files.

The UNIX file system allows you to group files logically, according to their use and relationship with other files. The key idea of the UNIX file system is that it is hierarchical, like a family tree—files are housed in directories (much like drawers in a filing cabinet), and each directory can contain both files and (sub)directories.

Another concern for the file system of a multiuser computer is who can access each file. In the UNIX system, each file has an access permission that determines who can access (and in what way) each file.

■ **Distributed file system** At the top of the UNIX file system hierarchy is a special directory called the *root directory*, denoted by the slash symbol (/). All directories appear underneath it. Each directory and its subdirectories may exist on a different device, yet they all appear as an integral part of the (logical) file system. Figure 1.2 illustrates a simple UNIX file system. In this example, the contents of /bin, /tmp, and /dev are on one hard drive whereas the contents of /usr are on a separate hard disk. However, UNIX doesn't care, and as far as the users are concerned, all files are located on the same device, and access to them is transparent.

FIGURE 1.2
A simplified diagram of a typical UNIX file system. Directories are shown in boxes, whereas files are shown without borders.

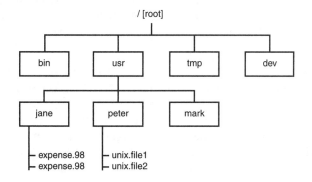

With the popularity of TCP/IP networking and using the NFS (Network File System) introduced by Sun Microsystems (and now a standard), a UNIX file system can be physically spread across multiple UNIX hosts, and not just different devices on the same host.

- File links   UNIX provides a method (known as *symbolic link*) to allow a given file to be accessed by means of two or more different names. The alternative name can be located in the same directory as the original file or in another directory. Links can be used to make the same file appear in several users' directories, enabling them to share the file easily.

- Electronic mail and Network News   UNIX was one of the first operating systems to have electronic mail (email) capability built-in. Using `mail` (and other popular mail programs), you can easily exchange electronic messages with users on the same UNIX system or other UNIX systems.

  UNIX also introduced the idea of electronic bulletin boards. However, instead of a user needing to access a central location for messages, the messages are delivered directly to the user's host. All the user has to do is use a reader program and select the particular groups for reading the associated messages, similar to your newspaper or magazine subscriptions. These message groups are known as *newsgroups*.

N O T E   Because of the volume of newsgroup messages and their varied contents, the system administrators will generally select to only retrieve messages from selected newsgroups from the Internet. ▓

- Networking support   UNIX "defined" the current state of TCP/IP networking as well as the technology available for the Internet today. Also included are UUCP (*UNIX-to-UNIX CoPy*) and its related utilities for (email) message and file transport between different UNIX hosts using modems and over network links.

UNIX Networking

When computers were first introduced, each could be used fully in isolation because there wasn't much need for information sharing. However, today, with the ever-increasing number of computers, it is important to be able to move data easily between computers. A *network* is a group of computers that have hardware and software that enable the computers to communicate with each other. There are generally two categories of networks—wide area networks and local area networks.

A *wide area network* (WAN) consists of computers that are far apart, perhaps separated by cities or even countries. Computer systems in a WAN typically communicate using the public telephone system, high-speed leased lines, or microwave or other types of communication links. One of the earliest, and perhaps the most famous, WANs is the Advanced Research Projects Agency Network (ARPAnet). Initially developed to support U.S. defense industry projects, ARPAnet was the precursor of the modern-day Internet. Most technology developed for the ARPANet and Internet were done using UNIX systems.

A *local area network* (LAN) consists of computers that are generally no farther apart than a couple of kilometers. Computer systems in a LAN environment typically are linked together using high-speed data links, such as coaxial cables or fiber optics.

N O T E There are also *metropolitan area networks* (MANs) where computer systems are distributed around a city's boundary. However, such networks are generally classified as WANs, and therefore you will not frequently encounter references to MANs. ▦

Today, UNIX systems include a rich set of networking tools and utilities that allow you to access remote systems over a both LANs and WANs. Besides the capability to send email easily to users on other machines, some of the capabilities offered to you by UNIX networking are as follows:

- Log in to remote systems as if your terminal were locally connected.
- Access files on disks or tapes mounted on other computers as if they were located on your own UNIX host and make your own files available to other computers in a similar manner.
- Easily copy files back and forth between different computer systems, either from local to remote or remote to remote.
- Run programs on other machines while displaying results back on your machine.
- Access the World Wide Web.
- Publish your home pages to the World Wide Web.
- Carry out video conferencing with people around the world as easily as making a telephone conference call.

UNIX Services in the Marketplace

You might not be aware that UNIX systems are used in just about every type of business today. Other than providing time sharing services to a group of users, the following are some examples of applications of UNIX systems:

- Accounting applications
- Advertising (computer-generated graphics in TV commercials and movies, for example)
- Computer-aided design and computer-aided manufacturing (CAD/CAM)
- Database servers (the UNIX operating system is a popular choice for client/server-type database applications such as Oracle and Sybase)
- Document management systems
- Manufacturing process control
- Network security (as in network firewalls and gateways)
- Imaging (such as those used in medical sciences)
- Point-of-sale (POS) systems
- Publishing (often used by newspaper and book publishers as part of the print process)
- Software development for other operating system platforms (using cross-compilers)
- Web servers

Because of the versatility of UNIX, its applications and uses are essentially unlimited.

Open Systems Standards

The UNIX industry developed most of today's networking standards including TCP/IP, Network File System (NFS), Web technologies, Java technology, Domain Name Service (DNS), and many more. UNIX systems were originally developed with the network in mind. The competitive environment of the UNIX operating systems is due to the open philosophy of the original UNIX design because you can easily add and extend the system. However, as a result, many variants of UNIX exist. Variety comes with a price—because there is no one UNIX standard, there are incompatibilities between different flavors of UNIX, and software vendors need to maintain different versions of their applications to support the different UNIX platforms.

Efforts have been made to combine, collate, and otherwise "condense" all variants of UNIX into a single, all-encompassing version of the operating system. Throughout the early and mid-1980s, the debate about the strengths and weaknesses of UNIX systems raged and often were fueled by the vendors themselves who fought to protect their profitable proprietary systems by talking UNIX systems down. In an effort to further differentiate their competing UNIX system products, vendors kept developing and adding features of their own.

In 1984, a group of vendors concerned about the continuing encroachment into their markets and control of system interfaces by the larger companies developed the concept of *open systems*. Open systems would meet agreed on specifications or standards. This resulted in the formation of X/Open Company, Ltd., (commonly known as X/Open), whose charter was to define a comprehensive open systems environment. Open systems, X/Open declared, would save on costs, attract a wider portfolio of applications, and keep competition on equal terms. X/Open chose the UNIX system as the platform for the basis of open systems.

At that time, although UNIX was still owned by AT&T, the company did little commercially with it until the mid-1980s. Then X/Open showed clearly that a single standard version of the UNIX system would be in the wider interests of the industry and its customers. The question now was, "Which version?"

In a move intended to unify the market in 1987, AT&T announced a pact with Sun Microsystems, the leading proponent of the Berkeley derivative of UNIX and the developer of NFS. However, the rest of the industry viewed the development with considerable concern. Believing that their own markets were under threat, they clubbed together in 1988 to develop their own "new" open systems operating system. Their new organization was called the Open Software Foundation (OSF). In response to this, the AT&T/Sun faction formed UNIX International.

The ensuing "UNIX wars" divided the system vendors between these two camps clustered around the two dominant UNIX system technologies: AT&T's System V and the OSF system called OSF/1. In the meantime, X/Open held a neutral position. X/Open continued the process of standardizing the APIs necessary for an open operating system specification.

In addition, X/Open looked at areas of the system beyond the operating system level where a standard approach would add value for supplier and customer alike: developing or adopting specifications for programming languages, database connectivity, networking, and mainframe interworking. The results of this work were published in successive X/Open Portability Guides (XPG).

XPG revision 4 (XPG4) was released in October 1992. During this time, X/Open had put in place a brand program based on vendor guarantees and supported by testing. Since the publication of XPG4, X/Open has continued to broaden the scope of open systems specifications in line with market requirements. As the benefits of the X/Open brand became known and understood, many large organizations began using X/Open as the basis for system design and procurement. By 1993, more than $7 billion had been spent on X/Open branded systems. By the start of 1997, that figure had risen to more than $23 billion. To date, procurements referencing the "Single UNIX Specification" amount to more than $5.2 billion.

In early 1993, AT&T sold its UNIX System Laboratories to Novell, Inc. At the same time, AT&T recognized that vesting control of the definition (specification) and trademark with a vendor-neutral organization would further facilitate the value of UNIX as a foundation of open systems. So the constituent parts of the UNIX System, previously owned by a single entity are now quite separate. In 1995, SCO bought the UNIX Systems business from Novell, and UNIX system source code and technology now continues to be developed by SCO.

In 1995, X/Open introduced the UNIX 95 brand for computer systems guaranteed to meet the *Single UNIX Specification.* The Single UNIX Specification brand program has now achieved critical mass: Vendors whose products have met the demanding criteria now account for the majority of UNIX systems by value.

For more than ten years, since the inception of X/Open, UNIX has been closely linked with open systems. X/Open, now part of The Open Group, continues to develop and evolve the Single UNIX Specification and associated brand program on behalf of the IT community.

The Open Group, a standards organization with offices around the world and a Web site at **http://www.opengroup.org**, owns the definition of the UNIX brand (obtained from Novell when Novell sold the UNIX technology to SCO). The UNIX vendors—SCO, Sun, DEC, IBM, HP, and so on—all provide input to The Open Group on the future direction of the UNIX operating system. The benefit to the industry is that all companies can create products that meet the definition of a UNIX operating system. Companies compete for business, forcing innovation and differentiation. Application developers can build products based on the standard definition of a UNIX operating system. You, the customer, can have a choice for your operating system vendor, yet at the same time have the confidence that your applications will be compatible with future versions of UNIX.

Table 1.3 shows a summary of timeline and milestones of UNIX development.

Table 1.3   UNIX Development Timeline and Milestones

1969   **The Beginning**. The history of UNIX started back in 1969, when Ken Thompson, Dennis Ritchie, and others started working on a "little-used PDP-7 in a corner" at Bell Labs and what was to become UNIX.

1971   **First Edition**. It had an assembler for a PDP-11/20, a file system, `fork()`, `off`, and `ed`. It was used for text processing of patent documents.

1973   **Fourth Edition**. It was rewritten in C. This made it portable and changed the history of operating systems.

1975   **Sixth Edition—UNIX leaves home**. Also widely known as Version 6, this was the first to be widely available outside Bell Labs.

1975   The first BSD version (1.x) was derived from v6.

1979   **Seventh Edition**. It was an "improvement over all preceding and following Unices." It had C, UUCP, and the Bourne shell. It was ported to the VAX, and the kernel was more than 40KB in size.

1980   **XENIX was born**. Microsoft introduced XENIX.

1980   32V and BSD 4.0 introduced by UC Berkeley.

1982   **System III**. AT&T's UNIX System Group (USG) released System III, the first public release outside Bell Laboratories.

1983   **System V**. AT&T's Computer Research Group (CRG), UNIX System Group (USG), and a third group merged to become UNIX System Development Lab. AT&T announced UNIX System V, the first supported release.

1984   **BSD 4.2**. University of California at Berkeley released BSD 4.2.

1984   **SVR2—System V Release 2 introduced by AT&T**. At this time, there were 100,000 UNIX installations around the world.

1984   **X/Open Company Ltd. was formed**.

1987   **SVR3**. System V Release 3 included STREAMS, TLI, and RFS. At this time, there were 750,000 UNIX installations around the world.

1988   **POSIX.1 (Portable Operating System Interface for Computing Environments, v1) published**. POSIX was largely based on AT&T's SVID (System V Interface Definition) and other earlier standardization efforts.

1988   Open Software Foundation (OSF) and UNIX International (UI) were formed.

1989   **AT&T UNIX Software Operation was formed in preparation for spin-off of USL**.

1989   **SVR4**. UNIX System V Release 4 shipped, unifying System V, BSD, and XENIX.

1990   **XPG3**. X/Open launched XPG3 Brand.

1991   **Formation of USL**. UNIX System Laboratories (USL) became a company—majority-owned by AT&T.

1992   **SVR4.2**. USL released UNIX System V Release 4.2 (codename Destiny).

1992   **October—XPG4 Brand launched by X/Open**.

1992   **December 22—Novell announced intent to acquire USL**.

1993   **BSD 4.4**. BSD 4.4, the final release from Berkeley.

1993   **June 16—Novell acquired USL**.

1993   **December—SVR4.2MP**. Novell shipped SVR4.2MP, the final USL OEM release of System V.

1993   **December—Novell transferred rights to the "UNIX" trademark and the Single UNIX Specification to X/Open**.

1995   **UNIX 95**. X/Open introduced the UNIX 95 branding program.

1995   **Novell sold UnixWare business to SCO**.

1996   **The Open Group**. The Open Group formed as a merger of OSF and X/Open.

1997   **Single UNIX Specification, Version 2**. The Open Group introduced Version 2 of the Single UNIX Specification, including support for real-time, threads, and 64-bit and larger processors.

1998   **UNIX 98**. The Open Group introduced the UNIX 98 family of brands, including Base, Workstation, and Server.

From Here...

This chapter introduced you to the UNIX operating system. The history, different flavors, and the big picture view of the UNIX operating system was presented. You learned about the key concepts and important terminology, such as kernel, multiuser, and multitasking, used in the UNIX world. An overview of the application of UNIX systems and the UNIX networking facilities was covered.

- For a discussion of UNIX shells, see Chapter 3, "UNIX Shells and System Commands."

- For a discussion of processes, see Chapter 6, "UNIX Processes."

- For a discussion of how hardware devices are handled by UNIX, see Chapter 12, "Device Management."

- For a discussion of networking basics, see Chapter 17, "Networking Essentials."

- For a discussion of TCP/IP and networking technologies, see Chapter 18, "Internetworking."

- For a discussion of how you can set up your own Web server on UNIX, see Chapter 24, "Apache Web Server."

Logging In

by Peter Kuo

In this chapter

Understanding the Login Process

The first thing a UNIX system requires you do is to *log in*. The purpose of logging in is twofold: to let the UNIX system verify you are who you say you are, and to set up your working environment. With today's technology where you can access a UNIX system from just about anywhere, such as over the telephone or over a network, it is important to restrict use to authorized people. In computer systems where people are billed for usage, it is also important to know who is using the system when and for how long so that accurate billing can be made.

> **N O T E** In most single-user or home personal computer systems, there is no login procedure because physical access to the hardware confirms your right to use the system. You can, however, use additional software to provide a formal login process so that you can track the usage. ▪

One feature of UNIX is *time sharing*, where multiple users share access to the computer. To do this, the UNIX system maintains a separate environment for each user. The UNIX system keeps track of who each user is, when each logged in, how much time each has used, what files each owns, what network resources each user is allowed to access, what type of terminal is being used, and so on.

Before you can log in for the first time, your UNIX system administrator must first create your account or user ID (also known as login name or username) and configure a (logical) working environment, such as your home directory and the default UNIX shell, for you.

▶ **See** "What Is a UNIX Shell?" **p. 46**

▶ **See** "Creating User Accounts," **p. 242**

▶ **See** "Deleting User Accounts," **p. 250**

▶ **See** "Modifying User Accounts," **p. 251**

User Login Names

The login name is the name that you provide the UNIX system to identify yourself. This name is predetermined by the UNIX system administrator when the account is created. Generally, the login name is your initials, nickname, or first name. Often, the name is in lowercase. For example, "peter," "pk," and "unixguy" are all acceptable login names. Because each login name must be unique, some installations (such as universities or companies where there are many users) will use your employee ID number, student ID number, or a combination of your first and last name (for example, "peterk") as your login name.

CAUTION

Names in UNIX systems are case-sensitive. Therefore, a user named *Peter* is different from *peter*, and a file named *UsingUNIX* is different from *usingunix*. Even passwords are case-sensitive.

 T I P If you have trouble logging into the system, check the Caps Lock key on your keyboard. Make sure that it is off.

The Superuser

At this point, you may be thinking about the age-old chicken-and-the-egg question: how can I create the login name for the system administrator so that other login names can be created? Fear not. When the UNIX operating system is installed, a special user called *root* is automatically created. The root user is also referred to as the *Superuser* and has extraordinary privileges—the root user has full and complete access to the UNIX system. When logged in as root, you can do the following and much more:

- Read from or write to any file on the system
- Execute programs that ordinary users cannot
- Reconfigure the UNIX operating system

> **CAUTION**
>
> You should safeguard root's password and change it frequently. Also, do not experiment with the system while you are logged in as root. The Superuser can do a lot of damage easily if not careful.

The Login Prompt

After you have the login name and its password, you are ready to log in to your UNIX system. After you have established a connection with the system, a login dialog similar to the following is displayed on your screen:

```
UNIX(r) System V Release 4.0 (sco1)
Welcome to Software Developement Server SCO1. Unauthorized access not permitted.

login:
```

 TIP If your screen does not have the `login:` prompt on it, check that the screen is powered on and press the Enter key a few times. If `login:` still does not appear, try pressing Ctrl+Q and then Enter.

The first line identifies the version of UNIX running on the system, and the second line is a system-specific banner message (defined by the system administrator).

At the `login:` prompt, enter your login name and press Enter. After a brief pause, the UNIX system asks for your password. Enter your password (if this the first time you are logging onto UNIX, your system administrator will provide you with the password) and press Enter. Note that your password is not echoed on the screen.

> **N O T E** Remember that UNIX passwords are case-sensitive, just like UNIX names. Therefore, make sure that you enter your password carefully with the proper casing. ■

In some rare instances, the login prompt appears in all uppercase letters, as in `LOGIN:`; then everything you enter will also appears in uppercase letters. This occurs when for some reason (perhaps due to configuration error), the UNIX system thinks you have a terminal that can display only uppercase characters. It sends uppercase letters to your screen and translates everything you enter to lowercase for its internal use. When this happens, you might not be able to log in if your login name and/or your password uses both upper- and lowercase characters. You will need to determine the cause and fix the problem before you can log in.

 TIP If your terminal is capable of displaying both upper- and lowercase characters, make sure that the Shift Lock or Caps Lock key on your keyboard is *off*.

After you have logged in, you can use the following command to inform UNIX that your terminal can display both upper- and lowercase characters:

```
$ STTY -LCASE
```

Then you should inform the system administrator that there is a possible misconfiguration causing UNIX to think that your particular terminal is only capable of displaying uppercase letters and have the problem rectified.

Incorrect Login

After you have entered your password, the system checks it. If it passes verification, then the login process continues. If the system displays the following message, after you have entered both your login name and password:

```
Login incorrect
```

then you have either entered your name or password incorrectly, or they are not valid. The message does not differentiate between an unknown login name or an incorrect password. This is to prevent unauthorized users from guessing login names and passwords to gain access to the system.

After the Login incorrect message is displayed, you are asked to enter your login name and password again. Most UNIX systems allow two or three incorrect login attempts before terminating the connection. Should the Login incorrect message persist, seek assistance from your UNIX system administrator.

After You Log In

After UNIX verifies your password, it may print several messages at the end of the login process. The messages are to provide information that might be of interest to you, such as news about system scheduling, availability of new programs, meetings, and so on. After the messages, UNIX prints a prompt to indicate that the system is ready to accept commands from you. The default prompt is usually a currency symbol ($) or a percent sign (%).

N O T E The system administrator can define news flash announcements by placing the necessary text messages in the /etc/mtod file or as files in the /var/news directory.

The following dialog shows the login process. In this dialog, user input is shown in bold (here the user input is the word *peter*):

```
UNIX(r) System V Release 4.0 (sco1)
Welcome to Software Developement Server SCO1. Unauthorized access not permitted.

login: peter
password:
Login incorrect

login: peter
password:
            Welcome to DreamLAN's Software Development System
                    Unauthorized Access is Forbidden

NOTICE: The system will be down between 9:00 pm - 11:00 pm
        for routine maintenance.

$
```

In this dialog, noticed that the login name, *peter*, is echoed on the screen, but the password is not.

Changing Your Password

If you were assigned a password by someone other than yourself (such is the case when you log on to UNIX for the first time), you should change that password immediately to ensure good security. The following shows the process of changing your password using the passwd utility. Depending on the version of UNIX you are using, the messages from passwd and the sequence of the interaction might differ slightly from the following dialog, but the gist of the interaction is the same.

```
$ passwd
New UNIX password:
Retype new UNIX password:
passwd: All authentication tokens updated successfully
```

Again, notice that because of security reasons, none of the passwords that you enter are ever displayed by this or any other utility.

T I P Give some thought to your password. Refer to the "UNIX Password Administration" section later in the chapter for some ideas and guidelines.

CAUTION

Because UNIX passwords are case-sensitive, you must always enter your password exactly the way you created it. If you forget your password, the Superuser can fix things for you. The Superuser cannot determine what your password is, but can change it and tell you your new password.

It is always a good idea to log out and try logging back in after you change your password to make sure that the new password works.

If you have access to another terminal or workstation connected to the same UNIX system, it is best not to log out of your current workstation to test the new password, but use another one to try logging in using the new password. This is in case the new password does not work; you can change it again because you are still logged in. Alas, this trick would not work on all systems. For example, Solaris 2.x requires you to enter your current password as part of the change password process; therefore, if you changed your password and could not log in from another terminal, you have no way to change the password again without assistance from your system administrator.

Logging Out

After you are finished using the UNIX system, you should always log out and not simply turn off your terminal or workstation. More often than not, turning off the terminal or workstation does not disconnect you from UNIX, and the next person using the terminal can gain access to your login session.

Depending on the UNIX shell you are using, you can log out using one of the following methods:

- Press Ctrl+D at the command prompt.
- Issue the exit command.
- Issue the logout command.
- Issue the bye command.
- Issue the quit command.

After a successful logout, you should generally see the login: prompt again.

NOTE You might see another shell prompt instead of the login: prompt after you issue the logout command. This is because you have started another UNIX shell from the current one. To fully log out of the system, continue issuing the logout command until you see the login: prompt.

UNIX Password Administration

A single UNIX system can support many users simultaneously. The only way UNIX can determine whether you are authorized to access the system and to level the access (such as reading a file or deleting a file) is through your (unique) login name. Unless you run a wide-open system where everyone can have full access to anyone's files, you should and need to implement password security.

Need for Security

If you are the UNIX system administrator or someone responsible for setting security policy, ask yourself the following questions to determine whether any security for your UNIX system is needed—and how much:

- Does the system contain vital company confidential information?
- Is the system connected to the outside world at all, either over a network connection or telephone connection?
- Should a user only have access to files and programs that are related to his job functions?

If your answer to any of the preceding questions is yes, then some level of security is warranted.

You can implement many types of security measures, and they vary in cost. For example, if your system is connected to the outside world (such as to the Internet) via a network connection, you can place a *firewall* (a network device that does filtering) between your UNIX system and the outside link. If you have telephone connections, you can implement dial-back security so that when the UNIX system receives a telephone connection, it prompts the user for a name and password, hangs up the phone, and based on the telephone number associated with the given name, calls the user back (so that a person cannot call in using someone else's name unless he is at that phone number for the call-back).

▶ **See** "Private Networks, Firewalls, and NAT," **p. 544**

One of the easiest security measures you can implement is password security. A good password security implementation is like having a good theft-deterrent on your door—the person doing the break-in would not want to spend more than a few minutes trying to crack your password (lock), and good passwords (locks) take a while to break. Best of all, password security is an inherent part of any UNIX system, therefore it's free!

N O T E When implementing a security measure—whether a hardware- or software-based solution— make sure that the measure does not inconvenience users. If it does, users will not use it, thus defeating the purpose of having security.

For example, a good theft-deterrent door is probably a door with a lot of fancy locks, just like a bank vault door. However, it is inconvenient to use, and as a result, most people will probably only use one of many the locks—and that defeats the purpose.

CAUTION

No system can be completely secure from outside attacks. The best thing you can do is to make it difficult to break into and be able to detect and report when your system has been attacked or an attack is underway.

The first part of keeping the system secure is making sure that the hardware cannot be tampered with—the computer must not be physically accessible to anyone without proper authorization. What good would the greatest password protection be if someone walked away with your UNIX system's hard drives and backup tapes? At a minimum, the system should be placed in a locked room.

Picking a Good Password

You should follow some basic rules and guidelines when implementing password security:

- A password should be at least six characters long; UNIX only recognizes the first eight characters in any password.
- Make sure that a password is required so that a user cannot select "blank" as a password.
- A password should not be a single word, such as *secret*, that you can easily find in the dictionary, yet it should be easily remembered. You can put two or more words together, such as *issecret* (is secret).

TIP In the late 1980s, a student from Cornell University released a worm program (not a virus because it does not make changes to files or the operating system) onto the Internet. This program contained a list of "commonly" used passwords that the student had used, with a more than 80 percent success rate, to break into UNIX systems. Table 2.1 shows this list, and you should *avoid* using these words for your passwords.

- When possible, a password should contain a mix of uppercase letters, lowercase letters, and digits. For example, *Secret45*.
- The password should not be similar to your login name.

TIP Not only should a good password not be similar to your login name, but it also should *not* be similar to your first or last name, your initials, your spouse's name, your pet's name, the model of your car, your child's name, your birthday, your employee ID number, or anything that is normally associated with you.

Table 2.1   Words to Avoid Using for Passwords

aaa	cornelius	guntis	noxious	simon
academia	couscous	hacker	nutrition	simple
aerobics	creation	hamlet	nyquist	singer
airplane	creosote	handily	oceanography	single
albany	cretin	happening	ocelot	smile
albatross	daemon	harmony	olivetti	smiles
albert	dancer	harold	olivia	smooch
alex	daniel	harvey	oracle	smother
alexander	danny	hebrides	orca	snatch
algebra	dave	heinlein	orwell	snoopy
aliases	december	hello	osiris	soap

alphabet	defoe	help	outlaw	socrates
ama	deluge	herbert	oxford	sossina
amorphous	desperate	hiawatha	pacific	sparrows
analog	develop	hibernia	painless	spit
anchor	dieter	honey	pakistan	spring
andromache	digital	horse	pam	springer
animals	discovery	horus	papers	squires
answer	disney	hutchins	password	strangle
anthropogenic	dog	imbroglio	patricia	stratford
anvils	drought	imperial	penguin	stuttgart
anything	duncan	include	peoria	subway
aria	eager	ingres	percolate	success
ariadne	easier	inna	persimmon	summer
arrow	edges	innocuous	persona	super
arthur	edinburgh	irishman	pete	superstage
athena	edwin	isis	peter	support
atmosphere	edwina	japan	philip	supported
aztecs	egghead	jessica	phoenix	surfer
azure	eiderdown	jester	pierre	suzanne
bacchus	eileen	jixian	pizza	swearer
bailey	einstein	johnny	plover	symmetry
banana	elephant	joseph	plymouth	tangerine
bananas	elizabeth	joshua	polynomial	tape
bandit	ellen	judith	pondering	target
banks	emerald	juggle	pork	tarragon
barber	engine	julia	poster	taylor
baritone	engineer	kathleen	praise	telephone
bass	enterprise	kermit	precious	temptation
bassoon	enzyme	kernel	prelude	thailand
batman	ersatz	kirkland	prince	tiger
beater	establish	knight	princeton	toggle

Part

I

Ch

2

continues

Table 2.1   Continued

beauty	estate	ladle	protect	tomato
beethoven	euclid	lambda	protozoa	topography
beloved	evelyn	lamination	pumpkin	tortoise
benz	extension	larkin	puneet	toyota
beowulf	fairway	larry	puppet	trails
berkeley	felicia	lazarus	rabbit	trivial
berliner	fender	lebesgue	rachmaninoff	trombone
beryl	fermat	lee	rainbow	tubas
beverly	fidelity	leland	raindrop	tuttle
bicameral	finite	leroy	raleigh	umesh
bob	fishers	lewis	random	unhappy
brenda	flakes	light	rascal	unicorn
brian	float	lisa	really	unknown
bridget	flower	louis	rebecca	urchin
broadway	flowers	lynne	remote	utility
bumbling	foolproof	macintosh	rick	vasant
burgess	football	mack	ripple	vertigo
campanile	foresight	maggot	robotics	vicky
cantor	format	magic	rochester	village
cardinal	forsythe	malcolm	rolex	virginia
carmen	fourier	mark	romano	warren
carolina	fred	markus	ronald	water
caroline	friend	marty	rosebud	weenie
cascades	frighten	marvin	rosemary	whatnot
castle	fun	master	roses	whiting
cat	fungible	maurice	ruben	whitney
cayuga	gabriel	mellon	rules	will
celtics	gardner	merlin	ruth	william
cerulean	garfield	mets	sal	williamsburg

change	gauss	michael	saxon	willie
charles	george	michelle	scamper	winston
charming	gertrude	mike	scheme	wisconsin
charon	ginger	minimum	scott	wizard
chester	glacier	minsky	scotty	wombat
cigar	gnu	moguls	secret	woodwind
classic	golfer	moose	sensor	wormwood
clusters	gorgeous	morley	serenity	yaco
coffee	gorges	mozart	sharks	yang
coke	gosling	nancy	sharon	yellowstone
collins	gouge	napoleon	sheffield	yosemite
commrades	graham	nepenthe	sheldon	zap
computer	gryphon	ness	shiva	zimmerman
condo	guest	network	shivers	
cookie	guitar	newton	shuttle	
cooper	gumption	next	signature	

Finally, regardless of how good you think your password is, change it regularly. This goes double for the Superuser password.

> **CAUTION**
>
> You often see in movies that computer hackers find important passwords taped to workstations and under keyboards. Don't laugh; it is true (and sad) that it does happen in the real world. A password should be remembered. It should never be written down—anywhere. On the other hand, if you are the system administrator, you should keep a written record of root's password in safe storage, such as a safe or in a bank vault where only upper management can have access. This way, should something happen to you, the root password is not entirely lost.

Implementing Password Aging

You can configure most UNIX systems so that users are required to change their passwords regularly. This is called *password aging*. With password aging enabled, if someone gains access by guessing a password, that person's access to the system is limited in the future to the time when the password changes.

One disadvantage of changing passwords is that users have to choose new passwords—and they might not be as conscientious as they ought to be about choosing good passwords after a few changes. You might even find users flipping back-and-forth between two passwords. This, unfortunately, is unavoidable, and user education is the best solution. ▦

From Here...

This chapter provided you with the basic login and logout procedures of the UNIX operating system. Password security essentials such as changing your password, selecting a good password, and password aging were covered.

■ For detailed information on how to create new user accounts and administer user passwords, see Chapter 10, "Administering User Accounts and Groups."

■ For a discussion of UNIX shells and commonly used commands and utilities, see Chapter 3, "UNIX Shells and System Commands."

■ For a discussion of network firewall devices, see Chapter 21, "Advanced Networking."

■ For a discussion of login security, secure administration, and data encryption, see Chapter 26, "Security."

UNIX Shells and System Commands

by Peter Kuo

What Is a UNIX Shell?

Computers are dumb. You need to tell the computer exactly what you want it to do for you. To communicate with the computer, people have developed *command languages* to control a computer's operation. Most command languages are designed so that easy commands specify command operations, such as copy or delete. However, computers do not have the capability to decipher the command you enter at the terminal; a *command interpreter* performs the translation from human-readable commands into computer-understood commands. Depending on the operating system, the command interpreter is known by different names. In UNIX, the command interpreter is called a *shell*.

The shell provides a wealth of functions and features that make it possible to specify powerful commands. Some people would like to think that, given the proper hardware, you could ask a UNIX shell to make coffee and eggs for you exactly the way you want them in the morning! To use the UNIX system effectively, you have to know how to enter shell commands, and the most commonly used shell commands are discussed in this chapter.

What Shell Am I Using?

After you log in to UNIX, the operating system places you in your home directory and runs a shell program. If you are using a version of UNIX that has a GUI, such as UnixWare, the graphical desktop starts up after you're logged in; you can get to a command line by starting a terminal session.

A number of different UNIX shells are available today. The most common shell programs are as follows:

- Bourne shell (sh), named after its developer Steven Bourne of AT&T Bell Labs.
- C shell (csh), by Bill Joy, was originally developed for the BSD UNIX distributions and is now part of System V.
- Korn shell (ksh), developed David Korn and is based on the Bourne shell but with C shell extensions.

You can do a lot without knowing or worrying about the shell you are using. But if you are curious, you can get a good idea of which shell you are currently running by noting the shell prompt. Although you can easily change the shell prompt, the default prompts are as follows:

- Bourne shell uses the dollar sign ($).
- C shell uses the percent sign (%).
- Korn shell uses the dollar sign ($).

There are other ways of finding out what your default shell is. Following are two of these methods:

- Examine the /etc/passwd file. Your default shell is listed in the last field (each field is separated by a colon). For example, the following sample /etc/password file shows that the default shell for root and Peter is the C shell, and for Sally it is the Korn shell:

```
root:*:0:0:Super User:/root:/bin/csh
peter:*:67:67:System Admin:/usr/home/peter:/csh
sally:*:777:777:System Backups:/usr/home/sally:/bin/ksh
```

▪ Issue the ps command (discussed in more detail later in this chapter) right after you log
   in. You should see two commands listed; one is your ps command, and the other is your
   shell:

```
% ps
  PID  TT  STAT     TIME COMMAND
29326  p5  Ss     0:00.06 -csh (csh)
29380  p5  R+     0:00.00 ps
%
```

Choosing a Shell

The UNIX shells available today are derived from either the Bourne Shell or the C Shell or a
combination of both, and these two designs were heavily influenced by the obsolete Version 6
shell. Therefore, in many areas all shells are similar. Their standard features, syntax, and nota-
tions are extremely close. However, the areas of difference are deep. For example, both the
Bourne shell and the C shell contain many of the features of a programming language, but
these features are totally incompatible. Another incompatibility is that the C shell has features
for interactive command entry, such as job control, aliases, and a command history mechanism, that are not found in the Bourne shell.

Many seasoned UNIX users recommend the C shell for interactive use and the Bourne shell
for writing shell command scripts. However, this means that you need to learn two separate
command sets. Fortunately, unless you plan to write many shell scripts, knowing just the C
shell is generally sufficient. However, if you do plan to write shell scripts that are highly portable, knowledge of Bourne shell is an asset because Bourne shell is widely available.

N O T E You can write shell scripts using the C shell, but because the complete C shell relies on
some of Berkeley's kernel modifications, implementations of it on other UNIX systems are
often slightly different. Your C shell scripts may not work perfectly on other systems. ▪

If available on your UNIX system, the Korn shell is probably your best alternative to the
Bourne/C shell dilemma. The Korn shell is compatible with the Bourne shell, but it contains
additional components that make it superior even to the C shell in its interactive capabilities. In
addition, the Korn shell is extremely efficient.

Other than the previously mentioned "standard" UNIX shells, a number of other shells also are
available. Without going into detail, the other shells are listed here for your reference because
you may encounter them in your travels:

▪ Bourne Again shell (bash), written by the Free Software Foundation as part of the GNU
   project.

▪ Pd-ksh (pdksh) is a public domain implementation of AT&T's Korn shell. Although a
   close clone of the Korn shell, Pd-ksh is missing some of the more advanced features that
   make the Korn shell a powerful language for writing shell scripts.

■ TC shell (tcsh), is an expanded version of the C shell. tcsh has a number of nice features not found in csh, such as command-line editing and spelling correction.

■ Z shell (zsh) combines many features of the Bourne Again shell, TC shell, and Korn shell and incorporates some new features. zsh most closely resembles the Korn shell.

N O T E Regardless of the UNIX shell you use, all the commands and concepts discussed in this chapter apply equally. However, the examples illustrated in this chapter use the C shell because it is available for every UNIX flavor. If you are using another shell, the behavior of the shell or the exact format or wording of the shell output may differ from what you see here. ■

You can easily switch from one shell to another. A UNIX shell is really a program, so to switch from, for example, C shell to Korn shell, you simply run the shell:

```
% ps
  PID  TT  STAT      TIME COMMAND
29326  p5  Ss     0:00.06 -csh (csh)
29380  p5  R+     0:00.00 ps
% ksh
$
```

In the preceding example, you are running the C shell (as indicated by the -csh. By typing ksh, you switch into the Korn shell (as indicated by the dollar sign prompt).

CAUTION

The invoking of another shell does not terminate the original shell. Therefore, in the preceding example, your "current" shell is Korn, but it is running under the C shell. When you type exit at the Korn shell prompt, you are returned to the C shell. Because UNIX multitasks, you can have many shells running without knowing it.

The best way to permanently change your default shell is to have the entry updated in the /etc/passwd file. This needs to be done by the system administrator because users don't normally have write access to the /etc directory.

▶ **See** "Modifying User Accounts," **p. 251**

Navigating Directories

On any system that supports a lot of storage capacity, it is always crucial to know how to navigate around the directory structures. UNIX provides two important commands that permit you to find out or change your current directory.

▶ **See** "The UNIX File and Directory Structure," **p. 112**

The *pwd* Command

The name of the current directory in which you are working is probably the most basic piece of information about your current environment. You can use the pwd (print current directory) command to show the name of your current (working) directory.

On a UNIX system, files are stored in various directories. At any given time, just one of these directories is your current working directory. And your shell commands affect the files and subdirectories in this working area. When you log on to the system, the current directory is your *home directory*, where you have full rights to do whatever you want to the files and subdirectories there. You can move from directory to directory using the cd command, discussed in a later section in this chapter. It is generally a good idea to make sure that you have landed in the desired directory before you start executing other commands.

> **CAUTION**
>
> Because UNIX filenames are case sensitive, it is possible—although not a good idea—to have one directory called `Projects` and another called `projects`. It is an easy mistake to move to the `projects` directory when you really want the `Projects` directory. Therefore, it is good practice to use the pwd command to verify that you are in the right directory before you start deleting any files. Better yet, establish a naming convention for your directories. For example, some people use uppercase letters for directory names and lowercase letters for all regular filenames.

Immediately after logging in, you're placed in your home directory. Let's say that your home directory is /usr/home/genuser. If you execute the pwd command immediately after logging in, then /usr/home/genuser is displayed:

```
% pwd
/usr/home/genuser
%
```

 T I P To help identify the directory you are currently in, you can modify your shell prompt to include the current directory name. For example, in C shell:

```
% set prompt="`pwd` %"
```

includes the name of your working directory as part of the shell prompt, and the prompt looks something like this:

```
/usr/home/peter %
```

▶ **See** "Shell Variables," **p. 163**

The *cd* Command

The cd (change directory) command changes the current working directory to the named directory. For example:

```
% pwd
/usr/home/peter
% cd /usr/home/sally
% pwd
/usr/home/sally
%
```

CAUTION

If you are familiar with DOS, you will find the cd command works exactly the same way in UNIX with two exceptions. In DOS, if you don't specify a directory name when you give the cd command, the current working directory's name is displayed (just like the UNIX pwd command). However, in UNIX, if you don't specify a directory name when you give the cd command, the new directory will be your home directory. The other exception is the use of slash ("/") versus backslash ("\") in the directory path as explained in the following Note.

N O T E You will no doubt notice by now that UNIX directory paths are specified using the forward slash ("/") rather than the backslash ("\") you're so accustomed to in DOS. Don't use the backslash lightly because backslashes in UNIX have special meaning. A backslash stops the shell from giving a special character (known as a metacharacter), such as "*", its special meaning (wildcard, in this case). See the "Special Characters" section later in this chapter for more information. ■

 You can create an alias for cd that prints your current directory name after you have changed directory. Place the command:

```
alias cd 'cd \!*;pwd'
```

in the .cshrc file, if you are using the C shell. If the UNIX shell you are using doesn't support aliases, you can create a shell script instead.

▶ **See** "Introduction to Shell Programming," **p. 154**

The pathname argument to cd may be either an absolute pathname (as shown in the preceding example) or a relative pathname, which is shown in the following example:

```
% pwd
/etc/home/sally
% cd ../peter
% pwd
/etc/home/peter
% cd Projects/UNIX.Book
% pwd
/etc/home/peter/Projects/UNIX.Book
%
```

The double dots ("..", a pseudonym for the parent directory) in the first cd command moves the working directory "up one level" and then "down" to a child directory called peter; you can move up multiple levels in the directory tree by specifying multiple ".." in the pathname (for example, cd ../.. moves you up two levels). The second cd command makes the current directory the child directory named UNIX.Book of the child directory named Projects. Note that the second cd path starts where the first one finished.

N O T E Although ".." is the pseudonym for the parent directory, "." is the pseudonym for the current directory. You may already be familiar with them from using DOS—DOS "borrowed" this naming convention from UNIX. ■

Listing Files and Directories

The vast majority of UNIX commands manipulate files and directories. The basic command to list files and directories is `ls`. The way `ls` displays file and directory names depends on what version of UNIX you are using and the `ls` command-line options used.

The *ls* Command

If you use the `ls` command in a pipe (pipe is explained later in this chapter), every name is displayed on a line by itself. This is also the default for some versions of UNIX such as SCO. Other versions of UNIX list files in several columns. For most uses, the columnar format is more convenient; systems that list names one per line often have an alternative command, usually named `lc`, for listing names in column format.

Each argument to the `ls` command is either the name of a file, the name of a directory, or one or more options. The options are used to control the ordering of the list of files and information that is printed for each file. For each file argument, the requested information is printed. For each directory argument the requested information is printed for all the files in the directory (unless the `-d` option is used).

Options used with the `ls` command can be listed separately or concatenated. This means the following commands are effectively identical:

```
ls -l -F
ls -lF
```

Table 3.1 shows some of the most frequently used `ls` command options.

Table 3.1   Frequently Used *ls* Command Options

Option	Description
-a	Lists all entries. By default, `ls` does not show any files whose names begin with a period ("."), and the `-a` option forces these files to be displayed.
-d	Forces `ls` to only print the requested information for a directory and not its contents. Normally, all the directories named in the argument list are searched, and the requested information is printed for all the files in those directories.
-F	Marks directories with a trailing slash ("/"), executable files with a trailing asterisk ("*"), and symbolic links with a trailing at sign ("@").
-i	Prints each file's inode number in the first column of the listing. If you list files that are linked, notice that both files have the same inode number.
-l	The long-list option is used to print detailed information (such as owner and size in bytes) about each listed file. The default is to only print the filenames.
-n	Lists the user and group ID numbers, instead of names, associated with each file and directory.

continues

Part

I

Ch

3

Table 3.1   Continued

Option	Description
-r	Reverses the order of sort.
-s	Gives the size of each file, including any indirect blocks used to map the file, in KB (Berkeley) or 512-byte blocks (System V).
-t	Lists the files sorted according to each file's modification date. The most recently modified files are printed first.
-u	Uses the last access time instead of modification time.

N O T E If a command takes a filename as its argument, you must specify any options before the filename. For example, `ls -l testfile` is valid, but `ls testfile -l` is not.

▶ **See** "Symbolic Links," **p. 120**

▶ **See** "The Inode Table," **p. 129**

▶ **See** "Understanding UIDs and GIDs," **p. 242**

If no files or directories are named in the arguments, then the contents of the current directory are listed. By default, the names are listed in alphabetical order. One thing that confuses many UNIX users, especially novices, is the difference between the `ls` command and the `ls *` command.

The `ls` command has no argument, so by default a list of files in the current directory is displayed. The `ls *` command uses the *metacharacter* (character that has a special meaning to the shell; see the "Special Characters" section later in the chapter) "*" to match the names of all files in the current directory, including directories. Therefore, this command provides the `ls` command with one argument for every file in the current directory. For ordinary files, the two commands produce the same output, but when subdirectories are present, the first command lists only the subdirectory name, whereas the second command lists the subdirectory's name and its contents (because the subdirectories are explicitly mentioned in the argument list). In the following example, `passwd_old` is a file, and the other three files are directories:

```
% ls
passwd_old        public_ftp      public_html     www_logs
% ls *
passwd_old

Files:
order.frm

public_ftp:
BETA              dsqmover.zip    mig2nds.zip     ndslogin.zip    script.zip
Freeware          etc             ndsadm2.zip     ndsright.zip    ssi-demo.zip
an304x.zip        fstrust.zip     ndscount.zip    ndstime.zip     toolkit.old
bin               incoming        ndsdir.zip      ndstree.zip     toolkit.zip
dspass.zip        makesu.zip      ndsedit.zip     outgoing
```

```
public_html:
NSC_SysOps       dsqmover.htm     money.gif        note.gif         safe.gif
an304x.zip       earth3s.gif      ncstool.gif      notice.gif       saw2.gif

www_logs:
www.980729       www.980803       www.980808       www.980813       www.980818
%
```

N O T E In multicolumn output mode, the files are listed column-wise and not row-wise as you
might expect. ▨

It is important to understand the wealth of information provided by the `-l` (lowercase L) option. This option is the only way to discover key information, such as file type, ownership, and
security, associated with each file. The long-format output of the `ls` command contains, typically, seven fields:

Part

I

Ch

3

- ▨ Mode   It shows both the file type and the privileges (such as read, write) associated
  with the file.
- ▨ Links   Number of names associated with the file.
- ▨ Owner   Name of file owner.
- ▨ Group   Name of the group that can access this file.
- ▨ File size   Size of file (in bytes if BSD or blocks if System V).
- ▨ Modification date   Time stamp of last file modification.
- ▨ Filename   Name of the file.

▶ **See** "Owners, Groups, and Permissions," **p. 122**

CAUTION

Do not confuse the `ls -l` (lowercase L) command with the `ls -1` (numeric one) command. On some
systems, the `-1` option is used to force a single-column output from `ls`.

N O T E The output of the `ls -l` command on your system might be somewhat different from the
example shown because the format varies slightly from system to system. For example, on
Berkeley systems, the group information isn't shown unless the `-g` option is specified. ▨

The following is a sample output of an `ls -l` command:

```
% ls -l /etc/passwd
-rw-r—r—  1 root  adm    19797 Aug 20 05:58 /etc/passwd
%
```

It is interesting to note that the modification date field does not contain "year" information.

Filename Generation

When you give the shell abbreviated filenames that contain special characters, or *metacharacters*, the shell can generate filenames that match the names of existing files. These special characters are also referred to as *wildcards* because they act as the jokers in a deck of cards in certain card games. When one of these special characters appears in a command's argument list, the shell expands that argument into a list of filenames and passes the list to the program that the command line calls.

N O T E   Filenames that contain metacharacters are sometimes called *ambiguous file references* because they do not refer to any one specific file. The process that the shell performs on these filenames is called *pathname expansion* or *globbing*. ■

The five special characters ("*", "?", "[", "]", and "-") used in filename generation and pathname expansion are discussed in the following sections.

The "*" Wildcard   The asterisk ("*") is the most universal wildcard and is often used. It simply means *any and all characters*. For example, the string "a*" means all files beginning with the letter "a". You can use as many asterisks in a single expression as you need to define a set of files. For example, the expression *xx*.dat defines any filename with the extension dat that has xx anywhere in the rest of the name. Matches include the filenames abxx.dat, 1xx33.dat, xxyyzz.dat, and the simple name xx.dat.

The "?" Wildcard   The question mark ("?") represents a *single* occurrence of any character. Thus the string "???" represents all files whose names consist of just three characters. You can generate a list of files with three-character extensions with the string *.???. For example, if you're searching a directory containing graphics images as well as other data, the following command lists all files with extensions such as tif, jpg, and gif as well as any other files with three-character extensions:

```
ls *.???
```

The "[]" Expression   Sometimes you might need to be more selective in generating the file or pathnames than either of the general-purpose wildcards allows. Suppose you that want to select the files job1, job2, and job4 but not job3 or any other jobx. It is not possible to accomplish this using the "?" wildcard because it represents one occurrence of any character. You can, however, use job[123]. Like the question mark, items inside the square brackets ("[]") represent exactly one character—a specific character.

Using the square brackets, you can select a discrete series of permissible values such as [124], which allows only the characters 1, 2, or 4. You can also describe a range of characters such as [A-Z], which represents any characters between uppercase A and uppercase Z, inclusive. You can also specify a set of ranges such as [1-3, 5-8, a-e, A-E].

CAUTION

When using ranges, remember that what is included in the range depends on the character set used. Most UNIX systems use the ASCII character set, but some systems use the IBM EBCDIC character set. The range you specify is between the characters specified by the character's sort sequence.

For instance, [9-B] in the ASCII character set specifies the following characters:

9 : ; < = > ? @ A B

However, in the EBCDIC character set, it is an invalid range, and the result is unpredictable.

It is interesting to note that the hyphen ("-") loses its role as a metacharacter when it is used outside the square brackets. Conversely, the asterisk and the question mark lose their power as metacharacters when they are used within the square brackets. For example, `-[*?]abc` matches exactly two filenames: `-*abc` and `-?abc`.

TIP Although possible, it is best to avoid creating filenames that contain dashes, asterisks, question marks, or other metacharacters.

Special Characters

Special characters, or metacharacters, are characters that have a special meaning to the shell. Avoid using any of these characters in a filename because files with metacharacters in their names are somewhat tricky to access, and certain programs might not be able to access them at all. The standard special characters are as follows:

& ; ¦ * ? ' " ` [ ] ( ) $ < > { } ^ # / \ % ! ~

N O T E The ~/ combination can be used to reference your home directory. Therefore, cd ~/ changes your working directory to that of your home directory.

Similarly, ~*username* can be used to reference that user's home directory. For example, cd ~peter changes your current directory to the home directory of user peter. Do keep in mind that not all UNIX utilities support this shortcut. ▣

Although not considered special characters, Return, Spacebar, and Tab also have special meaning to the shell. Return usually ends a command line and initiates execution of a command. The Space and Tab characters separate elements on the command line and are collectively known as *white spaces* or *blanks*.

In you need to use one of the metacharacters as a regular character, you can *quote* it. Another often used term with the same meaning as quote is *escape*: You can escape a metacharacter. The shell treats a quoted metacharacter as a regular character. There are three ways to quote, or escape, a character:

■ Precede it with a backslash ("\"). One backslash must precede each character that you are quoting. If you're using two or more metacharacters, you must precede each with a backslash. For example, ** must be entered as **. You can quote a backslash just as you would quote any other metacharacters—by preceding it with a backslash (for example, "\\").

■ Enclose the metacharacters between single quotation marks, for example '**'. You can quote many special and regular characters between a pair of single quotation marks, for example, '* and ? are wildcards'. The regular characters remain regular, and the shell also treats the special characters as regular characters.

■ Enclose the metacharacters between double quotation marks, for example, "**". As with single quotation marks, you can quote many meta and regular characters between a pair of double quotation marks.

> **CAUTION**
>
> The only way to quote control characters, such as Ctrl-h and Ctrl-m, is to precede each with a Ctrl-v. Quotation marks and backslashes don't work for control characters.

The most commonly used quoting method is to use backslashes.

Viewing Files

The UNIX system was originally designed with text-processing in mind. Therefore, it contains a rich set of utilities for manipulating text files. As a result, you can display a file on your terminal in more than one way.

Using *cat* to View Files

For displaying short ASCII files, the simplest command is cat. The name of the command is derived from *catenate*, which means to join together one after the other. The cat command takes a single file or a list of files and prints the contents unaltered on your screen:

```
% cat /etc/greeting
Welcome to BSD 4.3
% cat /etc/motd
The system will be unavailable between 9:00-10:00 pm
for regular system maintenance.
% cat /etc/greeting /etc/motd
Welcome to BSD 4.3
The system will be unavailable between 9:00-10:00 pm
for regular system maintenance.
%
```

The cat command may be used to display a file of arbitrary size. But it is generally used to send the contents of a *short* file to your screen. If you try to display a large file, the file will scroll past your screen as fast as the screen can handle the character stream without pausing. Unless you have a slow connection between your terminal and the UNIX host or you can read really fast, cat is not a suitable tool for displaying large files.

Using *more* to View Files

The more program displays one screenful of data at a time so it is much more suitable for displaying large files. It was first developed for the Berkeley UNIX, but it proved to be so useful that it has become a standard for all versions of UNIX. However, because more has been rewritten many times, its behavior on different versions of UNIX is slightly different.

Just like cat, more can display one or a list of files on your screen. The simplest form of the more command is more *filename*. It displays a screenful of data and then pauses (if the contents don't fit on one screen), and the name of the file is displayed on the last line of the screen (some implementations simply show "—more—") along with the percentage of the file displayed, as shown in Figure 3.1. To continue on to the next screenful, press the Spacebar; if you press Return, only the next line is displayed. To stop viewing the file, press "q".

FIGURE 3.1
Using more to display a large ASCII file.

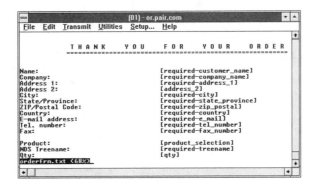

N O T E more determines how many lines your terminal can display using the $TERM variable and the information in the terminal database. ▪

▶ **See** "Terminal Settings," **p. 319**

The more program allows you to search for strings in the file being displayed. The search syntax is /*string*. If the string is found, a new page is displayed with the line containing the matching string at the top of the screen. Should the need arise, you can "jump" to the shell using the ! command. When you escape to the shell with the ! command, you are actually in a subshell; you must exit the subshell and return to more using either exit or Ctrl-d.

N O T E One serious disadvantage of using more instead of another viewer program, such as pg or less, is that many implementations of more allow you to only scroll and search forward in the file; you can't go back to a previous screen. ▪

Using *head* to Look at the Top of a File

There will be times that you simply want to check the beginning of a file to make sure that it is the file you want. The head program can be used to display the beginning of a file. The head utility displays the first ten lines of a file, by default. For instance, you have a file named months that contains the names of the 12 months of the year in order (one per line); the command head months displays January through October. You can also include a -*n* parameter in your head command to display the first *n* lines of a file. For example,

```
% head -1 months
January
%
```

displays only the first line of months.

N O T E   head is part of BSD UNIX and might not be available with your version of UNIX.

Using *tail* to Look at the End of a File

The tail program allows you to display the end of a large file without having to sit through a tedious display of the entire file. Similar to head, tail displays the last ten lines of a file by default. Therefore, the command tail months displays March through December. You can also include a -*n* parameter in your tail command to display the last *n* lines of a file. For example,

```
% tail -1 months
December
%
```

displays only the last line of months.

N O T E   There is a limit to how far tail can read back from the end of a file. In such cases, you can put a plus in front of *n* to cause tail to skip that many lines from the start of the file and then print the rest. For example, tail +10 months skips the first ten lines in the file and prints the last two lines of the file months.

Dumping Files

Occasionally, you want to know exactly what binary codes are contained in a file. For instance, a text file may contain an unprintable character, such as a tab, and causes some applications to misbehave when accessing this file. If you were to cat the file onto your screen or send the file to a printer, the UNIX device handler or your terminal or printer would automatically expand the tabs into the correct number of spaces. However, you can "dump" the contents of the file using one of the many file dump utilities, such as od or hexdump, supplied with UNIX and look for \t in the output that indicates a tab.

N O T E   The term "dump" originated many years ago when program debugging was usually performed by producing a printout of all the values in memory following a program failure. Because of the huge quantity of information, the printout was called a dump.

During a dump using od (octal dump), printable characters are displayed normally, and unprintable characters are printed in octal except for a few standard characters, which are represented as shown in Table 3.2.

Table 3.2 Special Character Representations Used by *od*

\b	Backspace	\r	Carriage Return
\t	Tab	\0	Null
\n	New Line	\f	Form Feed

The following is an example of how to use od and hexdump to dump a file called days in ASCII (by using the -c option) format:

```
% cat days
Monday          Tuesday
Wednesday       Thursday
Friday          Saturday
Sunday
% od -c days
0000000   M   o   n   d   a   y  \t  \t   T   u   e   s   d   a   y  \n
0000020   W   e   d   n   e   s   d   a   y  \t   T   h   u   r   s   d
0000040   a   y  \n   F   r   i   d   a   y  \t  \t   S   a   t   u   r
0000060   d   a   y  \n   S   u   n   d   a   y  \n
0000073
% hexdump -c days
0000000   M   o   n   d   a   y  \t  \t   T   u   e   s   d   a   y  \n
0000010   W   e   d   n   e   s   d   a   y  \t   T   h   u   r   s   d
0000020   a   y  \n   F   r   i   d   a   y  \t  \t   S   a   t   u   r
0000030   d   a   y  \n   S   u   n   d   a   y  \n
000003b
%
```

If you dump the file without using the -c option, the output is all in octal (if using od) or hexadecimal (if using hexdump) numbers and is rather useless:

```
% od days
0000000   067515 062156 074541 004411 072524 071545 060544 005171
0000020   062527 067144 071545 060544 004571 064124 071165 062163
0000040   074541 043012 064562 060544 004571 051411 072141 071165
0000060   060544 005171 072523 062156 074541 000012
0000073
% hexdump days
0000000 6f4d 646e 7961 0909 7554 7365 6164 0a79
0000010 6557 6e64 7365 6164 0979 6854 7275 6473
0000020 7961 460a 6972 6164 0979 5309 7461 7275
0000030 6164 0a79 7553 646e 7961 000a
000003b
%
```

Working with Files and Directories

UNIX provides a number of utilities for you to manipulate and organize the files you create. The utilities perform various tasks involving files and directories, including copying, moving, and deleting.

Copying Files and Directories with *cp*

The cp (copy) utility makes a copy of a file. It can copy any file, including text and executable program files. You must be able to read the file and have write access to the directory to which you are copying the file before cp can be executed successfully. If your cp command fails, check the rights to the source file and the destination directory using the ls -l command.

▶ **See** "Viewing Permissions," **p. 123**

N O T E If you are overwriting a file, you also need to have write access to the file. ▪

A cp command specifies source and destination files with the following syntax:

```
cp source-file destination-file
```

The *source-file* is the name of the file that cp is going to copy, and the *destination-file* is the name that cp assigns to the resulting copy of the file. If the *destination-file* is a directory, then cp copies the *source-file* into that directory:

```
% ls *
Backup          chapter3

Backup:
chapter1        chapter2
% cp chapter3 Backup
% ls *
Backup          chapter3

Backup:
chapter1        chapter2        chapter3
%
```

> **CAUTION**
>
> If the destination file exists before you give a cp command, cp overwrites it (thus destroying its content) without warning you. Therefore, take care not to cause cp to overwrite a file that you need. It is generally a good idea to include the -i option (interactive) in the cp command (for example, cp -i source-file destination-file) so that you are prompted before cp overwrites a file.

TIP You can create an alias for cp that includes the -i option. Place the command:

```
alias cp 'cp -i'
```

in the .cshrc file, if you are using the C shell.

You can copy several source files if (and only if) the destination file is a directory. The command `cp file1 file2 file3 mydir` copies all three source files into the `mydir` directory. If `mydir` is not a directory but a file, `cp` returns an error message.

> **CAUTION**
>
> You are not allowed to use a directory file as the source file for a copy operation.

Moving and Renaming Files with *mv*

In UNIX, moving and renaming files are accomplished with the same command, `mv`. The syntax and rules are the same for `mv` as they are for the copy command, `cp`. That is, you can move as many files as you want to a directory, but the directory name must be last in the list, and you must have write access to that directory.

One thing you can do with `mv` that you can't do with `cp` is move or rename directories. When you move or rename a file, the only thing that happens is that the entry in the directory table is changed (unless the new location is on another physical drive or partition, in which case the file and the contents of the directory are physically moved). For `mv` to rename directories, the source and target directory must have the same parent. If `mydir` is a directory, then the command `mv mydir mynewdir` is legal because both directories have the same parent directory (that is, both are at the same level within the directory tree structure). The command `mv mydir ../mynewdir` is illegal because they don't have the same parent directory. (Some versions of UNIX, such as BSD, may be more flexible than described here.)

N O T E The mv utility does not move directories from one file system to another. You can use `tar` or `cpio` for this purpose. ▨

▶ **See** "Using `tar`," **p. 387**

▶ **See** "Using `cpio`," **p. 389**

Deleting Files and Directories with *rm*

The `rm` (remove) UNIX command allows you to delete a file. To remove a file, you must have write rights in the directory containing the file, but you need neither read nor write access for the file itself. This is because removing a file actually removes an entry from a directory—thus, the write access to the directory governs your capability to create or delete files (in that directory).

N O T E If you don't have write access to the file you're deleting, rm may, as a precaution, ask whether you really want to remove that file:

```
% ls -l temp.*
-rw-r—r—  1 peter   users   59 Aug 23 13:51 temp.1
-r—r—r—   1 peter   users   59 Aug 23 13:52 temp.bak
% rm temp.bak
```

continues

continued

```
override r—r—r—  peter/users for temp.bak? y
% ls -l temp.*
-rw-r—r—  1 peter  users  59 Aug 23 13:51 temp.1
%
```

Some versions of UNIX show the permission in octal notation instead of the symbolic form, as in the preceding above. ▨

▶ **See** "Viewing Permissions," **p. 123**

Be careful when you use rm because removed files really are gone. The only way to recover a deleted file is to ask the system administrator to restore a copy from a recent backup, but you may not necessarily get the latest version of your file back. Therefore, whenever you're in doubt, refrain from deleting a file until you have a chance to double check first. Wildcards are useful in saving time typing a long list of filenames, but be *very* careful when using wildcards with the rm command.

▶ **See** "Implementing a Backup Strategy," **p. 380**

The command rm * removes all files (but not directories) in your current directory, without warning or prompting. Don't use this command unless you're clearing out a directory with certainty. Two frequently used options for the rm command are as follows:

▨ -i (interactive)   When this option is specified, rm asks whether you really want to remove every mentioned file:

```
% ls temp.*
temp.1     temp.bak
% rm -i temp.1 temp.bak
rm: remove temp.1?  y
rm: remove temp.bak?  n
% ls temp.*
temp.bak
%
```

Any reply starting with a "y" or "yes" causes the file to be removed; any other reply causes the file to be retained. The -i option is helpful in preventing you from deleting all files from a directory by mistake.

TIP

Just like cp, you can create an alias for rm that includes the -i option. Place the command:

```
alias rm 'rm -i'
```

in the .cshrc file, if you are using the C shell.

CAUTION

The -i option is implemented in Version 7, System V, and BSD UNIX systems. However, the option may not be present on older (or variant) UNIX systems. For example, on most Version 6 systems, rm -i * removes every file in the current directory and then complains that the file -i is not found.

■ -r (recursive) This option can be used to remove a directory, all its contents, and all the files and directories in that directory's subtree. For example, rm -r Backup removes the directory Backup and all its files, subdirectories, and so on.

N O T E There is also an -f (force) option that you can use. This forces the removal of a file without prompting you for confirmation—a dangerous feature. Don't use it if you can avoid it. ■

Creating and Removing Directories

There are no fixed rules in UNIX on organizing files. Unlike some operating systems, such as DOS or VMS, files do not have to have specific extensions (such as EXE for executable programs). Although they may not require it, applications encourage you to name files that you use with their applications with certain extensions. For example, WordPerfect for UNIX uses the .wp extension. When you are working on different projects, it is useful to create different directories to keep the files separate. In UNIX, you create directories with the mkdir command. Its syntax is simple:

mkdir *directory-name*

where *directory-name* is the name you want to assign to the new directory.

N O T E Just like creating files, you need to have write access to the directory before you can create a subdirectory. If you are making a subdirectory within your home directory, you should have no problem. ■

When the system creates a directory, it automatically inserts entries for the names "." and "..". The name "." is a pseudonym for the directory, and the name ".." is a pseudonym for its parent directory. All directories contain these entries, and ordinary users are prohibited from removing these entries. A directory that contains only the entries for "." and ".." is considered empty.

To remove a directory, you must first remove all its contents (including any subdirectories and their contents); then you can use the rmdir command to remove it:

rmdir *directory-name*

As discussed earlier, you can also use rm -r *directory-name* to remove a directory and all its contents.

Locating Files Using *find*

With the growing storage capacity supported by UNIX today, sometimes it is difficult to locate a file on the file system. Or there may be times that you need to locate duplicate files on your system as part of the housecleaning process. The find command, a powerful tool, can assist you in locating files. Because of its flexibility, find is one of the more difficult commands to master and use. Instead of explaining find in all its glory, the following three examples illustrate some of its capabilities—capabilities that most UNIX users will find useful.

It is useful to know that the `find` command has three main parts: where to look, what to look for, and what to do when you find it. This knowledge helps you to construct the `find` command line.

Finding Files by Name   Probably the most common use of `find` is to locate a file whose name (or part of whose name) is known. Unlike other programs, `find` searches through an entire file system subtree without you asking. The simplest case of the `find` command for searching a file by name is:

```
find / -name filename -print
```

 `find` can take a long time to search through a large subtree, therefore, if you run `find` routinely searching through entire large file systems, you should probably run it during the wee hours of the morning (say, as part of a `cron` job).

▶ **See** "Adding and Modifying `cron` Tasks," **p. 414**

Let's examine each argument to the preceding `find` command. The first argument specifies the subtree to be searched. In this case, it is `/`, which means start the search from the root of the file system; any directory name could have been supplied in place of the `/` (such as `/usr/home/peter`, or `/etc`). The second argument is `-name`, which tells `find` to search for files named in the following argument, and the following argument is *filename*, the target name; you can use wildcards to specify a group of files. The last argument is `-print`, which tells `find` to print the name of all found files. For example:

```
% find . -name chapter* -print
./chapter3
./Backup/chapter1
./Backup/chapter2
./Backup/chapter3
%
```

The following is a slightly more complicated example where filename generation technique is used, and the search is confined to the `/usr/home` subtree:

```
% find /usr/home -name 'z*[0-9]' -print
/usr/home/zenworks/z/z19
/usr/home/zenworks/zz/z19
/usr/home/zenworks/zz/z30
%
```

 You can precede the `-name` option with a "`!`" symbol (because `!` is a metacharacter, you need to escape it when using it as an argument to a command) to mean "not equal to." Therefore,

```
find / \! -name "*.c" -print
```

prints out a list of all the files whose names do not end in `.c`.

Finding Files by Size   Another common use of `find` is to search for files that are larger (or smaller) than a certain size. This is useful for system administrators who need to determine what is taking up the storage space. Instead of the `-name` option, the `-size` option is used. But other than that, the syntax is similar to the preceding examples. Following the `-size` option is a number that represents the size of files in blocks (each block is 512-byte in size); a "c" appended to the number means that the specified number is in bytes (characters) instead of blocks. A plus sign in front of the number means files larger than that size, and a minus size in front means files smaller than that size; if a plus or minus sign is not placed in front of the size specification, files that are exactly that size are found. Here are some examples:

- `find / -size +250 -print` produces a list of files that are greater than 250 blocks in size.
- `find / -size +250c -print` produces a list of files that are greater than 250 bytes in size.
- `find / -size -5 -print` produces a list of files that are less than 5 blocks in size.
- `find / -size 10 -print` lists all the files that are exactly 10 blocks in size.

Finding Files by Date   There are occasions when you need to locate files that have been recently modified. For this, `find` recognizes a number of time-related options:

- `-atime` (last accessed time)
- `-ctime` (last changed time)
- `-mtime` (modification time)

These options must be followed by a signed number, to indicate the number of days. The following command searches for files in the `/etc` subtree that have been modified within the last two days:

```
% find /etc -mtime -2 -print
/etc
/etc/utmp
/etc/wtmp
/etc/mnttab
%
```

If you use a plus sign for the time selection, `find` locates files older than that many days. This is useful when you want to clear out old files.

Many other uses of `find`, such as searching for files belonging to a specific user (using the `-user` option), are possible. However, the uses are too numerous to mention. Refer to your system manual for more advanced features.

Pipes, I/O Redirection, and Filters

Your terminal is the basic communication device between the UNIX host and you. The operating system makes it easy for programs to access the terminal because most utility programs need to interact with the users. UNIX provides a number of methods in which you can manipulate the flow of data from one utility to another.

Understanding I/O

Before going into detail on how you can manipulate data flow between programs, some background in how UNIX handles input/output (I/O) is in order. When a program types something to your terminal, the program is (usually) performing output operations to what is called the *standard output* "connection." When you type at your terminal, a program is (usually) reading your typed text from what is called the *standard input* connection. The standard input and the standard output are UNIX system conventions that simplify programming—interactive programs, such as the shell, read your commands from the standard input and write their responses to the standard output.

N O T E The qualifier "usually" is used in the preceding definitions of the standard input and output because it is possible to access the terminal without using the standard input and output. However, the great majority of the UNIX-supplied programs do use the standard input and output connections when they access the terminal.

In addition to standard input and output, a running program normally sends any error messages to the *standard error* connection. A program can send error messages to standard error to keep them from getting mixed up with the information it sends to standard output. By default, the shell sends the data for the standard error to the terminal, just as it does with standard output. Therefore, unless you redirect one or the other (as described in the "Using I/O Redirection" section later in the chapter), you may not know the difference between the output a command sends to standard output and the output it sends to standard error.

Understanding File Descriptors

In UNIX, each I/O connection available to a program is identified by a (small, positive integer) number known as a *file descriptor*. When a program wants to read or write to a file, it must first open that file. When it does so, UNIX associates a file descriptor with the file. Most UNIX systems allow each program to have between 10 and 20 files opened simultaneously, thus 10 to 20 file descriptors may be associated with a given running program. Each program has its own set of open files and its own file descriptors. After a program opens a file, it reads from and writes to that file by referring to it with the file descriptor. When the program no longer needs the file, it closes it, freeing the file descriptor.

Remember that in UNIX, a file can be either a disk file or a terminal or some other I/O device or even a connection to another program. When a typical UNIX program starts, it opens three "files": standard input, which has file descriptor 0; standard output, with file descriptor 1; and standard error, with file descriptor 2. By default, these three standard channels are connected to your terminal.

You normally don't need to worry about or deal with file descriptors, but knowing something about them helps your understanding of how I/O redirection works.

Using I/O Redirection

The standard input, output, and error are normally attached to the terminal. However, it is possible to reassign their "connections" to something else. The shell's capability to reassign these standard connections is one of the UNIX system's most important features—and the idea has been borrowed and implemented on several other operating systems.

Redirecting Standard Output   The *redirect output* (">") symbol instructs the shell to connect a command's standard output channel to the specified file instead of the terminal. The format of a command line that redirects standard output is as follows:

```
command [arguments] > filename
```

where `command` is any UNIX command or executable program, `arguments` are optional arguments for the program, and `filename` is the name of the file to which the shell redirects the output. The spaces surrounding the > are optional.

N O T E   The redirection is performed by the shell, not by the individual programs. ▪

CAUTION

Depending on what shell you are using and how your environment has been set up, the following command may display an error message and overwrite the contents of the file `apple`:

```
cat apple banana > apple
```

The `cat` command displays an error message, and you'll find the new apple file will have the same contents as banana. This is because the first action the shell takes when it sees the redirection symbol is to remove the contents of the original `apple` file.

CAUTION

Normal output redirection completely overwrites the output file without any warning. If you want to add the output to the end of the output file, use >> instead of just >. For example:

```
cat banana >> apple
```

adds the contents of the banana file to the end of the `apple` file.

The shell's capability for output redirection adds two uses to the `cat` command:

▪ You can catenate multiples files into a single file. For example:

```
% cat file1
This is file number 1.
% cat file2
This is file number 2.
% cat file3
This is file number 3.
% cat file? > file
```

```
% cat file
This is file number 1.
This is file number 2.
This is file number 3.
%
```

■ You can create a file without using an editor, such as vi:

```
% cat > new.file
This file is being created by entering
text at the keyboard. cat is copying it
to a file. Press CONTROL-D to indicate
the End-of-file.
<Ctrl-d>
% cat new.file
This file is being created by entering
text at the keyboard. cat is copying it
to a file. Press CONTROL-D to indicate
the End-of-file.
%
```

The redirect symbol on the command line causes the shell to associate cat's standard output with the file specified on the command line, new.file. As a result, any text up to the Ctrl-d character entered at the keyboard is redirected into the file.

N O T E   UNIX has a special device, /dev/null, commonly called a "bit-bucket." It is a place where you can redirect output from a program that you don't want; the output disappears without a trace:

```
ls -ald /tmp > /dev/null
```

Redirecting Standard Input   Just as you can redirect a program's standard output, you can redirect its standard input. The redirect input ("<") symbol instructs the shell to connect a command's standard input channel to the specified file instead of the terminal. The format of a command line that redirects standard input is as follows:

```
command [arguments] < filename
```

where command is any UNIX command or executable program, arguments are optional arguments for the program, and filename is the name of the file from which the shell redirects the input. The spaces surrounding the < are optional.

Many of the UNIX utilities, such as cat, first examine the command line you used to call them. If you include a filename on the command line, the utility takes its input from the filename. If you don't specify a filename, the utility takes its input from standard input. Therefore, for such utilities, the same result is obtained regardless of whether you used input redirection.

Redirecting Standard Error   To separate a program's error message output from its standard output, you can redirect the standard error to a file. The symbols 2> redirect standard error.

N O T E   Recall that a running program opens three file descriptors: 0 for standard input, 1 for standard output, and 2 for standard error. The redirect input symbol < is actually a shorthand for <0, and the redirect output symbol > is short for 1>. It easily follows that 2> is used to redirect standard error. ▓

CAUTION

Not all shells support standard error redirection. For example, in the C shell, you cannot redirect standard error to a file without also redirecting standard output; you can redirect standard output to a file and leave standard error to print to the terminal.

The following example (running under the Bourne shell) demonstrates how to redirect standard output and standard error to different files:

```
$ cat x y
This is file X.
cat: y: No such file or directory
$ cat x y > z1 2> z2
$ cat z1
This is file X.
$ cat z2
cat: y: No such file or directory
$
```

Using Pipes

The shell uses a *pipe* to connect standard output of one command directly to standard input of another command. A pipe is different from I/O redirection as discussed previously. Although the end result is the same as redirecting standard output of one command to a file and then using that file as standard input to another command, it does away with separate commands and the intermediate file. The symbol for a pipe is a vertical bar ("|"). The syntax for a command using a pipe is as follows:

```
command_a [arguments] ¦ command_b [arguments]
```

The preceding command line uses a pipe to achieve the same result as the following group of command lines:

```
command_a [arguments] > temp
command_b [arguments] < temp
rm temp
```

Although I/O redirection and pipes are separate UNIX shell functions, it is possible to use both in one command. You can pipe the output of one program to the input of another while simultaneously redirecting the input of the first (or the output of the second) to a file:

```
ls -l ¦ sort > sorted.list
```

The preceding command generates a file of sort list for a long-format directory listing of your current working directory. The spaces surrounding the ¦ are optional. The same result can be achieved without using pipes:

```
% ls -l > temp
% sort < temp > sorted.list
% rm temp
```

As you can easily see, pipes make many procedures conceptually easier.

N O T E   There is no limit on how many pipes you can have on a given command line.

Filtering Commands

A *filter* is a command that processes an input stream of data to produce an output stream of data. A command line that includes a filter uses a pipe to connect the filter's standard input to standard output of the previous command. The following sections discuss some often used filters.

Using *cut* and *paste*

If you need to rearrange columns within a file, the cut and paste utilities are the best tools to use. The cut program can be used to extract a vertical section from a file, whereas the paste program merges several vertical sections into one file. You can specify the positions within a file to cut by either character position or column (field) number:

```
cut -cposition filelist
cut -ffield filelist
```

The character position may be a list separated by commas, a range separated by dashes, or a combination. For example:

```
cut -c1,4,5 filename
cut -c1-4 filename
cut -c 1-4,5-10,25 filename
```

are all valid. Instead of specifying by character positions, you can use -f to specify columns. The syntax for -f is the same as -c; the two options are mutually exclusive.

The paste command can combine several vertical columns into a single file, and paste automatically separates each column with a tab character. Following is an example of how to use cut and paste to interchange the position of two columns of a file:

```
% cat numbers
555-1212        peter
555-1313        sally
555-1414        john
555-1414        jane
% cut -f1 numbers > telnos
% cut -f2 numbers > names
% paste names telnos > new.list
% cat new.list
peter   555-1212
sally   555-1313
```

```
john      555-1414
jane      555-1414
%
```

N O T E These programs are available in System V but are not standard utilities in Version 7 or BSD. ▨

The *sort* Utility

The sort command is used to sort and/or merge text files. sort outputs the rearranged lines in a file according to your command-line specifications; ordinarily, the input file is not changed. By default, the sorted output is sent to standard output, which you can redirect to a file.

Each line of the input can contain one or more fields. The fields are delimited by a field separator, usually a tab or a space. The portion of the input line that sort examines to determine the ordering for the file is called the *sort key*. The sort key can be one or more fields, or parts of fields, or the entire line.

sort supports a number of options, but the most important two are the options that specify the beginning and the end of the sort key:

```
sort +begin -end [filename]
```

+begin specifies that the sort key starts at field number *begin*; if no beginning number is specified, the beginning of the line is assumed. Fields start counting at zero, so the third field is 2. *-end* specifies up to (but not including) what field number the sort key ends; if no ending number is specified, the end of the line is assumed. For example, a file containing names and telephone numbers is sorted. The first sort command sorts the file by people's names as the arguments +0 and -1 limit the sort key to the first field (field 0). The second sort command performs a "two-way" sort: first by telephone number (field 1), and if there is a "tie," by name (field 0):

```
% cat numbers
peter     555-1212
sally     555-1313
john      555-1414
jane      555-1414
% sort +0 -1 numbers
jane      555-1414
john      555-1414
peter     555-1212
sally     555-1313
% sort +1 +0 -1 numbers
peter     555-1212
sally     555-1313
jane      555-1414
john      555-1414
%
```

Part

I

Ch

3

NOTE When multiple sort keys are specified, the keys specified later in the command line are compared only when the earlier keys yield an equal match. For example:

```
sort +2 -3 +5 -6
```

the key defined by field 6 is used only when the key defined by field 3 produces an equal match between two records. ■

The *tee* Utility

The tee program reads the standard input and sends the output to both the standard output and a file. It is an ideal tool for troubleshooting your pipes because you can capture the intermediate results for examination:

```
ls -l ¦ tee unsorted.list ¦ sort > sorted.list
```

You can also use tee to make a copy of a program's output in a file and also see it on your terminal:

```
% ls -l ¦ tee save.list
-rw-r—r—  1 root   adm    19796 Aug 20 05:58 passwd.bad
-rw-r—r—  1 root   adm    19797 Aug 20 05:58 passwd_new
-rw-r—r—  1 root   adm     9897 Aug 10 09:11 passwd.old
% cat save.list
-rw-r—r—  1 root   adm    19796 Aug 20 05:58 passwd.bad
-rw-r—r—  1 root   adm    19797 Aug 20 05:58 passwd_new
-rw-r—r—  1 root   adm     9897 Aug 10 09:11 passwd.old
%
```

The *grep* Command

You can use the grep program (and its relatives fgrep and egrep) to search for text patterns in files. Whenever the text pattern is matched on a line, that line of the file is displayed on the standard output. When compared with cut, you can think of the grep program as taking a horizontal section through a file based on a text-matching criterion.

NOTE grep stands for *global regular expression print*. ■

NOTE An entire chapter easily could be devoted just to discussing regular expressions. However, due to limited space, only the highlights are described here.

A *regular expression* specifies a set of character strings. A member of this set of strings is said to be matched by the regular expression. Some characters have special meaning when used in a regular expression; other characters stand for themselves. Learning regular expressions is an important concept of UNIX. Most of the commands in UNIX, even the vi editor, use regular expressions for searching or formatting text. A regular expression matches one or more character strings. Table 3.3 lists the regular expression characters. ■

Table 3.3   UNIX Regular Expression Characters

Expression	Description
c	The character c where c is not a special character.
\c	The character c where c is any character, except a digit in the range 1-9.
^	The beginning of the line being compared.
$	The end of the line being compared.
.	Any character in the input.
[s]	Any character in the set s, where s is a sequence of characters and/or a range of characters, for example, [a-f].
[^s]	Any character not in the set s, where s is defined as previously.
$r*$	Zero or more successive occurrences of the regular expression r. The longest leftmost match is chosen.
rx	The occurrence of regular expression r followed by the occurrence of regular expression x. (Concatenation)
$r\{m,n\}$	Any number of m through n successive occurrences of the regular expression r. The regular expression $r\{m\}$ matches exactly m occurrences; $r\{m,\}$ matches at least m occurrences.
\(r\)	The regular expression r. When \n (where n is a number greater than zero) appears in a constructed regular expression, it stands for the regular expression x where x is the nth regular expression enclosed in \(and \) that appeared earlier in the constructed regular expression. For example, \(r\)x\(y\)z\2 is the concatenation of regular expressions $rxyzy$.

Part

I

Ch

3

Characters that have special meaning except when they appear within square brackets ("[]") or are preceded by \ are: . , * , [, \. Other special characters such as $ have special meaning in more restricted contexts.

The character ^ at the beginning of an expression permits a successful match only immediately after a newline, and the character $ at the end of an expression requires a trailing newline.

Two characters have special meaning only when used within square brackets. The character - denotes a range, [c-c], unless it is just after the open bracket or before the closing bracket, [-c] or [c-], in which case it has no special meaning. When used within brackets, the character ^ has the meaning "complement of" if it immediately follows the open bracket (example: [^c]); elsewhere between brackets (example: [c^]) it stands for the ordinary character ^.

The special meaning of the \ operator can be escaped only by preceding it with another \, for example \\.

continues

continued

Using and understanding the preceding set of characters and rules does take some practice. To help you learn how regular expressions work, some examples are listed here (a forward slash, /, is used as a delimiter):

/^The/	Match the word "The" at the beginning of a line.
/help/	Match the word "help."
/W...d/	Match a "W," followed by exactly three characters, followed by a "d." This would match "World."
/^$/	Match a blank line.
/^[0-9]/	Match a line that starts with a numeric.
/\.$/	Match a line that ends with a period. Notice that the period is escaped using the \ character. This is required because the period is a regular expression character.

▶ **See** "Searching for Text," **p. 101**

The first argument to grep is the text pattern, and the following arguments specify the files that should be examined. Suppose that you want see a list of all the UNIX processes that the root user is currently running; you can use the grep command to filter out the unwanted information from the ps command:

```
% ps -aux ¦ grep root
root          1  0.0  0.1   344  112  ??  Is   Mon06AM    0:02.43 /sbin/init --
root          2  0.0  0.0     0   12  ??  DL   Mon06AM    0:00.00 (pagedaemon)
root          3  0.0  0.0     0   12  ??  DL   Mon06AM    0:00.00 (vmdaemon)
root          4  0.2  0.0     0   12  ??  DL   Mon06AM   13:31.02 (update)
root         22  0.0  0.0   196   44  ??  Is   Mon06AM    0:00.00 adjkerntz -i
root        375  0.0  0.3   188  316  ??  Ss   Mon10AM    0:32.69 syslogd
root        392  0.0  0.4   328  464  ??  S    Mon10AM    0:50.53 /usr/local/sbi
root        398  0.0  0.3   296  344  ??  Ss   Mon10AM    0:08.03 cron
root        402  0.0  0.3   800  388  ??  Ss   Mon10AM    0:25.12 sendmail: acce
root        447  0.0  1.1  1656 1388  ??  S<s  Mon10AM    4:06.24 /usr/pair/apac
root        448  0.0  0.5   604  600  ??- SN   Mon10AM    0:24.05 /usr/local/Min
root        449  0.0  1.0  1048 1252  ??- I<   Mon10AM    8:28.50 /usr/local/bin
root        454  0.0  0.1   136  148  ??  I    Mon10AM    0:00.01 /usr/local/etc
root        457  0.0  0.1   140  168  ??  IN   Mon10AM    0:00.05 /usr/pair/uu/u
root        458  0.0  0.7   672  892  ??- IN   Mon10AM    0:24.32 /usr/local/bin
root        459  0.0  0.7   672  892  ??- IN   Mon10AM    0:24.39 /usr/local/bin
root        465  0.0  0.3   156  404  v0  Is+  Mon10AM    0:00.01 /usr/libexec/g
root        466  0.0  0.3   156  404  v1  Is+  Mon10AM    0:00.01 /usr/libexec/g
root        467  0.0  0.3   156  404  v2  Is+  Mon10AM    0:00.01 /usr/libexec/g
root      24700  0.0  0.4   192  492  ??  S    Thu10AM    0:07.43 rlogind
root      24722  0.0  0.2   480  304  p4  I+   Thu10AM    0:00.06 -su (csh)
root      27691  0.0  0.4   192  488  ??  S    Thu12PM    0:07.23 rlogind
root      27704  0.0  0.2   464  268  p2  I    Thu12PM    0:00.04 -su (csh)
root      27708  0.0  0.7   640  952  p2  I+   Thu12PM    0:00.06 -csh (tcsh)
```

```
root      6106  0.0  5.2  6784 6644  ??  Ss   Thu04PM   6:36.44 /usr/sbin/name
root     10941  0.0  0.4   236  572  ??  S     1:14PM   0:02.26 telnetd
root      4241  0.0  0.8   564 1060  ??  SN    1:02AM   0:00.46 /usr/local/etc
root      4242  0.0  0.2   432  296  ??  IN    1:02AM   0:00.02 /usr/local/etc
root      4243  0.0  0.7   580  832  ??  IN    1:02AM   0:00.03 /usr/local/etc
root      4244  0.0  0.7   668  920  ??  IN    1:02AM   0:00.21 /usr/local/etc
root      4245  0.0  0.7   660  912  ??  IN    1:02AM   0:00.25 /usr/local/etc
root      4246  0.0  0.7   584  836  ??  IN    1:02AM   0:00.05 /usr/local/etc
root      4247  0.0  0.6   568  820  ??  IN    1:02AM   0:00.03 /usr/local/etc
root      7059  0.0  0.8   932 1012  ??  S     2:39AM   0:00.08 sendmail: BAA0
root      7186  0.0  0.4   232  572  ??  S     2:44AM   0:00.04 telnetd
root      7218  0.0  0.6   824  704  ??  I     2:45AM   0:00.01 sendmail: star
root         0  0.0  0.0     0    0  ??  DLs   -        0:00.00 (swapper)
%
```

The *awk* Command

The awk utility is a programmable, pattern-scanning and processing filter for text files. It searches one or more files to see whether they contain lines that match specified patterns and then performs actions, such as writing the line to standard output or incrementing a counter, each time it finds a match. You can use awk to generate reports or filter text. It works equally well with numbers and text; when you mix the two, awk almost always comes up with the right answer. The awk utility takes many of its constructs from the C programming language, including:

- Conditional execution
- Looping statement
- Numeric variables
- String variables
- Regular expressions
- C's printf

The awk utility takes its input from files you specify on the command line or from standard input.

N O T E awk was named after its developers: Alfredo V. Aho, Peter J. Weinberger, and Brian W. Kernighan. ▨

As with regular expressions, an entire chapter (or a whole book) could be devoted just to a discussion of awk. However, due to limited space, only a simple awk script is described here.

An awk script (also called a program) consists of two parts: *patterns* and *actions*. The patterns are regular expressions, and the actions bear some resemblance to the C language. In an awk program, patterns are followed by actions, with braces ("{}") surrounding each action. An action is performed if the pattern matches something in the current input line. If the pattern part of the script is absent, the action is performed for each line in the file. If the action is absent, then the default action is to print the line to standard output.

The following example shows a simple awk script that prints out any line containing the string "sday":

```
% cat days.2
Monday
Tuesday
Wednesday
Thursday
Friday
Saturday
Sunday
% cat days.2 | awk '/sday/ {print}'
Tuesday
Wednesday
Thursday
%
```

The quotes surrounding the awk script are necessary because the script contains blanks.

You can do much more with awk scripts; refer to either an awk book or your system documentation for more information.

N O T E   Although awk and the shell are both programmable, they are specialized for different applications. awk is best at manipulating text files, whereas the shell is best at managing UNIX commands. ▧

▶ **See** "Introduction to Shell Programming," **p. 154**

Working with Users

Previous sections in this chapter covered utilities for working with text files. This section focuses on the utilities that allow you to observe and interact with other users on your system.

Viewing Users Logged On

To find out who is using the computer system, you can use one of several utilities that vary in the details they provide and the options they support. The oldest utility, who, produces a short list (sorted according to terminal name) of usernames along with the terminal connection each person is using and the time the person logged on to the system:

```
% who
penpals   ttyp0    Aug 22 03:02    (pc1)
peter     ttyp1    Aug 22 03:59    (slip10-37-153-2)
hypno     ttyp2    Aug 20 12:04    (sco2)
dilbert   ttyp3    Aug 21 13:15    (10.154.63.187)
john      ttyp4    Aug 20 10:37    (nu)
%
```

The first column shows the names of the logged in users. The second column shows the designation of the terminal that each person is using. The third column shows the date and time the person logged in. The last column, if present, shows either the X display being used or the name of the remote system from where the person is logged in. People who are logged in at multiple terminals are listed multiple times.

Some systems allow you to find out which terminal you're using or what time you logged in using the who am i command:

```
% who am i
peter ttyp1    Aug 22 03:59    (slip10-37-153-2)
%
```

N O T E Some systems may use whoami instead of who am i. On systems that support both, whoami simply returns the name of your login name. ■

You can also use finger to display a list of the people currently using the system. In addition to login names, finger also shows some extra information, such as each user's full name:

```
% finger
Login     Name               TTY  Idle Login Time   Office      Office Phone
john      John Pence         *p4  12:13 Thu   10:37
dilbert   Dilbert            p3   11:04 Fri   13:15
peter     Peter Kuo          p1         Sat   03:59
hypno     Jacques Beland     p2   3d    Thu   12:04
penpals   Sandra             p0   55    Sat   03:02
%
```

Part
I
Ch
3

The star ("*") in front of John's terminal (TTY) line indicates that he has blocked others from sending messages directly to his terminal (using the mesg utility, described later).

The w utility also displays a sorted list (by terminal name) of the users currently logged in.

```
% w
 4:00AM   up 6 days, 17:26, 5 users, load averages: 0.00, 0.00, 0.00
USER      TTY FROM            LOGIN@  IDLE WHAT
penpals   p0  pc1             3:02AM    55 -csh (csh)
peter     p1  slip10-37-153-2 3:59AM     - w
hypno     p2  sco2            Thu12PM 3days -csh (tcsh)
dilbert   p3  10.154.63.187   Fri01PM 11:04 (pine)
john      p4  nu              Thu10AM     - -su (csh)
%
```

The first column shows the names of logged in users. The second column shows the designation of the terminal that each person is using. The third column shows where the user is logged in from or the X display that is being used; some versions of w don't show this column. The fourth column shows the date and time each person logged in. The fifth column indicates how long each person has been idle (that is, how many minutes have elapsed since a key was last pressed on the keyboard). The last column shows what program the person is currently running. On some versions of w, there are two columns (not shown in the preceding example) after the idle time to measure how much CPU time each person has used during the current login session and on the task that is currently running.

The first line that the w command displays includes the current time of day, how long the system has been running (in days, hours, and minutes), how many users are logged in, and how busy the system is (load average). The three load average numbers measure the number of processes waiting to run, averaged over the past minute, 5 minutes, and 15 minutes, respectively.

Getting User Information

`Finger` can also be used to learn more about a particular individual by specifying the username on the command line:

```
% finger peter
Login: peter                        Name: Peter Kuo
Directory: /usr/home/peter          Shell: /bin/csh
On since Sat Aug 22 03:59 (EDT) on ttyp1 from slip10-37-153-2
No Mail.
Mail forwarded to:
"|IFS=' ' && exec /usr/local/bin/procmail -f- || exit 75 #peter"
Project: Using UNIX SE, 3e
Plan: Finish with chapter 3 asap.
%
```

The user does not have to be logged in for the preceding command to work; if the user isn't logged in, `finger` reports the last time the user used the system. The preceding example shows that Peter is currently and actively using his terminal (if he were not, `finger` would report how long he had been idle). Most of the information reported by `finger` was collected from system files, such as `/etc/passwd`. The information shown after the headings `Project:` and `Plan:`, however, were supplied by Peter. The information is taken, respectively, from the `.project` and `.plan` files in Peter's home directory.

You might find it helpful to create a `.plan` file for yourself. It can contain any information you choose, such as your typical schedule or contact information.

If you don't know a person's login name, you can use `finger` to find out. You can use the `finger` command for a user's information using either login name, first name, or last name. Therefore, `finger peter` and `finger kuo` both return the same information.

Switching to Another User Using *su*

Because of the extensive powers of potential destruction you have with the root username, it is a good idea to become the Superuser only when necessary. If you are just doing your day-to-day work, log in as yourself. That way you will not easily erase someone else's files or shut down the system by mistake. When you need the power of the Superuser, use the `su` (substitute user) command—when you run `su` without any parameters, it defaults the username to root, and you are prompted for the root password.

N O T E   For you to be able to `su` to become root, you need to be in the group that has GID 0 (on BSD, this group is normally "wheel"). Otherwise, `su` gives you an error message:

```
% su
su: you are not in the correct group to su root.
%
```

▶ **See** "The group File," **p. 240**

If you need to become a specific user so that, for instance, you can access his files, include the username on the command line:

```
% su john
Password:
Sorry
%
```

You'll need to know the user's password to su successfully. However, if you are logged in as root, you can su to become any user without needing to know the user's password.

If the specified username is not valid (that is, not listed in the /etc/passwd file), you'll get an error message:

```
% su abcd
su: unknown login: abcd
%
```

Part

I

Ch

3

Sending a User a Message

You can use the write utility to send a message, one line at a time, to another user who is logged in. When the other user also uses write to send you a reply, you establish a two-way communication. When you give a write command, it displays a banner on the other user's terminal indicating that you are about to send a message: "Message from penpals on ttyp0 at 08:20 ...".

The syntax for the write command follows:

```
write destination-user [terminal-name]
```

where *destination-user* is the login name of the user to whom you want to send a message. The *terminal-name* is optional and is needed only when the *destination-user* is logged in on multiple terminals. The combination of *destination-user* and *terminal-name* uniquely identifies your target. You can find out the login and terminal names of the users who are logged in by using who, finger, and w as discussed previously.

When you're finished sending your message, press Ctrl-d at the beginning of a line to terminate your write session; the word EOF (End of File) is displayed on the other user's terminal to indicate you have terminated your session.

 When you have established a two-way communication with another user using write, it is best to observe the following convention to avoid confusion as to whose turn it is to send a message: type o (for over) when you're ready for the other person to type, and type oo (for over-and-out) when you're ready to terminate the session. This is very much like the protocol used by CB (Citizen Band) radio users.

Talking to Another User

talk is a "visual" version of the write communication program that copies lines from your terminal to that of another user. The talk command allows users on the same host to communicate with each other. The talk command requires that you specify the username you want to talk to. The user you want to talk to must be currently logged on. If the user is logged in on multiple terminals, you also need to specify a terminal name representing the user's session. You can find out the login and terminal names of the users who are logged in by using who, finger, and w as discussed previously.

To initiate a talk session with the user penpals, the talk command would be issued as follows:

% **talk penpals**

After you have executed the talk command, a message appears on penpals's screen. The message tells penpals that dilbert wants to talk. The message appearing on penpals's screen is similar to the following:

```
Message from TalkDaemon@sco1...
talk: connection requested by dilbert@sco1.
talk: respond with: talk dilbert@sco1
```

After penpals establishes the talk session, then both of the terminal screens are split in half, separated by a dashed line. The top half contains what you type; the bottom half contains what the other user types.

To terminate the talk session, just type Ctrl–d (Ctrl-c on some systems). Both users are terminated when either user terminates the talk session.

Sending All Users a Message

If you are logged in as the Superuser, you can broadcast a message to all logged in users on the system using the wall (write all) utility:

wall *message*

This allows you send a one-line message to all users. If you need to send a message that requires more than one line, put the message in a file and then use the following syntax:

wall *filename*

Restricting Messages

You might be in the middle of an editing session and don't want to be bothered by messages from another user using write or talk. Give the following command before you start the editor program:

% **mesg n**

Anyone who tries to send you a message after you have issued this message sees the following:

```
% write john
write: john has messages disabled
%
```

N O T E   mesg n does *not* block messages sent by the wall utility, because it is generally used by the Superuser for emergency announcements, such as he's about to bring the system down. ▨

To enable receiving of messages, issue this command:

% **mesg y**

You can check your current mesg setting simply by running the mesg program without any argument. The response Is y means that you can receive messages, and the response Is n means that you can't receive messages.

UNIX Processes

When a UNIX program is running, it is called a *process*. If several people are running the same program at about the same time, then there are several processes but only one program. When you execute a command line that has pipes, you have a number of processes running. For example, for the command ls -l ¦ tee unsorted.list ¦ sort > sorted.list you have three processes, one for each of the following commands:

▨ ls

▨ tee

▨ sort

Because a shell is also a UNIX program, it is a process as well. Therefore, as soon as you log in to the system, you have at least one process running. UNIX processes and their administration are discussed in detail in a later chapter.

▶ **See** "Process" **p. 132**

From Here...

This chapter presented an introduction to UNIX shells and introduced you to a number of the most commonly used shell commands that will get your daily chores done.

▨ To learn about editing files in the UNIX environment, see Chapter 4, "vi Editor."

▨ To get an understanding of UNIX file structures and file system security, see Chapter 5, "Files, Directories, and Permissions."

▨ For a detailed discussion about processes in UNIX, see Chapter 6, "UNIX Processes."

▨ To find out how you can automate some of your repetitive tasks through shell scripting, see Chapter 7, "Essential Shell Scripting."

vi Editor

by Peter Kuo and Jeff Robinson

In this chapter

Introducing *vi*

Before vi was developed, the standard UNIX system editor was ed, a line-oriented editor. It was replaced by ex, a superset of ed, which contains a full-screen editing mode. While using ex, you can switch into the full-screen mode using the vi command. People liked the full-screen mode so much that the developers of ex made it possible to start the editor so that you are in the full-screen mode without having to start ex and give it the vi command. As a result, they named the program vi. You can still call up the visual mode in ex, and you can still go back to ex (line-mode) while you are using vi.

Originally developed by University of California at Berkeley (UC Berkeley) for BSD UNIX, vi is now included as a standard feature with all versions of UNIX with the exception of Linux. This is because vi includes proprietary code from AT&T that is not compatible with the licensing terms under which Linux is distributed (see the Note box about GNU at the end of this chapter). However, a number of vi clones are available for Linux, such as elvis, ni, and vim.

vi does not require nor provide any support for graphics or the use of a mouse. The editor uses only the keyboard to perform all functions of editing, saving, and scrolling of files. The vi editor uses only letters, numbers, punctuation keys, and the **Esc** key on the keyboard for all its editing and navigation functions. The F1 through F12 keys that are commonly used by editors on PCs and on other operating systems are not functional in vi; the arrow (cursor) keys are only supported on some terminals.

In today's graphical this-and-mouse-that computing environment, vi seems rather archaic. However, because all keyboards have the standard keys used by vi, the editor can be used on nearly any terminal type and is one of the most favored editors by UNIX programmers. Because keyboard layouts are fairly standard, you have consistent key mappings regardless of your terminal type. When used in conjunction with remote access commands such as telnet or rlogin, you can easily remote-edit files over the network.

▶ **See** "Using telnet," **p. 426**

▶ **See** "The r-Utilities," **p. 436**

N O T E   Remember that vi is not a word processor or a desktop publishing system. It doesn't have menus and virtually no online help. Word processors usually offer screen and hard copy formatting and printing, such as representing text as **bold**, *italic*, or underline; vi doesn't. vi is strictly a text editor—a versatile and powerful one. ▪

The vi editor might appear a cryptic to you in the beginning; however, over time you will find the editor useful and powerful for many system tasks, and you'll come to like it and depend on it.

N O T E   The vi editor is not limited to just UNIX. It has been ported to many other operating systems, such as MS-DOS and DEC VMS. ▪

N O T E   Because of the rich feature set available in vi, it is impossible to cover all of it in the space available here. As a matter of fact, entire books are dedicated to vi. If you want to know more about advanced features of vi than is covered here, refer to the Reference Manual supplied with your system. ▧

Modes of Operation in *vi*

There are at least five (six according to some longtime vi users) different "modes" of operation available within the vi editor. The two most common modes are the *Command Mode* and the *Input* (or *Insert*) *Mode*. In the Command Mode, your keystrokes are interpreted as commands to vi—for example, to save a file, exit vi, move the cursor, delete text, and so on. You can also instruct vi to enter the Input Mode using several different commands, depending on what you want to do. For example, the i command allows you to insert text before the current cursor position, and the a command allows you to append text following the current cursor position.

> **CAUTION**
>
> The commands entered in the Command Mode are not echoed to the screen, and most commands are carried out as you enter each keystroke. As a result, be careful while entering vi commands because the keyboard is "live"—each keystroke is acted on immediately. For example, if you think vi is in Input Mode when it is actually in Command Mode, the result of typing in text can be confusing, and you could be inadvertently delete blocks of text without realizing it until it's too late.

Part

I

Ch

4

In Input Mode, vi accepts anything you type as text and displays it on the screen. Within the Input Mode, there are three types of insert (sub)modes: *Open, Insert*, and *Append*. The Open mode starts a new line to add text; the Insert mode starts adding text at the current cursor position; and the Append mode appends text to either the current cursor position or at the end of the line. Additionally, the Change and Replace commands combine Command and Input Modes. The Change command deletes the text you want to change and puts vi in the Input Mode. The Replace command deletes the character(s) you overwrite and inserts the new one(s) you entered. These various insert modes are further discussed in the "Text Editing Using vi" section later in this chapter. The Esc key puts vi back into Command Mode.

> **N O T E** If you enter a character as a command in the Command Mode but the character is not a valid command, vi beeps to warn you of the error. ▧

 If you are unsure what mode vi is in, press the **Esc** key a couple of times. This ensures that vi is placed in the Command Mode.

 You can use the :set showmode command from within vi to display the current mode on the status line (last line on the screen); the default is noshowmode. If you also issue a :set terse command, the mode is represented by a single character; the default is noterse.

vi also has *Last Line Mode*. This is a less frequently used way of entering vi commands. All Last Line commands start with a colon (:), such as the set command in the preceding Tip. The colon moves the cursor to the bottom of the screen, where you enter the rest of the command. In addition to the position of the cursor, there is another important difference between Last Line Mode and Command Mode. When you give a command in Command Mode, you don't need to press the Enter key at the end. However, you must press the Enter key at the end of each Last Line Mode command. Last Line Mode commands are discussed in the "Advanced vi Techniques" section later in the chapter. Figure 4.1 illustrates the different modes in vi as well as the methods of changing between them.

FIGURE 4.1

The various modes of operation in vi and how to change between them.

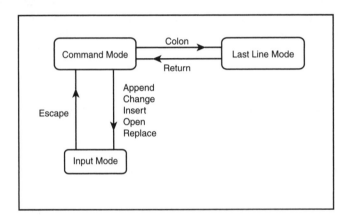

Because vi is part of the ex editor, the other operational modes available in vi are the ex Command Mode and the ex Input Mode. You don't normally need to use the ex modes, and they are not covered in this chapter. If you want to know more about ex, refer to the Reference Manual supplied with your system.

N O T E When this chapter refers to Input and Command Modes, it means the vi modes, not the ex modes. ▪

CAUTION

When issuing vi commands, it is important to remember that, like UNIX commands, the editor is case-sensitive. Because most commands differ only in their case (for example, a versus A), make sure that the Caps Lock or the SHIFTLOCK key on your keyboard is properly set.

The last mode of operation in vi (also available in ex) is the *Shell Escape Mode*. This mode allows you to "jump" out of your current vi editing session back to the UNIX shell, execute some commands, and then jump back into vi and resume your editing session. The Shell Escape Mode is discussed in the "Escaping to the Shell" section later in this chapter.

> **N O T E**   For those who are familiar with DOS, the Shell Escape Mode is similar to the Go to DOS
> option available in many DOS applications, such as WordPerfect. ▦

To summarize, the seven vi modes of operation are as follows:

- ▦ ex Command Mode
- ▦ ex Input Mode
- ▦ ex Shell Escape Mode
- ▦ vi Command Mode
- ▦ vi Input Mode
- ▦ vi Last Line Mode
- ▦ vi Shell Escape Mode

Text Editing Using *vi*

In this section, you learn about vi techniques for day-to-day editing needs, such as how to
move around within vi, save files, and so on. But before you start using vi to edit any text files,
you should have an understanding of how the vi editing process works and know about terminal type settings.

Understanding the Editing Process

The vi editor does all its work in the *Work Buffer* and not directly in your file that is stored on
disk. At the start of an editing session, vi reads the file you want to edit from disk into the
Work Buffer (memory). And during the editing session, all changes to this copy of the file are
done in memory. It does not change the disk file until you write the Work Buffer contents back
to the disk, which makes changes to the text final. When you edit a new file, vi does not create
the file until it writes the contents of the Work Buffer to disk, usually at the end of the editing
session or when you issue a write or save command from within vi.

> **N O T E**   Because vi does its work using memory, it can work with any file format and any size file
> provided that the length of a single "line" (that is, the characters between two NEWLINE,
> typically LineFeed, characters) can fit into available memory. The total length of the file is limited only
> by available disk space. ▦

The bottom line of the screen is referred to ask the *status line*. This line is used to display status such as error messages, information about addition or deletion of blocks of text, and file
status information. In addition, this line is also used to display the Last Line Mode commands.

vi also does file locking to prevent multiple users from editing the same file simultaneously.
When you edit an existing file, vi displays the lines on the screen and gives status information
about the file (such as character and line count) on the status line. It also "locks" the file so that
if someone tries to open the same file a second time (while you are still working on it), vi

allows the file to be opened only in the read-only mode. The second user gets a message similar to the following on his vi's status line:

```
filename already locked, session is read-only.
```

The second user can edit the file (because its content is retrieved into system memory) but has to save the changes to a different filename.

Terminal Type

Because vi is a screen-oriented editor, it has to be able to move the cursor to different positions on your screen and update the display correctly. Because there are a multitude of different terminals, each with its own control codes for cursor movements and screen update functions (such as underlining and reverse video), vi must be told what model of terminal you are using. You can do it in one of two ways: You can set it after starting up vi, or specify the terminal type in your shell's login script.

vi learns the name of your terminal from the $TERM shell environment variable. Using the terminal name in the $TERM variable, vi looks up the necessary cursor movement and screen display control codes for that terminal type from the termcap or terminfo file. Ordinarily, the system administrator makes sure that certain system shell variables, such as $TERM, are set correctly when your account is created. You can check to see whether $TERM is set correctly by entering the following command:

```
$ echo $TERM
vt220
$
```

▶ **See** "Shell Variables," **p. 163**

▶ **See** "Terminal Settings," **p. 319**

In the preceding example, vt220 is the name of the terminal. In this case, your terminal should be or emulate a DEC VT220 terminal; otherwise, you will find that you can't navigate the screen, and you might see blocks of strange characters overwriting blocks of legible text.

N O T E   UNIX assigns a name to each terminal type that it supports. Terminal names are typically in lowercase, they never contain spaces, and they don't usually contain punctuation (such as periods or commas)—hyphens are sometimes used. Typically a terminal's name consists of a few identifying characters followed by a model number. Some typical terminal names are: heathkit, hp2621, vt100, vt220, tvi925, adm3a, qume102, att630, and vc404. ▪

If the answer does not match the terminal type you are using, you can change it using one of the following methods:

- ▪ While inside vi, issue the Last Line Command :set term=*name* where *name* is the name of your terminal type, such as vt100 or vt220.
- ▪ Set the value of the $TERM variable at the shell prompt before starting vi. For example:
  ```
  $ TERM=vt220; export TERM
  ```

If you are using the Berkeley csh, the command would be:

```
$ setenv TERM vt220
```

■ The best way of setting the value for the $TERM variable is to do that in your shell's login script. This ensures that every time you log in, the variable is correctly set. (See Chapter 3, "UNIX Shells and System Commands," for a discussion of shell login scripts.)

TIP If you are unsure of the terminal name to use or which terminal type you have, you can try to look it up in the termcap or terminfo file, but it is best to simply ask your system administrator.

N O T E If for some reason your shell login script doesn't have the command to set the $TERM variable, you can use vi to update your shell's login script to include the command after you have learned to use vi. ▦

TROUBLESHOOTING

If your vi session doesn't appear to be working correctly with your terminal or screen, go into the Command Mode and try pressing Ctrl+r or Ctrl+l (lowercase L) to force a screen redraw and see whether the screen displays correctly. If not, exit to the shell prompt and check the setting for the $TERM variable. The $TERM variable must be set correctly for any UNIX screen-oriented programs, including vi, to function correctly.

Part

I

Ch

4

Starting *vi*

After the $TERM variable is properly defined, you can invoke the vi editor using the shell command:

```
$ vi [filename]
```

If vi was invoked without the *filename* parameter or if the file does not already exist, the message "new file" is displayed on the status line after the screen is cleared; otherwise, the file's name, number of lines in the file, and number of characters contained within the file are displayed on the status line as illustrated in Figure 4.2.

If the end-of-file is displayed on the screen, vi displays a tilde symbol (~) at the left of the screen for each line that would appear past the end-of-file, as shown in Figure 4.2. When a new file is started, the screen is filled with flush-left tildes (one per line) except for the very first line, where there is a flush-left blinking underscore or blinking block character to indicate the current cursor position.

N O T E Unlike most word processors, vi starts in Command Mode. Before you start entering text, you must first switch to the Input Mode. ▦

FIGURE 4.2

Sample opening
screens of vi. The
number of lines shown
here is fewer than you
see on your screen.

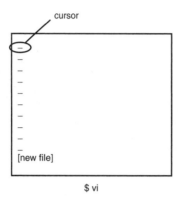

cursor

[new file]

$ vi

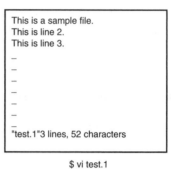

This is a sample file.
This is line 2.
This is line 3.

"test.1"3 lines, 52 characters

$ vi test.1

TROUBLESHOOTING

If your vi screen is garbled, or if on startup vi prints a warning message and then prompts you with a
:, chances are good that your $TERM variable is set incorrectly or not set at all. The "Terminal Type"
section earlier in the chapter shows you how to set $TERM correctly.

Exiting *vi*

You can exit vi in a number of ways, depending on what you want to do. The traditional command for exiting vi is ZZ. That is, while in the Command Mode, press capital "Z" twice. This
writes your Work Buffer to disk, updates the file content, and then exits you back to a shell
prompt. The other exit commands are discussed later.

N O T E   You might wonder why use this particular key combination for save-file-then-exit. It is a
matter of convenience: The ZZ command is easy to execute because you can simply use
the little finger of you left hand to hold down the Shift key and then use one of the other fingers of the
left hand to press the "Z" key. After a little practice, you can do it without even looking at the
keyboard. ▩

Creating Your First *vi* File

There is no better learning method than actual hands-on experience. So, let's create your first
vi file, and you can use it to practice the various commands discussed in this chapter. Follow
these steps to create your first vi file:

1. Enter the shell command:

    ```
    $ vi sample.vi
    ```

    The screen is filled with flush-left tildes with a blinking cursor on the first line.

2. Enter the vi command **a** (append) to switch into Input Mode. Do not press **Enter**.

3. Type the following three lines, pressing **Enter** at the end of the first and second lines but not at the end of the third line:

```
List of things to do today.
a. Read chapter 4.
b. Practice vi.
```

While you are entering a line, you can use the **Backspace** key to correct mistakes on the line you are typing, but don't bother to fix mistakes on any previous line for now. You learn how to make changes in later sections of this chapter.

4. Press the **Esc** key to return to the Command Mode.

5. Press ZZ to save your Work Buffer to the file named `sample.vi` and return to the shell. `vi` should print a message giving the size of the `sample.vi` file and then a shell prompt should appear on the bottom left of the screen.

N O T E You will use the preceding steps, or variations of them, for all your editing tasks. Remember the following things about `vi`:

- `vi` starts in Command Mode.

- To enter the Input Mode, press **a** or one of the other commands described in the "Adding and Inserting Text" section later in the chapter.

- Commands entered in the Command Mode are not echoed to the screen.

- You can add text only when you are in the Input Mode.

- You give commands (including Last Line Mode commands) only when you are in the Command Mode.

- Use **Esc** to return you from the Input Mode to the Command Mode.

- You give commands to save changes to a file and can quit only when you are in the Command Mode.

Just as a check, you might want to display your newly created file using the `cat` or `more` command:

```
$ cat sample.vi
List of things to do today.
a. Read chapter 4.
b. Practice vi.
$
```

▶ **See** "Using cat to View Files," **p. 56**

▶ **See** "Using more to View Files," **p. 57**

You are now ready to learn how to move from one place in the file to another.

Moving Around in *vi*

When you edit text, position the cursor to where you want to insert additional text, delete text, correct mistakes, change words, or append text to the end of existing text, you'll need to know the *cursor-positioning commands*.

Part
I

Ch
4

On some terminals and UNIX workstations (such as if you are running UnixWare on a PC), you can use the arrow keys, **Page Up**, and **Page Down** to move around in the file. However, some terminals don't have arrow keys, and even some that include arrow keys don't use them with vi. Therefore, to be usable on all terminal types, vi has adopted the convention of using the "hjkl" keys for moving the cursor. Notice that on a standard keyboard layout, the "hjkl" keys are next to each other. Figure 4.3 shows how these keys can position the cursor. The **h** key moves one character left, **j** moves one line down, **k** moves one line up, and **l** moves one character right.

FIGURE 4.3

The "hjkl" keys are in a convenient location for touch-typists.

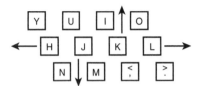

These four keys work on any terminal, and they are easy to use because you don't need to take your hands away from the main part of the keyboard. Here's an example showing simple cursor movements:

1. Bring up the sample.vi file you created earlier:

   ```
   $ vi sample.vi
   ```

   Notice that the cursor is on the letter **L** on the first line of the text.

2. Press the **j** key. The cursor moves down one line to the letter **a**.

3. Press **l, l, k**. Where is the cursor now? It should be on the letter **s** back on the first line of text.

Many commands can be performed repeatedly by prefixing the command with a number. For example, instead of pressing the "j" key three times, you can use **3j** instead. vi will not execute the command if the repeat numeric count puts the cursor outside the range of the buffer. For example, if a file has only ten lines and you issue a **11j**, vi gives you a beep, and the cursor stays where it is.

Most commands in vi can be prefixed by a number. This number causes the specified command to execute the specified number of times. This helps to reduce the number of keystrokes. It also makes a difference when it comes to undoing a command as discussed in the "Undoing Changes" section later in the chapter.

Following are some other keys that move the cursor:

■ Press the **Spacebar** to move the cursor to the right by one character (the same as **l**).

■ Press **Enter** or + to move the cursor to the first *non-blank* at beginning of the next line. (Note that the **j** key simply moves down one line but remains in the same column.)

- Press - to move the cursor to the first non-blank at the beginning of the previous line. (Note that the **k** key simply moves up one line but remains in the same column.)
- Press **0** to move the cursor to the beginning of the current line. Press ^ to move the cursor to the first non-blank on the current line.
- Press **$** to move the cursor to the end of the current line.
- Press **Ctrl+f** to move the cursor forward (down) by one screenful. You can use **Ctrl+d** to scroll down about half a screen.
- Press **Ctrl+b** to move the cursor backward (up) by one screenful. You can use **Ctrl+u** to scroll up about half a screen.
- Press *number* **G** to go to a specific line in the file. Press **G** alone to go to end of the file.
- Press **H** to move to the first line of the screen.
- Press **M** to move to the line in the middle of the screen.
- Press **L** to move to the last line on the screen.

`vi` also allows you to navigate the cursor relative to words on a line using the following three commands:

- **w** moves forward one word.
- **b** moves backward one word.
- **e** moves to the end of the current word.

A *word*, according to `vi`, is a sequence of characters separated from other characters by spaces, punctuation (such as ".", ",", "?", and "-"), or digits. For example, `vi` considers "4th" to be two words: the "4" and the "th"; similarly, "44?" is also considered to be two words: the "44" and the "?".

N O T E The W command also moves the cursor forward by one word, but for W a word is delimited by white space. Therefore, the W command often moves the cursor farther than the w command. Similarly, the B and E commands move the cursor to the beginning and end of the current word, respectively, using white spaces as delimiters. ▪

Adding and Inserting Text

When you first enter `vi`, you are always in the Command Mode. To be able to enter text into your document, you must issue a command. Several commands in `vi` will allow you to start inserting text. The two most often used commands are the letters **i** (insert) and **a** (append). The **i** command starts inserting text before the current character the cursor is on, and the **a** command starts inserting the text you want to type right after the cursor.

The capital letters **I** and **A** are also commonly used. The **I** command starts entering the text from the beginning of the current line regardless of your cursor location on the line. The **A** command starts entering the text at the end of the line. These two commands can save you a lot of time by not having to scroll to the beginning or end of the line and then inserting the text.

Part

I

Ch

4

The commands o and O stand for *open line*. The o command opens a new line directly below your current line. This line will be ready for text to be inserted. The O command opens a new line ready for inserting text directly above your current line. These commands also save you from constantly scrolling.

TIP Using commands in sequence can be powerful. For example say that you are at the top of a file, and you want to start adding text at the end of line 53. Simply type **53G** to take you to line 53, then type **A** to start adding text at the end of that line.

Remember to press **Esc** when you are finished adding text so that you are returned to the Command Mode.

Deleting Text

Making corrections or changes to a file might involve deleting text. You must be in the Command Mode to delete characters. With vi, you can delete a single character, a word, a number of consecutive words, all the text to the end of the line, or an entire line.

The x command can be used to erase a single character. The x command always erases the character to the right of the cursor. If you want to erase a character to the left of the cursor, use the X key. If you need to delete many characters, the x or X command can be prefixed with a number representing the number of characters to erase, such as **5x** to erase five characters.

If you need to delete a word, the dw command is most efficient. The dw command deletes a single word from the cursor position forward in the document. Prefixing dw with a numeric erases the specified number of words. The db command deletes a single word from the cursor position backward in the text.

Deleting all the text from the current cursor position to the end of the line is accomplished using the d$ or D command. **Ctrl+d** deletes all text from the current cursor position to the beginning of the line.

If you need to delete a line or line of text, use the dd command. The dd command deletes the current line that your cursor is positioned on. If you need to delete multiple lines of text, you can specify the number of lines to delete before the dd command. For example, 5dd deletes the line that your cursor is positioned on and the four lines below it.

N O T E When you delete two or more lines, the status line shows how many lines were deleted.

You can be more specific when deleting lines using Last Line Mode. The :d command deletes the current line. You can also pass line addresses to commands in Last Line Mode. For example, if your cursor were on line 30 of a file and you wanted to delete lines 5 through 10, you could use the following command:

```
Esc:5,10d
```

Addresses used in Last Line Mode can be absolute or relative. Say that you were currently on line 54 of a file, and you want to delete all the text from five lines above your cursor position to 8 lines below your current position. You could easily accomplish that using the :d command with the following relative addresses; the "." in an address represents your current line:

```
Esc:.-5,.+8d
```

The ^ and $ characters may be used in the line address used in Last Line Mode to represent the first and last line on the document, respectively. For example, if you need to delete all the text from you current line to the end of the document, use the following command:

```
Esc:.,$d
```

 TIP Most commands used in Last Line Mode can be used with an address. The address always is placed in front of the command and forces that command to act on the lines specified in the address.

 TIP You can use :set number or :set nu to ask vi to display line numbers. To turn off line numbering, use :set nonu.

Changing and Replacing Text

Part
I
Ch
4

Now that you have learned how to add and delete text, you can take a look at changing existing text. These next commands will help the keystrokes you need to type in vi.

First, the **r** (replace) command allows you to replace a single character at the current cursor location. Make sure that you are in Command Mode and place the cursor over the character you want to change. Type the letter **r** followed by the replacement letter. You are placed back in the Command Mode. The R command places vi into the overwrite mode; it continues to re-place the character under the cursor with the new one you enter until you press **Esc**.

If you want to change a particular word, you first must move to be beginning of the word and then type **cw** (change word) or **ce**. A "$" appears at the end of the word that will be changed. Type the new word followed by the **Esc** key. Notice that the editor automatically space the word properly, even if it is shorter or longer than the original word. The cb command changes a particular word that is before the current cursor position.

The C or c$ command replaces all the text from your current position to the end of the current line. Once again, a $ appears at the end of the line when the edit is being performed. When you are finished typing the replacement text, press the **Esc** key to return to Command Mode.

Joining a Line

Sometimes you might need to join two lines together, such as making two shorter lines into a single long line; this is similar to the cat command, which can string together the contents of more than one file. The J command can be used to have two consecutive lines joined into a single line. First, move to the line that will be having text joined to it. Once on the line, simply use the J command to have the line located directly below joined to the current line.

▶ **See** "Using cat to View Files," **p. 56**

Undoing Changes

Like many editors, vi allows you to undo edit changes. However, vi can only undo the last edit change for a given line. Two levels of undo are supported. The u command will undo the most recent change, and U will undo all recent changes on the current line. (Recent means since you last moved to the line. After you move away from the line, the U command won't work.)

As previously mentioned, you can type a number before a command to make the command repeat that many times. This feature is not only a keystroke-saver, but it also makes a big difference when it comes to undoing changes. When you place a number before a command, vi considers that a single command (but executed repeatedly). If you actually enter the command several times, each is considered a separate command. Therefore, xxxxx is five commands, whereas 5x is considered one command. You might wonder why this is important.

The difference between one command and several is important when you use the u command because the u command can only undo the last change. Therefore, if you used xxxxx to delete five characters, u will only undelete the last character deleted. However, if you used 5x, the u command can recover all five deleted characters.

Repeating Commands

When editing a file, a command might need to be executed many times. The . command can be used to repeat the last command. Suppose that you wanted to insert a # symbol at the beginning a several lines including the current line of text. You could first use the I command to begin inserting text at the beginning of the current line. You would then enter the # and press the **Esc** key. You now can scroll to the other lines that need the # at the beginning of the line and just push the . key. The period repeats the inserting of the # at the beginning of the line.

The . command can be used to repeat nearly any command executed in vi.

Managing Files

One way to tell vi which file you want to edit is to supply the filename as an argument when you start vi. Thus the shell command:

```
$ vi sample.vi
```

tells the system that you want to use vi to edit the file sample.vi. (If the file doesn't exist, it will be created.) When you are finished editing, you can use the ZZ command to save the changes and then exit from vi. This method is fine if all you want to do is edit a single file and then do something else, but it is clumsy if your needs are more complicated. vi contains several other file manipulation possibilities you should know about.

Saving Without Exiting   If you are working with a single file for an extended period of time, you should periodically save your work. This helps to prevent a loss of data should the machine crash or if you make a mistake. Because you are working with a copy of the original file in memory (the Work Buffer), you can force an update back to the original file using the :w (write) command.

N O T E   When you invoke the `:w` command, the command itself is displayed on the status line (because it is a Last Line Mode command), and then when the update is complete, the size of your file is printed on the status line. ▪

The `:w` command also allows you to specify a filename when you write the file, `:w filename`. This allows you to make copies of your text in several files.

Quitting Without Saving   Occasionally while editing you make a mess of the file. Your mistake might be an accidental deletion, an addition you don't like, or some other changes that are too pervasive to fix with a few moments of reediting. In these cases, it is sometimes better to abandon the file without updating the original copy and start over again. The `:q!` command quits an editing session without saving the Work Buffer to the original file.

The exclamation mark in the command says to `vi`, "Yes, I know what I am doing so let me quit," so `vi` will allow you to exit without printing a warning message. Without the exclamation mark (for example, `:q`), `vi` will warn you that the Work Buffer has been modified (since it was last saved) and refuse to quit.

T I P   Be careful when you quit without saving the changes. As a safety precaution, you might want to save the Work Buffer to a different file so that you have the original copy and the copy that you are abandoning.

CAUTION

There may be times when you open a file in `vi` that you get a message about "line too long" or you see some strange (control) characters on the screen. These might be results of you trying to open a file created by a word processor (such as WordPerfect) or any (binary) executable program. In these cases, use the `:q!` command to exit the file immediately. Otherwise, you might inadvertently write some changes to the file and corrupt it.

Editing a Different File   When you are working on a programming project, for example, there usually are a number of files that you need to constantly edit. It isn't necessary to leave `vi` to start working on a completely different file. All you need to do is first save your current work using `:w` and then tell `vi` that you want to edit a new file using the `:e filename` command. You must supply the filename for the new file. If the file doesn't exist, it will be created; otherwise, it will be read into the Work Buffer so that you can start working with it.

If you haven't saved your previous work, the `:e` command causes `vi` to print an error message as the new file will overwrite the contents of your Work Buffer. If you really want to start working on a new file without saving the changes, you must use the `:e!` command.

Adding One File to Another   At times, you might need to include the content of one file into another. The `:r filename` command allows you to do that—it takes the text from *filename* and adds it to another file after the current line.

One use of the :r command is to add standard boilerplate text to a document.

Recovering Text After a Crash

If the system crashes while you are editing a file with vi, you can often recover text that would otherwise be lost. If the system saved a copy of your Work Buffer, it might send you an email telling you so. However, even if you don't get an email from the system, give the following command a try to see whether the system saved the contents of your Work Buffer:

```
$ vi -r filename
```

where *filename* was the name of the file you were working on when the system crashed. If your work was saved, you will be editing a recent copy of your Work Buffer. After inspecting the text in the Work Buffer, you should immediately use :w to save the salvaged copy of the Work Buffer to disk before continuing editing.

 In case corrupted text is in the recovered Work Buffer, you might want to save the Work Buffer to a different filename and then use cut and paste to update the (yet) unchanged version of your file.

Basic *vi* Command Summary

At first glance, the vi command set appears to be a hopeless jumble. There are 128 separate codes in the ASCII character set, and vi has assigned a specific meaning to about 100 of them. One of the goals in the design of the vi command set was to make the commands mnemonic. With just a few exceptions, each command letter or symbol is reminiscent of the command name: a to append, i for insert, and so on. Table 4.1 summarizes the vi commands that have been presented in this section.

Table 4.1 Basic *vi* Commands

Cursor Movement Commands

h	Left one character
j	Down one line
k	Up one line
l, Spacebar	Right one character
Enter, +	First non-blank at beginning of next line
-	First non-blank at beginning of previous line
0, ^	Beginning of current line
$	End of current line
Ctrl+f	Forward (down) by one screen full

Cursor Movement Commands

Ctrl+d	Scroll down about half a screen
Ctrl+b	Backward (up) by one screen full
Ctrl+u	Scroll up about half a screen
*n*G	Goto line *n*.
H	First line of screen
M	Middle line of screen
L	Last line on screen
w, W	Forward one word
b, B	Backward one word
e, E	End of current word.i.vi:commands:summary tables;.i.commands:vi:summary tables;

Text Entry Commands

a, A	Append text
i, I	Insert text
o, O	Open new line and add text
Esc	Return to Command Mode

Text Deletion Commands

x, X	Delete character
dw	Delete word
db	Delete previous word
dd	Delete current line
d$, D	Delete to end of line
Ctrl+d	Delete to beginning of line
:*x*,*y*d	Delete line *x* to line *y* (using Last Line Command Mode)
J	Join lines together
u	Undo last change
U	Restore last deleted line

continues

Part

I

Ch

4

Table 4.1 Continued

Text Replacement Commands

r, R	Replace character
cw, ce	Change word
cb	Change word backward
c$, C	Change to end of line
cc	Change the entire line

File Manipulation Commands

:w	Write Work Buffer to original file
:w *filename*	Write Work Buffer to *filename*
:e *filename*	Start editing a new file named *filename*
:e! *filename*	Start editing a new file named *filename* without saving the previous content
:r *filename*	Read contents of *filename* into Work Buffer
:q	Quit, don't save changes (a warning is printed if a modified Work Buffer hasn't been saved yet)
:q!	Quit, don't save changes (no warning)
ZZ	Save Work Buffer and then quit

Other Commands

.	Repeat last executed command

Advanced *vi* Techniques

Although vi has hundreds of commands, you can easily get by with just a handful such as those presented in the previous section. In this section, you learn of a group of vi commands that enable you to perform sophisticated text editing functions.

Copying and Pasting Text

When you delete or cut characters, words, lines, or a portion of a line, the deleted data is saved in a *buffer* (much like the Clipboard you have in Microsoft Windows). This buffer is known as the *unnamed* buffer, but the name of this buffer isn't important; what is important is that you can put or paste the contents of that buffer anywhere in the text you're editing. You do that with the p or P (put, or paste) command. The p command pastes the data to the right of the cursor; the P command pastes the data to the left of the cursor.

TIP Both of the paste commands can be executed many times to paste the text in the buffer to multiple places throughout the document.

N O T E vi contains three sets of buffers: the *unnamed* buffer (due to lack of a better name), nine *numbered* buffers that contain the nine most recent line deletions, and 26 *named* buffers identified by "a" through "z." By default, the unnamed buffer is used for all deletion, copying, and pasting operations. The discussion of the use of named and numbered buffers is beyond the scope of this chapter. Refer to your vi manual included with your system for more information about using these buffers. ▪

You don't have to delete before you can paste. You can copy text first and then paste. In vi's parlance, the text copying operation is referred to as *yank*. The yanking of text is accomplished with the y or Y command. The yw command yanks the current word into the buffer. A number before the yw command represents the number of words to be yanked. For example, 5yw yanks five words into the buffer.

The yy command copies the current line of text into the buffer. The yy command can be prefixed by a number representing how many lines of text to yank into the copy buffer. For example, 5yy yanks the current line and the four lines following the current line into the buffer. The y or y$ command yanks text starting from the current cursor position to the end of the line.

Searching for Text

If you are editing a document that has more than a few dozen lines, it becomes difficult to find a word, phrase, or number in the file. vi has several ways to search for text patterns in your document. It has a single-character search for moving from one place on a line to another, and it has a more sophisticated search command for locating a text pattern anywhere in the file.

The single-character search is a speedy way to maneuver on a line. This f command followed by a character moves the cursor to the next occurrence of that character on the *current* line. For example, fa moves the cursor to the right to the next letter "a" on the line. The F command searches backward, toward the beginning of the line. You can use the ; command to repeat the last f or F command (or it can be repeated in the reversed direction using the , command).

> **CAUTION**
> The use of the , command may be confusing at times. If you have previously used a fa command to look for the next letter **a** to the right of the cursor, the , command looks for the next letter **a** in the opposite direction—to the left of the cursor.

The general text search capability of vi is invoked by the / command. To search for a pattern in a forward direction in the file, use the / command. A "/" appears at the bottom of the screen (just as with the ":" commands). Next, you must specify the pattern you are looking for—this can include a word, part of a word, or a regular expression. A regular expression is a pattern containing wildcard characters; the expression should end with another / character. When you press **Enter**, vi positions the cursor at the next occurrence of the pattern specified. If the pattern cannot be found, vi returns a message "pattern not found."

▶ **See** "Filtering Commands," **p. 70**

After finding the pattern, if you want to have vi find the next occurrence of the same pattern, the n command can be used instead of retyping the search command. If you need to search for the last search pattern in *reverse* direction, use the N command. If you want to search from the current position and proceed toward the top of the file, use the ? command rather than /. When the ? command is used, the n command continues the search up the file, and the N searches downward in the file.

N O T E   Searching in vi is case-sensitive. Therefore, make sure that you specify the proper case in the search pattern. ▪

Certain characters, such as "*", "[", "^", "$", "\", and ".", carry special meanings in vi, and when used in the search pattern, you might not get the results you wanted. For example, if you want to find a text string "end." (where there is a period at the end of the word), you must "escape" the period (that is, make a character lose its special meaning); to vi, the period means "any character." If you perform a search using /end., vi will locate *ending*, the word *end* followed by a space, other combinations of the word *end* with other characters, as well as the word *end* followed by a period. To find only "end.", enter /end\. (slash, end, backslash, period) as the search command.

Search and Replacing Text

Now that you know how to search for text patterns in vi, you can extend your knowledge to be able to perform complex search and replace routines.

The search and replace routines are performed in Last Line Mode, meaning that the **:** will be used before each search and replace routine. The syntax is as follows:

`:[address]s/pattern/newpattern/[g]`

The address specifies the lines that the search and replace will be performed against. The address is optional, and if not specified, the search and replace function will only be performed on the current line. The address is expressed in the form of [start_line,stop_line]. For example, the address 5,50 means lines 5 through 50. The address [.,100] means from your current line to line 100. The address 1,$ represents from line 1 through the last line of the document.

The "pattern" can be a fixed string or a regular expression. The "newpattern" can only be a fixed string and cannot contain any regular expressions.

The optional letter **g** can be included at the end of the expression, forcing the editor the search and replace in a global manner on a particular line of text. By default, vi only looks for the specified pattern once on any given line. Without the **g** option (default), vi only searches and replaces the first occurrence of the pattern on a given line.

TIP When addressing all the lines in the text file, you can use the address 1,$, or you can use the shortcut, the percent "%" symbol. For example, the following expression would search the entire file for the word "unix" and replace with the word "UNIX."

```
:%s/unix/UNIX/g
```

Some simple and complex examples of searching and replacing are shown here:

`:1,30s/users/people/`	Search for the first occurrence of the string "users" and replace with the string "people", only on lines 1 through 30.
`:1,30s/users/people/`	Search for the first occurrence of the word "users" and replace it with the word "people", on lines 1 through 30.
`:1.$s/^Unix$/UNIX/`	Search the entire file for the string "Unix" on a line by itself and replace it with the string "UNIX".
`:%s/[0-9][0-9]*\.//`	Remove all numbers followed by a period from the beginning of any line in the file.

Escaping to the Shell

Do you often find that you need to do other things while you are in the middle of a vi editing session? For example, you need to check or send an email or look up the correct name of a file that is being referenced in your document. Of course, you could save your vi file, exit from vi, and then attend to the interruption. However, it is usually easier to escape temporarily to a UNIX shell, do what needs to be done, and then resume your vi session where you left off.

You can "escape" to the UNIX shell from within vi in two ways. The first method is used if you want to run a single UNIX command, such as ls. To do this, enter :! followed by the UNIX command you want to execute, followed by an **Enter**. vi takes the command and hands it to a shell, the shell executes the command, and then vi resumes. In the example illustrated in Figure 4.4, the ls command is executed (using :!ls /usr/peter/report) from within vi. When ls has finished listing the files in the /usr/peter/report directory, vi regains control and prompts you to press **Enter** to continue. vi erases the screen, redraws the display of the file being edited, and returns the cursor to the original position.

Part
I

Ch
4

FIGURE 4.4

Obtaining a directory listing without exiting vi.

```
This is a sample file.
This is line 2.
This is line 3.

—

—
:!ls/etc./peter/report
usage.1998      usage.1999
projected.usage.2000
[Hit<CR>]
```

The second escape method is for when you need to execute several UNIX commands. Use the :!sh command to start a new shell that can be used for as long as you want. When you are ready to return to vi, enter the exit command or press **Ctrl+d**.

> **CAUTION**
>
> One common mistake often made by people using the : ! sh command is that they try to resume the original vi editing session by entering the vi command again. This brings up a new vi session and does not resuming the original one. Because UNIX multitasks, you can have multiple vi sessions running concurrently. Sometimes this is desirable, but most times not. If you become unsure on how many copies of vi are running, use the ps command (see Chapter 6, "UNIX Processes" for details).

> **N O T E**   You can also put vi to "sleep" using **Ctrl+z**, "spawn" a new process to perform the necessary tasks, and then return to vi. This technique is discussed in Chapter 16, "Automating Tasks." ▪

Advanced *vi* Command Summary

vi contains a wealth of other functions that are have not been touched upon in this chapter. For example, the use of named and numbered buffers, marking of text, macros, and buffer filtering have not be discussed. Table 4.2 summarizes the advanced vi commands that have been presented in this section.

Table 4.2   Advanced *vi* Commands

Buffer Manipulation Commands

p	Paste text from buffer to the right of cursor
P	Paste text from buffer to the left of cursor
y	Yank text into buffer (delete also saves text into buffer)
Y, y$	Yank from cursor position to end of line
yy	Yank the entire current line

Text Search Commands

fc	Intraline search forward for character *c*
Fc	Intraline search backward for character *c*
;	Repeat last intraline search
,	Repeat last intraline search in opposite direction
/pattern	Forward search for *pattern*
?pattern	Backward search for *pattern*
n	Repeat last search

Text Search Commands

N	Repeat last search in opposite direction
:[x,y]s/pattern/ newpattern/[g]	Search for *pattern* and replace with *newpattern* between lines x and y

Shell Escapes

:!command	Escape to perform one command
:!sh	Start a subshell. Use exit or **Ctrl+d** to return to vi.

Setting *vi* Options

The vi editor has several options you may or may not choose to use. Some of these options can be set on a system wide basis by the system administrator. You can customize your environment with a number of options that are in effect whenever you start vi.

Setting Options Inside *vi*

Many options can be configured in vi to alter its functionality. All the options are configured in the Last Line Mode using the :set command. To obtain a list of all the configurable options use the following command within vi:

`:set all`

You can see a list of the settings that differ from the defaults by entering the command:

`:set`

N O T E   Many of the setting names have abbreviations that you can use instead of their longer versions. ▨

Many of vi's settings are either on or off. For those settings, the mode is enabled with the command :set *modename* or unset by prefixing a no to the mode name, :set *nomodename*. The other options have values, which are set using the command:

`:set modename=modevalue`

T I P   You can set more than one option on the same line. Simply separate each option with a space, as in the following example:

`:set showmode report=3 warn wm=5`

Part

I

Ch

4

Option List

Table 4.3 lists some of the more commonly used vi set options. You can use either the full name of the option or the abbreviation shown in the parentheses. Consult your vi manual for more information about all vi options.

Table 4.3   Commonly used *vi* Set Options

Option	Function
autoindent (ai)	When autoindent is set, each newly appended line has the same amount of white space as the preceding line. (Default is noautoindent.)
errorbells (eb)	Ring the terminal's bell when there is a command error. (Default is noerrorbells.)
ignorecase (ic)	Causes vi to ignore case distinctions in searches and substitutions. (Default is noignorecase.)
list (li)	Causes vi to display tabs and end-of-line markers explicitly: Tabs are shown as ^I, and end-of-line markers as $. (Default is nolist.)
number (nu)	Turn on line numbering at the beginning of each line. (Default is nonumber.)
report=*n*	When a command modifies more than *n* lines, vi prints a message. (Default is 5.)
shell (sh)	Contains the name of the shell to use for the :! and :sh commands. The value of this option is taken, if possible, from the $SHELL environment variable when vi starts to run. Setting shell to /bin/csh makes the C shell your default shell from within vi.
shiftwidth (sw)	Specified the width of vi's software tab stop. This value is used when the autoindent mode is on. (Default is 8.)
showmode	This option turns on the mode display on the status line. (Default is noshowmode.)
term=*name*	Contains the name of the terminal. The value of this option is taken, if possible, from the $TERM environment variable when vi starts to run.
warn	When warn is set, vi warns you if you enter a :! (shell) command without first saving your Work Buffer. (Default is warn.)
wrapmargin=*n* (wm)	Specifies the number of columns from the right margin of the screen before which vi automatically moves the text down to the following line. A line break is automatically inserted between words. (Default is 0, which disables the wm feature.)

Setting Options Outside *vi*

Although any of the option settings can be changed while in vi, you might want to place your customary options into the vi startup file, .exrc, so that the various set commands are executed each time vi starts. The .exrc file can be in your home directory, your current directory, or both. Following is an example of a common .exrc file; note that the set commands start with the word set but no colon (:).

```
set showmode
set autoindent
set wm=5
set shell=/etc/ksh
```

Alternatively, you can set more than one option on the same line. Simply separate each option with a space, as shown in the following example:

```
set showmode autoindent wm=5 shell=/etc/ksh
```

N O T E   The .exrc file is read when you start vi. If you create or modify it while you're in vi, you must restart vi to have the (new) settings take effect. ▨

Other UNIX Editors

Throughout the UNIX system's history, there have been several common programs for text editing. The first UNIX text editor was ed, a line-oriented editor. Because it was the original editor, many other UNIX editors contain a syntax or command-line language that has many similarities to ed's. Some examples are sed (a stream editor), lex (lexicon analyzer, a programmer's utility), awk (a programmable text manipulation language), grep (a text searching program), and the edit-ex-vi family of text editors. Other commonly used UNIX text editors include Emacs (Editor MACroS), pico (Pine COmposer), and joe (Joe's Own Editor).

Emacs and its variants (such as Freemacs, by Russell Nelson and MicroEmacs, by Dave Conroy) are available for a wide variety of operating systems, ranging from DOS to MiNT (for Atari ST) to DEC VMS. Originally developed by Richard Stallman, the first Emacs was a set of macros written in 1976 at MIT for the editor TECO (Text Editor and COrrector, originally Tape Editor and COrrector) under the ITS operating system on a PDP-10. The Emacs program itself was started by Guy Steele as a project to unify the many divergent TECO command sets and key bindings at MIT. A number of Emacs versions are available for UNIX systems, and the most notable version is Stallman's GNU Emacs.

N O T E   Richard Stallman is a founder and proponent of the Free Software Foundation and the GNU project; GNU stands for "GNU is Not UNIX." The proponents of the GNU project believe very strongly that all software should be free and that computer systems should be open for use by anyone. Any software released under the GNU banner encourages users to take it for their own use, and users are encouraged to make modifications and share those changes with others. ▨

N O T E   All GNU software (such as Emacs and Linux) is distributed under the terms of the GNU
Public License Agreement (GPL). The GPL says that you have the right to copy, modify, and
redistribute the code covered by the agreement, but that when you redistribute the code, you must also
distribute the same license with the code, making the code and license inseparable. Because this is
the reverse of the way a normal copyright works (where GPL gives you rights instead of limiting them),
the GPL is often referred to as a "GNU copyleft," or simply copyleft.

The real legal meaning of the GNU General Public License (copyleft) will only be known if and when a
judge rules on its validity and scope. As of this writing, there has not yet been a copyright infringement
case involving the GPL to set any precedents. ◼

Unlike vi, the Emacs editor is *modeless*: Simply start up the editor, and everything you type
goes into the file buffer. Control+key sequences (such as Ctrl+x) and the **Esc** key are used to
save files, search for text, delete text, and so on. Emacs has built-in online help and can be accessed using **Ctrl+h h**.

pico, a trademark of the University of Washington, is the name for the Pine composer and is
available in two ways: It is compiled on its own to be a standalone editor or compiled as a library for Pine (an email system, also a trademark of the University of Washington) to support
composition of messages within Pine. pico is Pine's internal editor invoked when users need to
fill in header lines or type the text of an email message. pico is available as freeware and has
been ported to other operating systems such as DEC Ultrix, DEC VMS, NeXT, and DOS/
Windows. The program has extensive internal help files.

Developed by Joseph Allen, joe is a powerful ASCII-text screen editor, yet it is freeware. It has
a "modeless" user interface, which is similar to many user-friendly PC editors. If you are familiar with Micro-Pro's WordStar (remember it?) or Borland's "Turbo" languages (such as Turbo
Pascal), you will feel at home. joe is a full-featured UNIX screen editor, though, and has many
features for editing programs and text:

N O T E   At the time of writing, you can obtain the latest version by anonymous ftp from:
ftp://ftp.std.com. ◼

▶ **See** "Using ftp," **p. 430**

▶ **See** "The grep Command," **p. 72**

◼ Search and replace system, including powerful regular expressions, including matching
of balanced C expressions.

◼ Tags file search.

◼ Paragraph format.

◼ Undo and redo.

◼ Position history allows you to get back to previous editing contexts and allows you to
quickly flip between editing contexts.

◼ Multiple keyboard macros.

- Block move, copy, delete, and filtering.
- Rectangle (columnar) mode.
- Overtype and insert modes.
- Indent and unindent.
- Autoindent mode.
- Goto matching using "(", "[", and "{" (like in vi).

joe also supports many options:

- Can have Emacs-style cursor recentering on scrolls.
- Extended ASCII characters between 128-255 can be shown as-is for non-English character sets.
- Final NEWLINE (line-feed) can be forced on end-of-file.
- Can start with a help screen on.
- Left/Right margin settings.
- Adjustable tab width.
- Indentation step and fill character.

For UNIX systems that have a GUI desktop, such as UnixWare, you can find a graphical text editor. UnixWare's Text Editor is an example. UNIX versions of popular PC-based commercial word processors also are available. For example, you can purchase WordPerfect for UNIX, and it functions and behaves just like its DOS/Windows version.

Part

I

Ch

4

From Here...

The vi editor, as cryptic as it may sometimes seem, offers you a fast and well-supported method to make changes to text files. This chapter covered the most commonly used vi skills and commands that allow you to use vi effectively.

- For a discussion of UNIX shells and commonly used commands and utilities, see Chapter 3, "UNIX Shells and System Commands."
- To investigate and learn about the layout and structure of the UNIX file system, see Chapter 5, "Files, Directories, and Permissions."
- To learn how to create scripts to help automate repetitive tasks, see Chapter 7, "Essential Shell Scripting."
- To learn about printing in the UNIX environment, see Chapter 14, "Printing."
- For a discussion of networking basics, see Chapter 17, "Networking Essentials."

Files, Directories, and Permissions

by Sriranga Veeraraghavan and Jeff Robinson

In this chapter

The UNIX File and Directory Structure

UNIX uses a hierarchical structure for organizing files and directories that is often referred to as a *directory tree*. In this tree, there is a single root node, /, and all other directories are contained below it. This is slightly different from the multiroot hierarchical structure used by Windows and MacOS. In those operating systems, all devices (floppy disks, CD-ROMs, hard drives, and so on) are mounted at the highest directory level. The UNIX model is slightly different, but after a short time, most users find it extremely convenient.

▶ **See** "Mounting and Unmounting File Systems," **p. 336**

Every directory, including /, can be used to store files along with other directories. Every file is stored in a directory, and every directory except / is stored in another directory. This brings about the notion of "parent" directories and subdirectories. For example, consider two directories, where directory A contains directory B. In this case, A is called the parent of B, and B is called a subdirectory of A.

This arrangement of parent directories and subdirectories produces the tree structure of the UNIX directory tree. The depth of the directory tree is limited only by the fact that the *absolute* path to a file cannot have more than 1,024 characters.

File and Directory Names

In UNIX, every file and directory has a name associated with it. The name of a file or a directory is made up of its name along with its parent's name—its *pathname*. Two examples of pathnames are as follows:

```
/home/ranga/docs/book/ch5.doc
/usr/local/bin/
```

As you can see, each of these pathnames is a set of strings separated by the / character. In UNIX, the / character is used to separate directories, whereas the strings are used to name files or directories. The sum of all the strings and the / characters makes up the pathname.

The last set of characters in a pathname is the actual name of the file or directory; the rest of the characters represent its parent directories. In the first example, the filename is ch5.doc.

The name can be up to 255 characters long and can contain any ASCII character except /. Generally, the characters used in pathnames are the alphanumeric characters (a-z,A-Z,0-9) along with the characters '.','-','_'. Other characters are usually avoided because many programs cannot deal with them properly.

One thing to keep in mind about filenames is that two files in the same directory cannot have the same name. Thus both of the following filenames:

```
/home/ranga/docs/ch5.doc
/home/ranga/docs/ch5.doc
```

refer to the same file. But the following filenames:

```
/home/ranga/docs/ch5.doc
/home/ranga/docs/books/ch5.doc
```

refer to different files because they are located in different directories. Because UNIX is case-sensitive, it is possible to have two files in the same directory whose names differ only by case. The following:

```
/home/ranga/docs/ch5.doc
/home/ranga/docs/CH5.doc
```

are considered different files by UNIX. This is often a source of confusion for users coming from the Windows or DOS environment.

▶ **See** "Navigating Directories," **p. 48**

N O T E Files and directories that use the dot character, ".", as the first character in their name are considered "hidden" and are ignored by the ls command, even when shell metacharacters like "?" or "*" are used to list files. These files can be viewed by specifying the -a option with the ls command. Many programs, including the shell, store their startup information in hidden files. ■

Pathnames

To access a file or directory, you must specify its pathname. As you have seen, a pathname consists of two parts—the name of the directory and the names of its parents. In UNIX, there are two ways to specify the names of the parent directory. This leads to two types of pathnames:

- Absolute
- Relative

N O T E A good analogy for the difference between absolute and relative pathnames is the difference between the following statements:

"I live in San Jose."

"I live in San Jose, California, USA."

The first statement only gives the city in which I live. It does not give any more information, thus the location of my house is relative. The second statement fully qualifies the location of my house, thus it is an absolute location. ■

Absolute Pathnames   An absolute pathname represents the location of a file or directory starting from the root directory and listing all the directories between the root and the file or directory of interest.

Because absolute pathnames list the path from the root directory, they always start with the / character. Regardless of what the current directory is, an absolute path will point to an exact location of a file or directory. The following is an example of an absolute pathname:

```
/home/ranga/work/bugs.txt
```

CAUTION

A common problem encountered by new UNIX users is the removal of files with special characters as the first character in their filename.

Often files with names like "`-file`" are created accidentally, but the rm command gets confused and refuses to remove it. For example:

```
rm -file
```

Will report an error like the following:

```
rm: invalid option -- l
```

In this case, calling rm with the absolute pathname of the file causes it to be removed:

```
rm /home/ranga/-file
```

Relative Pathnames   Relative pathnames allow for accessing files and directories by specifying a path to them relative to your current directory. These pathnames are highly dependent on the directory that you are currently located in. To find out what the current directory is, use the pwd command, which prints the name of the directory in which you are currently located.

When specifying a relative pathname, the / character will not be present at the beginning of the pathname. This identifies that a relative pathname is being used instead of an absolute pathname. The relative pathname will be a list of the directories located between your current directory and the file or directory you are representing.

If in your pathname you are pointing to directories that are below your current one, then the directory names are used as normal. To access the current directory's parent directory or other directories at a higher level in the tree than the current level, the special name .. can be used.

The UNIX file system uses two dots, .., to represent the directory above you in the tree, and a single dot, ., to represent your current directory. For example, the relative pathname:

```
../docs/ch5.doc
```

represents the file:

```
/home/ranga/docs/ch5.doc
```

if the current directory was:

```
/home/ranga/work
```

N O T E   To make pathnames easier to remember for users, UNIX shells such as csh, tcsh, ksh, and bash support a special kind of relative pathname.

In these shells, files and directories can be referenced relative to the user's home directory by using the tilde character, '~' as the first character of a pathname. When these shells encounter the ~, they replace it with the absolute path to the user's home directory. The simplest use of this feature is as follows:

```
cd ~/
```

This puts me in my home directory. Tilde expansion is much more useful for changing into subdirectories below your home directory. For example, the command:

```
cd ~/docs
```

puts me in the directory:

```
/home/ranga/docs
```

In addition, if a username appears after the tilde, these shells replace this string with the absolute path to that user's home directory. For example, the command:

```
cat ~shannon/recipes/cake
```

Displays the contents of the file named cake, located in the subdirectory named recipes, of the user shannon's home directory. ▨

Organization of the Directory Tree

In comparison with most other operating systems, the UNIX directory tree tends to be well organized, with programs and files placed in logical subdirectories with short and easy to remember names.

Another feature of the UNIX directory tree is that most of the tree cannot be written to or deleted by ordinary users; only root can make important changes that affect the system. By centralizing the ability to make changes, UNIX adds security to a system and prevents unfortunate and costly mistakes. Because users cannot accidentally delete or modify essential files and directories, UNIX machines can be configured and then left to run without intervention for extended periods of time. This is one of the major advantages of a UNIX system over Windows or MacOS. Its file system security makes the job of administrators easier, but this security does not hinder the ability of users to accomplish their work.

▶ **See** "Working With Users," **p. 76**

Part

I

Ch

5

This section looks at the organization of a typical UNIX system starting from the root directory /.

The root directory

Usually the / directory is very clean and only holds the most essential files. For example, the / directory on my system looks something like the following:

```
dev/        mnt/        sbin/           tmp/
bin/        etc/        lib/            opt/        usr/
boot/       home/       lost+found/     proc/       var/
```

In addition to these files, on most systems, a few hidden files may be present in this directory. These are usually the initialization files for the root users, whose home directory is usually /.

System Directories

Located under the root directory are several system directories. This section looks at some of these directories.

/bin* and */sbin   Most of the essential programs for using and maintaining a UNIX system are stored in the /bin and /sbin directories. The bin in the names of these directories comes from the fact that executable programs in UNIX are binary files. The name sbin indicates that the directory contains system binaries.

The /bin directory is usually used to hold the most commonly used essential user programs, such as the following:

- login
- Shells (bash, ksh, csh)
- File manipulation utilities (cp, mv, rm, ln, tar)
- Editors (ed, vi)
- File system utilities (dd, df, mount, umount, sync)
- System utilities (uname, hostname, arch)

In addition to these types of programs, the /bin directory might also contain GNU utilities like gzip and gunzip. The /sbin directory, by comparison, is used to hold maintenance programs such as the following:

- fsck
- fdisk
- mkfs
- shutdown

/etc   Another important directory is /etc. This directory is normally used to store the systemwide configuration files required by programs. Some of the important files it contains are as follows:

- passwd   This file is the system's user database, and is used to allow users to log in.
- fstab   This file contains a list of all the hard drives and removable media the system can automatically mount.
- hosts   This file contains a list of IP addresses and their corresponding symbolic names.
- profile   This file is the systemwide shell configuration file. It can be used by a system administrator to make sure that all users have a common environment.

The /etc directory contains files necessary for system startup. The organization of these files varies between different versions of UNIX.

▶ **See** "The UNIX Boot Process," **p. 271**

N O T E Solaris has a standard System V setup for system initialization files, in that the /etc directory contains several directories with names like rcx.d, where x is a number between 1 and 6. Each of these numbers corresponds to a different "run level," and is accessed by the init program based on its initialization file /etc/inittab.

On FreeBSD, the /etc directory contains a script named rc, which controls the behavior of the system during boot time. This script often references another script called rc.local, to handle local startup issues. The BSD version of the init program does not use the /etc/inittab file.

Linux organizes its system initialization files in a manner similar to Solaris but allows for local changes via the rc.local file, in a manner similar to BSD. In Linux, the rcx.d directories are stored in the /etc/rc.d directory.

The AIX initialization system is based on a version of the init program that uses the /etc/inittab file, but it does not use the standard System V rcx.d directories. Like BSD, AIX relies on the script /etc/rc to handle the initialization process.

/home   The /home directory is where all the home directories for all the users on a system are stored. This includes home directories for actual users (people) along with users such as HTTPD and FTPD.

On some systems, root's home directory is also located under the /home directory in /home/root. Most of the advantages of this stem from a desire to keep the / directory clean and to avoid accidental mishaps with the rm command.

/mnt   By convention, the /mnt directory is the directory under which removable media such as CD-ROMs, floppy disks, ZIP disks, or JAZ disks are mounted. On some systems, the /mnt directory contains a number of subdirectories, each of which is a mount point for a particular device type. On my system, the /mnt directory looks like the following:

```
cdrom/    floppy/    jaz/    zip/
```

/tmp and /var   The /tmp and /var directories are used to hold temporary files or files with constantly varying content.

The /tmp directory is usually a dumping ground for files that only need to be used briefly and can afford to be deleted at any time. It usually is quite unstructured, but on a multiuser system, most users abide by the convention of creating a personal directory (named the same as their usernames) in /tmp for storing their temporary files.

The most common use of /tmp, other than as a location for throw-away files, is as a starting point for building and installing programs.

The /var directory is a bit more structured than /tmp and usually looks something like the following:

```
catman/    local/    log/     nis/        run/      tmp/
lib/       lock/     named/   preserve/   spool/    yp/
```

Part
I

Ch
5

Of these directories, the `/var/log` directory is one of the directories with which all users should be familiar because most of the messages generated by the system are stored in it. On my system, `/var/log` contains the following files:

```
./              dmesg         maillog        savacct        spooler        wtmp
../             httpd/        messages       secure         usracct
cron            lastlog       pacct          sendmail.st    uucp/
```

Of these files, the following are helpful when attempting to diagnose system problems:

- `dmesg` contains the messages displayed when the system was last booted.
- `messages` contains all the messages displayed at boot time since the system was first booted.

/usr   By convention, the `/usr` directory is where most programs and files directly relating to users of the system are stored. In some ways, it is a miniature version of the `/` directory. On my system, the `/usr` directory looks like the following:

```
X11/            etc/          libexec/       share/
X11R6/          games/        local/         src/
X386@           man/          tmp@
bin/            include/      openwin/
dict/           info/         opt/
doc/            lib/          sbin/
```

The `/usr/bin` and `/usr/sbin` directories hold the vast majority of the executables available on a system. The function and type of the executables placed into these directories follow the same general convention as for `/bin` and `/sbin`.

In this example, the `/usr/opt` directory server is the same as the `/opt` directory found in UNIX versions such as Solaris. It is the location where optional software packages are usually installed. For example, the Caldera Internet-Office Suite is usually installed into `/usr/opt`.

The `/usr/X11` and `/usr/X11R6` directories and their subdirectories contain the files related to X Window, such as man pages, libraries, and executables. Depending on the type of system you have, the X Window files may or may not exist.

The `/usr/local` directory is the location where local programs, man pages, and libraries are installed. At many sites, most of the directories in `/usr` are kept the same on every computer; but anything that needs to be installed on a particular machine is placed in `/usr/local`, thus identifying those files as local files. This makes maintenance of large numbers of systems easier.

File Types

There are several types of files on your UNIX system. Files can contain your important data, such as files from a word processor or graphics package, or they can be used to represent devices, directories, and symbolic links. This section looks at the different types of files available under UNIX.

Checking a File's Type

The main command used when checking a file's type is the ls command. Specifying the -1 option to ls lists the file type for the specified files. For example, the command:

```
ls -l /home/ranga/.profile
```

produces the following output:

```
-rwxr-xr-x   1 ranga    users        2368 Jul 11 15:57 .profile*
```

Here you see that the first character is a -. This indicates that the file is a regular file. For special files such as directories, the first character will be one of the letters given in Table 5.1.

To get file type information about a directory, the -d option must be specified also:

```
ls -ld /home/ranga
```

which produces the following output:

```
drwxr-xr-x  27 ranga    users        2048 Jul 23 23:49 /home/ranga/
```

Table 5.1   Special Characters for Different File Types

Character	File Type
-	Regular File
d	Directory File
c	Character Special
b	Block Special
l	Symbolic Link
p	Named Pipe
s	Socket

Part

I

Ch

5

The actual descriptions of each of these file types are given in the following sections.

Regular Files

The regular file type is the most common type that you will use. These files are used to store any kind of data. This data may be stored in plain text, an application-specific format, or a special binary format that can be executed by the system.

The data contained in a regular file does not have to be understood by UNIX. A regular file can be used to store any form of raw data because UNIX does not interpret the data that is in the file. UNIX provides many tools to interpret data that is in a file, but that data may be very application specific and therefore cannot be opened with any standard UNIX tools. For example, a file containing a Word Perfect 7.0 document could only be opened and interpreted by an application that understands the Word Perfect 7.0 format.

NOTE Often simply determining that a file is a regular file tells you little about it the file itself. Usually, you need to know whether a particular file is a binary program, a shell script, or a library. In these instances, the `file` program is useful. It is invoked as follows:

```
file [filename]
```

For example, the command:

```
file /bin/ash
```

produces the following output:

```
/bin/ash: ELF 32-bit LSB executable, Intel 80386, version 1, dynamically linked,
stripped
```

Here, you see that the file, `/bin/ash`, is an executable program. Try it out on a few files to get an idea of the kind of information that it can give you.

Directories

Directories are a special file type that serves as containers for files and directories. Internally, UNIX treats a directory as a table of filenames and reference numbers called *inode numbers*. Inodes are covered in great detail later in the chapter, but for now think of inodes as numbers that the kernel uses to locate files. To view the inode number for a file, specify the `-i` option for `ls`.

As new files are created in a directory, a unique inode number is assigned to that file by the kernel, and the directory keeps track of the filename and inode number. Next time you access the file by name, the inode number will be looked up, and the kernel can open the file for you.

Directories are stored in binary format because searching through a plain text file for a filename and inode numbers would be very slow on directories containing many files.

Symbolic Links

A *symbolic link* is a special file that points to another file on the system. When you access one of these files, it has a pathname stored inside it. This pathname is used to forward you to the file or directory on the system represented by the pathname stored in the symbolic link.

Symbolic links can be used to have a file appear as though it's located in many different places or has many different names in the file system. Symbolic links may point to any type of file or directory.

Symbolic links are created using the `ln` command with the `-s` option. The syntax is as follows:

```
ln -s [source path] [symbolic_link_name]
```

For example, the following command:

```
ln -s /home/httpd/html/users/ranga /home/ranga/public_html
```

creates a link in my home directory to my Web files. Using `ls` on a link produces output similar to the following:

```
lrwxrwxrwx   1 ranga   users   26 Nov  9  1997 public_html -> ../httpd/html/
users/ranga
```

This output indicates that the file is a link and also shows the file or directory that is pointed to by the link.

Device Files

UNIX devices are accessed through reading and writing to device files. These device files are access points to the device within the file systems. Later in the book when we cover adding new devices, we will look at creating device files.

Usually, device files are located under the /dev directory. The two main types of devices files are as follows:

- Character special
- Block special

Character Special Files   Character special files provide a mechanism for communicating with a device one character at a time. Usually, character devices are used to represent a "raw" device. The output of ls on a character special file looks like the following:

```
crw-------   1 ranga   users    4,   0 Feb  7 13:47 /dev/tty0
```

The first letter in the output is c, thus we know that this particular file is a character special file, but we also see that there are two extra numbers before the date. The first number is called the *major* number, and the second number is called the *minor* number. These two numbers are used by UNIX to identify the device driver that this file communicates with.

Block Special Files   Block special files also provide a mechanism for communicating with device drivers via the file system. These files are called block devices because they transfer large blocks of data at a time. This type of file is typically used to represent hard drives and removable media.

Let's look at the ls -l output for a typical block device. For example, /dev/sda:

```
brw-rw----   1 root    disk     8,   0 Feb  7 13:47 /dev/sda
```

In the preceding example, the first character is b, indicating that this file is a block special file. Just like the character special files, these files also have a major and a minor number.

Named Pipes

One of the greatest features of UNIX is that the output of one program can be redirected to the input of another program with very little work. For example, the command:

```
who | grep ranga
```

takes the output of the who command and makes it the input to the grep command. This is called *piping* the output of one command into another. On the command line, temporary anonymous pipes are used, but sometimes more control is needed than the command line provides. For such instances, UNIX provides a way to create a *named pipe*, so that two or more processes can communicate with each other via a file that acts like a pipe. Because these files allow processes to communicate with one another, they are one of the most popular forms of interprocess communication (IPC for short) available under UNIX.

Named pipes are created with the `mknod` program as follows:

```
mknod [filename] p
```

The syntax may vary slightly on some systems; check the man page for `mknod` for the exact syntax on your system. As a simple demonstration, let's rewrite the preceding command using a named pipe:

```
mknod /tmp/tmp_pipe p
who > /tmp/tmp_pipe &
grep ranga /tmp/tmp_pipe
rm /tmp/tmp_pipe
```

There are two important points to notice here. First, the process that is writing output into the pipe is placed in the background. This is done so that a command can be issued to read from the pipe before writing has completed. Second, we see that the last command removes the pipe. This is done because after the process that creates the pipe exits, the pipe becomes useless. We remove it to keep the system clean.

As you can see, using named pipes to do simple command-line input/output redirection is not very easy. For more complex redirection, it is useful. For example, you could easily use the named pipe to pipe in the output of several commands to a single `grep` command, something that is not possible on the command line.

Sockets   Socket files are another form of interprocess communication; however, sockets have the capability of passing data and information between two processes that are not running on the same machine. Socket files are created when communication to a process on another machine located on a network is required. Internet tools we use today, such as Web browsers, use sockets to make a connection to the Web server.

Owners, Groups, and Permissions

File ownership is a key component for UNIX to providing a secure method to store files in the file system. Every file in UNIX has the following attributes:

- Owner permissions
- Group permissions
- Other (World) permissions

The owner's permissions determine what actions the owner of the file can perform on the file. The group's permissions determine what actions a user, who is a member of the group that a file belongs to, can perform on the file. The permissions for "others," indicate what actions all other users can perform on the file.

The actions that can be performed on a file are as follows:

- Read
- Write
- Execute

If a user has read permissions, then he can view the contents of a file. A user with write permissions can edit the contents of a file, whereas a user with execute permissions can run a file as a program.

Viewing Permissions

The permissions of a file are displayed using the `ls -l` command. For example, the following command:

```
ls -l /home/ranga/.profile
```

produces the following output:

```
-rwxr-xr-x  1 ranga    users      2368 Jul 11 15:57 .profile*
```

Because the first character is a `-`, we know that this is a regular file. After the hyphen, there are several characters. The first three characters indicate the permissions for the owner of the file, the next three characters indicate the permissions for the group the file is associated with, and the last three characters indicate the permissions for all other users.

After the permissions block, the owner and the group are listed. For this file, the owner is `ranga` and the group is `users`. The permission block for this file indicates that the user has read, write, and execute permissions, whereas members of the group users and all other users have only read and execute permissions.

Permission Definitions

This section examines in greater detail the all the permissions that a file can have.

Understanding Read, Write, and Execute Permissions   Three basic permissions that can be granted or denied on a file are read, write, and execute. These permissions are defined in Table 5.2.

Table 5.2 Basic Permissions

Letter	Permission	Definition
r	Read	User is able to view the contents of the file.
w	Write	User is able to alter the contents of the file.
x	Execute	User is allowed to run the file, which is likely a program. For directories, the execute permission must be set for users to access the directory.

These three permissions may be different for the owner, users in the group that owns the file, and anyone who is not the owner or part of the group.

CAUTION

The "x" bit on a directory grants access to the directory. The read and write permissions have no value if the access bit is not set.

The read permission on a directory allows users to use the ls command to view files and their attributes that are located in the directory.

The write permission on a directory is the permission to watch out for because it allows a user to add and also remove files from the directory.

A directory that grants a user only execute permission will not allow the user to view the contents of the directory, nor add or delete any files from the directory, but will allow executable files located in the directory to be executed.

To make sure that your files are secure, check both the file permissions and the permissions of the directory that the file is located in. If a file has write permission for owner, group, and other, then the file is insecure. Inversely, if a file is in a directory that has write and execute for owner, group, and other, all files located in the directory are insecure, no matter what the permissions are on the files themselves.

SUID and SGID File Permission   Often when a command is executed it will have to be executed with special privileges to accomplish its task. An example of this is when you change your UNIX password. When you select a new password, it is written to and stored in the /etc/shadow system file. You as a regular user do not have read or write access to this file for security reasons; however, when you change your password, somehow you have to be given write permission to this file.

Additional permissions are available for executable program files. These permissions are known as Set User ID (SUID), and Set Group ID (SGID). Without SUID, or SGID bits set, an executable program can be executed with the permissions of the user who started it. When that SUID bit is enabled on an executable, rather than the process running with the permissions of the user who started it, the process runs the permissions of the owner of the executable program. Thus during the execution of this file, you inherit the permissions of the file's owner.

In the case of you changing your password, the passwd command is owned by root and has the set SUID bit enabled. When you execute the passwd command, you effectively become root during the passwd command's execution period.

The same applies for SGID. Normally, programs are executed with your group permissions; but instead, your group will be changed just for this program to the group owner of the program.

The SUID and SGID bits appear as the letter s if the permission is available. The SUID s bit will be located in the permission bits where the owner's execute permission would normally reside. If a capital letter S appears in the execute position, then the execute bit behind it is not set, but if a lowercase s appears, the execute permission is then set for the owner. For example, the command:

```
ls -l /usr/bin/passwd
```

produces the following output:

```
-r-sr-xr-x   1 root      bin           19031 Feb   7 13:47 /usr/bin/passwd*
```

which shows that the SUID bit is set, as well as shows the command owned by root.

Directories can take advantage of the SGID bit; however, it has an entirely different meaning than when applied on files. The letter s appears over the x in the group section of the permissions if this bit is enabled. If a directory has the SUID bit on, then any new files added to the directory automatically inherit the directory's group and are not set to the group of the user writing the file.

The SGID on a directory is very wise, and people from different groups can add files to it. All the files in your upload directory will automatically be chgrp'ed when a file is added.

The "sticky bit" is used to impose extra file removal permissions on a directory. A directory that has write permissions enabled for a user, allows that user to add, as well as delete any files from this directory. If the sticky bit enabled on is the directory, files may only be removed if you match any one credential in the list.

To remove a file from a directory with the sticky bit enabled, you must be one of the following users:

- The owner of the sticky directory
- The owner the file being removed
- The Superuser, root

Enabling the sticky bit for a directory should be considered for any directories that can be written to by nonprivileged users. Examples of such directories include temporary directories and public file upload sites.

Changing File and Directory Permissions

Changing file and directory permissions is always accomplished using the chmod command. The basic syntax is as follows:

```
chmod [expression]  files
```

Here *expression* is a statement of how to change the permissions. This expression can be of the following types:

- Symbolic
- Octal

Symbolic Method   The symbolic expression method uses letters to alter the permissions, and the octal expression method uses numbers. First we'll look at the symbolic method.

The symbolic expression has the following syntax:

```
(who)(action)(permissions)
```

Tables 5.5, 5.6, and 5.7 show the possible values for who, action, and permissions.

Table 5.2 Who

Letter	Represents
u	Owner
g	Group
o	Other
a	All

Table 5.3 Action

Symbol	Represents
+	Adding permissions to the file
-	Removing permission from the file
=	Explicitly set the file permissions

Table 5.4 Permissions

Letter	Represents
r	Read
w	Write
x	Execute
s	SUID or SGID

Using the three preceding reference tables, you can now build an expression. Following are a few examples to illustrate the use of chmod.

To give the "world" read access to all files in a directory, you can use one of the following commands:

```
chmod a=r *
```

or

```
chmod guo=r *
```

To stop anyone except the owner of the file .profile from writing to it, use this command:

```
chmod go-w .profile
```

Use the following command to be a "file miser":

```
chmod go= ~/*
```

or

```
chmod go-rwx ~/*
```

When specifying the users part or the permissions part, the order in which the letters are given is irrelevant. Thus the commands are equivalent:

```
chmod guo+rx *
chmod uog+xr *
```

If more than one set of permissions changes needs to be applied to a file or files, a comma-separated list can be used. For example:

```
chmod go-w,a+x a.out
```

removes the groups and "world" write permission on a.out, and adds the execute permission for everyone.

Octal Method   Changing permissions with an octal expression allows you only to explicitly set file permissions. This method uses a single number to assign the desired permission to each of the three categories of users (owner, group, and other). The read permission is valued at 4, the write permission at 2, and the execute permission at 1. Adding up the value of the permissions that you want to grant gives you a number between 0 and 7. This number between 0 and 7 is used to specify the permissions for the owner, group, and, finally, the other category. Setting SUID, SGID, and the sticky bit using the octal method places these bits out in front of the standard permissions. The permissions SUID, SGID, and the sticky bit take on the values 4-2-1 and add a fourth number at the beginning of the chmod expression.

Let's go through the some of the examples covered in the previous section to get an idea of how to use the octal method of changing permissions.

To set the "world" read access to all files in a directory, use the following command:

```
chmod 0444 *
```

To stop anyone except the owner of the file .profile from writing to it, use this command:

```
chmod 0600 .profile
```

Part

I

Ch

5

TROUBLESHOOTING

Many new users find the octal specification of file permissions confusing. The most important thing to keep in mind is that the octal method sets or assigns permissions to a file; it does not add or delete them.

This means that the octal mode does not have an equivalent to:

chmod u+rw .profile

The closest possible octal version would be:

chmod 0600 .profile

But this removes permissions for everyone except the user. It may also reduce the user's permissions, by removing his execute permission.

Remember that the octal mode is used to set the permissions of files, not to modify them.

Changing Owners and Groups

Two commands are available to change the owner and the group of files. These are:

- chown
- chgrp

The chown command, which stands for "change owner," is used to change the owner of a file. The chgrp command, which stands for "change group," is used to change the group of a file. On some systems, the chgrp command is unavailable, and the chown command must be used instead.

Changing Ownership

The chown command is used to change the ownership of a file. The basic syntax is as follows:

```
chown [options] [user]:[group] files
```

Here *options* can be one or more of the options listed in the man page for chown. Because there is considerable variation in the available options, consult the man page on your system for a complete list. The value of *user* can be either the name of a user on the system or the user ID (UID) of a user on the system. The value of *group* can be the name of a group on the system or the group ID (GID) of a group on the system. To just change the owner, the group value can be omitted. For example:

```
chown ranga: /home/httpd/html/users/ranga
```

changes the owner of the given directory to be the user ranga.

The Superuser, root, has the unrestricted ability to change the ownership of a file; however, there are some restrictions for normal users.

First, you can only change the owner of a file you own. This means that if you give another user ownership of a file, you cannot regain ownership of the file. The user that is now the owner of the file, or the Superuser, has to return the ownership to you.

On some systems, the chown command will be disabled for the normal user. This is generally done if the system is running disk quotas. Under a disk quota system, a user might only be allowed to store 100 megabytes of files, but if the user changes the ownership of some files, his free available disk space would increase, and he would still have access to the files.

Shell filename metacharacters can be used with the chown command to change the ownership of many files all at one time. For example:

```
chown  martha: *.c
```

changes the owner of all files in the current directory ending with .c to the user martha. The chown command recursively changes the ownership of all files when the -R option is included. For example, the command:

```
chown -R ranga: /home/httpd/html/users/ranga
```

changes the owner of all the files and subdirectories located under the given directory to the user `ranga`.

Changing Group Ownership

Changing group ownership of a file is done via the `chgrp` command. Its basic syntax is as follows:

```
chgrp [options] [group] files
```

Here `options` are one or more of the options listed in the man page for `chgrp`. The value of *group* can be either the name of a group or the GID of a group on the system. For example:

```
chgrp authors /home/ranga/docs/ch5.doc
```

changes the group of the given file to be the group `authors`. Similar to the `chown` command, the `chgrp` command can be used with shell metacharacters to change the name of more than one file. Just like `chown`, all versions of `chgrp` understand the `-R` option also.

On systems without this command, `chown` can be used to change the group of a file. For example, the command:

```
chown :authors /home/ranga/docs/ch5.doc
```

changes the group of the given file to the group `authors`.

The Inode Table

Files exist on the hard drive or other media; however, it is the users and administrators who access files and directories, not the hard drive directly.

Inodes are unique pieces of data for each file that resides in the file system on the hard drive. When you open a UNIX file, the kernel takes the filename you want to open and looks up the inode number for the file in the directory in which the file lives.

This unique inode number is used to reference an entry in the inode table located in the file system. These inode tables are created on the hard drive when you format the hard drive with a file system. We will look at creating file systems later in Chapter 15.

A single inode is 128 bytes in length and contains all file attributes, such as the owner, permissions, and group owner. The inode also includes a list of addresses to locations on the disk where the file data is actually stored.

Figure 5.1 illustrates the relationship between a filename in the a directory that points to an inode and the inode table containing the files attributes. The inode table points to the data area on the hard drive.

The first 12 addresses point directly to data blocks. These data blocks are usually 8192 bytes in size. These 12 addresses only can address a file of 96KB or (12 addresses ×8KB).

FIGURE 5.1

The directory, inode table, and data blocks.

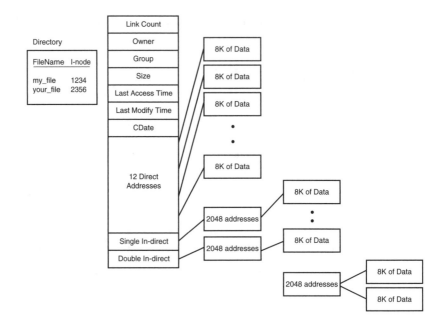

Addresses 13, 14, and 15 do not point directly to data stored in data blocks, but instead point to data blocks that contain more addresses. The single indirect block points to a data block that contains 2048 addresses to actual data and allows a file of 16 megabytes to be saved.

The double indirect block points to a data block that contains 2048 addresses of data blocks, which each contain 2048 addresses to the actual data blocks. Double indirect blocks allow a file size of 2 gigabytes with an 8KB data block size

From Here...

This chapter covered pathnames and the layout of the UNIX directory structure. You looked at file types and file permissions and examined changing and setting file and directory permissions. In addition, you briefly examined the inode table in which UNIX stores file information.

From here, you can proceed to the following topics:

- Chapter 12, "Device Management," provides information on how files and directories are stored on physical media such as hard disks.

- Chapter 13, "File Systems," covers the setup and maintenance of the file systems on which files and directories are stored.

- Chapter 15, "Backup and Recovery," explains methods of backing up your file system and recovering it when a problem occurs.

- Chapter 22, "NFS," introduces a method of making files and directories stored on remote machines appear to be stored on the local machine.

## CHAPTER 6

UNIX Processes

by Dan Wilson

In this chapter

Introduction

This chapter discusses what a process is and how it comes to life within the system. The chapter covers process scheduling, classes, and their life cycles. You will see an example of a program navigating through the various states that comprise a running program or process.

After you understand the "whats" and "hows" of processes, the chapter shows some examples of useful commands that help you find out information about your system's processes. The chapter also covers some commands that allow you to directly manipulate your processes as well.

Process

The UNIX operating system is a collection of software routines that manage users, programs, hardware, and the UNIX kernel itself. The kernel software is responsible for managing the four UNIX subsystems: memory management, I/O management, file management and process management. Depending on what you are trying to accomplish, each of the subsystems can be called into action by your programs. This chapter begins by explaining how a program becomes a UNIX process.

For the sake of discussion, let's say that your company is in desperate need of a program that displays the following message onscreen: "Hello World!" Being the versatile system administrator that you are, you come to the rescue. You start up your favorite editor (if you plan to use the vi editor and are unsure how to use it, consult the systems man page on vi(1).) and write the following program in the C programming language:

```
#include <stdio.h>
int main(void)
{
    printf("Hello World!!!\n");
    return 0;
}
```

You now have this text file called hello.c. Before you can display your message, you need to turn this text file into an executable program. To do this, you use the cc command. This command invokes the C compiler. (See the man page for the cc(1) command.)

```
# cc -o hello hello.c
```

You just told the C compiler to compile and link the text file hello.c and make an executable program named hello. This will be the program that you invoke to display the message "Hello World!!!". This, or a variation of this program, also serves as the example program we use to explain other UNIX process concepts for the remainder of the chapter.

> **N O T E** Even though you compile your source code into a UNIX executable file, you still must use the chmod command to make it executable for the UNIX shell to actually run the program. ■

▶ **See** "Files, Directories, and Permissions," **p. 122**

To invoke your program, type **hello** at the shell command line:

▶ **See** "UNIX Shells and System Commands," (Chapter 3)

```
# hello
```

And as long as no errors are in the program, you'll see

```
Hello World!!!
```

displayed on the screen.

An executable program can be broken down into the following parts:

- Text* This segment contains sharable program code (machine language).
- Data This segment contains initialized variables within the program.
- BSS This segment contains the uninitialized variables within the program.
- Stack This segment expands to handle the local variables and parameters passed via function calls.
- User area This area maintains process information used by the UNIX kernel

*This is the only part of a process that may be shared by other processes. The other segments are entirely local to each individual process.

For illustration, let's make a change to the hello.c program so that you can see how its process image looks when the program is run.

```c
#include <stdio.h>
#include"function_x.h"

int main(void)
{
    int i = 0;
    int x;
    char *ch_ptr;

    for (i=0;i<100;i++)
        printf("Hello World!!!\n");

    *ch_ptr = "Hello World!!!";
    for(x=0;x<100x++)
        printf("%s\n",ch_ptr)
    function_x(100);
    return 0;
}
```

From the preceding program, you see the following:

- Text This is the compiled hello.c in machine language format.
- Data int i = 0
- BSS int x and char *ch_ptr. (Later in the program, you assign this pointer the value of Hello World!!!)

■ Stack   Temporary data storage used by the process. The stack contains an entry of 100. This is the value you are passing to the function/subprogram *function_x*.

■ User area   Information such as real and effective user IDs, real and effective group IDs, pointers to additional process structures, and accounting information to name a few. This area is used by the UNIX kernel to manage the process during execution.

As you can now see, the UNIX kernel recognizes that it has five different areas to manage when executing a program. One advantage to note is that the Text segment of a process is sharable. This means that many users could execute the hello program simultaneously and still only have one copy of the Text portion in memory. This amounts to tremendous savings in memory usage. Keep in mind that although the Text segment is shared, the others are not. This is because as a program executes, each process can have different values assigned to the various variables and function call parameters.

We end this section by simply stating the differences between a process and a program. A *program* is a file stored in a form recognized by the UNIX kernel as an executable file. This file format is known as an a.out format. It contains executable instructions. When this file is executed, it is read into memory and executed by the kernel. An executing program is called a *process*. In the preceding example, hello.c is a text file that you turned into executable (a.out) file with the cc command. When you run hello, it becomes a UNIX process. Now you can take a look at UNIX process creation.

Process Creation

When the UNIX kernel creates a process, it assigns it a unique number. This number is called the process ID or PID. The kernel uses this unique process ID to manage each process within the system. You reference the process by its assigned name (for example, hello), but the system only recognizes the process by its unique PID.

Each process, except for PID 0, has a parent process. Process 0 is created during the system initialization process. All other processes are created or "spawned" by using the fork() (or vfork()) and exec() system calls. Let's take a look at each of these system calls.

■ The fork() system call creates a new process. The new (child) process is an exact copy of the calling (parent) process. This process is overlayed with the process defined by the exec() system call.

■ The vfork() system call also creates a new process. It does it in a more memory efficient manner. Unlike the fork() system call, vfork() does not make a complete copy of the parent process. The child process can share both the text and data of the parent. This is useful because the system doesn't incur the overhead of making a copy of a process that will more than likely be overlayed with another process when the program calls the exec() system call.

- The `exec()` system call is used to overlay the process's current image with that of a new one. This new process image is actually a new executable. The `exec()` system call has six forms. (Check your systems documentation for a more detailed explanation of each call type.):

```
execl()

execv()

execle()

execve()

execlp()

execvp()
```

Let's take a look at some pseudo-code that depicts how the `fork/vfork` and `exec` looks:

```
Print 'Setting at Current Process'
IF return code from fork() system call is greater than 0
    Then print 'This is the Current Process'
    Exit
    ELSE IF return code from fork() system call equals 0
        Then print 'This is the new child process'
        Print 'We are now ready to start a new program'
        exec('NEW_PROGRAM')
    ELSE print 'FORK SYSTEM CALL FAILED!!)
```

 T I P I was able to greatly improve the performance at one site by recommending that the company switch its `fork()` system calls to `vfork()`. They were spawning processes at such a high rate that the system just couldn't keep up.

Process States

Each process transitions through a series of states as it exists in the system. A series of queues keeps track of processes based upon their process ID (PID). A process resides on a specific queue according to its run state and priority classification. Process structure information resides in `/usr/include/sys/proc.h` and `/usr/include/sys/user.h` on the system. The following is an excerpt from header `proc.h` from a Sun Solaris 2.5.1 operating system. Take note of the structures and components that make up a process:

```
/*
 * One structure allocated per active process.  It contains all
 * data needed about the process while the process may be swapped
 * out.  Other per-process data (user.h) is also inside the proc structure.
 */
typedef struct     proc {
    /*
     * Fields requiring no explicit locking
     */
    struct    vnode *p_exec;        /* pointer to a.out vnode */
    struct    as *p_as;         /* process address space pointer */
```

```
struct    plock *p_lockp;         /* ptr to proc struct's mutex lock */
int    p_pad;              /* for backwards compatibility */
kmutex_t p_crlock;          /* lock for p_cred */
struct    cred    *p_cred;    /* process credentials */
/*
 * Fields protected by pidlock
 */
int    p_swapcnt;         /* number of swapped out lwps */
char    p_stat;              /* status of process */
char    p_wcode;          /* current wait code */
int    p_wdata;          /* current wait return value */
pid_t    p_ppid;            /* process id of parent */
struct    proc    *p_link;    /* forward link */
struct    proc    *p_parent;    /* ptr to parent process */
struct    proc    *p_child;    /* ptr to first child process */
struct    proc    *p_sibling;    /* ptr to next sibling proc on chain */
struct    proc    *p_psibling;    /* ptr to prev sibling proc on chain */
struct    proc    *p_sibling_ns;    /* ptr to siblings with new state */
struct    proc    *p_child_ns;    /* ptr to children with new state */
struct    proc    *p_next;    /* active chain link next */
struct    proc    *p_prev;    /* active chain link prev */
struct    proc    *p_nextofkin;    /* gets accounting info at exit */
struct    proc    *p_orphan;
struct    proc    *p_nextorph;
struct    proc    *p_pglink;    /* process group hash chain link next */
struct    proc    *p_ppglink;    /* process group hash chain link prev */
struct    sess    *p_sessp;    /* session information */
struct    pid    *p_pidp;    /* process ID info */
struct    pid    *p_pgidp;    /* process group ID info */
/*
 * Fields protected by p_lock
 */
kcondvar_t p_cv;          /* proc struct's condition variable */
kcondvar_t p_flag_cv;
kcondvar_t p_lwpexit;          /* waiting for some lwp to exit */
kcondvar_t p_holdlwps;          /* process is waiting for its lwps */
                /* to to be held.  */
kcondvar_t p_flock;          /* asleep in closef */
u_short    p_prwant;          /* /proc: process wanted for locking */
u_int    p_flag;          /* protected while set. */
                /* flags defined below */
clock_t    p_utime;          /* user time, this process */
clock_t    p_stime;                    /* system time, this process */
clock_t    p_cutime;          /* sum of children's user time */
clock_t    p_cstime;          /* sum of children's system time */
caddr_t *p_segacct;          /* segment accounting info */
caddr_t    p_brkbase;          /* base address of heap */
u_int    p_brksize;          /* heap size in bytes */
/*
 * Per process signal stuff.
 */
k_sigset_t p_sig;                    /* signals pending to this process */
k_sigset_t p_ignore;          /* ignore when generated */
k_sigset_t p_siginfo;          /* gets signal info with signal */
struct sigqueue *p_sigqueue;    /* queued siginfo structures */
```

```
struct sigqhdr *p_sigqhdr;        /* hdr to sigqueue structure pool */
u_char    p_stopsig;        /* jobcontrol stop signal */

/*
 * Special per-process flag when set will fix misaligned memory
 * references.
 */
char    p_fixalignment;

/*
 * Per process lwp and kernel thread stuff
 */
int    p_lwptotal;        /* total number of lwps created */
int    p_lwpcnt;        /* number of lwps in this process */
int    p_lwprcnt;        /* number of not stopped lwps */
int    p_lwpblocked;        /* number of blocked lwps. kept  */
                /*    consistent by sched_lock() */
int    p_zombcnt;        /* number of zombie LWPs */
kthread_t *p_tlist;        /* circular list of threads */
kthread_t *p_zomblist;        /* circular list of zombie LWPs */
/*
 * XXX Not sure what locks are needed here.
 */
k_sigset_t p_sigmask;        /* mask of traced signals (/proc) */
k_fltset_t p_fltmask;        /* mask of traced faults (/proc) */
struct    vnode *p_trace;        /* pointer to primary /proc vnode */
struct    vnode *p_plist;        /* list of /proc vnodes for process */

struct    proc *p_rlink;        /* linked list for server */
kcondvar_t p_srwchan_cv;
u_int    p_stksize;        /* process stack size in bytes */
/*
 * Microstate accounting, resource usage, and real-time profiling
 */
hrtime_t p_mstart;        /* hi-res process start time */
hrtime_t p_mterm;        /* hi-res process termination time */
hrtime_t p_mlreal;        /* elapsed time sum over defunct lwps */
hrtime_t p_acct[NMSTATES];        /* microstate sum over defunct lwps */
struct lrusage p_ru;        /* lrusage sum over defunct lwps */
struct itimerval p_rprof_timer;        /* ITIMER_REALPROF interval timer */
int    p_rprof_timerid;        /* interval timer's timeout id */
u_int    p_defunct;        /* number of defunct lwps */
/*
 * profiling. A lock is used in the event of multiple lwp's
 * using the same profiling base/size.
 */
kmutex_t p_pflock;        /* protects user pr_base in lwp */

/*
 * The user structure
 */
struct user p_user;        /* (see sys/user.h) */

/*
 * Doors.
```

Part

I

Ch

6

```
     */
    kthread_t          *p_server_threads;
    struct door_node   *p_unref_list;
    kcondvar_t         p_server_cv;
    char               p_unref_thread;     /* unref thread created */


    /*
     * Kernel probes
     */
    u_char             p_tnf_flags;


    /*
     * C2 Security  (C2_AUDIT)
     */
    caddr_t p_audit_data;           /* per process audit structure */
    kthread_t   *p_aslwptp;     /* thread ptr representing "aslwp" */
#if defined(i386) ¦¦ defined(__i386)
    /*
     * LDT support.
     */
    kmutex_t p_ldtlock;         /* protects the following fields */
    struct seg_desc *p_ldt;         /* Pointer to private LDT */
    struct seg_desc p_ldt_desc;     /* segment descriptor for private LDT */
    int p_ldtlimit;             /* highest selector used */
#endif
    u_int p_swrss;              /* resident set size before last swap */
    struct aio     *p_aio;          /* pointer to async I/O struct */
    struct timerstr    *p_itimer;    /* posix timers */
    k_sigset_t    p_notifsigs;     /* signals in notification set */
    kcondvar_t    p_notifcv;     /* notif cv to synchronize with aslwp */
    int          p_alarmid;      /* alarm's timeout id */
    struct lwpchan_data    *p_lcp; /* lwpchan cache */
} proc_t;
```

Code Removed for Brevity

```
/*
 * Stuff to keep track of the number of processes each uid has.
 *
 * A structure is allocated when a new uid shows up
 * There is a hash to find each uid's structure.
 */
struct    upcount     {
    struct    upcount    *up_next;
    uid_t        up_uid;
    u_long        up_count;
};


/* process ID info */

struct pid {
    unsigned int pid_prinactive :1;
    unsigned int pid_pgorphaned :1;
    unsigned int pid_padding :6;      /* used to be pid_ref, now an int */
    unsigned int pid_prslot :24;
```

```
    pid_t pid_id;
    struct proc *pid_pglink;
    struct pid *pid_link;
    u_int pid_ref;
};
```

As you can see from this header file excerpt, the kernel must track and maintain numerous structural and management issues for the system to run smoothly. Take a look at your `proc.h` header file on your system to see the kernel structures and flags it uses to manage processes. You should also familiarize yourself with the other header files (`*.h`) that reside on your system. As a system administrator, you should realize that some of your best systems documentation resides on the system in the `/usr/include` directory.

 TIP One of the best places to look for UNIX errors is the `errno.h` file. This header file lists the standard errors returned by the system. You can find information here that you wouldn't normally find in the printed materials. So learn to take advantage of your header files.

The following list presents process states:

- **SIDL** (idle)   A new UNIX process is created by a call to `fork`, `vfork`, and `exec`. The process is available to be scheduled to run.
- **SRUN** (run)   The process exists on a run queue.
- **SSLEEP** (sleep)   A process is "put to sleep" or suspended. This usually occurs when the process is waiting on a system resource (for example, disk subsystem).
- **SSTOP** (stopped)   An executing process is stopped. (Either by a signal or the parent process).
- **SZOMB** (zombie)   Having exited, the process no longer exists but leaves behind for the parent process some record of its termination status.

Let's use our program `hello` to show how a process would transition through the preceding states. When the kernel starts up `hello` (a.k.a. the process `hello`), it allocates a `proc` structure for it from the process table (as long as the system has not reached the maximum amount of allowable processes configured for the system—see Chapter 27, "Performance Tuning,"). The process is now in the idle (SIDL) state, ready for the kernel to load and execute it. After the kernel has available resources, the process is linked onto a run queue and made runnable (SRUN). When the process acquires a time-slice, it runs, switching as necessary between kernel mode and user mode. If a running process receives a SIGSTOP signal (that is, Ctrl+Z) or is being traced, it enters a stop state (SSTOP). On receiving a SIGCONT signal, the process returns to a run queue (SRUN). If a running process must wait for a resource (for example, disk subsystem), the process goes on a sleep queue (SSLEEP) until obtaining the resource. After the resource is made available, the kernel wakes up the process and puts it on a run queue (SRUN). A sleeping process might also be swapped out, until the kernel grants it the resource it's blocking on (the process can be runnable [SRUN], but still swapped out). The swapped out process is swapped in and put on a run queue. When the process is finished, it exits into a zombie (SZOMB) state—possibly returning a return code to the parent process.

Part
I
Ch
6

Each process is subject to the scheduler. The scheduler sees to it that all processes have access to the CPU. A user process can be classified as either timeshare or real-time. A process falls into the timeshare classification by default. The primary goal of the timeshare classification with regards to the scheduler is to fairly apportion the system resources to all the processes. This classification uses a round-robin method to schedule and run all the timeshare processes within the system. As a process runs, it accumulates system time. The scheduler algorithms use this as a basis for determining when to grant a process future use of the CPU. This way, the scheduler attempts to balance how the system resources are utilized.

> **CAUTION**
>
> Be extra careful when adjusting process priorities. Certain products expect to run as a normal timeshare process. For example, the background processes of an Oracle database should not have their priority levels altered because they work in concert with one another. Make sure that you understand the side effects of altering the way commercial products run on your system.

Generally, processes fall into a priority class range from which the scheduler grants them system time. After their time-slice has expired (or the process blocks for system resources), the kernel saves certain process-specific information and performs a context switch. A *context switch* is where the kernel stops (preempts) the current process from running, saves certain process information (see the proc.h header for details), and starts or restarts another process that is ready to run and residing on one of the various run queues. A timeshare process can have its classification changed to real-time by using the priocntl system call. Unless you have specific timing constraints, the timeshare classification almost always suffices.

A real-time classification is usually reserved for processes that either must run through to completion without being preempted by another process or are not suitable for the timeshare classification. A real-time process runs until either it finishes or its time-slice expires. Keep in mind that a real-time process can have a time-slice that is set to infinity. As you can see, unless a process with this classification is handled with care, you can crash the system by executing a real-time process. Remember the kernel needs to execute to maintain the system. Kernel processes fall into the system classification. If the kernel cannot gain control of the CPU because of a real-time process, everything comes crashing down. So remember, a real-time classification means that the process's priority supersedes that of even the kernel.

 If you must run a real-time process, be sure to establish your current shell (PID) with a higher real-time priority than the real-time process you are going to start. This enables you to interrupt or kill the real-time process so that it won't run away with your system.

Now that you know what a process is and how it's created, scheduled, and executed, let's look at some UNIX commands that show useful information and how system administrators can manage processes.

N O T E When a parent process of a child process issues a wait() system call, it is telling the kernel that it wants to be notified of the child process's termination status. If the parent of the child process does not call the wait() system call and it does not have the SIGCLD (death of a child) signal set to ignore the signal, the child process becomes a zombie process at termination. The parent process (PPID) is set to 1 for all the parent process's existing children and zombie processes. PID 1 (init) inherits each of the child processes because every process must have a parent process—except for PID 0. ■

Commands to View Process/Program Information

The first command we will look at is the ps command. This command tells the status of every process currently in the system. The ps command has several options that you can use to display various amounts of information. See your systems man page for the exact syntax and description of the command.

At the prompt, type the following:

```
$ ps -ef
```

UID	PID	PPID	C	STIME	TTY	TIME	CMD
root	0	0	0	Aug 09	?	0:01	sched
root	1	0	0	Aug 09	?	0:20	/etc/init -
root	2	0	0	Aug 09	?	0:00	pageout
root	3	0	0	Aug 09	?	9:44	fsflush
root	927	1	0	Aug 09	?	0:00	/usr/lib/saf/sac -t 300
root	930	927	0	Aug 09	?	0:00	/usr/lib/saf/listen tcp
root	742	1	0	Aug 09	?	0:00	/usr/sbin/kerbd
root	9	1	0	Aug 09	?	0:08	vxconfigd -m boot
root	736	1	0	Aug 09	?	0:00	/usr/sbin/keyserv
root	754	1	0	Aug 09	?	0:00	/usr/lib/nfs/statd
root	751	1	0	Aug 09	?	0:03	/usr/sbin/inetd -s
root	822	813	0	Aug 09	?	0:00	lpNet
root	756	1	0	Aug 09	?	0:01	/usr/lib/nfs/lockd
root	734	1	0	Aug 09	?	1:37	/usr/sbin/rpcbind
root	780	1	0	Aug 09	?	0:01	/usr/lib/autofs/automountd
root	841	1	0	Aug 09	?	0:00	/usr/lib/utmpd
root	813	1	0	Aug 09	?	0:00	/usr/lib/lpsched
root	803	1	0	Aug 09	?	0:04	/usr/sbin/nscd
root	784	1	0	Aug 09	?	0:01	/usr/sbin/syslogd
root	797	1	0	Aug 09	?	0:10	/usr/sbin/cron
oracle	5591	1	0	Aug 10	?	0:00	ora_pmon_test
oracle	5593	1	0	Aug 10	?	0:01	ora_dbwr_test
oracle	5595	1	0	Aug 10	?	0:01	ora_lgwr_test
oracle	5597	1	0	Aug 10	?	0:32	ora_smon_test
oracle	5599	1	0	Aug 10	?	0:00	ora_reco_test

Notice the additional information that the ef options provide. This information is extremely valuable to administrators. You can use this command to find out not only what active jobs are

Part
I

Ch
6

on the system, but also which ones are running and by whom. Let's look at using the ps command to see process classes.

At the system prompt, type the following:

```
$ ps -efc
```

```
UID    PID  PPID  CLS PRI    STIME TTY      TIME CMD
       root    0     0  SYS 96   Aug 09 ?        0:01 sched
       root    1     0   TS 58   Aug 09 ?        0:20 /etc/init -
       root    2     0  SYS 98   Aug 09 ?        0:00 pageout
       root    3     0  SYS 60   Aug 09 ?        9:45 fsflush
       root  927     1   TS 58   Aug 09 ?        0:00 /usr/lib/saf/sac -t 300
       root  930   927   TS 58   Aug 09 ?        0:00 /usr/lib/saf/listen tcp
       root  742     1   TS 50   Aug 09 ?        0:00 /usr/sbin/kerbd
       root    9     1   TS 59   Aug 09 ?        0:08 vxconfigd -m boot
       root  736     1   TS 22   Aug 09 ?        0:00 /usr/sbin/keyserv
       root  754     1   TS 58   Aug 09 ?        0:00 /usr/lib/nfs/statd
       root  751     1   TS 48   Aug 09 ?        0:03 /usr/sbin/inetd -s
       root  822   813   TS 43   Aug 09 ?        0:00 lpNet
       root  756     1   TS 58   Aug 09 ?        0:01 /usr/lib/nfs/lockd
       root  734     1   TS 58   Aug 09 ?        1:37 /usr/sbin/rpcbind
       root  780     1   TS 48   Aug 09 ?        0:01 /usr/lib/autofs/automountd
       root  841     1   TS 58   Aug 09 ?        0:00 /usr/lib/utmpd
       root  813     1   TS 58   Aug 09 ?        0:00 /usr/lib/lpsched
       root  803     1   TS 22   Aug 09 ?        0:04 /usr/sbin/nscd
       root  784     1   TS 58   Aug 09 ?        0:01 /usr/sbin/syslogd
       root  797     1   TS 48   Aug 09 ?        0:10 /usr/sbin/cron
    cspretnj 1797     1   TS 48   Aug 09 ?        0:10 /home/cspretnj/
➥kill_users

     oracle 5591     1   TS 59   Aug 10 ?        0:00 ora_pmon_test
     oracle 5593     1   TS 59   Aug 10 ?        0:01 ora_dbwr_test
     oracle 5595     1   TS 59   Aug 10 ?        0:01 ora_lgwr_test
     oracle 5597     1   TS 58   Aug 10 ?        0:32 ora_smon_test
     oracle 5599     1   TS 58   Aug 10 ?        0:00 ora_reco_test
```

As you can see, the command returned the processes' classifications. Notice the processes with the SYS classification. Those are the kernel processes that help to maintain the system. If these processes were not able to gain CPU time due to a real-time process, the system would crash.

Remember the hello program? You are going to use the truss command to see a trace of the system calls it performs, the signals it receives, and the machine faults it incurs.

```
$ truss hello
```

```
execve("./hello", 0xEFFFFB80, 0xEFFFFB88)  argc = 1
open("/dev/zero", O_RDONLY)                      = 3
mmap(0x00000000, 8192, PROT_READ¦PROT_WRITE¦PROT_EXEC, MAP_PRIVATE, 3, 0) = 0xEF
➥7C0000
open("/usr/dt/lib/libucb.so.1", O_RDONLY)        Err#2 ENOENT
open("/u01/oracle/product/7.3.2/lib/libucb.so.1", O_RDONLY) Err#2 ENOENT
open("/usr/openwin/lib/libucb.so.1", O_RDONLY)   Err#2 ENOENT
open("/usr/ucblib/libucb.so.1", O_RDONLY)        = 4
```

```
fstat(4, 0xEFFFF798)                                      = 0
mmap(0x00000000, 8192, PROT_READ|PROT_EXEC, MAP_SHARED, 4, 0) = 0xEF7B0000
mmap(0x00000000, 106496, PROT_READ|PROT_EXEC, MAP_PRIVATE, 4, 0) = 0xEF790000
munmap(0xEF798000, 57344)                                 = 0
mmap(0xEF7A6000, 10289, PROT_READ|PROT_WRITE|PROT_EXEC, MAP_PRIVATE|MAP_FIXED, 4,
➡24576) = 0xEF7A6000
close(4)                                                  = 0
open("/usr/dt/lib/libsocket.so.1", O_RDONLY)     Err#2 ENOENT
open("/u01/oracle/product/7.3.2/lib/libsocket.so.1", O_RDONLY) Err#2 ENOENT
open("/usr/openwin/lib/libsocket.so.1", O_RDONLY) Err#2 ENOENT
open("/usr/ucblib/libsocket.so.1", O_RDONLY)     Err#2 ENOENT
open("/usr/lib/libsocket.so.1", O_RDONLY)         = 4
fstat(4, 0xEFFFF798)                                      = 0
mmap(0xEF7B0000, 8192, PROT_READ|PROT_EXEC, MAP_SHARED|MAP_FIXED, 4, 0) = 0xEF7B
➡0000
mmap(0x00000000, 122880, PROT_READ|PROT_EXEC, MAP_PRIVATE, 4, 0) = 0xEF760000
munmap(0xEF76E000, 57344)                                 = 0
mmap(0xEF77C000, 5393, PROT_READ|PROT_WRITE|PROT_EXEC, MAP_PRIVATE|MAP_FIXED, 4,
➡49152) = 0xEF77C000
close(4)                                                  = 0
open("/usr/dt/lib/libnsl.so.1", O_RDONLY)         Err#2 ENOENT
open("/u01/oracle/product/7.3.2/lib/libnsl.so.1", O_RDONLY) Err#2 ENOENT
open("/usr/openwin/lib/libnsl.so.1", O_RDONLY)   Err#2 ENOENT
open("/usr/ucblib/libnsl.so.1", O_RDONLY)         Err#2 ENOENT
open("/usr/lib/libnsl.so.1", O_RDONLY)            = 4 fstat(4, 0xEFFFF798)
➡= 0
mmap(0xEF7B0000, 8192, PROT_READ|PROT_EXEC, MAP_SHARED|MAP_FIXED, 4, 0) = 0xEF7B
0000
mmap(0x00000000, 532480, PROT_READ|PROT_EXEC, MAP_PRIVATE, 4, 0) = 0xEF680000
munmap(0xEF6E2000, 57344)                                 = 0
mmap(0xEF6F0000, 38765, PROT_READ|PROT_WRITE|PROT_EXEC, MAP_PRIVATE|MAP_FIXED, 4,
➡393216) = 0xEF6F0000
mmap(0xEF6FA000, 29832, PROT_READ|PROT_WRITE|PROT_EXEC, MAP_PRIVATE|MAP_FIXED, 3,
➡0) = 0xEF6FA000
close(4)                                                  = 0
open("/usr/dt/lib/libelf.so.1", O_RDONLY)         Err#2 ENOENT
open("/u01/oracle/product/7.3.2/lib/libelf.so.1", O_RDONLY) Err#2 ENOENT
open("/usr/openwin/lib/libelf.so.1", O_RDONLY)   Err#2 ENOENT
open("/usr/ucblib/libelf.so.1", O_RDONLY)         Err#2 ENOENT
open("/usr/lib/libelf.so.1", O_RDONLY)            = 4
fstat(4, 0xEFFFF798)                                      = 0
mmap(0xEF7B0000, 8192, PROT_READ|PROT_EXEC, MAP_SHARED|MAP_FIXED, 4, 0) = 0xEF7B
➡0000
mmap(0x00000000, 131072, PROT_READ|PROT_EXEC, MAP_PRIVATE, 4, 0) = 0xEF730000
munmap(0xEF740000, 57344)                                 = 0
mmap(0xEF74E000, 5328, PROT_READ|PROT_WRITE|PROT_EXEC, MAP_PRIVATE|MAP_FIXED, 4,
➡57344) = 0xEF74E000
close(4)                                                  = 0
open("/usr/dt/lib/libaio.so.1", O_RDONLY)         Err#2 ENOENT
open("/u01/oracle/product/7.3.2/lib/libaio.so.1", O_RDONLY) Err#2 ENOENT
open("/usr/openwin/lib/libaio.so.1", O_RDONLY)   Err#2 ENOENT
open("/usr/ucblib/libaio.so.1", O_RDONLY)         Err#2 ENOENT
open("/usr/lib/libaio.so.1", O_RDONLY)            = 4
fstat(4, 0xEFFFF798)                                      = 0
```

```
mmap(0xEF7B0000, 8192, PROT_READ|PROT_EXEC, MAP_SHARED|MAP_FIXED, 4, 0) = 0xEF7B
➥0000
mmap(0x00000000, 90112, PROT_READ|PROT_EXEC, MAP_PRIVATE, 4, 0) = 0xEF710000
munmap(0xEF716000, 57344)                         = 0
mmap(0xEF724000, 2735, PROT_READ|PROT_WRITE|PROT_EXEC, MAP_PRIVATE|MAP_FIXED, 4,
➥16384) = 0xEF724000 close(4)                                             = 0
open("/usr/dt/lib/libc.so.1", O_RDONLY)          Err#2 ENOENT
open("/u01/oracle/product/7.3.2/lib/libc.so.1", O_RDONLY) Err#2 ENOENT
open("/usr/openwin/lib/libc.so.1", O_RDONLY)     Err#2 ENOENT
open("/usr/ucblib/libc.so.1", O_RDONLY)          Err#2 ENOENT
open("/usr/lib/libc.so.1", O_RDONLY)             = 4
fstat(4, 0xEFFFF798)                             = 0
mmap(0xEF7B0000, 8192, PROT_READ|PROT_EXEC, MAP_SHARED|MAP_FIXED, 4, 0) = 0xEF7B
➥0000
mmap(0x00000000, 622592, PROT_READ|PROT_EXEC, MAP_PRIVATE, 4, 0) = 0xEF580000
munmap(0xEF600000, 57344)                        = 0
mmap(0xEF60E000, 28888, PROT_READ|PROT_WRITE|PROT_EXEC, MAP_PRIVATE|MAP_FIXED, 4,
➥516096) = 0xEF60E000
mmap(0xEF616000, 4904, PROT_READ|PROT_WRITE|PROT_EXEC, MAP_PRIVATE|MAP_FIXED, 3,
➥0) = 0xEF616000
close(4)                                         = 0
open("/usr/dt/lib/libdl.so.1", O_RDONLY)         Err#2 ENOENT
open("/u01/oracle/product/7.3.2/lib/libdl.so.1", O_RDONLY) Err#2 ENOENT
open("/usr/openwin/lib/libdl.so.1", O_RDONLY)    Err#2 ENOENT
open("/usr/lib/libdl.so.1", O_RDONLY)            = 4
fstat(4, 0xEFFFF798)                             = 0
mmap(0xEF7B0000, 8192, PROT_READ|PROT_EXEC, MAP_SHARED|MAP_FIXED, 4, 0) = 0xEF7B
➥0000
close(4)                                         = 0
open("/usr/dt/lib/libintl.so.1", O_RDONLY)       Err#2 ENOENT
open("/u01/oracle/product/7.3.2/lib/libintl.so.1", O_RDONLY) Err#2 ENOENT
open("/usr/openwin/lib/libintl.so.1", O_RDONLY) Err#2 ENOENT
open("/usr/lib/libintl.so.1", O_RDONLY)          = 4
fstat(4, 0xEFFFF798)                             = 0
mmap(0x00000000, 8192, PROT_READ|PROT_EXEC, MAP_SHARED, 4, 0) = 0xEF670000
mmap(0x00000000, 81920, PROT_READ|PROT_EXEC, MAP_PRIVATE, 4, 0) = 0xEF650000
munmap(0xEF654000, 57344)                        = 0
mmap(0xEF662000, 3040, PROT_READ|PROT_WRITE|PROT_EXEC, MAP_PRIVATE|MAP_FIXED, 4,
➥8192) = 0xEF662000
close(4)                                         = 0
open("/usr/dt/lib/libw.so.1", O_RDONLY)          Err#2 ENOENT
open("/u01/oracle/product/7.3.2/lib/libw.so.1", O_RDONLY) Err#2 ENOENT
open("/usr/openwin/lib/libw.so.1", O_RDONLY)     Err#2 ENOENT
open("/usr/lib/libw.so.1", O_RDONLY)             = 4
fstat(4, 0xEFFFF798)                             = 0
mmap(0xEF670000, 8192, PROT_READ|PROT_EXEC, MAP_SHARED|MAP_FIXED, 4, 0) = 0xEF67
➥0000
mmap(0x00000000, 98304, PROT_READ|PROT_EXEC, MAP_PRIVATE, 4, 0) = 0xEF560000
munmap(0xEF568000, 57344)                        = 0
mmap(0xEF576000, 3568, PROT_READ|PROT_WRITE|PROT_EXEC, MAP_PRIVATE|MAP_FIXED, 4,
➥24576) = 0xEF576000
close(4)                                         = 0
open("/usr/platform/SUNW,Ultra-Enterprise/lib/libc_psr.so.1", O_RDONLY) = 4
fstat(4, 0xEFFFF5C0)                             = 0
```

```
mmap(0xEF670000, 8192, PROT_READ¦PROT_EXEC, MAP_SHARED¦MAP_FIXED, 4, 0) = 0xEF67
0000
mmap(0x00000000, 81920, PROT_READ¦PROT_EXEC, MAP_PRIVATE, 4, 0) = 0xEF540000
munmap(0xEF544000, 57344)                        = 0
mmap(0xEF552000, 5440, PROT_READ¦PROT_WRITE¦PROT_EXEC, MAP_PRIVATE¦MAP_FIXED, 4,
➡8192) = 0xEF552000
close(4)                                         = 0
close(3)                                         = 0
munmap(0xEF670000, 8192)                         = 0
ioctl(1, TCGETA, 0xEFFFF76C)                     = 0
Hello World!!!
write(1, " H e l l o   W o r l d !".., 15)       = 15
lseek(0, 0, SEEK_CUR)                            = 37116
_exit(0)
```

I realize that this is a long listing. But given the fact that not all UNIX systems support the `truss` command, it is worth seeing how much is involved in such a small program as `hello`. It should give you some appreciation of complexity of the UNIX environment. Note the first line. See how the system invokes the `execve` system call without the `hello` program being passed as a parameter? Also, note the line `write(1, " H e l l o W o r l d !".., 15) = 15`. UNIX automatically opens (and closes at process termination) three files for each process 0, 1, 2. That is `stdin`, `stdout`, and `stderr`, respectively.

If you know the PID of a process you want to monitor, you can use the following command to watch it run. (Note—You must be root to do this; otherwise, you'll get `truss: cannot control process <PID>`.)

```
$ truss -p PID
```

```
Received signal #14, SIGALRM, in semop() [caught]
semop(1, 0xEFFFE850, 1)                          Err#91 ERESTART
getcontext(0xEFFFE2B8)
setcontext(0xEFFFE2B8)
times(0xEFFFE9C8)                                = 34205494
getcontext(0xEFFFE698)
setitimer(ITIMER_REAL, 0xEFFFE848, 0x00000000)   = 0
```

TIP

The `truss` command is a great tool to use when debugging client/server problems. You can use it on your server or client programs to see what's going on inside the program while it's communicating with its client or server counterpart over the network. If you see a lot of "sleeping" going on, then you can usually feel confident that the process is either waiting on some system resource or there is very little activity. I use the `truss` command in conjunction with `ping` and Oracle's `tnsping` (a `ping` against an Oracle database that tests connectivity with a specific database) to get an idea of how the network and system are functioning. Beware of comparing these two times against each other solely to gauge network performance.

Part

I

Ch

6

The crash command is useful in examining the system memory image of a running system or a crashed system by formatting and printing control structures, tables, and other system information. Run this command as root and on a live system to see a snapshot of process information:

```
# crash
dumpfile = /dev/mem, namelist = /dev/ksyms, outfile = stdout
>p -w /tmp/proc.out          ( at the crash prompt, this command will
                              write process information to the file '/tmp/proc.out' )

>q          ( Enter 'q' to quit or '?' to see the available crash commands)
```

Following is the proc.out file:

```
PROC TABLE SIZE = 16266
SLOT ST   PID  PPID  PGID   SID  UID PRI    NAME         FLAGS
   0 t     0     0     0     0    0  96 sched          load sys lock
   1 s     1     0     0     0    0  58 init           load
   2 s     2     0     0     0    0  98 pageout        load sys lock nowait
   3 s     3     0     0     0    0  60 fsflush        load sys lock nowait
   4 s   925     1   925   925    0  58 sac            load jctl
   5 s   928   925   925   925    0  58 listen         load nowait jctl
   6 s   747     1   747   747    0  50 kerbd          load
   7 s     9     1     9     9    0  59 vxconfigd      load nowait
   8 s   782     1   782   782    0  58 automountd     load
   9 s   756     1   756   756    0  58 inetd          load
  10 s   739     1   739   739    0  58 rpcbind        load
  11 s   741     1   741   741    0  22 keyserv        load
  12 s   759     1   759   759    0  32 statd          load jctl
  13 s   761     1   761   761    0  25 lockd          load
  14 s   839     1     0     0    0  59 lmgrd.ste      load
  15 s   805     1   805   805    0  52 nscd           load
  16 s   786     1   786   786    0  58 syslogd        load nowait
  17 s   799     1   799   799    0  58 cron           load
  18 s   821   815   815   815    0  48 lpNet          load nowait jctl
  19 s   815     1   815   815    0  58 lpsched        load nowait
  20 s   829     1   829   829    0  58 sendmail       load jctl
  21 s   840     1   840   840    0  58 utmpd          load
  22 s 25822     1 25951 25951  200  58 oracle         load
  24 s   844   839   844   844    0  59 suntechd       load
  25 s   851     1   851   851    0  42 vold           load jctl


  98 s 25853  1424  1424   926    0  31 sleep          load
 101 s 12608     1 12608 12608  200  11 oracle         load
 103 p 25862 25859 25862 11974    0  41 crash          load
 106 s 11974 11972 11974 11974 1255  48 ksh            load
 108 s 12404     1 12404 12404  200  59 oracle         load
 109 s 10506     1 10506 10506  200  24 oracle         load
 112 s 25380     1 25380 25380  200  58 oracle         load
 115 s 25719     1 25719 25719  200  54 oracle         load
 118 s 22980     1 22980 22980  200  59 oracle         load
```

Notice that you caught one process sleeping. It's probably waiting for a system resource or another process to free up a system resource.

You can learn a lot about your system by using the `crash` command. Be sure to read your system documentation on this command so that you'll be able to make full use of it.

You can use the `size` command to display the size of the text, data, and BSS (uninitialized data) segments (or sections) and their totals.

```
$ size -f hello
```

```
17(.interp) + 332(.hash) + 800(.dynsym) + 348(.dynstr) + 24(.rela.ex_shared) + 4
8(.rela.plt) + 400(.text) + 56(.init) + 56(.fini) + 4(.exception_ranges) +
4(.rodata) + 4(.got) + 184(.dynamic) + 100(.plt) + 32(.ex_shared) + 40(.data) +
16(.data1) + 0(.bss) = 2465
```

The `-f` option gives us the size and name of each section that comprises `hello`.

The `ldd` command can tell you what shared libraries your program requires when it is executed.

```
$ ldd hello
```

```
        libucb.so.1 =>    /usr/ucblib/libucb.so.1
        libsocket.so.1 =>          /usr/lib/libsocket.so.1
        libnsl.so.1 =>    /usr/lib/libnsl.so.1
        libelf.so.1 =>    /usr/lib/libelf.so.1
        libaio.so.1 =>    /usr/lib/libaio.so.1
        libc.so.1 =>      /usr/lib/libc.so.1
        libdl.so.1 =>     /usr/lib/libdl.so.1
        libintl.so.1 =>   /usr/lib/libintl.so.1
        libmp.so.1 =>     /usr/lib/libmp.so.1
        libw.so.1 =>      /usr/lib/libw.so.1
```

It is also useful in allowing the system administrator a peek into the location of the libraries a compiled program is using as well.

The `priocntl` command can be used to modify or display the CPU scheduling settings for a process.

> **CAUTION**
>
> Keep in mind that on some systems the order in which you list the options to modify a process may be critical. Check your system's documentation.

```
$ priocntl -l
```

```
CONFIGURED CLASSES
==================
```

```
SYS (System Class)
```

```
TS (Time Sharing)
        Configured TS User Priority Range: -60 through 60

RT (Real Time)
        Maximum Configured RT Priority: 59

IA (Interactive)
        Configured IA User Priority Range: -60 through 60
```

Notice on this system, Sun Solaris, there is an additional class called IA. The intent of this classification is to allow interactive users better system response times. Again, the reader is reminded to check his or her system for what classes are configured on the system before altering a process's default scheduling policy.

Next we'll take a look at what some systems call the *proc tools*. These commands enable you to display detailed information about your systems processes. The proc tools utilize the /proc file system, which contains one file for every active process. The filename is the PID number of each process. These files are actually the logical address space representations for each process. That is why you cannot cat, rm, pg, or use the file command on them. Any user command that you would normally use on a regular file doesn't work here.

The ps command takes advantage of the /proc file system. That's why you get such a quick response when you issue it. The read(2) and write(2) system calls can be used to read and/ or write these files. However, although numerous programs can read any /proc file, only one program can write to it. The process writing to a /proc file is called the *controlling* process.

The first command we will run is the pflags command to display signal and flag information for a specific process. (Use the ps command to find a PID you want to use these tools on.)

```
# pflags 396
396:    ora_pmon_D2K
  /1:   flags = PR_PCINVAL¦PR_ASLEEP [ semsys(0x2,0x0,0xefffe948,0x1,0x0) ]
#
```

The pcred command prints the effective, real, and saved UIDs and GIDs for each process.

```
# pcred 396
396:    e/r/suid=200  e/r/sgid=200
#
```

The pmap command prints the address space map for each process:

```
# pmap 396
396:    ora_pmon_D2K
00010000 9880K read/exec          dev:  32,136 ino: 123689
009C4000  192K read/write/exec    dev:  32,136 ino: 123689
009F4000   80K read/write/exec
009F8000   64K    [ heap ]
E0000000100000K read/write/exec/shared
EF560000   32K read/exec          /usr/lib/libw.so.1
EF576000    8K read/write/exec    /usr/lib/libw.so.1
EF580000  512K read/exec          /usr/lib/libc.so.1
EF60E000   32K read/write/exec    /usr/lib/libc.so.1
EF616000    8K read/write/exec
```

```
EF620000   16K read/exec          /usr/platform/SUNW,Ultra-2/lib/libc_psr.so.1
EF632000    8K read/write/exec    /usr/platform/SUNW,Ultra-2/lib/libc_psr.so.1
EF640000   16K read/exec          /usr/lib/libmp.so.1
EF652000    8K read/write/exec    /usr/lib/libmp.so.1
EF660000   16K read/exec          /usr/lib/libintl.so.1
EF672000    8K read/write/exec    /usr/lib/libintl.so.1
EF680000  392K read/exec          /usr/lib/libnsl.so.1
EF6F0000   40K read/write/exec    /usr/lib/libnsl.so.1
EF6FA000   32K read/write/exec
EF720000   24K read/exec          /usr/lib/libaio.so.1
EF734000    8K read/write/exec    /usr/lib/libaio.so.1
EF750000   88K read/exec          /usr/lib/libm.so.1
EF774000    8K read/write/exec    /usr/lib/libm.so.1
EF780000   56K read/exec          /usr/lib/libsocket.so.1
EF79C000    8K read/write/exec    /usr/lib/libsocket.so.1
EF7B0000    8K read/exec/shared   /usr/lib/libdl.so.1
EF7C0000    8K read/write/exec
EF7D0000  104K read/exec          /usr/lib/ld.so.1
EF7F8000    8K read/write/exec    /usr/lib/ld.so.1
EFFFC000   16K read/write/exec
EFFFC000   16K     [ stack ]
#
```

The `pldd` command displays the dynamic libraries linked into each process:

```
# pldd 396
396:    ora_pmon_D2K
/usr/lib/libsocket.so.1
/usr/lib/libnsl.so.1
/usr/lib/libm.so.1
/usr/lib/libdl.so.1
/usr/lib/libaio.so.1
/usr/lib/libc.so.1
/usr/lib/libintl.so.1
/usr/lib/libmp.so.1
/usr/lib/libw.so.1
/usr/platform/SUNW,Ultra-2/lib/libc_psr.so.1
#
```

The `psig` command displays the signal actions of each process:

N O T E You might want to review the signal(5) man page for more information about signals. ▪

```
# psig 396
396:    ora_pmon_D2K
HUP    default
INT    default
QUIT   caught  RESTART,SIGINFO
ILL    caught  RESTART,SIGINFO
TRAP   caught  RESTART,SIGINFO
ABRT   caught  RESTART,SIGINFO
EMT    default
FPE    caught  RESTART,SIGINFO
KILL   default
```

```
BUS      caught  RESTART,SIGINFO
SEGV     caught  RESTART,SIGINFO
SYS      caught  RESTART,SIGINFO
PIPE     default
ALRM     caught  RESTART,SIGINFO
TERM     default
USR1     default
USR2     caught  RESTART,SIGINFO
CLD      default
PWR      default
WINCH    default
URG      default
POLL     default
STOP     default
TSTP     ignored
CONT     default
TTIN     default
TTOU     default
VTALRM   default
PROF     default
XCPU     caught  RESTART,SIGINFO
XFSZ     caught  RESTART,SIGINFO
WAITING  default
LWP      default
FREEZE   default
THAW     default
CANCEL   default
RTMIN    default
RTMIN+1  default
RTMIN+2  default
RTMIN+3  default
RTMAX-3  default
RTMAX-2  default
RTMAX-1  default
RTMAX    default
#
```

The pfiles command reports status and control information for all open files associated with a process:

 Sometimes you might not be able to remove a file from the system because it is in use by a process. You can use the pfiles command to see what files are being used by your processes and either wait for the job to finish or use the kill command to end the job.

> **CAUTION**
>
> Some UNIX background jobs or commercial products place a hidden file in a directory that you may be cleaning out. Be careful when removing these files because they will more than likely cause these jobs or products to fail.

```
# pfiles 396
396:    ora_pmon_D2K
  Current rlimit: 1024 file descriptors
   0: S_IFCHR mode:0666 dev:32,120 ino:28516 uid:0 gid:3 rdev:13,2
      O_RDONLY
   1: S_IFCHR mode:0666 dev:32,120 ino:28516 uid:0 gid:3 rdev:13,2
      O_RDONLY
   2: S_IFCHR mode:0666 dev:32,120 ino:28516 uid:0 gid:3 rdev:13,2
      O_RDONLY
   3: S_IFREG mode:0666 dev:32,136 ino:677128 uid:200 gid:200 size:356400
      O_RDWR
   4: S_IFREG mode:0666 dev:32,136 ino:677128 uid:200 gid:200 size:356400
      O_RDWR
   5: S_IFREG mode:0666 dev:32,136 ino:677130 uid:200 gid:200 size:29404
      O_RDWR
   6: S_IFREG mode:0666 dev:32,136 ino:677129 uid:200 gid:200 size:5448
      O_RDWR
   7: S_IFREG mode:0666 dev:32,136 ino:677130 uid:200 gid:200 size:29404
      O_RDWR
   8: S_IFIFO mode:0000 dev:158,0 ino:166 uid:200 gid:200 size:0
      O_RDWR
   9: S_IFREG mode:0666 dev:32,136 ino:677129 uid:200 gid:200 size:5448
      O_RDWR
  10: 0xd000  mode:0444 dev:165,0 ino:2 uid:0 gid:0 size:0
      O_RDONLY close-on-exec
  11: S_IFIFO mode:0000 dev:158,0 ino:167 uid:200 gid:200 size:0
      O_RDWR
  12: S_IFREG mode:0640 dev:32,136 ino:506480 uid:200 gid:200 size:830
      O_RDWR
  13: S_IFREG mode:0444 dev:32,136 ino:153089 uid:200 gid:200 size:196096
      O_RDONLY close-on-exec
#
```

The pwdx command prints the current working directory of a process:

```
# pwdx 396
396:    /u01/oracle/product/7.3.2/dbs
#
```

And finally, the ptree command displays a tree representation of a process and its children. Notice that the child processes are indented:

T I P The ptree command is useful in helping you to determine which processes are the parents of other processes. You can use this information to see which processes were started by your users. This simplifies the task of hunting down runaway user jobs so that you can kill the appropriate process.

```
# ptree 24992
153    /usr/sbin/inetd -s
  24979 in.telnetd
    24981 -ksh
      24992 man proc
        24998 sh -c more -s /tmp/mpa0066W
          24999 more -s /tmp/mpa0066W
#
```

From Here...

In this chapter, you learned what a process is and how UNIX creates one. You saw an example of the proc.h header file, which the system uses to define certain process structures. You also saw commands that you can use to query the system for information and manipulate your system processes. The system administrator and/or system programmer needs to become familiar with how his system specifically creates, schedules, and manages processes. UNIX basically revolves around two main flavors: System V Release 4 (SVR4) or the Berkeley Standard Distribution (BSD). Most releases, however, are hybrids of both, taking the best services and practices from each flavor. Whether you are using HP/UX, SUN Solaris, DEC UNIX, or Linux, the principles and concepts you learned here will help you to understand and master your particular version of UNIX.

- To learn more about the UNIX shell, see Chapter 3, "UNIX Shells and System Commands."
- For information on files and permissions, see Chapter 5, "Files, Directories, and Permissions."
- To learn about UNIX shell programming and scripting, see Chapter 7, "Essential Shell Scripting."
- To see how you can improve your system's performance, see Chapter 27, "Performance Tuning."

Essential Shell Scripting

by Sriranga Veeraraghavan

In this chapter

Introduction to Shell Programming

Many tasks that users and administrators perform on the UNIX system are repeated several times. Tasks and groups of commands can be executed repeatedly using shell scripts. The UNIX system also configures itself through the use of shell scripts; therefore, understanding shell scripts is an essential part of the administrative process.

This chapter covers the basics of Bourne shell (sh) programming. It also introduces some useful programming constructs from the Korn shell (ksh). All the examples in this chapter are compatible with the Bourne Again shell (bash) because it provides feature compatibility with both the Korn and Bourne shells.

▶ **See** "Choosing a Shell," **p. 47**

Because a shell script is nothing more than a set of commands placed into a file, this chapter looks first at the types of commands that can be used:

- Pipelines
- Lists
- Redirection

The chapter also examines the following topics, which are important for shell script programming:

- Subshells
- Comments

The Korn Shell

The Korn shell (ksh) is a Bourne shell (sh) compatible UNIX shell. It was written by David Korn of AT&T Bell Labs to make interactive use of the shell easier for users. It also introduced several useful shell programming constructs.

In general, ksh can be treated as fully compatible with sh, but there are some differences that prevent scripts from functioning correctly. These exceptions are noted in this chapter.

Three major versions of ksh are available:

- The Official version (ksh)
- The Public Domain version (pdksh)
- The Desktop version (dtksh)

The Official version is available in binary format (no sources) from:

```
http://www.kornshell.com
```

The Public Domain version is available in both binary and source format from:

```
ftp://ftp.cs.mun.ca:/pub/pdksh
```

For the shell programmer, there is no difference between the Official and the Public Domain versions of `ksh`; all scripts that run in one version will run in the other.

For shell users, the Official version provides a few nice features such as command-line completion with the Tab key rather than the Esc key.

The Desktop version comes with all major implementations of CDE. This version provides the capability to create and display Graphical User Interfaces (GUIs) using `ksh` syntax. Scripts written for the other two versions of `ksh` run correctly under this version.

▶ **See** "Overview of the Common Desktop Environment," **p. 198**

Pipes

One of the most common tasks in UNIX is to have one program manipulate the output of another program. This is accomplished by using a *pipeline*, which connects several commands together with *pipes* as follows:

```
command1 ¦ command2 ¦ ...
```

The pipe character, ¦, connects the standard output of *command1* to the standard input of *command2*, and so on. The commands can be as simple or complex as required.

Following are some examples of pipeline commands:

```
tail -f /var/adm/messages ¦ more

ps -ael ¦ grep "$UID" ¦ more

tar -cf - ./foo ¦ { cd /tmp; tar -xf - }
```

In the first example, the standard output of the `tail` command is piped into the standard input of the `more` command, which allows the output to be viewed one screen at a time.

In the second example, the standard output of `ps` is connected to the standard input of `grep`, and the standard output of `grep` is connected to the standard input of `more`, so that the output of `grep` can be viewed one screen at a time.

The third example is an obscure but somewhat useful way for root to copy files without changing their ownership.

▶ **See** "Pipes, I/O Redirection, and Filters," **p. 65**

CAUTION

One important thing about pipelines is that each command is executed as a separate process, and the exit status of a pipeline is the exit status of the last command.

It is vital to remember this fact when writing scripts that must do error handling.

Lists

In addition to pipelines, commands can be executed as *lists*. Lists are a sequence of one or more commands or pipelines:

```
command1; command2; command3 ...
command1 | command2; command3 | command4 ...
```

Lists are commonly used for tasks that cannot be executed in a single pipeline or command. Some examples are as follows:

```
lpr homework.txt; lpq;
ps -ael | head -1; ps -ael | grep "$UID"
```

The first example submits a printer request and then checks its status. The second example runs the ps command twice. The first time you use it to get the headers for the table that is produced. The second time it is used to grep for the value of the variable UID. Both of these can be accomplished only by using a list.

Lists can also be used to execute commands based on the exit status of previous commands using the logical AND or the logical OR operators:

```
command1 && command2
command1 || command2
```

TIP The use of the logical AND and the logical OR operators is similar to their use in the C programming language. Because these operators use the exit codes to determine the next action, they are called "lazy" logical operators.

If the logical AND operator is used, as in the first case, *command2* is executed only if *command1* returns an exit status of 0.

If the logical OR operator is used, as in the second case, *command2* is executed only if *command1* returns with a nonzero exit status.

A common use of the && operator is in situations like the following:

```
mkdir docs && cd docs
```

Here, a directory change is appropriate only if the directory was successfully created.

An example using the || operator follows:

```
grep root /etc/passwd || echo "Help! No one in charge!"
```

Redirection

Lists can also include redirection of input and output using the < and > operators. By default < redirects the standard input, and > redirects the standard output, but the redirection operators can also be used to open and close files. In general, output redirection is either:

```
command > file
list > file
```

The first form redirects the output of the specified *command* to specified *file*, whereas the second redirects the output of specified *list* to specified *file*. In the following example:

```
date > now
```

the output of the date command is redirected into the file now. The output of lists can also be redirected:

```
{ date; uptime; who ; } > mylog
```

The preceding example redirects the output of all the commands date, uptime, and who into the file mylog.

In addition to this form output redirection, which overwrites the output file, there is appended output redirection:

```
command >> file
list >> file
```

In these examples, form output is appended to the end of the specified *file*, or the specified *file* is created if it does not exist. For example, if the file mylog (in the previous example) shouldn't be erased each time data is added, the following could be used:

```
{ date; uptime; who ; } >> mylog
```

In addition to redirecting only standard output, you can redirect both standard output and standard error together. In general, this is done by:

```
command > file 2>&1
list > file 2>&1
```

Here, the standard output (file descriptor 1) and standard error (file descriptor 2) are redirected into the specified *file*. A situation where it is necessary to redirect both the standard output and the standard error is as follows:

```
rm -rf /tmp/my_tmp_dir > /dev/null 2>&1 ; mkdir /tmp/my_tmp_dir
```

Here, you are not interested in the error message or the informational message printed by the rm command; you only want to remove the directory. Thus its output or any error message it prints out is redirected to /dev/null.

If you had one command that should append its standard error and standard output to a file, use the following form:

```
command >> file 2>&1
list >> file 2>&1
```

The following is an example of a command that might require this:

```
rdate -s ntp.nasa.gov >> /var/log/rdate.log 2>&1
```

This example uses the rdate command to synchronize the time of the local machine to that of an Internet time server, and you want to keep a log of all the messages.

Part

I

Ch

7

The input can also be redirected in a similar fashion. In general, input redirection is as follows:

```
command < file
```

In this example, the contents of `file` becomes the input to `command`. For example, the following would be an excellent use of redirection:

```
Mail ranga@soda.berkeley.edu < Final_Exam_Answers
```

Here the input to the `Mail` command, which becomes the body of the mail message, is the file `Final_Exam_Answers`. This particular example is best performed by a professor, and the file should contain the answers to a current final exam.

An additional use of input redirection is in the creation of Here documents. The general form for a Here document is as follows:

```
command << delimiter
document
delimiter
```

The shell interprets the << operator as an instruction to read input until a line containing the specified *delimiter* is found. All the input lines up to the line containing the *delimiter* are fed into the standard input of the *command*. For example, to print out a quick list of URLs, the following Here document could be used:

```
lpr << MYURLS
     http://www.csua.berkeley.edu/~ranga/
     http://www.cisco.com/
     http://www.marathon.org/story/
     http://www.gnu.org/
MYURLS
```

This provides a handy alternative to creating temporary files. To strip the tabs in this example, the << operator can be given a - option.

▶ **See** "Pipes, I/O Redirection, and Filters," **p. 65**

Subshells

Any list can be executed either in the current shell environment or in a subshell. A *list* enclosed in braces:

```
{ list; }
```

is executed in the current shell environment, whereas a list enclosed in parentheses:

```
(list;)
```

is executed in a subshell. For example, the following command runs a list in the current shell:

```
{ ps -ael ¦ head -1; ps -ael ¦ grep " $UID " ; } ¦ more
```

This example generates a table of all the processes running under the current user ID and then pipes the output to the `more` command. Every command is executed in the context of the current shell. The same list could be run in a subshell:

```
( ps -ael ¦ head -1; ps -ael ¦ grep " $UID " ; ) ¦ more
```

This is probably not a good idea because each subshell that runs takes up more system resources. When possible, it is more efficient to run all the programs in the current shell.

There are instances where using subshells is useful or required. One reason to use subshells is because they effectively make all variables local. This is illustrated by the following command:

```
FRUIT="bannana" ; ( FRUIT="watermelon" ; echo $FRUIT; ) ; echo $FRUIT ;
```

The output is:

```
watermelon
banana
```

You can see that the value of the variable FRUIT was changed only in the subshell. You'll learn more about variables later in the chapter.

In addition to localizing variables, subshells also have their own working directories. This is illustrated by the following example:

```
pwd; ( cd /tmp ; pwd ) ; pwd;
```

The output is similar to the following:

```
/home/ranga
/tmp
/home/ranga
```

As you can see, the current working directory is only changed for the subshell.

Comments

In shell scripts, comments start with the # character. Every character between the # and end of the line is considered part of the comment and is ignored.

Variables

Variables are "words" that hold a value. They are defined as follows:

name=value

Here *name* is the name of the variable, and *value* is the value it should hold. For example:

```
FRUIT=peach
```

defines the variable FRUIT and assigns it the value peach.

To access the value stored in a variable, prefix its name with the dollar sign, $. For example, the command:

```
echo $FRUIT
```

prints out the value stored in the variable FRUIT. A common mistake made by new users is to access variables as follows:

```
echo FRUIT
```

This command simply prints out FRUIT, not the value of the variable FRUIT. Another common mistake is to define variables as follows:

```
$FRUIT=apple
```

If FRUIT is defined as in the preceding line, this results in the warning:

```
sh: peach=apple: not found
```

If the variable FRUIT was undefined, the error would be:

```
sh: =apple: not found
```

Remember that when the dollar character, $, precedes a variable name, the value of the variable is substituted.

▶ **See** "Special Variables," **p. 177**

▶ **See** "Variable Substitution," **p. 182**

Array Variables

The Bourne shell only supports "scalar" variables, whose use is demonstrated in the preceding section. The Korn shell extends this to include array variables. Current versions of the Bourne Again shell also support array variables.

Array variables can be set in two ways. The first form sets a single element:

```
name[index]=value
```

Here *name* is the name of the array; *index* is the index of the item in the array. For example, the following commands:

```
FRUIT[0]=apple
FRUIT[1]=banana
FRUIT[2]=orange
```

set the values of the first three items in the array named FRUIT. In this example, we set the array indices in sequence, but this is not necessary. For example, you can issue the following command:

```
FRUIT[10]=plum
```

This sets the value of the item at index 10 in the array FRUIT to plum.

CAUTION

In ksh, numerical indices for arrays must be between 0 and 1023. In bash, there is no such requirement.

In addition, both ksh and bash support only integer array indices. This means that floating point or decimal numbers such as "10.3" cannot be used.

Additionally, you do not need to use numeric indices for arrays. Strings can be used in their place:

```
FRUIT[apple]=10
```

Here, the value of the item apple in the array FRUIT is set to 10.

If an array variable with the same name as a scalar variable is defined, then the value of the scalar variable becomes the value of the element of the array at index 0. For example, if the following commands are executed:

```
FRUIT=apple
FRUIT[1]=peach
```

The element FRUIT[0] will have the value apple.

The second form of array initialization is used to set multiple elements at once. In ksh, this is done as follows:

```
set -A name value1 value2 ... valuen
```

In bash, the multiple elements are set as follows:

```
name=(value1 ... valuen)
```

In both forms, *name* is the name of the array, and the values, 1 to n, are the values of the items to be set. When setting multiple elements at once, both ksh and bash use consecutive array indices beginning at 0. For example, the ksh command:

```
set -A band derri terry mike gene
```

is equivalent to the commands:

```
band[0]=derri
band[1]=terry
band[2]=mike
band[3]=gene
```

TIP When setting multiple array elements in bash, an array index can be placed before the value:

```
myarray=([0]=derri [3]=gene [2]=mike [1]=terry)
```

There are no requirements that the array indices be in order, as shown in the preceding example, or that the indices be integers.

This feature is not present in ksh.

After any array variable has been set, you access it as follows:

```
${name[index]}
```

Here, *name* is the name of the array, and *index* is the index you are interested in. If the array FRUIT was initialized as given previously, then the command:

```
echo ${FRUIT[2]}
```

produces the following output:

```
orange
```

All the items in an array can be accessed in one of the following ways:

```
${name[*]}
${name[@]}
```

Here, *name* is the name of the array you are interested in. If the FRUIT array was initialized as given previously, the command:

```
echo ${FRUIT[*]}
```

produces the following output:

```
apple banana orange
```

If any of the array items held values with spaces, then this form of array access would not work, and you would need to use the second form. The second from quotes all the array entries so that embedded spaces are preserved.

Environment Variables

An environment variable is a variable available to any child process of the shell. Variables are placed in the environment by *exporting* them. Exporting can be done in two ways:

```
export name
export name=value
```

The first form marks the variable with the specified *name* for export. This is the only form supported by sh, thus it is the most commonly encountered form. A common use is as follows:

```
PATH=/sbin:/bin ; export PATH
```

This example sets the value of the variable PATH and then exports it. This is done in a list to make the commands more readable. The export command can be used to export more than one variable to the environment. For example:

```
export PATH HOME UID
```

exports the variables PATH, HOME, and UID to the environment.

The second form for exporting variables is supported by ksh and bash. In this form, the given *value* to the variable is specified by *name*, and then marks that variable for export. In this form, the previous example can be written as:

```
export PATH=/sbin:/bin
```

In bash and ksh, any combination of *name* or *name=value* pairs can be given to the export command. For example, the command:

```
export FMHOME=/usr/frame CLEARHOME=/usr/atria PATH
```

assigns the given values to the variables FMHOME and CLEARHOME, and then exports the variables FMHOME, CLEARHOME, and PATH.

Shell Variables

The variables examined so far have all been user variables. A user variable is one that the user can set and reset manually.

This section looks at shell variables, which are variables that the shell sets during initialization and uses internally. Users have the ability to modify the value of these variables.

Table 7.1 gives a partial list of these shell variables. In addition to these variables, several special variables are covered in the sections "Special Variables" and "Variable Substitution" in Chapter 8. Unless noted, all the variables given in Table 7.1 are available in sh, ksh, and bash.

Table 7.1 Shell Variables

Variable	Description
PWD	The current working directory as set by the cd command.
UID	Expands to the numeric user ID of the current user, initialized at shell startup.
SHLVL	Incremented by one each time an instance of bash is started. This variable is useful for determining whether the built-in exit command ends the current session.
REPLY	Expands to the last input line read by the read built-in command when it is given no arguments. This variable is not available in sh.
RANDOM	This parameter generates a random integer between 0 and 32767 each time it is referenced. The sequence of random numbers can be initialized by assigning a value to $RANDOM. If $RANDOM is unset, it loses its special properties, even if it is subsequently reset. This variable is not available in sh.
SECONDS	Each time this parameter is referenced, the number of seconds since shell invocation is returned. If a value is assigned to $SECONDS, the value returned on subsequent references is the number of seconds since the assignment plus the value assigned. If $SECONDS is unset, it loses its special properties, even if it is subsequently reset. This variable is not available in sh.
IFS	The Internal Field Separator that is used by the parser for word splitting after expansion. $IFS is also used to split lines into words with the read built-in command. The default value is the string, " \t\n", where " " is the SPACE character, \t is the Tab character, and \n is the newline character.
PATH	The search path for commands. It is a colon-separated list of directories in which the shell looks for commands. A common value is PATH=/bin:/sbin:/usr/bin:/usr/sbin:/usr/local/bin:/usr/ucb
HOME	The home directory of the current user; the default argument for the cd built-in command.

Part

I

Ch

7

Unsetting Variables

Unsetting a variable tells the shell to remove the variable from the list of variables that it tracks. It is like asking the shell to forget a piece of information because it is no longer required.

Both scalar and array variables are unset using the `unset` command:

```
unset name
unset -v name
```

Here, `name` is the name of the variable to unset. For example:

```
unset FRUIT
```

unsets the variable FRUIT.

The `-v` option in the second form is used to indicate to `unset` that `name` is a shell variable. It is not required.

Substitution and Quoting

One of the most powerful features of the shell is its capability to substitute the output of commands and variables on demand. This section looks at the different types of substitution and quoting available in the shell.

Command Substitution

Command substitution is the mechanism by which the shell performs a given set of commands and then substitutes their output in the place of the commands. Command substitution is performed when a command is given as:

```
`command`
```

Here `command` can be a simple command, a pipeline, or a list. Command substitution is generally used to assign the output of a command to a variable. Each of the following examples demonstrates command substitution:

```
DATE=`date`
USERS=`who ¦ wc -l`
UP=`date ; uptime`
```

In the first example, the output of the `date` command becomes the value for the variable DATE. In the second example, the output of the pipeline becomes the value of the variable USERS. In the last example, the output of the list becomes the value of the variable UP.

Command substitution can also be used to provide arguments for other commands. For example:

```
grep `id -un` /etc/passwd
```

Looks through the file /etc/passwd for the output of the command:

```
id -un
```

In my case, the command substitution results in the string ranga, and thus grep returns the entry in the passwd file for my username.

Arithmetic Substitution

In ksh and bash, the shell allows for integer arithmetic to be performed. This avoids having to run an extra program such as expr or bc to do math in a shell script.

Arithmetic substitution is performed when the following form of command is given:

```
$((expression))
```

Expressions are evaluated according to the C programming language rules, and the result is substituted. For example:

```
foo=$(( ((5 + 3*2) - 4) / 2 ))
```

sets the value of foo to 3. Because this is integer arithmetic, the value is not 3.5, and because of operator precedence, the value is not 6.

The following short script demonstrates the use of arithmetic substitution (it uses the shell variable SECONDS to get the number of seconds since the shell was started):

```
hrs=$(($SECONDS/3600));

# if the hours are greater than 24, then initialize
# day to the number of days since shell was started
if [ $hrs -ge 24 ]; then day=$(($hrs/24)); fi;

# get the number of minutes and seconds
min=$((($SECONDS/60)-($hrs*60)));
sec=$(($SECONDS - ($min*60) - ($hrs*3600)));

# format the minutes and seconds
if [ $sec -le 9 ]; then sec="0$sec"; fi;
if [ $min -le 9 ]; then min="0$min"; fi;

# output the results
if [ -n "$day" ]; then
    hrs=$(($hrs - ($day*24)));
    echo $day days $hrs:$min:$sec;
else
    echo $hrs:$min:$sec;
fi
```

Part
I

Ch
7

This script uses some flow control commands such as if-then-else, which are explained later in this chapter. To run this script, type the commands into a file called `howlong`, and then run it as follows:

```
. ./howlong
```

This assumes that the file you used is in the current directory and that your current shell is either `ksh` or `bash`. This script does not work correctly with other shells. The output looks something like the following:

```
4:31:35
```

Here we also demonstrate the use of the dot, ., command. This command is used in `sh`, `ksh`, and `bash` to read in scripts and execute them in the context of the current shell. Normally, scripts are executed in the context of a subshell. In large shell script based programs, "libraries" of shell functions often are "imported" or "included" into a shell script by using the . command. For those familiar with the C programming language, the . command can be used in a manner similar to the C preprocessor directive `#include`.

Quoting

Quoting is used to disable the meaning of certain characters that the shell treats in a special way. Strings can be quoted by surrounding them in single quotes (') or double quotes ("), whereas single characters can be quoted by preceding them with a backslash (\). Some characters whose meanings are disabled by quoting are as follows:

```
` ~ ! # $ % ^ & * ( ) - + = \ ¦ ; ` " , . < > ?
```

Strings enclosed in single quotes, `'string'`, have all the special characters in them disabled. Strings enclosed in double quotes, `"string"`, have all the special characters except !, $, `, \, and { disabled. Characters preceded by a backslash (\)have their special meaning disabled.

In addition to quoting, several standard escape sequences familiar to C language programmers, such as `\t` for tab and `\n` for newline, are recognized.

Control Structures

The Bourne shell provides a host of powerful flow control and looping structures. This section first looks at flow control structures and then considers looping structures.

Flow Control

Two powerful flow control mechanics are available in the shell:

- The `if-fi` block
- The `case-esac` block

The `if` statement is normally used for the conditional execution of commands, whereas `case` statements allow any of a number of command sequences to be executed depending on which one of several patterns matches a variable first. It is often easier to write `if` statements as `case` statements if they involve matching a variable to a pattern.

The *if-fi* block

The basic `if` statement syntax:

```
if list1 ; then
    list2
elif list3 ; then
    list4
else
    list5
fi
```

Both the `elif` and the `else` statements are optional. An `if` statement can be written with any number of `elif` statements, and `if` statements can contain just the `if` and `fi` statements.

In the general `if` statement, shown previously, first `list1` is evaluated. If the exit code of `list1` is 0, indicating a true condition, `list2` is evaluated, and the `if` statement exits. Otherwise, `list3` is executed and then its exit code is checked. If `list3` returns a 0, then `list4` is executed, and the `if` statement exits. If `list3` does not return a 0, `list5` is executed. A simple use of the `if` statement is as follows:

```
if uuencode koala.gif koala.gif > koala.uu ; then
    echo "Encoded koala.gif to koala.uu"
else
    echo "Error encoding koala.gif"
fi
```

The message:

```
"Encoded koala.gif to koala.uu"
```

is echoed if the `uuencode` command exits with a 0, indicating success. Otherwise, the error is reported.

Most often, the `list` given to an `if` statement is one or more `test` commands, which can be invoked by calling the `test` command as follows:

```
test expression
[ expression ]
```

Here, `expression` is constructed using one of the special options to the `test` command.

The `test` command returns either a 0 (true) or a 1 (false) after evaluating an expression. Table 7.2 lists the commonly used options for `test`.

Table 7.2 Options for the *test* Command

Option	Description
-d *file*	True if *file* exists and is a directory.
-e *file*	True if *file* exists.
-f *file*	True if *file* exists and is a regular file.
-k *file*	True if *file* exists has its sticky bit set.
-L *file*	True if *file* exists and is a symbolic link.
-r *file*	True if *file* exists and is readable.
-s *file*	True if *file* exists and has a size greater than zero.
-t fd	True if fd is opened on a terminal.
-w *file*	True if *file* exists and is writable.
-x *file*	True if *file* exists and is executable.
-O file	True if file exists and is owned by the effective user ID.
file1 -nt *file2*	True if *file1* is newer (according to modification date) than *file2*.
file1 -ot *file2*	True if *file1* is older than *file2*.
-z *string*	True if the length of *string* is zero.
-n *string*	True if the length of *string* is non-zero.
string1 = *string2*	
string1 == *string2*	True if the strings are equal.
string1 != *string2*	True if the strings are not equal.
! expr	True if expr is false. The expr can be any of the tests given previously.
expr1 -a *expr2*	True if both *expr1* AND *expr2* are true.
expr1 -o *expr2*	True if either *expr1* OR *expr2* is true.
arg1 OP *arg2*	OP is one of -eq, -ne, -lt, -le, - gt, or - ge. These arithmetic binary operators return true if *arg1* is equal to, not equal to, less than, less than or equal to, greater than, or greater than or equal to *arg2*, respectively. *Arg1* and *arg2* can be positive or negative integers.

Examples of common uses of a simple if statement in conjunction with a test are as follows:

```
if [ -d $HOME/bin ] ; then PATH="$PATH:$HOME/bin" ; fi
if [ -s $HOME/.bash_aliai ] ; then . $HOME/.bash_aliai ; fi
```

In the first example, `test` is used to determine whether a directory exists and then some action is taken. In the second example, `test` is used to determine whether a file exists and has non-zero size before any action is taken.

Here are two more equivalent examples that demonstrate how to combine tests:

```
if [ -z "$DTHOME" ] && [ -d /usr/dt ] ; then DTHOME=/usr/dt ; fi

if [ -z "$DTHOME" -a -d /usr/dt ] ; then DTHOME=/usr/dt ; fi
```

Some users prefer the first form because it is obvious what tests are being done and what the evaluation criteria are. Other users prefer the second form because it only invokes the `[` command once and may be marginally more efficient.

The *case-esac* Block

The other form of flow control is the `case-esac` block. The basic syntax is as follows:

```
case word in
     pattern)
             list
             ;;
     pattern2)
             list2
             ;;
esac
```

In this form, *word* is either a string or a variable, whose value is compared against each *pattern* until a match is found. The *list* following the matching *pattern* is executed. After a list is executed, the command `;;` indicates that program flow should jump to the end of the entire `case` statement. This is similar to `break` in the C programming language.

If no matches are found, the `case` statement exits without performing any action. Some default actions can be performed by giving the `*` pattern, which matches anything.

There is no maximum number of patterns, but the minimum is one. The patterns can use the same special characters as patterns for pathname expansion, along with the OR operator, `¦`. The `;;` signifies to `bash` that the list has concluded.

An example of a simple `case` statement is as follows:

```
case "$TERM" in
     *term)
             TERM=xterm ;;
network¦dialup¦unknown¦vt[0-9]*)
             TERM=vt100 ;;
Esac
```

Reading User Input   A common task in shell scripts is to prompt the user for input and then read the user's response. This is done by using the read command to set the value of a variable and then evaluating the value of the variable using a case statement.

The `read` command works as follows:

```
read name
```

It reads the entire line of user input until the user presses Enter and makes that line the value of the variable specified by `name`.

A example of this is as follows:

```
YN=yes
printf "Do you want to play a game [$YN]? "
read YN
: ${YN:=yes}
case $YN in
    [yY]¦[yY][eE][sS]) exec xblast ;;
    *) echo "Maybe later." ;;
esac
```

Here we prompt the user and provide a default response. Then we read and evaluate the user's answer using a case statement.

Many more extensive examples of using case statements are given in the sections "Special Variables" and "Variable Substitution" in Chapter 8.

Loops

Two main types of loops available in `sh` are as follows:

- The `for` loop
- The `while` loop

In addition to these two types of loops, `ksh` and `bash` add two more types:

- The `until` loop
- The `select` loop

A `for` loop is used when a set of commands needs to be executed repeatedly. A `while` loop is used when a set of commands needs to be executed while a certain condition is true. A common use for a `select` loop is to provide a convenient selection interface.

This section examines each of these in turn.

The *for* Loop   The basic `for` loop syntax is as follows:

```
for name in list1
do
    list2
done
```

In the `for` loop, the variable specified by `name` is set to each element in `list1`, and `list2` is executed for each element of `list1`. A simple `for` loop example is as follows:

```
for i in 1 2 3 4 5 6 7 8 9 10 ; do echo $i ; done
```

A more common use of the `for` loop follows:

```
for files in ~/.bash_*
do
    echo "<HTML>" > ${files}.html
    echo "<HEAD><TITLE>$files</TITLE></HEAD>" >> ${files}.html
    echo "<BODY><PRE>" >> ${files}.html
    cat $files >> ${files}.html
    echo "</PRE></BODY>" >> ${files}.html
    echo "</HTML>" >> ${files}.html
    chmod guo+r ${files}.html
done
```

The *while* Loop   The basic `while` loop syntax is as follows:

```
while list1
do
    list2
done
```

In the `while` loop, *list1* is evaluated each time, and as long as it is true, *list2* is executed. This allows for infinite loops to be written with `/bin/true` or `:` as *list1*.

A simple `while` loop example follows:

```
x=1
while [ $x -lt 10 ]
do
    echo $x
    x=$(($x+1))
done
```

This `while` loop copies its input to its output, like the `cat` program:

```
while read
do
    echo $REPLY;
done
```

If input redirection is used, this loop writes the contents of the input file to the standard output, similar to `cat`.

▶ **See** "Option Parsing in Shell Scripts," **p. 186**

The *until* Loop   A variation on the `while` loop is the `until` loop:

```
until list1
do
    list2
done
```

In the until loop, *list2* is executed until *list1* is true. The following while and until loops are equivalent:

```
x=1; while ! [ $x -ge 10 ]
do
    echo $x
    x=$(($x+1))
done

x=1; until [ $x -ge 10 ]
do
    echo $x
    x=$(($x+1))
done
```

In general, the until loop is not favored because it can be written as the negation of a while loop.

The *select* Loop   The select loop is an easy way to create a numbered menu from which users can select options. The basic select syntax is:

```
select name in list1
do
    list2
done
```

In the select loop, the items in *list1* are printed onto the standard error preceded by a number. A prompt is then displayed, and a line is read in. If $REPLY, the variable containing the value of the line that is read, contains a number of a displayed item, then *list2* is executed. Otherwise, the list of items in *list1* is displayed again. The select loop ends if an EOF (end of file) is read.

The following select loop displays a number list of the files in the directory /tmp and runs an ls -l on files that exist:

```
select file in /tmp/* QUIT
do
    if [ -e $file ] ; then
        ls -l $file
    else
        break
    fi
done
```

The output is similar to the following:

```
1) /tmp/.                    6) /tmp/job.control.ms
2) /tmp/..                   7) /tmp/job.control.ps
3) /tmp/.X11-unix            8) /tmp/ps_data
4) /tmp/intro7.html          9) /tmp/sunpro.c.1.157.3.00
5) /tmp/java                10) QUIT
#?
```

where #? is the prompt at which a number is typed by the user.

The *break* Command   All loops in `bash` can be exited immediately by giving the built-in `break` command. This command also accepts as an argument an integer, greater or equal to 1, that indicates the number of levels to break out of. This feature is useful when nested loops are being used.

From Here...

This chapter looked at the basics of shell programming. The chapter covered the different types of commands and introduced variables and substitution. It also examined the control structures available to shell programmers. Using this material, you can start writing shell scripts of your own. To further understand scripting and its applications, take a look at the following chapters:

- Chapter 8, "Advanced Shell Scripting," explores the material covered in this chapter to a greater degree, giving examples of advanced topics that are required by shell programmers.

- Chapter 11, "Startup and Shutdown," provides information on the startup and shutdown of UNIX systems. This is an area where shell scripts are used heavily and gives you a good idea of the kinds of scripts system administrators maintain.

- Chapter 16, "Automating Tasks," introduces the capability to schedule programs and scripts to run at given intervals. Shell scripts are one of the most important components in UNIX task automation.

## CHAPTER 8

Advanced Shell Scripting

by Sriranga Veeraraghavan

In this chapter

Making Shell Scripts Executable

The Bourne Shell, sh, is a powerful and portable tool for writing programs in the UNIX environment. Though developed in the early seventies, sh remains a tool of choice for programs, such as system initialization scripts and product install scripts, which must run under various flavors of UNIX.

> **CAUTION**
>
> One important fact to keep in mind while programming with the Bourne shell is that several slightly incompatible versions exist.
>
> The major commercial UNIX flavors—Solaris, HP/UX, and AIX—use a derivative of the original version written by Steve Bourne for the very first version of UNIX. With effectively no difference between these versions, scripts can be easily transferred and run on any of these systems.
>
> The free UNIX flavors, notably FreeBSD and Linux, do not use a derivative of the original Bourne shell. Instead they use either ash (A Shell) or bash (Bourne Again Shell) as a replacement. Some system administrators on free UNIX flavors use ksh (Korn Shell) as a replacement.
>
> In general, these shells are a little more forgiving of syntax errors than the original Bourne shell, but the biggest pitfall of these shells is that they will enable the programmer to use shell-specific constructs without warnings. This requires the programmer to stick to the standard constructs.
>
> ▶ **See** "Introduction to Shell Programming," **p. 154**

One of the most important tasks in writing shell scripts is making the shell scripts executable and making sure that the right shell is invoked on the script. Let's start with the following command line and make it a script:

```
echo `who ¦ wc -l` Users
```

This command returns the number of users currently logged on. For example, on my system the output looks like the following:

```
5 Users
```

To make this a shell script called countusers, open a file called countusers in an editor and type in the above command. After the file is saved, the command can be run as the following (assuming that the file is located in the current directory):

```
sh ./countusers
```

If we want to run the script by just typing its name, we need to give the script execute permissions and to make sure that the right shell is used when the script is run. To give this shell script execute permissions, do the following:

```
chmod a+x ./countusers
```

▶ For more detail on changing permissions with the chmod command, **see** "Changing File and Directory Permissions," **p. 125**

In order to ensure that the correct shell is used to run the script, we must add the following "magic" line to the beginning of the script:

```
#!/bin/sh
```

So our script would have two lines:

```
#/bin/sh

echo `who ¦ wc -l` Users
```

Without the magic line, the current shell will be used to evaluate the script. Thus, csh and tcsh users might not get the script to run correctly.

N O T E   The #!/bin/sh must be the first line of a shell script in order for sh to run the script. If this appears on any other line, it is treated as a comment and ignored by all shells. ▪

Special Variables and Variable Substitution

In this section, we will demonstrate the use of special variables that the shell defines and show how to use variable substitution.

Special variables are set automatically by the shell and are available to the shell programmer on a read-only basis. Thus the programmer can read the value stored in these variables, but he cannot set their values.

Variable substitution enables the shell programmer to manipulate the value of a variable based on its state. Variable substitution falls into two categories:

- Actions taken when a variable is set
- Actions taken when a variable is unset

The actions range from one-time value substitution to aborting the script.

Special Variables

The shell sh defines several special variables. These variables, described in Table 8.1, are used heavily in shell scripting. In this section, we will construct a simple yet useful shell script that illustrates the use of these variables.

Table 8.1   Special Shell Variables

Variable	Description
$0	The name of the command being executed. For shell scripts, this is the path with which it was invoked.
$n	These variables correspond to the arguments with which a script was invoked. Here n is a positive decimal number corresponding to the position of an argument. (The first argument is $1, the second argument is $2, and so on.)

continues

Table 8.1 Continued

Variable	Description
$#	The number of "positional" parameters supplied to a script.
$*	All the arguments double quoted. If a script receives two arguments, "$*" is equivalent to "$1 $2".
$@	All the arguments individually double quoted. If a script receives two arguments, "$@" is equivalent to "$1" "$2".
$?	The exit status of the last command executed.
$$	The process number of the current shell. For shell scripts, this is the process ID under which they are being executed.
$!	The process number of the last background command.

Using $0 Let's start by looking at $0. This variable is commonly used to determine the behavior of scripts that can be invoked with more than one name. Consider the following script:

```
#!/bin/sh
case $0 in
    *listtar) TARGS="-tvf $1" ;;
    *maketar) TARGS="-cvf $1.tar $1" ;;
esac
tar $TARGS
```

This script can be used to list the contents of a tar file or to create a tar file based on the name with which the script is invoked. The tar file to read or create is specified as the first argument, $1.

I called this script mytar and made two symbolic links to it called listtar and maketar as follows:

```
ln -s mytar listtar ; ln -s mytar maketar ;
```

If the script is invoked with the name maketar and a directory or filename to make a tar file from, a tar file will be created. If we have a directory called test with the following contents:

```
test
test/foo
test/bar
test/blatz
```

we can invoke the script as maketar to get a tar file called test.tar containing this directory:

```
maketar test
```

If we want to list the contents of this tar file, we can invoke the script as follows:

```
listtar test.tar
```

This gives us the following output:

```
drwxr-xr-x  ranga/users      0 Jun 27 23:25 1998 test/
-rw-r--r--  ranga/users      0 Jun 27 23:25 1998 test/foo
-rw-r--r--  ranga/users      0 Jun 27 23:25 1998 test/bar
-rw-r--r--  ranga/users      0 Jun 27 23:25 1998 test/blatz
```

For this example, the output that you will encounter depends on the version of tar that is installed on your machine.

 TIP

Using $0 as previously illustrated is encountered in the install and the uninstall scripts of some software packages.

Because these scripts share many of the same routines and global variables, it is desirable, for ease of maintenance, to merge them into a single script having different behaviors depending on the name with which it is invoked.

If you write scripts that need to share many routines, consider using such a scheme to simplify maintenance.

Another common use for $0 is in the "usage statement" for a script. The usage statement is a short message informing the user how to properly invoke the script. In general, it is something like the following:

```
echo "Usage: $0 [options][files]"
```

If we consider the previous mytar script, a usage statement would be a helpful addition, in the case that the script was called with a name other than the two names that it knows about. The case statement then becomes the following:

```
case $0 in
    *listtar) TARGS="-tvf $1" ;;
    *maketar) TARGS="-cvf $1.tar $1" ;;
    *) echo "Usage: $0 [file¦directory]" ; exit 0 ;;
```

Thus if the script was invoked as just mytar, we get following message:

```
Usage: mytar [file¦directory]
```

That is not what we really want because it does not give the user any idea that the problem encountered was that the name of the script was wrong. We can change this by hard coding the valid names in the usage statement or we can change the script to use its arguments to decide in which mode it should run. In order to demonstrate the use of arguments, the next section will do the latter.

Arguments   To illustrate the use of arguments, let's change the script to use its first argument, $1, as the mode argument and $2 as the tar file to read or create. Our case statement becomes the following:

```
USAGE="Usage: $0 [-c¦-t] [file¦directory]"
case "$1" in
    -t) TARGS="-tvf $2" ;;
    -c) TARGS="-cvf $2.tar $2" ;;
    *) echo "$USAGE" ; exit 0 ;;
esac
```

In addition to changing all the references to $1 to $2, `listtar` has been replaced by `-t` and `maketar` has been replaced by `-c`. Now running `mytar` produces the correct output:

```
Usage: ./mytar [-c¦-t] [file¦directory]
```

basename We can make one more improvement on the preceding message using the `basename` command. Currently, the message is displaying the entire path with which the shell script was invoked, but what is really required is just the name of the shell script. So we can change the variable $USAGE to the following:

```
USAGE="Usage: `basename $0` [-c¦-t] [file¦directory]"
```

Which will produce the following output:

```
Usage: mytar [-c¦-t] [file¦directory]
```

TIP The basename command might also have been used in the first version of the script to avoid using the * wildcard character in the case statement as follows:

```
#!/bin/sh
case `basename $0` in
    listtar) TARGS="-tvf $1" ;;
    maketar) TARGS="-cvf $1.tar $1" ;;
esac
tar $TARGS
```

In this version, the basename command enables us to match the exact names that the script can be called with. This simplifies the possible user interactions and is preferred for that reason.

As an illustration of a potential problem with the original version, we can see that if the script was called as:

```
makelisttar
```

the original version would use the first case statement, though it was incorrect, but the new version would fall through and report an error.

Now that we have the script using options to set the mode, we have another problem to solve. Namely, what should the script do if the second argument, $2, is not provided? We don't have to worry about what happens if the first argument, $1, is not provided because the case statement deals with this situation via the default case, *.

The simplest method for checking the necessary number of arguments is to see if the number of given arguments, $#, matches the number of required arguments. Let's add this check to the script:

```
#!/bin/sh
USAGE="Usage: `basename $0` [-c¦-t] [file¦directory]"
if [ $# -lt 2 ] ; then echo "$USAGE" ; exit 1 ; fi
case "$1" in
    -t) TARGS="-tvf $2" ;;
    -c) TARGS="-cvf $2.tar $2" ;;
    *) echo "$USAGE" ; exit 0 ;;
esac
tar $TARGS
```

This short script is mostly finished, but a few improvements can still be done. For example, the script deals only with the first file that is given as an argument and does not check if the file argument is really a file.

We can add the processing of all file arguments by using the special shell variable $@. Let's start with the -t (list contents) option. The case statement now becomes the following:

```
case "$1" in
    -t) TARGS="-tvf"
        for i in "$@" ; do
            if [ -f "$i" ] ; then tar "$TARGS" "$i" ; fi ;
        done ;;
    -c) TARGS="-cvf $2.tar $2" ;
        tar "$TARGS" ;;
     *) echo "$USAGE" ; exit 0 ;;
esac
```

The main change is that the -t case now includes a for loop that cycles through the arguments and checks if each one is a file. If an argument is a file, tar is invoked on that file.

> **CAUTION**
>
> When examining the arguments passed to a script, two special variables are available for inspection, $* and $@.
>
> The main difference between these two is how they expand arguments. When $* is used, it simply expands each argument without preserving quoting. This can sometimes cause a problem. If our script was given a filename containing spaces as an argument as follows:
>
> `mytar -t "my tar file.tar"`
>
> using $* would mean that the for loop would call tar three times for files named my, tar, and file.tar, instead of just once for the file we requested, my tar file.tar.
>
> By using $@, we avoid this problem because it expands each argument as it was quoted on the command line.

We should deal with a few more minor issues that we should deal with. Looking closely, we see that all the arguments given to the script, including the first argument, $1, are considered as files.

If we are using the first argument as the flag to indicate the mode in which the script runs, we should not consider it. Not only does this reduce the number of times the for loop runs, but it also prevents the script from accidentally trying to run tar on a file with the name "-t". To remove the first argument from the list of arguments, we use the shift command. A similar change to the make mode of the script is also required.

Another issue is what the script should do when an operation fails. In the case of the listing operation, if tar cannot list the contents of a file, skipping the file and printing an error would be a reasonable operation. Because the shell sets the variable $? to the exit status of the most recent command, we can use that to determine if a tar operation failed.

Resolving the above issues, our script is as follows:

```
#!/bin/sh
USAGE="Usage: `basename $0` [-c|-t] [file|directory]"
if [ $# -lt 2 ] ; then echo "$USAGE" ; exit 1 ; fi
case "$1" in
    -t) shift ; TARGS="-tvf" ;
        for i in "$@" ; do
            if [ -f "$i" ] ; then
                FILES=`tar "$TARGS" "$i" 2>/dev/null`
                if [ $? -eq 0 ] ; then
                    echo ; echo "$i" ; echo "$FILES"
                else
                    echo "ERROR: $i not a tar file."
                fi
            else
                echo "ERROR: $i not a file."
            fi
        done ;;
    -c) shift ; TARGS="-cvf" ;
        tar "$TARGS" archive.tar "$@" ;;
     *) echo "$USAGE" ; exit 0 ;;
esac
exit $?
```

Variable Substitution

Variable substitution enables the shell programmer to manipulate the value of a variable based on its state. Variable substitution falls into two categories:

- Actions taken when a variable is set
- Actions taken when a variable is unset

These categories are broken down into four forms of variable substitution. We can use variable substitutions as shorthand forms of expressions that would have to be written as explicit if-then-else statements.

The first form allows for a default value to be substituted when a variable is unset or null. This is formally described as the following:

${parameter:-word}

Here *parameter* is the name of the variable and *word* is the default value. A simple example of its use is as follows:

PS1=${HOST:-localhost}"$ " ; export PS1 ;

This can be used in a user's .profile to make sure that the prompt is always set correctly. This form of variable substitution does not affect the value of the variable. It performs substitution only when the variable is unset.

To actually set the value of a variable, the second form of variable substitution must be used. This form is formally described as:

```
${parameter:=word}
```

Here *parameter* is the name of the variable, and *word* is the default value to set the variable to if it is unset. Appending the previous example, we have the following:

```
PS1=${HOST:=`uname -n`}"$ " ; export PS1 HOST ;
```

After the execution of this statement, both HOST and PS1 will be set. This example also demonstrates that the default string to use does not have to be a fixed string but can be the output of a command. If this substitution did not exist in the shell, the same line would have to be written as follows:

```
if [ -z "$HOST" ] ; then HOST=`uname -n` ; fi ; PS1="$HOST$ "; export PS1 HOST ;
```

As we can see, the variable substitution form is shorter and clearer than the explicit form.

Sometimes substituting default values can hide problems; thus sh supports a third form of variable substitution that allows for a message to be written to standard error, when a variable is unset. This form is formally described as follows:

```
${parameter:?message}
```

A common use of this is in shell scripts and shell functions requiring certain variables to be set for proper execution. For example, we can rewrite the parameter check in the mytar script from the previous sections as follows:

```
: ${2:?"Insufficient Arguments, $USAGE"}
```

In addition to using the variable substitution form previously described, we also are making use of a feature of the no operation command, `:`. This command simply evaluates the arguments passed to it. In this case, we pass the second argument of the script to it. If the second argument of the script is unset, an appropriate message prints to the screen and the script exits.

The final form of variable substitution is used to print messages when a variable is set. Formally this is described as follows:

```
${parameter:+word}
```

Here *parameter* is the name of the variable, and *word* is the value to substitute if the variable is set. This form does not alter the value of the variable, it alters only what is substituted. A frequent use is to indicate when a script is running in debug mode:

```
echo ${DEBUG:+"Debug is active."}
```

A summary of all these variable substitution methods is given in Table 8.2.

Table 8.2   Variable Substitution

Form	Description
`${parameter:-word}`	If *parameter* is null or unset, *word* is substituted for *parameter*. The value of *parameter* does not change.
`${parameter:=word}`	If *parameter* is null or unset, *parameter* is set to the value of *word*.
`${parameter:?message}`	If *parameter* is null or unset, *message* is printed to standard error. This is used to check that variables are set correctly.
`${parameter:+word}`	If *parameter* is set, then *word* is substituted for *parameter*. The value of *parameter* does not change.

Functions

Shell functions in scripts are similar to functions and procedures in other languages. They can also be thought of as mini shell scripts that enable a name to be associated with a set of commands. The formal definition of a shell function is as follows:

name () { *list* ; }

A function binds a *name* to the *list* of commands that compose the body of the function. The "()" are required in the function definition. The following examples illustrate valid and invalid function definitions:

```
lsl() { ls -l ; }    # valid
lsl { ls -l ; }       # invalid
```

In this example, the first definition is valid, but the second one is not because it omits the parentheses after the string "lsl".

This example also demonstrates a common use of functions. Because the original shell, sh, did not have the alias keyword common to more recent shells, all aliases were defined in terms of shell functions. A frequently encountered example of this is the source command. The sh equivalent is the `.` command. Many converts from csh use the following function to simulate source:

```
source() { . "$@" ; }
```

▶ For more information about aliases and their function in shells, **see** "Choosing a Shell," **p. 47**

An important feature of shell functions is that they can be used to replace binaries or shell built-ins of the same name.

An example of this is as follows:

cd () { chdir ${1:-$HOME} ; PS1="`pwd`$ " ; export PS1 ; }

This function replaces the cd command with a function that changes directories but also sets the primary shell prompt, $PS1, to include the current directory.

To invoke a function only its name is required, thus typing:

```
$ lsl
```

on the command line causes the lsl() function given previously to be executed, but

```
$ lsl()
```

will not work because sh interprets this to be a redefinition of the function by the name lsl.

The functions seen so far operate independent of one another, but in most shell scripts, functions either are dependent on or share data with other functions. In the following example, we will look at three functions that work together and share data between them to provide an equivalent to the popd, pushd, and dirs commands in csh.

These commands allow for quick moving around in the UNIX file system.

▶ For more information about moving around in the UNIX file system, **see** "Navigating Directories," **p. 48**

These commands maintain a stack of directories internally and enable the user to add and remove directories from the stack, along with listing the contents of the stack. In csh, the stack is maintained within the shell, but in our shell function based implementation, we have to maintain the stack as an exported environment variable in order for all three functions to have access to it. Let's look at the simplest of the three functions, the dirs() function. Because it lists only the contents of the stack, it is a simple function:

```
dirs() { echo $DIRSTACK; }
```

Now let's look at the popd() function. This function removes the first entry from the directory stack variable and then sets it to reflect this. When the stack has been pop'ed, the function tries to cd to that directory and if it is successful, the full path of the current directory is displayed. The function is as follows:

```
popd() {
    # pop the stack
    POPD="`echo $DIRSTACK ¦ awk '{ print $1; }'`"
    # update the stack
    DIR_STACK="`echo $DIRSTACK ¦ awk '{ ORS=\" \" ; for (i=2;i<=NF;i++) { print
➥$i; } }'`"
    # if what was pop'ed is a dir, cd there
    if [ -d "$POPD" ] ; then cd "$POPD" ; pwd ; fi
    export DIRSTACK
    unset POPD
}
```

One of the last operations performed by this function is exporting the DIRSTACK variable. This is required in order to ensure that the other functions access a current version of the variable.

N O T E As we can see, the function popd() unsets its internal variable POPD. It is a good habit to unset all variables that should not be exported.

In some languages, this is not an issue because local variables disappear when execution leaves the scope of the function. In other languages, variables can be marked for local scope only, but in shell all variables are of global scope. This means that the programmer has to take care in managing variables. ■

In order to facilitate the manipulation of the directory stack, the popd() function uses a few simple awk statements.

▶ For more information on awk, **see** "Filtering Commands," **p. 70**

Let's now look at the pushd() function. This function is slightly more complicated than the popd() function because it must deal with arguments. The simplest case is the case of a directory that is named explicitly. In addition to this case, three special cases of arguments must be dealt with. These are the case of no arguments, the case of the '.' argument, and the case of the '..' argument.

In the case of no arguments or the `.' argument, the present working directory is pushed onto the stack. In the case of '..', the function starts a subshell, cd's into the parent directory, and pushes the full path to that directory onto the directory stack. After the directory stack is updated, its current value is printed out using the dirs() function. The complete function is as follows:

```
pushd() {
    REQ=${1:-.};
    case "$REQ" in
        .) DIRSTACK="`pwd` $DIRSTACK" ;;
        ..) DIRSTACK="`( cd .. ; pwd; )` $DIRSTACK" ;;
        *) if [ -d "$REQ" ] ; then DIRSTACK="$REQ $DIRSTACK" ; fi ;;
    esac
    export DIRSTACK
    unset REQ
    dirs
}
```

Option Parsing in Shell Scripts

The general format for the invocation of programs in UNIX is as follows:

```
command [options] [file/parameters]
```

In shell scripts, it is desirable to adhere to this format. This means that a shell script that can have options specified must be able to parse them correctly.

You can handle the parsing of options passed to a shell script in two common ways. The first one is to manually deal with the options using a case statement. This method was used in the mytar script presented earlier in the chapter. The second method is to use the getopts command.

The *getopts* Command

The syntax of the getopts command is as follows:

```
getopts option-string variable
```

Here *option-string* is a string consisting of all the single character options getopts should consider, and *variable* is the name of the variable that the option should be set to. Usually the *variable* used is named OPTION.

The process by which `getopts` parses the options given on the command line is the following:

1. It looks through all the command line arguments for the '-' character.
2. If the '-' character is found, it compares the characters following the '-' to the characters given in the *option-string*.
3. If a match is found, *variable* is set to the option. Otherwise *variable* is set to the '?' character.
4. Steps one through three are repeated until all the options have been considered. When parsing has finished, `getopts` returns a nonzero exit code. This allows it to be easily used in loops. Also when `getopts` has finished, it sets the variable OPTIND to the index of the last argument.

Another feature of `getopts` is the ability to indicate options requiring an additional parameter. This is accomplished by following the option with a ':' character. In this case, after an option is parsed, the additional parameter is set to the value of the variable named OPTARG.

An Example of Using *getopts*

To get a feeling for how `getopts` works and how to deal with options, let's write a script that simplifies the task of uunening a file.

I will first describe the interface of this script, which will make it easier to understand the implementation.

This script should accept the following options:

- -f to indicate the input filename
- -o to indicate the output filename
- -v to indicate the script should be verbose

Here's the command to implement these requirements:

```
getopts e:o:v OPTION
```

This indicates that all the options except for -v require an additional parameter. The variables we need require are as follows:

- VERBOSE, which stores the value of the verbose flag. By default this will be false.
- INFILE, which stores the name of the input file.
- OUTFILE, which stores the name of the output file name. If this value is unset, decode uses the name supplied in the input file, and encode uses the name of the supplied input file and appends to it the .uu extension.

The loop to implement these requirements is as follows:

```
VERBOSE=false
while getopts f:o:v OPTION ; do
    case "$OPTION" in
        f) INFILE="$OPTARG" ;;
        o) OUTFILE="$OPTARG" ;;
```

```
        v) VERBOSE=true ;;
        \?) echo "$USAGE" ; exit 1 ;;
    esac
done
```

The nice thing about using getopts is that if options requiring an additional parameter are missing this parameter, getopts reports the error automatically and exits. Our script is much simpler because we don't have to explicitly do all the error checking.

Just using getopts doesn't relieve us of all error checking however. For example, what should our script do if the input file is not specified? The simplest answer would be to exit with an error, but with a little more work, we can make the script much more user friendly.

If we use the fact that getopts sets the variable OPTIND to the value of the last option that it scanned, we can have the script assume that the first argument after this is the input filename. If in this case the argument is not given, we should exit. Our error checking consists of the following lines:

```
shift `echo "$OPTIND - 1" ¦ bc`
: ${INFILE:=${1:?"Input file not specified."}}
```

Here we shift the arguments given to the script by one minus the last argument processed by getopts. Strictly speaking, we do not have to shift the arguments, but it makes the output consistent in every error case. Also, we are using variable substitution to make sure that the input file is set or that an error is generated. The reason that we precede the checks with the ':' command is to avoid having the result of the variable substitution be interpreted as a command.

In addition to these two checks, we also need to set the output filename, in case the -o option was not specified. To do this, we add the following variable substitution argument to the ':' command:

```
: ${INFILE:=${1:?"Input file not specified."}} ${OUTFILE:=${INFILE}.uu}
```

After we make sure that all the inputs are correct, the actually work is quite simple. The uuencode command that we use is as follows:

```
uuencode $INFILE $INFILE > $OUTFILE ;
```

We should also check if the input file is really a file, before doing this command, so the actual body is as follows:

```
if [ -f "$INFILE" ] ; then uuencode $INFILE $INFILE > $OUTFILE ; fi
```

At this point, the script is fully functional, but we still need to add the verbose reporting. This changes the previous if statement to the following:

```
if [ -f "$INFILE" ] ; then
    if [ "$VERBOSE" = "true" ] ; then
        echo "uuencoding $INFILE to $OUTFILE... \c"
    fi
    uuencode $INFILE $INFILE > $OUTFILE ; RET=$? ;
    if [ "$VERBOSE" = "true" ] ; then
```

```
        MSG="Failed" ; if [ $RET -eq 0 ] ; then MSG="Done." ; fi
        echo $MSG
    fi
fi
```

We can simplify the verbose reporting to print a statement when the uuencode completes, but issuing two statements, one before the operation starts and one after the operation completes, is much more user friendly. This method clearly indicates that the operation is being performed.

The complete script is as follows:

```
#!/bin/sh
USAGE="Usage: `basename $0` [-v] [-f] [filename] [-o] [filename]";
VERBOSE=false
while getopts f:o:v OPTION ; do
    case "$OPTION" in
        f)  INFILE="$OPTARG" ;;
        o)  OUTFILE="$OPTARG" ;;
        v)  VERBOSE=true ;;
        \?) echo "$USAGE" ; exit 1 ;;
    esac
done
shift `echo "$OPTIND - 1" ¦ bc`
: ${INFILE:=${1:?"Input file not specified."}} ${OUTFILE:=${INFILE}.uu}
if [ -f "$INFILE" ] ; then
    if [ "$VERBOSE" = "true" ] ; then
        printf "uuencoding $INFILE to $OUTFILE... \c"
    fi
    uuencode $INFILE $INFILE > $OUTFILE ; RET=$?
    if [ "$VERBOSE" = "true" ] ; then
        MSG="Failed" ; if [ $RET -eq 0 ] ; then MSG="Done." ; fi
        echo $MSG
    fi
fi
```

With this script, we can uuencode files in all the following ways (assuming the script is called uu):

```
uu ch8.doc
uu -f ch8.doc
uu -f ch8.doc -o ch8.uu
```

In each of the previous examples file ch8.doc is uuencoded. The last one will place the result into the file ch8.uu instead of the default ch8.doc.uu, which might be required if the document needs to go to a DOS or Windows system. Because this script uses getopts, any of the commands given above can run in verbose mode by simply specifying the -v option.

Dealing with Signals

Signals are "software interrupts" that are sent to a program to indicate that an important "event" has occurred. These events are a notification to the program that an unexpected problem has occurred or that a user has asked the program to do something that is not usually in the flow of control. Due to their asynchronous nature, signals are one of the more complicated tasks of shell programming.

Signals

In UNIX, signals are represented by small positive integers, with each integer representing a specific type of event. The signals most commonly encountered in shell script programming are given in Table 8.3. These signals listed are available on all versions of UNIX. The complete list of all signals understood by the system are usually listed in the file /usr/include/signal.h. Some vendors provide a man page for this file that is viewable by doing a man signal.

Table 8.3   Important Signals for Shell Scripts

Name	Value	Description
SIGHUP	1	Hangup detected on controlling terminal or death of controlling process
SIGINT	2	Interrupt from keyboard
SIGQUIT	3	Quit from keyboard
SIGKILL	9	Kill signal
SIGTERM	15	Termination signal

A signal can be handled by a program or script receiving it in three different ways. The simplest way for a program or a script to handle a signal is to do nothing. In this case the default action for a signal is taken by the system. Usually this is the termination of the program or script.

The second way to deal with signals is to ignore them. This is different from doing nothing because it requires that the program or script has code that explicitly ignores the signals.

The third method to deal with a signal is to "catch" it. This means that the program or script receiving the signal must have a routine that will take the appropriate actions. Except for SIGKILL, all other signals can be caught. This signal cannot be caught because it is used to terminate programs "with extreme prejudice." This means that a process receiving this signal cannot cleanly exit and might leave data it was using in a corrupted state. This signal should only be used to terminate a process when all the other signals fail to do so.

The *trap* Command

The trap command is used to set and unset the actions taken when a signal is received. The syntax of this command is as follows:

```
trap name signals
```

Here *name* is the set of commands or the shell function to execute when a signal in the list of specified *signals* is received. If *name* is not given, trap resets the action for the given signals to be the default.

Here are three common uses for trap in shell scripts:

- Clean up temporary files
- Always ignore signals
- Ignore signals only during critical operations

Most shell scripts that create temporary files use a trap command similar to the following:

```
trap "rm -f $TMPF; exit 2" 1 2 3 15
```

Sometimes when more complicated clean up is required, a shell function might be used. In order to make the uu script given in the pervious section signal safe, we can add something similar to the following to the beginning of the script:

```
CleanUp() {
    if [ -f "$OUTFILE" ] ; then
        printf "Cleaning Up… ";
        rm -f "$OUTFILE" 2> /dev/null ;
        echo "Done." ;
    fi
}
trap CleanUp 1 2 3 15
```

N O T E The main reason to use functions to handle signals is that it is more convenient to have a shell function invoked when a signal is received than to write in the appropriate code inline.

Also, the commands that should be executed when a signal is received might be different depending on which point in the script the signal was received. In many cases, it is difficult to capture that logic in a few commands, thus is it necessary to use a shell function as the signal handling routine.

Sometimes there is no intelligent or easy way to clean up if a signal is received. In these cases, it is better to ignore signals than to deal with them. There are two methods of ignoring signals:

```
trap `` signals
trap : signals
```

Here *signals* is the list of signals to ignore. The only difference between these two forms is that the first form passes a special argument, ' ' or null, to the trap command, and the second uses the ':' command. The form to use is largely based on programmer style.

If we want the uu script to simply ignore all signals, instead of cleaning up when a signal is received, we can add the following to the beginning of the script:

```
trap `` 1 2 15
```

If the preceding command is so given in a script, all signals will be ignored by the script until it exits. This is not always the most user-friendly behavior. A better idea is to have only critical sections of code ignore traps. This can be achieved by unsetting the signal handler after the critical code has finished executing.

As an illustration, say we have a shell script with a shell function called `DoImportantStuff()`. This routine should not be interrupted. In order to ensure this, we can install the signal handler before the function is called and reset it after the call finishes:

```
trap `` 1 2 3 15
DoImportantStuff
trap 1 2 3 15
```

The second call to `trap` has only signal arguments. This causes `trap` to reset the handler for each of the signals to the default. By doing this, we allow the user to still terminate the script, and we ensure that critical operations are performed without interruption.

In the examples that we have looked at so far, the signal handler has been the same for each signal. This is not required, and frequently different signals have different handlers. The following set of trap declarations is completely valid:

```
trap : 3
trap CleanUp 2 15
trap Init 1
```

These declarations indicate that the script ignores the SIGQUIT signals, calls a clean-up routine when a SIGINT or SIGTERM is received, and calls its initialization routine when a SIGHUP is received. Declarations such as these are common in scripts that run as daemons.

Debugging and Logging Shell Scripts

For larger shell scripts, especially the kind that change system configurations, it is essential that the script produce logs of its activity. Also, during the development of such scripts, it is necessary to be able to debug them without having to wait for the script to finish executing. In this section we cover a few simple, yet powerful, techniques for debugging and logging shell scripts.

Debugging

You can use a few common techniques in shell script debugging. In order to activate debugging, use one of the following methods:

```
sh [option] [script]
set [option]
```

Table 8.4 gives the debugging *options*. The only difference between these two is that the first version can be used only when the script is first invoked. By using the `set` command, the debugging flags can be altered as part of the execution of the script.

Usually the first test of a shell script (other than running it) is to make sure that `sh -n script` does not fail. By using this option, most syntax problems such as mismatched parentheses or unset variables are easily detected and fixable. It is always better to know that a script does not have any syntax problems because then you can concentrate on the real bugs.

Table 8.4 Debugging Options for Shell Scripts

Option	Description
-e	Exits if a command fails
-n	Reads all commands, but does not execute them
-u	Treats all unset variables as an error when performing variable substitution
-v	Prints all lines as they are read
-x	Prints all commands and their arguments as they are executed
-	Turns off all debugging flags

The -e and -u options are not heavily used because they tell you only what command failed, not why the command failed. In order to determine why something failed, an execution trace is required. Both the -v and -x options produce such a trace. Most shell programmers prefer the -x option for generating traces because it shows the results of every variable and command substitution. In order to demonstrate the difference, I ran the uu script using both options. Using the -v option:

```
sh -v ./uu test.tar
```

basically produces a listing of the script with a few of the commands expanded in place as follows:

```
#!/bin/sh

USAGE="Usage: `basename $0` [-v] [-f] [filename] [-o] [filename]";
basename $0
VERBOSE=false

while getopts f:o:v OPTION ; do
    case "$OPTION" in
        f) INFILE="$OPTARG" ;;
        o) OUTFILE="$OPTARG" ;;
        v) VERBOSE=true ;;
        \?) echo "$USAGE" ; exit 1 ;;
    esac
done

shift `echo "$OPTIND - 1" | bc`
echo "$OPTIND - 1" | bc
: ${INFILE:=${1:?"Input file not specified."}} ${OUTFILE:=${INFILE}.uu}
if [ -f "$INFILE" ] ; then
    if [ "$VERBOSE" = "true" ] ; then
        printf "uuencoding $INFILE to $OUTFILE... "
    fi
    uuencode $INFILE $INFILE > $OUTFILE ; RET=$?
    if [ "$VERBOSE" = "true" ] ; then
        MSG="Failed" ; if [ $RET -eq 0 ] ; then MSG="Done." ; fi
        echo $MSG
    fi
fi
```

However, using the -x option:

```
sh -x ./uu test.tar
```

produces a trace of how each of the commands were executed as follows:

```
++ basename ./myuu.sh
+ USAGE=Usage: myuu.sh [-v] [-f] [filename] [-o] [filename]
+ VERBOSE=false
+ getopts f:o:v OPTION
++ echo 1 - 1
++ bc
+ shift 0
+ : test.tar test.tar.uu
+ [ -f test.tar ]
+ [ false = true ]
+ uuencode test.tar test.tar
+ RET=0
+ [ false = true ]
```

The '+' character preceding a line indicates the shell level in which each command was run. Thus command substitution and commands run in subshells will be preceded by extra '+' characters. To track down many complicated bugs involving redirection and substitution, this type of trace is extremely helpful.

The examples so far have shown how to activate debugging at script invocation time, but it is equally easy to turn on and off debugging during the execution of the script. This is often encountered when the bulk of a large script is operating properly but a few functions are not. For example, if we have a function called BuggyFunction(), and we want to trace only while that function executed, the following would be one approach:

```
set -x ; BuggyFunction; set - ;
```

Here tracing is turned on just before the function is called, and then all debugging flags are deactivated.

Logging

Often large shell scripts are required to produce a log file of their activities. For interactive scripts, the log file cannot be the output redirected to a file and it cannot be the same as the output from one of the debugging options. For such scripts, you have two common techniques used to produce log files.

The first technique is based on the tee command. This command pipes the output to the screen and to a file. The simplest way to implement this is as follows:

```
if [ "$LOGGING" != "true" ] ; then
    LOGGING="true" ; export LOGGING ;
    exec $0 ¦ tee $LOGFILE
fi
```

Here we check to see if a variable indicates logging is turned on; if it is, the script will continue. Otherwise the script will rerun itself and tee the output to a log file. In order to record all the output from a script, this if statement is usually one of the first commands in a script.

The second technique is based on using the `script` command. This command is invoked as follows:

```
script [filename]
```

When `script` is run, it creates a new shell and records all the input and output that happens in that shell. To determine which shell to use, it examines the value of the variable SHELL. To use `script` for logging, we trick it to use our script as the shell:

```
if [ "$LOGGING" != "true" ] ; then
    LOGGING="true" ; export LOGGING ;
    exec script $0 $LOGFILE
fi
```

From Here...

In this chapter, we examined some of the advanced shell programming techniques. We started with making shell scripts executable and covered special variables, variable substitution, shell functions, option parsing, signal handling along with debugging and logging of shell scripts. With the material covered here you are on the way to writing fully functional and robust shell scripts.

Chapter 11, "Startup and Shutdown," provides information on the startup and shutdown of UNIX systems. This is an area where shell scripts are used heavily and will give you a good idea of the kinds of scripts system administrators maintain.

Chapter 15, "Backup and Recovery," demonstrates how to handle the routine task of backing up your system along with introducing the tools for recovering your system from a backup. You will see how having robust shell scripts is required for these tasks.

Chapter 16, "Automating Tasks," introduces the ability to schedule programs and scripts to run at given intervals. Shell scripts are one of the most important components in UNIX task automation.

UNIX Windowing Systems

by Sriranga Veeraraghavan

In this chapter

Overview of the Common Desktop Environment

Until recently, every version of UNIX had a different windowing system. For users that had to use more than one version of UNIX this often caused severe problems because they would have to remember the nuances of each system in order to function efficiently.

Though there was a standard called Motif, its implementation differed between vendors. Configurations and the look and feel of Motif based systems were often similar, but slightly different, causing confusion to users as well as system administrators. In addition, not all vendors supported Motif as the default windowing system, meaning that applications programmers could not count on its availability on a user's system.

In order to solve these problems and provide a common user experience and applications programming environment, the Common Open Software Environment (COSE) initiative was started in 1993 by Hewlett-Packard, IBM, Novell, and SunSoft. Digital, Fujitsu, and Hitachi eventually joined the COSE initiative. The outcome of this project was the Common Desktop Environment (CDE) 1.0.

CDE is a standard desktop for UNIX that provides many basic applications with a common look and feel across all the supported platforms. It also provides many common services for system administrators and applications programmers.

The most recent version of CDE released to the public, as of this writing, is 1.0.10. Work is currently progressing on CDE version 1.1. CDE Version 1.0.x is available on the following operating systems:

- Sun Solaris
- Hewlett-Packard HP/UX
- Digital UNIX
- IBM AIX
- FreeBSD
- Linux

Except for FreeBSD and Linux, CDE is installed and configured by default on the latest versions of the operating systems listed here.

For Linux and FreeBSD, CDE is available as an add-on application package. It is available from the following vendors:

- TriTeal
- Work Group Solutions (WGS)
- X Inside

TriTeal's implementation, called the TriTeal Enhanced Desktop (TED), contains many additions to the standard CDE, and is the most common version found on Linux and FreeBSD systems.

CDE Features

In this section, we look at logging in to CDE along with the main features of the desktop environment.

Logging In

The login process on a machine with CDE is handled by the program `dtlogin`, which is based on an X Window program called `xdm`. By using dtlogin, CDE enables users to directly log in X Window without having to run a program such as `xinit` or a shell script such as `startx`. Every user had separate configurations for X Window, and these configurations were invoked by the X Window startup programs, either `xinit` or `startx`. In those days, using X Window meant that you had to log in on the console of the machine, make sure your environment was correct, and then issue the X Window startup command.

Because each user would have customized X Window to their needs, each and every problem encountered in starting and using X Window required administrative help. This translated to an enormous workload for system administrators because each new user configuration potentially required system wide changes. Additionally, the system administrators also had to maintain site specific stub scripts to give to new users in order to allow them to use X Window.

In CDE, every user is automatically logged in to X Window, and the base environment is always the same. This is an asset to users because they no longer have to maintain X Window configuration files. It is also an asset to system administrators because no matter what customizations the user has made, an administrator can easily access standard CDE functionality.

To log in the CDE environment, a user first enters his user name into a text field. After a user hits Enter, this text field changes to prompt for the user's password. After the password is entered, the user is logged in to a CDE session.

Usually the session that a user logs in to is the same session that was running when he last logged out. Almost always this is desirable, but occasionally another session is required. CDE accommodates this by allowing the user to choose the required session before logging in. The sessions available are as follows:

- Standard CDE Session
- Vendor Specific Session
- Fail Safe
- Command Line

The standard CDE session is identical to the session that the user is given with a standard login. The vendor specific session is usually an X Window session running under a vendor specific window manager. On Solaris, this is the Open Windows session. Under Linux or FreeBSD, the vendor specific session is usually a FVWM session.

The Fail Safe session is a single `xterm` with no window manager. This session is mainly used to fix configuration problems or to restore the last CDE session from its system location.

RESTORING AN OLD SESSION

TROUBLESHOOTING: Occasionally, a serious problem, such as a power outage or a disk crash, will occur. Such problems can corrupt your CDE session. In such an instance, it is possible to restore the last session so that you can get back to work quickly.

To restore the last CDE session, the following command is commonly used:

```
cd $HOME/.dt/sessions ; cp -r current.old current
```

In this command, change directories to the .dt/sessions directory located in the home directory of the user. This directory holds the information about the current session and about the last session. In CDE terms, a session is the set of programs that were running when you last logged out.

When in the sessions directory, copy the contents of the last session stored in the directory current.old into the directory for the current session. This process restores the environment that was present before the last logout.

The Command Line session is used when an X Window environment is not required. This is usually used before shutdowns and reboots of the machine.

In addition to these sessions, some systems such as Solaris and Linux also offer a twm session.

Overview of the CDE Front Panel

After the login is complete, the CDE desktop loads. For those users familiar with Motif's MWM, the CDE desktop appears very familiar. The main difference is the Front Panel, shown in Figure 9.1. This screen shot is from the Solaris version of CDE. Depending on the vendor, the appearance might vary slightly.

FIGURE 9.1
The CDE Front Panel on Solaris.

The CDE desktop is controlled by the CDE window manager, dtwm. At first, many users conclude that the Front Panel is just another program launcher. In fact, the Front Panel is really a subprogram that runs within dtwm and provides much more functionality than a simple program launcher.

It provides the user with pop-up program menus, a virtual workspace manager, and a trash can (like Windows and Mac OS) along with access to a file manager, a mail reader, printing tools, and the on-line help system. It also provides buttons for logging out and locking the display.

Each of the buttons, icons, and pop-up menus are a distinct type of component. The CDE has five different types of components:

- panel
- box

- control
- sub-panel
- switch

A `panel` is always the outer-most component. In general, all the other components are placed inside `panels`. The Front Panel's outer-most frame is its `panel`. Most panels also have a frame, a title bar, and minimize and maximize buttons. In the case of the Front Panel, these are turned off.

Inside the Front Panel are several icons and buttons that correspond to different programs and functions. All these items are contained within a `box` component. A box component can hold one or more control, sub-panel, or switch components.

Each of the icons in the Front Panel is a *control* component. These components associate an icon with a program or set of commands. Often control components and the programs that they execute are referred to as one unit called an *action*. We will look at creating actions in the "Customizing the Window Environment" section.

Looking closely as the Front Panel reveals that some of the icons also have small arrows above them. Clicking these arrows allows for access to a pop-up menu. These menus are called *sub-panel* components. Sub-panel components are slightly different than the other components in that they can be "torn" from their parent panels and placed into separate windows. In general, any control in the Front Panel can have sub-panels, and the contents of these sub-panels can be customized. Creating and customizing sub-panels is covered in the "Customizing the Window Environment" section. In other windowing environments sub-panels are referred to as drop-down or pop-up menus.

Several buttons are in the middle of the Front Panel. Each of these buttons is a special type of component known as a *switch*. These components allow for switching between virtual workspaces. They are covered in the next section.

The Graphical Workspace Manager

Four large buttons and two smaller buttons are in the center of the Front Panel. This part of the Front Panel is the Graphical Workspace Manager (GWM), which is responsible for controlling the virtual workspaces as well as providing a central location for logging out and locking the console.

The four large buttons in the GWM, usually labeled One, Two, Three, and Four, each correspond to one of the four virtual workspaces that CDE starts by default. Clicking one of these buttons causes the display to switch to that virtual workspace.

Think of each virtual workspace as a separate desktop in which windows can be opened and programs can be run. This allows for many windows to be open while ensuring that screen space is never cluttered.

PROBLEMS WITH STARTING SHELLS

TROUBLESHOOTING: On some systems, notably AIX and Solaris, users who have bash or tcsh as their default shell encounter problems starting xterms and dtterms in the virtual desktops. On AIX systems, users with ksh as their default shell may encounter this problem as well.

The most common cause of this is that the operating system has placed a '-' character in front of your shell's name, thus when the default application tries to run a shell with this modified name, it fails.

You have three solutions to this; the first is to simply make a link from your shell to a name containing the extra '-', for example:

Cd /usr/local/bin ; ln –s bash \-bash ;

In this example, we cd to the directory containing the bash binary and then make the appropriate link.

For more information on making links, consult the section titled "Different File Types" in Chapter 5.

The second method is to create an alternative to the default dtterm or xterm actions that take arguments indicating which shell to run. We will cover the commands necessary to do this in a later section.

The third method is to get your system administrator to change your shell to either sh or csh and then run the correct shell from your shell startup script.

The number of virtual consoles can be easily increased or decreased by clicking in this panel and then holding the second mouse button down. This produces a pop-up menu that allows for adding and deleting virtual consoles. Most versions of CDE also allow for the virtual consoles to be renamed by clicking their names.

The two smaller buttons in this panel correspond to the terminal lock function (the lock button) and the logout function (the exit button). Also in this panel is a small yellow icon that is located above the exit button. This is the "busy light." It can be seen blinking when CDE is trying to run a program or is busy with some task.

CDE Front Panel Features

In addition to Graphical Workspace Manager, several icons are in the Front Panel. These icons provide access to important CDE tools. Some also feature pop-up menus that allow additional programs and features to be accessed.

Let's look at each of the icons in the Front Panel. The leftmost icon is an analog clock. It allows the user to automatically tell the time without having to issue a date command in a terminal, or having to run a program such as xlock. For those readers unfamiliar with the xlock program, it is a password protected screen saver. After you start xlock, it locks the console, displays a screen saver, and waits for the password of the user who locked the screen to be entered.

The next icon always shows the current date and enables the user to access the CDE Calendar Manager. The Calendar Manager is really a sophisticated appointment manager that allows the user to manage appointments and To Do lists in a variety of formats. In addition, it enables any CDE users to share their schedules. We will look at some of the basic features of the Calendar Manager in the CDE Tools section.

Next to the Calendar icon is the icon that provides access to the CDE File Manager. The File Manager is an interface for browsing, copying, and moving files along with running programs. Apart from the icons used, this File Manager's look and feel is similar to that of the Mac OS Finder and the Windows Explorer. The File Manager is covered in greater detail in the section on CDE Tools.

The icon next to the File Manager is usually the Terminal icon. It provides access to the CDE terminal, dtterm. This terminal is far more advanced that the traditional xterm and allows for menu-based customization.

This icon always has a small up arrow above it, which allows for access to a subpanel or pop-up menu. In this menu the user can access several additional CDE tools such as a graphical text editor and an icon editor. On most systems this menu also contains an entry that allows xterm to be launched.

N O T E On Linux and AIX systems, the icon for the graphical text editor is located where the dtterm icon is located. On those versions, clicking this icon launches the CDE editor, dtpad, not the terminal dtterm. To access dtterm on these systems, the terminal icon from the submenu must be used.

The next icon is the Mailer icon. It is always to the immediate left of the GWM panel. The CDE mailer provides a powerful mail reading and sending agent with an easy-to-use GUI interface. The Mailer supports templates, mail folders, searches, and mailing lists.

Immediately to the right of the GWM panel is the Printer Control. This tool allows for manipulating and monitoring the printing queue on a particular printer, as well as supporting drag-and-drop printing of documents from the File Manager.

Next to this icon is the Style Manager icon. It enables the user to customize the various aspects of the CDE interface on-the-fly. It simplifies tasks such as setting the desktop background, window colors, and mouse response time. The Style Manager is covered in greater detail in the "Customizing the Windows Environment" section.

To the right of the Style Manager icon is the Application Manager icon. This icon uses the File Manager interface and enables users to launch programs by clicking on them, similar to Mac OS and Windows.

Next to this icon is the Help System icon. It enables the user to view and search the extensive CDE help system. All the help topics are set up as books in a hierarchical structure that makes locating the correct material very easy. Also most of the help pages have embedded hyperlinks that allow related materials to be browsed quickly.

At the far right of the Front Panel is the Trashcan icon. It enables users to discard files and applications by dragging them from the File Manager or the Application Manager and dropping them onto the Trashcan icon. This method of disposing files is very similar to Windows and the Mac OS. Also, items in the trash are deleted only when the user requests it. Thus accidentally trashed files can be recovered simply by dragging them out of the trash.

CDE Tools

In this section, we will examine four of the most useful CDE tools in greater depth. We will give examples of standard uses as well as show some common customizations. Here are the tools covered in this section:

- `dtterm`
- `dtpad`
- File Manager (`dtfile`)
- Calender Manager (`dtcm`)

dtterm

The `dtterm` program is intended as a replacement for `xterm`. It provides the same type of terminal environment as `xterm`, but adds several improvements that make it easier to use and customize. The standard `dtterm` window is shown in Figure 9.2.

FIGURE 9.2

A standard `dtterm` window.

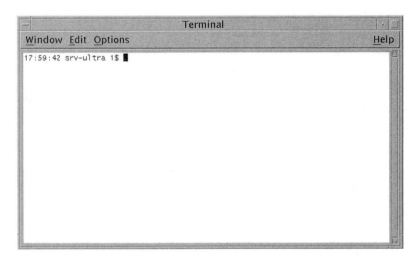

N O T E New CDE users who are familiar with Windows or the Mac OS often note that the dtterm looks just like a telnet window. This was one of the goals of the CDE design team. They wanted to provide a more intuitive look and feel to the traditional UNIX tools.

By preserving the power of xterm, the CDE design team kept traditional UNIX users happy but also allowed many users who were not familiar with UNIX to get acquainted with the environment using a familiar GUI.

Usually dtterm is accessed from the Front Panel by clicking its icon, but it can also be launched from the command line as follows:

```
$ dtterm &
```

Strictly speaking, the '&' is not required but is nice to use because it puts dtterm in the background and restores the prompt so that other commands can be issued. If the shell responds to this command with a message like the following:

```
bash: dtterm: command not found
```

it means that the CDE binaries could not be found in the current binary search path specified by the environment variable PATH. The CDE binaries are usually located in the directory /usr/dt/bin, though some system administrators might relocate them. To add this directory to the PATH variable use one of the following methods:

Part
I
Ch
9

- Under csh/tcsh: setenv PATH ($PATH /usr/dt/bin)
- Under sh/ksh/bash: PATH="$PATH:/usr/dt/bin" ; export PATH

The most obvious difference that xterm users will notice upon accessing dtterm is the presence of the menu bar. The other main difference is that the scrollbar is located on the right side of the window instead of on the left side like xterm. This will feel familiar to users from Mac OS or Windows but often confuses xterm users.

In dtterm, the following four menus are displayed for every new terminal window:

- Window
- Edit
- Options
- Help

The Window menu has two items, New and Close, which allow for a new dtterm to be created or for the existing dtterm to be closed.

The Edit menu also has two items, Copy and Paste, which allow for copying and pasting text between windows. These items are very useful when dtterm is displayed remotely on a Windows or Mac OS system that does not support the standard X copy and paste mouse functions.

The next menu is the Options menu. It enables the user to extensively customize the appearance and behavior of dtterm. The sub menus available are as follows:

- Menu Bar
- Scroll Bar
- Global
- Terminal
- Window Size
- Font Size
- Reset

The Menu Bar item allows the menu bar to be hidden. This is often required to maximize terminal space when running dtterm on smaller monitors. The menu bar can be restored by using a pop-up menu that appears when the second mouse button is clicked in the dtterm window.

The Scroll Bar item toggles the state of the scrollbar. If the scrollbar is showing, selecting this item will hide it. If the scrollbar is hidden, selecting this item will cause it to be displayed.

The Global item brings up the Global Options window, shown in Figure 9.3, for dtterm. This window allows for customizing the Cursor, Color, Scroll Behavior, and Bell sounds. Clicking the Help button brings up the help page for this window. It contains detailed information about all the options available in this window.

FIGURE 9.3

The Global Options window for dtterm.

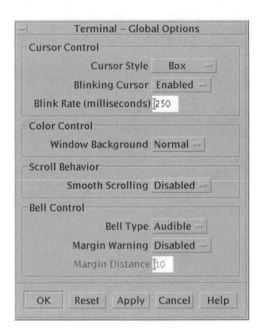

Upon selecting a set of options, click the OK button, apply the changes to every dtterm. In order to preview the settings on the current window, click on the Apply button. To reset dtterm to its original factory settings, click the Reset button.

The Terminal item brings up the Terminal Options window shown in Figure 9.4. From this window various aspects of keyboard and screen controls can be customized. In most cases, the defaults function quite well. In order for some programs and shell scripts to function properly, sometimes the Newline Sequence setting needs to be changed to Return/Line Feed. A description of each item is available in the online help.

The Window Size item displays a submenu that enables the user to chose between two terminal sizes, 80×24 and 132×24. This menu is useful when viewing files with long lines. It is also useful when running dtterm remotely on a Windows or Mac OS system whose X server does not allow windows to be resized.

FIGURE 9.4
The Terminal Options
window for dtterm.

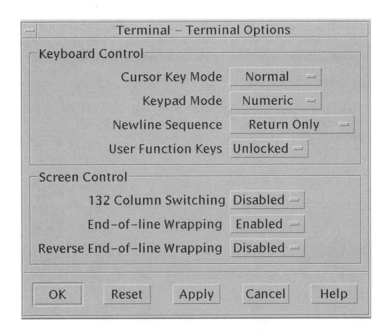

The Font Size item also displays a sub menu allowing the user to chose a font size, between 8 and 24 point, for the terminal's output. The default for most systems is 10 or 12 point.

One of the most useful items in the Options menu is the last item, Reset. This item displays a submenu with the items Soft Reset and Hard Reset. Performing a soft reset means that the terminal characteristics are reset. This is useful when control character in a file or in the output of a program corrupt the terminal display. In some cases, this is not enough to recover the display. The hard reset is provided for those instances. It causes dtterm to reinitialize itself, thus correcting almost all problems. Usually the soft reset is preferred to the hard reset because a hard reset tends to lose history information in some shells.

N O T E A considerable difference exists between the UNIX definition of a hard reset and the Windows/PC definition.

The Windows definition usually means a hard reset of the computer, which is powering it off and the powering it on. The UNIX notion is completely different and has nothing to do with the actual hardware itself. When UNIX performs a hard reset on a terminal or shell, it just causes that shell to start over like it had just been invoked. ▦

On the far right of the menu bar is the Help menu. This menu is a standard feature in all CDE applications and, in this case, enables the user to access the extensive documentation of dtterm. The help docs are also available by clicking the Help button in any of the configuration screens.

In addition to menu-based customization, dtterm also supports numerous command line options and x-resources. The x-resources can be configured in the standard ~/.Xdefaults file. Table 9.1 gives a list of the common command line options along with their x-resource equivalents.

Table 9.1 *dtterm* options

Option	X-Resource	Description
-bg		
-background	*background	Specifies the background color for dtterm.
-fg		
-foreground	*foreground	Specifies the foreground color for dtterm. This is the color the text will be displayed in.
-fn or -font	*font	Specifies the font for the terminal.
-geometry	*geometry	Specifies the onscreen size of the terminal.
-title	*title	Specifies the string that dtterm displays for new windows.
+sb or -sb	*scrollbar	Specifies whether the scrollbar should be displayed.

In addition to these options, dtterm also accepts the following options:

- -display [*display*]
- -e [*command*]

The -display option allows the dtterm to start on the specified display without setting the environment variable DISPLAY. As an example, the command:

dtterm -d kanchi:0.1

starts a dtterm on the second monitor of the computer called kanchi.

The -e (short for exec) option starts a new dtterm and runs the specified command in that terminal. For example, the command:

dtterm -e rsh soda

starts a dtterm and runs the given rsh command in it.

dtpad

The dtpad application is an easy-to-use graphical text editor. In CDE, it is used as the default text file viewer and editor. Though it is not meant to replace editors such as vi and emacs, dtpad is small and fast and thus can be used for many quick editing tasks. In addition, it supports the drag-and-drop feature of files for editing and inserting. In this section, we look at some of the features of dtpad. For those users familiar with Windows, the dtpad can be thought of as the CDE equivalent to NotePad.

Usually `dtpad` is launched from the Front Panel by clicking its icon, but it can also be launched from the command line as follows:

```
$ dtpad &
```

The `dtpad` will start in a separate window as shown in Figure 9.5. By default this window consists of two parts: the menu bar and the text area. The text area behaves normally in that it allows for inserting, appending, mouse select, and editing in a manner consistent with similar applications on other platforms.

FIGURE 9.5

The main window of dtpad.

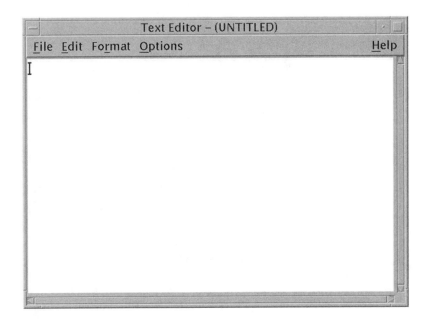

The menu bar for `dtpad` contains the following menus:

- File
- Edit
- Format
- Options
- Help

TIP   All the menus in dtpad support the CDE tear-off feature that allows them to be torn off and placed in separate windows. To tear off a menu, select the menu item that looks like a series of dashes. This feature of menus will be familiar to Windows and Mac OS users.

Part

I

Ch

9

The first menu item is the File item. This menu is used for opening other files, creating new files, saving the current file, printing the current file, and inserting files into the current file. These are standard features that should be familiar to most users.

The Edit menu item provides the standard document editing commands such as undo, cut, copy, paste, select all, and delete. Also accessible from this menu is the Find/Change feature. It allows for finding and changing strings in the current file, via an easy-to-use GUI. Many users find it extremely useful because they do not have to remember complicated editor commands in order to accomplish this task. The Find/Change window of dtpad is shown in Figure 9.6.

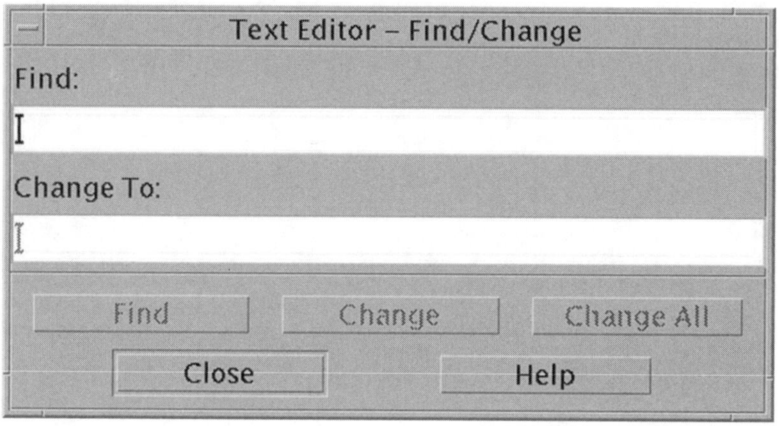

FIGURE 9.6

The Find/Change window of dtpad.

An extension of the Find/Change feature, the Check Spelling feature, is also available from the Edit menu. This feature checks the current documents for misspelling and then presents the user with a list of errors to correct. It is very handy for short emails and memos because it points out all obvious spelling errors. This window is shown in Figure 9.7.

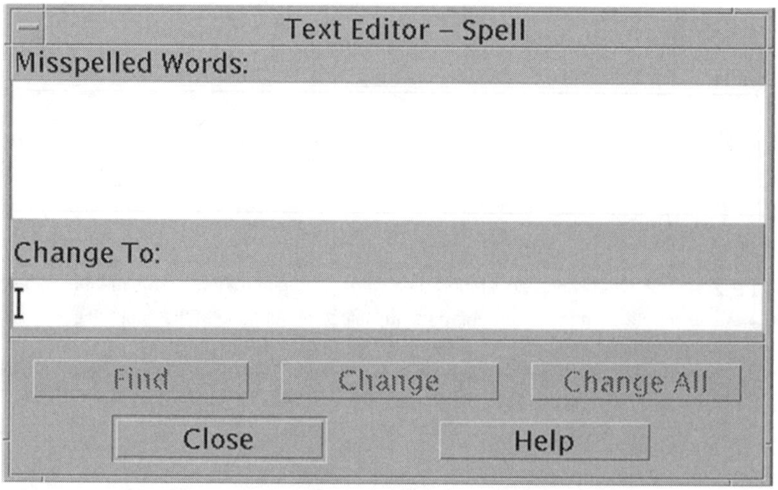

FIGURE 9.7

The Check Spelling window of dtpad.

The Format menu allows for changing the alignment and the margins of a document. The settings for the margins and the alignment are configured using the Settings window that pops up when the Settings menu item is chosen. This window is shown in Figure 9.8.

FIGURE 9.8
The Settings window of dtpad.

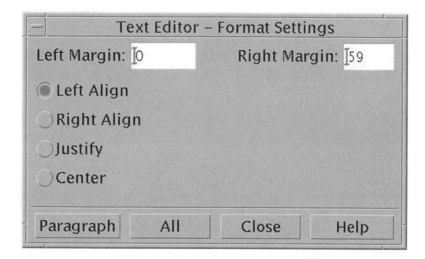

The settings chosen in this window can be applied to the entire document by choosing the All menu item. To apply the selected settings to only one paragraph, choose the menu item Paragraph.

The next menu is the Options menu. This allows the following features to be toggled on and off:

- Overstrike
- Wrap to Fit
- Status Line

When the Overstrike mode is enabled, typing while text is selected causes the selected text to be overwritten with the text that was just typed. When the Wrap to Fit mode is enabled, any line containing more characters than the right margin limit will have the last word on that line automatically wrapped to the next line. This is similar to almost all word processors.

The last option, Status Line, is even more useful than the other two options. Enabling this option places a small status bar across the bottom of the dtpad window. In this bar, the current line and the total number of lines in the document are displayed. What is useful about the status line is that by entering a number in the current line text field, you can go to any line within the current document. The dtpad window with the status line displayed is shown in Figure 9.9.

The File Manager

The CDE File Manager is a file browser that is similar to the Mac OS Finder and the Windows Explorer. It enables users to browser the contents of the computer and interact with files and applications using a simple point-and-click interface. The main window of the CDE File Manager is shown in Figure 9.10.

FIGURE 9.9

The main window of dtpad with the status line displayed.

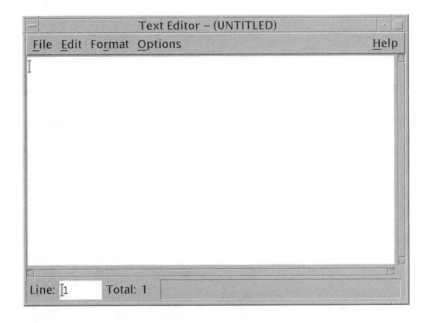

FIGURE 9.10

The main window of the CDE File Manager.

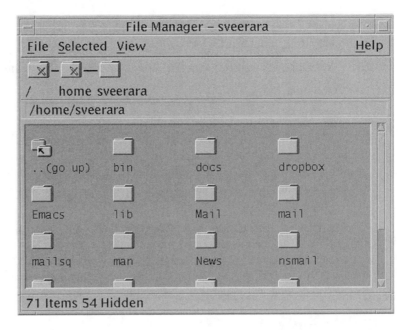

Typically the File Manager is launched when its icon is clicked in the Front Panel. It can also be launched from the command line as follows:

```
$ dtfile &
```

When the File Manager first starts, it always displays the contents of the current directory. If the File Manager is launched from the Front Panel, this directory is usually the user's home directory.

As is shown in Figure 9.10, the main File Manager window is divided into four parts. At the top is the menu bar. Just below this is a panel that shows the current directory path and allows a new directory to be entered. Under this is the main panel that displays the contents of the directory. At the bottom is the status line that displays the number of files in the current directory.

In this section, we will look at using the File Manager to accomplish the following tasks:

- Changing directories
- Creating files and folders
- Renaming files and folders
- Moving and copying files and folders
- Finding files and folders
- Changing permissions

The first task that most users perform with the File Manager is changing directories. Clicking any folder icon changes to that directory. In addition to the standard folder icon, you always have a double folder icon with the name .. (go up). Clicking this icon will change to the parent directory of the current directory. This icon is available in every directory except '/' because '/' has no parent. Sometimes a directory will have its icon marked with a crossed-out pencil. This indicates that the user cannot write in those directories.

▶ For more information about access permissions for files and directories, **see** the section titled "Owners, Groups, and Permissions" in Chapter 5.

To change directly to a given directory, use the text field located above the directory display to enter the required path.

The File Manager also simplifies the process of creating files and folders by presenting the user with a GUI interface. To create a new file, select the item New File from the File menu. A dialog box similar to the one shown in Figure 9.11 will be presented. After entering a filename in the text field, click either the OK or the Apply button to create the new file and update the main window. To create a new folder, select the item New Folder from the File menu.

Changing the name of a file or a folder is equally easy. First click the name of the file or folder. The name appears highlighted. At this point, you can change the name by typing in the new name.

FIGURE 9.11

The New File dialog box.

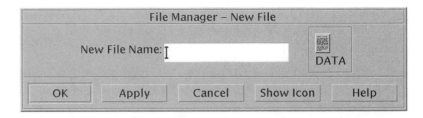

Moving and copying files and folders is equally easy. To move a file or folder, first click it. Then choose the Move To item from the Selected menu. The Move Object dialog box, shown in Figure 9.12, will appear. Enter the destination directory and press return. The selected item will be moved and the main window will be updated appropriately.

FIGURE 9.12

The Move Object dialog box.

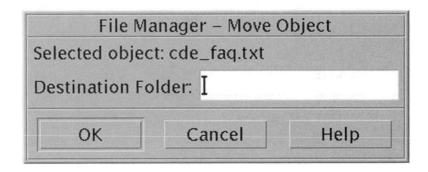

To copy files, select the Copy To item from the Selected menu. This will produce the Copy Object dialog box shown in Figure 9.13. In this dialog box both the destination and the name of the copy in the destination can be set. After the OK button is clicked, a status dialog box will be displayed. The Copy Object dialog box and the status dialog box disappears when the copy finishes.

FIGURE 9.13

The Copy Object dialog box.

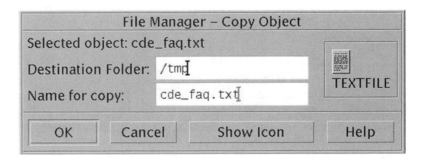

More than one file and folder can be acted on at once by first using the mouse to draw a selection rectangle around the required items, and then choosing the required action from the Selected menu.

Often it becomes necessary to find a file or a folder. The traditional method for this is to use the find program. Though it is a very powerful program, for many new users it is hard to use and often fails to produces the results that were intended. The File Manager provides an easy-to-use GUI front end to the find program. To search for a file, select the Find item from the File menu. This produces the Find window shown in Figure 9.14.

FIGURE 9.14

The Find window.

In this window, a search can be conducted for a file based on its name or contents. In addition, any starting directory can be specified. To start a search, enter the required file name in the text field labeled "File or Folder Name:". Then enter the starting folder. The matching files will be displayed in the bottom text area.

▶ For more information on using the find command directly please **see** the section titled "Working with Files and Directories" in Chapter 3.

The last task that we will look at is changing the permissions on files and folders. The first step is to select the items whose permissions need to be change. Then select the Change Permissions item from the Selected menu. This will produce the Permissions window shown in Figure 9.15. From this window, the owner and group of a file can be changed along with the read, write, and execute permissions for the file. After the required changes are selected, clicking the OK button applies the changes.

▶ For more information on file permissions **see** the section titled "Changing File and Directory Permissions" in Chapter 5.

Part

I

Ch

9

FIGURE 9.15

The Permissions window.

So far, we have looked at some of the common tasks that can be performed using the File Manager. Let's now look at some of the customization options for the display. To customize the display, select the Set View Options item from the View menu. The Set View Options window shown in Figure 9.16 will appear.

FIGURE 9.16

The Set View Options window.

From this window you can change the following parameters:

- The placement of icons
- The items to display
- The information displayed for each item
- The sorting order for items

These parameters can be customized on a per window basis or for every File Manager. In fact, the File Manager can be changed to display files and folders in a manner similar to the Windows Explorer. This can be accomplished as follows:

- In the Show panel select the By Tree option.
- Select the suboption Folders and Files.
- In the Representation panel select the By Name, Date, Size option.
- Click the OK or the Apply button.

The view changes to a tree-based view similar to the one shown in Figure 9.17.

FIGURE 9.17
The File Manager main window in tree mode.

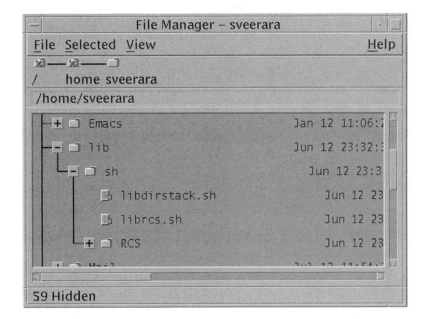

Calendar Manager

The CDE Calendar Manager is a sophisticated appointment scheduler and To Do list manager. In this section, we give an overview of the functions available in the Calendar Manager and show how to create an appointment.

The Calendar Manager is normally started by clicking its Front Panel icon, but it can also be started by issuing the following command:

```
$ dtcm &
```

When the Calendar Manager loads, a view of the current month appears. The main window is shown in Figure 9.18. The main window is divided into three panels: the menu bar, the button bar, and the calendar display.

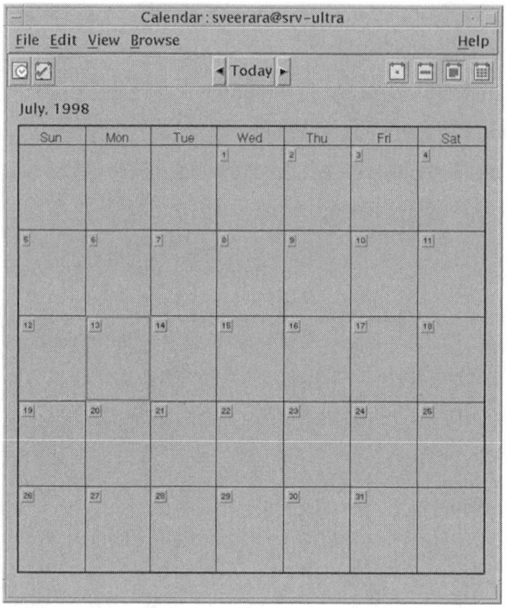

FIGURE 9.18

The Calendar Manager main window.

The available menus are:

- File
- Edit
- View
- Browse

The File menu allows for printing the current calendar, along with changing some options and exiting the program. The Edit menu allows for new appointments and To Do items to be created.

The View menu allows the calendar display mode to be changed and allows for the current appointments and To Do items to be listed. There are four available display modes: Single Day, Single Week, Single Month, and Single Year.

In the Single Day mode, shown in Figure 9.19, a breakdown of events occurring on the selected day is given. Clicking any of the given time intervals allows for an appointment to be scheduled at that time.

FIGURE 9.19

The Calendar Manager
in Single Day mode.

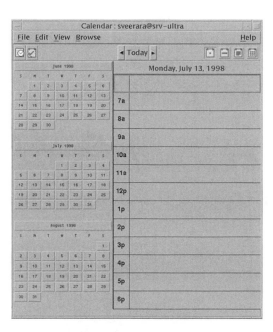

In the Single Week mode, shown in Figure 9.20, a breakdown of an entire week's appointments appears. An appointment can be scheduled for any time period on any day of the week by clicking the appropriate rectangle in the lower-left grid.

FIGURE 9.20

The Calendar Manager
in Single Week mode.

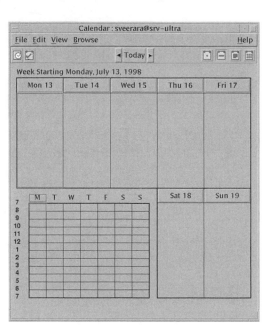

The Single Month mode is the default and is the view presented on initial startup. Clicking a given day invokes the Single Day mode and lists the appointments for that day.

In the Single Year mode, a list of all the months appears. The appointments for a particular month can be displayed by clicking the button with the name of the month.

Most of the tasks in the Edit and the View menus are accessible from the buttons in the button bar.

Finally, the Browse menu allows for browsing the schedules of other CDE users. This feature is only available if you are connected to a network with other CDE users.

In order to create a new appointment, click the leftmost button in the button bar. This is the button used to invoke the appointment editor shown in Figure 9.21. In this window, an appointment can be scheduled for any given time on any given day.

FIGURE 9.21

The Appointment Editor window.

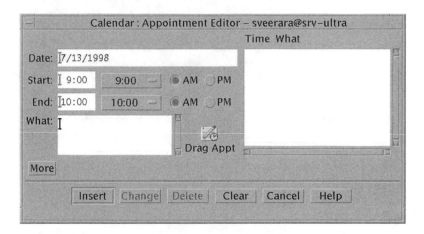

As an example, let's schedule an appointment that occurs once a week on every Tuesday from 11:30 a.m. to 1:00 p.m., starting on the 14th of July. This type of appointment might represent a status meeting or lunch appointment that occurs weekly.

The first step is to select the 14th of July. Start by clicking the rightmost button in the button bar. This switches the calendar to Single Year mode, and the calendar for the entire year appears. Now click the button for July. This produces a calendar for July. In this calendar, click the 14th and then press the leftmost button in the button bar. The Appointment Editor window shown in Figure 9.21 appears.

In the text field marked Start:, enter the value 11:30 and click the AM button. In the text field marked End:, enter the value 1:00 and click the PM button. The drop-down menus next to these text fields can also be used to enter these values.

In the text area, enter a description. Clicking the Insert button creates this appointment, but simply creating the appointment for this date is only part of our task. We still need to mark the event as occurring once a week. In order to do this, click the "More button. This expands the window and offers more choices for this event. The expanded window is shown in Figure 9.22.

FIGURE 9.22

The expanded Appointment Editor window.

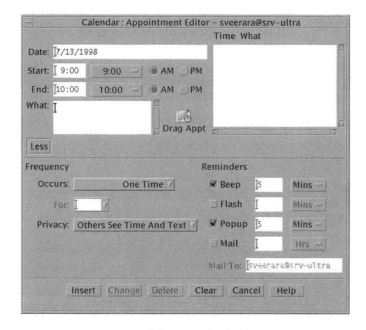

In the extended view, click the Occurs drop-down menu and select Weekly. As you can see, several options are available for scheduling flexibility. Some of the other options available are the number of weeks the event is valid, the privacy level of the event, and the notification that should be given for the event. In our case, the defaults for these parameters are fine.

Clicking the Insert button at this point creates the event and places it in the calendar.

Customizing the Window Environment

In the previous section, we looked at some of the common CDE tools. In this section, we look at customizing CDE by using the Style Manager and by editing configuration files.

The Style Manager

The Style Manager is a powerful program that allows many aspects of the CDE environment to be customized. Usually it is launched when its Front Panel icon is clicked, but it can also be launched from the command line as follows:

```
$ dtstyle &
```

After the Style Manager loads, a window containing several icons will be presented. This window is shown in Figure 9.23.

FIGURE 9.23

The Style Manager window.

Each of the icons in this window corresponds to a different CDE attribute that can be configured. The configuration windows are referred to as Managers. Thus the window that allows the color attribute to be changed is called the Color Manager.

You can modify the following attributes:

- Color
- Font
- Backdrop
- Keyboard
- Mouse
- Beep
- Screen
- Window
- Startup

Because the actual configuration is straightforward, we will just give an overview of the function of each item.

Clicking the Color icon produces the Color Palette Manager. The Color Palette Manager enables you to choose from over 30 predefined color schemes. You can also add, delete, and modify color schemes and test them on-the-fly.

The Font icon gives you access to the Font Manager, which enables you chose the default font for terminal output, window decorations, and icon text.

The Backdrop icon enables you to access the Backdrop Manager where you choose one of 26 backdrops for each virtual console. It also enables you to deactivate backdrops by choosing the No Backdrops option. This is required to allow for programs such as xsetroot or xv to set the background.

The buttons for Mouse, Keyboard, and Beep allow various attributes such as the key repeat rate, the mouse threshold, and the keyboard beep to be set. These Managers provide the same functionality as the program xset, but are much easier to use.

The Screen button enables you to configure the delay for the screen saver. It also lets you to pick one of several predefined screen savers. The screen saver can be activated either by leaving the machine idle for the given delay or by clicking the Lock icon in the Front Panel.

The Window button allows for configuring the behavior of windows, such as auto-raise or click-to-raise. It also lets you enable the icon box for storing icons. This feature will be familiar to MWM users. Normally CDE stores the icons of running programs on the desktop. If the icon box is enabled, CDE stores the icons for running programs in this window, freeing up desktop space.

The last button, Startup, controls the startup behavior of CDE. Usually the behavior is to restore the last session or to restore a baseline session called the Home Session. This behavior can be changed using the Startup Manager.

Creating and Installing New Actions and Subpanels

By default, the Front Panel contains several subpanels. Often, it is useful to create new subpanels for programs or *actions* of a specific type. We will first look at creating a new subpanel. Then we will create a new action and install it in this subpanel.

Creating a new subpanel is very easy. To add a panel, first right- click top of the Control (icon) that you want the subpanel to appear above. If you want a subpanel above the Clock icon, right-click on top of the clock.

When you right-click, a small menu with three items will be presented. In this menu, choose the Add Subpanel option. This creates the small arrow above the control along with a subpanel. A newly created subpanel will contain an item labeled Install Icon. This item will be used to install actions into the subpanel.

Actions are created using the Create Action program which is located in the Desktop Apps folder of the Application launcher, or it can be launched from the command line as follows:

```
$ dtcreate &
```

When the program finishes loading, the Create Action window shown in Figure 9.24 appears.

FIGURE 9.24
The Create Action
window.

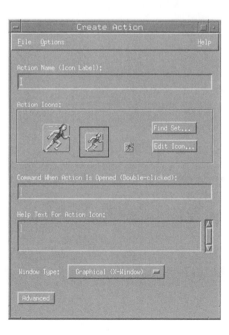

As an example of creating a new action, we can create an action for xterm and install it. The same process can be used to create and install actions for any program or command. Here are the steps:

1. Enter the name the action should be given in the text field labeled Action Name (Icon Label):. This name can be anything you want. It does not have to be the same as the name of the program that will be executed. In this case, I entered xTerm.

2. Enter the command that should be run for this action in the text field labeled Command When Action is Opened (Double Clicked):. This must be the exact command to run. Including the full path to a program is recommended because the Front Panel may or may not have the same search path as your shells. In this case, I entered /usr/X11R6/ bin/xterm.

3. Enter the help text for this action in the text area labeled Help Text For Action. If you do not want any help text to appear, just leave this area blank.

4. Choose the type of window for the action by selecting one of the choices in the drop-down menu labeled Window Type:. For xterm, the default was adequate.

At this point, you can select Save from the File menu and save the action. But before we do that, let's change the icon for this action.

To change the icon for an action, click either the Find Set or the Edit Icon button. The Edit Icon button enables you to edit each of the icon images in detail using a graphical bitmap editor as shown in Figure 9.25.

FIGURE 9.25

The Edit Icon window.

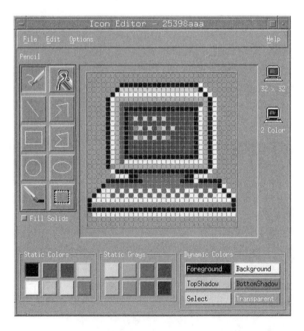

The Find Set enables you to search through a list of your icons, the local system icons, and the distribution icons in order to locate the icon you want. For `xterm`, I used the Find Set command to select the Fpterm icon from the directory `/usr/dt/apps/icons`, as shown in Figure 9.26.

FIGURE 9.26

The Find Set Window.

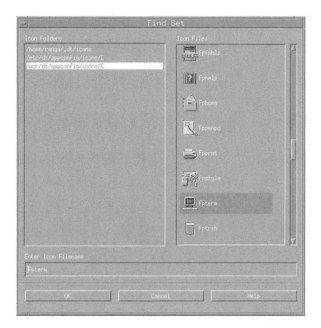

After the required icon is found, save the action by selecting Save from the File menu. When the action is saved, its location will appear in a dialog box. Usually actions created by a user are stored in one of the following locations:

`$HOME`

`$HOME/.dt/appmanager`

Now that we have created an action, let's install it in a submenu. Here are the steps:

1. Use the arrow above the `dtterm` icon to display the Personal Applications sub-panel.
2. Using the File Manager, `dtfile`, go to the directory containing your actions. In my case, the actions were saved in `$HOME`.
3. Click the icon for the action and drag it onto the Install Icon item in the Personal Applications subpanel.

The action will be installed in this subpanel. Clicking it will launch the specified program.

Editing Configuration Files

CDE has many customizations that cannot be done using the GUI tools that are provided. These customizations often improve the usability and the efficiency of the environment for power users. In this section, we look customizing the following files:

- .dtprofile
- sessionetc
- sessionexit

In addition to these files, the standard X resources configuration file, .Xdefaults, can be used to configure the appearance of individual CDE applications. See the section on dtterm for information about this.

The .dtprofile is the file that controls the behavior of shells that are started while running under CDE. This file allows for standard shell initialization files to remain CDE-independent and provides for a method to integrate shell initialization and CDE initialization.

When CDE starts, it does not read the .profile (for sh/ksh/bash) or .login (for csh) file. This is in order to present all new users with the same environment. For users who have extensively modified their shell initialization scripts, this may cause confusion. To make sure that CDE always runs these scripts, add the following line to the file $HOME/.dtprofile:

DTSOURCEPROFILE=true

If this file doesn't exist, you need to make a copy of either the local system version or the distribution version of this script. The local system version is stored in the file /etc/dt/config/sys.dtprofile. The distribution version is usually stored in /usr/dt/config/sys.dtprofile.

These locations are typical for all CDE applications. The local system versions of the configuration scripts are stored in the directory /etc/dt/config, whereas the distribution versions are usually stored in the directory /usr/dt/config.

The order in which CDE searches for its configuration files is as follows:

- $HOME/.dt
- /etc/dt/config
- /usr/dt/config

Thus a user always gets his customization before local system customization. Also, the user is always guaranteed to get the distribution versions of the configurations files in case that neither personal or local system versions of the configuration files exist.

For system administrators who want to customize CDE for all the users of a system, changes should be made to the files in /etc/dt/config and not the files in /usr/dt/config because upgrades to CDE will overwrite files in /usr/dt but not in /etc/dt.

An additional feature that can be configured in the .dtprofile is session logging. Unlike standard X Window, where output from programs is written to the console, under CDE, output generated by programs running under CDE is usually discarded. In order to view the output or to pipe the output to a file, set the variable `dt_sessionlogfile` in the `.dtprofile` as follows:

```
dt_sessionlogfile=$HOME/.dt/session-$$.log
```

In this case, the session log file is set to the file `session-$$.log` located in the users `.dt` directory. In general any filename can be used. The above filename was chosen because it differentiates each session log by its process ID.

Some users also use the `.dtprofile` to start X Window programs. Although this works, CDE provides the `sessionetc` file in order to accomplish this task. As with the `.dtprofile`, CDE searches for the user's copy of this file; then the local system copy, and finally the distribution copy.

The `sessionetc` file is a standard Bourne shell script similar to the `.Xinitrc` or `.Xclients` files used in X Window. Some common uses of this file are to start up programs such as `xload` or `xlock` and to set the background. A sample `sessionetc` is as follows:

```
#!/bin/sh

xmodmap $HOME/.xmodmap-`uname -n`

xsetroot -solid mediumseagreen

xclock -digital -update 1 -geometry 230x30+780+5 &

procmeter -vertical -geometry 120x120+5+615  cpu load disk mem-free &
```

The first time that a user logs into CDE, this file is copied to the user's home directory from the file `/usr/dt/config/locale/sys.session`. Here `locale` is the language format that should be used. For the United States, the `locale` is C. The distribution version starts a few desktop applications along with a help viewer. If you are a system administrator who wants to extend or modify this, copy the distribution version to `/etc/dt/config` directory and modify the copied version.

CDE also provides an equivalent of the `.logout` script in `csh`. This script is called the `sessionexit`. Unlike the other initialization scripts, there are not default and system-wide copies of this script. It exists on a per-user basis. Usually it is used to clean up temporary files or to make backups of critical data. Some users just use it to clear the screen as follows:

```
#!/bin/sh

clear
```

Other Window Systems

In addition to CDE, several other window systems are available for UNIX systems. In this section, we briefly look at the following window systems:

- OpenWindows
- HP-VUE
- KDE

Part I

Ch 9

To obtain more information about a particular window system, please visit the URL's given in its section.

 T I P   Many, many windowing systems are available for UNIX machines. They vary from small and simple to large and extremely customizable. To take a look at window systems not covered in this chapter, try the following site:

http://www.plig.org/xwinman/

This site contains a large selection of screen shots and descriptions about all the major window systems available for UNIX systems.

OpenWindows

OpenWindows is a graphical windowing system developed by Sun Microsystems. OpenWindows is an implementation of the OPEN LOOK graphical user interface specification. Until the Solaris 2.5 release, OpenWindows was the standard window system for all versions of Solaris and SunOS. Currently, OpenWindows is being phased out in favor of CDE.

HP-VUE

Hewlett-Packard's Visual User Environment (HP-VUE) is a window system available for computers that run HP's HP/UX version of UNIX. It provides the user with a graphical desktop with which they can interact. Some of the nicer features of HP-VUE, namely the login manager, the Front Panel, and the Style Manager, were integrated into CDE.

HP-VUE also provides virtual screen functionality like CDE along with providing a standard set of tools for all users. Currently, HP-VUE is being phased out in favor of CDE on all HP/UX computers.

For more information about HP-VUE, please check the following Web site:

http://www.hp.com/xwindow/viaFrames/windowmgrs

KDE

The K Desktop Environment (KDE) is a free window system available for all major UNIX platforms. As of this writing, the newest available version is 1.0.

KDE is similar to CDE in that it provides both programmers and users with a common environment and services. KDE in some ways is closer to Windows than CDE in its look and feel.

KDE is also the first UNIX windowing system that treats the desktop in a manner similar to Mac OS and Windows. It also incorporates a Web browser-based interface for the file manager which allows not only the local desktop to be browsed but also remote sites. In addition to the features of its File Manager, KDE also supports many applications and includes integration with the Koffice, which is a suite of office applications written to run under KDE.

KDE has a strong user base in the Linux and FreeBSD communities, but due to its strengths, it is being used on some commercial systems such as Solaris.

Screenshots and more information along with the links to download KDE are available on the KDE home page:

```
http://www.kde.org
```

From Here...

In this chapter, we looked at the common desktop environment. We covered logging in, using the Front Panel and many of the tools that are available in CDE. We also looked at customizing the look of CDE via the Style Manager along with creating new actions for use in the Front Panel. The configuration files that users and system administrators can customize for their needs were also covered. From here, you will be ready to use CDE and utilize all the features that make it one of the most productive tools available for UNIX workstations.

From here, you can go on to the following topics:

Chapter 11, "Startup and Shutdown", introduces the process by which UNIX systems are started and stopped safely. After reading this chapter you will be familiar with the mechanisms used to initiate CDE at boot time.

Chapter 14, "Printing", introduces the printing model used in UNIX systems. After reading this chapter you will be able to explore the printing system used by CDE.

Chapter 17, "Networking Essentials", covers the basic networking commands required to get the most out of UNIX and CDE.

Part
I
Ch
9

System Administration

## CHAPTER 10

Administering User Accounts and Groups

by Bill Wood

Understanding Users and Groups

User account and group account management is a common responsibility of the system administrator. This chapter discusses the components of a user account and a group account, as well as the process of creating, modifying, and properly deleting accounts. Readers will be familiar with user and group configuration files and systems tools that should be used to properly administer accounts.

You, as the system administrator, control access to your UNIX box by user account management. UNIX was designed to share files, devices, and resources easily between the users on a system. Your users can be other computers, daemon processes, or just regular persons owning files and executing programs. Groups of users can be assigned control access to functions and resources within the computers system. I have separate groups for operators, programmers, data entry staff, and of course administrators. However, this chapter is only concerned with the common user—the one who will be logging in, running programs, and saving and editing files.

 TIP   Remember, the more secure a UNIX system is, the more difficult the administrator's job. So keep in mind that the more secure your company wants its systems, the bigger the pay raise.

The systems that you support are multiuser, meaning that more than one person will share their resources. After a user logs on, he is assigned a workspace for file storage, and certain system resources are dedicated to him. All users have to contend with sharing the power of the UNIX system between fellow users and applications. As system administrator, you are required to balance users' demands to prevent any one user from hogging all the resources.

Each user of the computer system is assigned a username that identifies him to other users and to the computer system. Groups of users are designed to allow for the sharing of files and resources between certain individuals. By controlling how users are added to the system and what groups they belong to, you have effective control over access rights and system resources.

The *passwd* File

The passwd file is the first file used to authenticate and grant access to the users of your system. Each line contains entries in fields separated by colons that define a user and his default environment. The first field is the login name of the user. The second field contains either an encrypted password or a placeholder to reference the /etc/shadow file. The third and fourth fields assign a unique user ID number and a group number that the user belongs to. The fifth field contains the GECOS/CGOS user information. The sixth field is the default home directory, and the seventh field is the initial startup program.

▶ **See** "Understanding the Login Process," **p. 34**

The following is a sample line of an /etc/passwd file:

```
login_name:password_field:user_UID:group_GID:freeform_text:home_directory:default_shell
```

A sample /etc/passwd file follows:

```
root:x:0:1:Super-User:/:/usr/bin/ksh
daemon:x:1:1::/:
bin:x:2:2::/usr/bin:
sys:x:3:3::/:
adm:x:4:4:Admin:/var/adm:
lp:x:71:8:Line Printer Admin:/usr/spool/lp:
smtp:x:0:0:Mail Daemon User:/:
uucp:x:5:5:uucp Admin:/usr/lib/uucp:
nuucp:x:9:9:uucp Admin:/var/spool/uucppublic:/usr/lib/uucp/uucico
listen:x:37:4:Network Admin:/usr/net/nls:
woodwd:x:200:1000:William Wood,,,,:/usr/bin/ksh
wilsondj:x:201:1000:Dan Wilson,,,,:/usr/bin/csh
piercebw:x:202:1050:Bill Pierce,,,,:/usr/bin/bash
cornidw:x:350:2001:David Corni,,,,:/usr/bin/sh
```

Table 10.1 Field Descriptions for the */etc/passwd* File

Field	Description
login_name	Unique login name for this user, also referred to as the username.
password_field	User's encrypted password or security marker (see further definition later of the password field).
user_UID	This field is a "unique" number between 0 and 60,000. This is how UNIX relates the username to the kernel.
group_GID	A unique number to relate the default group to which the user is assigned.
freeform_text	This is the GECOS or CGOS field. Commonly used to store user information for the `finger` command or just the user's full name.
home_directory	Default directory that the user should keep his files in.
default_shell or startup command	What UNIX executes after the user has been authenticated as having access to the operating system. This is normally the default shell for the user, but you can use it to restrict user access by automatically starting a program for him.

Part

II

Ch

10

N O T E The 0–60,000 UIDs and GIDs are a limitation imposed by 32-bit operating systems. With the advent of the new 64-bit systems, this limitation is increased to 2,147,483,647. As you can see, this number can become unwieldy. I would recommend that you keep your UIDs and GIDs to the 32-bit limitation. Output from commands such as `ls` is formatted for a 32-bit UID and GID. The larger 64-bit numbers will skew the table output and make it more difficult to read.

When all operating systems are 64-bit and the UNIX commands are formatted to handle larger numbers in their output fields, then I would change to 64-bit addressing. ▨

The login name can be anywhere from one to eight characters and is case-sensitive. Try to use a combination of upper- and lowercase letters and numbers for a username. Most systems cannot handle a number as the first character of a login name, so avoid this. Login names should be easy to remember and have a standard companywide format. UNIX uses this login name for email addresses, system logs, and file ownership, which makes it such that you and other users can easily guess who the user is.

One convention I often see is the user's initials followed by the first six letters of his last name. When you have a duplicate (and you will), replace the middle initial with an x or some other letter. You could also do this in reverse, using the first six letters of the last name first and then the initials.

For example:

    Name: William Dale Wood   Username: wdwood or woodwd

    Name: William David Wood   Username: wxwood or woodwx

The password field is now a placeholder for either the password or a pointer to a shadow file. Never edit this field yourself. There are four possible entries in the password field: an encrypted password, an "x," the bang (!), or an asterisk. You generally will only find the encrypted password on systems that do not run some form of security that requires a separate file for the passwords—more on the /etc/shadow file later. The asterisk means an account that is "locked" or barred from logging into the system until the system administrator releases it. The "x" or (!) bang character in this field means to look in the /etc/shadow file for the encrypted password.

> **CAUTION**
>
> The pwconv command creates and updates the /etc/shadow file from the information contained in the /etc/passwd file. When updating the /etc/shadow file, pwconv looks for the special value of "x" in the password field of /etc/passwd for a user account. When the password field has the value of "x" in it, this informs the program that the user is already in the /etc/shadow file and should not be modified at this time.

The next field is the User Identification (UID) field, a unique number for the operating system. This number is between 0 and 60,000 on 32-bit systems (remember that 64-bit systems are higher but not recommended). On all systems, the root username is always assigned the number 0, usually followed by bin as UID 2 and daemon as UID 3. Other system UIDs are always assigned the first and lowest numbers at the head of the /etc/passwd file. You should start human UIDs at 200 or greater to leave yourself room when applications want to assign their own administrator's ID in the /etc/passwd username system.

The next field is the Group Identification (GID) field, a unique number for the operating system for controlling access to resources by multiple users. The GID field follows the same conventions as the UID field. It must be a unique number between 0 and 60,000, and it must be defined in the /etc/group file. The only real difference between the UID and GID is that multiple users can belong to a GID, but there can be only one UID per user. Remember, this is the DEFAULT group that the user belongs to on login. You can assign a user to more than one group.

The next field is the GECOS/GCOS free-form text field. GECOS/GCOS was originally assigned to hold login information to submit batch jobs in a mainframe environment running GECOS/GCOS. Because GECOS/GCOS was developed by Bell Labs, and UNIX was developed there too, now only the name remains. Now this field is more commonly known as the user information field and is used for personal information on each user. The `finger` command uses the information in this field for useful output if you follow this comma-separated format. Remember, if you use commas, you include all of them regardless of whether they are empty.

- Full Name
- Office Location
- Telephone number
- Any other number

The next field is the HOME DIRECTORY and represents where the user starts out after a successful login attempt. A user's home directory is normally where files are located that set up the user's environment and are owned by the user. If a home directory is not available at login time, the system normally places the user in either the root directory or a directory called `/home/guest`.

The last field is the default SHELL or initial startup program at login for the user. A number of shells can be used by users; a few are presented in the following list. Anybody who uses UNIX will usually have a favorite. I don't recommend arguing with them about it; it's like politics—just give them what they ask for. I prefer the Korn shell just because that's what I cut my system administrator teeth on.

▶ **See** "Choosing a Shell," **p. 47**

Bourne shell	`/usr/bin/sh`
Korn shell	`/usr/bin/ksh`
C shell	`/usr/bin/csh`
TC shell	`/usr/bin/tcsh`—not available on all systems
BASH Shell	`/usr/bin/bash`—Bourne Again shell—popular on Linux systems

Part

II

Ch

10

> **CAUTION**
>
> The `passwd` file is not a "space delimited" file; it is a colon- delimited file. This can present problems if you have a space at the end of the line. UNIX will try to find a shell that actually ends with a space as part of its filename. To see whether this is the case, `vi` the password file and turn on the option `set list`. This shows you whether a space is at the end of the user's line. UNIX systems immediately log out a user when she tries logging in if she has a space at the end of her `/etc/passwd` entry. This is very frustrating to troubleshoot—I know from personal experience. (For more on `vi`, see Chapter 4, "`vi` Editor.")

The *shadow* File

The `/etc/shadow` file is designed to remove the capability of users (read hackers) to have access to the encrypted passwords on a system. This file has its read access restricted to the root user only, meaning that no other user can read the file or see the encrypted passwords. Most system administrators try to keep the /etc/passwd and /etc/shadow entries in the same order. This makes system administration more manageable. As long as you are using the commands to enter users and are not trying to add users manually, this should not be a problem.

The following is a sample line of the /etc/shadow file:

```
login_name:encrypted_password:last_change:min:max:warn:inactive:expire:reserved
```

An example of an /etc/shadow file follows:

```
root:YVLdVLweC59ws:10393:0:0::::
daemon:NP:6445::::::
bin:NP:6445::::::
sys:NP:6445::::::
adm:NP:6445::::::
lp:NP:6445::::::
smtp:NP:6445::::::
uucp:NP:6445::::::
nuucp:NP:6445::::::
listen:*LK*:::::::
woodwd:x:10401:7:35:7:40::
wilsondj:x:10401:7:35:7:40::
piercebw:x:10410:7:35:7:40::
cornide:x:10425:7:35:7:40::
nobody:NP:6445::::::
noaccess:NP:6445:::::::
nobody4:NP:6445::::::
```

Table 10.2   Field Descriptions of the */etc/shadow* File

Field	Description
login_name	Unique login name for this user, also referred to as the username (see /etc/passwd).
encrypted_password	A 13-character encrypted password for the user.
last_change	The number of days since January 1, 1970, the date that the password was last modified.
min	The minimum number of days required between password changes.
max	The maximum number of days the password is valid.
warn	The number of days before a password expires that a warning is issued to the user when he logs in.
inactive	The number of days an account can be inactive before being barred from logging in.
expire	The absolute date that the username will become inactive and will not be allowed to log in.
reserved	This field is currently reserved for future use; leave blank.

The field for the `login_name` is the same as the field in the `/etc/passwd` file. When a user logs into the system, a match is made between the password file and the shadow file. Should the user's name not be in the shadow file, then the user is barred from logging in.

The second field is the encrypted password field and is always comprised of 13 characters generated from a 64-character alphabet (., /, 0–9, A–Z, a–z). This is a system-generated encrypted string; you should never attempt to edit it. If this field must be updated, use the `passwd` command. This field can also contain a lock string to indicate that the login is not accessible, or no string, which shows that there is no password for the login.

▶ **See** "UNIX Password Administration," **p. 38**

The third field, `last_change`, is the number of days that have passed since January 1, 1970, and the date the password was last modified. This field is a numeric representation of the days and is not formatted out as a date field. This field is a good one to include in your year 2000 test plans.

The fourth field represents the minimum number of days between password changes. This field is commonly used to force users to select a new password and use it. You should set it for at least seven days. This discourages users from immediately setting a password back to what it was before they changed it.

The fifth field, `max`, sets the number of days a password is valid for a user before forcing the user to change it. The common practice for this field is 30–45 days between forced password changes.

▶ **See** "Implementing Password Aging," **p. 43**

The sixth field, `warn`, is used to notify the user when her password is about to expire and she must select a new one. This is a highly annoying message, and most administrators set it between one and seven days. I have found that any more than four days and the users will ignore it, and you will end up resetting their passwords for them.

The seventh field, `expire`, represents the absolute date that the username becomes inactive and the user will not be allowed to log in. This field is generally left blank unless you can tell exactly when a username will be removed from the system. I recommend leaving this field blank unless you have contractors working for you—generally, they have an end date.

AIX Differences

AIX does not use the `/etc/shadow` file system for storing passwords. The file `/etc/security/passwd` is used for storing the encrypted password of a user. The AIX security setup stores these passwords encrypted like the `/etc/passwd`, but instead of on a single line, it does it in a stanza. Stanzas, in the AIX world, mean that a block of multiple lines represents user attributes instead of a colon-delimited single-line system such as the `/etc/shadow` file on other systems. Using stanzas means that more information can be stored for a user than a single line allows. You'll see this when we get to groups later in the chapter.

```
example /etc/security/passwd file
```

Part

II

Ch

10

woodwd:

```
password = uzLabsSq2kxKK
lastupdate = 898112198
flags = ADMIN,NOCHECK
```

piercewd:

```
password = VnLzcmSq3LxKK
lastupdate = 898112198
flags =
```

Table 10.3   Field Definitions for the AIX /etc/security Stanza File

Field	Definitions
password	The 13-character encrypted representation of the user's password.
lastupdate	Specifies the time (in seconds!) since the epoch (00:00:00 GMT, January 1, 1970) when the password was last changed.
flags	Applies restrictions to the login, passwd, and su commands for the user. Restrictions can be a comma-separated listing of: ADMIN, ADMCHG, NOCHECK, or blank (which is the default).

The *group* File

The /etc/group file is used to group users into common areas of the computer system. You can control access to file systems and resources at the group level in the /etc/group file. Each group has a unique name and a unique GID (Group Identification) number. A user can be a member of multiple groups or just one. A group of users can share filebs between each other, and you control that access through the group system files.

The group file contains a one-line entry for each group recognized by the system, of the form:

```
groupname:password: gid:user-list
```

The following is an example of an /etc/group file:

```
root::0:root
other::1:
bin::2:root,bin,daemon
sys::3:root,bin,sys,adm
adm::4:root,adm,daemon
uucp::5:root,uucp
mail::6:root
tty::7:root,tty,adm
lp::8:root,lp,adm
nuucp::9:root,nuucp
staff::10:
daemon::12:root,daemon
sysadmin::14:
```

```
operator::1000:piercewd,wilsondj,woodbm
admin::2000:woodwd,cornide,woodkv
nobody::60001:
noaccess::60002:
```

Table 10.4   Field Definitions of the */etc/group* File

Field	Description
groupname	Unique group name also referred to just as the group.
password	An encrypted password for this group.
gid	A unique number that represents the group name to the operating system.
user-list	This is a comma-separated listing of all users allowed access to this group.

The first field, groupname, represents a human understandable listing of the GID. To assign a group name, follow the same conventions as the username field in the /etc/passwd file.

The second field, password, is a user-assignable password that must be entered before access to a group is granted. This password is encrypted, and if you leave world readable permissions on the file, all users will be able to see it. When the password field is empty, users are prompted to gain access to a group they belong to.

The third field, gid, is the group's unique numerical ID (GID) within the system. The maximum value of the GID field is 2137483647 on 64-bit systems; however, to keep yourself away from upgrade nightmares, GIDs have a recommended threshold of 60,000 and below (remember this is a 32-bit operating system limitation). This field is user-assignable, and I recommend that you follow the same format for UID in the /etc/passwd here.

The fourth field, user-list, is a comma-separated list of users who are allowed access to the resources shared by any particular group. This being a comma-separated listing, you must allow the line of usernames to wrap at the end of the screen.

AIX uses the /etc/group file for only basic group definitions, but it has a secondary file for extended definitions. The file /etc/security/group is used to enhance the standard /etc/group file for the AIX system.

Sample /etc/security/group file:

sys:

admin = true

adm:

admin = true
adms = ppadmn,ftp02

dmdusers

admin = false

Part

II

Ch

10

Table 10.5 The AIX /etc/security/group Enhanced Field Definitions

Fields	Definitions
admin	Possible values:
	true: Sets up the group as an administrative group and only the root user can modify it.
	false: default value used to define a standard user group. This group can be modified by the root user or another user listed in the security group.
adms	Users who can perform administrative tasks for the group.

Understanding UIDs and GIDs

Every username on your system is assigned a UID (User Identification number). These numbers will fall in the range of 0–60,000. A UID is used by the system to equate a username with an operating system identification method. A computer does not understand human names as well as it can process numbers, hence the need for a unique UID. When setting up users, you must ensure that each one has a unique UID number assigned to them. Should you find yourself running in a networked environment, such as NIS, all UIDs must be unique. Reusing a UID causes confusion when file systems must be restored from a previous user. The new user will end up owning the files. One way to avoid this is to leave the username in the system files and assign an invalid password to the new account.

Groups follow a similar format for the GID (Group Identification number) as the UID. These numbers also fall within the range of 0–60,000. All users will be assigned to at least one group and so will have a GID assigned to them. Groups are a way of logically associating users; just remember, don't reuse a GID. This could open up a security hole in the computer. Avoid this by leaving in defined groups without users assigned to them.

Creating User Accounts

After your new UNIX system is set up, it is time to create user accounts for access to it. We are concerned with using the commands that add the users for you, instead of manually editing the system files. Making use of the UNIX commands for the affected users will protect you from making a mistake during an editing session of the system files. I recommend using the commands. They will make all appropriate changes to all necessary files and notify you when something is wrong.

Table 10.6 Commands Used to Affect Users

Command	Definition
Useradd	
AIX - `mkuser`	Used to add users and change user attributes
Usermod	
AIX - `chuser`	Used to modify user accounts without having to edit the system files
Userdel	
AIX - `rmuser`	Used to delete user accounts and all associated files within the user's home directory
Groupadd	
AIX - `mkgroup`	Used to add new groups to the system
Groupmod	
AIX - `chgroup`	Used to modify just the information about the group
Groupdel	
AIX - `rmgroup`	Used to completely delete a group from the system
AIX only	
`chgrpmem`	Used to modify the group membership or the userlist of the group

Part
II

Ch
10

Creating User Accounts with *useradd*

Use the program `useradd` to add a new user entry to basically the `/etc/passwd`, `/etc/shadow`, and `/etc/group` files—the main user account files. This program can also be used to set up the default user environment and allow for activation of password aging. I use this program not only to add users, but also to add users to groups and change their account information. With a little bit of planning, you could develop a script to automate your task of adding users.

▶ **See** Chapter 7, "Essential Shell Scripting," **p. 153**

The command structure for `useradd` is as follows:

```
useradd [ -c comment ] [ -d dir ] [ -e expire ] [ -f inactive ] [ -g group ]
  [ -G group [, group...]][ -m [ -k skeldir ]] [ -u uid [ -o]] [ -s shell ] login
```

Following are some sample `useradd` commands:

```
useradd -c "Dan Wilson, Bldg P, 2455,555-5555" -d /home/wilsondj -e 070799 -f 200
-g admin -m -k /usr/local/bin/skel -u 2001 -s /bin/ksh wilsondj
```

Table 10.7   Option Definitions for the *useradd* Command

Available Options	Description
–c comment	Any text string. It is generally a short description of the login and is currently used as the field for the user's full name. This information is stored in the user's /etc/passwd entry.
– d dir	The home directory of the new user. It defaults to /base_dir/login, where base_dir is the base directory for new login home directories, and login is the new login name.
–e expire	Specify the expiration date for a login. After this date, no user can access this login. Expire is a date entered in any format, except a Julian date. If the date format you choose includes spaces, it must be quoted. For example, you may enter 10/6/90 or "October 6, 1990." A null value (" ") defeats the status of the expired date. This option is useful for creating temporary logins.
–f inactive	The maximum number of days allowed between uses of a login ID before that login ID is declared invalid. Normal values are positive integers. A value of 0 defeats the status.
–g group	An existing group's integer ID or character-string name. Without the – D option, it defines the new user's primary group membership and defaults to the default group. You can reset this default value by invoking: useradd – D – g group.
–G group	An existing group's integer ID or character-string name. It defines the new user's supplementary group membership. Duplicates between groups with the –g and –G options are ignored.
–k skel_dir	A directory that contains skeleton information (such as .profile) that can be copied into a new user's home directory. This directory must already exist. Most systems provide a sample skel directory for creating users, normally located in /etc/skel.
–m	Creates the new user's home directory if it does not already exist. If the directory already exists, it must have read, write, and execute permissions by group, where group is the user's primary group.
–s shell	Full pathname of the program used as the user's shell on login. It defaults to an empty field causing the system to use /sbin/sh as the default. The value of shell must be a valid executable file.
–u uid	The UID of the new user. This UID must be a non-negative decimal integer below MAXUID as defined in <sys/param.h>. The UID defaults to the next available (unique) number above the highest number currently assigned. For example, if UIDs 100, 105, and 200 are assigned, the next default UID number will be 201.

The following are some common error messages displayed when you try to create a new user, and `useradd` encounters a problem adding a new user:

```
UX: useradd: ERROR: login is already in use.  Choose another.
    The login specified is already in use.

UX: useradd: ERROR: uid is already in use.  Choose another.
    The uid specified with the -u option is not unique.

UX: useradd: ERROR: group does not exist.  Choose another.
    The group specified  with the -g option is already in
    use.
```

CAUTION

The entries used with this command have a limit of 512 characters per command line. Specifying long arguments to several options on the command line may exceed this limit.

AIX uses a completely different command for adding users to the operating system, `mkuser`. This can be run from the command line, but until you have your defaults set up in `/etc/security`, I recommend using the SMIT interface. By using the SMIT interface, you ensure that each user's access file is updated appropriately. Another benefit of using SMIT is the F6 key function that shows you want the command string it's using to make a user. This is helpful for developing your own scripts.

Table 10.8   User Account System Files for AIX

File Location	Definition
`/etc/passwd`	This is the system password file and holds the master list of all user accounts.
`/etc/security/passwd`	This is AIX's equivalent of the `/etc/shadow` file.
`/etc/group`	Holds the basic attributes of groups.
`/etc/security/group`	Holds the extended attributes of groups.
`/etc/security/user`	Holds the user account attributes.
`/etc/security/limits`	Controls system resource usage for the users.
`/etc/security/environ`	Like the `/etc/profile`—sets up the initial user environment.
`/etc/security/audit/config`	Holds user audit configuration attributes.
`/usr/lib/security/mkuser.default`	Default values used to set up users into distinct groups.

Part

II

Ch

10

N O T E AIX can make the task of adding users simple. All it takes is knowing how to modify the user account system files. Take the time to learn how these files work together and how to modify them. ■

▶ **See** "Viewing Files," **p. 56**

When running `mkuser`, the `/etc/security/user` file will be scanned for a stanza of default. You can modify this file to include other group stanzas with different default values. You can also define classes of users in the `/usr/lib/security/mkuser.default file`. The AIX default classes are user and admin. The first represents a regular user, and the latter represents an administrative user. If you take the time to understand and modify the default attribute files for adding users to an AIX system, you can reduce the command-line string for adding a user to just a command and the new username.

The following is a sample command syntax for the `mkuser` command:

```
mkuser cornidw
```

Sometimes your users will need a different default value than what is predefined. AIX allows for this by accepting *attribute=value* modifiers to the `mkuser` command that override the default value for just that specified attribute.

A sample command syntax follows:

```
mkuser gecos="David Corni" home=/admin cornidw
```

Table 10.9 Default Values for AIX *mkuser* Command Defined in the File /etc/security/user

Field	Definition
admin = false	Used to indicate whether this is an administrative user account.
login = true	Set whether the user can log in.
su = true	Used to control users' abilities to su to this account.
sugroups = ALL	Controls a group's ability to su to this account.
daemon = true	Sets the accept or deny access to the cron functions.
rlogin = true	Sets whether the user can use remote logins to access this account.
ttys = ALL	Used to control what TTYs will grant access to this user.
umask = 022	Sets the default file creation mask.
expires = 0	Uses the format of *mmddtimeyy* to set when this user account will expire and be barred from access to the computer. (0 means never to expire.)

A small sample of the /etc/security user file will attribute definitions.

N O T E This is just a list of the attributes defined in the default version of /etc/security/user shipped with AIX. For more in-depth definitions, see the actual file and read the man page for /etc/security/user. This file is also a good example of how much more information a stanza can assign for a user versus a single-line entry only.

Here is a sample /etc/security/user file with notes indicating what each field is used for. At the end of the file are defined users and options showing how you change the default attributes for any given user.

```
#VALID USER ATTRIBUTES FOR /ETC/SECURITY/USER:
#
default:
```

admin = false	# Defines the administrative status of the user.
login = true	# Defines whether the user can log in.
su = true	# Defines whether other users can switch to this user account.
daemon = true	# Defines whether the user can execute programs using the cron daemon or the system resource controller (SRC).
rlogin = true	# Defines whether the user account can be accessed by remote.
sugroups =	# ALL Defines which groups can switch to this user account.
admgroups =	# Lists the groups that the user administers.
ttys = ALL	# Defines which terminals can access the user account.
auth1 = SYSTEM	# Defines primary authentication methods for a user.
auth2 = NONE	# Defines the secondary authentication methods for a user.
tpath = nosak	# Defines the user's trusted path characteristics.
umask = 022	# Defines the default umask for the user.
expires = 0	# Defines the expiration time for the user account.
SYSTEM = "compat"	# Describes Version 4 authentication requirements.
logintimes =	# Defines the times a user can log in.
pwdwarntime = 0	# The number of days before a forced password change.
account_locked = false	# Defines whether the account is locked.
loginretries = 0	# The number of invalid login attempts before a user is not allowed to log in.
histexpire = 0	# Defines the period of time in weeks that a user will not be able to reuse a password.
histsize = 0	# Defines the number of previous passwords that cannot be reused.

Part

II

Ch

10

```
    minage = 0
```
\# Defines the minimum number of weeks between password changes. The default is 0. Range: 0 to 52.

```
    maxage = 0
```
\# Defines the maximum number of weeks a password is valid.

```
    maxexpired = -1
```
\# Defines the maximum number of weeks after `maxage` that an expired password can be changed by a user.

```
    minalpha = 0
```
\# Defines the minimum number of alphabetic characters in a password. The default is 0. Range: 0 to 8.

```
    minother = 0
```
\# Defines the minimum number of nonalphabetic characters in a password.

```
    minlen = 0
```
\# Defines the minimum length of a password. The default is 0. Range: 0 to 8.

```
    mindiff = 0
```
\# Defines the minimum number of characters in the new password that were not in the old password.

```
    maxrepeats = 8
```
\# Defines the maximum number of times a given character can appear in a password.

```
    dictionlist =
```
\# Defines the password dictionaries used when checking new passwords.

```
    pwdchecks =
```
\# Defines external password restriction methods used when checking new passwords.

```
root:

admin = true
SYSTEM = "compat"
loginretries = 0
account_locked = false
login = true
    rlogin = false

daemon:

admin = true
expires = 0101000070

woodwd:

admin = false
minother = 1
minlen = 6
minage = 0
maxage = 4
histsize = 3
pwdwarntime = 5
```

Table 10.10   Default Values for AIX *mkuser* as Defined in the */usr/lib/ security/mkuser.default* Class File

Field	Definition
pgrp	Primary Group this class of user belongs to.
groups	Secondary groups this class of user belongs to.
shell	Default shell program.
home	Home directory location.
su	Specifies whether other users can su to this user account.
loginretries	Sets how may times a user of this class can try logging in before being barred from system access.
pwdwarntime	Number of days a user receives a warning prior to his password expiring.
histsize	Size of the shell command history file.
maxage	Sets number of weeks a password is valid.
minage	Sets number of weeks before a password can be changed.
minlen	Sets the minimum length of a password.
minother	Defines the minimum number of nonalphabetic characters that must be in a new password.
maxrepeats	Defines the maximum number of times a character can be repeated in a new password. Because a value of 0 is meaningless, the default value of 8 indicates that there is no maximum number.

Part
II

Ch
10

I have included a sample copy of one of our /usr/lib/security/mkuser.default files:

```
user:

pgrp = staff
groups = dwdusers,staff,printq
shell = /usr/bin/ksh
home = /home/$USER
su = false
loginretries = 5
pwdwarntime = 5
histsize = 3
maxage = 4
minage = 1
minlen = 6
minother = 1
maxrepeats = 8
```

```
admin:

pgrp = system
groups = system
shell = /usr/bin/ksh
home = /home/$USER
```

TIP

The `mkuser` command does nothing more than run a shell script, `/usr/lib/security/mkuser.sys`, which is what actually creates a user account for you. Because this is an editable shell script, you should modify it to fit the requirements of your environment.

▶ **See** "Introduction to Shell Programming," **p. 154**

TIP

In AIX, when using the SMIT interface, shell scripts are automatically created for you. SMIT creates two log files, smit.log and smit.script. The smit.log file is a step-by-step listing of everything you do with smit. The smit.script file actually stores the commands that were run when you requested SMIT to accomplish some task. By using the smit.script file, you can easily create your own custom scripts and have SMIT develop the correct syntax for you.

▶ **See** "Advanced Shell Scripting," **p. 175**

CAUTION

The logs created by SMIT can become very large, very quickly if you do not manually trim them every now and then. Don't trim them with a `cron` job; these files not only show you how to do what you are doing but also can save you when you need to know what someone has changed.

▶ **See** "Filtering Commands," **p. 70**
▶ **See** "The `cron` Process," **p. 409**

Deleting User Accounts

When a user no longer requires access to your computer system, you should delete the user's account or at least disable the user from being able to log in. Disabling a user account is preferable over just deleting it. This provides the capability to track what files the user owned and duplicate this setup should someone take that user's place. A section in Chapter 3 describes what happens when you use a command to remove a user and the options you can select with them. These commands can delete the user's login along with the user's home directory and all files inside it, if you want.

▶ **See** "Locating Files Using Find," **p. 63**

CAUTION

Removing a user can delete the user's home directory. If you need any files out of it, get a good backup of the files or copy them to another location

Use the following command structure to delete user accounts:

```
Solaris / HP / Linux        userdel [ -r ] login
AIX                    rmuser [-p] login
```

Command Sample

```
Solaris / HP / Linux        userdel -r wilsondj
AIX               rmuser -p wilsondj
```

Table 10.11 Option Definitions for the *userdel* Command

Available Options	Description
-r	Removes the user's home directory and all subdirectories from the system
-p (AIX only)	Removes the password information from the /etc/security/passwd file
login	The username of the account to be deleted

Return codes for shell programming of userdel

```
    0    Success.
    2    Invalid command syntax.  A usage message for the userdel command is
➥displayed.
    6    The login to be removed does not exist.
    8    The login to be removed is in use.
    10   Cannot update the /etc/group file but the login is removed from the
➥/etc/passwd file.
    12   Cannot remove or otherwise modify the home directory.
```

Modifying User Accounts

The command usermod allows you to modify user information without having to manually edit the system files. This is a preferred method because it changes all login system files and file systems as needed. You also can use usermod to change the user's login name. This changes all system files and files owned by the user.

The command structure for the usermod command follows:

```
usermod [ -u uid] [ -g group ] [ -G group [ , group ... ] ] [ -d dir [ -m ] ] [ -
s shell ] [ -c comment ]   [ -l new_logname ] [ -f inactive ] [ -e expire ] login
```

The following is a sample usermod command:

```
usermod -u 1214 -g staff -d /staff/woodsa -s /bin/ksh woodsa
```

> **CAUTION**
>
> The entries used to create this command-line string have a limit of 512 characters per line. Specifying long arguments in the string to several options might exceed this single line limit.

Part
II

Ch
10

Table 10.12   Option Definitions for the *usermod* Command

Available Options	Description
-u uid	Specify a new UID for the user. It must be a non-negative decimal integer less than MAX-UID as defined in <param.h>. Note that the UID associated with the user's home directory is not modified with this option; a user will not have access to his home directory until the UID is manually reassigned using chown(1M).
-g group	Specify an existing group's integer ID or character-string name. It redefines the user's primary group membership.
-G group	Specify an existing group's integer ID "," or character string name. It redefines the user's supplementary group membership. Duplicates between group with the -g and -G options are ignored.
-d dir	Specify the new home directory of the user. It defaults to base_dir/ login, where base_dir is the base directory for new login home directories, and login is the new login.
-m	Move the user's home directory to the new directory specified with the -d option. If the directory already exists, it must have permissions read/write/execute by group, where group is the user's primary group.
-s shell	Specify the full pathname of the program used as the user's shell on login. The value of shell must be a valid executable file.
-c comment	Specify a comment string. The comment can be any text string. It is generally a short description of the login and is currently used as the field for the user's full name. This information is stored in the user's /etc/passwd entry.
-l new_logname	Specify a string of printable characters that specifies the new login name for the user.
-e expire	Specify the future date on which a login can no longer be used; after this date, no user can access this login. You may type the value of the argument expire (which is a date) in any format you want (except a Julian date). For example, you may enter 10/6/90 or "October 6, 1990." A value of " " (null) defeats the status of the expired date.
-f inactive	Specify the maximum number of days allowed between uses of a login ID before that login ID is declared invalid. Normal values are positive integers. A value of 0 defeats the status.

Return codes for shell programming of usermod

```
2    The command syntax was invalid.
3    An invalid argument was provided to an option.
4    The uid given with the -u option is already in use.
5    The password files contain an error.
```

```
      6    The login to be modified does not exist, the group does not exist, or
➥the login shell does not exist.
      8    The login to be modified is in use.
      9    The new_logname is already in use.
     10    Cannot update the /etc/group file. Other update requests will be
➥implemented.
     11    Insufficient space to move the home directory  ( - m option).  All the
➥other update requests however will be processed
     12    Unable to complete the move of the home directory to the new home
➥directory.
```

For the AIX world, `chuser` works like the `usermod` command, except in syntax. The `chuser` command modifies values for an existing user by using the *attribute=value* parameters with it. The `mkuser` and `chuser` commands both use the same syntax to add or modify a user's attributes. There are so many different attributes for `mkuser` and `chuser` commands that I could write a whole chapter on just these two commands. I strongly recommend that you at least see the man pages for more in-depth information.

Writing Shell Scripts to Create User Accounts

The best way to write a shell script to create a user account is to find a shell script that is already written and then modify it to your needs. Hundreds of programs currently are available, so why re-create the wheel? I have a script that I use to add users. I have stripped out the company proprietary stuff and added some comments to it. This is just a sample script, and it shows you what steps to follow when creating your own script for your company.

▶ **See** "Introduction to Shell Programming," **p. 154**

This script performs the rudimentary steps of creating a new user on a UNIX system. The script prompts the root user to enter the new user's information and then perform error checking on the system files. It then installs the new user in the `/etc/passwd`, `/etc/shadow`, and `/etc/group` files. The new user program then creates a home directory for the user in the format of `/home/{username}`. Default `.profile` and `.login` files are also copied into their home directories and made accessible to the user for editing. A default section in the front of the program allows you to set predefined answers to some of the questions if you leave them blank when prompted for them. Some simple checks are built in for validation of the data that is input by the root user. You can expand on these to fit your environment.

Here is a sample of a script that we use to add users to our systems:

```
#!/bin/sh
#
#      Script to add new users
#
LeaveScript()
{
    echo "Script has been interrupted, leaving now..."
    diff ${PASSWDDIR}/passwd  etc/ptmp

  # we do not want to leave any copies of passwd or shadow files around!
  rm -i /etc/ptmp /etc/stmp
```

Part

II

Ch

10

```
        exit 1
}

trap LeaveScript INT

#
#    Assign default required values.
#

ALIASDIR="/etc/mail"
PASSWDDIR="/etc"
TMPDIR="/var/tmp"
PASSWD="/usr/bin/passwd"

# Set the default shell as bourne shell.
DSHELL="/usr/bin/sh"

# Set the default group as other.
DGROUP="other"

# Set the default home directory
DHOME="/home"

#
#   Test the usage of the command.
#

if [ $# -eq 0 ]
then
    echo "usage: add_user requires username as an argument"
    exit
fi

#
#   Test to determine if program is being run by root user.
#

if [ "`/usr/ucb/whoami`" != "root" ]
then
    echo "You must be root to run this program."
    exit
fi

#
#   Use the vipw locking
#

if [ -f /etc/ptmp ]
then
    echo "The passwd file is in use."
    exit
else
    cp ${PASSWDDIR}/passwd /etc/ptmp
    cp ${PASSWDDIR}/shadow /etc/stmp
    chmod --- /etc/stmp
    rm -f /tmp/change.passwords
fi

for username in $*
do
```

```
#
# Assign the userid.
#
    echo "Select User ID for ${username}:"
    read nuid

#
# Assign the user's full name.
#
    echo "${username}'s full name: \c"
    read fullname

#
# Assign the user's default group.
#
    echo "default group for ${username}: (${DGROUP}): \c"
    read group

    if [  -z "${group}" ]
    then
        group=${DGROUP}
    else
        DGROUP=${group}
    fi

#
# Assign the user's home directory.
#
    echo "default home directory for ${username}: (${DHOME}): \c"
    read home

    if [ -z "${home}" ]
    then
        home=${DHOME}
    else
        DHOME=${home}
    fi

#   Is a home directory already there?

    if [ -d ${DHOME}/${username} ]
    then
            echo "${username}'s home directory already exists, skipping."
            continue
    else
            mkdir ${DHOME}/${username}
            cp /etc/skel/local.profile ${DHOME}/${username}/.profile
            cp /etc/skel/local.login ${DHOME}/${username}
            chown ${nuid} ${DHOME}/${username}
            chgrp ${DGROUP} ${DHOME}/${username}
            chown ${nuid} ${DHOME}/${username}/.profile
            chgrp ${DGROUP} ${DHOME}/${username}/.profile
            chown ${nuid} ${DHOME}/${username}/.login
            chgrp ${DGROUP} ${DHOME}/${username}/.login
    fi

#
#   Test to determine if user is in the passwd file already
#
```

```
        if [ `grep "^${username}:" /etc/ptmp ¦wc -l ` -gt 0 ]
        then
            echo "${username} already exists in the file.  Choose another."
            rm -i /etc/ptmp /etc/stmp
            exit 1
        fi

#
#   Test to determine if group is okay
#

        gid=`grep "^${group}:"  /etc/group ¦ awk -F: ' {print $3}'`

        if [ -z "${gid}" ]
        then
            echo "${group} is not a reasonable group"
            rm -i /etc/ptmp /etc/stmp
            exit
        fi

#
#   Add an entry to password file
#

    echo "${username}:x:${nuid}:${gid}:${fullname}:${home}/${username}:${DSHELL}"
➡>> /etc/ptmp

        echo "${username}:.Cl4oC4GX7dfoi:9999::::::" >> /etc/stmp

#
# Save information for mail alias
#

    first_name=`echo ${fullname} ¦ awk '{print $1}' ¦ tr '[A-Z]' '[a-z]'`
    passwd="${first_name}`date +%d`"
    echo "${username}:${passwd}:${fullname}" >> /tmp/change.passwords
done

#
# Make copies of current passwd and shadow files
#

cp ${PASSWDDIR}/passwd ${PASSWDDIR}/passwd.`date "+%y%m%d"`
cp ${PASSWDDIR}/shadow ${PASSWDDIR}/shadow.`date "+%y%m%d"`

#
# Copy the ptmp onto passwd and stmp onto shadow.
#

cp /etc/ptmp ${PASSWDDIR}/passwd
cp /etc/stmp ${PASSWDDIR}/shadow

#
# Remove the temporary files.
#

rm -f /etc/ptmp etc/stmp

#
#   Assign a password
#
```

```
for username in `cat /tmp/change.passwords ¦ awk -F: '{print $1}' `
do

echo "Password for ${username} should be \c"
#grep"^${username}:" /tmp/change.passwords ¦awk -F: '{print $2}'

${PASSWD} ${username}

done

#
#  Add an entry to the system mail alias
#

echo " "
echo "Now making entry for mail alias."
#
cat /tmp/change.passwords ¦ awk -F: '{print $1 ":" $3"@smtplink"}' >>
➥${ALIASDIR}/aliases

rm -f /tmp/change.passwords

exit 0
```

Chapter 7, "Essential Shell Scripting," and Chapter 8, "Advanced Shell Scripting," show you
how to write a script like the preceding sample, "adduser script."

Creating Groups

Groups are just a subset of users for the entire system. The system file /etc/group (and /etc/
security/group for AIX) uses a format similar to the /etc/passwd file. This is why you should
always use the groupadd command to create a new group definition in the /etc/group file. The
groupadd ensures all appropriate changes to the /etc/group file are made as required and
ensures that you do not duplicate the GID between groups.

The command structure of the groupadd command is as follows:

```
groupadd [-g gid ] group
```

Following is a sample groupadd command:

```
groupadd -g 3001 babylon
```

Table 10.13 Option Definitions for the *groupadd* Command

Available Options	Description
-g gid	The group ID for the new group. This group ID must be a non-negative decimal integer. The group ID defaults to the next available (unique) number above the highest number currently assigned. For example, if groups 100, 105, and 200 are assigned as groups, the next default group number is 201.
group	A string of printable characters that specifies the name of the new group, up to a maximum of eight characters.

Part
II

Ch
10

Return codes for shell programming of `groupadd`

```
0    Success.
2    Invalid  command  syntax.
3    An invalid argument was provided to an option.
4    gid is not unique (when -o option is not used).
9    group is not unique.
10   Cannot update the /etc/group file.
```

The AIX world uses the `mkgroup` command rather than the `groupadd` command. It also uses the *attribute=value* syntax to set group information upon creation. See the man page on `chgroup` for a complete listing of all the attributes you can set for a group. This command adds a new twist by allowing you to define a group as administrative or just standard.

The command syntax for the `mkgroup` command follows:

```
mkgroup [ -a ] [ -A ] [ Attribute=Value ... ] Group
```

The following is a sample `mkgroup` command:

```
mkgroup operators
```

or

```
mkgroup -a users=woodwd,wilsondj operators
```

Table 10.14   Option Definitions for the *mkgroup* Command

Available Options	Descriptions
-a	Creates an administrative group
-A	Sets the group administrator
attribute=value	Sets attributes for the new group

Modifying Groups

The `groupmod` command modifies the definition of the specified group by making changes to the group's entry in the /etc/group file. The `groupmod` command makes all appropriate changes to the /etc/group file as required and ensures that you will not duplicate the GID between groups. With this command, you can modify the group name or GID number or both.

The command structure for the `groupmod` command is as follows:

```
groupmod [ -g gid ] [ -n name ] group
```

Following is a sample `groupmod` command:

```
groupmod -g 3001 -n ark noah
```

Table 10.15   Option Definitions for the *groupmod* Command

Available Options	Description
-g gid	The group ID for the new group. This group ID must be a non-negative decimal integer. The group ID defaults to the next available (unique) number above 99.
-n name	A string of printable characters that specify a new name for the group.
group	The current name of the group to be modified.

Return codes foe shell programming of groupmod

```
0    Success.
2    Invalid command syntax.
3    An invalid argument was provided to an option.
4    gid is not unique
6    group does not exist.
9    name already exists as a group name.
10   Cannot update the /etc/group file.
```

When using the AIX operating system, you can use the chgroup command to modify the attributes for any group. chgroup also has the advantage of being able to remove users from and add users to a group, whereas with the other operating system you have to manually edit the /etc/group file. Anytime you use the chgroup command, you should be the root user; this ensures that you have the proper authority for modifying group attributes.

The command syntax for the chgroup command follows:

```
chgroup Attribute=Value ... Group
```

A sample chgroup command follows:

To add cornide and woodwd to the operator group, which only wilsondj is a member of, use the following command:

```
chgroup users=cornide,woodwd,wilsondj  operator
```

To remove woodwd from the administer group, but retain cornide and wilsondj, and remove any of the administrators from the group, use this command:

```
chgroup users=cornide,wilsondj adms= administer
```

N O T E   I wanted to show these two examples to point out something to you. Each time you change a group's user list, you have to specify all the members for that group in the new list. The chgroup command rebuilds the user list each time you want to modify the user's attribute. This would be a good place to create a script that would grep the group and pull the user list and then let you edit it offline.

▶ **See** "The grep Command," **p. 72**

Table 10.16 shows the attributes that the chgroup command can modify for groups.

Part

II

Ch

10

Table 10.16   Option Definitions for the *chgroup* Command

Available Options	Description
adms	Defines the users who can perform administrative tasks for the group, such as setting the members and administrators of the group. The Value parameter is a list of comma-separated user login names. If you do not specify a Value parameter, all the administrators are removed.
admin	Defines the administrative status of the group. Possible values are:
true	Defines the group as administrative. Only the root user can change the attributes of groups defined as administrative.
false	Defines a standard group. The attributes of these groups can be changed by the root user or a member of the security group. This is the default value.
id	The group ID. The Value parameter is a unique integer string.
users	A list of one or more users in the form: User1,User2,...,Usern. When working with a user list, all the users in the list must already have an account. chgroup does not allow you to remove users from their primary group.

N O T E   The adms and admin attributes are set in the /etc/security/group file. The remaining attributes are set in the /etc/group file. If any of the attributes you specify with the chgroup command are invalid, the command makes no changes at all. ■

AIX gives you the capability to change the members or administrators of groups that you have already defined without the need to manually edit the system files. This command, chgrpmem, allows you to add members to or delete members from a group or modify the administrators of a group.

The command syntax of the chgrpmem command follows:

```
chgrpmem [ { { -a ¦ -m } { + ¦ - ¦ = } User ... } ] Group
```

A sample chgrpmem command is as follows:

```
chgrpmem -m + vickerkx,nagykv pizza
chgrpmem -a -woodbm1 operator
```

Table 10.17   Option Definitions for the *chgrpmem* Command

Available Options	Description
-a	Sets the administrators of a group
-m	Sets the users of a group
+ (modifier to -a or -m)	Adds the user to the group depending on whether you've used -a or -m option

Available Options	Description
– (modifier to –a or –m)	Deletes the user from the group depending on whether you've used the –a or –m option
= (modifier to –a or –m)	Used to pass a new listing of users or administrators to a group depending on whether you've used the –a or –m option

Deleting Groups

Always use the groupdel command to delete a group definition in the /etc/group system file. The groupdel command makes all appropriate changes to the /etc/group file as required. This is one way of making sure that you do not accidentally delete the wrong group or mess up the /etc/group file.

The command structure for the groupdel command follows:

groupdel group

A sample groupdel command follows:

groupdel noah

Part
II
Ch
10

Table 10.18 Option Definitions for the *groupdel* Command

Available Options	Description
group	A string of printable characters that specify the group to be deleted.

Return codes for shell programming of groupdel

```
0    Success.
2    Invalid command syntax.
6    group does not exist.
10   Cannot update the /etc/group file.
```

AIX uses the rmgroup command to remove a group from the system. This command removes all users from the group but does not delete the actual users' accounts from the system.

The command syntax for the rmgroup command follows:

rmgroup Name

A sample rmgroup command follows:

rmgroup operator

CAUTION

If the group is the primary group (or default group) for any user, you cannot remove it unless you redefine that user's primary group. This effectively empties the user list for this group and then allows you to remove it.

Customizing the User Environment

You can customize a user's environment by editing certain configuration files depending on what shell the user starts by default when logging in. When explaining the user environment setup files to users, I contrast these files to the DOS files of `autoexec.bat` and `config.sys`. I know it's crude, but you would be surprised how that little example turns on the light and makes the system more friendly to the users.

▶ **See** "Understanding the Login Process," **p. 34**

Next, you need to understand the login process to correctly modify a user's environment versus the entire computer system for everyone. The UNIX system is designed to execute certain system environment scripts during the login session. What gets read/executed basically depends on what shell your users want to work in when they log into the computer system. I have included a simple flowchart of what is happening during the login process for any given "human" user (see Figure 10.1).

The system has files that execute first, `/etc/profile` and `/etc/login` (AIX—`/etc/environment`). Modifying these files globally changes how every user's environment is defined upon login. To override these system settings and to enhance them, a user will modify files within her home directory. These files are referred to as "dot" files because they start with a "dot" (.). Examples are `/home/$USER/.profile` and `/home/$USER/.chsrc` to name two. Table 10.18 shows you what most users use each file for. Table 10.18 also includes some extra "dot" files that are used to further customize the user's environment but are not necessary during login.

Table 10.18 Environment Shells

Shell	Filename	Environment Setup
csh	.login	Defining terminal attributes
		Defining initial global environment for the user
	.cshrc	Personal command aliases
		Environment pathing statements
		Modifying the default file creation mask (umask)
		Defining system variables
	.logout	Closing files
		Cleaning up after a session
sh		
ksh	.profile	Multipurpose used for setting up any environment for a user who is different from the system default

continues on page 264

FIGURE 10.1
System scripts read
during user login.

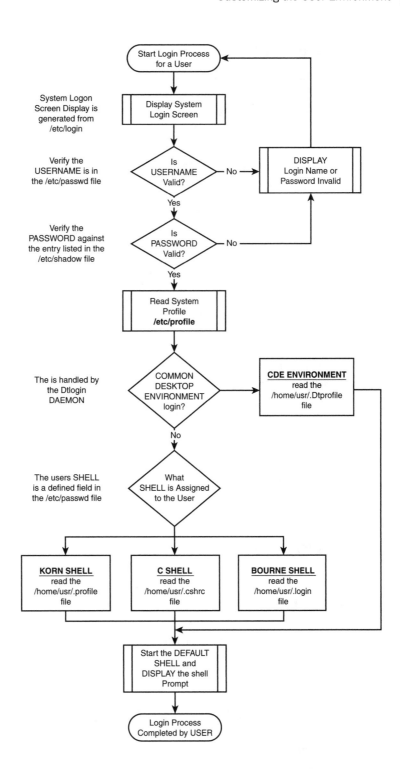

Table 10.18   Continued

Shell	Filename	Environment Setup
dtterm	.Dtprofile	Sets options for the Common Desktop Environment. This system startup file does not reference any other dot (.) file unless set to do so with the attribute settings inside it. (source /home/$USER/.profile)

Additional User Environment Shells

Program	Filename	Environment Setup
vi	.exrc	Sets up the vi editor option preferences for a user
emacs	.emacs_pro	Used to set emacs editor options and key defaults
rn	.newsrc	Sets up the default newsgroups a user wants to belong to
xrdb	.Xdefaults	Sets up the X11/CDE terminal configurations
startx	.xinitrc	Sets a user's default X11/CDE environment upon startup of the Xterminal session

All system environment and user startup files are in a text format and easy for you to use your favorite editor on for customization. Viewing the configuration files involves the use of a text viewer such as cat, pg, or more. I prefer the more file viewer. It's basic, and when I more a file that is a binary (I do this every now and then by mistake, when I'm too lazy to use the file command first), I can easily quit from it, without having to wait for the entire file to dump to the screen.

N O T E   Any time you have to edit a system environment or user startup file, make a backup copy of it. I just make a copy of the file in the directory it's in and append a date to it, as in this example:

```
cp /home/woodwd/.profile /home/woodwd/.profile.980701
```

Sample User Profiles

The following is a sample /home/.profile file:

```
# @(#)local.profile 1.4 93/09/15 SMI#
➥######################################################  System Variables
➥Initialized Here
#
######################################################
export EDITOR=vi
export VISUAL=vim
export HISTSIZE=500
export EXINIT="set noautoindent tabstop=3 ts=4 sw=4 ai"
export TERM=vt100
PATH=.:$HOME/bin:/usr/bin:/usr/sbin:/usr/ucb:/etc:/usr/openwin/bin:/usr/local/bin
export PATH

LD_LIBRARY_PATH=/usr/dt/lib:/usr/openwin/lib; export LD_LIBRARY_PATH
```

```
TMPDIR=/var/tmp; export TMPDIR

# set manpath to include openwin man pages
export MANPATH=/usr/share/man:/usr/openwin/share/man

PS1=`hostname`:$PWD'> `
export PS1

LPDEST=lineprt1; export LPDEST

DISPLAY=206.30.231.74:0; export DISPLAYalias cls=clearalias vi=/usr/local/bin/
➥vimalias load='uptime¦cut -d, -f4,5,6'umask 002set -o vi
```

UNIX Passwords

This is your first line of defense against unauthorized access to a UNIX system—read this as first line of defense against hackers internal and external to your company. I cannot stress enough that you must keep the root password a secret and limit the number of users who have access to it. Keep in mind that if someone else has access to your root password that is one person too many. I seal the root passwords in an envelope and send them to the vault with my disaster recovery safe box.

The Superuser account may change any password; hence, the `passwd` command will not prompt root for the old password. The root user account is one account not affected by password aging and password requirements or even recommendations. One neat trick the root user can do is create a null password by just pressing Enter in response to the prompt for a new password. Now you can see why this super user account and all Superuser accounts must be protected from unauthorized access.

A new user's account has the password field locked and is barred from login until you set a password for the user. Of course, the user, upon login will be forced to change the password immediately after login. This is where you have the chance to enforce (suggest) some ideas for a password.

- The user's password must be at least six characters long. UNIX only considers the first eight characters to have significance. The user can have a password longer than eight, but UNIX only cares about the first eight. You can also enforce this by setting the PASSLENGTH field in the /etc/default/passwd file to be six characters.

- A password must be made up of at least two alphabetic characters and at least one numeric character for a total of six characters. When using the alphabetic characters, upper- and lowercase are valid characters.

- Suggest that a password be different from the user's login name and any reverse or circular reference to the user's username.

- Passwords should not be the name of a spouse, child, or pet. Basically, real words are the easiest for a password cracking program to break; teach your users to avoid them.

TIP Get a password cracking program and run it against your system. This will surprise your users when you send them an email message with their password in it. This will help to drive home the point of not using passwords that are easy to guess.

▪ New passwords must differ from the old, and this can be enforced by using the min and max fields in the /etc/shadow file.

▪ Don't make passwords so difficult that you have to write them down to remember them. Try and help your users to select a password schema that is easy for them to remember.

Setting passwords

The passwd command changes the password or lists the password attributes associated with the user's login name. The root user can use this command to install or change passwords and attributes associated with any user's account. We will not discuss what a user must do when using passwd to change his password, but we will concentrate on what the root user can do with the passwd command. (For further discussion of using the passwd command as a user, see Chapter 2, "Logging in.")

The command syntax for the passwd command is as follows:

```
passwd -s [ -d ¦ -l ] [ -f ] [ -n min ] [ -w warn ] [ -x max ]   username
```

A sample passwd command follows:

```
passwd -n 35 -x 65 -w 7   woodwd
```

Table 10.20   Privileged User Options for the *passwd* Command

Available Options	Description
-s	Shows the current password attributes assigned to a user account.
	Sample output of the passwd -s username command:
	`username status mm/dd/yy min max warn`
	`woodwd  PS  06/16/98  1 4  1`
-f	Forces the password to expire immediately when the user logs in next.
-l	Locks password and bars the user from logging in.
-n min	Sets the minimum number of days between password changes for user.
-w warn	Sets "your password is going to expire in X days" warning field in the /etc/shadow file.
-x max	Sets the maximum number a days a password is valid for user.
-d	Deletes the password associated for a user to log in. Stops the user from being prompted for a password when he logs in.
-a	This option shows the password attributes for all entries and only works with the -s option.

CAUTION

Should the min field in the /etc/shadow file be greater than the max field, the user will not be able to change his password. To avoid this confusion when you use the -n min option, always use the -x max option.

Return codes for shell programming of passwd

```
0    success.
1    Permission denied.
2    Invalid combination of options.
3    Unexpected failure.  Password file unchanged.
4    Unexpected failure.  Password file(s) missing.
5    Password file(s) busy.  Try again later.
6    Invalid argument to option.
7    Aging option is disabled.
```

 TIP Remember that password aging does not follow your system clock's time zone but is calculated from Greenwich Mean Time (GMT).

Part
II

Ch
10

From Here...

You have now learned how to add and delete users and groups to and from your systems. The real trick in managing user access to your system is in how you set up default user attributes and file permissions (see Chapter 5, "Files, Directories, and Permissions"). There are a few things I want you to get out of this chapter.

1. Keep your UIDs and GID numbers between 200 and 60,000. This reduces upgrade hassles and keeps UNIX output neat and readable.

2. Learn the default values for adding users and the process for modifying them to your environment.

3. Automate the process of working with adding and deleting users. This allows you to pass this burden off to a junior level administrator and free you up for the real system problems.

Your first line of defense against destructive use of your computer systems is in how you control user access. By planning and setting system defaults, you control exactly what a user can and cannot do on your system.

■ Chapter 2, "Logging In," assists you with following the path a user goes through when logging in and executing startup files.

■ Chapter 3, "UNIX Shells and System Commands," provides information on the UNIX shells and how they work.

■ Chapter 4, "vi editor," discusses the basic editor. When you are setting up a user's environment, you will use it.

■ Chapter 5, "Files, Directories, and Permissions," provides you with the capability to control user access to resources on your computer systems.

■ Chapter 7, "Essential Shell Scripting," shows you how to write a script like the previous sample "adduser script."

■ Chapter 8, "Advanced Shell Scripting," builds on Chapter 7.

■ Chapter 26, "Security," assists you with setting login defaults.

## CHAPTER 11

Startup and Shutdown

by Bill Wood

In this chapter

The UNIX Startup Process

The UNIX startup process often requires alteration as new applications and programs become available on the system. This chapter details the entire startup process, allowing the reader to modify and troubleshoot the system. The UNIX shutdown process is equally important because the administrator must go through proper channels to ensure data integrity, a content user community, and proper termination of system processes.

You need to understand the startup and shutdown processes to begin troubleshooting a system failure during these processes. A good knowledge of what the computer is doing during these processes enables you to go straight to the problem when it occurs. After I learned the processes, I was much more comfortable during a crisis and was able to reassure users that the system was back online and okay.

The three types of system startups or boots are as follows:

■ Hard disk boot   A machine is started for normal operations by finding a locally installed hard disk with a boot partition on it, loading this, and then passing control to the UNIX kernel. From this point forward on the system, this hard disk is generally referred to as the root disk because it has all of the UNIX operating system on it.

■ Diskless network boot   A diskless workstation does not have a root drive and must get its kernel remotely over a network. One or more remote file servers are designated as boot servers and provide the files and programs that a diskless workstation needs to boot. These files are then stored in RAM instead of on a hard disk. Diskless network clients have no local file systems and get all their information by way of this network remote access.

■ Single-User/maintenance boot   A machine is started or restarted from a hard disk, network, tape, or CD-ROM and placed into the single-user mode. This condition is also called maintenance mode. In maintenance mode, you can perform tasks such as installing new or updated software and running diagnostic checks.

Shutting down a UNIX system is a lot like flying an airplane—takeoffs are optional; landings are mandatory. How you choose to shut down a running operating system determines whether you land or crash. UNIX systems should be shut down in an orderly manner. Whenever a system is up and running in multiuser mode or single-user mode, it is always working, so keep these things in mind as you plan a shutdown:

■ A number of background processes and daemons are always running.

■ An active system usually has a number of open files. These can be files used by an individual or by the system itself.

■ Your system is probably running an application or database. It's possible for these to have open files that would be corrupted if not shut down properly.

■ The UNIX file systems do not write changes to the disks immediately on request, so at any given moment the file systems do not reflect the actual contents on a disk. Updates to the disks are stored in memory and written at later times to improve the efficiency of access to the disks.

Should you decide that your shutdown method is to just turn off the power or press the reset button, you run the risk of damaging your files and directories beyond the hope of manual repair. This is never the recommended way to shut down an operating system and should only be done in extreme circumstances.

Now for the good news: Stopping and starting a UNIX system is the easiest task a system administrator has to do. The bad news is that it can be the most difficult thing to troubleshoot if you don't know what the computer is doing during the startup and shutdown processes. You have to gain a considerable understanding of all the hardware system processes and the system configuration files being activated during these steps to figure out where it went wrong. And that is where this chapter is going to help you the most.

The UNIX Boot Process

All systems come with some intelligence built into their computer chips. Whenever you turn a unit on, it executes vendor code to ensure that its components are functioning correctly. Special chips in the system hold the code in nonvolatile memory for execution during the initial power-on phase. Vendors refer to this kind of memory as ROM (Read Only Memory) or NVRAM (nonvolatile random access memory); however, you the most common user term is *firmware*. Firmware is basically a program that your vendor has included to allow its systems to verify themselves. Firmware is basic, machine dependent, and designed only to discover the hardware devices installed with the system and then find the bootable media. After the bootable media (remember the three boot phases from earlier?) are found, the bootstrap is initiated, and control is then passed to it.

After the firmware has executed and confirmed that the system is ready to continue, it then passes control to the bootstrap program. Generally, you always boot from a disk. This is normally referred to as your boot device and usually is the first disk seen by your computer system. After firmware has located the "root" disk or the bootable disk and passed control to the bootstrap, its job is finished. The bootstrap has only one job, and that is to load the kernel into RAM and pass the device listing found earlier to it. When the bootstrap is finished loading the kernel in memory, it relinquishes control of the boot process to it, and the bootstrap's job is finished.

The kernel queries the hardware, checking for all its memory and ensuring that all peripheral devices function correctly.

➤ **See** "The UNIX Kernel," **p. 20**

Remember, the NVRAM phase just checks whether the devices are there; the kernel ensures that the devices can actually function by performing additional hardware checking. When the kernel is satisfied with those checks, it starts up system services based on the system configuration files and the computer's requested run level. When the kernel has completed starting all processes, it then grants access to users for login. There is one unique thing about the kernel from the bootstrap and the firmware; it stays in memory and executes user requests for processes until you shut down the system, whereas the bootstrap and firmware turn over control to the next phase and stop executing.

Part

II

Ch

11

The three phases of the boot process are as follows:

- Phase 1   Firmware executes and checks basic system functionality.
- Phase 2   Firmware turns over control to the bootstrap to load the kernel.
- Phase 3   The kernel takes control of the system and brings it to a user-defined run level.

NOTE After the kernel is finished executing, it will fork and create another process, the init process. So the kernel then becomes process ID 0, and the init process is assigned process ID 1. On some systems, the process ID 0 is not listed, and on other systems, when process ID 0 is listed, it is referred to as the daemon. ▨

➤ **See** "Process" **p. 132**

➤ **See** "Process Creation" **p. 134**

Following is a sample process status listing from a Solaris 2.4 system; you can see that process 0 is the sched process.

```
UID    PID  PPID  C    STIME TTY    TIME COMD
root     0     0 80    Feb 21 ?     0:01 sched
root     1     0 80    Feb 21 ?     7:02 /etc/init -s
root     2     0 80    Feb 21 ?     0:05 pageout
root     3     0 80    Feb 21 ?   940:33 fsflush
root   259     1 75    Feb 21 ?     0:01 /usr/lib/saf/sac -t 300
root   209   200 22    Feb 21 ?     0:00 lpNet
root    87     1 80    Feb 21 ?     2:59 /usr/sbin/rpcbind
root   136     1 80    Feb 21 ?     0:07 /usr/sbin/inetd -s
root    89     1  1    Feb 21 ?     0:00 /usr/sbin/keyserv
root   113     1 47    Feb 21 ?     0:00 /usr/lib/netsvc/yp/ypbind
root   109     1 80    Feb 21 ?     6:39 /usr/lib/netsvc/yp/ypserv -d
root   121     1 80    Feb 21 ?     2:15 /usr/lib/netsvc/yp/ypxfrd
root   111   109 70    Feb 21 ?     0:01 rpc.nisd_resolv -F -C 8 -p 107374
root   128     1 26    Feb 21 ?     0:00 /usr/sbin/kerbd
root   126     1 80    Feb 21 ?     3:08 /usr/lib/netsvc/yp/rpc.yppasswdd
root   139     1 80    Feb 21 ?     0:01 /usr/lib/nfs/statd
root   141     1 80    Feb 21 ?     0:03 /usr/lib/nfs/lockd
—More—
```

Run Levels

After the kernel has loaded into memory, it executes the init daemon process to move the system from a powered down state to a user-definable run level. Run levels determine what resources are made available and how the computer system is to behave in your environment. The resources for each run level are governed by the /etc/inittab file, which the init daemon uses to determine a run level definition. Generally, the init daemon executes scripts defined by the /etc/inittab file for each run level. After the kernel has determined that all systems devices are ready, subsystems are then activated by the init daemon as it moves through each run level until coming to the assigned default multiuser mode or run level.

There is also a new twist added to the run levels by having four additional ones named by letters of the alphabet for a total of ten run levels and four additional run states. These run states do not represent distinct system run levels but rather function as ways of getting the init daemon to perform certain tasks on demand. For example, run state q or Q tells init to reread its configuration files, starting with the /etc/inittab. The run states a, b, and c exist to allow you to define other inittab actions without having to actually change a run level (see Table 11.1).

Table 11.1 Run Level Definitions

Run Level	Description
0	Powerdown state.
1 or S	Single-user state.
2	Multiuser mode: The normal operating state for isolated, non-networked systems, nonserver systems, depending on the version of UNIX.
3	Remote file sharing state: defined as the normal operating state for server systems on networks that share their local resources with other systems.
4	Administrator-definable system state: a currently unused run level, which can be set up and defined locally.
5	Firmware state: used for some types of maintenance activities, running diagnostics, and booting from an alternative disk.
6	Shutdown and reboot state: used to reboot the system from some running state. Moving to this state causes the system to be taken down (to run level 0) and then immediately rebooted back to its normal operating state.
a,b,c	When the init command requests a change to run state a, b, or c, it does not kill processes at the current run level; it simply starts any processes assigned with the new run states.
q or Q	Instructs the init daemon process to reread and execute the inittab file.

N O T E Run level 5 generally powers down a computer system for you after it halts the operating system. This is a good run level to remember if you ever have to remotely log in to a computer system to shut it down. ■

AIX has added additional numeric run levels instead of just the seven listed previously, as shown in Table 11.2. AIX has a total of ten states identified by alphabet charaters, a, b, c, and q/Q. The run states a, b, and c allow you to define other inittab actions without having to actually change a run level. This can be helpful because when the init command changes to run levels 0-9 in the AIX world, it kills all processes at the current run level and then restarts all processes at the current run level and then restarts all processes associated with the new run levels. See where having these four run states could come in handy? This allows you to start a process on demand through the `init` program without restarting your system.

Table 11.2 AIX Run Level Descriptions

Run Level	Description
0–1	Reserved for the future use of the operating system.
2	Default run level.
3–9	Can be defined according to the user's preferences.
a,b,c	When the `init` command requests a change to run state a, b, or c, it does not kill processes at the current run level; it simply starts any processes assigned with the new run states.
q or Q	Instructs the `init` daemon process to reread and execute the `/etc/inittab` file.

N O T E When you execute the shutdown command from any of the run levels in AIX (not run states), the system powers itself down. This requires you to manually press the power switch or reset switch on the physical unit itself. ▪

Boot Phases

Three distinct phases take place whenever you start up or "boot" a UNIX system (see Figure 11.1). The first two phases are generally user transparent and are not shown on the console computer screen, unless you take special steps to see them. The first test that any computer system conducts from the lowly PCs to big multiuser ones is a power on self-test. This is how the computer determines that all systems are "available." It doesn't check to see whether the systems function; it just makes sure that they are there. These tests are developed by the vendor and vary from platform to platform; consult your guide for further information on the self-tests.

The next thing a computer system does is "pull itself up by its bootstraps" (as many people like to say). The computer must load the kernel into memory before it can boot up; but, if it's not in memory, how can it boot up? This is where the bootstrap program comes into play. It is just smart enough to find the kernel, pass it the device listings from phase I, and load it into memory.

➤ **See** "The UNIX Operating System," **p. 19**

After the kernel is loaded into memory, you start to see information about the boot process displayed on the console computer screen. Now that the kernel is available, it starts the process of defining a run level and activating all resources for you. After the kernel has passed execution off to the system, you are now in a usable state and are presented with the login prompt.

The three boot phases are as follows:

- Phase 1 POST is a set of boot PROM resident firmware programs that run independently of the UNIX operating system.

- Phase 2 Conducts a probe across the system to detect all the peripherals that make up the computer system's resources.

- Phase 3 Activates the console port and sends all messages to the screen for the rest of the boot process. This phase also conducts further tests on the peripherals to determine whether they are "working" versus just "there."

The *init* Process

When you do a process listing, you always see process number as the init process. The init daemon is responsible for the process of moving the computer system between run levels. When init is first activated by starting a system up, it scans the /etc/inittab file for the boot and bootwait entries for execution. These actions define what run level init is to bring the system to and must be performed before any other entries are processed. After init has determined the default run level, it begins to process each entry in the /etc/inittab file for execution at the default run level. As each process is executed, init forks a child process for it; this is why processes on your system have the parent process ID of 1. After all entries are processed, init waits for a run level change, a child process to die, or a power failure. When one of these conditions occurs, init then reexamines the /etc/inittab file.

Entries can be added or modified in your /etc/inittab file at any time; however, init still waits for one of the preceding three conditions to occur before reexamining /etc/inittab. To manually make the init daemon reexamine the /etc/inittab file, you can use the command init Q, which makes it process the /etc/inittab immediately.

➤ **See** "Text Editing Using vi," **p. 187**

How init handles its three conditions:

Part II · Ch 11

- Run level change request When a run level change request is made, init sends the warning signal (SIGTERM) to all processes that are undefined in the target run level. The init process then waits five seconds before forcibly terminating these processes by sending a kill signal (SIGKILL).

- Child process of init dies When init receives the signal telling it that a process it spawned has died, it records the facts and the reason it died in /var/adm/utmp and /var/adm/wtmp, if it exists. A history of the processes spawned is kept in /var/adm/wtmp.

- init receives a power failure signal When init receives a powerfail signal (SIGPWR) it reexamines the /etc/inittab for special entries with the action of powerfail and/or powerwait. These entries are invoked before any further processing takes place. In this way, init can perform various cleanup and recording functions during the powerdown of the operating system.

FIGURE 11.1

A breakdown of the three-phase boot process.

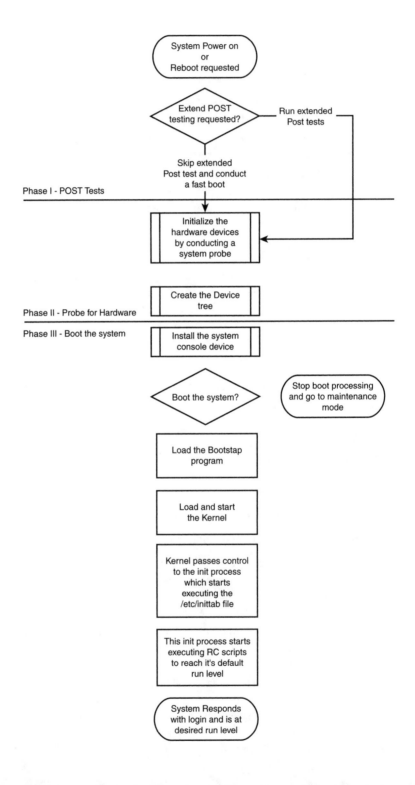

N O T E When init receives a request to enter single-user mode, the terminal that requested this mode becomes the system console. Single-user mode is the only run level that doesn't require the existence of a properly formatted /etc/inittab file (or one at all) for the init daemon to examine. When your system is booted into single-user mode, file systems for the users are not mounted, and only the essential kernel processes are activated. When the init command receives the signal to go to single-user mode, all mounted file systems remain mounted, and all processes started by init that should only be running in multiuser mode are killed. In addition, any process that has a /var/adm/utmp entry is killed. This last condition ensures that all port monitors are killed, and all services spawned by them, including ttymon login services. Other processes not started directly by init remain running; for example, cron remains running. ▩

The *inittab* File

The first two lines identify scripts that are run before init tries to enter any run level (this is specified with the sysinit action). The next four lines are some of those used to control the definitions of the run levels. Note that all of the script's I/O must be redirected to the console if the operator is to see the output and respond to any queries.

➤ **See** "Pipes, I/O Redirection, and Filters," **p. 65**

The line that has the initdefault action in it specifies that the default run level for this machine is run level 3. Whenever the init daemon reads the /etc/inittab file, it looks for the line with the initdefault action and brings the system to the run level indicated.

The /etc/inittab file format is as follows:

```
identifier:Run Level:Action:Command
```

In some cases, you might need to add, change, list, and remove records in the /etc/inittab file. The /etc/inittab file defines which processes to start at each run level. When you run the init command, it reads the records in the /etc/inittab file. Each record consists of one line, defines a run level for the specific process, and contains only four parameters. The four parameters and their associated keywords or defined attributes are as follows:

- ▩ Identifier   Identifies unique objects in 1–14 characters. The identifier is a unique, case-sensitive label identifying each entry. Many systems limit its length to four characters, but a few allow labels of up to 14 characters.

- ▩ Run level   Defines the run levels in which the object can be processed in 1–20 characters. Run level is a list of run levels to which the entry applies; if run levels is blank, the entry applies to all of them.

- ▩ Action   Defines what action the init command should take for this process. The following actions can be specified:

  - ● respawn   Start the process and automatically restart it when it dies.
  - ● wait   Start the process and wait for it to finish before going on to the next entry for this run state.
  - ● once   Start the process if it's not already running but don't wait for it to finish before continuing.

- `boot` Only execute entry at boot time but don't wait for it to finish.
- `bootwait` Only execute entry at boot time and wait for it to finish.
- `powerfail` Executed when the system receives a `powerfailure` signal.
- `powerwait` Executed when the system receives a `powerfailure` signal but waits for execution to finish.
- `off` If the process associated with this entry is running, kill it. Also used to comment out unused terminal lines.
- `ondemand` Like `respawn` but used only with run levels a, b, and c.
- `initdefault` Specify the default run level; must be the first line and have only one run level listed.
- `sysinit` Used for activities that need to be performed before `init` tries to access the system console.

▓ Command Contains the `shell` command to be executed.

N O T E If you have subsequent entries with duplicate labels, the `init` daemon only executes the first one in the `/etc/inittab` file; all other entries are ignored. ▓

SCO UNIX:

▓ `smmck:` Run before the system enters single-user mode; it checks the security-related databases and notes any missing or problem files. If such exist, the system administrator may have to restore them before the system proceedd to multiuser mode.

▓ `authckrc:` Multiuser security check script that verifies that any deficiencies found during the earlier phase have been corrected. It also performs integrity checks on some of the database files themselves.

▓ `asktimerc:` Prompts user for the current time, continuing automatically after a 30-second timeout.

▓ `scologin:` Initializes SCO UNIX's graphical login manager.

AIX is the only system that has designed programs to modify the `/etc/inittab` file without having to use `vi`. The following commands are what AIX gives you for modifying the records in the `/etc/inittab` file:

▓ `chitab` Changes records in the `/etc/inittab` file.
▓ `lsitab` Lists records in the `/etc/inittab` file.
▓ `mkitab` Adds records to the `/etc/inittab` file.
▓ `rmitab` Removes records from the `/etc/inittab` file.

These are sample `/etc/inittab` files; some lines have been removed for clarity and briefness. Your actual files will be much larger than these. I have also added comments to each line so that you can get a feel for what the `/etc/inittab` entries are used for.

Sample Solaris /etc/inittab file:

```
is:3:initdefault:                                        # default run level 3
p3:s1234:powerfail:/usr/sbin/shutdown -y -i5 -g0 >/dev/console 2>&1
                                                         # powerfailure
➥shutdown to
                                                          # maintenance run
➥level 5
s0:0:wait:/sbin/rc0  >/dev/console 2>&1 </dev/console     # execute during run
➥level 0
s1:1:wait:/usr/sbin/shutdown -y -iS -g0 >/dev/console 2>&1 </dev/console
                                                         # When requested run
➥level 1
                                                         # reboot into single
➥user mode
s2:23:wait:/sbin/rc2 >/dev/console 2>&1 </dev/console     # execute during run
➥level 2 & 3
s3:3:wait:/sbin/rc3  >/dev/console 2>&1 </dev/console     # execute during run
➥level 3
s5:5:wait:/sbin/rc5  >/dev/console 2>&1 </dev/console     # execute during run
➥level 5
s6:6:wait:/sbin/rc6  >/dev/console 2>&1 </dev/console     # execute during run
➥level 6
sc:234:respawn:/usr/lib/saf/sac -t 300                    # execute system
➥accounting ****
co:234:respawn:/usr/lib/saf/ttymon -g -h -p "`uname -n` console login: " -T sun
-d /dev/console -l console -m ldterm,ttcompat             # start the console
➥port
```

Sample AIX /etc/inittab file:

```
init:2:initdefault:                                      # default run level 2
brc::sysinit:/sbin/rc.boot 3 >/dev/console 2>&1          # Phase 3 of system
➥boot
powerfail::powerfail:/etc/rc.powerfail 2>&1 ¦ alog -tboot > /dev/console # Power
➥Failure Detection
rc:2:wait:/etc/rc 2>&1 ¦ alog -tboot > /dev/console       # Multi-User checks
srcmstr:2:respawn:/usr/sbin/srcmstr                      # System Resource
➥Controller
rctcpip:2:wait:/etc/rc.tcpip > /dev/console 2>&1         # Start TCP/IP
➥daemons
rcnfs:2:wait:/etc/rc.nfs > /dev/console 2>&1             # Start NFS Daemons
rcx25:2:wait:/etc/rc.net.x25 > /dev/console 2>&1         # Load X.25
➥translation table
cron:2:respawn:/usr/sbin/cron                            # Start the crontab
➥daemon
piobe:2:wait:/usr/lib/lpd/pio/etc/pioinit >/dev/null 2>&1 # pb cleanup
qdaemon:2:wait:/usr/bin/startsrc -sqdaemon               # Print job schedular
uprintfd:2:respawn:/usr/sbin/uprintfd                    # Kernel message
➥handler
logsymp:2:once:/usr/lib/ras/logsymptom                   # for system dumps
cfgmceh:2:once:/usr/lib/methods/cfgmceh >/dev/console 2>&1 # Configure Machine
➥Check Error Handler
dt:2:wait:/etc/rc.dt                                     # starts the
➥Xterminal server
```

Part

II

Ch

11

```
cons:0123456789:respawn:/usr/sbin/getty /dev/console      # starts the console
➥port
tty0:2:off:/usr/sbin/getty /dev/tty0                      # removes unused
➥terminal line
tty1:2:off:/usr/sbin/getty /dev/tty1                      # removes unused
➥terminal line
```

Sample HP/UX `/etc/inittab` file:

```
init:4:initdefault:                                       # default run level
➥4
ioin::sysinit:/sbin/ioinitrc >/dev/console 2>&1           #
tape::sysinit:/sbin/mtinit > /dev/console 2>&1            #
stty::sysinit:/sbin/stty 9600 clocal icanon echo opost onlcr ixon icrnl ignpar <
➥/dev/systty
                                                          #
brc1::bootwait:/sbin/bcheckrc </dev/console >/dev/console 2>&1
                                                          # fsck, etc.
cprt::bootwait:/sbin/cat /etc/copyright >/dev/syscon      # legal req
sqnc::wait:/sbin/rc </dev/console >/dev/console 2>&1      # system init
cons:123456:respawn:/usr/sbin/getty console              # system console
vue :4:respawn:/usr/vue/bin/vuerc                         # VUE invocation
ShPr::respawn:/opt/sharedprint/bin/spserver              #
a0:4:respawn:/usr/lbin/uucp/uugetty -r -t60 -h ttyd0p0 19200 #
```

Run Control Scripts

When the init daemon is activated and it reads the `/etc/inittab` file, it executes run control scripts that will program what services are available at each run level. These scripts are commonly referred to as RC shell scripts and can usually be found in the `/etc` directory or the `/sbin` directory.

➤ **See** "Working with Files and Directories," **p. 60**

Run control scripts are executed during the boot process and are called as each run level is accessed. When you see a file that begins with rc followed by a number, that is the run control script for that run level.

The run control script's primary function is to execute the scripts required to start services for the selected run level. These scripts are generally located in a directory structure under `/etc/ rc#.d`, where # equals the run level. For example, when a system is booted, the init daemon reads the `/etc/inittab` file, which tells it to execute `/etc/rc0`, then `/etc/rc1`, then `/etc/rc2`, and then stop after the running of `/etc/rc3` because the default run level is 3. Now if you were to tell the system to reboot to run level 2, it would execute `/etc/rc6`, then `/etc/rc0`, then `/etc/rc1`, and then stop after running `/etc/rc2`, which is the new default run level.

N O T E   AIX is completely different at this point. It controls the run levels and what rc scripts are executed by the `/etc/inittab` file only. Instead of `/etc/rc2.d` being executed for run level 2, the `/etc/inittab` file indicates the need to execute a single script in the `/etc` directory. For example, to start networking services, AIX executes the `/etc/rc.net` run control script—more on this later. Just remember that when you see an `rc.{}` script in the `/etc` directory in AIX, you can bet it's a run control script. ■

TIP When tracing a run level for AIX, check the /etc/inittab file. This is the only place that shows you what gets called first when changing run levels.

init typically executes a script named rcn when entering run level *n* (rc2 for state 2, for example). Although the boot process to each system state is controlled by the associated rc script, the actual commands to be executed are stored in a series of files in the directory /etc/rcn.d. Thus, when the system enters state 0, init runs rc0 (as directed in the inittab file), which in turn runs the scripts in rc0.d.

NOTE On HP/UX systems, all run control scripts and directories are stored in the /sbin directory. HP/UX follows the same layout here, but remember to replace the /etc directory listing with /sbin. ■

Following are some things that the rc scripts do when your system is booting:

- Set the name and IP address of the computer
- Set the time zone
- Check the file systems with FSCK
- Mount the file systems
- Remove files from the /tmp directory
- Configure network interfaces
- Start up daemons and network services
- Start up your applications

Run Control Directories

The run control scripts are kept in the /etc directory, and the scripts for each run level are kept in a special directory called /etc/rc#/rc#.d. Where the # sign equals the run level just like its corresponding run control script. There is one run control directory per run level. Inside this directory are the scripts that will start and stop services pertaining to that single run level. For example, when the init daemon is told to execute the /etc/rc3 run control script, rc3 executes the files in the /etc/rc3.d directory only. Each directory /etc/rcN.d contains all the startup and shutdown scripts associated with that particular run level N. The rc scripts are designed to be passed the argument start or stop depending on which one you want it to do. When you call a script with start, the script starts the service in question, and when called with stop, the script kills the service. By utilizing this, you have the capability to program functions to start or stop at specific points in the boot or shutdown sequence.

There is a possible total of seven run control directories although not all will be present. That depends on whether you have customized your environment. The directories are as follows:

- /etc/rc0.d   Scripts for halting the system
- /etc/rc1.d   Scripts for single-user mode or maintenance mode
- /etc/rc2.d   Scripts to enter the multiuser mode

Part
II

Ch
11

- `/etc/rc3.d` Scripts to start the remote file sharing multiuser mode
- `/etc/rc4.d` Scripts to enter system maintenance mode by vendor
- `/etc/rc5.d` Not used—user-definable
- `/etc/rc6.d` Scripts for rebooting the system

NOTE The HP/UX operating system follows this format of run control directories, but the run control scripts and directories are in the `/sbin` directory rather than `/etc`.

AIX on the other hand follows the format of all run control scripts being in the `/etc/rc.{}` variety. This means that there are no `rc#.d` directories only `/etc/rc.{}` files.

Start and Kill Scripts

We have discussed how the `rc` scripts execute scripts in the `rc` directory for that run level. This section covers those scripts and how they are executed. These scripts have the name of start and kill scripts because they will start with either an S or K. The S tells the run control script to "start" this process, and the K tells it to "kill" this process. When the `rc` script calls an S file it passes the parameter `start` to it as an argument; when the K file is executed, the parameter `stop` is passed in as its argument.

➤ **See** "Control Structures," **p. 166**

These files are executed in an alphanumeric order, with the K files running first and the S files running second.

To control the startup and shutdown process, the start and kill scripts must be able to execute in a certain order each and every time. To achieve this, all filenames begin with either S or K, followed by a two-digit number, and they all end with a descriptive process name. The `rcn` scripts execute the K files in numeric order, followed by the S files in numeric order. The only rule to ensure this works is that all numbers must be the same length (for example, 01, 02, 45, 67, 99).

An example format of a run control script filename is as follows:

`S##xxxxx or K##xxxxx`

I have included a listing of the `/etc/rc2.d` directory showing the run control scripts in real-time format and in order executed. As you can see, the K scripts are executed first and then the S scripts are executed. Following is an example listing of the `rc2.d` run level directory:

```
K20lp
K22acct
K25snmpd
K60nfs.server
K65nfs.client
K85xntp
K92volmgt
S01MOUNTFSYS
S05RMTMPFILES
S20sysetup
```

```
S21perf
S22acct
S30sysid.net
S69inet
S70uucp
S71rpc
S71sysid.sys
S71yp
S72autoinstall
S72inetsvc
S73nfs.client
S74autofs
S74syslog
S75cron
S80PRESERVE
S80lp
S85xntp
S88sendmail
S88utmpd
S90hpnpd
S92volmgt
S95SUNWmd.sync
S99audit
```

N O T E   As you have probably noticed, some scripts in this listing have duplicate numbers. When this is encountered, the scripts are then executed with the process name in alphabetic order. Hence, S80PRESERVE executes before S80lp because capital letters come before lowercase ones.

If README files are located in the rc#.d directories, they will contain a guideline for selecting sequence numbers for any S or K scripts. If there are not any README files in the directory, then you are free to choose whatever sequence you deem appropriate. ▪

The */etc/init.d* directory

The /etc/init.d directory contains initialization and termination scripts for handling processes on the system. I like to think of this directory as the human readable directory of start and kill scripts. You use these scripts to pass the start or stop parameter for a process on your system.

➤ See "Variables," **p. 159**

These scripts will use the appropriate files in the rc#.d directories to start or kill a process. Using these scripts helps you by reducing the amount of time you spend searching for a certain S or K script to execute.

Each script in the /etc/init.d directory has a case statement that will accept the arguments start or stop. Assume that you were to execute the file /etc/init.d/networker with the parameter start (/etc/init.d/networker start) to initiate the networker program. When you execute this script with the argument start, the case statement links to the /etc/rc2.d/ S90networker, or to the /etc/rc0.d/K90networker if you were to pass it stop.

Part

II

Ch

11

A sample `/etc/init.d` directory from Solaris 2.4 follows:

```
ANNOUNCE      autoinstall    inetsvc       rpc             syslog.orig
MOUNTFSYS     buildmnttab    lp            sendmail        ufs_quota
PRESERVE      cron           mkdtab        standardmounts  utmpd
README        devlinks       networker     sysetup         volmgt
RMTMPFILES    drvconfig      nfs.client    sysetup.orig    yp
acct          esmrc          nfs.server    sysid.net       yp.orig
audit         hpnpd          perf          sysid.sys
autofs        inetinit       rootusr       syslog
```

HP does not have the `/etc/init.d` directory. Instead, it has all of its run control scripts under the `/etc/rc.config.d` directory system. You use these scripts just like you would use ones from the `/etc/init.d` directory on other systems. You manually call the script you want to activate and pass it the `start` or `stop` parameter, depending on what you want to do.

For example:

```
/etc/rc.config.d/mailservs stop
```

HP `/etc/rc.config.d`

```
LANG          auditing       dfs           mailservs       nfsconf         swcluster
SnmpHpunix    clean          hparray       namesvrs        ptydaemon       swconfig
SnmpMaster    clean_tmps     hpetherconf   ncs             savecore        syncer
SnmpMib2      clean_uucp     i4lmd         netconf         set_date        vt
acct          cron           list_mode     netdaemons      spa             xfs
audio         dce            lp            nettl           supprtinfo
```

AIX does not have an `/etc/init.d` directory concept at all. Instead, it has all its run control scripts under the `/etc` directory starting with `rc`. You use these scripts just like you would use scripts from the `/etc/init.d` directory on other systems. You manually call the `rc` (run control) script you want to activate and pass it the `start` or `stop` parameter, depending on what you want to do—although AIX prefers for you to use the `startsrc` and `stopsrc` commands for turning on and off subsystem processes.

> **CAUTION**
>
> If you do not use the `startsrc` and `stopsrc` commands, you run the risk of starting or stopping more processes than you want by manually executing a run control script. AIX uses the run control script to combine many start and stop features into one file. Passing the `start` or `stop` parameter to one of these files will affect more than one process.

➤ **See** "Variables," **p. 159**

Example:

```
/etc/rc.tcpip start
```

Better option:

```
startsrc -s tcpip
```

The `/etc/rc*` directory file listings for an AIX system:

```
/etc/rc            /etc/rc.net         /etc/rc.ntp        /etc/rc.tcpip
/etc/rc.adsmhsm    /etc/rc.net.serial  /etc/rc.ntp.old
/etc/rc.bsdnet     /etc/rc.net.x25     /etc/rc.powerfail
/etc/rc.dt         /etc/rc.netls       /etc/rc.sap
/etc/rc.ncs        /etc/rc.nfs         /etc/rc.sp
```

Changing Run Levels

At any given time, you might have to change run levels on your computer system, especially to perform system maintenance. UNIX allows you to change your run level (see Figure 11.2) without having to modify the `/etc/inittab` default run level entry and then reboot. UNIX allows you to use the `init` command to change between run levels, without the need to shut down and restart in a new run level. By using the `init` command, after you have finished performing necessary system administration tasks, you can change back to any multiuser mode without having to cycle power on your equipment.

You are required to change run levels whenever you have created new run levels or changed which processes will be run at a certain level. Modifying a predefined run level by adding a new entry or changing an existing entry in `/etc/inittab` also forces the need to change a run level. Remember the `/etc/inittab` file defines how you want the system to operate when in, or at, a specific run level.

System administrators always find creative ways to use the startup/shutdown process to control their environments. In most cases, you will be adding system and company specific applications and standards. When adding an application such as a database, you are required to add a `start` and `kill` script to a run level for it. By knowing how the computer is changing levels, you can modify your run levels (see Figure 11.2) and test them without having to wait for a reboot cycle each time you make a change.

Verifying Run Level

An interesting thing happened as I was writing this. I had a system that was not running quite right. For some reason, the Xserver environment was locking up, and the process table did not have everything running in it. After beating my head against this, I verified the run level, and sure enough, I was in the wrong level. I then used the `init` command to move the system up one level. This saved me half an hour for a reboot, and the users were back on the system in a few minutes. I should ask for my pay raise now.

➤ **See** "UNIX Windowing Systems," **p. 197**

Anytime you have to verify the run level that your computer system is at, use the `who -r` UNIX command. This command shows you the current and previous run levels and also shows you the date and time that the system's run level was last changed.

Example:

```
$who -r
.   run level 2   Dec 12 18:30   2   0   3 <- previous run level
```

Part

II

Ch

11

FIGURE 11.2

System process for changing from run level 2 to run level 3.

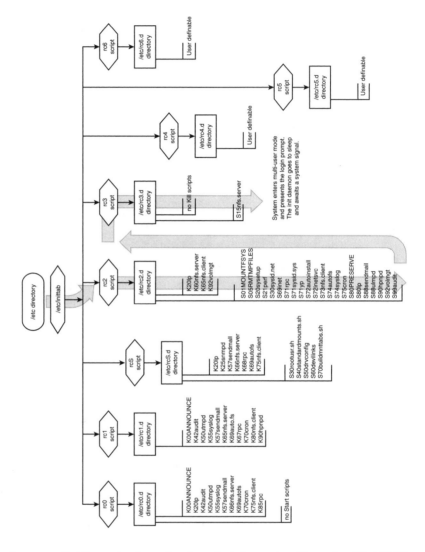

This example shows you that the system's run level was last changed on December 12 at 18:30 or 6:30pm. It also shows you that the previous run level was 3, and the current run level is 2.

AIX lets you see additional information about your system state changes. You can display a history of previous run levels using the `fwtmp` command. This shows you when a run level was changed.

To display the history of previous run levels, enter the following command:

```
/usr/lib/acct/fwtmp </var/adm/wtmp |grep run-level
```

Sample output follows:

```
run-level 2    1    0 0062 0123    883774309    Fri Jan  2 15:51:49 EST 1998
run-level 3    1    0 0062 0123    884708001    Tue Jan 13 11:13:21 EST 1998
run-level 2    1    0 0062 0123    884787851    Wed Jan 14 09:24:11 EST 1998
run-level 2    1    0 0062 0123    886520063    Tue Feb  3 10:34:23 EST 1998
run-level 3    1    0 0062 0123    887144595    Tue Feb 10 16:03:15 EST 1998
run-level 2    1    0 0062 0123    888430365    Wed Feb 25 13:12:45 EST 1998
run-level S    1    0 0062 0123    896285500    Wed May 27 11:11:40 EST 1998
run-level 3    1    0 0062 0123    896394524    Thu May 28 17:28:44 EST 1998
run-level 2    1    0 0062 0123    900623303    Thu Jul 16 16:08:23 EST 1998
run-level 2    1    0 0062 0123    900627411    Thu Jul 16 17:16:51 EST 1998
run-level 0    1    0 0060 0062    900684639    Fri Jul 17 09:10:39 EST 1998
run-level 2    1    0 0062 0123    900698247    Fri Jul 17 12:57:27 EST 1998
```

The *init* Command

When you must change run levels on a system that is already up and running, you use the `init` command. Instead of changing the `/etc/inittab` `initdefault` entry and then rebooting the system, you can use the `init` command to move from one run level to another. When the `init` command is given a new run level, it reads the `/etc/inittab` file and executes all run control scripts for that particular run level.

Command synopsis:

```
init  0 ¦ 1 ¦ 2 ¦ 3 ¦ 4 ¦ 5 ¦ 6 ¦ a ¦ b ¦ c ¦ Q ¦ S
```

> **N O T E** You may use either `init` or `telinit` to change the run level of the system. The command `telinit` is linked to the `init` command and uses the same command format as `init`. What to watch out for is if the `/etc/inittab` file does not exist, the system only boots to single-user mode. ■

The Shutdown Process

When it becomes time for you to shut down your system, you really only have three options: shutdown, power off, or reboot. The shutdown process allows the computer system to sync its file systems and buffers and gracefully shut down services in an orderly manner, versus just throwing the power switch. There are several controlled situations in which you might want to shut down your system:

- ■ After installing new software (for example, patches, applications, and run level scripts)
- ■ After changing the configuration of existing software
- ■ When a hardware problem exists
- ■ When the system is irrevocably hung
- ■ When system performance is degraded
- ■ When the file system is possibly corrupt

All UNIX systems use the `shutdown` command to bring the operating system down gracefully. Only the user with root Superuser authority should be allowed to run this command. When using the default shutdown, all users on the system are notified (by the wall command) to log off because of the impending system shutdown. The shutdown process first kicks all users off by killing their processes before continuing with stopping system services. After it has removed all users from the system, it then starts to execute the kill scripts from the /etc/ inittab file and run level 0. During this process, any attempt to restart or turn off the system results in file system corruption or damage.

N O T E The halt completed message is displayed on the console terminal. If you start shutdown from a remote location, it is not displayed on the remote terminal. Always run the shutdown commands from the console terminal. It is designed to receive all error messages and to show that the system is truly in a down state for you. ■

You can give the system a number of options when you use the shutdown command. The nicest thing you can do is give a short length of time for users to log off before the shutdown actually starts. The default is 60 seconds, but, I prefer to give my users 5 minutes before kicking them off, when I can. Table 11.3 shows the different formats for the shutdown command on different operating systems.

Table 11.3   Shutdown Options for Various Operating Systems

UNIX	Pathname	Time	Reboot	Halt
AIX	/usr/sbin/shutdown	+(# of mins)	-r	-v
Solaris	/usr/sbin/shutdown	-g(# of secs)	-i6	-i0
SunOS	/usr/etc/shutdown	+(# of mins)	-r	-h
HP/UX	/etc/shutdown	(# of secs)	-r	-h

SunOS shutdown example:

```
/usr/sbin/shutdown -g300 -i0
```

After the specified number of seconds, 300 seconds equal 5 minutes, the system stops the accounting and error logging processes and writes an entry to /var/adm/messages. The shutdown command then runs the kill scripts for run level 0 thus killing any remaining processes (see Figure 11.3). Next, to ensure that all pending updates to the file systems have been written, it runs the sync command flushing all memory-resident disk blocks; it unmounts the file systems. The last thing it does is call the halt command to bring the system gracefully into a shutdown mode.

 T I P You can see startup and shutdown messages last displayed on the console system on AIX units with the dmesg command.

FIGURE 11.3

The process of shutdown as it goes through the run levels in /etc.

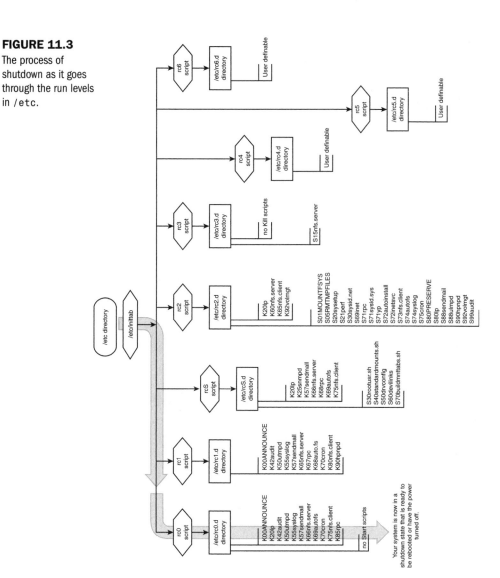

CAUTION

Some system administrators use the `halt` command to bring down a system when no users are on it. The `halt` command performs the essential duties required to bring down the system. This command is called by `shutdown` but can also be used by itself to halt logs, kill nonessential processes, and halt the kernel. Keep in mind that if you use `halt` rather than `shutdown`, you run the risk of conducting a nongraceful shutdown. If you use `halt -q`, you will instigate an almost immediate system halt, without synchronization, killing of processes, or writing of logs. Why on earth you would want to do this, I don't know. You might as well just turn off the power switch—it's just as good.

The last option that you can give the shutdown command is an option to reboot or boot to a new run level. When shutdown is executed with this option, it performs an orderly shutdown and then starts the boot process for you automatically. The only difference between the boot process and the reboot process is that the start and kill scripts in run level 6 are used during a reboot (see Figures 11.3 and 11.4). I have included a figure (see Figure 11.4) that shows the path the system takes during a shutdown cycle with a reboot requested.

Troubleshooting the Boot and Startup Process

This is the time when your job as a system administrator becomes the most difficult. You have a system that won't boot into multiuser mode. What do you do? Don't worry; believe it or not, the computer is going to try to help you figure out what is wrong. You just have to know where to start. Your system will fail during one of the three phases discussed earlier: phase 1—POST testing, phase 2—Bootstrap, and phase 3—conducting a boot to multiuser mode.

Some problems that could cause your system not to boot are as follows:

- Hardware problems
- Damaged file systems
- Improperly configured kernel
- Errors in the run control scripts

Phase I—POST Test Boot Errors—Hardware Problems

Whenever the computer cannot pass the POST testing, you have a hardware problem. Most systems will try and tell you what is failing by displaying information to the console port, LED sequences, or like AIX systems, a three-digit LED display. You must check all these to see what the computer is trying to tell you might be wrong. If you still cannot determine what is wrong from system diagnostics, here are a few steps to try:

- Start with the basics. Check all power supplies. Are all power cords plugged into the sockets, both ends, all the way? I've been bitten by this one before.
- Check the status lights on all equipment; be sure to include the peripherals. Do all system components show power, and do their status lights indicate no problems?
- Check all the cables to make sure that each one is tight and secure. I have had a problem with a node on an RS6000 system in which the cable was not screwed in. It was connected but not tight, and the node kept rebooting. I did not find this error until I physically checked each cable, so don't just look and say it's okay—check.
- When you've checked all the preceding items and nothing seems wrong, power down all the computer equipment. Wait about a minute and then power up all the peripherals first. Wait for the peripherals to come online and then power up the CPU itself last.

When you have checked everything that you can and the system will still not boot, it's time to call your service representative. Be sure to inform him of each step you have accomplished and what you have already tried. Also let him know about any diagnostics that the system is showing; this could help him solve the problem over the phone, or at least bring the right part on the first visit.

FIGURE 11.4

Reboot process path during a shutdown request.

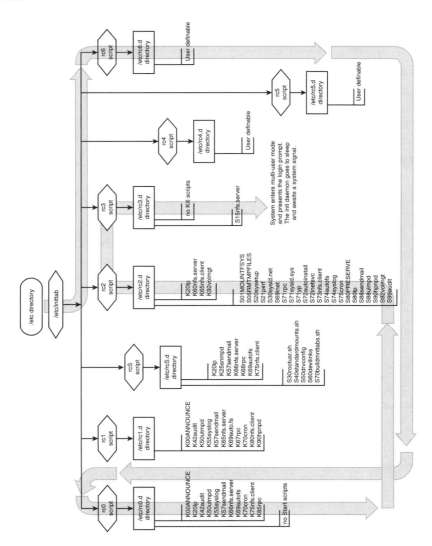

Phase II—Bootstrap Errors

After the POST test is complete, control is passed to the PROM level to find the bootable media and load the bootstrap program. The firmware (NVRAM) then reads into memory a bootable file system that contains the kernel, thus passing control to the kernel. Only a few things can go wrong at this level in the boot process.

■ The firmware could be damaged and not be able to load the bootstrap program, although normally the POST test finds this problem.

Part

II

Ch

11

■ The bootstrap program cannot find the bootable media on the hard drive. This can be caused by a corrupt disk or file system. Try booting from the installation disk and rebuilding the boot blocks on the boot drive.

Phase III—Conducting the Boot to Multiuser Mode

Now we have come to the last phase in the boot process. This is the stage where if things are going to go wrong, they will. You should have a good understanding now of the boot process and what the computer is doing at each step in it. This is a big help when the computer hangs while booting.

One of the easiest ways to troubleshoot a hung boot process is to follow the run levels. Whenever I have a hung system, I first boot to single-user mode, or run level 1. Because this is the first run level and doesn't really start anything, it is easy to run diagnostics from this level and almost always is guaranteed to start. After I am in run level 1, I try using the `init` command and switching to run level 2. If this works, I go to run level 3. Somewhere during this process the system will hang, and then I will know what run level to start doing diagnostics on.

For example, say that the system hangs during run level 2. I would then restart to single-user mode and run diagnostics again if I have an idea what failed. Now here is something most people won't think to do. Remember earlier we discussed that all the system is doing when changing run levels is executing scripts for each level. You can execute those scripts manually to change run levels. That's what I do. When in run level 1, I start executing the scripts to get to run level 2 one at a time, just like the system would. Finally, I get to the single script that is causing the system to hang. I reboot to single-user mode, and analize the script to see why it is hanging. Nine times out of ten someone changed something.

TIP All the scripts to boot your system are simple shell scripts. This means that you can follow the shell routines during a boot process and find the single command that is causing your system to hang. After you have found this, you can edit the script to bypass the problem or fix the problem. This allows the computer to finish the boot process. Remember this important rule: If you can edit the code, you own the code. So be careful what you do to the run control scripts and always make a backup.

Table 11.4 lists commands that are helpful when troubleshooting a system that is not responding correctly. These commands should be part of any system administrator's tool bag when working on UNIX. You can tell a good system administrator from a bad one by just asking whether he or she knows how to use some of these commands.

Table 11.4 System Administrator Troubleshooting Commands

Command Tool	Usage
adb	Analyze dumps on a running system
crash	Analyze crash dumps
diff	Compare file contents
dmesg	Analyze recent log messages

Command Tool	Usage
eeprom	Analyze and change boot PROM settings
file	Determine a file's type
find	Look for specific files in the file systems
format	Analyze or modify disk partition information
grep	Analyze file contents, look for specific patterns
ifconfig	Analyze the status of network interfaces
kadb	Analyze trap and low-level faults
ls	Analyze file properties
modinfo	Lists modules loaded into a kernel
pkgchk	Check file integrity and accuracy of installation
prtconf -v	Get system device information from POST probe
ps	Analyze properties of running processes
strings	Analyze object and binary files for ASCII strings
sysdef	Analyze device and software configuration information
truss	Trace system calls used by a process

From Here...

You have now gone through the entire boot and shutdown processes. You should now be able to boot a system, know which phase it is in, and watch it change through its run levels. The boot process is always the scariest for junior system administrators, but learning what the system is doing and how can eliminate those fears. The most important thing for you to get from this is that the computer is running scripts for you (the init daemon), and you have control over those scripts. You control when they are executed (run levels) and how they are executed (start and kill scripts and the inittab file).

When you have problem, and it's not hardware, you can bet it is just a script that is hanging your system. Now that you know how to manually run the computer one step at a time to bring it into multiuser mode, you can step through the process and find that one command that is hanging your system. When troubleshooting, you can also use the same technique to find the exact location in code where the computer system is hanging.

- Chapter 1, "UNIX Environment Overview," provides information on the UNIX kernel and how it relates to the operating system.

- Chapter 3, "UNIX Shells and System Commands," provides information on the UNIX shells and how they work.

- Chapter 6, "UNIX Processes," provides information on how UNIX creates a process and the life cycle of the processes.

- Chapter 7, "Essential Shell Scripting," provides directions on how the best shell scripts work.

Part
II

Ch
11

Device Management

by Gordon Marler

What Is Device Management?

Device management can be defined as the process you have to go through to add, remove, or change the behavior of a piece of hardware in your UNIX computer. To make such changes to your system, you need to understand the following concepts:

- What kinds of hardware you can physically connect to your particular computer and how that connection is made.
- Whether your flavor of UNIX already has a *device driver* that supports the hardware you want to add, or whether you need to install one that the vendor provides for you.
- What features of the hardware you can turn on or off by communicating with its device driver.

Here are some scenarios where such information will be invaluable to you:

- You've run out of hard disk space, and you want to install that new 18GB SCSI hard drive you just bought to give you more space.
- Your network interface is capable of operating at 10 or 100 Mbps. You want to force it to operate at 100 Mpbs at all times.
- You need to upgrade from a single tape drive on your backup server to a multidrive tape jukebox to more efficiently handle your backup needs.

This chapter helps you get a feel for how UNIX handles device interaction. It also examines some troubleshooting techniques and offers a few device management tips.

Device Files

The UNIX kernel allows direct access to most devices in the system through a special kind of file known as a device file. These are not files in the normal sense because they don't contain data and don't really have any size. But they are convenient in that they allow UNIX system programmers to refer to devices by filename instead of forcing you to know the exact memory location of every device in the system. Any requests passed to these files are transparently sent on to the proper device driver in the kernel.

In short, UNIX tries to allow you to access *anything* in the system through some kind of file, whether it be a simple file, a directory (yes, a directory is really a file), or a device.

▶ **See** "Device Files," **p. 121**

As you already know from Chapter 5, device files come in two flavors: character and block. The character flavor allows you to send or fetch data from a device one character (or byte) at a time. The block flavor allows you to send or fetch data from a device one block at a time. Usually a block is about 512 bytes but can vary between UNIX flavors. Block device files are used when you want to transfer large chunks of data with the device. Most disk and tape devices have both character and block device files, whereas serial ports (which you use to talk with terminals and modems) usually only have character device files.

If you look at a long listing of a device file, you'll notice that it is marked as a character (c) or a block (b) file by the first letter in the permissions field. It also has two comma-separated numbers in the place you would normally see the size of a regular file (in this example 32, 0):

```
brw-r-----   1 root     sys     32,  0 Apr 30  1996 sd@0,0:a
crw-r-----   1 root     sys     32,  0 Sep  1  1997 sd@0,0:a,raw
```

The comma-separated numbers are known as the *major* and *minor* device numbers. The major number refers to the device driver that the kernel uses when talking to this device. The minor number refers to the location of this particular device in the system; it can also be used to activate or deactivate certain features of a device. Because the major and minor numbers of the preceding device files are the same, they must refer to the exact same device, with the first device file referring to the device in block mode, and the other referring to the device in character mode. From this discussion, you can see that it is possible to have many different names for the same device.

Device files are created on a UNIX system in a couple of different ways, depending on the flavor you have. On older BSD and System V derived UNIX systems, you have to create each device file manually using the mknod command. On BSD systems, you are usually given a script, /dev/MAKEDEV, which creates all the device files for any device you specify. You might have to read this script to see what arguments you need to call it with, or you might have to edit it to support your device if it is extremely unusual. On newer System V releases, you can use the add_drv command, which actually scans the device configuration files and creates the device files you need.

Most of the device drivers you will ever need are already configured in your UNIX kernel. However, you may purchase a device that has added features not available when your UNIX kernel was compiled. The vendor of that device needs to provide you with the necessary driver module and instructions on how to insert that driver into your UNIX kernel and create the device files you will need. Always verify that any third-party vendor actually supports your version of UNIX before purchasing its products.

CAUTION

A danger with adding or upgrading a driver is a system *panic*, which is when the kernel itself crashes due to an event that should never happen. This usually occurs because some piece of hardware in your computer is going bad. However, because drivers are actually part of the kernel, they have total access to it and the rest of the machine. If a driver has a bug in it, it might try to modify memory contents that the kernel wasn't expecting to change. If you experience this, unload the driver and report the problem to the driver vendor.

Part
II

Ch
12

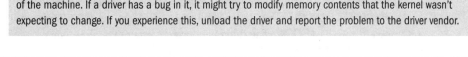

Most modern flavors of UNIX support a form of loadable device driver that you can activate or deactivate without rebooting your computer. Instead of forcing you to recompile the kernel itself, this facility allows you to load and unload the device driver into the kernel on-the-fly. This allows you to attach the new piece of hardware you want to use, turn on the computer, and then activate the device driver whenever you want. It's most useful when you want to upgrade the driver to get new features. You just unload it from the kernel, load the new one, and you never had to reboot.

▶ **See** "The UNIX Kernel," **p. 20**

Hard Disks and CD-ROMs

Almost all hard disks and CD-ROMs on UNIX today are SCSI (Small Computer Systems Interface) devices. A few old machines around still use IPI (Intelligent Peripheral Interface) or SMD (Storage Module Disk) disks, but they are increasingly rare. This chapter considers SCSI only.

First, we should discuss the different types of SCSI interfaces available so that you'll know what you've got when you see it. The problem you will encounter in practice is that products are usually simply referred to as "SCSI," so you have to know what SCSI features you're looking for when you're examining a product.

- SCSI-1 was the original standard, with transfer speeds of 3–5MB per second. You don't see many of these anymore.

- SCSI-2 was the next step, improving the cables and connectors. This variation is also known as Slow Narrow SCSI-2, to differentiate it from later Fast Wide SCSI-2.

- Wide SCSI-2 uses a wider cable and allows you to pump twice as much data through the interface as Narrow SCSI-2. This gives you a maximum transfer rate of 10MB per second. It also increases the number of devices you could attach to the bus from 7 to 15.

- Fast SCSI-2 doubles the speed of the plain SCSI-2 bus to give you a transfer rate of 10MB per second. You'll normally never see a SCSI interface that's just Fast or just Wide. They are usually combined to produce Fast Wide SCSI-2, which gives you a 20MB per second transfer rate and access to 15 devices on the SCSI bus.

- SCSI-3 is the next enhancement to the standard and is not completely accepted as of this writing. It is to increase the number of devices you can access on the bus from 15 to 32, provide error correction, and use the same cable as Wide SCSI-2.

- Ultra SCSI is a subset of the proposed SCSI-3 standard that actually exists today. It is sometimes referred to as SCSI FAST-20. It doubles the speed of Fast SCSI-2 to give you speeds of 20MB per second using the same cables as Fast Narrow SCSI-2.

- Ultra Wide SCSI has the same characteristics as Ultra SCSI except for the wider cable, which is the same as that used by Fast Wide SCSI-2. This wider data path gives you transfer rates of 40MB per second.

- Another variation you might see on Fast Wide SCSI-2 and Ultra SCSI interfaces is differential SCSI. The purpose of differential SCSI is to allow longer cable lengths. The length of each SCSI chain can now be up to 25 meters instead of the 3 meters you are limited to with Fast SCSI-2. The thing you have to remember about this variation is that it is electrically different from all other forms of SCSI. Differential and single-ended (nondifferential) devices cannot be mixed on the same SCSI bus, even if they use the same kind of cables, without some kind of electrical converter. The terminator for a differential SCSI bus is also different from that for a nondifferential bus. If a terminator is not clearly marked as differential, it's not.

CAUTION

Because the voltages and currents for differential and single-ended SCSI devices are different, you run the risk of burning up your host adapter or hard disks if you try to connect a differential host adapter to single-ended drives, or vice versa.

Be *very* sure what every type of device is on any SCSI chain before you power them up. This includes terminators!

Now a word about SCSI cables and their connectors. Narrow (Slow/Fast) SCSI-2 cables usually have the 50-pin male-to-male connectors shown in Figure 12.1. Wide (Slow/Fast) SCSI-2, differential, and Ultra SCSI cables usually have the 68-pin male-to-male connectors shown in Figure 12.2. If you are using nondifferential drives, you have to make the total length of your SCSI chain as short as possible; you are limited to 3 meters. This does not mean that the cables for any type of Wide SCSI are different from those for differential SCSI, they just need to be shorter. In practice, it's better to get the highest quality cables you can because they have better shielding. Anything marked SCSI-3 should be suitable for any drives that are Wide, Ultra, or differential SCSI, but not mixed on the same bus, of course.

SCSI disks are each assigned a SCSI ID and an LUN (logical unit number) so that they have a unique identity on the SCSI bus. Most vendors only assign LUN 0 for each SCSI ID, ignoring LUNs 1–7, which means that you can only have as many disks as you have SCSI IDs, as shown in Figure 12.1, 7 for Narrow SCSI, and 15 for Wide. However, you can manually adjust your drives to use LUNs 0–7 for each SCSI ID, giving you many more devices per bus, as shown in Figure 12.1. You may have to configure the kernel to recognize these drives with LUNs 1–7 however. The SCSI controller (also known as a SCSI host adapter) also uses up a SCSI ID, usually 7, although your vendor may provide a way to change this if you want. Most vendors also assign a standard SCSI ID for CD-ROM drives, usually 6.

Figure 12.1 shows how SCSI devices are arranged on the SCSI bus, assuming that you are using LUNs 0–7 for each SCSI ID.

FIGURE 12.1

Using all the LUNs for each SCSI target ID.

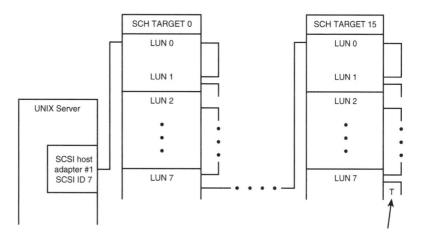

Part
II

Ch
12

Figure 12.2 shows what kind of cabling you'll have to use to attach drives of different wide-ness and differential-ness to the same SCSI bus.

FIGURE 12.2

Using all SCSI types on a single SCSI bus.

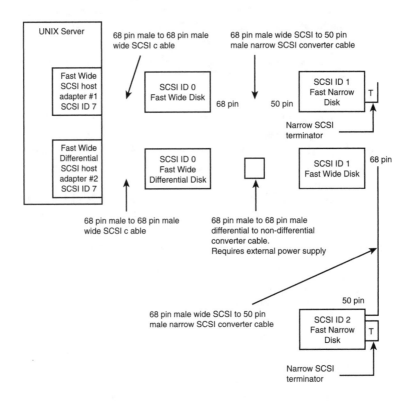

Tape Devices

Almost all tape drives on UNIX are also SCSI devices and follow the same installation principles that SCSI hard drives do. The difference is that there are several types of tape media, and you need to get the tape drive that writes to the medium you want to use. Common media types are QIC-150, also known as Quarter Inch Cartridges, DAT (4 mm), Exabyte 8mm, DLT, and the venerable 9-track half-inch reel-to-reel tapes. In many sites, you'll see a machine set aside with one SCSI tape drive of each type attached to it, so that you can read any of these tape types that a vendor might send you. Today, vendors distribute on any of Exabyte 8mm, 4mm DAT, or QIC-150. Over time, each tape technology has increased the amount of data you can store on a tape by increasing the density of the medium. Therefore, tape drives can often read and write several different densities of tape for backward compatibility. Some drives can even compress data internally just before it is written to the tape. All these capabilities have to be accessible in some way through device files, and each vendor has its own special device file naming convention to clue you into the capabilities that will be turned on if you use that device file. One thing you will want to note is that data compression is usually lumped into the tape density category because it does allow you to put more data on the tape.

Tape drives all have a common set of activities, regardless of the media type, so you can't tell what media type (DAT, 8mm, and so on) you're writing to merely from the name of the device file. And depending on the flavor of UNIX you're running, there may or may not be a mapping between the SCSI ID of the tape drive and the name of the device file that controls it. You'll see a bit later how to be sure which tape device file maps to what tape device. At least you can be sure that the tape device file naming convention is different from the naming convention for all other SCSI devices on a particular UNIX flavor. The following sections discuss what it is on the four flavors of UNIX we're considering in this chapter.

SunOS 4.x   See the st(4S) man page for a full discussion of all the device filenames for all tape drives and all tape densities. The short description is that there are four groups of device files that autorewind the tape after you've accessed it, and four groups of device files that don't rewind the tape after you've accessed it. Table 12.1 shows what they look like.

Table 12.1   SunOS 4.x SCSI Tape Device Files

Rewinding	Nonrewinding
/dev/rst[0-7]	/dev/nrst[0-7]
/dev/rst[8-15]	/dev/nrst[8-15]
/dev/rst[16-23]	/dev/nrst[16-23]
/dev/rst[24-31]	/dev/nrst[24-31]

Each group of numbers in a column refers to the same drives, just different characteristics of those drives. Thus, /dev/rst0, /dev/rst8, /dev/rst16, and /dev/rst24 all refer to the exact same drive but just access different characteristics of that drive. The differences, in this case, deal mostly with tape densities.

Solaris 2.x   See the st(7D) man page for a full description of all the device filenames for all tape drive types and their characteristics. The Solaris 2.x device filenames for tape drives take the following form:

/dev/rmt/[0- 127][l,m,h,u,c][b][n]

Where [0-127] picks the tape drive itself, [l,m,h,u,c] picks the density of the tape media, [b] picks optional BSD behavior, and [n] picks the nonautomatic rewind of the tape after you've accessed it. Solaris also automatically creates compatibility device files that look like the SunOS 4.x device files, in case you're more familiar with them.

HP/UX 10/11:   See the HP/UX manual "Configuring HP/UX for Peripherals" for a full discussion of this topic. SCSI tape device filenames take the following form:

/dev/rmt/c#t#d#BEST[b¦n¦nb]

Where c# denotes the SCSI host adapter card the device is attached to, t# denotes the SCSI ID (or target), of the tape drive, and d# denotes what HP/UX calls a device number—we call it a LUN. BEST is used to denote the highest density that this drive supports, and [b¦n¦nb] denotes BSD behavior, nonrewinding behavior, and nonrewinding BSD behavior, respectively.

Part

II

Ch

12

AIX 4.x The AIX System Management Guide provides a full discussion of this topic. Tape device filenames take the following form:

```
/dev/rmt[0-15][.X]
```

where 0–15 is the tape drive number, and .x has a special meaning if it is used. Table 12.2 shows all possible permutations for tape drive 0. Auto Rewind, if yes, automatically rewinds the tape after any command you use on it completes. Retention, if yes, runs the tape to the end and then rewinds it before performing any action on the tape. Density is only used if you are writing to the tape. By convention, #1 is usually the highest possible density setting for the tape media, and #2 is the next highest. Not everyone follows this convention, however.

Table 12.2 AIX Tape Drive Device File Permutations

Special file	Auto Rewind?	Retention?	Density
/dev/rmt0	Yes	No	#1
/dev/rmt0.1	No	No	#1
/dev/rmt0.2	Yes	Yes	#1
/dev/rmt0.3	No	Yes	#1
/dev/rmt0.4	Yes	No	#2
/dev/rmt0.5	No	No	#2
/dev/rmt0.6	Yes	Yes	#2
/dev/rmt0.7	No	Yes	#2

Serial Ports/Pseudo Ports

UNIX systems will have at least two serial ports available for you to attach modems, terminals, and other serial devices to. Sometimes you'll find a system that seemingly has only one serial port, such as Sun's SparcStation 20. That system's single serial port is special in that it is wired differently than a regular RS-232 serial port, and you can connect a special Y-cable to it that has two regular RS-232 ports on the end.

Depending on the system you're using, the serial ports on the back of your machine could have 9 pins or 25 pins, and could be male or female connectors. The 9-pin connectors are referred to as DB9[M,F] depending on whether the connector is male or female, respectively, and the 25-pin connectors are referred to as DB25[M,F]—more on this and serial cables in the section, "Terminals and Modems" later in the chapter.

TIP The quality of the built-in serial ports in your UNIX system can be pretty poor and in most cases can only be relied on for speeds up to 38,400 bps, unless your vendor swears otherwise. If you want to use higher speeds, it might be best to get a third-party serial port expansion device and install it. These devices can give speeds up to 128,000 bps per port.

Another special type of device available in UNIX is known as a "pseudo" port. In the distant past, you would normally have a single large UNIX server, and everyone would have a character terminal on his or her desk to access the server through. This meant that the server would need as many serial ports as there were terminals, and each serial port would need a UNIX device file to reference that particular port (and thus, the character terminal) through. In our current day of graphical user interfaces, however, each user can run multiple instances of programs such as xterm, each one of which emulates a single old character terminal. UNIX needs a way to reference each of these xterms uniquely, just as it used to reference each character terminal uniquely. This is done through the pseudo ports, or pseudo ttys. Anyone logging in to the UNIX machine via the network using programs such as telnet or rlogin rather than through a modem or terminal directly connected to the machine's serial ports will also use up a pseudo tty.

TIP A certain number of pseudo ports are already configured into your UNIX kernel, so you won't have to worry about them unless you run out. If this happens, see your OS documentation to find out how to increase the number of pseudo ttys to support your needs. Just knowing that you *can* increase the number of pseudo ports is half the battle.

Other Peripherals

Other peripherals you might have to configure for your workstation/server are discussed in the following sections.

Tape and CD-ROM Jukeboxes   To keep an online catalog of large amounts of data, you might need to have a tape or CD-ROM jukebox, which can have one or multiple drives, a large number of slots to store media in, and some sort of robotic device to move media between the slots and the drives. The drives themselves will show up as normal tape or CD-ROM drives, but you'll usually have to load a special device driver to control the robotics in the jukebox. There isn't anything special about these setups as far as UNIX is concerned. Everything shows up as a SCSI device.

Unusual SCSI Devices   SCSI was meant to control pretty much any device, not just hard drives. So if you use your machine to develop hardware or software, you may run into hardware emulators or debuggers that plug into your SCSI bus, using SCSI to transfer data to and from UNIX. Again, these look like regular SCSI devices to UNIX. Just don't try formatting them.

Part
II

Ch
12

Adding Hard Disk Devices

Adding a hard disk to your system consists of the following general steps:

1. Determine whether you can attach the disk to an already existing disk bus, or install a new host adapter to attach the disk to.

2. Determine where on the disk bus the hard disk can appear and configure the hard disk appropriately.

3. Cable and terminate the disk bus properly.

4. Verify that the system hardware can see the new disk device.

5. Create a partition table for the disk.

6. Create file system(s) on the disk and mount it.

Because each flavor of UNIX handles the addition of peripherals slightly differently, we will be considering these steps for SunOS 4.x, SPARC Solaris 2.x, HP/UX 10/11, and AIX.

 Unlike a lot of other UNIX flavors, Sun doesn't provide a way to easily see the host adapters and SCSI devices connected to the system from inside UNIX. You normally have to shut down the operating system and use the OpenBoot PROM monitor to perform a `probe-scsi-all`. This gives you a listing of all the host adapters in the system and all the devices attached to each one. However, a utility is available that probes the SCSI buses and provides reports that are even more informative than the `probe-scsi-all` command. It's called `scsiinfo` and can be found at the following URL: **ftp:// ftp.cdf.toronto.edu/pub/scsiinfo/**. You'll find precompiled binaries there for most versions of SunOS 4.x and Solaris 2.x. Using the -p option to the command gives you output similar to what you would have received from the `probe-scsi-all` command. On Solaris 2.x, you will have to temporarily deactivate the `vold` program if you want `scsiinfo` to be able to query your CD-ROM drives.

To attach your new hard disk, you need to follow the preceding steps 1–3 for your particular flavor of UNIX.

For step 1, you'll need to determine whether you have a host adapter in your machine that matches the kind of drive you're going to attach. If you have a differential SCSI drive and a regular SCSI host adapter in your machine, you're going to have to install a differential host adapter in your machine before you even begin. After you've verified that you have the proper host adapter, you can move on to the OS specific steps.

SunOS 4.x

You need to see what SCSI host adapters are available in the system, and which SCSI IDs are free for you to use on each one.

1. Run `scsiinfo -p`. You'll get output that looks similar to the following:

```
# scsiinfo -p
esp0: sd0 tgt 3 lun 0:
        Synchronous(10.0MB/sec) Clean CanReconnect
        Non-removable Disk:     SEAGATE   ST32430W SUN2.1G 0508        [ST]
esp1: sd6 tgt 2 lun 0:
        Synchronous(10.0MB/sec) Clean CanReconnect
        Non-removable Disk:     SEAGATE   ST15230N SUN4.2G 0702        [ST]
esp1: sd5 tgt 1 lun 0:
        Synchronous(10.0MB/sec) Clean CanReconnect
        Non-removable Disk:     SEAGATE   ST15230N SUN4.2G 0702        [ST]
esp1: sd4 tgt 3 lun 0:
        Synchronous(10.0MB/sec) Clean CanReconnect
        Non-removable Disk:     SEAGATE   ST15230N SUN4.2G 0702        [ST]
```

From this, you can see that there are two SCSI host adapters: the host adapter on the motherboard (esp0) and an additional host adapter (esp1). Host adapter esp0 reports that only SCSI ID 3 (tgt 3), LUN 0 is taken. Of course the host adapter takes SCSI ID 7 for itself. Host adapter esp1 reports that SCSI IDs (tgt) 1, 2, and 3 are taken; the host adapter takes SCSI ID 7 for itself. Note that scsiinfo doesn't list the targets in numerical order, not that it matters.

For this example, you want to add a 4.2GB SEAGATE disk just like the ones already attached to esp1.

2. So we have SCSI IDs 0, 4, 5, and 6 free. We'll use 0. Following the disk manufacturer's instructions, we set the SCSI ID of the drive to 0. This may involve rotating a dial on the back of the drive enclosure, or actually taking the drive out and changing jumper settings on it, depending on where you got the drive from.

3. As root, shutdown the system by running shutdown now. Then power off the system. Because this disk is narrow and fast SCSI, just like the host adapter, you need a 50-pin to 50-pin narrow SCSI-2 cable. Remove the terminator from the last disk in the current SCSI chain hanging off of esp1, plug one end of the new cable where the terminator was, and then plug the other end of the cable into one of the ports on the back of the new disk. Then put the terminator in the remaining port on the new disk. Power up the disks first and then turn on the power to the machine. SunOS usually creates all the device files you'll ever need for the first four host adapters you'll plug into the system, so you won't have to create device files in this instance. If you ever do need to create more disk devices, you can read the man page for MAKEDEV.

Solaris 2.x

You need to see what SCSI host adapters are available in the system and which SCSI IDs are free for you to use on each one—but first a word about the host adapters you're going to see here. esp is the name for Narrow Fast SCSI-2 host adapters. fas is the name for Fast Wide SCSI-2 host adapters. Another one, isp, is used to denote Fast Wide Differential and Ultra Wide Differential host adapters. Other names may become common in future.

1. Run scsiinfo -p. You'll get output that looks similar to the following:

```
# scsiinfo -p
esp0: sd0,0 tgt 0 lun 0:
        Synchronous(10.0MB/sec) Clean CanReconnect
        Non-removable Disk:      SEAGATE  ST32550N SUN2.1G 0416      [SLT]
esp0: sd1,0 tgt 1 lun 0:
        Synchronous(10.0MB/sec) Clean CanReconnect
        Non-removable Disk:      SEAGATE  ST32550N SUN2.1G 0414      [SLT]
esp0: sd2,0 tgt 2 lun 0:
        Synchronous(10.0MB/sec) Clean CanReconnect
        Non-removable Disk:      SEAGATE  ST32550N SUN2.1G 0416      [SLT]
esp0: sd3,0 tgt 3 lun 0:
        Synchronous(10.0MB/sec) Clean CanReconnect
        Non-removable Disk:      SEAGATE  ST32550N SUN2.1G 0416      [SLT]
esp0: sd4,0 tgt 4 lun 0:
        Synchronous(10.0MB/sec) Clean CanReconnect
```

Part
II

Ch
12

```
          Non-removable Disk:     SEAGATE  ST32550N SUN2.1G 0416          [SLT]
esp0: sd5,0 tgt 5 lun 0:
          Synchronous(10.0MB/sec) Clean CanReconnect
          Non-removable Disk:     SEAGATE  ST32550N SUN2.1G 0416          [SLT]
fas0: sd0,0 tgt 0 lun 0:
          Synchronous(2.667MB/sec) Clean NoTaggedQueuing Narrow
          Non-removable Disk:     SEAGATE  ST32550W SUN2.1G 0414          [SLT]
fas0: sd1,0 tgt 1 lun 0:
          Synchronous(10.0MB/sec) Clean NoTaggedQueuing Narrow
          Non-removable Disk:     SEAGATE  ST32550W SUN2.1G 0416          [SLT]
fas0: sd6,0 tgt 6 lun 0:
          Asynchronous Clean NoTaggedQueuing Narrow
          Removable CD-ROM:       TOSHIBA  XM-5401TASUN4XCD 2565         [ASL]
```

In this particular machine, the `fas0` host adapter is on the motherboard, and `esp0` is an additional host adapter. Note that the drive with SCSI ID 0 (`tgt 0`) already attached to the host adapter `fas0` is marked with the `Narrow` keyword. This means that the drive that is already there is a Narrow SCSI drive being attached to a Wide host adapter. If you examine the cable between `fas0` and this drive, you'll either see that it is a 68-pin (wide) to 50-pin (narrow) SCSI cable, or that it is a 68-pin to 68-pin cable, and the drive connector itself converts to Narrow SCSI inside the disk enclosure. In this case, it turns out that the cable is a 68-pin to 50-pin Wide to Narrow SCSI converter cable. We want to add another 2.1GB SCSI disk drive to the SCSI chain attached to the `fas0` host adapter.

2. SCSI IDs 1–6 and 8–15 are available on this host adapter, but because you already have a narrow drive attached to the host adapter, you are restricted to using SCSI IDs 1–6. So let's pick 1. Following the disk manufacturer's instructions, set the SCSI ID of the drive to 1. This may involve rotating a dial on the back of the drive enclosure, or actually taking the drive out and changing jumper settings on it, depending on where you got the drive.

3. Shut down UNIX and turn off the power to the machine by running `init 5` as root. Because you are connecting to an already narrow SCSI chain and the drive you are adding is also narrow, you need a 50-pin to 50-pin narrow SCSI cable. Remove the terminator from the last drive in the current SCSI chain and attach one end of the cable to that port. Attach the other end of the cable to the new drive and put the terminator on the remaining port of the new drive. Power up the drives and then the system. Before the kernel gets a chance to come up, hold down the `Stop` and `A` keys at the same time on the keyboard. This takes you to the `OpenBoot` PROM monitor, and you should see an `ok` prompt. Type the following:

```
boot -r
```

This causes the kernel to scan all the devices in the system and automatically create any device files you might need to access this drive.

HP/UX 10/11

You need to see what SCSI host adapters are available in the system and which SCSI IDs are free for you to use on each one. You can use the `ioscan` utility on HP/UX to tell you about the devices present in the system, including SCSI ones.

1. Run `/usr/sbin/ioscan -k`. Your output will look like this:

```
# /usr/sbin/ioscan -k
H/W Path    Class            Description
=========================================
56/52            ext_bus           HP 28655A - SCSI Interface
56/52.1          target
56/52.1.0            disk       HP C2247M1 - SCSI Disk
56/52.2          target
56/52.2.0            disk       HP C2247M1 - SCSI Disk
56/52.7          target
56/52.7.0              ctl          Initiator
```

From this output, you can tell that the HP 28655A SCSI host adapter is located at hardware path 56/52 on this particular machine, so all devices on that bus will have hardware paths that start with 56/52. For SCSI devices, the hardware path will be deciphered like this: `56/52.X.Y`, where X is the SCSI ID (or target), and Y is the SCSI LUN. So on this machine, you have SCSI IDs 1, 2, and 7 taken (the SCSI host adapter takes ID 7; `ioscan` lists it as the SCSI "Initiator"). Only LUN 0 is used for each SCSI ID in this example. You want to add another HP C2247M1 SCSI disk to the bus.

2. From the information you already know, SCSI IDs 0, 3–6, and 8–15 are available for use because this is a Fast Wide SCSI bus. If the bus were Narrow, you would only be able to use IDs 0 and 3–6. In this case, add the drive as SCSI ID 3, LUN 0. Following the disk manufacturer's instructions, set the SCSI ID of the drive to 3. This may involve rotating a dial on the back of the drive enclosure or actually taking out the drive and changing jumper settings on it, depending on where you got the drive.

3. Shut down HP/UX by running `shutdown -h` and turn off the power to the system. Because this host adapter is Fast Wide SCSI, and so is the new drive, you'll need a 68-pin male to 68-pin male SCSI cable. Remove the terminator from the last drive in the current SCSI chain and plug one end of the cable into the port where the terminator was. Plug the other end of the cable into the new drive and put the terminator on the remaining port on that drive. Power up the drives and then the system. If this had been the first drive attached to the host adapter, you would have had to purchase a Fast Wide SCSI terminator, attach it to a port on the new drive, and then run the cable from the host adapter to the remaining port on the new drive. Turn on all the drives; then turn on the computer. As it boots, HP/UX creates the device files for the new disk automatically.

AIX 4.x

You need to see what SCSI host adapters are available in the system and which SCSI IDs are free for you to use on each one. You can first look on the back of the machine to find the port labeled SCSI if it is present. This shows up as the host adapter on the motherboard. You can also look for extra host adapters marked with numbers that look like 4-X. Each adapter slot is also marked with a number. Table 12.3 gives the possible types of host adapters that you may encounter.

Table 12.3 AIX SCSI Host Adapter Types

Type Number	Interface Type
4–1	Slow Narrow SCSI–2
4–2	Fast Narrow Differential SCSI–2
4–4	Fast Narrow SCSI–2
4–6	Fast Wide Differential SCSI–2
4–7	Fast Wide SCSI–2
4–C	Fast Wide Differential SCSI–2

1. You can now have AIX list the SCSI devices in the system by running `lsdev -C -s scsi -H`. You get output similar to the following:

```
# lsdev -C -s scsi -H
name      status       location       description

hdisk0    Available    00-01-00-0,0   2.1GB SCSI Disk Drive
hdisk1    Available    00-01-00-1,0   2.1GB SCSI Disk Drive
rmt1      Available    00-00-0S-1,0   2.3GB 8mm Tape Drive
```

In the location field, the first four digits (`00-01`) tell you which adapter slot the host adapter is in. In this case, it is in adapter slot 1. If the first six digits are `00-00-0S`, then this is the host adapter built into the motherboard. The seventh and eighth digits are the SCSI IDs and LUNs of each device, respectively. So in this case, `hdisk0` is attached to the host adapter in slot 1, its SCSI ID is 0, and its LUN is 0. `hdisk1` is also attached to the host adapter in slot 1, with SCSI ID 1, and LUN 0. Therefore, on this machine, you have the host adapter in slot 1 with SCSI IDs 0 and 1 taken, and the host adapter on the motherboard with SCSI ID 1 taken.

2. You want to add another 2.1GB disk drive to the SCSI chain attached to the host adapter in slot 1. Look at the back of the machine and see that the host adapter is marked as a type 4–7, a Fast Wide SCSI-2 host adapter. The drive you want to add is also Fast Wide SCSI-2. SCSI IDs 2–6 and 8–15 are available because drives are taking IDs 0 and 1, and the host adapter is taking ID 7 for itself. Let's choose ID 2. Following the disk manufacturer's instructions, set the SCSI ID of the drive to 2. This may involve rotating a dial on the back of the drive enclosure or actually taking out the drive and changing jumper settings on it, depending on where you got the drive.

3. Shut down AIX by running `shutdown -h` and turn off the power to the system. Because the host adapter is Fast Wide SCSI, and so is the new drive, you'll need a 68-pin male to 68-pin male SCSI cable, unless IBM has put one of its proprietary SCSI connectors on the host adapter and drive. In that case, you'll need to purchase the SCSI cable they specify. If you already have a drive with a terminator on this SCSI bus, remove the terminator, and attach one end of the cable to the port where the terminator was. Attach the other end of the cable to the new drive and put the terminator on the remaining port

on the new drive. Turn on the drives; then the computer. AIX creates the necessary device files automatically as it boots up.

Verifying the Presence of the Hard Disk

Even though you've taken all the preceding necessary steps, you still need to verify that the hardware and the operating system can see the new device.

SunOS 4.x

Now that the system is back up, you can run the scsiinfo command again to see whether the new drive shows up:

```
# scsiinfo -p
esp0: sd0 tgt 3 lun 0:
        Synchronous(10.0MB/sec) Clean CanReconnect
        Non-removable Disk:     SEAGATE   ST32430W SUN2.1G 0508        [ST]
esp1: sd7 tgt 0 lun 0:
        Synchronous(10.0MB/sec) Clean CanReconnect
        Non-removable Disk:     SEAGATE   ST15230N SUN4.2G 0702        [ST]
esp1: sd6 tgt 2 lun 0:
        Synchronous(10.0MB/sec) Clean CanReconnect
        Non-removable Disk:     SEAGATE   ST15230N SUN4.2G 0702        [ST]
esp1: sd5 tgt 1 lun 0:
        Synchronous(10.0MB/sec) Clean CanReconnect
        Non-removable Disk:     SEAGATE   ST15230N SUN4.2G 0702        [ST]
esp1: sd4 tgt 3 lun 0:
        Synchronous(10.0MB/sec) Clean CanReconnect
        Non-removable Disk:     SEAGATE   ST15230N SUN4.2G 0702        [ST]
```

From this output, you can see that it's been given a device name of sd7.

Solaris 2.x

Now that the system is back up, you can run the scsiinfo command again to see whether the new drive at SCSI ID 1 on host adapter fas0 shows up:

```
# scsiinfo -p
esp0: sd0,0 tgt 0 lun 0:
        Synchronous(10.0MB/sec) Clean CanReconnect
        Non-removable Disk:     SEAGATE   ST32550N SUN2.1G 0416        [SLT]
esp0: sd1,0 tgt 1 lun 0:
        Synchronous(10.0MB/sec) Clean CanReconnect
        Non-removable Disk:     SEAGATE   ST32550N SUN2.1G 0414        [SLT]
esp0: sd2,0 tgt 2 lun 0:
        Synchronous(10.0MB/sec) Clean CanReconnect
        Non-removable Disk:     SEAGATE   ST32550N SUN2.1G 0416        [SLT]
esp0: sd3,0 tgt 3 lun 0:
        Synchronous(10.0MB/sec) Clean CanReconnect
        Non-removable Disk:     SEAGATE   ST32550N SUN2.1G 0416        [SLT]
esp0: sd4,0 tgt 4 lun 0:
        Synchronous(10.0MB/sec) Clean CanReconnect
        Non-removable Disk:     SEAGATE   ST32550N SUN2.1G 0416        [SLT]
```

Part

II

Ch

12

```
esp0: sd5,0 tgt 5 lun 0:
        Synchronous(10.0MB/sec) Clean CanReconnect
        Non-removable Disk:      SEAGATE  ST32550N SUN2.1G 0416          [SLT]
fas0: sd0,0 tgt 0 lun 0:
        Synchronous(2.667MB/sec) Clean NoTaggedQueuing Narrow
        Non-removable Disk:      SEAGATE  ST32550W SUN2.1G 0414          [SLT]
fas0: sd1,0 tgt 1 lun 0:
        Synchronous(10.0MB/sec) Clean NoTaggedQueuing Narrow
        Non-removable Disk:      SEAGATE  ST32550W SUN2.1G 0416          [SLT]
```

You can see that it does, as the last entry in the scsiinfo output.

HP/UX 10/11

Now that you've brought the system back up, you can run /usr/sbin/ioscan -k again to see whether the new disk at SCSI ID 3 shows up:

```
# /usr/sbin/ioscan -k
H/W Path    Class             Description
==============================================
56/52               ext_bus       HP 28655A - SCSI Interface
56/52.1             target
56/52.1.0             disk      HP C2247M1 - SCSI Disk
56/52.2             target
56/52.2.0             disk      HP C2247M1 - SCSI Disk
56/52.3             target
56/52.3.0             disk      HP C2247M1 - SCSI Disk
56/52.7             target
56/52.7.0              ctl          Initiator
```

From this output, you can see that it does, as the device with hardware path 56/52.3.0.

AIX 4.x

Now that the system has come back up, you can run lsdev -C -s scsi -H again and see what name the system gave to our new drive.

```
# lsdev -C -s scsi -H
name       status      location       description

hdisk0     Available   00-01-00-0,0   320MB SCSI Disk Drive
hdisk1     Available   00-01-00-1,0   320MB SCSI Disk Drive
hdisk2     Available   00-01-00-2,0   320MB SCSI Disk Drive
rmt1       Available   00-00-0S-1,0   2.3GB 8mm Tape Drive
```

From this output, you see that the new drive is called hdisk2.

Configuring the Device

Configuring the device consists of making sure that all the necessary device files exist for the device; then you create or modify the partition table to your liking and create a file system on it.

▶ **See** "Creating File Systems," **p. 330**

SunOS 4.x

1. Run the format command to examine and modify the partition table. You want to use the whole disk as a single file system. On SunOS, partition c of any disk is the entire disk and is used as a standard reference point that you can always look at if you forget exactly how large the disk is. Never change it. Just pick another partition and make it identical in size to partition c because we want to use the whole disk for this example. In this case, make it partition a. After you've changed the partition layout, label the disk and quit the format program.

```
# format
Searching for disks...done

AVAILABLE DISK SELECTIONS:
        0. sd0 at esp0 slave 24
           sd0: <SUN2.1G cyl 2733 alt 2 hd 19 sec 80>
        1. sd4 at esp1 slave 24
           sd4: <SUN4.2G cyl 3880 alt 2 hd 16 sec 135>
        2. sd5 at esp1 slave 8
           sd5: <SUN4.2G cyl 3880 alt 2 hd 16 sec 135>
        3. sd6 at esp1 slave 16
           sd6: <SUN4.2G cyl 3880 alt 2 hd 16 sec 135>
        4. sd7 at esp1 slave 0
           sd7: <SUN4.2G cyl 3880 alt 2 hd 16 sec 135>
Specify disk (enter its number): 4
FORMAT MENU:
        disk       - select a disk
        type       - select (define) a disk type
        partition  - select (define) a partition table
        current    - describe the current disk
        format     - format and analyze the disk
        repair     - repair a defective sector
        show       - translate a disk address
        label      - write label to the disk
        analyze    - surface analysis
        defect     - defect list management
        backup     - search for backup labels
        quit
format> p
PARTITION MENU:
        a      - change 'a' partition
        b      - change 'b' partition
        c      - change 'c' partition
        d      - change 'd' partition
        e      - change 'e' partition
        f      - change 'f' partition
        g      - change 'g' partition
        h      - change 'h' partition
        select - select a predefined table
        name   - name the current table
        print  - display the current table
        label  - write partition map and label to the disk
        quit
partition> p
Current partition table (original sd7):
```

```
          partition a - starting cyl      0, # blocks   4097520 (1897/0/0)
          partition b - starting cyl      0, # blocks         0 (0/0/0)
          partition c - starting cyl      0, # blocks   8380800 (3880/0/0)
          partition d - starting cyl      0, # blocks         0 (0/0/0)
          partition e - starting cyl   1897, # blocks   4097520 (1897/0/0)
          partition f - starting cyl      0, # blocks         0 (0/0/0)
          partition g - starting cyl      0, # blocks         0 (0/0/0)
          partition h - starting cyl      0, # blocks         0 (0/0/0)

partition> a

          partition a - starting cyl      0, # blocks   4097520 (1897/0/0)

Enter new starting cyl [0]:
Enter new # blocks [4097520, 1897/0/0]: 3880/0/0
partition> q

FORMAT MENU:
        disk        - select a disk
        type        - select (define) a disk type
        partition   - select (define) a partition table
        current     - describe the current disk
        format      - format and analyze the disk
        repair      - repair a defective sector
        show        - translate a disk address
        label       - write label to the disk
        analyze     - surface analysis
        defect      - defect list management
        backup      - search for backup labels
        quit
format> label
format> quit
```

2. The device file for each partition of sd7 is going to be `/dev/sd7[a-h]` and `/dev/rsd7`
    `[a-h]`. To create a new file system on partition a of this disk, issue the following com-
    mand:

    ```
    # /usr/etc/newfs /dev/rsd7a
    ```

Solaris 2.x

1. Run the format command to examine and modify the partition table. We want to use the
    whole disk as a single file system. On Solaris, partition (or slice) 2 of any disk is the
    entire disk. Never change it. Just use another partition and make it identical in size to
    partition 2. In this case, make it partition 0. Each disk in the output of format is listed in
    `c#t#d#` format, where `c#` is the controller number dynamically assigned by Solaris, `t#` is
    the SCSI ID number, and `d#` is the SCSI LUN. Because the disk you added was SCSI ID
    1, you only have two options—number 1 and number 3—because they have t1 parts to
    their names. However, you attached the disk to the `fas0` bus, and only number 1 has a
    `fas` part in its name, so pick that one.

    ```
    # format
    AVAILABLE DISK SELECTIONS:
           0. c0t0d0 <SUN2.1G cyl 2733 alt 2 hd 19 sec 80>
              /sbus@1f,0/SUNW,fas@e,8800000/sd@0,0
    ```

```
        1. c0t1d0 <SUN2.1G cyl 2733 alt 2 hd 19 sec 80>
           /sbus@1f,0/SUNW,fas@e,8800000/sd@1,0
        2. c1t0d0 <SUN2.1G cyl 2733 alt 2 hd 19 sec 80>
           /sbus@1f,0/dma@0,81000/esp@0,80000/sd@0,0
        3. c1t1d0 <SUN2.1G cyl 2733 alt 2 hd 19 sec 80>
           /sbus@1f,0/dma@0,81000/esp@0,80000/sd@1,0
        4. c1t2d0 <SUN2.1G cyl 2733 alt 2 hd 19 sec 80>
           /sbus@1f,0/dma@0,81000/esp@0,80000/sd@2,0
        5. c1t3d0 <SUN2.1G cyl 2733 alt 2 hd 19 sec 80>
           /sbus@1f,0/dma@0,81000/esp@0,80000/sd@3,0
        6. c1t4d0 <SUN2.1G cyl 2733 alt 2 hd 19 sec 80>
           /sbus@1f,0/dma@0,81000/esp@0,80000/sd@4,0
        7. c1t5d0 <SUN2.1G cyl 2733 alt 2 hd 19 sec 80>
           /sbus@1f,0/dma@0,81000/esp@0,80000/sd@5,0
Specify disk (enter its number): 1
selecting c0t1d0
[disk formatted]

FORMAT MENU:
        disk       - select a disk
        type       - select (define) a disk type
        partition  - select (define) a partition table
        current    - describe the current disk
        format     - format and analyze the disk
        repair     - repair a defective sector
        label      - write label to the disk
        analyze    - surface analysis
        defect     - defect list management
        backup     - search for backup labels
        verify     - read and display labels
        save       - save new disk/partition definitions
        inquiry    - show vendor, product and revision
        volname    - set 8-character volume name
        quit
format> p
PARTITION MENU:
        0      - change '0' partition
        1      - change '1' partition
        2      - change '2' partition
        3      - change '3' partition
        4      - change '4' partition
        5      - change '5' partition
        6      - change '6' partition
        7      - change '7' partition
        select - select a predefined table
        modify - modify a predefined partition table
        name   - name the current table
        print  - display the current table
        label  - write partition map and label to the disk
        quit
partition> p
Current partition table (SUN2.1G):
Total disk cylinders available: 2733 + 2 (reserved cylinders)

Part    Tag    Flag    Cylinders       Size          Blocks
 0      root    wm      0 -   40      30.43MB    (41/0/0)      62320
```

```
1       swap    wu      41 -  170       96.48MB    (130/0/0)    197600
2       backup  wu       0 - 2732        1.98GB   (2733/0/0)  4154160
3   unassigned  wm       0                    0      (0/0/0)         0
4   unassigned  wm       0                    0      (0/0/0)         0
5   unassigned  wm       0                    0      (0/0/0)         0
6       usr     wm     171 - 2732        1.86GB   (2562/0/0)  3894240
7   unassigned  wm       0                    0      (0/0/0)         0

partition> 0
Part     Tag    Flag   Cylinders        Size          Blocks
  0      root    wm       0 -   40     30.43MB    (41/0/0)       62320

Enter partition id tag[root]:
Enter partition permission flags[wm]:
Enter new starting cyl[0]:
Enter partition size[62320b, 41c, 30.43mb]: 2733c
partition> q
FORMAT MENU:
        disk       - select a disk
        type       - select (define) a disk type
        partition  - select (define) a partition table
        current    - describe the current disk
        format     - format and analyze the disk
        repair     - repair a defective sector
        label      - write label to the disk
        analyze    - surface analysis
        defect     - defect list management
        backup     - search for backup labels
        verify     - read and display labels
        save       - save new disk/partition definitions
        inquiry    - show vendor, product and revision
        volname    - set 8-character volume name
        quit
format> label
format> quit
```

2. The device files for this disk are /dev/[r]dsk/c0t1d0s[0-7]. Create a file system .i.Solaris 2.x:SCSI:configuring devices;.i.SCSI:devices:configuring in Solaris 2.x;.i.configuring:SCSI devices:Solaris 2.x;on partition 0 of the disk.

```
/usr/sbin/newfs /dev/rdsk/c0t1d0s0
```

HP/UX 10/11

1. HP/UX, starting with version 10.00, uses a Logical Volume Manager (LVM) to manage hard disks. The example given here is simple. Read the HP/UX System Administration Tasks Manual, Chapter 3—Managing Disks Using the Logical Volume Manager, for a more complete coverage of this subject. In the example, you added a disk with SCSI ID 3. This shows up as the device files /dev/[r]dsk/c0t3d0. Initialize this disk for use by the volume manager.

```
pvcreate /dev/rdsk/c0t3d0
```

2. Now create a test volume group.

```
mkdir /dev/vg89
```

3. Create a device file named *group* in the directory you just created, using the number 89 that we pulled out of the air in two locations. Everything else in the command will always be the same.

```
mknod /dev/vg89/group c 64 0x890000
```

4. Create a volume group, listing all the disks that will be part of it; in this case, just the one—c0t3d0. Then create the logical volume with the `lvcreate` command. This step creates the device file `/dev/vg89/[r]lvol1`, which allows you to access the disk through the volume manager. The number 1 in `lvol1` is assigned because this is the first logical volume to be created in this volume group.

```
vgcreate /dev/vg89 /dev/dsk/c0t3d0
lvcreate /dev/vg89
```

5. Now create an HFS file system on the logical volume just created.

```
newfs -F hfs /dev/vg89/rlvol1
```

AIX 4.x

Like HP/UX, AIX also uses a volume manager rather than a standard UNIX file system. Again, the example given here is extremely simple. For complete details on handling volumes and file systems on AIX, see the AIX Version 4.X System Management Guide: Operating System and Devices, Chapter 6 —Logical Volumes.

1. Create a volume group to put your logical volume in and associate the new disk, hdisk2, with it. The -y option lets you name this volume group testvg.

```
mkvg -y testvg hdisk2
```

2. Now create a logical volume to put the file system on, using the disks in volume group testvg.

```
mklv testvg 1
```

3. Finally, create a Journaling File System (jfs) on the logical volume, specifying that it will be mounted at /test, and that it will never be automatically mounted at boot time.

```
crfs -A no -g testvg -m /test -v jfs
```

Testing the Device

An adequate test of the new hard drive would be to mount the file system just created on it. If anything is going to go wrong, it should have happened already, but this test will remove all doubt. For each OS, we will mount the disk's file system at /test.

▶ **See** "Mounting and Unmounting File Systems," **p. 336**

SunOS 4.x

```
mkdir /test
mount /dev/sd7a /test
```

Part

II

Ch

12

Solaris 2.x

```
mkdir /test
mount /dev/dsk/c0t3d0s0 /test
```

HP/UX 10/11

```
mkdir /test
mount /dev/vg89/lvol1 /test
```

AIX 4.x

Because we specified the mount point when we created the file system on the volume, the necessary lines were placed in /etc/filesystems. All we have to do is create a mount point and let mount take care of the rest. You might want to edit /etc/filesystems and remove the lines dealing with the /test mount point after this exercise.

```
mkdir /test
mount /test
```

Adding a CD-ROM

Because a CD-ROM drive is a read-only device, there are fewer steps to consider in configuring it than adding a hard disk. Here is the list of general steps to use when adding one of these:

1. Determine whether you can attach the disk to an already existing disk bus, or install a new host adapter to attach the disk to.
2. Determine where on the disk bus you want the hard disk to appear and configure the hard disk appropriately.
3. Cable and terminate the disk bus properly.
4. Verify that the system hardware can see the new disk device.

As before, we will be covering this information as it applies to SunOS 4.x, Solaris 2.x, HP/UX 10/11, and AIX.

 One point you have to remember about CD-ROM drives is that you have no control over how the disks you put in them are partitioned. There are several CD-ROM formats and several ways to partition the CD to write data on it. You either have to have an OS-based utility (such as Solaris's Volume Manager) that automatically examines the partition table on the CD and mounts the proper partition at a predefined location in the file system, or the vendor you received that particular CD from has provide you with instructions on how to manually mount the file system contained on the CD.

SunOS 4.x and Solaris 2.x

1. On SunOS 4.x and Solaris 2.x, SCSI ID 6 is reserved for CD-ROM drives. Therefore if running scsiinfo -p shows no other devices with this SCSI ID, then make sure that the CD-ROM drive's SCSI ID is set to 6.

2. On SunOS 4.x, run `shutdown now` and turn off the power. On Solaris 2.x, run `init 5`, and the system should power itself down.

3. Attach the CD-ROM drive to the end of the SCSI chain with the correct cable.

4. If the CD-ROM drive is the last device in the SCSI chain, make sure to put a terminator on the remaining port.

5. Power on the drives and then the UNIX server.

HP/UX 10/11 and AIX 4.x

1. In previous examples on these system types, SCSI ID 2 was free to be used. On either of these systems, set the SCSI ID of the CD-ROM drive to 2 using the manufacturer's instructions.

2. Shut down the machines using the `shutdown -h` command. Turn off the power.

3. Attach the CD-ROM drive to the SCSI bus, using an appropriate cable. Don't forget to put a terminator on the last device in the SCSI bus.

4. Turn on the drives; then turn on the workstation.

Verifying the Presence of the CD-ROM

SunOS 4.x

The output of `scsiinfo -p` should contain an entry similar to the following:

```
esp0: sr0 tgt 6 lun 0:
        Synchronous(4.0MB/sec) Clean CanReconnect
    Removable CD-ROM:       TOSHIBA   XM-5401TASUN4XCD 2565
```

Solaris 2.x

The output of `scsiinfo -p` should contain an entry similar to the following:

```
fas0: sd6,0 tgt 6 lun 0:
      Asynchronous Clean NoTaggedQueuing Narrow
      Removable CD-ROM:       TOSHIBA   XM-5401TASUN4XCD 2565          [ASL]
```

HP/UX 10/11

The output of /usr/sbin/ioscan -k should contain lines similar to the following:

```
H/W Path          Class       Description
=================================================
8/16/5            ext_bus     Built-in SCSI
8/16/5.2          target
8/16/5.2.0          disk      TOSHIBA CD-ROM XM-5701TA
8/16/5.7          target
8/16/5.7.0           ctl      Initiator
```

AIX 4.x

The output of `lsdev -C -s scsi -H` should look similar to the following:

```
name      status      location        description

hdisk0    Available   00-01-00-0,0    320MB SCSI Disk Drive
hdisk1    Available   00-01-00-1,0    320MB SCSI Disk Drive
hdisk2    Available   00-01-00-2,0    320MB SCSI Disk Drive
cd0       Defined     00-02-00-2,0    CD ROM Drive
rmt1      Available   00-00-0S-1,0    2.3GB 8mm Tape Drive
```

 To test the device, you can use a CD with a UNIX file system on it. The best thing to use would be a CD containing your operating system. It comes with instructions on how to mount the CD so that you can access it. If that works, you're done.

Terminals and Modems

If you don't have a graphics card in your UNIX machine, known as a "headless" system, or if you have users that don't need graphical interfaces, then connecting a few terminals to the system's serial ports is the way to go.

You might also want to allow access to your machine remotely via a modem, or allow someone logged in to your machine to call a remote site via a modem. You might even want to allow both (but not simultaneously).

> **CAUTION**
>
> A warning about using terminals on Suns: Any terminal you plug into the first serial port (port A) is considered to be the system console. If you turn the terminal's power off while it is connected to the Sun, you've just killed the machine! It is safe, however, to disconnect the serial cable from the Sun while the terminal is still powered on.

Most versions of UNIX run a program called `getty` for every single port that has a terminal or modem connected to it. `getty`, using options you specify, sets up the serial characteristics of the port in preparation for the use that you have in mind, whether that is to connect a terminal or a modem to it. This program also has to be told something about how you expect it to communicate with the terminal or modem you plan to attach.

The Solaris flavor of UNIX strives to be different when dealing with serial devices. It uses a *tty monitor*, called `ttymon` to set up and control the configuration of a serial port. You then have to set up a *port monitor* to monitor the status of the tty monitor. We'll show how this works in the following examples. For complete documentation and many examples of configuring this service, go to **http://docs.sun.com** and search for Managing Terminals and Modems.

Terminal Settings

The most widely supported terminal settings on UNIX are 8 bits, no parity, 1 stop bit. These settings are sometimes abbreviated to 8,N,1. The manual that comes with the terminal you have tells you how to change these settings. Another setting you'll need to verify is that the terminal is speaking full duplex, not half. Also, if you're going to use the terminal at speeds higher than 9600 baud, you should turn off software flow control and turn on hardware flow control. In the terminal setup menus, these flow control settings are sometimes referred to as XON/XOFF and RTS/CTS, respectively. Finally, most terminals are capable of acting like, or emulating, several different standard terminals, such as Wyse 50 or DEC VT-100. Because VT-100 is probably the most recognized terminal type, go ahead and tell all your terminals to emulate it.

Attaching Terminal Devices

Connecting a terminal device can be the most difficult or the easiest task you encounter in UNIX device management. It will be extremely difficult if you just try to connect the device to the computer and expect it to just work. There are many different settings for serial devices, and you can never be sure what a vendor had in mind when it programmed the initial settings into the device you want to attach to. It will be the easiest if you take a little time to understand the device (with help from the vendor), manually verify its settings, and make sure that UNIX will be expecting those settings so that it can communicate with the device.

DTE   A DTE (Data Terminal Equipment) device is an RS-232 designation given to a computer, terminal, or printer. All it really does is tell you which RS-232 signals the device expects on particular pins of the RS-232 connector.

DCE   A DCE (Data Communications Equipment) is an RS-232 designation reserved almost exclusively for modems. Again, the designation just specifies what signals are expected by the device on the pins of the RS-232 connector.

Now that you know what a DTE and a DCE are, you should know that when you connect a DTE to a DCE (like connecting a modem to a serial port on your computer), the cable you use should be a *straight though* RS-232 cable. However, when you connect a DTE to a DTE (like connecting a terminal to the serial port on your computer), or a DCE to a DCE (connecting a modem to another modem via their serial ports), you have to use a modification of the cable known as a *null modem* cable. Essentially, this is a rewiring of the pins in the cable to fool the equipment into thinking that the connection is a DTE to a DCE.

But what about all those different serial port connector types and the fact that you can never tell what sex the port connector will be? You could buy a quality breakout box, cable, and connectors and build your own custom cables for each instance, but frankly this is a waste of time. It's easier and sometimes cheaper to figure out what kind of cable and connectors you need and then call your nearest computer shop and see whether they have the part in stock. If the cable is very unusual, there are companies that do nothing but build unusual cables to your specifications.

The rule of thumb is that any serial cable with DB25 or DB9 connectors can be found off the shelf. You'll discover that cables with the same sex on both ends (male to male, female to female) are much more common than those of mixed sex (male to female). Not to worry; most places sell null modem gender changers. Connecting this to the end of a straight through cable turns it into a null modem cable, and lets you change the sex of the connector at the same time. If you need RJ-45 connectors (which look like large phone plugs), you might have to look around or have them custom built.

Following is an example of the process you would go through to determine what cable you're going to need:

1. You have a UNIX workstation with DB25F serial ports and a modem with a DB25F serial port.

2. Because this is an example of connecting a DTE (your workstation) to a DCE (your modem), you need a straight through cable.

3. Because the connectors on the serial ports of both devices are DB25F, you need a cable that has DB25M connectors on both ends.

4. Purchase a DB25M to DB25M straight through RS-232 cable.

Here's a more complicated example:

1. You have a UNIX workstation with DB9F serial ports and a terminal with a DB25M serial port.

2. This is an example of connecting a DTE (your workstation), with another DTE (your terminal). You need a null modem cable.

3. Your workstation's serial port is DB9F, so that end of the cable needs to be DB9M.

4. Your terminal's serial port is DB25M, so that end of the cable needs to be DB25F.

5. Purchase a DB9M to DB25F null modem cable, if you can find one. Or, purchase a DB9M to DB25M straight through cable and a DB25M to DB25F null modem gender changer.

Now let's examine how to attach a terminal to a serial port on several flavors of UNIX. In this example, we will make a few assumptions:

1. The terminal will be set to emulate a VT-100.

2. The terminal will be set to run at 38400 baud, with 8 data bits, no parity, 1 stop bit, and hardware flow control.

3. All the commands mentioned will have to be run as root.

SunOS 4.x

You will attach the terminal to the first serial port, known as /dev/ttya on SunOS.

1. Make sure that /etc/gettytab contains an entry that sets up getty to speak to the terminal with the settings specified. If you look at this file, you'll see that Sun has provided a default entry that looks like this:

```
h¦std.38400¦38400-baud:\
        :sp#38400:ms=crtscts:
```

This entry has three aliases: h, std.38400, and 38400-baud. The sp#38400 entry specifies that this setting will have a speed of 38400 baud, and the mode setting entry, ms=crtscts, turns on hardware flow control (RTS/CTS). If you don't specify differently, an entry in this file will default to 8 data bits, no parity, 1 stop bit. So we'll use this entry for our purposes.

2. Turn off any getty that might be running on ttya already, so that you can reconfigure it. If you don't take this step, you might end up having to reboot. The file /etc/ttytab lists all serial and pseudo ports in the system and tells getty how to manage the port. Here's the line as it looks in the file now:

```
ttya    "/usr/etc/getty std.19200"    wyse50         on local
```

The first field says that this line is for /dev/ttya. The second field says that /usr/etc/ getty should run on this port, using the std.19200 entry from the /etc/gettytab file. The third field says to expect a terminal emulating wyse50 to be connected to the port. The fourth field says that getty should actually be "on" or running. The final field says that this is a local terminal; that is, it is directly connected to the machine and is not a modem. To turn getty off, change the line to read:

```
ttya    "/usr/etc/getty std.19200"    wyse50         off       local
```

Then signal the init process to let it know that you have made this change:

```
# kill -HUP 1
```

3. Set up /dev/ttya to properly use software carrier detection because this is a terminal and not a modem:

```
# ttysoftcar -y ttya
```

4. Unfortunately, on SunOS the getty process is not fully capable of directly changing some of the settings of the serial ports on the motherboard. Some of these settings can only be changed from the OpenBoot PROM monitor, which is accessible from the eeprom command. For the settings you want, issue the following commands:

```
# eeprom ttya-rts-dtr-off=false
# eeprom ttya-ignore-cd=false
# eeprom ttya-mode=38400,8,n,1,h
```

The first command tells the /dev/ttya not to disable hardware flow control. The second command tells the /dev/ttya to use software carrier detect. The third command tells /dev/ttya to talk at 38400 baud, using 8 data bits, no parity, 1 stop bit, and hardware flow control.

5. Edit the /etc/ttytab file again and change the line for /dev/ttya to do what you want. In this case, it looks like the following:

```
ttya    "/usr/etc/getty std.38400"    vt100          on        local
```

As you can see, we just changed the baud rate and the terminal emulation.

6. Tell the init process that you have made this change by running the following:

```
# kill -HUP 1
```

7. Turn on your terminal and connect it to serial port A on the Sun using a null modem cable. You should now see a login prompt. Press Enter a couple of times if you don't.

Part
II

Ch
12

Solaris 2.x

You will attach the terminal to the first serial port, known as /dev/term/a on Solaris 2.x. You should be logged in as root to perform the following tasks.

1. Make sure that /etc/ttytab contains an entry that sets up the tty monitor on /dev/term/a so that it can talk to your terminal. If you look at this file, you'll notice that the last line comes just short of what you need:

    ```
    contty5H:19200 opost onlcr:19200 hupcl sane::conttyH
    ```

    This entry unfortunately has the wrong baud rate, the wrong parity, and no flow control. So create an entry named contty6H with the parameters you want.

    ```
    contty6H:38400 -parity opost onlcr:38400 sane -parity crtscts
    hupcl::contty6H
    ```

    This entry runs at 38400 baud, 8 bits, no parity (the -parity option), and 1 stop bit, and uses hardware flow control (the crtscts option).

2. Make sure the tty monitor, ttymon is running. Execute the following:

    ```
    # sacadm -l -t ttymon
    ```

    If the answer is something like:

    ```
    PMTAG        PMTYPE       FLGS RCNT STATUS    COMMAND
    zsmon        ttymon       -    0    ENABLED   /usr/lib/saf/ttymon #
    ```

    then proceed to the next step. However, if the answer is something like:

    ```
    "Invalid request, ttymon does not exist"
    ```

    you need to activate the tty monitor with the following command:

    ```
    # sacadm -a -p zsmon -t ttymon -c /usr/lib/saf/ttymon -v `ttyadm -V`
    ```

3. You need to know whether there is already a service active on the port you are going to attach the terminal to, /dev/term/a. Run the following command:

    ```
    # pmadm -l
    ```

    If the answer that comes back has an entry with /dev/term/a in it, like the following one does:

    ```
    PMTAG        PMTYPE       SVCTAG       FLGS ID      <PMSPECIFIC>
    zsmon        ttymon       ttya         u    root    /dev/term/a I -
    ➥/usr/bin/login - 9600 ldterm,ttcompat ttya login:  - tvi925 y  #
    ```

    then you will have to remove that service before you can proceed. Do so with this command:

    ```
    # pmadm -r -p <PMTAG> -s <SVCTAG>
    ```

    Where <PMTAG> and <SVCTAG> are from those respective columns in the pmadm -l command you just ran. In this case, the command would be as follows:

    ```
    # pmadm -r -p zsmon -s ttya
    ```

4. Activate the port monitor /dev/term/a with the options you want in the contty6H entry from /etc/ttytab. Here's the command that does it:

```
# /usr/sbin/pmadm -a -p zsmon -s ttya -i root -fu -v `/usr/sbin/ttyadm -V`
-m "`/usr/sbin/ttyadm -l contty6H -p "login:" -d /dev/term/a -T vt100 -i
'terminal disabled' -s /usr/bin/login -S y``"
```

5. Now that Solaris is ready, turn on your terminal, make sure that it has been set to 38400 baud, 8 data bits, no parity, 1 stop bit, hardware flow control, and VT-100 emulation. Then using a null modem cable, plug it into serial port A of your Solaris. Press Enter a few times if you don't see a `login:` prompt immediately.

HP/UX 10/11

You'll use SAM to configure the onboard serial port to be used with a terminal.

1. As root, run SAM. Select Peripheral Devices->Terminals and Modems.
2. Select the Actions menu and then choose Add Terminal.
3. Select asio0, the Built-in RS-232 Interface.
4. Select port 0.
5. Select Speed (baud rate) of 38400.
6. Connect your terminal to the workstation using a null modem cable. Press Enter a couple of times to see the login prompt.

AIX 4.x

In AIX, you can use SMIT to activate the two onboard serial ports. You can configure all the settings so that the server recognizes your terminal's settings when you plug it in.

Terminal Handling

Connecting a modem to a UNIX machine doesn't have to be difficult, but it often is because people don't know how to configure the modem properly. One word of advice: Pay a little more for your modem and ask whether the vendor can give you exact instructions on how to configure the modem to work with your exact hardware and software flavor of UNIX. You'd be amazed at how some have no idea how to do it, whereas others have exacting documents that explain every little detail.

Dial In   Configuring a modem to let you dial in means that some program has to be watching the port your modem is plugged into. Usually this is getty (except on Solaris), which preprograms your modem, waits for you to dial in, and then causes the modem to pick up. And when you hang up, this same program makes sure that the modem is reset and ready for you to dial in again.

Dial Out   Configuring a modem to let you dial out means that you don't want a program sitting on the serial port all the time. This way, you can use programs such as tip, cu, and kermit to tell the modem to dial up a remote system so that you can log in.

Part
II

Ch
12

TIP The best tutorial for everything you ever want to know about configuring modems and terminals for serial ports on SunOS 4.x and Solaris 2.x can be located at

`http://www.stokely.com/unix.serial.port.resources/tutorials.html`

Give it a try, it will save you hours of time.

Configuring modems on HP/UX 10/11 and AIX 4.x can be done through the SAM and SMIT tools, respectively. They cover pretty much all the modem and terminal setup scenarios you're likely to need.

Troubleshooting Terminal Problems

If you connect a terminal to your workstation and can't get any output, try the following:

1. Make sure that you're using the correct kind of cable. Having a null modem converter handy is a good idea.

2. Make sure that the settings on your terminal match what UNIX is expecting on that serial port.

3. Make sure that you are not in Local or Half Duplex mode on your terminal.

If you see garbage on your terminal, try this:

1. Make sure that the baud rate on the terminal matches what UNIX is expecting.

2. Make sure that the number of data bits, parity, and stop bits on the terminal are the same that UNIX is expecting.

   If you are communicating at speeds greater than 9600 baud, then make sure that you don't have software flow control on, that you do have hardware flow control on, and that UNIX is configured to use hardware flow control.

From Here...

Now that you have a basic understanding of how to attach various devices to your UNIX machine, you might want to read the following chapters to get a deeper understanding of how UNIX deals with devices:

- Chapter 2, "Logging In," gives you insight into how the UNIX kernel actually works and handles devices.

- Chapter 5, "Files, Directories, and Permissions", contains more in-depth information on special files, including device files, and how UNIX handles them.

- Chapter 13, "File Systems," gives you more information on how to create, check the integrity of, and use UNIX file systems on hard disks and CD-ROM drives you attach to your system.

- Chapter 19, "Configuring TCP/IP,"describes networking devices you might run into and have to configure; the section "Working with Network Interfaces" describes how to manipulate the networking devices using UNIX commands.

- Chapter 21, "Advanced Networking," gives you information on how to use TCP/IP over a modem connection. This is useful if you can't afford a direct network connection to a site you want to have a network connection with.

## CHAPTER 13

File Systems

by Sriranga Veeraraghavan

In this chapter

Introduction

Data stored on media, such as hard disks and CD-ROMs, are located in a file system. File systems are a method of organizing data so that data retrieval is fast, easy, and secure.

This chapter examines the tasks of creating, maintaining, monitoring, and repairing file systems. This chapter assumes that you have a good understanding of the UNIX directory tree structure and its components.

Though numerous file systems are available in the UNIX environment, this chapter concentrates on the most common ones:

- `ufs`
- `iso9660`
- `msdos`
- `ext2`

All the preceding file systems, except `ext2`, are available on the following flavors of UNIX:

- Sun Solaris
- FreeBSD
- Linux

In general, even if you are not using one of these flavors, the operations and commands given in this chapter still apply. The differences you are likely to encounter are usually in the specification of options to commands.

> **CAUTION**
>
> When dealing with file systems, use caution. A few wrong commands can lead to a file system or disk that cannot be recovered.
>
> Before proceeding with any of the operations given in this chapter, make sure that you understand them thoroughly.
>
> If you are unsure about issuing any of the commands or doing any of the operations given in this chapter, consult the online help and the manufacturer's documentation for your system before proceeding.

Understanding File Systems

UNIX uses file systems as the primary method of storing files and directories. A file system is a group of directories and files that can be placed anywhere in the UNIX directory tree.

The UNIX directory tree, unlike the directory trees used in Windows or the MacOS, is singly rooted. This means that all files and directories are stored under the topmost level of the tree, which is called `/`. The tree can be as deep as required. The only limitation is that the absolute path to a file does not exceed 1,024 characters.

▷ For more information on the directory structure of UNIX systems, **see** "UNIX Files and Directory Structure," **p. 112**

Regardless of their location in the UNIX directory tree, file systems are generally located on disks or disk partitions.

Each disk drive contains some number of file systems. Disk partitions are a method of dividing larger disks into a smaller and more manageable size. In UNIX, all disks have at least one partition. For disks containing only one partition, it is common for people to refer to the disk and the file system residing on that disk as the same entity.

File Types

Now that you have an idea of what file systems are, let's look at the types of files that can be stored in a file system. There are eight different types of files in UNIX:

- Normal files
- Directories
- Hard links
- Symbolic links
- Sockets
- Named pipes
- Character devices
- Block devices

Most of these file types are covered in other chapters and are not covered here.

▷ For a full description of each file type, **see** "File Types," **p. 118**

While this chapter does cover block devices, it is essential to know what these files are and how they are related to file systems.

Let's look at the ls –1 output for a typical block device. For example, /dev/sda:

```
brw-rw----  1 root     disk      8,   0 Feb  7 13:47 /dev/sda
```

Here the letter b in the first position of the permissions listing indicates that the file /dev/sda is a block device. This example has used /dev/sda, and in general most block devices are stored in the /dev directory. The variations for the names of these files are covered in a later section.

Block devices are special files that provide a mechanism for communicating with device drivers via the file system. Each block device contains a major and a minor number. Together these numbers represent the device driver with which the file communicates. In the preceding example, the major number is 8, and the minor number is 0.

These files are called block devices because they transfer large blocks of data at a time. Because this is the manner in which hard drives and floppy drives work, you need to be familiar with this type of file.

inodes and *superblocks*

In addition to containing the previously mentioned file types, UNIX file systems also keep track of essential information about the files and about the file system itself. This information is stored in `inodes` and `superblocks`.

The information about the file system is stored in the `superblock`. Depending on the type of file system, this information varies, but commonly it consists of information about the physical media the file system is on along with the total size of the file system. Because this information is critical to the operation of a file system, multiple copies of it are stored on the disk. In general, the only time you have to deal with the superblock for a file system is when the file system becomes heavily corrupted.

All the information about a file, except for its name, is stored in the file's `inode`. The name of a file is stored in its directory. The directory entry for a file consists of its name and the number of its `inode`. In general, most of the information stored in an `inode` is useful only to the kernel. The information that is useful for us is the following:

- `mode`   Describes the file's permissions
- `uid`   The user ID of the file's owner
- `gid`   The group ID of the file
- `size`   The file's size in bytes
- `atime`   The last time the file was accessed
- `mtime`   The last time the file was modified

This is information is displayed by the `ls -l` command:

```
-rwxr-xr-x  1 ranga    users       2780 Jul  3 10:48 .profile
```

▶ For more information about `inodes` and the `inode` table, **see** "The inode Table," **p. 129**

Different Types of File Systems

To better understand the differences and features of the file systems mentioned earlier, let's examine each of them in turn.

The *ext2* File System

The `ext2` file system is the native Linux file system and is available only in FreeBSD and Linux. If you are running a Linux system, this should be your file system of choice. Despite the extensive support for varied types of file systems, `ext2` should be used for all primary partitions. If you are running FreeBSD, you can use `ext2` partitions, but the `ufs` partition should be used for your boot partition.

The *ufs* File System

The ufs file system, is sometimes referred to as Berkeley Fast File System or the 4.2 file system depending on the version of UNIX. A disk containing a ufs format file system can be used on all the versions of UNIX mentioned previously, although Linux currently only supports reading of ufs partitions.

The *iso9660* File System

The iso9660 file system is the standard file system for CD-ROMs. It is often called the High Sierra file system. On Linux, it is referred to as the iso9660 file system. On FreeBSD, it is called the cd9660 file system. Under Solaris, it is called the hsfs. Because this file system is a cross-platform CD-ROM format standard, it is limited to the capabilities of the msdos file system. This means that all filenames must adhere to the 8.3 filename notation.

 T I P There are extensions to the iso9660 file system called the Rockridge Extensions, which allow for UNIX-style pathnames instead of the 8.3 notation used on iso9660 CD-ROMs. A regular iso9660 CD-ROM and one with Rockridge Extensions can be mounted using the iso9660 file system.

The *msdos* File System

The msdos file system is one file system commonly found on computers running Windows. In the UNIX world, it is usually found only on floppy disks. Due to limitations in the naming of files, DOS is mostly used to transfer small files between a UNIX machine and a Windows machine. This file system is referred to as the pcfs under SunOS and Solaris.

N O T E Under older versions of Solaris and SunOS, a special package known as pctools or dostools was required to access msdos file systems. In the current releases of Solaris (2.5.1 and 2.6), this is no longer the case. Both FreeBSD and Linux have built-in support for the msdos file system.

The *proc* and *swap* File Systems

In addition to these file systems, two more file systems available on all the platforms being discussed— proc and swap.

The *proc* File System The proc file system, which is usually mounted on /proc, is not a regular file system in the sense that it does not physically exist on a disk. Rather, it is a file system representation of the system memory and the UNIX kernel's state. The amount of information stored in the proc file system varies between the different versions of UNIX. In general, most versions of UNIX store files and directories in /proc for each running process. The exception is Linux, which stores much more information, much of which is in human-readable form.

Part
II

Ch

13

The proc file system is created by the UNIX kernel itself and is never directly created by the system administrator. In general, it is used as a reference to track down problems when some process is running away or behaving badly.

The *swap* File System   The swap file system is the location or locations on a disk that are used for virtual memory by UNIX. Most versions of UNIX do not allow a swap file system to be mounted as part of the directory tree, thus users generally never interact with a swap partition. The exception to this is Solaris, which uses a special file system called tmpfs.

N O T E   Under Solaris, all partitions of type tmpfs get mapped to /tmp along with the all the available RAM. Thus machines with a lot of RAM and swap have large /tmp directories.

One nice side effect of /tmp being partially in RAM is that compiling and running programs from /tmp on Solaris machines is incredibly fast because the computer does not have to read the disk to access program information.

Creating File Systems

This section looks at how devices are addressed and gives an example of creating a file system. This process applies to the swap file system as well as to the other file systems mentioned in the previous section.

Addressing Disks—The Device Entries

During boot time, most versions of UNIX detect any disks that have been added and will record the appropriate device entries. These entries are a special type of file known as a *block device*.

Addressing Disks Under Linux   Under Linux, hard disks are addressed as follows:

```
/dev/hd[letter][partition]
```

```
/dev/sd[letter][partition]
```

The first form is used to address an IDE disk, and the second form is used to address a SCSI disk. The *letter* following hd or sd refers to the disk's location in the chain. The first disk on a chain is a, the second is b, and so on. For example, /dev/hdd4 refers to the fourth partition of the fourth IDE disk, and /dev/sda2 refers to the second partition of the first SCSI disk. If a partition number is not present, the entire disk is accessed.

Addressing Disks Under Solaris   Under Solaris, hard disks are addressed as follows:

```
/dev/rdsk/c[C]t[T]d0s[S]
```

Here *C* stands for the controller the disk is on, *T* stands for the SCSI ID of the disk, and *S* stands for the partition number. So /dev/rdsk/c0t3d0s5 refers to the fifth partition of the disk on controller 0 with a SCSI ID of 3. If the partition number specified is 2 then the whole disk is addressed.

Addressing Disks Under FreeBSD   Under FreeBSD, hard disks are addressed as follows:

```
/dev/sd[T]s1[letter]
```

Here *T* stands for the SCSI ID of the disk, and *letter* stands for the partition. Usually, the root partition is letter a, and the swap partition is letter b. In FreeBSD, you are limited to partitions a–f.

Formatting and Partitioning a Disk

When a new disk is added or an old disk needs to be wiped clean, the disk is formatted and partitioned to serve its new purpose. Because the general principle is the same for all the systems discussed in this chapter, we will look at the partitioning of a disk under Linux using the `fdisk` command and partitioning a disk under Solaris using the `format` command.

> **CAUTION**
>
> All the commands and procedures demonstrated in this section can only be performed on unmounted file systems. Attempting to modify or format a mounted file system not only damages the contents of the disk but also may damage the physical medium of the disk and crash your system.
>
> The modern tools, especially those demonstrated in this section, do not allow you to modify a mounted file system. This prevents accidental mishaps that were common in UNIX system administration a decade ago.

Formatting and Partitioning Under Linux   This example looks at formatting and partitioning a brand-new zip disk that will be used as an archive under Linux. In this case, the zip drive is the second SCSI device, so issue the following command:

```
# fdisk /dev/sdb
```

> **CAUTION**
>
> When issuing the `fdisk` command, make sure that you specify the device name you want to partition correctly. Simply issuing the `fdisk` command will result in it using `/dev/hda` as the default. Because this usually points to the boot device on which `/` is mounted, this is rarely what you want.

The following prompt appears:

```
Command (m for help):
```

Type **M** and the following list of commands appears followed by a new prompt:

```
Command action
   a   toggle a bootable flag
   b   edit bsd disklabel
   c   toggle the dos compatibility flag
   d   delete a partition
   l   list known partition types
```

```
m   print this menu

n   add a new partition

p   print the partition table

q   quit without saving changes

t   change a partition's system id

u   change display/entry units

v   verify the partition table

w   write table to disk and exit

x   extra functionality (experts only)

Command (m for help):
```

The first thing you always want to do when formatting a disk is to look at the partition table to make sure that the disk being formatted is the correct one. To do this, type **p** at the prompt:

```
Command (m for help): p
```

This produces the following output:

```
Disk /dev/sdb: 64 heads, 32 sectors, 96 cylinders
Units = cylinders of 2048 * 512 bytes

    Device Boot    Begin    Start    End    Blocks    Id    System
```

Because there are no partitions on this disk, it is safe to proceed.

 TIP If there are partitions on a disk, pressing Ctrl+C exits the fdisk program, and no damage is done to the partitions. In fact, pressing Ctrl+C at any step in the process before the system writes the partition table to disk prevents any changes from being made.

Now add a partition. To do this, type **n** at the prompt:

```
Command (m for help): n
```

This produces the following prompt:

```
Command action
    e   extended
    p   primary partition (1-4)
```

Because no partitions are on the disk, you are creating a primary partition. You indicate this by typing **p**. This produces the following prompt:

```
Partition number (1-4):
```

You only require one partition, so make it partition 1 by entering **1**. This produces the following prompt:

```
First cylinder (1-96):
```

Here you are asked for the starting cylinder for the partition. You can pick any cylinder between 1 and 96 for this disk (one cylinder is roughly a megabyte). Because this is the first partition, pick cylinder 1. This produces the following prompt:

```
Last cylinder or +size or +sizeM or +sizeK ([1]-96):
```

In this case, you want the partition to occupy the entire disk, so enter **96**. If other partitions need to be created, then the desired size of this partition could be given instead. I did not specify a size because I want the partition to occupy the entire disk. In this case, if a size in KB or MB is given, a portion of the disk might not be present in the partition. In this case, that portion will be inaccessible.

After you have entered the size you want, you are returned to the following prompt:

```
command (m for help):
```

Print the partition table to see whether the partitioning you requested resulted in the correct partitioning of the disk. Typing **p** produces the following:

```
Disk /dev/sdb: 64 heads, 32 sectors, 96 cylinders
Units = cylinders of 2048 * 512 bytes

   Device Boot   Begin    Start    End   Blocks   Id  System
/dev/sdb1            1        1     96    98288   83  Linux native
```

This looks okay. You can now type **w** to write the partition and exit.

After you have created a partition, you need to create a file system on that partition to be able to use it. To do this, use the mkfs command:

```
# mkfs /dev/sdb1
```

Usually this program takes a few minutes to run and outputs a list of superblocks for the file system. In this case, the output is as follows:

```
mke2fs 1.10, 24-Apr-97 for EXT2 FS 0.5b, 95/08/09
Linux ext2 filesystem format
Filesystem label=
24576 inodes, 98288 blocks
4914 blocks (5.00%) reserved for the super user
First data block=1
Block size=1024 (log=0)
Fragment size=1024 (log=0)
12 block groups
8192 blocks per group, 8192 fragments per group
2048 inodes per group
Superblock backups stored on blocks:
        8193, 16385, 24577, 32769, 40961, 49153, 57345, 65537, 73729,
        81921, 90113

Writing inode tables: done
Writing superblocks and filesystem accounting information: done
```

While mkfs is working, it will print out a list of the superblocks on the disk. It is a good idea to make a note of these superblocks in case the file system becomes corrupted. Without a list of the alternative superblocks, when the first superblock becomes corrupted, it will be impossible to recover the disk.

Formatting and Partitioning Under Solaris   Under Solaris, the process of formatting and partitioning a disk is similar to Linux. In this example, you are creating the boot disk for a workstation. To partition the disk, use the `format` command:

```
# format
```

This produces the following list:

```
AVAILABLE DISK SELECTIONS:
       0. c0t3d0 <Andataco Quantium LPS1080S cyl 2895 alt 2 hd 8 sec 91>
          /sbus@1,f8000000/esp@0,800000/sd@3,0
Specify disk (enter its number):
```

If more than one disk is available, all of them are listed in order. This makes it easier for the user because you don't have to know ahead of time the device name of the disk you want to format. It is also safer because you can always exit at this stage if you ran the `format` command by mistake.

Because only one disk is available, select that one. This produces the following menu:

```
FORMAT MENU:
        disk       - select a disk
        type       - select (define) a disk type
        partition  - select (define) a partition table
        current    - describe the current disk
        format     - format and analyze the disk
        repair     - repair a defective sector
        label      - write label to the disk
        analyze    - surface analysis
        defect     - defect list management
        backup     - search for backup labels
        verify     - read and display labels
        save       - save new disk/partition definitions
        inquiry    - show vendor, product and revision
        volname    - set 8-character volume name
        !<cmd>     - execute <cmd>, then return
        quit
```

To partition the disk, enter `partition`:

```
format> partition
```

This produces the following menu:

```
PARTITION MENU:
        0      - change '0' partition
        1      - change '1' partition
        2      - change '2' partition
        3      - change '3' partition
        4      - change '4' partition
        5      - change '5' partition
        6      - change '6' partition
        7      - change '7' partition
        select - select a predefined table
        modify - modify a predefined partition table
        name   - name the current table
        print  - display the current table
        label  - write partition map and label to the disk
        !<cmd> - execute <cmd>, then return
        quit
```

Here, you can modify each partition manually, select a predefined partition table, or modify a predefined partition table. The easiest of these options to use is the `modify` option because it provides a base to work from. This provides the following options:

```
Select partitioning base:
        0. Current partition table (unnamed)
        1. All Free Hog
Choose base (enter number)[0]?
```

Choose the `All Free Hog` method because it provides an easy way to have one partition receive all the available space after you have allocated the space required of the other partitions. After you make this choice, you are prompted for the partition that you want to hog all the available space:

```
Free Hog Partition[6]?
```

In our case, pick partition 0 for the hog partition. Entering this results in a prompt for each of the other possible partitions in turn. After this process, you can print the result of the partitioning by typing **print** at the partition prompt:

```
partition> print
```

Part

II

Ch

13

This produces a table with the result of the partitioning:

```
Total disk cylinders available: 2895 + 2 (reserved cylinders)

Part     Tag   Flag    Cylinders        Size          Blocks
  0      root   wm      0 - 2329       828.24MB   (2330/0/0) 1696240
  1      swap   wu   2330 - 2611       100.24MB    (282/0/0)  205296
  2    backup   wm      0 - 2894         1.00GB   (2895/0/0) 2107560
  3       var   wm   2612 - 2893       100.24MB    (282/0/0)  205296
  4 unassigned  wm      0                    0      (0/0/0)        0
  5 unassigned  wm      0                    0      (0/0/0)        0
  6 unassigned  wm      0                    0      (0/0/0)        0
  7 unassigned  wm      0                    0      (0/0/0)        0
```

Because the partition table looks okay, you can write it to the disk and exit, which is done by issuing the `label` command.

```
partition> label
Ready to label disk, continue?
```

Typing **y** here writes the partition table to the disk. To exit the format program, type **quit** twice.

After you have partitioned the disk, the `newfs` command is used to make the file system. In this case, you need to make two file systems—one for / and one for /var. Run the `newfs` command twice:

```
newfs /dev/dsk/c0t3d0s0
newfs /dev/dsk/c0t3d0s3
```

N O T E Commands given in this section assume that the currently mounted root file system is on a device other than the one that you are formatting because it is not possible to format a mounted file system.

In this example, I was using a CD-ROM. In general, the process for installing a root file system involves booting with a CD-ROM as the root file system and then formatting and partitioning the appropriate hard drive.

Mounting and Unmounting File Systems

Before a file system can be used, it must be mounted. Because all files in UNIX are in a single directory tree, the mount operation makes it look like the contents of the new file system are the contents of an existing directory.

Mounting a File System

A file system is mounted using the `mount` command. The general syntax is as follows:

```
mount device directory
```

Here *device* is the name of the block device you want to mount, and *directory* is the directory you want to overlay with the file system contained on the given *device*. For example the following:

```
mount /dev/sdb1 /usr/archive
```

mounts the device `/dev/sdb1` on the directory `/usr/archive`. Under Linux, this command would have mounted the `ext2` file system located on the first partition of the second SCSI drive. To mount the same device under Solaris, the command would be:

```
mount /dev/dsk/c0t2d0s1 /usr/archive
```

As you can see, other than the device specification, the general syntax of the `mount` command is the same between the different versions of UNIX.

Keep in mind two things when mounting a file system. First, the destination directory must exist before the mount can take place. For example, if the directory `/usr/archive` did not exist, `mount` would complain as follows:

```
mount: mount point /usr/archive/ does not exist
```

Second, `mount` overlays the directory specified with the contents of the file system just mounted. In the preceding example, this would mean that if the `/usr/archive` directory had the following contents before a mount command:

```
/           archive/  bin/      etc/      include/  lib/      sbin/     src/
../         atalk/    doc/      gimp/     info/     man/      share/
```

after the `mount` command, those files would no longer be visible. Instead, only the files in the mounted file system would be seen. In this case:

```
./          ../                 archive/    lost+found/  old/
```

Mount Options

In addition to simply mounting devices, it is possible to specify options to `mount` by giving the `-o` flag. For example, the following command:

```
mount -o ro /dev/dsk/c0t6d0s2 /mnt/cdrom
```

mounts the specified device (in this example a CD) as read-only on the mount point `/mnt/cdrom` under Solaris. Although the `-o ro` option is not required for CD-ROMs, it is sometimes handy to use for removable disks being used to store backups. To specify more than one option, the required options can be separated with commas. For example:

```
mount -o ro,exec /dev/dsk/c0t6d0s2 /mnt/cdrom
```

This allows for the execution of binaries from the CD-ROM after it is mounted. Table 13.1 lists the common options understood by `mount`. These options can be specified on the command line as well as in `mount`'s configuration file.

Other than the options specified with the `-o` flag, `mount` understands three other options. These are the `-a`, `-t`, and `-v` flags.

mount -a   The -a flag indicates to mount that it should mount all the file systems that it knows about. In this case, no device or mount point is given. This information is obtained from mount's configuration file. The configuration file is discussed in a subsequent section. Usually the command:

```
mount -a
```

is never directly given by an administrator; it is issued by a script during the system startup.

mount -t   The -t flag indicates to the mount command the type of file system that the target device has on it. This flag is most often encountered when mounting a file system that is not the main file system for your version of UNIX. The following command mounts an MS-DOS floppy disk under Linux or FreeBSD:

```
mount -t msdos /dev/fd0 /mnt/floppy
```

On newer versions of Solaris, the -t flag has been changed to the -F flag.

mount -v   The -v flag indicates to the mount command that it should be verbose. Depending on the version of mount, this can be anything from echoing the command line it was invoked with to displaying an execution trace. Because the output varies considerably, type:

```
$ mount -v
```

to get an idea of what the verbose reporting looks like on your system.

Table 13.1   *mount* Options

Option	Description
async	Specifies that all I/O to the file system should be done asynchronously.
auto	Allows the device to be mounted with the -a option.
defaults	Use default options: rw, suid, dev, exec, auto, nouser, and async.
dev	Interprets character or block devices on the file system. For security reasons, this option is given only for the device mounted on /.
exec	Permits execution of binaries.
noauto	Specifies that device can only be mounted explicitly. The command mount -a skips file systems marked as noauto.
nodev	This is the opposite of dev option. This option prevents character or block devices on the file system from being used.
noexec	This is the opposite of exec option. This option prevents the execution of any binaries on the mounted file system. This option might be useful for a server that has file systems containing binaries for types of hardware.
nosuid	Prevents the set-user-identifier or set-group-identifier bits from taking effect.
nouser	Allows only root to mount the file system. For security reasons, this is the default.

Option	Description
remount	This option indicates to mount that it should attempt to remount an already-mounted file system. This is commonly used to change the mount flags for a file system, especially to make a read-only file system writable.
ro	Mounts a file system read-only.
rw	Mounts a file system read-write.
suid	This is the opposite of the nosuid option. It allows the set-user-identifier or set-group-identifier bits to take effect.
sync	All I/O to the file system should be done synchronously.
user	This option allows an ordinary user to mount the file system. This option implies the options noexec, nosuid, and nodev, unless they are overridden by subsequent options, as follows: mount -o user,exec,dev,suid.

Unmounting a File System

A file system is unmounted using the umount command. The general syntax is as follows:

umount *device*

umount *directory*

In the first form, umount attempts to unmount the file system that is mounted on the specified *directory*. In the second form, umount attempts to unmount the file system that is located on the specified *device*. The second form is mainly used when more than one file system can be mounted on a single directory.

For example, the following command:

umount /usr/archive

will unmount the file system that was mounted on /usr/archive and reveal the directory structure that existed before the mount.

Keep in mind one important thing when using umount. If the directory used as a mount point or any subdirectory in the mounted file system is in use by a user or a process, umount will not allow the file system to be unmounted. For example, if I was in the directory /usr/archive:

cd /usr/archive ; umount /usr/archive

produces the following error:

umount: /dev/sda4: device is busy

On FreeBSD and Solaris, umount can be forced to unmount file systems by specifying the -f option. In general, it is better to find the offending process or user and stop them from using the file system rather than to use the umount -f command on a file system. This is because a forced unmount will leave processes in a confused state and may cause the file system to become corrupted.

Configuration Files

The `mount` and `umount` commands both use the same configuration file. On Linux and FreeBSD, this file is called `/etc/fstab`. On Solaris, this file is called `/etc/vfstab`.

The configuration file lists all the partitions that need to be mounted at boot time along with the directory where they are to be mounted. This file also allows the system administrator to specify the options for a file system. It also gives the system administrator the ability to mount files simply by giving either the device of the file system or the destination directory.

Let's first look at the format of this file and then look at a few examples of how it eases the process of mounting and unmounting file systems.

The basic format of the `fstab` file is as follows:

```
<device> <dir> <fs> <options> <dump> <fsckps>
```

The definition of these parameters is given in Table 13.2.

Table 13.2 Parameters in the *fstab* File

Parameter	Description
`device`	This is the block device on which the file system is located.
`dir`	This is the destination directory where the file system is to be mounted.
`fs`	This is the type of file system located on the device.
`options`	These are the options that should be used when mounting the device. These options can be any of the options given in Table 13.1.
`dump`	This field is used by the `dump` program for backups.
`fsckps`	This is a field used at boot time by the `fsck` program.

A sample entry on Linux or FreeBSD looks like the following:

```
/dev/hda1        /                  ext2    defaults 1 1
```

This entry corresponds to the first partition of the first IDE drive in the system and tells the `mount` command that the file system located on that partition is an `ext2` file system and should be mounted with the default permissions on `/`. A similar entry on Solaris looks like this:

```
/dev/dsk/c0t2d0s6    /dev/rdsk/c0t2d0s6    /external2 ufs    1    no    -
```

As you can see, the Solaris format is slightly different and includes a second field that is not the destination directory. This field is a reference to the raw device and for the purposes of `mount` is the same as the device entry, except that the `/dsk/` is `/rdsk/` for the raw device.

In all `fstab` files, there are two entries that do not adhere to the format given previously. These are the entries for `swap` and `proc`. These file systems appear as follows on Linux and FreeBSD:

```
none         /proc       proc     defaults
/dev/hda2    none        swap     sw
```

Under Solaris, these entries look like the following:

```
/proc      -      /proc  proc    -    no      -
/dev/dsk/c0t0d0s1          -      -    swap    -    no      -
```

These entries should not be removed. Though swap entries can be added by hand, they are not mounted using the mount command. Instead you must use the swap -a command on Solaris and the swapon command under Linux and FreeBSD. During boot time, one or more of the system initialization scripts issues this command to ensure that all the swap partitions are activated by the time the system is ready for users.

▶ For more information about the boot process and the mounting of file systems and swap partitions during the boot process, **see** "The Boot Process," **p. xx** (Chapter 11)

In addition to file system entries, you can add comments to this file by entering lines that start with the # character.

Monitoring File Systems

Now that you have looked at creating and mounting file systems, it is important to know how to monitor and maintain these file systems. This section examines monitoring overall usage, monitoring and limiting usage on a per-user basis, and maintaining a file system.

Monitoring Overall Usage

Two main commands are used in the monitoring of overall file system usage—df and du.

df   The df command summarizes the free disk space on a system on a per-file system basis. The basic syntax is as follows:

```
df [options] [directory]
```

Here *options* is one of the choices listed in Table 13.2, and *directory* is the name of a directory. If the df command is given by itself, it outputs information for every mounted file system. On a Linux or FreeBSD system, the output looks like the following:

```
Filesystem        1024-blocks  Used  Available Capacity Mounted on
/dev/hda1          1190014   704847    423681     62%    /
/dev/hdd1          4128240   867508   3047117     22%    /internal
/dev/hdb1          1521567   807897    635048     56%    /store
/dev/hda3           320086    28586    274969      9%    /tmp
/dev/sda4          1011823   202615    756934     21%    /mnt/jaz
```

Table 13.3 describes each of the columns in the output of the df command on AIX, FreeBSD, and Linux. On a Solaris system (or any SVR4 system), the output looks more like this:

```
/                    (/dev/dsk/c0t0d0s0 ): 3115278 blocks    474622 files
/proc                (/proc            ):       0 blocks      1977 files
/dev/fd              (fd               ):       0 blocks         0 files
/var                 (/dev/dsk/c0t0d0s1 ):  940114 blocks    237306 files
/export              (/dev/dsk/c0t0d0s6 ): 9594934 blocks    720937 files
/tmp                 (swap             ):  727064 blocks     15369 files
```

Part

II

Ch

13

As you can see, the differences between the two versions are mainly in the formatting of the output. The Solaris output can be made to match the output of Linux or FreeBSD by specifying the -k option to df.

Table 13.3   Descriptions of the Columns in the Output of *df*

Column	Description
Filesystem	The device on which the file system is located.
x-blocks	The number of total blocks, where x is the number of bytes per block. This is usually either 1024 or 512.
Used	The number of blocks currently in use.
Available	The number of blocks currently free.
Capacity	A percentage indicating how full a file system is.
Mounted On	The directory where the file system is mounted.

If a directory argument is given, then df lists the output for the file system that the directory is a part of. In the system whose df output is given previously, the following command:

```
df /usr/local
```

results in the following output:

```
Filesystem         1024-blocks  Used Available Capacity Mounted on
/dev/hda1             1190014  704847    423681      62%   /
```

In this case, /usr/local is a subdirectory of /, thus df reports information about the file system in which the requested directory is located. The output of df for a directory is the same on Linux, FreeBSD, and AIX machines, but as noted earlier, the output differs slightly on a Solaris machine. The command may produce output like the following:

```
/export        (/dev/dsk/c0t0d0s6 ): 9594934 blocks   720937 files
```

Here, you can see that the directory /usr/local is mounted on /export. The rest of the output displays information about the disk on which /export is located.

TROUBLESHOOTING

In general, it is a bad idea to have a file system become completely full. Not only does this slow down the machine for all users, it can also prevent users from using the machine. In the worst case, if the root file system mounted on / fills up, it could crash your computer.

For these reasons, many system administrators have cron jobs that parse the output of df every hour or every day and then send mail to the administrator if file systems start filling up. Depending on the requirements of your system, you might need to implement such a system.

▶ For more information on how to use cron for this task, **see** "The cron Process," **p. 409**

Table 13.4 *df* **Options**

Option	Description
-a	Specifies that all currently mounted file systems, including /proc and swap, should be displayed.
-i	Specifies that inodes should be reported instead of blocks.
-k	Specifies that the output should be in 1KB blocks instead of the default. Depending on your system, this option may have no effect. On Solaris systems, this option makes the output of df match the output of df on AIX, Linux, and FreeBSD systems.
-t [fstype]	This option specifies that only mounted file systems of the type fstype should be reported. On Solaris, the -t option is not available; the -F option should be used instead.

du   In many instances, the size of individual directories or entire directory trees is required. Here df is of little help because it reports only the information for an entire file system. The command to use when the disk usage of a directory is required is the du command. The basic syntax of du is similar to df:

```
du [options] [directory]
```

Here *options* is one of the options given in Table 13.3, and *directory* is the name of a directory to report usage on. Running du without any arguments, as follows:

```
# du
```

produces a size listing for each directory under the current directory. If there are many subdirectories, the output can easily scroll off the screen. Usually, du is running with a directory name, as follows:

```
# du /usr/local
```

By default, du lists size information for each directory, but often only the total size is required. The -s option provides this functionality:

```
# du -s /usr/local
```

This produces the following output:

```
91052    /usr/local
```

In this case, the output indicates that this directory occupies 91052 blocks.

Part

II

Ch

13

Table 13.5 *du* Options

Option	Description
-a	Specifies that disk usage information for every file and directory should be listed.
-s	Specifies that only the total usage should be listed.
-k	Specifies that the output should be in kilobytes instead of blocks. Depending on your system, this option may have no effect.
-b	Specifies that the output should be in bytes rather than blocks. This option is restricted to FreeBSD and Linux systems.

Disk Quotas

On a single user system or a system with few users, a disk quota system is often not required. But at most sites where tens or hundreds of users will be using a single machine, a per-user quota system is required.

A quota system is basically a method of giving each user a limited amount of disk space that is available for his or her use. It also ensures that no one user can fill up the disk and thus make it impossible for other users to use their accounts on that system.

The minimum amount of information required to implement a quota system is as follows:

- The amount of disk space available
- The number of current and future users that need to be supported
- The volumes on which quotas are required

In addition to these considerations, the hard limit and the soft limit must also be determined.

A *soft limit* is a level at which a warning is issued to the user that he is exceeding the disk space allotted to him. When the soft limit is reached, the user is prompted that he has exceeded his quota by a prompt like the following:

```
/home: warning, user disk quota exceeded
```

If this message is generated, the user must reduce his disk usage to below the soft limit. This message continues to appear at every login until the user reduces his disk usage. The soft limit also carries with it a timeout, after which any further disk usage generates the following message:

```
/home: warning, user disk quota exceeded
No space left on device.
```

Exceeding the hard limit causes a message similar to the preceding message.

To define the available disk space for a user, the edquota command is used. The basic syntax is as follows:

```
edquota [username]
```

To edit the quota for the user ranga, the command is as follows:

```
edquota ranga
```

This brings up an editor (usually vi) that allows for the setting of the hard and soft limits for the user.

N O T E Before edquota can be used to edit the quota for a file system, a file called quotas must exist at the root of the file system. Some versions of edquota will create this file if it does not exist. Other versions require that you manually create it. A simple way to do this is to use the touch command. Refer to the man page for touch, if you are unfamiliar with its use.

After an entry is made for a single user, the -p option can be used to duplicate it for other users. For example, the command:

```
edquota -p ranga vathsa
```

sets the quota of the user vathsa to be the same as that of the user ranga. Issuing the edquota command with the name of a user whose quota is already defined allows the quota for that user to be redefined.

To check the quota for a username, use the quota command. The basic syntax is as follows:

```
quota [-v] [username]
```

Here the -v option indicates that the current usage limits for the specified *username* should be listed. If this option is not given, then quota produces output only if the specified *username* has exceeded its limits. As an example, on my system, the command:

```
quota -v ranga
```

produces the following output:

```
Disk quotas for user ranga (uid 13043):
   Filesystem blocks   quota   limit    grace   files   quota   limit   grace
    /var/mail      0    4096   10240               1       0       0
        /csua      0       0       0               0       0       0
        /home   8409   15360   20480             470       0       0
```

This shows that I am under the quota limits. If I had exceeded the soft limit, then an entry with the amount of time left in the soft limit timeout would appear in the grace column.

To get a report of the quota limits of every user on a system, use the repquota command. The output looks like the following:

User	used	Block limits			used	File limits		
		soft	hard	grace		soft	hard	grace
patrick	- -	67	15360	20480		33	0	0
wend	- -	714	15360	20480		69	0	0
cvieri	- -	11	15360	20480		10	0	0
sg	- -	4695	15360	20480		85	0	0

In addition to editing the quotas for users, the accounting must be turned on for each file system that quotas are required on. This is done with the quotaon command:

```
quotaon [file system]
```

Part II
Ch 13

Here *file system* is the file system for which user quotas should be enforced. For example:

```
quotaon /home
```

activates quotas for the /home file system.

In addition to running the quotaon command, the entries in the /etc/fstab for the file systems on which quotas are required must have either the userquota or the groupquota option specified. These options are ignored by mount, but are used by quotaon.

To turn quotas off for a file system, use the command quotaoff :

```
quotaoff [file system]
```

For example:

```
quotaoff /home
```

deactivates quotas on the /home file system.

Maintaining File Systems with *fsck*

Eventually, it becomes necessary to manually maintain and fix a file system. The need arises when someone turns off the power, hits the reset button, or if the power goes out unexpectedly.

When something unexpected occurs and a UNIX machine is not shutdown properly, chances are that a file system on the machine is corrupted. In this case, the system administrator has to manually confirm that each of the file systems is clean. This is done with the fsck command.

The fsck command is used to verify that all the inodes and superblocks have correct information stored in them. This command runs in five stages, where each stage verifies a different piece of information about the file system. After all the stages are complete, the file system should be okay. But it is common practice to run fsck until it reports that a file system is okay in a single step.

Due to the high overhead of maintaining file systems manually using fsck, a new type of file system known as a Journalling File System (JFS) is becoming popular.

 TIP A JFS writes all modifications into a circular log prior to (or instead of) committing them on disk. This file system is available on the following platforms:

- IBM AIX (JFS)
- Digital OSF/1 (Advanced File System)
- Silicon Graphics IRIX (XFS)

FreeBSD has a file system similar to JFS called Log-Based File System (LFS). This file system stores all its information in logs.

The primary advantage of JFS is that it can use the information from the log to recover from a system crash. Post-crash checking is only dependent on the number of active processes at crash time, not on the size of the file system.

File system checking time can become a significant factor in large installations. For installations with hundreds of gigabytes of storage, fsck can run for hours or even days before it recovers the file system, whereas systems with JFS can be recovered in minutes.

Another problem with modern file systems is the metadata update (*metadata* are things like directory entries and inodes), which has to be done synchronously or at least in a somewhat orderly fashion to keep the file system in a consistent state. This turns out to be a major performance bottleneck, which can be worked around with a log.

▷ For more information on what metadata are and why they need to be kept in a consistent state, **see** "The Inode Table," **p. 129**

The Phases of *fsck*

The five phases of fsck are as follows:

- Check Blocks and Sizes
- Check Pathnames
- Check Connectivity
- Check Reference Counts
- Check Cylinder Groups

In the first phase, every inode is checked to make sure that there are no invalid entries. If an invalid entry is found, it prompts for an action. A sample question could look like the following:

```
PARTIALLY TRUNCATED INODE I=<number> (SALVAGE)?
```

Here you are asked whether you want to salvage a damaged inode. The correct answer is yes, which is the default. Most of the questions can be answered with common sense.

In the second phase, directory entries are removed from bad inodes found in phase 1. If you encounter a question like the following:

```
ROOT INODE NOT A DIRECTORY (FIX)?
```

you should let fsck fix the problem, but be aware that this means significant damage has occurred to the file system. All other questions indicate that the file system has suffered only minor damage that can be recovered.

In the third phase, fsck looks for directories on the file system that are not referenced by any other directory on the file system. It places all such directories into the directory lost+found at the root of the file system.

In the fourth phase, fsck uses the information from phases 2 and 3 to check for any files not properly referenced by the file system. Usually problems in this phase can be corrected, but occasionally fsck asks you to clear a file.

Part

II

Ch

13

In the fifth and final step, fsck checks the free block and unused inode count to make sure that they are correct. If they aren't, fsck attempts to correct the problem.

After these phases have completed, the file system should be okay, but usually fsck is run several times on a damaged file system until it responds as follows:

```
/home: clean
```

If a message like this appears, then the file system is usable.

Running *fsck*

Normally, the system runs fsck automatically during the system boot to make sure that all the file systems being mounted are okay. If you need to run it manually, invoke it as follows:

```
fsck [-b] [device]
```

Here *device* is the block device corresponding to the file system you want to check. The -b option is used to tell fsck to use an alternative superblock. This is useful if the first superblock has become severely corrupted. One alternative superblock that is available for all file systems is 32.

If fsck is invoked with no options, it checks all the file systems in /etc/fstab that are not mounted.

If you need to check a file system, it must be unmounted. This is to prevent file system corruption. Usually, this is not a problem because fsck is normally run in single user mode.

From Here...

In this chapter, you looked at creating, managing, and maintaining file systems. The chapter discussed the most common UNIX file systems and covered the creation of file systems on both Linux and Solaris. In addition, the chapter explained mounting and unmounting file systems, along with monitoring the usage of mounted file systems. With the information covered, you should be ready to handle using and maintaining file systems on your own systems.

From here, you can start on the following topics:

- Chapter 15, "Backup and Recovery," gives you information on how to implement a comprehensive method of backing up your file systems and how to recover them in the case of a disk crash.
- Chapter 16, "Automating Tasks," gives you the necessary information to implement a monitoring system for disk quotas and file system capacity.
- Chapter 22, "NFS," introduces you to one of the most useful file systems available to networked computers. Using the network file system (NFS), you can access data stored on an NFS server as if it were stored on one of the local file systems discussed in this chapter.
- Chapter 27, "Performance and Tuning," demonstrates how to tune your file systems to increase their performance and the performance of your system.

## CHAPTER 14

Printing

by Terry W. Ogiltree

In this chapter

Introduction

Two printing models are used by most UNIX implementations—the BSD spooling system and the SVR4 spooling system. Although in some UNIX versions the manufacturer has chosen to use a proprietary solution, the two methods discussed in this chapter are the most widespread.

The BSD system uses the lpr program and the lpd daemon to send files to printers, using the /etc/printcap text file to determine individual printer characteristics. The terms lpr and lpd are short for line printer remote and line printer daemon, respectively. The SVR4 system uses the lp ("line printer") program and the lpsched daemon (printer scheduler) to print files. Although the SVR4 system is considered more sophisticated in that it has a number of utility commands for managing the system, the BSD system is better able to cope with printing in a networked environment.

Some versions of UNIX support both types of printing, but you should also note that the syntax for the applicable commands can differ slightly from version to version. In all cases, consult the man pages on your system to get the exact syntax for examples shown in this chapter.

Although you will find many people who still think that UNIX is the solution to the problem of a proliferation of operating systems, would it surprise you to know that there are several major variants of the operating system (System V and BSD), and several hundred different implementations? Go to the Web site at:

http://www.ntlug.org/~cbbrowne/unix11.html

and you will find a list of more UNIX variants than you will ever need to know about. You can also search the Web to find vendor-specific sites that can give you details about any add-ons (such as unique printing systems) that a particular vendor has implemented.

The BSD (*lpr/lpd*) Print System

The user interface to this printing system is the lpr command. In Figure 14.1, you can see how the process continues after the user has submitted a file to print using this command. The lpr program communicates with the lpd daemon, which then creates a copy of the file that is to be printed in the spooling directory for the particular printer.

When the daemon receives a print request from lpr, it spawns a new instance of itself and that process is then responsible for overseeing the process of formatting the file and sending it to the correct print device. The file /etc/printcap is used by lpd to get specific characteristics of the printer, such as the special device file to send the data to.

lpd doesn't perform the actual task of sending the user's file to the printer device. Instead an input filter is used. An input filter is a program that manipulates the data to be printed and put into a format that the printer can understand to achieve the desired print. When the lpd daemon runs the filter program, it sets the filter program's standard input to the file to be printed and standard output to the device specified by the lp symbol in the /etc/printcap file. The filter program then processes the data and sends it to the printer.

FIGURE 14.1
Overview of printing under the BSD system.

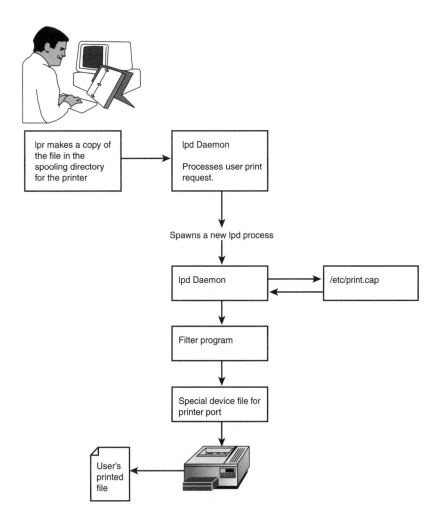

In the next few sections, the lpr and lpd programs are discussed in further detail, along with several other programs used for managing the printing system.

The *lpr* Command: Sending Files to Print

The lpr command sends files to print. The syntax for the command is as follows:

```
lpr [-parameters][filename...]
```

As you can see, everything is optional. If you omit a filename, then input is taken from *standard input*. You can specify more than one file to print on the command line. You can use parameters to select a specific printer and to specify document or printer characteristics.

Part
II

Ch
14

In its simplest form, you can just enter the lpr command followed only by the name of a file to be printed. This causes the file to be printed on the default printer. To specify that the file be printed on a specific printer, use the -P option. For example:

```
lpr -Plaser1 report03.txt report04.txt
```

sends the files report03.txt and report04.txt to the printer named laser1. When you use more than one filename on the print command line, you should separate each filename by a space.

The parameters that you can use with this command vary among different versions of UNIX. Some of the more common command-line parameters that you can use with the lpr command are as follows:

- # Number of copies to print.
- c Indicates that the date file(s) to be printed were created by the cifplot filter.
- C Job classification. Text following the C character is printed on the burst page for the print job.
- d Indicates that the data file(s) to be printed contain data created by the tex command (DVI format from Stanford University).
- f For printing FORTRAN files. Indicates that the first character in each line is to be interpreted as a FORTRAN carriage control character.
- g Indicates that the data file(s) to be printed contain data created by a program using the standard plot routines.
- h Suppress printing a burst page.
- i Indent. By default a job is printed with an indent of eight spaces. You can change that with this parameter. This value is passed to the input filter, which does the actual formatting of the data to be printed.
- J Job. Text following the J character is printed on the burst page for the print job. The default is the name of the first file on the print command line.
- l Causes control characters to be printed and suppresses page breaks.
- m Sends a mail message after the job is printed.
- n Indicates that the data file(s) to be printed contain data created by the ditroff command.
- p Uses the pr command as the filter to process the print job.
- P Name of the destination printer.
- r Removes the file when spooling (or printing using the -s parameter).
- s Indicates that the file should not be spooled. Instead, a symbolic link is used. This is a good option to use when printing large files, or a large number of files, to minimize consumption of disk space.
- T Title. This parameter is used with the -p option, which causes the pr command to be used to format the file to be printed. The text specified with this parameter is passed to

pr. If blank spaces or special characters are used, then the text should be enclosed by single-quotes (").

- t   Indicates that the data file(s) to be printed contains binary data created by the troff command.

- v   Indicates that the data file(s) to be printed is in raster image format.

- w   Number of columns. This parameter specifies the number of characters on the page (width).

When the lpr command is invoked to send a file to print, it first determines the destination printer. If the command-line parameter -P was used, then lpr uses that printer selected by the user. If this parameter was not used, the environment variable PRINTER is evaluated, and the printer referenced by it is used. Finally, if the PRINTER variable is null, the system default printer is used.

Next lpr scans the /etc/printcap file to get information about the printer, such as the spooling directory path. Before it notifies the lpd daemon that a file needs to be printed, it creates several temporary files in the spooling directory.

Data Files Created in the Spooling Directory: *cf**, *df**

When lpr makes a copy in the spooler directory of the file to be printed, it actually creates two different files. The first file has a filename that begins with the letters "cf" and is a *control file* that contains the name of the file to be printed and certain options for the print job. Each line in the file begins with a character that indicates how to interpret the remainder of the line. For example, a line beginning with the letter N contains the name of the file to print. If the line beginning with N is blank, then standard-input is assumed.

> **N O T E** The lpr command copies the file to be printed to the spooling directory for the destination printer. In some situations, this might not be practical. If you regularly print large reports that consume a lot of disk space, you can edit the /etc/printcap entry for the printer and tell it to use a symbolic link to the file instead (see "The /etc/printcap File" later in this chapter). You can also do this on a job-by-job basis by using the -s parameter with the lpr command.

Most of the other character key-codes are equivalent or similar to the command-line parameters used with the lpr command. The lowercase letter t indicates a file created by troff, whereas the uppercase letter I designates the indent value. A few additional characters are used that do not directly relate to identical lpr command-line parameters. For example, the uppercase letter H is used to specify the hostname of the machine from which the lpr command was executed.

> **N O T E** Don't get confused by the old interpreted BASIC programming language command called troff (and its counterpart, tron). These commands were used to turn on/off tracing to assist in debugging a program. In the UNIX world, troff is a utility used for text formatting and typesetting chores.

Part
II

Ch
14

▶ To read more about `troff` and other filters used in UNIX, **see** Chapter 3, "UNIX Shells and System Commands"

The name of the actual *data file* that will be printed, as specified by the N key in the `cf` control file, will begin with the letters "df" and will also be found in the spooling directory. If `lpd` was set to use symbolic links when it was started, or if the `-s` parameter was used by the `lpr` program, then the control file will contain a symbolic link to the file to be printed.

The *lpd* Daemon: Controlling the Printing Process

The background `lpd` daemon is usually started when the system is booted by commands placed in one of the `rc` files. Depending on the version of UNIX, there are only a few parameters you can use when starting up `lpd`. The syntax for the `lpd` command is as follows:

```
lpd [-l][-Llogfile] [port#]
```

The `-l` parameter causes valid requests from the network to be recorded in a log file. In some versions of UNIX, you can use the uppercase letter L to designate the name of the log file to use. You can also specify the Internet port number to use for process-to-process communication by specifying it on the command line.

When `lpd` is first started, it immediately reads the `/etc/printcap` file to get information about printers on the system. The daemon then proceeds to print any files left unprinted before the system was rebooted. Finally, the `lpd` daemon uses the system calls `listen` and `accept` to communicate with `lpr` and other programs in the printing system.

After the `lpr` command notifies the `lpd` daemon that files are ready to be printed, the `lpd` daemon checks to see whether another `lpd` process is already handling print processing for the specified print queue. If no process is running, then `lpd` spawns a copy of itself to handle the job. This process continues to process files in the specific spooler directory until there are no more jobs to print. The original `lpd` daemon that was started at system boot time continues then to listen for other print-related requests.

When the printer becomes available, the `lpd` process for the printer queue causes an input filter program to be run. The input filter is the program that actually sends data to the printer to get the print job completed. In some situations, the input filter also formats the data to make it compatible with the printer.

The Lock File When running in a multiuser environment, precautions must be taken to prevent one process from accessing a resource already in use by another process. The `lpd` daemon uses a lock file (created by the system call `flock`) in the spooling directory for this purpose. When a new `lpd` daemon is spawned to perform a printing function, it first scans the spooling directory to see whether a lock file exists. If one is not found, then the daemon creates one, thus taking "ownership" of the queue for the moment.

N O T E Locking is an important concept in UNIX, especially if you plan to write script files that write to a file and send it to print. Chapter 8, "Advanced Shell Scripting," sheds more light on this topic. ▪

The lock file is a simple ASCII text file consisting of only two lines. The first line contains the process ID (PID) of the lpd daemon that created the lock, and the second line contains the name of the control file for the current print job. In some versions of UNIX, the second line is used to show the current status of the print job. Another file, named *status*, is used by some versions for this purpose. In either case, other print-related commands can use this information to report the status of a print job when the user requests it.

Remote Printing By putting the appropriate entries in the /etc/printcap file, you can configure a printer on another computer system to be the destination of a particular print queue. When this is the case, the lpd daemon copies the control and data files to the remote system, and the lpd daemon on that system becomes responsible for seeing that the file is printed. The lpd daemon on the originating computer then immediately deletes the files from its spooling directory as they are no longer needed.

Managing Print Queues

In addition to the lpr and lpd programs, the BSD printing system includes several utilities that can be used to view information about print jobs and to manipulate the print queues. The most often used command from a user standpoint is the lpq command, which displays information about the print queue. The lprm command allows you to remove print jobs from the queue. The lpc command, which is usually used by administrators only, can be used to enable or disable printers, or to move jobs around in the queue.

Using the *lpq* Command to View Print Queues

To show information about jobs waiting to print in a print queue, use the lpq command. In Listing 14.1, you can see that the information displayed consists of the order of jobs in the queue, name of the user who submitted the print job, the job identification number, the files to be printed, and the total size of the files in bytes. In the case where the data to be printed is not in a file but is being redirected via a pipe, the Files column in the display shows the words *standard input* because no filename is applicable.

Listing 14.1 Output from the *lpq* Command

```
Rank    Owner      Job  Files             Total Size
active  harris     136  letter            1550 bytes
1st     brown      154  ch1003            9856 bytes
2nd     sogletree  116  appdocument       8847 bytes
3rd     norton     335  wnt50srvadm       857 bytes
4th     sowell     212  progasmb          4293 bytes
```

Part
II

Ch
14

In a manner similar to the lpr command, you can use the -P command-line parameter to specify a printer. If you omit this parameter, then the environment variable PRINTER is used, and if it is null, then the system default printer is used. The syntax for the lpq command is as follows:

```
lpq [-Pprinter][-l][+[interval]][job#...][username...]
```

The -l parameter will cause a "long" listing to be displayed. If you do not specify this parameter, then only as much information as will fit on a single line is displayed for each job. The plus sign (+) can be used by itself, or with a numeric value, and causes the command to continuously display the status until the print queue empties. If specified, the numeric value is the number of seconds the command waits before refreshing the display.

You can place one or more job identification numbers or usernames on the command line (separated by spaces) if you only want to display information about specific jobs or jobs for a specific user. For example, if user Harris only wanted to see status about her print jobs queued to a printer named laser1, she could enter:

```
lpq -Plaser1 harris
```

The job identification number that you can get from the lpq display can be used as input to the lpq command itself (lpq 545, to show only job number 545, for example), as well as other queue management commands such as lprm and lpc. Indeed, because the job number uniquely identifies a job on the system, it is common to use the lpq command before executing other queue management commands just so that you can obtain the job ID for the object to be managed.

The *lprm* Command: Removing Files from a Print Queue

A user can remove her own files from the print queue to prevent them from printing by using the lprm command. A superuser can remove files from the print queue that belong to other users. The syntax for the lprm command is as follows:

```
lprm [-Pprinter][-][job#...][username...]
```

As with other BSD print commands, lprm uses the -P command line parameter, the environment variable PRINTER, and the system default printer to determine the actual print queue to act on.

You can remove a job from the queue by specifying its job identification number (which you can get by using the lpq command or the lpstat command). If a user wants to remove all her print jobs from the queue, then the hyphen character by itself causes this to happen. A superuser can specify a username, in which case all jobs in the queue for that user are removed.

Following are some examples involving the lprm command:

```
lprm -
```

All files in the queue (either the system default printer or the printer specified by the PRINTER variable) for the user issuing the command are removed. If the user is a superuser, then all files in the spooling directory, no matter who submitted them, are removed.

```
lprm -Plaser1 513 566
```

> The files in the laser1 print queue that are associated with the job numbers 513 and 566 are removed from the queue, provided that the user issuing the command is the user who submitted them to print, or the user has Superuser authority.

```
lprm -Plaser1 555
```

> This command causes the files associated with print job 555 in the queue for laser1 to be removed, provided that the user is the same user who submitted the job or is a Superuser.

When the lprm command is executed, it actually kills the lpd daemon that is active for the selected print queue. After lprm removes the files it needs to, it restarts the daemon so that it can continue to process other jobs in the queue.

Using the *lpc* Command

The lpc command (line printer control program) is used by the administrator to control the local printing system. This command can be used to enable or disable print queues, flush queues, and move jobs around in the order they will print. It can also be used to inquire about the status of print queues.

The syntax for the lpc command is as follows:

```
lpc [command [parameters...]]
```

Each *command* that you use with the lpc command performs a specific management function and may or may not require additional command-line parameters. If you enter just the lpc command by itself, it prompts (using standard input) for additional data. The first parameter is interpreted by the program as a command, and any additional text is interpreted as parameter(s) for that particular command.

> **N O T E** The lpc command is used to administer only the local printing system. If you have set up remote printers in the /etc/printcap file, then you can manage the local queue for that printer but not the remote queue or spooling directory on the remote machine that actually controls the printer. ▓

The commands that can be used as the first parameter to the lpc command are as follows:

- abort [all ¦ *printer*...]
  This kills the active lpd daemon and then disables printing for the specified printers. This command stops the print job that is currently printing. After this, lpr cannot activate a new lpd daemon for the specified printers.
- clean [all ¦ *printer*...]
  This removes any temporary files (including control and data files) from the specified printer's spooling directory when the files do not form a complete print job.

▪ disable [all ¦ *printer*...]
Use this command to prevent lpr from submitting new print jobs to the specified print queue. This command turns off printing for the specified queue.

▪ down [all ¦ *printer*...] *message*...
Use this command to turn off the specified print queue(s) and disable printing. The text supplied as message... is entered into the printer's status file so that lpq can report it. You do not need to put quotes around the text of the message.

▪ enable [all ¦ *printer*...]
This command enables spooling on the printers specified so that users can once again use the lpr command to submit print jobs to the queue.

▪ restart [all ¦ *printer*...]
When a printer daemon dies unexpectedly, you can use this command to start a new daemon for the queue. The jobs currently existing in the queue will be printed by the new daemon. Perform this command when the lpq command gives you the "no daemon present" message.

▪ start [all ¦ *printer*...]
This command enables printing and starts a spooling daemon for the printers specified. This command (along with the stop command) changes the owner's execute permission on the lock file to accomplish its tasks.

▪ status [all ¦ *printer*...]
Use this command to get the status of printer daemons and queues. This command shows whether the queue is enabled or disabled, whether printing is enabled or disabled, the number of entries in the queue, and the status of the printer's lpd daemon.

▪ stop [all ¦ *printer*...]
Use this command to stop a spooling daemon and disable printing. The daemon stops after it finishes printing the current job. Use the abort command if you want to stop the daemon and kill the current job that is printing.

▪ topq *printer* [*job#*.. .][*username*...]
By default, entries into a queue are printed on a first-in, first-out (FIFO) basis. This command can be used to move print jobs to the top of the queue. You can specify one or more job numbers as an argument to this command. The print jobs specified by those job numbers are moved to the top of the queue. If you specify a username as an argument, then all pending jobs in the specified printer queue for that user are moved to the top of the queue.

▪ up [all ¦ *printer*...]
This command is the opposite of the down command. It enables all printing and starts a new printer daemon.

▪ exit or quit
These commands cause the lpc program to exit.

▪ ? [*command*] or help [*command*]
These commands can be used to get a short help text for each *command*. If no command is specified after the help command, then a list of all commands that the lpc program recognizes is displayed.

Although the lpc program is usually used by an administrator (Superuser), ordinary users can use the restart and status commands.

In Listing 14.2, you can see an example of using the lpc command to get the status of a printer named laser1. In this example, the queue is enabled and printing. There is only one job in the queue.

Listing 14.2 Using the *lpc* Command to Get the Status of a Printer

```
% /usr/sbin/lpc
lpc> status laser1
laser1:
        printer is on device '/dev/tty01' speed 9600
        queuing is enabled
        printing is enabled
        1 entry in spool area

lpc>
```

In Listing 14.3, you can see that although three jobs are waiting to print, the spooler daemon is not present. For some mysterious reason (yes, it happens), the daemon has died. When this happens, you can use the lpc restart laser1 command to create a new daemon for the queue, as shown in Listing 14.3. Note that although you must be a superuser to use the lpc start command, a regular user can use the lpc restart command. This is because the start command is used with the stop command by an administrator to control the queue, whereas the restart command is used when a malfunction has occurred, and the command only puts back into action what was supposed to be.

Listing 14.3 Restarting the *lpd* Daemon Using the *lpc* Command

```
% /usr/sbin/lpc
lpc> status laser2
laser2:
        printer is on device '/dev/tty02' speed 9600
        queuing is enabled
        printing is enabled
        3 entries in spool area
        no daemon present

lpc> restart laser1
```

If you see from the lpc status command that no daemon is present, but there are also no entries waiting to print, you do not have to restart the daemon. That is because a daemon is spawned by the original lpd process only when a queue has something to print. When all print jobs in a spooling directory have been printed and the directory becomes empty, the lpd daemon created for that queue terminates. When a user again sends a file to the queue to print, a new daemon is created automatically.

Gathering Print Statistics Using the *pac* Command

You can specify in the /etc/printcap file that accounting be enabled for one or more printers. This can be useful in an environment where chargeback mechanisms are in place for different departments, or for tracking usage for a specific user. The pac command can be used to report accounting data for queues for which it has been enabled.

The output of the pac command is a simple report with four columns, showing the user (and host computer) from which the print job was submitted, the number of units printed (in pages or feet), the number of times the printer was used, and finally, the computed price of the print job. Listing 14.4 shows a sample of output from the pac command. You should note that in this report the price column is merely the number of units times the cost, which defaults to two cents per unit if you do not specify it on the command line. The units are either the number of pages printed (for text files) or the number of feet of paper used (for raster devices).

Listing 14.4 Accounting Report Output from the *pac* Command

```
Login             pages/feet      runs     price
atlunix1:harris   14.00           1        $ 0.28
atlunix1:brown    3.00            2        $ 0.06
pluto:ogletree    21.00           3        $ 0.42
```

By default, the pac command outputs accounting information on all print jobs, in alphabetical order using the computer name and username that originated the print request. You can alter the report by using the command-line parameters. The syntax for the pac command is:

```
pac [-Pprinter][-cmrs][-pprice][username]
```

As is the custom with other printing commands, the -P parameter allows you to specify a printer. If you do not, the value of PRINTER is used, or the system default printer is assumed. The other parameters you can use are as follows:

- c   Sort the output report by cost instead of machine/username.

- m   Accounting charges are grouped by username with no regard to the hostname of the computer from which the job(s) were submitted. Effectively causes pac to ignore the computer hostname in the accounting file.

- r   Reverse the sort order for the report output. This would cause the listing to be in reverse order by the hostname or username in a normal sort. When used with the -c parameter, causes the output to be sorted by cost, in reverse order, with the highest cost first.

- s   This causes pac to summarize the accounting and write it to a summary file. The summary file is usually in the form of *printer*.acct_sum.

- p*price*   This allows you to specify the cost per unit (foot or page) for print jobs. The default, if not specified, is two cents per unit.

- *username*   If you supply usernames at the end of the command, then only statistics for print jobs for those users are output.

If your situation requires extensive accounting reporting, you can use the `pac` command in script files to automate the job.

Installing and Configuring a Printer Under the BSD System

To add a printer to your UNIX system, you have to perform several steps. The most logical step, of course, is to attach the printer to the computer. You must then create the special device file to be used by the operating system to access the device. Entries need to be made in the printer configuration file (`/etc/printcap`), and you have to create the spooling directories used for the print queue. Finally, you have to make sure that the `lpd` daemon is started by placing an entry into the appropriate `rc` startup file.

> **NOTE** Some versions of UNIX come with a program or script file that can be used to automate the setup process for printers. For example, Digital UNIX uses the `lprsetup` program to guide the user through the process. ▦

Before you begin the process of setting up a printer, be sure to have on hand all the information you need to complete the process. For most typical setups, you need the following:

- A name for the printer along with alias names that you will allow.
- The type of printer (for example, HP LaserJet V).
- The name of the printer device created by MAKEDEV for the port the printer is attached to.
- Accounting information. If you are going to enable accounting for the printer, do you want to use the standard two-cent price?
- Pathname for the spooler directory.
- Pathname and filenames for any log files or accounting files.
- Baud rate and port type (serial or parallel) for the printer port.

Using *MAKEDEV* to Create the Special Device File   After you have attached the printer to a port on the computer, you must use the MAKEDEV script to create the special device file that the operating system uses to communicate with the device. Create these files under the `/dev` directory. For example:

```
# cd /dev
# ./MAKEDEV port
```

where *port* is the name of the physical port to which the printer is attached. In general, device names for parallel ports (sometimes called Centronics after the printer manufacturer that devised the concept) are in the form of `lptn` where *n* ranges from zero for the first port (`lpt0`), one for the second (`lpt1`), and so on. For devices connected to a serial port, the naming convention is generally `ttynn` (`tty01`, `tty02`, and so on). You might need to consult the documentation that comes with your system to determine the correct port designation.

Depending on the version of UNIX you are running, you might have to further configure the printer port. Consult your documentation for information.

Part
II

Ch
14

You can use the lptest command to send a pattern of characters (including all 96 printable ASCII characters) to the printer port to test whether it is working properly. Invoke the command (with or without arguments) and redirect the output to the printer port:

```
# lptest > /dev/lpt01
```

The syntax for the lptest command is as follows:

```
lptest [length [count]]
```

The value you specify for *length* determines the length of the output line, and the value of *count* indicates the number of lines to output. The default for length is 79, and the default for count is 200.

After executing the command, check the printer to see whether the pattern of ASCII characters printed correctly.

Creating the Spooler Directory   For each printer, create a separate directory to be used to spool the files waiting to print. It is customary to put the spooling directories for all printers on the system under another directory to make them easier to manage. For example, you could use the directory path /var/spool/lpd and place subdirectories under this path for each printer you create:

```
# cd /var/spool/lpd# mkdir laser1
```

After you create the spooling directory, change the directory's group and ownership to daemon and set the permission mode.

```
# chmod 775 laser1
# chgrp daemon laser1
# chown daemon laser
```

The /etc/printcap File   The line printer daemon (lpd) uses the control file /etc/printcap to determine characteristics for each printer on the system. This file is similar to the /etc/termcap file in syntax, using two-character symbols to define characteristics. Each printer in this file is identified by a name and a number of aliases, each separated by the vertical-bar character ("|"). The remaining entries consist of the two-character codes with corresponding values, each separated using the colon character. Listing 14.5 shows a simple entry in /etc/printcap for a printer. In this listing, the only symbols defined are sd and lp.

Listing 14.5   Simple /etc/printcap Entry

```
laser¦laser1¦lp¦lp0¦HP Laser Printer 3rd floor:\
     :sd=/var/spool/lpd/laser:\
     :lp=/dev/tty01:
```

In this example, the first line contains the name of the printer ("laser") followed by several alias names that users can use to access the printer. Each alias is separated from the others by the vertical-bar character. The last alias on the first line shows a common technique used by many administrators: Describe the printer and/or its location. You can also put comments into the /etc/printcap file by using the pound sign character (#) as the first character in the line.

N O T E Although you only need a single colon character to separate paired-values within an `/etc/printcap` entry, it is customary when using multiple lines to place a colon at the start of the definition as well as after it to make it easier to read. For example, `:sd=/var/spool/lpd/laser1:br#9600:` could be written on a single line, or you could write it on multiple lines as follows:

```
:sd=/var/spool/lpd/laser1:\
:br#9600:
```

Note that the backslash character (\) is used to indicate continuation of the entry. ■

In Listing 14.5 the `sd` symbol is followed by a directory path. This is used to specify the spooling directory that `lpd` uses to store files waiting to be printed. Multiple users can send files to the printer using the `lpr` command, and copies of the files to be printed are created by the `lpd` daemon in the spooling directory and remain there until they are printed, at which time the `lpd` daemon deletes them.

The `lp` symbol indicates the special device file for the printer. The `makdev` command creates the device file just as for any other device attached to the system. In the case of a remote printer, you would use the hostname/queue name on the remote system for this value.

The other symbols that you can use in the `/etc/printcap` file are listed in Table 14.1.

N O T E In Listing 14.1, the equal sign operator was used to assign values to the `sd` and `lp` symbols. This operator is used to assign string values to `/etc/printcap` symbols. In Table 14.1, you find other symbols that are not string types. These are either boolean, which are indicated by their presence and take no value, or by the pound sign (#), used to assign numeric values. ■

Table 14.1 Symbols Used in the */etc/printcap* File

Symbol	Type	Default Value	Description
af	string	NULL	Name of accounting file
br	numeric	no default	Baud rate if `lp` is a `tty`
cf	string	NULL	The `cifplot` data filter
df	string	NULL	The `TeX` data filter (DVI format)
du	string	no default	Used to specify a nonstandard user ID for the daemon
fc	numeric	0	If `lp` is a `tty`, clear flag bits
ff	string	/f	String to send to printer for form feed
fo	boolean	false	Print a form feed when device is opened
fs	numeric	0	If `lp` is a `tty`, set flag bits
gf	string	NULL	Graph data filter (plot format)

Part

II

Ch

14

continues

Table 14.1 Continued

Symbol	Type	Default Value	Description
hl	boolean	`false`	Print the burst header page last
ic	boolean	`false`	Driver supports (nonstandard) `ioctl` to indent on printout
if	string	`NULL`	Accounting text filter
lf	string	`/dev/console`	Name of error logging file
lo	string	`lock`	Name of lock file
lp	string	`/dev/lp`	Output device
mc	numeric	`0`	Maximum number of copies allowed
mx	numeric	`1000`	Maximum file size (in BUFSIZ blocks)— zero means unlimited
nf	string	`NULL`	The `ditroff` data filter (device independent `troff`)
of	string	`NULL`	Output filtering program
pc	numeric	`200`	Price per foot or page (in hundredths of cents)
pl	numeric	`66`	Page length in lines
pw	numeric	`132`	Page width in characters
px	numeric	`0`	Page width in pixels (horizontal)
py	numeric	`0`	Page length in pixels (vertical)
rf	string	`NULL`	The FORTRAN-style text file filter
rg	string	`NULL`	Restricted group. Only members of this group are allowed access to the printer
rm	string	`NULL`	Machine name for remote printer
rp	string	`lp`	Remote printer name argument
rs	boolean	`false`	Restrict remote users to only those who have local accounts
rw	boolean	`false`	Open the print device for read/write
sb	boolean	`false`	Short (one line) banner
sc	boolean	`false`	Suppress multiple copies
sd	string	`/usr/spool/lpd` or `/var/spool/lpd`	Spooling directory
sf	boolean	`false`	Suppress form feeds
sh	boolean	`false`	Suppress printing of burst page header

Symbol	Type	Default Value	Description
st	string	status	Name of status file
tf	string	NULL	Name of `troff` data filter (cat phototypesetter)
tr	string	NULL	Trailer string to print when queue is emptied (that is, form feeds or escape characters)
vf	string	NULL	Raster image filter
xc	numeric	0	If `lp` is a `tty`, clear local mode bits
xs	numeric	0	If `lp` is a `tty`, set local mode bits

When assigning values to symbols in the `/etc/printcap` file, be careful and test small changes instead of trying to create a large file all at once and hoping it works.

When using the symbols `fs`, `fc`, `xs`, and `xc` to set or clear flag bits, consult the `tty(7)` man page and the manual that comes with the printer to get the appropriate values. These symbols are used to set up or clear flag masks, with different bit combinations representing specific printer characteristics. The flag mask is a 16-bit octal value preceded with the number zero.

In Listing 14.6, you see a more complex `/etc/printcap` entry.

Listing 14.6 Another Example of an */etc/printcap* Entry

```
lp¦lp0¦Default Laser: \
     :af=/usr/adm/printer/lp.acct:\
     :br#9600:\
     :lf=/usr/adm/lpterror:\
     :lp=/dev/tty03:\
     :mx#0:\
     :sd=/var/spool/lpd:\
```

In this example, the spooling directory, log file, and accounting file have been specified. The `mx#0` entry is used to allow files of unlimited size to be printed.

In Listing 14.7, the `/etc/printcap` entry has been set up to use a printer on another computer. In this instance the `/etc/printcap` file must be set up to provide the name of the remote computer host and the print queue on that system.

Listing 14.7 Example of */etc/printcap* Entry for a Remote Printer

```
bigprint¦laser12¦Laser at Administration:\
     :lp=:\
     :rm=admnunix:\
     :rp=lp:\
     :sd=/var/spool/lpd/bigprint:\
     :mx#0:\
```

Part
II

Ch
14

Note that in this example of remote printing, the lp symbol is set to null because the print device is not on this system, and you don't want to assume the default value. The rm symbol is used to define the remote hostname, and the rp symbol is used to define the name of the remote printer. Also, even though the actual printing is done on the remote computer, you must still specify a spooling directory because files submitted to the queue still need to be temporarily stored before being copied to the remote system.

The SVR4 Print System

The SVR4 printing system is a little more involved than the BSD printing system. The lp command is used to send files to be printed to a queue, and the lpsched daemon is responsible for finishing the process. Sounds just like lpr and lpd, doesn't it? However, you don't have to edit the /etc/printcap file to define printer characteristics; you use the lpadmin utility instead. Spooling directories hold documents for *classes* of printers rather than individual printers.

The lp command accepts input from the user (either a filename or text from standard input) and makes a copy of it in the appropriate spool directory. The lpsched daemon then functions similarly to the lpd daemon by executing another program to format and print the file.

What Are Destinations and Classes?

The spooling directory that holds the file, however, need not be used for only a printer. Instead, the term *destination* is used for the end point of the printing process. A destination (whose name can be up to 14 characters long) can be a printer, or it can be a file that is appended to by multiple users via the lp printing system.

Destinations can be grouped into *classes*. A class functions almost like a printer pool, where printers of like kind are grouped together and used as if they were one printer. When a print job is sent to a class, the lpsched daemon directs it to an available printer in the class rather than a specific printer each time. For example, if you had three similar printers in a room with users and designated the printers to be in the same class, if three users all send print jobs in a short period of time, each could possibly print on a different printer. If all three printers are busy, the print job is held in the spooling directory and sent to the first one to become free.

N O T E The SRV4 printing system uses the term "destination" rather than "printer." The commands use the -d parameter to specify the destination rather than the -P parameter used by lpr and lpd to specify a printer. If the -d parameter is not specified, the environment variable LPDEST is checked. If it is not defined, the print job is sent to the default device if one has been set up by the administrator. If there is no default device, the print job is rejected.

Using the *lp* and *cancel* Commands to Print Files

The lp command is the general user interface into the lp printing system. The lp command can be used to submit files to be printed or to modify or remove files in the print queue. Because of this multifunctionality, the syntax for the command comes in two distinct forms:

```
lp [-c][-m][-p][-s][-w][-d dest]
   [-f form-name [-d any]][-H special-handling]
   [-n number][-o option][-P page-list]
   [-q priority-level][-S character-set][-d any]]
   [-S print-wheel[-d any]][-t title]
   [-T content-type][-r]][-y mode-list]
   [filename...]

lp -i request-id ... [-c][-m][-p][-s][-w]
   [-d dest][-f form-name[-d any]]
   [-H special-handling][-n number][-o option]
   [-P page-list][-q priority-level]
   [-S character-set[-d any]]]
   [-t title][-T content-type[-r]]
   [-y mode-list]
```

The first version of this syntax is used to send files to print. The second version is used to modify a print request that has already been submitted, by referencing it using the request-id assigned to the print job. If you attempt to modify a print job that is already printing, it will be stopped and restarted with the modifications.

The cancel command is used to remove jobs waiting to print. It also comes in two flavors:

```
cancel [request-id...][printer...]
cancel -u login-ID-list [printer...]
```

The first instance of the cancel command can be used to remove print request(s) by referencing their request-ids. The second can be used to remove print requests associated with a particular user by referencing the user's login-ID. If the login-ID-list contains blank characters, enclose it in quotes. Note that ordinary users can only cancel their own print requests. Administrators can cancel any job.

When using the lp command to submit a file to print, or when using it to modify an existing print job, the command-line parameters function the same. Following is a description of the parameters you can use when submitting or modifying a print job:

- c   This parameter causes a copy of the file to be made before it is printed. The default action is to create a link to the file. It should be obvious that if you use the -c parameter, then you should not remove (delete) the file before it is printed. Also, any changes you make to the file after submitting the print request are not reflected in the output if you use this parameter to create a copy of the file to be printed.

- d *dest*   Use this parameter to specify the destination printer or class for the print job.

- f *form-name*   This specifies a form to be mounted on the printer to process the print request. If the printer does not support the form, the request is rejected. Note that if you use the -d any parameter with this one, the print request can be sent to any printer that supports the form.

- H *special-handling*   You can use this parameter to put print requests on hold, resume requests that are holding, or, if you are an LP administrator, to cause a specific request to be the next one to print. The terms you use for *special-handling* are hold, resume, and immediate, respectively.

Part

II

Ch

14

■ m   Send mail after the print job has finished.

■ n *number*   Number of copies to print.

■ o *option*   This is used to specify printer-dependent options. You can specify more than one option by using the –o parameter more than once. You can also include multiple options by enclosing them in quotes, for example: -o "option1 option2".

Terms you can use for the *option* are as follows:

nobanner   Do not print banner page.

nofilebreak   When submitting more than one file to print, this tells the printer not to insert a form feed character between files.

length=scaled-decimal-number   Used to specify page length. You can specify it in lines, inches, or centimeters. Length=66 specifies 66 lines per page, whereas length=11I specifies 11 inches per page, for example.

width=scaled-decimal-number   Similar to the length option just discussed, use this format to specify page width in columns, inches, or centimeters.

lpi=scaled-decimal-number   Like length and width, use this to specify line pitch (lines per inch).

cpi=scaled-decimal-number   Like length and width, use this to specify characters per inch. You can also use the terms pica (10 characters per inch), elite (12 characters per inch), or compressed, to allow the printer to fit as many characters on a line as it can.

stty='stty-option-list'   You can use this to specify options for the stty command. Enclose the list with single quotes if it contains blank characters.

■ P *page-list*   If the filter can handle it, this causes only the pages specified by *page-list* to be printed. You can specify single pages or a range of pages.

■ p   Enables notification on completion of the print request.

■ q *priority-level*   Priority levels range from 0 (highest) to 39 (lowest). Use this parameter to change the print priority of a print request. Giving a request a higher priority causes it to print before requests with a lower priority.

■ s   Suppresses messages from lp.

■ S *character-set* or S *print-wheel*   This is used to select a character set or print wheel to be used on the printer for the request. If the character set or print wheel is not available, the request is rejected.

■ t *title*   Prints *title* on the banner page. Use quotes around the text if it contains blank spaces.

■ T *content-type*   Causes the request to be printed on a printer that supports *content-type* if available, or to use a filter to convert the content in to the appropriate type. If you specify -r with this option, a filter is not used. The request is rejected if no printer for this type is available and/or a filter cannot be used.

■ w   Sends a message to the user's terminal after the print request completes. If the user is not currently logged in, a mail message is sent.

■ y *mode-list*   Use *mode-list* options to print. The allowed values for *mode-list* are locally defined, and the job is rejected if there is no filter to handle the request.

The *lpadmin* Command

This command is used by administrators to set up printers for the printing system. The lpadmin command actually creates text files in the spooling directory that you should not directly edit yourself. Instead, use the lpadmin command to add or modify printers on your system. You can use the command to add printers, remove printers, or modify their characteristics. It can also be used to set up alerts for printer faults and to mount print wheels, among other things.

The syntax for the command is as follows:

```
lpadmin -p printer-options
lpadmin -x dest
lpadmin -d [dest]
lpadmin -S print-wheel -A alert-type [-W minutes]
        [-Q requests]
lpadmin -M -f form-name [-a [-o filebreak]
        [-t tray-number]
```

How to Add a Printer Using *lpadmin*   The first form of the lpadmin syntax is used to add printers to the system. A simple example of this is as follows:

```
lpadmin -plaser1 -v/dev/tty04 -mdumb -cpr
```

This creates a printer named laser1 (-p is the option, followed by pr8, the printer name). The printer is attached to the device /dev/tty04, uses the "dumb" printer interface, and is a member of the pr class of printers (-cpr).

The options you can use to add a printer are numerous. Consult the man pages for your system to get a full listing. Following are some basic options:

■ A *alert-type* [-W *minutes*]   Use this parameter to set up an alert action that will be performed when a printer fault occurs. The *alert-type* can be mail or write (puts a message on an administrator's terminal). You can also use *quiet*, to suppress alerts, *showfault* to execute a fault-handling procedure, or *none* to remove alerts. You can also specify a shell command to be executed. Using the term list, you can see the type of alert currently set up for the printer.

■ c *class*   Puts the printer into the named *class*. If *class* does not yet exist, it is created. The -r parameter can be used to remove a printer from a specific class.

■ D *comment*   Used to set up text displayed when the user requests a full description of the printer.

■ e *printername*   Use this parameter to copy the interface program used by an existing printer (*printername*) to use with the printer being created. This allows you to quickly clone entries when adding a printer of a type you already have.

■ i *interface*   Use this to specify the interface program for the printer. See -e earlier in this list to copy an interface from an existing printer.

- ■ m *model* Selects the *model* interface program that comes with the lp print service. You cannot use -e or -i with this option.

- ■ s *system-name* [!*printer-name*] Use this option to create a remote printer, one that resides on a remote system that you want your users to be able to access. The *system-name* should be the name of the computer on which the printer resides and !*printer-name* is the name the printer uses on the remote system. Note that the printer name on your system does not have to be the same as the name on the remote system.

Using *lpadmin* to Remove a Printer Removing a printer from the lp printing system is simple. Use the -x command-line parameter:

```
lpadmin -xlaser1
```

This command removes the printer laser1 from the system. If laser1 is the only printer in its class, the class also is removed.

Starting the Print Scheduler: The *lpsched* Command The printer scheduler is a daemon usually started at boot time (see the /etc/init.d/lp file). The command used to start the scheduler is lpsched. You can execute this command online to start the scheduler if it has died or if you have used the lpshut command to stop the scheduler. The syntax for the command is as follows:

```
lpsched [-nofork][-debug][-nobsd]
```

Similar to the lpr daemon, the lpsched daemon creates a new copy of itself to handle the actual printing so that it can leave the original daemon free to respond to requests. You can use the -nofork parameter to suppress the creation of a separate process. This is recommended to be used during debugging. Use the -debug parameter to put the daemon into "verbose" mode, which is to display debugging messages.

The -nobsd parameter tells lpsched to ignore the BSD spooler's well-known port. This can prevent conflicts when the lpd daemon is also running and is using that port to receive print requests from remote systems.

Using *lpshut* to Shut Down the Printer Scheduler If it becomes necessary to stop all printing, you can use the lpshut command. This causes the scheduler to shut down. Jobs that are currently printing will stop but will be reprinted in their entirety after the printer scheduling system is once again started. The lpsched command is used to start the printer scheduler after you have executed lpshut.

Although the printer scheduling system is completely shut down by this command, users can still use the regular commands to send files to print. You can use lpshut in situations where you are having major problems with the printer devices themselves but cannot afford to interrupt your users' workflow. If you used the accept command (described in the next section), then print requests would be rejected, possibly causing users problems. For example, the accounting department could be running batch files to produce end-of-month reports that would bomb if you removed the ability for them to submit reports to print. By using lpshut you can take care of major printer problems while still allowing reports to be readied for the printing process. When you restart the printer scheduling system, the reports produced will print out as if nothing had taken place.

Using *accept* and *reject* to Allow or Disallow Print Queuing to a Destination   There may be times when a printer is going to be out of service for a while and you do not want users to continue to queue files to print. Instead of removing the printer from the system (using `lpadmin -x`), you can use the `accept` and `reject` commands to allow or disallow queuing to the particular destination (printer or class).

To disallow queuing for a destination, use the `reject` command:

```
reject -r"Printer out of service today" laser1
```

The `-r` option is used to give setup a "reason" text that is displayed to users via the `lpstat -a` command. It is optional, but is helpful in an environment with man users where word of mouth does not suffice to get the message out. You can use a printer name (such as `laser1`) or a class of printers for the target of this command.

When the printer or class of printers becomes available again, use the `accept` command with the destination to allow printing again:

```
accept laser1
```

> **N O T E**   When you first create a printer using `lpadmin`, you should use the `accept` command to enable printing. Printers are created by default to reject print requests. This is to prevent users from attempting to send print requests to a printer you have created but are not finished modifying yet.

Using *enable* and *disable* to Disable Printing for a Destination   The `enable` and `disable` commands work like the `accept` and `reject` commands but with an important difference. If you use `disable` for a print destination, it causes printing to stop. However, users can still send documents to the print queue that can be printed later after you issue the `enable` command. You can use the `-r` parameter to specify a reason text when using the `disable` command just as with the `reject` command. The `enable` command needs only the print destination for an argument.

Moving Files to a Different Printer   When a printer malfunctions, users have to wait for their documents. In most business environments, users need quick access to their printed documents and do not appreciate downtime. The ability to move documents from one printer queue to another allows the administrator to cope with this problem. The `lpmove` command can be used to move all print requests from one queue to another, or to move individual print requests.

The `lpmove` command has two forms. The first is used to move particular print requests to another printer:

```
lpmove laser1-123 laser1-124 laser2
```

The print requests that have request IDs of 123 and 124 would be moved from `laser1` to the queue for `laser2`. You can specify only the queue names if you want to move all the documents currently waiting to print. The following command accomplishes this task:

Part
II

Ch
14

```
Lpmove laser1 laser2
```

Note that the lpmove command does not check the accept status of the queue that you are moving documents to, thus some requests may fail.

Using *lpstat* to Obtain Print Queue and Print Job Status The lpstat command can be used to show the status of the print system. Most ordinary users will execute the command without any parameters to get the status of print jobs that belong to them. However, the syntax is flexible to allow users or administrators the ability to inquire into the status of many different aspects of the system. The syntax for the lpstat command is as follows:

```
lpstat [-d] [-r] [-R] [-s] [-t] [-a [list]]
    [-c [list]] [-o [list]]
    [-p [list]] [-P] [-s [list] [-l]]
    [-u [login-ID-list]] [-v [list]]
```

In this syntax *list* can be either a comma-delimited list or a series of items separated by spaces and enclosed in quotes. You can omit a list or use the keyword *all* in most instances to get the status of all the requested objects. The parameters for this command are as follows:

- a [*list*] Tells whether print destinations (printers or classes) are accepting print requests.
- c [*list*] This prints the name of all classes and the members of the each class. Specify classes using *list*.
- d Shows the system's default print destination.
- o [*list*] Shows the status of output requests. *list* can be printer or class names or request IDs.
- p [*list*] Shows the status of printers. Use *list* to specify printer names.
- r Shows the status of the print scheduler daemon (lpsched).
- s Shows summary information for the print system.
- t Shows all the status information available for the printing system.
- u [*login-ID-list*] Shows the status of requests for the users listed in *login-ID-list*.
- v [*list*] Shows the pathnames of the output devices for printers specified in *list*. If the printer is a remote printer, then the remote system name is shown instead.

For example, to show the status of the lpsched daemon, enter the following:

```
lpstat -r
```

To show the status of a particular printer, use:

```
lpstat -plaser1
```

where laser1 is the name of the printer you need information about.

From Here...

The two main printing systems that you will find in UNIX variants today are the BSD spooling system (lpr/lpd) and the SVR4 system (lp/lpsched). Although both perform the same basic functions, the lpr/lpd system works best in networked environments, whereas the lp/lpsched system is more flexible and easier to manage. The lpr/lpd method has also been used in some other operating systems for compatibility with UNIX network hosts. Printers are sold by several manufacturers network-ready to accept requests using lpr/lpd. You will even find some versions of UNIX that take the best from both systems to form a hybrid printing system.

Printing is a major function of any operating system and is closely related to other topics covered in this book:

- Chapter 3, "UNIX Shells and System Commands," discusses using filters and redirection, powerful tools in automating system functions, as well as utilities you can use to format data to be sent to the printing system.

- No discussion of printing would be complete without making reference to other major tools that user will use to create printable output. See Chapter 4, "The vi Editor," for more information about text editing on UNIX systems.

- Chapter 26, "Security," is useful if you want to protect important printers (the one with the payroll checks loaded in it, for example), or if you want to perform auditing to track usage of your printing resources.

## CHAPTER 15

Backup and Recovery

by Peter Kuo

In this chapter

Understanding the Importance of Data

No matter what the operating system or the type of hardware the OS runs on—be it MVS on a mainframe, UNIX on an HP mini, or DOS on a workstation—few system administrative issues are as important as backup or archiving.

Data comes in different forms. A computer system might store important financial data, such as accounts receivable and payroll information. With the increase of computer-automation in manufacturing environments, such as automobile assembly lines, computer systems are used to store and run mission-critical applications, such as manufacturing process-control software. In a research environment, computers are routinely used to store and manipulate vast amounts of experimental data, some of which takes months or even years to accumulate and millions of dollars to produce.

N O T E Sometimes the cost of lost data cannot be measured only in monetary terms such as the dollar amount spent in recovering it. Other costs are lost productivity (people sitting around doing nothing) and potential loss of sales due to the inability to access inventory or sales entry systems in a timely manner. Worst of all is the potential loss of customer confidence, which might take months or years to rebuild. ▨

A typical computer system uses hard drives for online data storage. Hard drives are electro-magnetic devices, and like any man-made devices, they *will* fail at some time. Most new hard drives have a rated MTBF (mean time between failure) of about 50,000 hours (a little less than six years), but that is just a statistical average. MTBF means that *most* hard drives will operate for at least 50,000 hours, some will work for more than ten years (highly unlikely), and some will fail in *less* than 50,000 hours of use. You are taking a risk if you only occasionally back up your systems, and you take an even greater chance if you do not verify the validity of the data of your backups. An administrator can lose his or her job or a company can fail because of the loss of valuable data due to lack of proper backups.

To err is human—even the most experienced users and system administrators make mistakes. Deleting the wrong file or mistyping information into a file (such as /etc/passwd) can cause unwarranted headaches and additional work for yourself or coworkers who need to access the data, or in the worst case, render the whole system unusable. In the unfortunate event that you encounter a disgruntled user or a malevolent hacker who has deliberately removed essential data or system files, having up-to-date backups would be a lifesaver. Data lost can also be caused by events beyond your control, such as an accidental fire or a natural disaster. (Remember the Los Angeles earthquake or the New York World Trade Center bombing?)

N O T E It *cannot* be emphasized enough that frequent and verified backups are essential. You can never have too many backups. ▨

You need to make some decisions about the frequency of backup, reuse of backup media, and storage requirements. Your choice of the method of backup and integrity checks would be dependent on how big your backup window is and how long it would take you to reconstruct the entire system, if necessary. These topics, along with discussions on some available backup tools are covered in this chapter.

A Look at Backup Strategies

The purpose of performing backups is to be able to restore individual files or complete file systems. How often to perform backups, what data should be backed up, and how to rotate backup media are issues that can be confusing.

Exactly how often you should back up which files depends on your system hardware configuration and particular needs. The criterion is, "If the system crashes, how much work are you willing to lose?" Ideally, you would want to back up all files on all file systems every few minutes so that you would never lose more than a few minutes of work. However, this approach is not practical, and there are other ways in which you can achieve this near real-time redundancy without doing backups (they are discussed in the "Selecting Appropriate Backup Devices" section later in this chapter).

To examine the problem another way, "How often should you back up the files?" The more users you have on the system, the more often you should back up the file systems. A common schedule is to perform a full backup once or twice a week and partial backups daily.

N O T E   A *full backup* is when every single file on every file system is backed up, regardless of its creation or modification time. A *partial*, or *incremental*, *backup* backs up only the files that have been created or modified since the last full backup.

Your backup strategy should be based on a rotation scheme that guarantees complete recovery in case of a disaster, within a reasonable amount of time. The following discussion is based on tape rotation because the most commonly used backup medium today is tape; however, the same principle applies to other storage media, such as CD-ROMs.

A rotation system distributes both old and new information across several tapes to reduce the risk of data being lost due to media failure. (Tapes have a limited lifetime and constant use of the same tape would shorten its life span.) The backup and storage media type and media rotation method you choose should take the following into consideration:

- Speed of backup device and amount of data to back up   Both the amount of data to back up and the speed at which it can be backed up will have an impact on your choice of backup methods. For example, if you have 20GB of data to be backed up daily and your backup device is only capable of backing up 1GB per hour, it will take at least 20 hours to perform a full backup. In such a case, doing a daily full backup is probably not a good option, and an incremental backup is more appropriate.

- File restoration decision   How many tapes (thus, how much time) will you need to restore information in the event of a complete system failure? (Always plan for the worst case.) Also, the procedure to restore your file systems back to a known-state (for example, last night) should be as straightforward as possible; you should not have to run through 20 tapes for the task.

■ Storage facilities   How many tapes are you physically capable of storing safely and securely onsite? For example, your backup tapes should be locked in a fire-resistant safe (specifically designed for tapes and magnetic storage media). That way, should there be an accidental small fire, the safe can keep the tapes from melting for a couple of hours, and at the same time secure them from theft. However, a typical safe (22×17×18 inches) only has a small usable storage space due to the thick walls.

■ Aging process   How long must you keep the files archived? For example, you might need to keep company accounting data around for a number of years or certain research material indefinitely.

You can choose from a number of commonly used media rotation schemes for your backup needs. Two of them, the Grandfather-Father-Son and the Tower of Hanoi methods are discussed in detail in the "Implementing a Backup Strategy" section later in the chapter.

Selecting Appropriate Backup Devices

With the first PCs, floppy diskettes were the norm for backup media. With the introduction of large hard drives and the typical disk space on a UNIX system (1GB or higher), it is no longer practical to use diskettes. For example, to fully back up a 1GB file system, you would need more than 700 diskettes! And the amount of time involved in writing to and swapping that many diskettes in and out of the disk drive also makes it impractical. However, for small amounts of personal data and specific (small) system files, such as /etc/passwd, /etc/hosts, and so on, diskette storage is a viable option. Other backup media options include:

■ Tape drives (various format)

■ (Removable) hard drives

■ Magneto-optical cartridges (optical jukebox)

■ ZIP and JAZ drives

■ WORM drives (Write Once, Read Many)

Tape Drives

The most commonly used backup devices are tape drives. Magnetic tapes are available in different sizes (ranging from 9-track reel-to-reel tapes to 1/4-inch tape cartridges, QICs, and 4mm and 8mm DAT tapes) and different capacities (ranging from about 100MB for QIC to more than 10GB for 8mm DAT). Tapes are popular backup media for two reasons: They are cost-effective and relatively fast. You can get an 8mm DAT tape (14GB capacity) for less than $20, and depending on the type of tape drive and software used, a peak throughput of 100MB/ minute is not uncommon.

 Some backup software, such as ARCserve/Open from Cheyenne (http://www.cheyenne.com), has a feature called *parallel streaming*. This enables you to perform simultaneous processing of backup and/or restore operations to separate tape devices attached to the same server.

For systems with large disk capacity, having an auto-tape changer is desirable. An autochanger holds multiple tapes and contains a mechanism for automatically loading and unloading them into a tape drive. This makes unattended backup and restoration of large file systems possible—otherwise, an operator would need to be available to change tapes manually. For those who are familiar with mainframe backup operations, autochangers function similarly to the "tape silos" used by mainframes but on a much smaller scale.

Hard Disks

The use of removable hard drives as a backup medium has the advantage in speed. However, to fully back up your system, you basically need to more than double up on your disk capacity (so that you have a "multigeneration" backup), which can be expensive. However, many UNIX systems support *disk mirroring* and/or *disk duplexing*—on some systems it is known as *shadowing*. Disk mirroring means to have one or more hard drives duplicating the data of the primary drive, and all these drives are connected to the same controller. When the operating system does a write-to-disk, data is written to both the primary and secondary drives. When a read operation takes place, the data is supplied from either the primary or the secondary drive because they contain the same information. In the event that the primary drive fails, the mirror (secondary) drive takes over transparently without any loss of data or downtime—you can limp along until the end of the day before taking the system down to effect repairs. In this configuration, however, the single point of failure is the hard drive controller.

Alternatively, you can put the secondary mirror drive(s) on a separate controller so that even if the controller of the primary drive fails, it does not affect the secondary drive(s). This is known as duplexing. Another advantage of duplexing is that because you now have two disk channels to the same data, disk I/O performance is increased, especially in terms of file reads.

A third way of using hard drives is more of a redundancy than a backup—but the end result is the same: preventing data loss. Instead of standard hard drive controllers you can use RAID (Redundant Array of Inexpensive Disks) controllers. There are different levels of RAID, and RAID-1 is equivalent to disk mirroring. It is common for high-performance UNIX systems or UNIX systems holding important data to use RAID-5, where three or more disks are used to form an array (a single logical disk). In the event of a single disk failure, RAID-5 can rebuild the data from the remaining disks (while running at a degraded performance).

 TIP Disks that can be physically mounted and left dormant in the array are sometimes used with RAID-5. If any disk in the array fails, the dormant disk automatically starts and rebuilds the data.

Other Media

The other backup media, such as WORM drives (in essence, CD-ROMs), optical jukeboxes (where the cartridges are written to magnetically and read optically), and ZIP and JAZ drives (from Iomega, `http://www.iomega.com`), are not as popular on large systems due to their limited capacity. The typical capacity is about 650MB, and in some cases with such a slow speed it would take minutes for a jukebox to cycle through all its platters. Although these media are not as cost effective or capable of storing as much data as tapes, they do, however, offer convenience and improved performance over using tapes.

 TIP Some companies use WORM/CD-ROMs to back up their financial data so that the recorded information cannot be modified and serves as reliable audit data.

In terms of access, it is faster using CD-ROMs, JAZ, and so on than tapes. This is because tapes need to be accessed sequentially, whereas CD-ROMs and other storage media can be accessed randomly. What's more, tapes have a relatively short "shelf-life" as compared to the other storage media (except for floppy diskettes)—years versus decades for CD-ROMs. So, if you have data that needs to be archived for an extended period (typically more than three years), consider moving them to CD-ROMs or JAZ cartridges.

Implementing a Backup Strategy

As previously mentioned, the ideal backup strategy is to do a full backup of all the file systems frequently (which would require 365 tapes, or more if you require more than one tape or do more than one full backup per day). This way, should you need to restore a single file or the whole system, you only need to access the latest backup tape and go from there. Unfortunately, daily full backups are not possible except for small systems where you have enough of a low system-usage time (a backup "window") to effect a complete backup, and it also becomes expensive to keep purchasing new tapes (none are reused during the retaining time period). For most systems, a combination of full and differential backups coupled with a tape rotation scheme, where a given set of tapes is reused, is the best option.

NOTE Always schedule your system backup during a time of little or no user activity—for two reasons. First, backup procedures take up system resources such as CPU cycles and put a high demand on hard disk access. This could degrade the system performance. Second, when users are on the system, there will always be opened files, which do not get backed up. Therefore, to back up as many changed files as possible, during the time that you perform your backup you should shut down any applications, such as inventory database programs, that keep files open constantly and also restrict user access to files.

The main drawback of doing differential backups is when you need to restore. You need to first restore the last full backup and then apply all the incremental backups from that point on. Therefore, you save some time during the backup process, but the restore phase takes a little longer.

There are two types of incremental backups—incremental to the last complete backup (call it Incremental Backup Type 1, IBL1), or incremental to the last incremental backup (call it Incremental Backup Type 2, IBL2). Assuming that you have set up the following backup schedule:

Sunday   FB, Full backup

Monday   IBL1, incremental backup of files changed since Sunday's full backup

Tuesday	IBL1, incremental backup of files changed since Sunday's full backup
Wednesday	IBL1, incremental backup of files changed since Sunday's full backup
Thursday	IBL1, incremental backup of files changed since Sunday's full backup
Friday	IBL1, incremental backup of files changed since Sunday's full backup
Saturday	No backup (assuming that no one uses the system on weekends)

If you need to restore a file lost on Thursday, you only need to access one tape—either the IBL1 tape created on Wednesday (if the file was changed during the current week) or the FB tape created on Sunday (if the file was not changed during the current week). To fully restore the system, you will only need two tapes—the FB tape and the latest IBL1 tape. Under this schedule, the backup time gets longer as the week progresses because more and more files need to be backed up. However, it makes file restore simple. This is a simplification of the Grandfather-Father-Son rotation method.

Consider the following schedule, which does a full backup at the beginning of the month (using January as an example), a weekly incremental (IBL1) on Mondays, and daily incremental (IBL2):

January 1	FB, Full backup
Every Monday	IBL1, incremental backup of files changed since FB
Tuesday	IBL2, incremental backup of files changed since Monday
Wednesday	IBL2, incremental backup of files changed since Tuesday
Thursday	IBL2, incremental backup of files changed since Wednesday
Friday	IBL2, incremental backup of files changed since Thursday
Saturday	No backup
Sunday	No backup

Using this schedule, file restore is a little more complicated than the previous example. For example, to restore a file you lost, you need to do the following:

- Use the FB tape, if the file wasn't changed during the month.
- Use the latest IBL1 tape, if the file was changed the previous week but not during the current week.
- Use the appropriate IBL2 tape from the current week, if the file was changed this week.

The advantage of this example schedule is that it takes less time per day for the backups.

The preceding two examples do not take into account multiple tape sets so that you can go back to data from the previous week or month. The Grandfather-Father-Son and Tower of Hanoi rotation schemes described in the following sections, on the other hand, use multiple tape sets. These two rotation methods are among the most often used by backup software.

Grandfather-Father-Son Method

The *Grandfather-Father-Son tape rotation scheme* uses three "generations" of tapes, as illustrated in Table 15.1. It uses a total of 21 tapes. Of these 21 tapes, four are daily tape sets labeled

Monday, Tuesday, Wednesday, and Thursday. Another four tapes are weekly tape sets labeled Friday1, Friday2, Friday3, and Friday4; for months that have five Fridays, a fifth weekly tape set labeled Friday5 is used. Also, 12 tapes labeled January, February,…December act as monthly tapes.

Table 15.1   Grandfather-Father-Son Tape Rotation Scheme

	Week1	Week2	Week3	Week4
Daily	Monday	Monday	Monday	Monday
Daily	Tuesday	Tuesday	Tuesday	Tuesday
Daily	Wednesday	Wednesday	Wednesday	Wednesday
Daily	Thursday	Thursday	Thursday	Thursday
Weekly	Friday1	Friday2	Friday3	Friday4
Monthly				January
	Week5	Week6	Week7	Week8
Daily	Monday	Monday	Monday	Monday
Daily	Tuesday	Tuesday	Tuesday	Tuesday
Daily	Wednesday	Wednesday	Wednesday	Wednesday
Daily	Thursday	Thursday	Thursday	Thursday
Weekly	Friday1	Friday2	Friday3	Friday4
Monthly				February

This rotation scheme recycles the daily tapes the following week (they are sometimes known as the "sons" because they have the shortest life span), the weekly backup tapes after five weeks (the "fathers"), and the monthly tapes the following year (the "grandfathers").

N O T E   The monthly backups are full backups, whereas the daily and weekly backups are incremental backups. As to which type of incremental backup (IBL1 or IBL2), the choice is yours. However, you should base your decision on these factors—how large a backup window you have, the amount of data to back up, and the throughput of your backup device. ▪

N O T E   Notice that the daily tapes get the most use, therefore, they are most prone to failure. Check these tapes often for wear-and-tear before using them. ▪

Tower of Hanoi

The *Tower of Hanoi rotation scheme* is named after an ancient mathematical game of the same name. This rotation scheme is sometimes referred to as the *ABACABA* rotation method, based on the frequency tapes are rotated. Five or more tapes are needed in its implementation. To simplify the discussion here, five tapes labeled A, B, C, D, and E are used.

N O T E The Tower of Hanoi (sometimes referred to as the Tower of Brahma or the End of the World Puzzle) was invented by the French mathematician, Edouard Lucas, in 1883. ■

The basic idea is that each tape is used at different rotation intervals. For example, tape A is used every other day, tape B every fourth day, tape C every eighth day, tapes D and E every sixteenth day. The rotation pattern is shown in Table 15.2. Uppercase letters represent the first use of the tape.

Table 15.2   Tower of Hanoi Tape Rotation Scheme

Week1	Week2	Week3	Week4
M,T,W,Th,F	M,T,W,Th,F	M,T,W,Th,F	M,T,W,Th,F
A,B,a,C,a	b,a,D,a,b	a,c,a,b,a	E,a,b,a,c
Week5	Week6	Week7	Week8
M,T,W,Th,F	M,T,W,Th,F	M,T,W,Th,F	M,T,W,Th,F
a,b,a,**d**,a	b,a,c,a,b	a,**e**,a,b,a	c,a,b,a,**d**
Week9	Week10	Week11	Week12
M,T,W,Th,F	M,T,W,Th,F	M,T,W,Th,F	M,T,W,Th,F
a,b,a,c,a	b,a,**d**,a,b	a,c,a,b,a	**e**,a,b,a,c

N O T E Notice that the pattern recycles itself every 31 days (one month), with the use of either tape D or E between the cycles. If you use less than five tapes, the cycle repeats itself every 15 days, which does not "map" nicely to the requirement of monthly backups.

In the case where five tapes are used, tapes D and E are alternated in their usage within the cycle (so they are used once every 16 days). This difference is shown in bold in Table 15.2. ■

Tips and Tricks

Choosing a backup storage medium and a media rotation scheme does not make a backup strategy. You also need to decide what to back up, decide how often to back up, and keep track of your backup tapes. The following are some points to consider:

- Automate your backup   Most backup software allows you to set up a schedule so that the process initiates itself periodically without manual intervention. This is important because if you need to manually start the backup procedure daily, inevitably there will be a day that you forget, you didn't have time, or something happened to prevent you from doing it, and, as Murphy's Law will have it, that is the one day you will need a backup!

If you are using one of the UNIX utilities, such as tar, for your backup, you can always automate it using one of the other UNIX utilities, such as at or cron. Topics about scheduling frequently executed tasks are discussed later in the book.

▶ **See** "The at Command" and "The cron Process," **p. 403, 409**

T I P You might want to get a backup device that holds about twice as much tape (or whatever medium) as you require for a backup job so that you have the option of not changing the tapes for one day.

■ Back up every hard disk   Every hard disk contains data that you need, either today or some time down the road—that's why you installed that hard disk, isn't it? Therefore, make sure that every file system is included in the full backup.

■ Back up every file   Do not limit backups to just documents or certain files—you will inevitably need one that was not backed up. Also, having a backup of every file, especially the system files, allows you to rebuild your entire system quickly, should there be a need. You can, however, just back up documents and files that change frequently in your daily incremental backup and include everything during the full backup.

You can, however, safely exclude /tmp, /var/tmp, and /usr/var/tmp from being backed up because they generally only contain temporary files. You should also exclude /proc, if it exists, because it is not a disk file system but is really just a way for the kernel to provide you with information about the operating system and system memory.

■ Make copies of your backup   As pointed out earlier, storage media will fail, especially tapes, after prolonged use. It does not hurt to have multiple copies (or generations) of your backups, even if they are older copies. Often, even an old copy is better than no copy at all.

Some tape backup software has a tape-to-tape copy feature that you can use to make a duplicate of your backup without having to do another backup.

■ Keep a backup offsite   You never know when a fire, flood, theft, or earthquake will make your offsite copy your only copy. One option is to keep your current weekly backup onsite (in a fire-resistant safe, for example) and send the previous week's backup to a secure offsite location.

■ Verify your backup   You need to know whether you can ever restore from your backups. Most backup software has a verification feature; use it whenever possible. Also restore a few files at random and verify them yourself.

Create the backups so that the files can be restored to anywhere on the file system, onto a different file system, or even onto another (UNIX) computer system.

■ Label all media   Be sure to label all media—tapes, disks, whatever—used in a backup. If you have to use multiple items, make sure that they are numbered sequentially and dated. If you send backups offsite, document them.

■ Keep track of where your backups are   As you can see from the Tower of Hanoi discussion, it can be complicated to keep track of which tape to use when. Labeling all your media is certainly a starting point. Fortunately, many backup programs logically labels the media so that they can detect whether the right one has been inserted. At the same time, the backup software keeps track of what files have been backed up on which tape using its own database. Make sure that the database is backed up as well.

■ Back up your system before making changes   When you upgrade your system, you should definitely make a backup of at least the root and /usr file systems, if not a full backup. Although it doesn't happen often, it is possible for a critical library or program not to upgrade properly, crippling your machine.

Backup and Restore Tools

A number of utilities are included with UNIX to help you back up your system, and most work with the media discussed earlier in this chapter. UNIX supports two major utilities designed expressly for backups:

■ volcopy and labelit

■ dump and restore

Also, the general-purpose utilities such as tar, cpio, and dd are often used for backups. Some backup utilities, such as ctar and BRU, use either tar or cpio as the "engine" and argument them by adding some user interface and bookkeeping capability for managing the backups.

Also available are third-party commercial products that are not necessarily dependent on tar or cpio or any of the previously mentioned UNIX utilities.

Using *volcopy* and *labelit*

The volcopy program makes a literal (image) copy of the file system from one location to another. The program requests length and density information if this is not given on the command line or if it is not recorded on a label on the input medium. If the file system is too large to fit on one tape, volcopy prompts for additional tapes as needed. Labels of all media (both input and output) are checked to make sure that the correct media (disk or tape) are in place before performing the copy operation. Tapes can be mounted alternatively on two or more drives. If volcopy is interrupted, it asks whether the user wants to quit or wants to escape to a shell. In the latter case, the user can perform other operations (for example, labelit) and then return to volcopy by exiting the shell.

N O T E   The labelit program is a supplementary utility to volcopy. labelit is used to write labels on unmounted disk file systems or file systems being copied to tape. Such labels can be used to uniquely identify volumes and are used by volume-oriented programs such as volcopy. ■

The advantage of using volcopy is that the entire file system is saved every time a backup is performed, and volcopy does it very efficiently. The other advantage of the volcopy system is that it can be used to make copies to either disks or tapes. A disk-to-disk backup operation, which is extremely fast, is often preferred for the most frequent backups or backups that have a small time window—you can first do a disk-to-disk copy during this available (small) time window to save the important data and then at your leisure do a (slower) disk-to-tape copy later.

The third advantage of using volcopy is that it is useful for recovering lost files. Because an entire file system is saved, it is possible to mount the saved file system to recover a single file, or to copy the file system back from the backup medium to recover an entire file system.

The advantage of volcopy's image backup is also its disadvantage. Because it backs up the whole file system every time, and if the file system is not very busy (that is, files are not being changed frequently), you are spending time backing up mostly unchanged data. This is where the dump/restore system offers a better alternative.

Using *dump* and *restore*

The dump program performs an incremental file system save operation. dump can back up all specified files (normally either a whole file system or files within a file system changed after a certain date or since the last backup) to magnetic tape, diskette, or a disk file (a "dump"). The restore program can examine the dumps created by the dump program to recover individual files or an entire file system.

N O T E Depending on the version of UNIX, restore is sometimes referred to as restor or ufsrestore; dump is sometimes called ufsdump. On HP/UX, you can also use fbackup, which performs similar functions to dump.

On AIX systems, you can use its proprietary backup and restore commands that provide file system dumps and recovery as well as backup of individual files and directories; these commands resemble the standard UNIX dump and restore utilities. ■

Incremental backups by dump are controlled by assigning a dump level to a particular backup. The dump levels range from 0 through 9. When a dump of a certain level N is performed, all files that have changed since the last dump of level $N-1$ or lower are backed up. For instance, if a "level 2" dump was done on Monday, followed by a "level 4" dump on Tuesday, a subsequent "level 3" dump on Wednesday would contain all files modified or added since the "level 2" (Monday) backup.

N O T E A "level 0" dump copies the entire file system. ■

The one major drawback of using dump/restore for backup is the lack of log files telling you what files are on which tape; there is, however, an entry made to /etc/dumpdates for each file system successfully dumped that includes the file system name, date, and dump level. As previously discussed in the "Implementing a Backup Strategy" section, recovering individual files from incremental backups can be time consuming—the missing file might be on any of several tapes depending on when the file was last modified, and without a log file to work with, the restore program will have to scan through the set of dump tapes to figure out which tape contains the missing file.

The other major drawback of using dump to back up your system is that when running dump, the file system must be inactive; otherwise, the dump output might be inconsistent, and restore can get confused when doing incremental restores from dump tapes that were made on active file systems. A file system is inactive when it is unmounted or the system is in single-user mode. This requirement of an inactive file system makes using dump on a 7x24 system impossible.

N O T E   A file system is not considered inactive if one tree branch of the file system is quiescent while another tree branch has files or directories being modified. ■

Using *tar*

The tar (*t*ape *ar*chive) utility was originally designed to create a tape archive (a large file that contains, or "archives," other files). In addition to file contents, an archive includes header information to each file inside it. This header data can be used when extracting files from the archive to restore information such as file permissions, ownerships, and modification dates. An archive file can be saved to disk (and later copied to tape or transferred to another storage medium), written directly to tape, or transmitted across the network while it is being created.

N O T E   The archive file is also known as a *tarfile*. ■

Although many command-line options are available with tar, Table 15.3 is a list of the most commonly used options (notice that all options are in lowercase).

Table 15.3   Commonly Used Options for *tar*

Option	Description
c	Create a new archive. This option implies the r option.
f *device*	This causes tar to use the *device* argument as the name of the tarfile. If the name of the tarfile is '-', tar writes to the standard output or reads from the standard input, whichever is appropriate. Thus, tar can be used as the head or tail of a pipeline. If f is omitted, tar uses the device indicated by the TAPE environment variable, if set; otherwise, it uses the default values defined in /etc/default/tar.
r	Append files to an archive.
t	Table of Contents. The names of the specified files are listed each time they occur on the tarfile. If no file arguments are given, all the names on the tarfile are listed. With the v function modifier, additional information for the specified files is displayed. The listing is similar to the format produced by the ls -l command.
u	Update an archive. The named files are added to the tarfile if they are not already there or have been modified since last written on that tarfile. This option implies the r option.

continues

Table 15.3   Commonly Used Options for *tar*.

Option	Description
v	Verbose. Normally, tar does its work silently. This option causes tar to show the name of each file it treats, preceded by the function letter. With the t option specified, v gives more information about the tape entries than just the name.
x *filenames*	Extract, or restore, files from an archive. The named files are extracted from the tarfile and written to the current directory. If a named file matches a directory whose contents had been written onto the tarfile, this directory is (recursively) extracted. Use the file or directory's relative path when appropriate, or tar will not find a match. The owner, modification time, and mode are restored (if possible); otherwise, to restore owner, you must be the superuser. If no filename argument is given, the entire content of the tarfile is extracted.

N O T E   The r option and the u option cannot be used with many tape drives due to limitations in the drive such as the absence of backspace or append capability.

N O T E   Some implementations of UNIX require you to prefix the options with a hyphen, such as tar -x rather than tar x.

The general syntax for the tar command is as follows:

```
tar [options] filename
```

Following are some examples of the use of tar in backing up and restoring files:

- tar cv /usr/peter tar.backup   Copies all files in /usr/peter and below to the archive file called tar.backup on the default device; the verbose mode is on.

- (cd /home; tar cf - peter) ¦ tar xf -   Creates the directory /home/peter as a subdirectory in the directory where you invoked the command. It preserves file permissions and ownerships.

- tar cvf /dev/rmt/0 /usr/lib   Copies all files in /usr/lib and below to the archive file created on device /dev/rmt/0; the verbose mode is on.

- tar tvf /dev/rmt/0   Reads the table of contents from the archive file on device /dev/rmt/0.

- tar xvf /dev/rmt/0   Extracts *all* files from the archive on device /dev/rmt/0.

- tar xvf /dev/rmt/0 /usr/lib/chapter.15   Extracts only the file called chapter.15 from the archive on device /dev/rmt/0. Note that you need to specify the complete filename.

You can include one or more `tar` commands in the system `cron` file so that the file systems frequently are backed up automatically. For example, the following entry performs a backup of `/usr/unix.project` every day at 3:00AM to:

```
00 03 * * * tar cvf /usr/unix.project > /home/peter/tar.log
```

▶ For more information about using `cron`, **see** "The `cron` Process" **p. 409**

`tar` is available for many different operating systems, including DOS. Therefore, you can use a tarfile for file distribution to other sites.

Using *cpio*

The `cpio` (*co*py *in-o*ut) program is similar to `tar` in that it is a general-purpose utility for copying (`cpio`) file archives. However, it can use archive files in many different formats, including the format used by `tar`, and a `cpio` archive can span multiple tapes or disks.

`cpio` operates in one of three modes:

- Copy In Mode `cpio -i` (copy in) extracts files from the standard input, which is assumed to be the product of a previous `cpio -o`. Only files with names that match patterns are selected. Extracted files are conditionally created and copied into the current directory tree based on the specified command-line options. The permissions of the files are those of the previous `cpio -o`. Owner and group are the same as the current user unless the current user is *root*. If this is true, owner and group are the same as those resulting from the previous `cpio -o`. Note that if `cpio -i` tries to create a file that already exists and the existing file is the same age or younger (newer), `cpio` outputs a warning message not to replace the file. (The `-u` option can be used to overwrite, unconditionally, the existing file.)

- Copy Out Mode `cpio -o` (copy out) reads the standard input to obtain a list of pathnames and copies those files onto the standard output together with pathname and status information. Output is padded to a 512-byte boundary by default or to the user-specified block size or to some device-dependent block size, where necessary (as with certain types of tape).

- Pass Mode `cpio -p` (pass) reads the standard input to obtain a list of pathnames of files that are conditionally created and copied into the destination directory tree based on the specified command-line options.

Similar to `tar`, many command-line options are available with `cpio`; Table 15.4 is a list of the most commonly used options (notice that the options are case-sensitive).

The general syntax for the `cpio` command is as follows:

```
cpio [options] [filename]
```

Table 15.4 Commonly Used Options for *cpio*

Option	Description
-B	Block input/output 5120 bytes to the record. The default buffer size is 512 bytes when this and the -C options are not used. -B does not apply to the pass option; -B is meaningful only with data directed to or from a character special device, for example, /dev/rmt/0m.
-C *bufsize*	Block input/output *bufsize* bytes to the record, where *bufsize* is replaced by a positive integer. The default buffer size is 512 bytes when this and -B options are not used. (-C does not apply to the pass option; -C is meaningful only with data directed to or from a character special device, for example, /dev/rmt/0m.)
-i	(copy in) cpio -i extracts files from the standard input.
-I *file*	Reads the contents of *file* as an input archive. If *file* is a character special device and the current medium has been completely read, replace the medium and press carriage return to continue to the next medium. This option is used only with the -i option.
-o	(copy out) cpio -o reads the standard input to obtain a list of pathnames and copies those files onto the standard output.
-O *file*	Direct the output of cpio to *file*. If *file* is a character special device and the current medium is full, replace the medium and type a carriage return to continue to the next medium. Use only with the -o option.
-p	(pass) cpio -p reads the standard input to obtain a list of pathnames of files. Used mainly to copy directory trees.
-t	Print a table of contents of the input. No files are created (mutually exclusive with -v).
-v	Verbose. Print a list of filenames. When used with the -t option, the table of contents looks like the output of an ls -l command.
-V	Special verbose. Print a dot for each file read or written. Useful to assure the user that cpio is working without printing out all filenames.

Following are some examples of using cpio in backing up and restoring files:

- ■ ls ¦ cpio -oO newfile   Copies the files in the current directory to a cpio archive file called newfile.

- ■ cpio -itI newfile   Extracts all the files in newfile and generates a table of contents.

- ■ find . -depth -print ¦ cpio -pdlmv newdir   cpio -p takes the filenames piped to it (from find) and copies or links (-l option) those files to another directory (newdir in the example). The -d option says to create directories as needed. The -m option says retain the modification time. The -v option turns on the verbose mode. (It is important to use the -depth option of find to generate pathnames for cpio.) Note that the destination directory, newdir, must exist.

TIP Similar to `tar`, you can include one or more `cpio` commands in the system `cron` file so that the file systems frequently are backed up automatically. For example, the following entry performs a backup of `/home/peter` every day at 3:00AM:

```
00 03 * * * (cd /home/peter; ls ¦ cpio -oVO /usr/unix.project.backup) >
/home/peter/cpio.log
```

▶ For more information about using `cron`, **see** "The `cron` Process" **p. 409**

The choice between using `cpio` or `tar` to perform backups is largely a matter of preference. However, because of the simpler command syntax and wide availability on other operating systems, `tar` seems to be the more popular choice.

N O T E Many UNIX system vendors include their own backup software. For example, with `IBM`'s `AIX` system, you can easily back up and restore individual files or the entire system using `AIX SYSBACK`, a backup software that interfaces with AIX's System Management Interface Tool (SMIT) to provide you with a menu; `HP/UX` comes with fbackup and `frecover`, which allows you to back up and restore files selectively in ways similar to dump. ▓

Using *dd*

The `dd` program is a general-purpose data conversion and transfer utility. It was originally designed for importing mainframe data to UNIX systems. On the mainframe, the data are transferred to tape using the EBCDIC character coding system. To use such data on most UNIX systems, use `dd` to change the coding to ASCII. However, with the availability of TCP/IP on mainframes, `dd` is no longer needed because FTP can do the same job over the network (and eliminate the need for tapes).

Because of system administrators' possible familiarity with `dd` (from doing the data conversion), `dd` can be used to perform file system backups because it can copy entire file systems from one place to another like `volcopy`. However, unlike `volcopy`, `dd` does not perform any label checking, but it does offer many more options than `volcopy` for managing the transfer.

Commercial Backup Products

A number of commercial backup products for UNIX systems are available. Some notable mentions follow:

- CTAR   CTAR is an unattended backup/preconfigured command scheduler, based on nonproprietary industry standard `tar` format. It is available for more than 20 flavors of UNIX. Contact UniTrends Software (`http://www.unitrends.com/ctar.htm`) for more information.

- BRU 2000   BRU (Backup and Restore Utility) is strongly based on `tar` but adds many more features. It runs a daemon that manages the backup schedule. It is available for more than a dozen different versions of UNIX. Contact Enhanced Software Technologies (`http://www.estinc.com`) for more information.

- PerfectBACKUP+ PerfectBACKUP+ began life as the UNIX version of DOS FAST-BACK PLUS (from Fifth Generation). It comes with menu-driven ASCII and Motif GUI interfaces, networking support, and scheduling and is compatible with both `tar` and `cpio`. Figure 15.1 shows the main screen of PerfectBACKUP+. Contact UniSource Systems (`http://www.unisrc.com`) for more information.

FIGURE 15.1

PerfectBACKUP+ main screen.

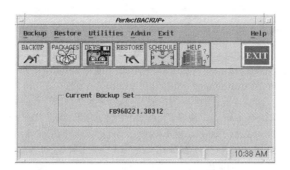

- ARCserve/Open ARCserve/Open is an easy-to-use, high performance, comprehensive data management tool for enterprise networks. Utilizing an intuitive Motif interface, ARCserve/Open makes managing the backup of large servers and heterogeneous networks simple. Ease-of-use is enhanced by the Auto Pilot feature, which provides full automation of the data management process, including tape rotation. High throughput is provided by an efficient backup engine that optimizes performance of each tape drive, giving every ounce of performance your device can deliver. Even greater throughput is achieved with the Parallel Streaming feature, which supports simultaneous backup to multiple tape devices.

  Figures 15.2 and 15.3 show, respectively, a sample ARCserve/Open restore option screen and a sample ARCserve/Open report option screen. Support is available for IBM AIX, HP/UX, SCO, and Solaris (SPARC, x86 and SunOS). Contact Cheyenne (`http://www.cheyenne.com`) for more details.

Maintaining File Systems with *fsck*

A file system can be compared to a general ledger, and like a ledger, a file system should be consistent. There are many causes for a file system becoming corrupted—for example, hardware failure, problems with the disk media, or turning off the system without first executing the `sync` command. In a corrupt file system, something (perhaps a block of data) is not accounted for, or perhaps it is counted twice. Fixing a corrupt file system removes the inconsistencies. File systems should be checked often. They are checked every time your system is booted up, and they should always be fixed as soon as a problem is noticed.

CAUTION

All (except for root) file system checking and repairing should be done on *unmounted* (or inactive) file systems. Otherwise, you could cause more problems than you fix.

FIGURE 15.2

ARCserve/Open restore option screen.

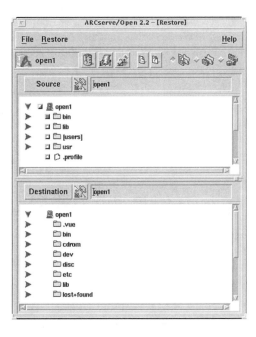

FIGURE 15.3

ARCserve/Open report option screen.

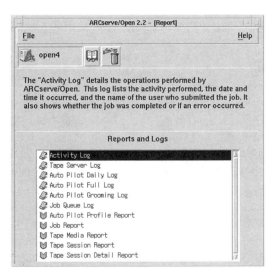

UNIX originally had a suite of programs for repairing file systems, but on modern systems the `fsck` program is predominant. Fixing file systems using the predecessors of `fsck` is difficult because you need to use several programs and good judgment to repair a corrupt file system. Using `fsck` is much easier and faster because it recommends solutions when it discover problems with a file system.

> **N O T E**   Many UNIX systems, such as SCO and HP/UX, include a file system debugger (`fsdb`). It
> can be used to patch up a damaged file system after a crash. However, because `fsdb`
> works directly with the disk, you need to exercise great care when using it because you can potentially
> cause more problems than you fixing if you write to the wrong location on the disk. ▦

> **N O T E**   The philosophy of `fsck` is to prune the dead or "dying" files. Pruning is simple and effective
> but usually results in loss of data. An adequate backup makes data loss less painful. ▦

The */etc/fstab* File

The `/etc/fstab` file contains the list of file systems that `fsck` checks by default. It is also used by `mount` and `umount` to obtain information about the file systems they are to mount and unmount. Each record in the file can have from four to six fields, with each field separated by spaces or tabs. From left to right, the fields specify:

1. Block device name giving the physical location of the file system
2. The mountpoint for the file system
3. The device or file system type
4. Any options to be used by `mount` when mounting the file system
5. A number used to determine when the `dump` utility is to back up the file system (optional)
6. A number used by `fsck` to determine the order in which file systems are to be checked (optional).

Following are two example entries:

```
/dev/hdb1     /    ext2     defaults 1 1
/dev/cdrom    /mnt/cdrom    iso9660    noauto,ro    0 0
```

The first entry indicates that the root file system (`/`) is located on the disk partition identified as the device `/etc/hdb1`, and the file system is type `ext2`. The second entry indicates that a CD-ROM (file system type `iso9660`) is present as device `/dev/cdrom`, that it should not be mounted automatically when the system boots, and that the device should be mounted as a read-only file system.

Running *fsck*

The `fsck` (file system check) utility verifies the integrity of a file system and reports any problems it finds. For each problem it finds, `fsck` asks whether you want to attempt to fix the problem or ignore it; always answer yes unless there is a strong reason not to. The command syntax for `fsck` is as follows:

```
fsck [options] filesystem-list
```

The `filesystem-list` is required unless you use the `-A` option, in which case `fsck` checks all the file systems listed in the `/etc/fstab` file.

N O T E On some UNIX systems, running fsck without the filesystem-list has the same effect as running fsck with the -A option. On those systems, the file /etc/checklist is used instead. ■

There are two ways to list the file systems you want fsck to check on the command line:

- ■ Specify the device name on which the file system resides—for example, /dev/hda1.
- ■ If the file system is listed in the /etc/fstab file, specify the mount point (for example, /usr2) for the file system, and fsck looks up the corresponding device name from /etc/fstab.

You will see messages similar to the following when fsck checks a file system:

```
** Phase 1 - Check Blocks and Sizes
** Phase 2 - Check Pathnames
** Phase 3 - Check Connectivity
** Phase 4 - Check Reference Counts
** Phase 5 - Check Free List
1185 files 382074 blocks 511984 free
```

During phase 1, the inode list is checked to make sure that there are no *orphaned* files (files without names) and that no one disk block is associated to more than one inode. Phase 2 removes directory entries pointing to bad inodes found in phase 1. In Phase 3, fsck looks for unreferenced directories and a nonexistent or full lost+found directory. Phase 4 checks for unreferenced files, a nonexistent or full lost+found directory, bad link counts, bad blocks, duplicated blocks, and incorrect inode counts. The last phase, phase 5, checks to see that the free list and other file system structures are okay. If any problems are found with the free list, phase 6 (Salvage free list) is run.

After fsck has repaired the file system, it informs you of the status of the file system and any action you need to take. If the file system was repaired, fsck displays the following message:

```
*****Filesystem Was Modified*****
```

fsck displays the following message when it has modified a mounted file system (including the root):

```
*****REBOOT SYSTEM*****
```

Upon seeing this message, you must reboot the system immediately, without using sync. For example, use halt -n.

N O T E In addition to the standard UNIX utilities fsck and fsdb, SCO CMW+ (a trusted, X Window System-based, multilevel system software product based on technology that has been officially evaluated by the National Computer Security Center, NCSC, and the Defense Intelligence Agency, DIA, at the B3 level) includes a sophisticated program, Trusted Recovery, trec, that ensures all sensitivity and information labels are consistent. ■

p_fsck—Parallel *fsck*

Whereas fsck checks one file system at a time, p_fsck allows several file systems to be checked in parallel by running a number of fsck processes simultaneously. When the system goes to multiuser mode, mountall uses p_fsck to check the file systems before mounting them.

p_fsck never checks two file systems on the same disk at the same time because this would require time-consuming seek operations by the drive heads. These file systems are checked in sequence instead. There is virtually no limit to the number of file systems on different disks that p_fsck can repair in parallel.

N O T E Do *not* use p_fsck to check the root file system. ▦

Recovering the Root File System

A corrupted system-related file (such as /etc/passwd) prevents you from logging in to your system. Or if your root file system is so corrupted that fsck cannot run when you boot the system, or the system displays error messages that make no sense, you must resort to using the hardware's built-in bootstrap process, a rescue disk, or an emergency boot floppy disk set.

N O T E A *rescue disk* is a floppy disk or a set of disks that contains a bare-bones working version of the UNIX kernel, the correct tape drivers, and perhaps a few basic system administration utilities. This allows you to boot your system from the diskette even if you have a totally destroyed root file system. ▦

Most systems either provide a rescue disk or include instructions on how to create one as part of the installation instructions. Refer to your documentation for details.

N O T E Many non-Intel UNIX systems, such as HP, come with their own bootstrap microcode built into the hardware. Therefore, there is no need for an emergency boot disk.

For example, by pressing and holding down the Esc key during an HP host's power-on sequence, you gain access to the Boot Console User Interface main menu from which you can perform a manual boot. ▦

N O T E To perform a standalone boot of an AIX system, you can boot from a local disk or tape, but most commonly it is done with diskettes. Four diskettes are used in this process: a boot diskette, two display diskettes, and an installation/maintenance diskette.

To boot an AIX system into the standalone (single-user) mode, you need to first switch the key in the front panel to Service Position (all the way to the right) before you insert the boot diskette into the floppy drive and power up the system. ▦

> **TIP** AIX provides a means to create a bootable tape containing an image of the root volume group using the `smit mksysb` command. This can be a lifesaver for single-disk systems in that you have a quick means of recovery in case of disk failure, provided, of course, that your `mksysb` image is fairly current.

The exact steps for recovering a lost root file system vary depending on the flavor of UNIX. However, the general procedure is as follows:

1. Boot up your system using the rescue disk.

2. The system loads a rudimentary root file system into memory. After you see the startup messages that list the devices configured into the kernel, the root prompt (#) is displayed. Try to run `fsck` on your root file system, for example:

   ```
   fsck /dev/hd0
   ```

   If `fsck` appears to be successful, shut down the system and try booting from the hard disk. If the check fails, continue with the next step.

3. If necessary, reconfigure your root disk from scratch, which might include running `fdisk` to (re)partition your disk, map bad blocks, and re-create the file systems and swap space. If the hard disk or file system information is still valid, you can skip to the next step.

4. Mount the root file system on the hard disk.

5. Insert the first volume of the root file system backup and restore the file system.

6. After the restore is complete, unmount and `fsck` the newly restored file system.

7. Restart the system using the new root disk.

8. Restore other file systems from backups as necessary.

If for any reason that you are unable to restore from the backup—perhaps you don't have a backup of the root file system—all is not lost. If the crashed disk contains data that are not easily replaced, you can consider sending the drive out to a hard disk recovery company, such as Ontrack Data International (http://www.ontrack.com) or Data Recovery Labs (http://www.datarec.com).

From Here...

A computer system generally contains important data. A fundamental responsibility of the system administrator (regardless of the operating system involved) is the implementation of a reliable backup and recovery strategy. This chapter provided information on how to develop a backup and recovery procedure. You now can make sound judgments on the selection of an appropriate backup device and backup tools for your UNIX system.

- For detailed information on how UNIX file systems are structured, see Chapter 5, "Files, Directories, and Permissions."

- For detailed information on shell scripting, see Chapter 7, "Essential Shell Scripting."

- For detailed information on how to use the `at` and `cron` facilities in UNIX to automate your system backup, see Chapter 16, "Automating Tasks."

## CHAPTER 16

Automating Tasks

by Peter Kuo

In this chapter

Introduction

You can run commands and programs that normally consume a lot of system resources—such as a CPU-intensive application like a Monte Carlo simulation—at a lower priority or during off-hours so that other users can get their work done during normal office hours.

For system administrators, administrative tasks often need to be executed when you are not present or during off-hours, or tasks or programs might need to be run on an ongoing basis at regular time intervals. For example:

- Clearing out the /tmp directory every Sunday evening
- Daily usage reports
- Backing up system and user files and directories (see Chapter 15, "Backup and Recovery")
- Large file transfers

In this chapter, you learn how to use some of the UNIX commands, such as at, batch, and cron, that allow you to automate task execution and scheduling to make your life easier and more productive.

Running Multiple Jobs

Whenever you give UNIX a command (for example, the ps command), you are running a "job." It is important that you understand the difference between a job and a process. A *job* consists of one or more processes. And a *process* is created for each UNIX command issued within a job. For example, when you use multiple UNIX commands on a single command line, such as the following:

```
$ find . -print ¦ sort ¦ lpr
```

you create a job with three processes—find, sort, and lpr, connected by pipes.

Given the multitasking capability of UNIX, you can execute multiple jobs concurrently, rather than sequentially (one at a time) provided that the jobs are not dependent on each other. You can run multiple jobs by adding a trailing & character to the preceding command. For example:

```
$ find . -print ¦ sort ¦ lpr &
```

This places the job to be executed in the background, thus freeing up the console for other commands. You can also create several background jobs on a single command line. For example, the following command creates two separate and *independent* jobs, which are executed concurrently:

```
$ find . -print ¦ sort ¦ lpr & ls  -l /etc/bin > /tmp/dir_listing &
```

Both jobs are placed into the background for execution by the trailing & characters, so the shell does not wait for them to complete before it gives you a prompt and waits for further instructions. Before the prompt, the shell displays the job number in square brackets followed by the PID (process ID) of the *last* process in the job:

```
$ find . -print ¦ sort ¦ lpr & ls  -l /etc/bin > /tmp/dir_listing &
[1] 13456
[2] 13470
```

Compare the following command with the preceding example:

```
$ (find . -print ¦ sort ¦ lpr ; ls  -l /etc/bin > /tmp/dir_listing)&
```

This command executes `ls` *after* the `find-sort-lpr` task has completed and is considered to be a single job. Using this technique, you can easily "schedule" one job to start running after another one is finished.

When a background job is completed, a message similar to the following is displayed:

```
[2]   Done                    find . -print ¦ sort ¦ lpr
```

The job number is displayed as well as the command associated with the job.

Using the job numbers, you can move commands from the background and suspend a job temporarily, as discussed in the following sections.

The *jobs* Command

If you forget how many jobs you have running in the background, you can use the `jobs` command to display a list of all background jobs currently running:

```
$ jobs
[1]   Running                 find / -name core -print >/tmp/core.listing
[2]+  Stopped                 vi ndstool-kit.doc
[3]-  Stopped (tty input)     cat >/tmp/this.is.a.test
[4]-  Stopped (tty output)    /usr/bin/RayTrace
```

In the preceding example, jobs 3 and 4 are shown to be temporarily suspended from execution because job 3 needs to read input from the console, and job 4 has output to the console pending.

If no jobs are running in the background, no message is displayed.

> **N O T E** Keep in mind that the background job list is associated with each shell. Therefore, if your default shell is `sh` and started a `csh` process, a `jobs` command issued while in `csh` will not show any background jobs that were initiated while you were in `sh`. ▦

Bringing a Job to the Foreground

To move a background job into the foreground, use the `fg` command followed by the job number as an argument. The following example moves job 2 into the foreground:

```
$ fg 2
```

You can also refer to a job by a string that uniquely identifies the beginning of the command line used to start the job. For example, instead of using `fg 2`, you can use either `fg vi` or just `fg v` because either one uniquely identifies job 2.

TIP You can also use a question mark followed by a string. The `fg` command matches the string anywhere on the command line. For example, `fg ?kit` also refers to job 2.

On some versions of UNIX, you might need to precede the job number or the string with a percent sign (%), for example:

```
$ fg %2
```

If you simply issue the `fg` command without an argument, the job with the "+" in the job list is brought to the foreground. In the case where only one job is running in the background, you can also use `fg` without any argument to bring it to the foreground.

Putting a Job into the Background

You can put a job into the background in three ways:

- Place an & character at the end of the command line.
- Press Ctrl+Z while in the program. This stops (suspends) the job immediately.
- Press Ctrl+Y while in the program. This puts the job running in the background until it tries to read input from the console, at which point it is suspended. (This feature might not work on some UNIX systems, such as IBM's AIX or Sun Solaris. And some systems, such as HP/UX, use Ctrl+D instead.)

After a job has been suspended (by pressing Ctrl+Y or Ctrl+Z), you can then use the `bg` command to resume execution of the job, in the background.

> **CAUTION**
> If you try to leave a shell while there are stopped jobs, the shell gives you a warning message that "There are stopped (running) jobs" and does not allow you to exit. If you then issue a `jobs` command followed immediately by `exit`, or immediately try to exit the shell again, the shell terminates all stopped jobs and allows you to leave. Jobs running in the background (not stopped) will, depending on the shell used, continue to run until completion.

Execute a Command at a Time You Specify

There are certainly times when you want to execute a command at a particular time instead of right away. For example, your Monte Carlo calculation needs 75 percent of the available system memory and will run for 6 CPU hours. If you run this program during the day, not only will the calculation not finish in 6 hours because of other users also needing access to CPU and memory resources, but because of the load this program poses on the system, the overall system response will be poor during the normal hours, and you and your coworkers will all suffer. Instead, you can use the at command to schedule the program to run in the evening when the system is mostly idle, and your application can have access to all the system memory and CPU cycles it needs.

The *at* Command

The at UNIX utility causes the operating system to execute commands it receives from standard input or a script file. The commands are executed under /bin/sh, by default, at the time you specify. Standard output and standard error output are sent to the user via email; if the output is redirected, no email is sent.

> **N O T E** The shell saves the environment variables (except for TERM, DISPLAY and _), current working directory, umask, and ulimit that are in effect at the time you submit the at job, so that they are available when it executes the command.

The at jobs are run by cron (discussed later in this chapter) and a program called atrun. The frequency with which cron executes atrun is based on the atrun entry in crontab and is normally every 5 minutes. You can increase or decrease this time interval by changing the entry in crontab, the schedule file used by cron. Some systems (such as AIX or Solaris) use a separate atd daemon to handle at jobs instead of using cron; in such cases, you will not find an atrun entry in the crontab file. ■

The at command requires one argument (time) and accepts a number of options. The common options are as follows:

```
at [-q queue] [-bdlmr] [-f filename] time [date ¦ +increment]
```

The syntax for the time argument and the options are discussed in the following section.

Specifying Execution Time　The time argument of the at command lists the time of day you want at to execute the job. The time can be specified as one, two, or four digits (you cannot use three digits because a three-digit number such as 115 can be interpreted as either 1:15 or 11:05, thus leading to confusion). One- and two-digit numbers are taken to be hours, and four-digits numbers are taken to be hours and minutes. The time can alternatively be specified as two (one or two digits) numbers separated by a colon, meaning *hour:minute*. A 24-hour clock time is assumed unless you specify am or pm immediately after the number, in which case at uses a 12-hour clock. Some UNIX versions (such as SCO and Linux) also support the use of the suffix *utc* to indicate Universal Time Coordinated (also known as Greenwich Mean Time, GMT), and the special names *noon*, *midnight*, and *now* (not supported by Linux).

Some UNIX versions, such as RedHat Linux 5.0, also support the use of *teatime* (4 pm) in the time specification.

HP/UX and System V support the use of *zulu* as a time suffix to indicate GMT.

N O T E If you use the word *now* in specifying time, you must also specify a date or an increment. For example, at now is not valid but at now sunday is.

The date specifies the day of the week (such as Sunday) or date of the month on which you want at to execute the command; when using the date-of-month format, you can either spell it out in full (such as December) or abbreviate it to three characters (such as Dec); an optional year number (preceded by a comma) can be specified when using the date-of-month format. Also recognized are two special "days," *today* and *tomorrow*.

When no date is given, today is assumed if the given hour is greater than the current hour, and tomorrow is assumed if it is less. If the given month is less than the current month (and no year is given), next year is assumed.

You can also specify the date in the form of *MMDDYY*, *MM/DD/YY*, or *DD.MM.YY* on some UNIX systems, such as HP/UX and Linux.

HP/UX and some UNIX systems also support the words *today, tomorrow, noon, midnight, now, minutes, hours, days, weeks, months, years,* and their singular forms in languages other than English, provided that the LANG variable has been properly defined.

> **CAUTION**
>
> The date specification must come after the time specification. For example, at 11:00am Dec 25 is valid, but at Dec 25 11:00am is not.

The time and optional date arguments can be modified with an increment argument of the form *+n units*, where *n* is an integer, and *units* is one of the following: minutes, hours, days, weeks, months, or years. The singular form is also accepted, and *next unit* (such as next month) can be used to denote *+1 unit* (+1 month).

Some versions of UNIX, such as SCO, allow an alternative format for specifying time using two-digit codes, such as at -t [CC][YY]MMDDhhmm.[SS], where:

- CC = century
- YY = year
- MM = month
- DD = day
- hh = hours
- mm = minutes
- SS = seconds

For example, at -t 9906021200.30 schedules a job for 12:00:30 (30 seconds after noon) on June 2, 1999.

Some examples of legitimate at time specifications include the following:

```
$ at 0900am Dec 24, 1999
$ at 0900am December 24
$ at 9:00am December 24, 1999
$ at 2:00am Sunday
$ at now tomorrow
$ at 1700 Friday next week
$ at teatime +3 days
```

The last example (which only works under Linux) runs an at job at 4 pm (teatime) three days from now.

Listing *at* Jobs When an at job is submitted and queued for execution, the system displays a job number (job ID, and its format varies depending on the version of UNIX). For example:

```
$ at 5pm friday < generate.report
Job 123 will be executed using /bin/sh
```

N O T E The at job ID is assigned sequentially and is not tied to a process ID. On some UNIX systems, this is controlled by the content of the /var/spool/at/.SEQ file. ▪

You can use at -l or atq to get a list of all pending jobs—in order of scheduled executing times—that you have submitted using the at command. For example:

```
$ atq
123     1998-09-15 03:15 a
124     1998-12-24 13:00 a
127     1999-01-01 00:01 a
```

(The output format varies depending on the version of UNIX. The "a" in the output indicates the job is in the at queue; see "Selecting an at Job Queue" later in the chapter for more details.)

You can optionally include a list of job IDs (separating each with a space) on the command line.

N O T E You can only see your own jobs unless you are logged in as *root*. ▪

Removing *at* Jobs Should you change your mind about a scheduled at job, you can delete it from the queue using either at -d or atrm:

```
at -d [job-id ...]
atrm [job-id ...]
```

For example:

```
$ atq
123     1998-09-15 03:15 a
124     1998-12-24 13:00 a
127     1999-01-01 00:01 a
$ atrm 124
```

Part
II

Ch
16

```
$ atq
123     1998-09-15 03:15 a
127     1999-01-01 00:01 a
```

N O T E You can only cancel your own jobs unless you are logged in as *root*. ■

Some UNIX versions, such as SCO and HP/UX, use at -r instead.

Job Completion Notification   As mentioned previously, at sends the standard output and standard error data to you via email, and no email is sent if the outputs are redirected. You can include the -m option in the at command, such as:

```
$ at -m 5pm friday < generate.report
```

An email is sent to you after the job is run. The email contains the content of standard error and/or standard output (depending on the version of UNIX) if there was any; otherwise, it contains a short message informing you that no errors occurred.

> **CAUTION**
>
> Depending on the version of UNIX, if you use the -m option, your output redirection in the command might not work, and the standard output result will end up in the notification email message instead.

N O T E If at is executed from a su shell, the owner of the login shell receives the mail notification. For example:

```
login: root
# su peter
$ at -m 09:00am < generate.report
```

results in the user *peter* receiving the email and not the user *root*. ■

The -m option is not available for all flavors of UNIX. For example, it is not supported by HP/UX and System V.

Specifying the Source of an *at* Job   The at utility gets the commands from the keyboard (standard input). Generally, this is not desirable because it is risky (you can easily issue a dangerous command, such as rm *, before you realize it), and it is difficult to correct typing mistakes. Therefore, it is recommended that you create a file (using, for example, cat or vi; see the section in Chapter 3 entitled, "Using cat to View Files" and in Chapter 4, "Text Editing with vi," respectively) containing the desired commands, one per line, and then pass its content to at:

```
$ at -m 5pm friday < /etc/usr/peter/generate.report
```

or

```
$ at -m -f /etc/usr/peter/generate.report 5pm friday
```

T I P　On some versions of UNIX, you can use `at -c job-id` to print out, to standard output, the commands that will be executed by the job identified by `job-id`.

Running When System Load Is Low　By default, all `at` jobs run at the designated time regardless of the system load. However, this might not be desirable in some cases. For example, there may be times that you want your job to start execution only if the system is mostly idle. You can submit such an `at` job in one of two commands: `at -b` or `batch`.

The `at` system examines the system load and runs the job when the load average falls below a certain predetermined value. For example, in RedHat Linux, the `at` system looks at `/proc/loadavg` and runs the job when the past minute's load average value is either 0.8 or lower, or equals the value specified at the invocation of `atrun`.

If you omit the time and date specifications when using `at -b` or `batch`, then the job is queued immediately and runs as soon as the system load permits. If you included a time specification, the job runs as soon as after the specified time as the load average permits.

N O T E　Some versions of UNIX, such as SCO, HP/UX, UnixWare, and RedHat Linux, do not permit the use of a time specification with the `batch` command and do not support the `-b` option in `at` (meaning that you need to use the `batch` command instead). ▪

Generally, `batch` jobs runs at a slightly lower priority than `at` and `cron` jobs.

Selecting an *at* Job Queue　The clock daemon, `cron`, and `atrun` use information associated with job queues to control how jobs submitted with `at`, `batch`, and `crontab` are executed. Every job submitted by one of these programs is placed in a certain queue, and the behavior of these queues is defined (under SCO, for example) in `/usr/lib/cron/queuedefs`.

For a given queue, the `queuedefs` file specifies the maximum number of jobs that may be executing at one time (*njobs*), the priority at which jobs will execute (*nice*), and how long `cron` will wait between attempts to run a job (*wait*). If *njobs* jobs are already running in a given queue when a new job is scheduled to begin execution, `cron` reschedules the job to execute *wait* seconds later.

Each line of `queuedefs` gives parameters for one queue. The line must begin with a letter designating a queue, followed by a period (.). This is followed by the numeric values for *njobs*, *nice*, and *wait*, followed by the letters "j," "n," and "w," respectively. The values must appear in this order, although a value and its corresponding letter may be omitted entirely, in which case a default value is used. The default values for *njobs*, *nice*, and *wait* are, respectively, 100, 2, and 60.

The value for *nice* is added to the default priority of the job (a higher numerical priority results in a lower scheduling priority). Note that the *nice* value does not apply when the command is run by *root*.

A typical `queuedefs` file might look like this:

```
a.4j1n
b.2j2n90w
```

Part

II

Ch

16

The preceding example shows that the a queue (used for at jobs) is allowed to run four jobs at a time with a *nice* value of 1. Jobs will be rescheduled to run 60 seconds later (default) if there is no room in the run queue. The b queue (used for batch jobs) can run two jobs at a time with a *nice* value of 2, and a rescheduling period of 90 seconds.

Queues are designated by a single letter, generally in lowercase; however, some UNIX versions (such as Linux) support uppercase queue names as well.

N O T E Queues with higher letters run with increased "niceness" (that is, lower priority). Therefore, a job running in the b (batch) queue runs at a lower priority (higher niceness level) than an equivalent job running in the a (at) queue.

Under Linux, when a job is submitted to a queue designated with an uppercase letter, it is treated as if it has been submitted to the batch queue.

The following queues have special significance:

- a   at queue
- b   batch queue
- c   cron queue
- =   currently running queue

For example,

```
$ atq
129      1998-07-01 00:01 =
123      1998-09-15 03:15 a
127      1999-01-01 00:01 a
142      1999-04-01 09:00 b
```

shows that job 129 is currently running, jobs 123 and 127 are at jobs, and job 142 is a batch job.

When you submit an at job for scheduling, the default queue used is a; if batch or at -b is used, the default queue used is b. You can select a different queue using the -q option:

```
$ at -m -q K 5pm friday < generate.report
$ batch -m -q K friday < generate.report
```

Both of the preceding examples submit the job to a queue designated as K.

You can also use the -q option with the atq or at -l command to list jobs in a particular queue. For example, the atq -v a command lists jobs that are in the at queue only:

```
$ atq
129      1998-07-01 00:01 =
123      1998-09-15 03:15 a
127      1999-01-01 00:01 a
142      1999-04-01 09:00 b
$ at -lq a
123      1998-09-15 03:15 a
127      1999-01-01 00:01 a
```

Controlling Access to *at*

Sometimes it is desirable to limit the use of the at and batch commands to a certain group of users. Depending on the version of at that you are using, you might be able to restrict user access to the at facility by using the at.allow and at.deny files.

> **N O T E** Depending on the version of UNIX, the at.* files are located in different directories. For example, SCO and HP/UX store the at.allow and at.deny files in the /usr/lib/ cron directory, whereas RedHat Linux uses the /etc directory, and some other versions of Linux use /usr/etc to hold these two files. ▨

If the file at.allow exists, then only those usernames listed in it are permitted to use at. If at.allow does not exist, the at.deny is checked; any usernames *not* listed in at.deny are granted access to at. If at.deny exists but is empty (default configuration), then all users on your system can use at. If neither at.allow nor at.deny exists, only the superuser (root) can use at.

> **CAUTION**
> If both at.allow and at.deny exist, only at.allow is consulted; the at.deny file is ignored.

Schedule a Command to Run at Regular Intervals

The at command is designed to schedule a command for execution at a future time, once. Although it is possible to have an at job reschedule itself by invoking at from within the job, it is not as flexible as using the clock daemon, cron (or crond on some systems), to schedule a job to run repeatedly at regular time intervals.

> **N O T E** The added benefit of using cron over at is that cron has a logging feature, whereas at does not. ▨

The *cron* Process

Upon system boot, the cron daemon process is automatically started by /etc/rc.d/rc., /etc/rc.d/rc.local, or /etc/rc.2 among other system daemons (such as lpd for printing and inetd for networking functions). The cron process executes commands at specified dates and times. Using the crontab utility, system administrators and users (subject to restrictions outlined in the "Controlling Access to cron" section later in the chapter) may submit a list of commands in a format that can be read and executed by cron.

> **CAUTION**
>
> To ensure correct scheduling and prevent conflicts, only one instance of cron should be running on the system at any given time. The script that starts cron (/etc/rc.d/init.d/crond) during system boot generally has this safeguard built-in, but it is worth noting.

▶ **See** "The init Process," **p. 275**

The cron process "wakes up" once every minute, examining all stored crontab files and checking each command to see whether it should be run in the current minute. When executing commands, such as the at command, any undirected output is emailed to the owner of the crontab file (or to the user named in the MAILTO environment variable in the crontab, if defined).

N O T E Because the cron process only runs once per minute, the smallest time interval between command execution is, thus, one minute. ■

The *cron* Configuration Files

cron uses a number of configuration files and directories (and their names and locations vary depending on the UNIX version):

- ■ usr/lib/cron, /etc, /etc/cron.d   main cron and system crontab directory
- ■ /usr/spool/cron/crontabs, /var/spool/cron   user crontab directory
- ■ /usr/lib/cron/cron.allow, /etc/cron.allow, /usr/spool/cron/allow   list of allowed users
- ■ /usr/lib/cron/cron.deny, /etc/cron.deny, /usr/spool/cron/deny   list of denied users
- ■ /usr/lib/cron/queuedefs, /usr/cron.d/queuedefs   queue description file
- ■ /etc/default/cron   file containing cron default settings
- ■ /usr/lib/cron/log, /var/cron/log, /var/log/cron   log file containing cron actions
- ■ /usr/lib/cron/olog, /var/cron/olog   when the log file size exceeds system ulimit, it is moved to olog

The most frequently encountered files, such as crontab, are discussed in the following sections.

***crontab* Files**   The command files created (and maintained) by the crontab utility are known as crontab files. There are two types of crontab files—system crontab and user crontab files.

The system crontab file contains regularly scheduled system-administration related commands, such as backup and temp file cleanups. This file, /etc/crontab (/usr/lib/crontab on some systems) is generally maintained by the system administrator.

Users can (subject to restrictions imposed by the system administrator) submit their own crontab files using the crontab command. User crontab files are named after their usernames as found in /etc/passwd and are stored in /var/spool/cron/crontabs, /usr/spool/cron/ crontabs, or /var/spool/cron. For example, the crontab file for user peter is /var/spool/ cron/peter.

TIP When a change is made to a crontab file, it is not necessary to restart cron for the change to take effect. At the same time, when cron checks for commands to execute, it also checks the modification time stamp of the crontab files for changes and reloads those that have changed.

The crontab files typically consist of lines of six fields each. The fields are separated by one or more spaces or one or more tabs. The first five fields are time and date fields and are integer patterns that specify, in order listed:

1. Minute (0–59)
2. Hour (0–23)
3. Day of the month (1–31)
4. Month of the year (1–12)—some systems allow you to use a name, the first three characters of the month, instead; for example, jan, and case is not important
5. Day of the week (0–6, with 0=Sunday)—some systems allow you to use a name, the first three characters of the day of the week, instead; for example, mon, and case is not important

Each of these patterns may contain:

- A number in the (respective) range indicated above; two numbers separated by a minus (indicating an inclusive range). For example, "2-5" means 2, 3, 4, and 5.
- A list of numbers separated by commas (meaning all these numbers or ranges of these number). For example, "1,3,5,7" and "2-5, 9-13"; note that AT&T and BSD UNIX do not support mixing list and ranges within the same field.
- An asterisk (*—meaning all legal values).

N O T E Note that the day of a command's execution can be specified by two fields—day of the month and day of the week. If both are specified as a list of elements (that is, not *), the command will be executed when *either* field matches the current time. For example, "0 0 1,15 * 1" would run a command at midnight on the first and fifteenth of each month, as well as on every Monday.

The sixth field is a string executed by the shell at the specified time. A % in this field is translated into a new line character (unless escaped by a backslash). Only the first line (up to a % or end-of-line) of the command field is executed by the shell. All data after that is sent to the command as standard input.

N O T E   Berkeley and its variants use 1–7 with Sunday as 7 for the day-of-week field. Linux actually
allows you to use 0–7 with Sunday as either 0 or 7 for the day-of-week field. ■

A sample `crontab` file follows:

```
#Sample crontab file
#
#mm hh dd mm ww command
  5  0  *  *  * echo "Runs 5 minutes after midnight, daily"
 45 16  1  *  * echo "Runs at 4:45pm (16:45) on the first of every month"
  0 22  *  * 1-5 echo "Runs at 10pm on weekdays"
 55 16  *  * fri echo "TGIF! (runs every Friday at 4:55pm)"
```

N O T E   If your system does not use `atd` and does not have an entry for `atrun` in the system
`crontab` file, you can add a line with "`* * * * * /usr/sbin/atrun`" to the file. This
line runs the `atrun` utility every minute, which checks for any `at` jobs scheduled to execute. Because
the output of `atrun` is not redirected, it is automatically emailed to the root user.

If your system does not have either `atd` or `atrun` then functionality is already included within the
clock daemon. ■

Some versions of UNIX, such as Berkeley 4.3, have an additional field following the date field
that specifies which username to use when running the command. For example:

```
#mm hh dd mm ww username command
  5  0  *  *  * peter    echo "Runs 5 minutes after midnight, daily"
```

N O T E   It is interesting that in RedHat Linux 5.0, the system `crontab` file, `/etc/crontab`, uses
the preceding format, whereas the user `crontab` files, located in `/var/spool/cron`,
do not. ■

cron Defaults   Depending on the implementation, `cron` may or may not generate a log file by
default. To keep a log of all actions taken by `cron`, make sure that `CRONLOG=YES` is specified in
the `/etc/default/cron` file. If `CRONLOG=NO` is specified, no logging is done.

> **CAUTION**
>
> If you enabled action logging, you should keep a constant watch on the log files because `cron` usually
> creates huge log files—a record is generated *every time* a command is executed, when `cron` is started, and
> when `cron` is shut down.

If logging is turned on, you can use the variable `MAXLOGSIZE` defined in `/etc/default/cron` to
limit the size in 512-byte blocks to which the log file will grow. If it exceeds this limit, its contents are moved to `olog`. The default value of `MAXLOGSIZE` is 2048 blocks. If this variable is not
specified, `ulimit` is used.

The PATH for user cron jobs can be set using PATH= in /etc/default/cron. The PATH for root cron jobs can be set using SUPATH= in /etc/default/cron. Following is a sample /etc/default/cron file:

```
CRONLOG=YES
PATH=/usr/bin:/usr/ucb:
```

This example enables logging and sets the default PATH used by non-root jobs to /usr/bin:/usr/ucb:. Root jobs will continue to use /usr/sbin:/usr/bin.

> **N O T E** Some systems, such as Sun Solaris, come with logchecker, which is a script that checks to see whether the log file has exceeded the system ulimit setting (maximum size to which a file can grow to). If so, the log file is moved to olog. ▧

T I P If your system does not have logchecker, you can set the length of the log file to zero every once in a while (say, using cron) without running into trouble. Simply do an echo -n > /var/cron/log (or the path and filename appropriate to your system). You should not use rm to delete this file. This is because syslogd will not know to reopen the log file and will try to log to the deleted file, thus causing problems.

The variable MAXCRON, if set in /etc/default/cron, controls the maximum number of running processes that cron can own at any one time. The default value is 100. (See the section in Chapter 7 titled, "Shell Variables," for information about setting shell variables.)

***cron* Log Files**   As mentioned earlier, if logging is enabled, all cron actions are logged into the log file. The following is a sample log file from RedHat Linux:

```
CRON (06/26-22:04:22-155) STARTUP (fork ok)
root (06/26-23:01:00-256) CMD (run-parts /etc/cron.hourly)
root (06/27-00:01:00-382) CMD (run-parts /etc/cron.hourly)
*system* (06/30-10:20:00-155) RELOAD (/etc/crontab)
root (06/30-10:21:01-4871) CMD (/etc/bin/RunEveryMinute)
root (06/30-10:22:00-4886) CMD (/etc/bin/RunEveryMinute)
CRON (06/30-10:22:38-4894) DEATH (can't lock /var/run/crond.pid, otherpid maybe
155: Resource temporarily unavailable)
```

As you can see, the file details every action taken by cron, starting with the loading of the cron daemon (STARTUP), to the execution of commands (CMD), to using the new system crontab file (RELOAD), to the shutdown of cron (DEATH).

The cron log file is useful for tracking "who did what when" using cron. It is also useful for troubleshooting any crontab syntax errors leading to commands being executed at the wrong time (by looking at the time stamps) or not at all (by the lack of CMD entry for the bad command).

Part

II

Ch

16

Advanced Time Specification According to *cron*

The time specification for cron can be sophisticated. As discussed earlier, you can specify ranges of numbers as well as lists of numbers for the time and date fields. Some versions of UNIX, such as Linux, allow you to also specify step values in conjunction with ranges.

The syntax for step values is to follow a range with a /*number*, where *number* specifies how a number's value is skipped through the range. For example, 0-23/2 (in the hours field) means execute the command every other hour, starting from midnight. The alternative, for UNIX versions that do not support step values, is 0, 2, 4, 6, 8, 10, 12, 14, 16, 18, 20, 22.

 You can also use a step value after an asterisk. Therefore, another way of specifying every other hour is */2.

Adding and Modifying *cron* Tasks

You can add a task to cron in two ways:

- Manually edit the crontab file using a text editor such as vi.
▶ **See** the section in Chapter 4 titled, "Text Editing with vi", for detailed procedures on using vi
- Use the crontab utility to edit and update the crontab file.

The advantage of using the crontab utility is that it works with a copy of the crontab file instead of working directly with the installed copy. The copy is edited and then checked for validity before it replaces the installed crontab file. The other advantage of using the crontab utility is that you do not need to know where your user crontab file is located on the system; the utility takes care of it for you. If you manually edit the crontab file, you need to know where it is stored.

N O T E The crontab utility works only with the user crontab files and not the system one. To update the system crontab file, you need to edit it directly. ■

 If you are going to manually edit your user crontab file or going to update the system crontab file, make two copies of the file first (using cp) and work with one copy (keeping the other copy as a backup). When you are finished editing, you can then overwrite the installed copy with the updated version (while you still have the other copy as a backup in case something goes wrong).

You can use the crontab utility in two ways to add to or update your crontab file. The first method is to use a text editor (such as vi) to create a text file (*filename*) containing the desired entries for cron. Then you use

```
$ crontab filename
```

to verify its contents for validity before applying the changes.

Alternatively, on some UNIX systems you can use `crontab -e` to work with a copy of your `crontab` file (so that you need not create a separate file first).

You can get a listing of your `crontab` file using the `crontab -1` command. The output is sent to standard output, so you can redirect it to a file for later editing, if you want.

Removing Tasks from *cron*

You can remove `cron` tasks in three ways:

- If you have your original file that contains the `cron` commands, edit it to delete the lines containing the tasks you want removed and then apply the updated file using `crontab` *filename*.

- Use `crontab -e` (if supported, or use a text editor such as `vi`) to edit your `crontab` file to delete the lines containing the tasks you want removed and then apply the updated file.

- You can remove all the tasks by deleting the entire `crontab` file using `crontab -r` (`crontab -d` on some systems).

Controlling Access to *cron*

Similar to the `at` command discussed earlier, you can also limit the use of `cron` (or `crond`) to a certain group of users. Depending on the version of `at` that you are using, you might be able to restrict user access to the `cron` facility by using the `cron.allow` and `cron.deny` files.

> **N O T E** Depending on the version of UNIX, the `allow` and `deny` files may be named differently and placed in different directories. For example, SCO uses `/usr/lib/cron/cron.allow` and `/usr/lib/cron/at.deny`; RedHat Linux uses the `/etc` directory for the same files; some versions of Linux use the `allow` and `deny` files in the `/usr/spool/cron` directory instead, whereas UnixWare uses `/etc/cron.d/cron.allow` and `/etc/cron.d/deny`. ▪

If the file `cron.allow` exists, then only those usernames listed in it are permitted to use `cron`. If `cron.allow` does not exist, the `cron.deny` is checked; any username not listed in `cron.deny` is granted access to cron. If `cron.deny` exists but is empty (default configuration), then all users on your system can use `at`. If neither `cron.allow` nor `cron.deny` exists, only the superuser (*root*) can use `cron`.

> **CAUTION**
> If both `cron.allow` and `cron.deny` exist, only `cron.allow` is consulted; the `cron.deny` file is ignored.

Part
II

Ch
16

The users authorized to use `cron` might need access to the `crontab` utility to manipulate their `crontab` files, you might need to perform the following tasks:

1. Create a special group (by making an entry in the `/etc/groups` file) for all users who are to be allowed to use `crontab`. Often the name of this group is called `cron`.

▶ **See** "Creating Groups," **p. 257**

2. Change the group for the `crontab` utility to match this new group.

3. Set the executable permission on `crontab` to allow members of this group, but not others, to execute `crontab`. You also need to turn on the set user ID mode bit (+s) so that `crontab` runs with root permission. This permission is required so that `crontab` can read from and write files to the directory where the user `crontab` files are stored. For example:

```
$ chgrp cron /usr/bin/crontab
$ chmod u+s,g=rx,o=-rwx /usr/bin/crontab
```

▶ For more information about file permissions and ownerships, **see** the section in Chapter 5 titled, "Owners, Groups and Permissions."

Troubleshooting *cron*

`cron` is simply a scheduler that takes commands from a `crontab` file and executes the commands at the times specified. It is a straightforward utility, and troubleshooting `cron` problems is relatively easy. The following are some commonly encountered `cron`–related issues along with their resolutions:

▪ crontab changes not taking place   crontab commands are executed by `cron(C)`. Some UNIX implementations of `cron` read the files in the `crontab` directory only on system startup or when a new `crontab` is submitted with the `crontab` command. Consequently, changes made to these files manually do not take effect until the system is rebooted. Changes submitted with the `crontab` command take effect as soon as `cron` is free to read them (that is, when `cron` is not in the process of running a scheduled job or reading another newly submitted at or `crontab` job).

▪ cron jobs skipped   Care should be taken when scheduling commands to run during time zone changes from the standard time to the daylight savings time. This is because when the clocks go forward, certain times cease to exist. For example, when the clocks go forward an hour at 2 am, all times between 2 am and 3 am (including 2 am) cease to exist. If commands are sched   uled to run in this time period, then `cron` still executes them at their scheduled time in the standard time zone, which will be later than expected in the local time zone. `cron` generally warns the user of this by email and gives the exact local time that the command will be executed. It is then the user's responsibility to reschedule the job if required.

- Certain `cron` jobs not running   If it seems that some `cron` jobs are not being scheduled, there are two ways to debug this problem. First, manually run the command to see whether there are any errors. Second, substitute the command with `echo "This is a debug test"` and see whether an email is generated at the scheduled time; or use `echo "This is a debug test" > /dev/console` and see whether the message is being displayed on the console at the scheduled time.

- `cron` does not reschedule jobs if time of day is moved back   Some `cron` implementations have a bug that if the system time is put back to before `cron`'s start-time, then `cron` jobs are not rescheduled correctly. Generally, this should not happen but if it does, it usually is during the time change from daylight savings time back to standard time where the clock moves back by an hour. The workaround is to stop `cron` before the time change and restart it afterward.

- Shell scripts not working   Some shell scripts depend on specific environments and/or shells to function correctly; the default shell is `/bin/sh`. To specify a different environment, the command specified in the `crontab` entry should be an executable shell script that sets the environment explicitly.

- No output display on console or terminal when using `at` or `cron` for automatic task execution   By default, the output of `at` and `cron` commands is sent to the user's mailbox, therefore, you cannot see the output display on the screen. However, you can use redirection command to redirect the output to `/dev/console`; then you can receive the output on the console screen.

- `cron may not be running`—`call your system administrator`   If for some reason `cron` is not running and you try to submit a job with `at` or `crontab`, the system displays the preceding message. You can use `ps -ef ¦ grep cron` to see whether the `cron` daemon is running. If there is no `cron` process, then the daemon is not running. You can try to restart `cron` by logging in as root and issue the `sd cron` (`/etc/rc.d/init.d/cron start` on some systems) command. If this does not start the `cron` process, simply reboot the system because `cron` is started by the startup scripts.

- `at: you are not authorized to use at. Sorry.` Or `cron: you are not authorized to use cron. Sorry.`   Check whether the user is listed in the `at.deny` or `cron.deny` files. Also in the case of `cron`, check to see whether the user is a member of the group that has access to the `crontab` utility.

One of the best `cron` troubleshooting tools is the `cron` log file. Looking at the time stamp of a command or the lack of `CMD` entry for a given command gives you clues to whether a job is being improperly scheduled or not being executed at all.

Part
II

Ch
16

From Here...

In this chapter, you read about how to use some of the UNIX commands, such as `at`, `batch`, and `cron`, which allow automated task execution and scheduling to make your life easier and more productive. You can use these utilities to schedule tasks that you need to perform at regular intervals to run automatically without manual intervention.

- For detailed information on various system utility programs, see Chapter 3, "UNIX Shells and System Commands."

- For detailed information on using the `vi` text editor, see Chapter 4, "`vi` Editor."

- For detailed information on processes in UNIX, see Chapter 6, "UNIX Processes."

- For detailed information on shell scripting, see Chapter 7, "Essential Shell Scripting."

TCP/IP Network Administration

## CHAPTER 17

Networking Essentials

by Peter Kuo and Jeff Robinson

In this chapter

Overview of Networking

Computer networks are an important part of many information systems and have become an essential part of many businesses, regardless of the company's size. Networks allow you to share application programs, data files, and system resources such as modems and printers, and to exchange mail and other information. Say that you have 20 PCs at your location. How much time would it take for you to install 20 copies of, for example, Corel WordPerfect, one copy on each workstation? If you have a network, you can simply install one copy of WordPerfect on the central server (with the proper number of licenses, of course) and have it accessed by all 20 users. Imagine the time and trouble that would save you—not to mention the time it would save you in the future when you need to upgrade the software. You only have to do that once, instead of 20 times.

How does a network apply to your UNIX environment? If you have only one UNIX host and no workstations (PCs or otherwise) and no other (UNIX or non-UNIX) hosts, then you don't need a network. But, if you are not using dumb terminals (such as VT-100 or Wyse terminals) for your UNIX access but are using workstations, such as PCs, then you already have a network, whether you know it or not. If you have more than one host system (UNIX or not), you definitely want to have them connected to a network, if they are not already. Because this book's focus is on UNIX, we'll talk about networking UNIX hosts and accessing UNIX hosts over networks. Nonetheless, the concepts and commands discussed in this chapter and the rest of Part 3 of this book apply equally to all networks.

A *network* is a collection of computer systems that communicate with each other in a cooperative manner. Although these systems need not run the same operating system, they do need to communicate with each other using a common *protocol* (a "language" or set of rules). In the UNIX world, the predominant common protocol is the Transmission Control Protocol/Internet Protocol (TCP/IP). As Internet access from home becomes more popular, you will also encounter references to other protocols such as SLIP (Serial Line IP) and PPP (Point-to-Point Protocol). Although TCP/IP is used mostly with LANs and WANs, SLIP and PPP both provide effective serial line point-to-point connections (through compression) that support the standard Internet Protocol. Because SLIP and PPP were designed to support IP, any IP-based service runs successfully and transparently over these connections.

▶ **See** "Examining the DoD Model," **p. 454**

▶ **See** "What is PPP?" **p. 541**

N O T E Compared to PPP, SLIP is an older standard and is slowly being phased out in favor of PPP. Today, almost all home connections to the Internet (through an Internet service provider [ISP]) are made using PPP connections. ▪

In the UNIX environment, most processing is done on the UNIX host itself. So why the need to communicate with other machines? As previously mentioned, one advantage of having your UNIX host on the network is the capability to share system resources and files, perform remote administration of your UNIX host from anywhere on the network, and communicate with other users. Often, information you seek is not available locally. Suppose that you need to work with a sales database that someone at another location in your company has created. If you obtain a copy of that database locally, the two copies can easily get out of sync and out of date. If you could access the original database on the other host *transparently*, life would be easy. Transparent access of remote resources is one of the many reasons why networking is becoming popular and important today.

N O T E   In TCP/IP terminology, each computer is called a *node*, but most often it is called a *host*. Your workstation is also referred to as a host because it has its own local intelligence.   ▪

This chapter explores many different tools that you can use to accomplish tasks such as transferring files reliably between hosts over the network and performing remote access to UNIX hosts, as well as communicating, such as sending messages, with other users on the network.

N O T E   One type of network that used to be prevalent on UNIX systems was a *UUCP network*. UUCP stands for *UNIX-to-UNIX CoPy*. Originally, UUCP was used to distribute files and email messages between UNIX systems using UUCP commands over serial communication connections, such as modem links. You could also connect systems over local area networks using UUCP, but it is not as efficient as using TCP/IP.

The primary advantage of a UUCP network is its low cost. The only special equipment required is a modem—cabling costs are minimal. The main disadvantage is that transmission speed over the network is limited by the speed of serial connections, which are generally *much* slower than transmission speeds on other types of networks. In addition, to make each connection efficient, files are often put into a queue to be transferred to another system only once or twice a day. Today, the use of UUCP networks has all but disappeared except in remote regions of the globe because most parts of the world are now connected through the Internet. Therefore, in this book, UUCP networks are not covered: instead we will cover the use of TCP/IP.   ▪

Hostnames and IP Addresses

Each computer is identified by a unique address on its network, and if a system is attached to more than one network (such as a router), it has multiple unique addresses—one for each network. For two devices to communicate with each other, each must know the other's address. Just like when you need to call someone on the telephone, you need to know that person's phone number. In the TCP/IP world, each host is assigned a host number known as the Internet Protocol address, or *IP address*. To connect to a host using TCP/IP, you need to know the IP address of the destination machine.

▶ **See** "What Is a Router?" **p. 477**

> **CAUTION**
>
> Without going into detail in this chapter, if you are not familiar with the IP address schemes, you should *not* change the IP address associated with your host without first consulting with someone familiar with IP addressing. Otherwise, you can potentially make your host's TCP/IP function stop working and may cause other hosts' network access not to function properly as well. This is, in a way, analogous to telephone numbers. You are assigned one by some authority that manages these numbers, and you should not change your assigned number without being asked.

▶ **See** "IP Addresses," **p. 468**

People generally remember names better than numbers. Therefore, a hostname can be used instead of an IP number to connect to a remote host. However, if a hostname is used, your host will have to resolve (look up) the name to get the corresponding IP address because IP services use IP addresses. This resolution process can be done in two ways. One way is by performing a lookup in your machine's /etc/hosts file. Generally, this text file is maintained by the system administrator. Another method, which is generally used on medium-size and large networks, is to use a name service such as *Domain Name Service* (DNS).

▶ **See** "Overview of the Domain Name Service," **p. 593**

Because detailed information about DNS is being covered in Chapter 23, "DNS," only the hosts file is discussed here. A hosts file is simply an ASCII text file that contains a list of hostnames and their corresponding IP numbers. The following is a sample hosts file:

```
# This is a sample hosts file.
# Updated by Peter, Aug 1, 1998 @ 12:30pm
10.1.123.45    SCO1
10.1.123.46    SCO2    peter    testbox    #sco-database-server
10.2.11.45     linux1
10.2.11.46     vms     database
10.3.83.14     Router
```

> **N O T E** On UNIX systems, the hosts file must be placed in the /etc directory. On other systems, check your TCP/IP documentation on where the file should be located. ▪

> **CAUTION**
>
> Keep in mind that the filename is hosts: often people mistakenly name it "host" (the singular form) instead.

The syntax used by the hosts file is straightforward. As with all UNIX script files, any text after the hash symbol (#) is treated as comment and is ignored. The IP address and its corresponding hostname are listed one set per line: starting with the IP address (which is four sets of numbers, separated by a period), followed by a tab or one or more spaces, followed by the hostname. For example, in the sample hosts file listed previously:

```
10.1.123.45    SCO1
```

`10.1.123.45` is the IP address and `SCO1` is the hostname. You can list more than one hostname per IP address. The first one listed is known as the official hostname, and the rest are referred to as aliases. For example:

```
10.1.123.46   SCO2    peter    testbox    #sco-database-server
10.2.11.46    vms     database
```

both have multiple hostnames per IP address listed. You can use either `vms` or `database` to access the host whose IP address is `10.2.11.46`. Similarly, you can use `SCO2`, `peter`, or `testbox` to access the host whose IP address is `10.1.123.46`. However, you *cannot* use `sco-database-server` to access the IP address `10.1.123.46` because this name is placed behind the `#` symbol, which causes the name to be treated as a comment.

TIP Generally, hostnames are not case sensitive. Therefore, `vms`, `Vms`, and `VMS` all refer to the same host. However, to avoid confusion and to save yourself from any trouble, it is best to use only lowercase for your hostnames.

Because the `hosts` file is located in the `/etc` directory where normal users generally have no write-access, it is the responsibility of the system administrator to keep this file accurate and up-to-date.

Network Connectivity Commands

Many commands, such as those discussed in Chapter 3, "UNIX Shells and System Commands," that you can use to communicate with other users on a single host have been extended so that they work over the network. The `finger` and `talk` utilities are examples of such extended commands. These utilities understand a common convention for the format of network addresses: `username@hostname` (often read as *username at hostname*). When you use the "@" symbol in the command-line argument to one of these commands, the utility interprets the text that follows as the name of a remote host. When your command-line argument does not include the "@" symbol or hostname, it assumes you are requesting information or corresponding with someone on your local host. Networks also introduce the need for some new connectivity tools, such as `telnet` and `ftp`. Unlike the extended utilities mentioned previously, some of these tools are useless without a network.

▶ **See** "Working with Users," **p. 76**

Many people (wrongly) think the term "TCP/IP" implies only two protocols—TCP (Transmission Control Protocol) and IP (Internet Protocol). Actually, TCP/IP is a suite of more than 100 protocols, many of which provide services such as terminal emulation and file transfer. The following sections discuss six commonly used TCP/IP services and commands:

- TELNET, which provides terminal emulation services
- FTP, which provides file transfer facilities
- r-utilities, which provide remote access
- PING, which provides network diagnostic information

Part
III

Ch
17

- FINGER, which looks up user information
- TALK, which allows you to communicate with other users in real-time

N O T E Confusion sometimes arises when discussing TCP/IP protocols when the name of the application that provides a service is the same as the name of the protocol being used. For example, `telnet` is *often* (but not always) the name of the program that implements the TELNET protocol. However, the context in which the term is used should indicate whether the protocol is being referenced or an application implementing that protocol is being discussed. ■

Using *telnet*

Often, you need to access a remote UNIX host over a network to perform some task. For example, you have three UNIX hosts in your company that you manage, and it would be inconvenient to have three terminals on your desk, each connected to one UNIX host, to do your job. With the help of the TELNET protocol, you can easily use your workstation to establish a terminal session to any remote computer, allowing you to execute commands as though your workstation were locally connected to the host.

The `telnet` application is probably the most common tool used for remote login to UNIX and other TCP/IP hosts. To provide security, `telnet` requires you to know a valid username and password on the remote machine that you are logging in to. Some UNIX systems do provide guest login capabilities. These logins usually restrict the user from executing many commands, or provide them with a menu interface, allowing them to only perform a fixed set of tasks such as using `vi`, accessing printing resources, or looking up information. For example, the U.S. Library of Congress offers Internet TELNET access to one of its hosts (`locis.loc.gov`) so that you can search for publication-related information:

```
$ telnet locis.loc.gov
Trying 140.147.254.3...
Connected to locis.loc.gov.
Escape character is '^]'.
          L O C I S :  LIBRARY OF CONGRESS INFORMATION SYSTEM

          To make a choice: type a number, then press ENTER

    1   Library of Congress Catalog        4   Braille and Audio
    2   Federal Legislation                5   Foreign Law
    3   Copyright Information
    *    *    *    *    *    *    *    *    *    *    *    *
    7   Searching Hours and Basic Search Commands
    8   Documentation and Classes
    9   Library of Congress General Information
    10  Library of Congress Fast Facts
    11  * * Announcements * *

        The Organizations (NRCM) file is no longer created or supported by LC.
        It has been removed from LOCIS.

    12  Comments and Logoff
        Choice:
```

▶ **See** "Introducing vi," **p. 84**

▶ **See** "Printing," **p. 349**

After you are logged in, telnet allows you to run any *text-based* application, such as vi to edit files, more to view files, and mail to read your email, and to execute programs. Programs executed on the remote host must not use any type of graphic or require mouse support, such as X Window applications. telnet only supports (dumb) terminal types such as DEC VT-100, Data General DG-210, Wyse 60, and so on.

> **N O T E** If the application you run on the remote host requires graphical or mouse support, you need to use an X Window application and not telnet. ■

After you are logged in under your own username and password, you have the same user privileges that you would normally have when logged in without using telnet. Usually, the only losses in capability are slower access and having to use a terminal-type (text) environment rather than a window-type environment (if that was available on the host).

A Sample *telnet* Session   The following is a sample telnet session from a (FreeBSD) UNIX host to another (SCO) UNIX host where user-entered commands are shown in **bold**:

```
peter@pc1 %> telnet sco1
Trying 10.1.123.45...
Connected to sco1.
Escape character is '^]'.

UNIX(r) System V Release 4.0 (sco1)
Welcome to Software Development Server SCO1. Unauthorized access not permitted.
login: develop
Password: (not echoed)
Last login: Sun Jul 27 20:33:33 from pc1
You have new mail.
develop@sco1 $> who
hypno     ttyp0    Jul 29 15:51    (gamma)
lrr       ttyp1    Aug  7 20:49    (beta)
cart      ttyp2    Jul  2 10:26    (alpha)
hypno     ttyp3    Jul  9 13:25    (delta)
matt      ttyp4    Jul  2 11:05    (phi)
cap       ttyp5    Aug 10 15:04    (beta3)
sigma     ttyp6    Jul 14 16:54    (sigma)
puppy     ttyp7    Jul 13 22:44    (pc5)
au        ttyp8    Aug  6 19:22    (10.24.37.28)
dob       ttyp9    Aug 16 12:12    (10.154.63.239)
develop   ttypa    Aug 16 21:29    (pc1)
develop@sco1 $> wall Reminder: Please logout from sco1 by 21:00 for schedule
maintenance.
...
develop@sco1 $> exit
Connection closed by foreign host.
peter@pc1 %>
```

The telnet program is invoked with the hostname (sco1) as the command-line option. Using the information in the /etc/hosts file, telnet looks up the IP address of sco1 (10.1.123.45)

Part

III

Ch

17

and connects the user to that host. After the connection is established, the remote host displays its banner messages and then prompts the user to log in as if the connection were from a locally attached terminal. The user can perform any task (such as checking who is logged on, editing a file, and so on) without knowing it is being done over a network connection rather than a direct-cabled connection: the only telltale sign might be the occasional slow response from the remote host due to network traffic.

The `exit` or `logout` command terminates the remote session. `telnet` always reports that the connection has been `closed by foreign host` before returning you to a shell prompt on the machine from which you originally invoked the `telnet`.

TIP If you appear to be "hung" on a remote system for an extended period of time and want to abort the `telnet` session, use the escape character, usually the "^]" (Ctrl+], Control_right square bracket) to transfer control back to your local `telnet` application: the escape character is always displayed by the `telnet` program after the connection to the remote host is established. After you are in `telnet`'s interactive mode, use the `close` or `quit` command to terminate the session.

CAUTION

The `telnet` escape character shouldn't be confused with the ASCII escape character (Esc).

Figure 17.1 shows a sample TELNET login session using the TELNET emulator (`TELNET.EXE`) included with Microsoft Windows NT Workstation 4. Although it is an MS Windows application—but because the TELNET protocol is character-based—the resulting session is text mode only.

N O T E Many operating systems that support TCP/IP include a TELNET application. For example, a TELNET application called `TELNET.EXE` is included with Windows NT 4. ▨

***telnet* Command Summary** Although `telnet` supports many command-line options, the most commonly used command syntax for `telnet` is as follows:

`telnet [hostname]`

where *hostname* is the hostname or IP address of the remote computer. If you do not provide a hostname, `telnet` opens into an interactive mode. The interactive mode provides you with the `telnet>` prompt and expects you to use interactive commands to establish a connection. If you provide a hostname or IP address, `telnet` attempts to connect directly to the hostname or IP address specified on the command line.

`telnet` accepts many command-line arguments that can be used to alter the connection behavior to the remote host. Table 17.1 shows a list of commonly supported arguments for `telnet`.

FIGURE 17.1

A sample `telnet` session using Windows NT Workstation 4's `TELNET.EXE` to log in to a remote UNIX host.

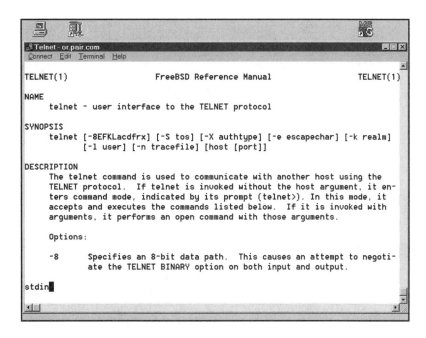

Part
III

Ch
17

Table 17.1   Command-Line Arguments for the *telnet* Command

Argument	Description
-d	Turns on debugging
-e [escape_char]	Sets the initial escape character to *escape_char*
-l [user]	Sends the username for login on the remote system
-n [trace_file]	Opens `trace_file` for recording your information
port [port_number]	Indicates that `telnet` should connect on a different port than the default (23)

You enter `telnet`'s interactive command mode if you use the `telnet` escape character (default is Ctrl+]), or if you open `telnet` without specifying a hostname or IP address. Table 17.2 lists the commands that you can execute when using `telnet` in interactive mode.

Table 17.2   Common *telnet* Interactive Commands

Command	Description
open [host] [port]	The command allows you to connect to a host. [port] allows you to connect to a port number other than the default (23)
close	Close the current connection

continues

Table 17.2 Continued

Command	Description
status	Shows the current status of telnet. This includes the machine that you are connected to
quit	Quits interactive telnet mode
?	Get help

N O T E No single standard set of commands exists for telnet. The command set and issues such as case-sensitivity vary from system to system. It is best to use the ? command to determine what commands are supported by your particular telnet implementation. ■

Using *ftp*

FTP (File Transfer Protocol) is the standard method of transferring files reliably across a TCP/IP network. FTP is designed to simplify file access between computers. You can use the ftp command to navigate between directories on a remote host, examine the contents of remote directories, transfer both text and binary files from the remote system to your computer, and put files from your local computer to the remote host. It does not matter whether the computer systems involved are of completely different architectures.

N O T E As the name of the protocol implies, you can't use ftp to perform non-file-oriented operations on a remote host. For example, ftp has commands to rename and delete files on the remote computer, but you can't run programs, such as vi, on the remote machine. ■

To retrieve a file from a remote host, you are required, as part of the security system, to have a valid username and password on the remote host. If you don't have an account on the remote system, some hosts offer "anonymous FTP" (which is discussed later in this chapter), which allows you to log in essentially as a guest user. ftp uses the get and put commands to transfer files to and from your host to the remote system. The following example demonstrates a sample FTP session from a UNIX host to a non-UNIX system (user-entered information is shown in **bold**). Notice that although the hostname database is used in the command line, the remote host identifies itself as vms—this is because the local /etc/hosts file (presented earlier) has both vms and database (with database being the alias) pointing to the same IP address:

```
$ ftp database
Connected to vms.
220 vms MultiNet FTP Server Process V4.0(15) at Wed 15-Aug-98 2:49PM
-EDT
Name (developer): peter
331 User name (peter) ok. Password, please.
Password: (not echoed)
230 User PETER logged into DISK1:[CS.PETER] at Wed 19-Aug-98 2:52PM-EDT, job
37cd2
```

```
.
Remote system type is VMS.
ftp>
```

The example illustrates that ftp can work between any operating systems, as long as TCP/IP is used, and not just between UNIX machines.

CAUTION

Be aware that no single standard way exists to implement the FTP protocol. The ftp program you run on one computer may appear (and behave) differently from the one you use on a different machine. Even between UNIX versions, although the ftp implementations are similar, differences exist.

A Sample *ftp* Session   The following example illustrates how easy it is to use ftp to get files from remote machines. In the example, ftp connects to one of InterNIC's hosts and retrieves the template file (domain-template.txt) that is used for domain registration and modification.

N O T E   InterNIC is the central authority that handles all non-military Internet domain registrations. ▥

The following example is an actual ftp session and preserves all text appearing onscreen during the session. User-entered information is shown in **bold**. All other text is generated by either the local or the remote system. First, the ftp program connects the local machine to the remote host named rs.internic.net. Because you don't have a valid account on this host, anonymous access is used:

```
dreamlan@or% ftp rs.internic.net
Connected to rs.internic.net.
220-*****Welcome to the InterNIC Registration Host*****
*****Login with username "anonymous"
*****You may change directories to the following:
      policy            - Registration Policies
      templates         - Registration Templates
      netinfo           - NIC Information Files
      domain            - Root Domain Zone Files
220 And more!
Name (rs.internic.net;dreamlan): anonymous
331 Guest login ok, send your complete e-mail address as password.
Password: (not echoed)
230 Guest login ok, access restrictions apply.
Remote system type is UNIX.
Using binary mode to transfer files.
```

N O T E   Notice that most ftp responses are prefixed by a number. They are used to identify the type of message, as defined in the RFC for FTP (RFC 959). ▥

The welcome message indicates the various documents available from this FTP server. Because you're interested in the domain registration template, a directory listing of the templates directory is obtained to determine the exact filename—you can use either the `dir` command or the `ls` command:

```
ftp> cd templates
250 CWD command successful.
ftp> dir
200 PORT command successful.
150 Opening ASCII mode data connection for /bin/ls.
total 136
drwxr-xr-x   3 60      1        1024 Aug 19 17:08 .
drwxr-xr-x  19 0       1         512 Feb 19  1997 ..
lrwxrwxrwx   1 60      1          31 Nov 21  1996 account-template.txt -> ..
/billing/account-template.txt
-rw-r--r--   1 60     10        2540 Sep  9  1996 contact-parser-errors.txt
-rw-r--r--   1 60     10       16299 May  2  1996 contact-template-examples.
txt
-rw-r--r--   1 60     10       14940 Jun 15  1996 contact-template.txt
-rw-r--r--   1 0      10        4932 Feb 26 19:48 domain-parser-errors.txt
-rw-r--r--   1 60     10       10008 Mar 30 20:31 domain-template.txt
-rw-r--r--   1 60      1       16376 Jul 15 19:09 host-template.txt
drwx------   2 60      1         512 Aug 19 17:08 old-templates
lrwxrwxrwx   1 60      1          27 Nov 21  1996 pmt-template.txt -> ..
/billing/pmt-template.txt
226 Transfer complete.
```

Because the file you're interested in is a text file, the file transfer type is set to ASCII. And to monitor the file transfer progress, the hash mark is turned on—a "#" symbol is displayed on the screen for each 1KB of data transferred:

```
ftp> ascii
200 Type set to A.
ftp> hash
Hash mark printing on (1024 bytes/hash mark).
ftp> get domain-template.txt
local: domain-template.txt remote: domain-template.txt
200 PORT command successful.
150 Opening ASCII mode data connection for domain-template.txt (10008 bytes).
##########
226 Transfer complete.
10237 bytes received in 2.37 seconds (4.22 Kbytes/s)
```

The `hash` command is a handy tool especially if you have a busy network or there is a slow link between your machine and the remote host. The visual indication it gives provides you with instant feedback on how the data transfer is going.

Finally, the `ftp` session is terminated, and control is returned to the local machine:

```
ftp> bye
221 Goodbye.
dreamlan@or%
```

The `domain-template.txt` file should now be in the default directory on the local system.

N O T E   It is common to include `ftp` in the name of the FTP server so that it is obvious. However, it is not necessary. Any host (as is the case shown by the preceding example) can be an FTP server provided that it has the `ftp` daemon running. ■

Anonymous FTP   When you try to connect to a remote computer using `ftp`, you are required, as part of the security system, to have a valid username and password on the remote host. Many facilities have information that they want to allow people without accounts on their computers to be able to access. For example, a software vendor might make updates and patches to its software available for download via FTP. In such situations, these sites enable *anonymous FTP* access on their FTP servers.

Anonymous FTP simply means that you enter "anonymous" (sometimes "ftp") as the username, and the FTP server allows you to use nearly any string as the password to gain FTP access. Often, you are asked to use either "guest" or your Internet email address for the password. In the Anonymous FTP mode, the FTP host does not allow you to access its entire directory structure, and often does not allow the uploading of files for security reasons.

Other than the use of a specific username and restricted access, anonymous FTP functions exactly the same as "normal" FTP.

Trivial FTP   Contrary to FTP where username and password authentication is required before file transfer can take place, Trivial FTP (TFTP) doesn't require any username/password authentication. To download a file, you simply need to know the name of the host, the location of the file, and the exact filename you want to retrieve. However, without this information, you can't download a file using TFTP because it doesn't provide any commands for generating directory listings. Although it is mostly used for file downloads, you can also upload files using TFTP.

N O T E   TFTP is used mostly by automated procedures, such as a router getting firmware updates or a smart hub getting management information. ■

FTP Command Summary   After a connection to an FTP server is established, the `ftp` command waits in interactive mode for you to enter commands. Table 17.3 lists some commonly used FTP commands that you need to know. Some commands are part of your local `ftp` command: others are executed on the server. Some servers do not support, or may restrict the use of, some of the commands listed in Table 17.3.

Part III

Ch 17

Table 17.3   Commonly Used FTP Commands

Command	Description
`![command]`	Allows you to run a command on your local machine without quitting ftp: this is much like the Shell Escape Mode in `vi`.

continues

Table 17.3 Continued

Command	Description
append *local-file* [*remote-file*]	This appends a specified local file to a remote file on the server. If you do not specify a remote file, then the remote file name is the same as the local filename.
ascii	This option must be set if you are going to transfer a text file. Your host converts the incoming text into ASCII format that is legible on your host.
bell	A bell sound occurs after a file transfer is complete.
binary	This option must be set if you are going to transfer a binary file. Your host does not convert any of the incoming data to any other format.
bye	This command is used to terminate a connection with an FTP server (does not exit from the ftp program).
cd *remote-directory*	Changing from one directory to another on the remote host.
close	This command is used to terminate a connection with an FTP server. Same as bye.
delete *remote-file*	Deletes the *remote-file* on the remote machine.
dir [*remote-directory*]	Prints a listing of the contents in the *remote-directory*. The output is similar to the ls -l command.
disconnect	The same as bye and close.
get *remote-file* [*local-file*]	Transfers a file named *remote-file* to your local machine and stores it in a file named *local-file*. If a local file is not specified, the *remote-file* name is used to store the file on your host.
hash	This prints a hash-symbol (#) for every xKB of data transferred. (The value varies between 1KB and 8KB depending on the implementation.)
help [*command*]	Shows help for the specified command.
lcd [*directory*]	This changes the directory on your local host, as opposed to cd, which changes directories on the server you are connected to.

Command	Description
Ls [-al] [*remote-directory*]	Lists the files in the remote directory specified. If no *remote-directory* is specified, then the current directory is assumed. The -l option lists files and their attributes, such as owner, group, and permissions. The -a option displays hidden files on the server.
mdelete *remote-files*	This allows you to delete multiple files from the server. Wildcard characters may be used to represent the multiple files.
mdir *remote-files*	The same as dir except that you can list multiple directories.
mget *remote-files*	This option allows you to transfer multiple files. Wildcard characters are supported. You are prompted to answer whether each file should be transferred. This can be disabled with the prompt command.
mkdir *directory-name*	Creates a directory on the remote machine.
open *host* [*port*]	This allows you to open a connection to a remote host while in ftp interactive mode. The *host* is the remote host's name or IP address. The port number is required if you need to connect to a nonstandard FTP port.
prompt	This toggles the prompting for confirming individual file transfers.
put *local-file* [*remote-file*]	Transfers a file named *local-file* from your local machine to the server and names it *remote-file*. If a *remote-file* is not specified, the *local-file* name is used to store the file on the server.
pwd	Displays your present working directory on the server.
quit	Same as the bye command.
recv *remote-file* [*local-file*]	Same as the get command.
rename *file-name* *new-file-name*	Allows you to rename a file on the server.
rmdir *directory-name*	Allows you to delete an existing directory from the server.

Part
III

Ch
17

continues

Table 17.3 Continued

Command	Description
runique	Toggles the capability to prevent overwriting a file on your host with one that is being downloaded. ftp renames an existing file about to be overwritten with the filename with a .1 at the end. If a .1 file exists, then ftp names that file .2, and so on.
send *local-file* [*remote-file*]	Same as the put command.
status	This command provides information about your ftp session.
user *user-name*	Specify your username to the FTP server that you are connected to. Useful if you mistype your username or password when authenticating to the server. You do not have to re-establish the connection to the server.
? [*command*]	The same as help command.

▶ **See** "The ls Command," **p. 51**

▶ **See** "Escaping to the Shell," **p. 103**

N O T E No single standard set of commands exists for ftp. The command set and issues such as case-sensitivity vary from system to system. It is best to use the ? command to determine what commands are supported by your particular ftp implementation. UNIX is case-sensitive, so you must enter the filenames used in ftp with this in mind. ▨

 T I P Often, if the remote host is not running UNIX, you can use either upper- or lowercase letters to reference a file. However, if in doubt, try lowercase first.

The *r*-Utilities

The remote utilities (better known as the r-utilities because they all start with the letter "r") are a set of commands that allow you to log in, copy, print, or execute commands on remote machines without being prompted for a password. This can be convenient when working in an environment with many machines or when you frequently run jobs on other systems. In all cases, you must have an account (or know of a valid username) on the remote server and a trust relationship established to avoid being prompted for a password.

N O T E To be a trusted host means that a system believes your computer is not pretending to be a different machine and that your login name on both systems (but not necessarily passwords) is the same. ▨

For the r-utilities to function, they require the following:

- A remote shell server program (`rshd`) on the remote host
- An entry in the `/etc/hosts` file on the remote host
- An entry in either the `.rhosts` or the `/etc/hosts.equiv` file on the remote host

Typically, only a privileged user or the system administrator can make the entry in the `/etc/hosts` and `/etc/hosts.equiv` files and start `rshd`. Coordinate requirements for remote server programs with the system administrator of the remote host.

> **N O T E** For UNIX, the filenames are `/etc/hosts`, `/etc/hosts.equiv`, and `.rhosts`. The names may vary for other operating systems.

The /etc/hosts.equiv File The `/etc/hosts.equiv` file is used to identify remote hosts and users that are trusted. This is useful for sites where it is common for users to have accounts on different machines, and it eliminates the security risk of sending your plain text password over the network where it might be "sniffed." Computer systems listed in the `/etc/hosts.equiv` file are considered as secure as your local machine. For security reasons, the `/etc/hosts.equiv` file is not consulted if the remote connection is trying to connect as the root (Superuser) account. Only a `/.rhosts` file (see the following section) works if you are trying to connect as root.

The `/etc/hosts.equiv` file is made up of entries (one line per host) that may consist of one or two fields, separated by a tab or one or more spaces, on each line:

```
Hostname    [username]
```

The first field is the hostname that you trust: the second (optional) field is the username that you trust. If only a hostname is specified, then any user from the named host is trusted. That means that every user from the named host is a trusted user and can access any account, provided that the account names are known by the trusted user. If you specify both a hostname and a username, then only the named user, from the named host, can access the accounts on the system.

> **N O T E** The hostnames must exist in the `/etc/hosts` file and must be an official name, not an alias.

A "+" symbol (rather than a "*" symbol) acts as a wildcard character in the file. If used by itself in the hostname field, it allows all specified user accounts on any host to connect without a password. If used in the username field, any user is allowed to connect from the specified host. A hostname with a leading "+" accepts all matching hosts and all their users. A username with a leading "+" accepts all matching users from matching hosts. Conversely, a hostname with a leading "-" rejects all matching hosts and all their users, and a username with a leading "-" rejects all matching users from matching hosts.

In the following sample `/etc/hosts.equiv`, (ignoring the comment line) the first line allows `sally` access to any user account on `SC01` if she is connecting from a host named `dallas7`: the

Part

III

Ch

17

second line trusts all users from a host named accounting except for user george: the last line trusts all users from the host named magic to connect as any user on SCO1 without needing a password:

```
# Sample /etc/hosts.equiv file from SCO1
dallas7 sally
+accounting    -george
magic    +
```

The $HOME/.rhosts File   The $HOME/.rhosts file is used to identify hosts and users that can be trusted by a single user, instead of all users on the host. When the .rhosts file is properly configured, specified users from particular hosts are not prompted when connecting to the host and account. For example, the following .rhosts file (located in $HOME where $HOME points to the home directory of user peter) permits user sally from host dallas7 to log in as user peter without requiring his password:

```
#Sample .rhosts file in /usr/home/peter
dallas7 sally
```

N O T E   The $HOME is a shell environment variable that points to the home directory of the user.

The syntax of the .rhosts file is the same as the /etc/hostname.equiv.

N O T E   For security reasons, a user's .rhosts file is ignored if it is not a regular text file, if it is not readable and writable by only the owner (mode 600), or if it is not owned by the user.

CAUTION

An .rhosts file allows someone to log in as you from a (trusted) remote system by just knowing your username on the local system without knowing your password. This is a potential security risk. The alternative file, /etc/hosts.equiv, introduces a much larger potential security risk because it permits not just a single user but any user from the trusted host to access your files by just knowing your username on the local machine. Therefore, being the lesser of two evils, the .rhosts file is the preferred authorization file for the r-utilities.

---

rhosts Authorization Mechanism   Servers accepting connections from clients using the r-utilities, such as rlogin, rcp, and rsh, do not ask for a password if you have an account on the server and can match the client hostname and the username in one of two files—/etc/hosts.equiv or $HOME/.rhosts.

Figure 17.2 illustrates the process that takes place when you use r-utilities to access your account on a remote host. The following steps explain the validation process:

1. An r-utility (rsh sco1 dates in the example), is executed on a client machine. (The syntax of the command is of the form: r_cmd remote_hostname remote_command.)

2. The client system checks its local hosts file for the remote hostname. If the name doesn't exist in the hosts file and no DNS is set up, the command is aborted.

3. The system sends the local hostname and the username (set in the $USER shell environment variable) to the remote host.

4. Upon receiving the request from the client machine, the remote host checks its hosts file to see whether the hostname is known.

5. The remote host then checks the /etc/hosts.equiv authentication file for a hostname/username match. If there is no match, the $HOME/.rhosts file is then checked. If there is no match, the request is denied: otherwise, the command is executed and the result returned to the client machine.

FIGURE 17.2

Flow chart illustrating the steps taken in r-utilities permission checking.

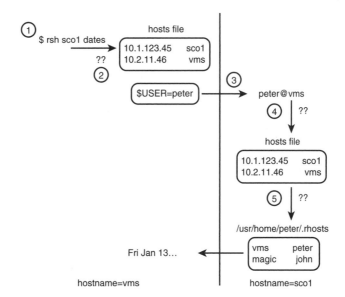

The *rlogin* Command   The rlogin command establishes a remote login session, similar to that of a telnet session, to a remote system if you have an account on that system. Instead of using the current username (as defined in $USER), you can use the -l option to specify a different username for the remote login session. For example, if you are logged in as user peter but want to access a remote host as user john, the rlogin command is as follows:

```
pc1 $> rlogin -l john sco2
Last login: Sun Jul 27 20:33:33 from pc1
You have new mail.
sco2 $> exit
rlogin: connection close.
pc1 $>
```

Generally, rlogin is only used between UNIX systems because not all TCP/IP-capable hosts support remote access via rlogin: it is best to use telnet for all remote access needs.

The *rsh* Command The rsh command allows you to execute a program or a shell script on a remote system without logging in: if you need to run multiple commands, it is usually easier to simply log in (using telnet or rlogin) and then run the commands. Like the other r-utilities, the rsh command requires you to specify the hostname or IP address of the remote host, and the command to execute. The rsh command is useful for performing basic tasks such as obtaining a directory listing from a remote host as follows:

```
$ rsh sco1 ls /usr/home/projects/chapter.*
chapter.01
chapter.02
chapter.04
chapter.15
chapter.16
chapter.17
chapter.in-progress
$
```

rsh can also be used to perform more complex tasks. The following example performs a backup of the /opt directory using the tar command. The - option used in the tar command forces tar to send the resulting archive to standard output: in this case the pipe. The output is then transferred across the network using rsh to a host named sco1, where the dd command is used to send the data to the device file /dev/rmt/0, a DAT tape drive:

```
$ tar cvf - /opt ¦ rsh sco1 dd of=/dev/rmt/0
```

▶ **See** "Using tar," **p. 387**

▶ **See** "Using dd," **p. 391**

The *rcp* Command You can use the rcp command to copy files to and from a remote machine using a syntax similar to the regular UNIX cp command. Using the rcp command involves less work to transfer a file than using ftp: however, more initial setup (such as establishing the trust relationship) is required on the server's side.

▶ **See** "Copying Files and Directories with cp," **p. 60**

The rcp command treats a filename as a local file, unless a machine name prefixes the filename. The following example copies a file named jokes.txt from the local host to a host named mickey and places the file in its /tmp directory:

```
$ rcp jokes.txt mickey:/tmp
```

As in cp, the -r option can be used to recursively copy a directory structure to or from a remote host. The following example copies the entire /opt/jokes directory and all subdirectories from the host mickey to the local machine and places the files and subdirectories in the /usr/home/peter/funny_jokes directory:

```
$ rcp -r mickey:/opt/jokes /usr/home/peter/jokes_funny
```

Using *ping*

When you can't communicate or have slow performance issues in a networked environment, it is sometimes difficult to determine where the problem lies. Fortunately, the ping (*Packet Internet Groper*) utility can be used to help troubleshoot network communication problems. The ping command tests connectivity between hosts by sending out a particular kind of IP packet (known as *Internet Control Message Protocol* packets, often referred to simply as ICMP packets) to the remote host that causes the remote system to send back a reply. This is a quick way to determine that there is a valid path between your machine and remote host, as well to check how well the network is operating by timing the ping response time and whether the network is dropping (losing) data packets.

> **N O T E** A lack of response from the remote host does *not* necessarily mean the remote host is down unless both systems are on the same network. A lack of ping response may mean the network path between your system and the remote host is down, rather than the remote host is down. ▪

Part
III
Ch
17

In the simplest form, the ping command accepts a single host name (or IP address) as an argument. ping sends a series of messages, once per second, to the host. If the host replies to the message, ping advises you that the host is alive. An example of pinging a host follows:

```
$ ping mickey
mickey is alive
$
```

If you need more detail about a network connection between two hosts, you can use the -s option. This option sends continuous 64-byte messages (56 data bytes and 8 bytes of protocol header information) to the remote host. The extreme right field of the output shows the round-trip time (in milliseconds) that elapsed from when the packet was sent to the remote host until the reply was received by the local system. This time is affected by the distance between the two systems as well as by other network traffic, the load on both computers, and the type of network links (such as LAN and WAN) involved. If the "time" values are very high (say, a few hundred milliseconds), this can indicate a large volume of data on the network:

```
$ ping -s mickey
PING mickey: 56 data bytes
64 bytes from mickey (10.5.12.4): icmp_seq=0. time=2. ms
64 bytes from mickey (10.5.12.4): icmp_seq=1. time=1. ms
64 bytes from mickey (10.5.12.4): icmp_seq=2. time=0. ms
64 bytes from mickey (10.5.12.4): icmp_seq=4. time=0. ms
64 bytes from mickey (10.5.12.4): icmp_seq=5. time=0. ms
64 bytes from mickey (10.5.12.4): icmp_seq=6. time=0. ms
64 bytes from mickey (10.5.12.4): icmp_seq=8. time=0. ms
64 bytes from mickey (10.5.12.4): icmp_seq=9. time=0. ms
^C
---- mickey ping statistics----
10 packets transmitted, 8 packets received, 20% packet loss
round-trip (ms)  min/avg/max = 0/0/2
$
```

N O T E   One reason that 64 bytes is used for the `ping` command is that TCP/IP was first implemented on Ethernet networks, and the minimum Ethernet packet size is 64 bytes. ▪

A Ctrl-c can be used to terminate the `ping`. After the `ping` command has terminated, some overall `ping` statistics are listed—how many packets were sent and received, as well as the minimum, average, and maximum round-trip delays it measured. A packet sequence number (`icmp_seq`) is given. If a packet is dropped, a gap occurs in the sequence number (packets 3 and 7 in the previous example). You might want to keep an eye on the percentage of packet loss. A network that consistently drops lots of packets is inefficient, and you should look into why packets are being lost.

N O T E   Some implementations of `ping` will continue to send the `ping` without the `-s` option until you abort the execution with Ctrl-c. ▪

TROUBLESHOOTING

If `ping` cannot contact the remote host, it continues trying and appears to be "hung." You can interrupt it with Ctrl-c and try again with the `-s` option to get more information.

You can use other command-line options (such as `-c`) with `ping`, but because they are seldom used, they are not discussed here. Refer to your online documentation (that is, `man ping`) for the various `ping` options supported by your system.

Using *finger*

As previously discussed in Chapter 3, `finger` can be used to display a list of the people currently using the system. With the advent of networks, the `finger` facility has been extended so that it can collect information from remote hosts. The command syntax to get a list of all users logged in to a given remote host is:

```
finger @hostname
```

where *hostname* is the name of the remote host listed either in your `/etc/hosts` file or known to your DNS. In the following example, `finger` displays information about all the users logged in on the system named `sco1`:

```
$ finger @sco1
[sco1]

Login    Name              TTY  Idle  Login Time   Office     Office Phone
sally    Sally Ann          3  21:40  Tue   10:03
root     Superuser         p0  11:13  Mon   17:04   Rm111      x123
develop  Peter             p2         Wed   07:48
```

A user's name (or login name) in front of the "@" symbol causes `finger` to look up the information from the remote system only for the user you have specified. If there are multiple matches for that name on the remote host, `finger` displays the results for all of them:

```
$ finger root@sco1
[sco1]
Login name: root                        In real life: System Admin.
Directory: /home/root                   Shell: /bin/sh
Last login Mon Aug 17 13:00 on ttyp0 from pc5
No unread mail
Plan:
Read "Using UNIX, Special Edition" from cover-to-cover.
```

Notice that the information displayed by `finger` for a remote host looks much the same as it does when `finger` runs on your local system, with one small difference: Before displaying the results, `finger` reports the name of the remote host that answered the query (sco1, as shown in the square brackets in the preceding example).

▶ **See** "Viewing Users Logged On," **p. 76**

Part

III

Ch

17

N O T E Depending on how the remote `finger` daemon is configured, the name of the host that answers might be different from the system name you specified on the command line. In some cases, you might see multiple hostnames listed if one `finger` daemon contacts another to retrieve the information. ▨

T I P To maintain privacy or some level of security (as it is, often people will list they are away on holidays or such in their `.plan` file), you might choose not to run the `finger` daemon. Alternatively, you can block the port used by `finger` (79) on your router that connects to the outside world. This way, your internal users will still have access to the `finger` facility but outside users will not.

Some sites on the Internet use `finger` as a means to provide special information. For example, you can use `finger` to retrieve information about recent earthquakes from the U.S. Geological Survey:

```
$ finger quake@gldfs.cr.usgs.gov
[gldfs.cr.usgs.gov]
Login name: quake                       In real life: see Ray Buland
Directory: /home/quake                  Shell: /home/quake/run_quake
Last login Tue Aug 18 13:00 on ttyp0 from mhaga.production
No unread mail
Plan:
The following near-real-time Earthquake Bulletin is provided by the National
Earthquake Information Service (NEIS) of the U. S. Geological Survey as part of
a cooperative project of the Council of the National Seismic System.  For
a description of the earthquake parameters listed below, the availability of
additional information, and our publication criteria, please finger
qk_info@gldfs.cr.usgs.gov.
Updated as of Tue Aug 18 15:02:20 MDT 1998.

   DATE-(UTC)-TIME     LAT    LON     DEP   MAG  Q  COMMENTS
  yy/mm/dd hh;mm;ss    deg.   deg.    km
  98/08/16 19:25:14   50.21N 131.47W  10.0 3.8Mb C  VANCOUVER ISLAND REGION
  98/08/17 01:15:09   36.40N 137.57E  33.0 4.5Mb B  EASTERN HONSHU, JAPAN
  98/08/17 05:57:26   40.65N 124.12W  22.5 3.3Ml    NEAR COAST OF NORTHERN CALIF.
  98/08/17 06:06:37   57.38N 153.88W  33.0 4.6Mb A  KODIAK ISLAND REGION
```

```
98/08/17 06:36:26    9.97S  77.43W   92.3 4.7Mb B   CENTRAL PERU
98/08/17 08:02:03    3.32S  12.12W   10.0 5.0Mb B   NORTH OF ASCENSION ISLAND
98/08/17 09:44:49   34.27N 117.21W    7.4 3.5Ml     SOUTHERN CALIFORNIA
98/08/17 12:43:35    7.40S 107.09E   33.0 5.4Mb B   JAWA, INDONESIA
98/08/17 19:38:16   19.52S 175.52W  142.8 4.6Mb B   TONGA ISLANDS
98/08/17 19:55:40   57.74N 162.94E   33.0 4.6Mb B   NEAR EAST COAST OF KAMCHATKA
98/08/17 23:18:01   34.11N 116.93W    4.7 3.0Ml     SOUTHERN CALIFORNIA
98/08/18 00:54:19   36.75N 121.45W    8.9 3.3Ml     CENTRAL CALIFORNIA
98/08/18 04:10:23   27.70N  90.95E   33.0 5.2Mb B   BHUTAN
98/08/18 05:01:10   30.07S 178.61W   56.8 5.0Mb C   KERMADEC ISLANDS, NEW ZEALAND
98/08/18 06:07:43   57.34N 156.79W   99.7 3.9Mb B   ALASKA PENINSULA
98/08/18 06:30:34   14.16S 166.77E   33.0 5.1Mb C   VANUATU ISLANDS
98/08/18 07:02:16   28.58N 130.10E   33.0 4.5Mb C   RYUKYU ISLANDS
98/08/18 08:18:17   17.46S 179.03W  500.0 4.4Mb C   FIJI ISLANDS REGION
98/08/18 10:50:33   43.34S  14.87W   10.0 4.8Mb C   SOUTHERN MID-ATLANTIC RIDGE
98/08/18 11:25:23   61.49N 148.34W   10.0 4.6Mb A   SOUTHERN ALASKA
98/08/18 18:00:12   45.87N 149.11E  116.6 5.4Mb A   KURIL ISLANDS
```

Using *talk*

The `talk` facility allows you to chat in real-time with other users on the same or remote host by copying lines from your terminal to the other user's. The syntax for the `talk` command is as follows:

```
talk username [tty_name]
```

where *username* is the login name of the person you want to communicate with. If this user is on another host, then *username* is of the form `username@hostname` or `hostname!username`, or `hostname;username`, depending on the implementation: the most commonly used form is `username@hostname`.

If you want to talk to a user who is logged in more than once, the optional *tty_name* argument may be used to indicate the appropriate terminal name, where *tty_name* is generally of the form "tty##". You can use the `finger` command, as discussed in the previous section, to find out whether the user is logged in and his or her terminal name.

N O T E   The version of `talk` released with BSD 4.3 uses a protocol that is incompatible with the protocol used in the version released with BSD 4.2. Therefore, `talk` between the two systems is not possible. ▪

From Here...

This chapter provided a brief overview of networking in the UNIX environment and explored a number of tools that you can use to accomplish tasks such as transferring files reliably between hosts over the network, performing remote access to UNIX hosts, and communicating, such as sending messages, with other users on the network.

▪ For information about connecting hosts together to establish network connectivity, see Chapter 18, "Internetworking."

- To learn about setting up TCP/IP on your UNIX system, see Chapter 19, "Configuring TCP/IP."

- To find out about IP routing protocols, see Chapter 20, "IP Routing."

- For an overview of advanced networking components and some future technologies, see Chapter 21, "Advanced Networking."

- To learn how to set up and configure network file systems to provide file sharing throughout a network, see Chapter 22, "NFS."

- For information about Internet host naming and domain name configuration, see Chapter 23, "DNS."

Part

III

Ch

17

## CHAPTER 18

Internetworking

by Peter Kuo and Jeff Robinson

Defining Connectivity

As defined previously, a *network* is a collection of computer systems that communicate with each other in a cooperative manner transparent to the users. These systems need not run the same operating system, but they do need to communicate with each other using a common *protocol* (a "language," or set of rules). In the UNIX world, this common protocol is most often TCP/IP.

To have a basic understanding of how networks function, you must learn some networking buzzwords. First, you need to know of two communication models that describe how computers communicate with each other: the Open Systems Interconnection (OSI) model and the Department of Defense (DoD), or the Internet, model.

N O T E   The design of TCP/IP is based on the DoD model. Because TCP/IP is the preferred networking protocol for UNIX systems, the discussions in this chapter are centered on the DoD model, not the OSI model. ▓

Different Networking Models

When dealing with computer networking, it is important to understand the different networking models involved. The models organize the various concepts involved and give you insights into the function of different protocols, as well as the order in which communication processes take place. A computer network can be organized into three major network elements:

- Physical connections
- Protocols
- Applications

The physical connections provide the medium over which the data can be transmitted. There are many choices for the physical connections of a network. They could be coaxial cable, twisted-pair wiring (shielded or unshielded), fiber optics, microwave links, and so on. You must make your choice based on factors such as bandwidth of medium, ease of installation, maintenance, media cost, and end-equipment cost.

The physical connections represent the lowest level of logical functionality needed by the network. To operate the network, you need to have a standard set of rules and regulations that all devices must obey to be able to communicate and interoperate with each other. The rules and regulations by which networking devices communicate are called *protocols*. A variety of such rules and regulations (protocols) exist, and these rules provide different types of functions for a network.

Network applications use the underlying network protocols to communicate with network applications running on other network devices. The network protocol in turn uses the network's physical connections to transmit the data.

When you consider that network operations consist of physical connections, protocols, and applications, you can see that these network elements form a hierarchy: the application at the top and the physical connections at the bottom. The protocols provide the bridge between the applications and the physical connections. To understand the hierarchy between the network elements and the functions that they perform, you need a "yard stick," or a model, for defining these functions.

Over the years, different vendors have developed different networking models specifically for their own networking protocols. For example:

- Systems Network Architecture (SNA) from IBM
- Digital Network Architecture (DNA) from Digital Equipment Corporation

Depending on the scope of the discussion, a network architecture may refer to a model that encompasses an entire computing environment (such as SNA from IBM) or one that specifies just low-level features (cabling, packet structure, and media access, such as the Ethernet specification from Xerox) of a network.

Of particular interest to UNIX networking are two (high-level) networking models:

- The Open Systems Interconnection (OSI) model, which deals with general multivendor interoperability
- The (U.S.) Department of Defense (DoD) model, which was developed for TCP/IP networking

The OSI model is the most widely accepted network model and is discussed next; the DoD model is discussed in another section later in this chapter.

Part
III

Ch
18

Exploring the OSI Model

Many different types of computers are used today. These systems differ in operating system, CPU type, network interface, and many other variables. These differences make the problem of communication between diverse computer systems nontrivial. In 1977, the International Organization for Standardization (ISO) created a subcommittee to develop data communication standards to promote multivendor interoperability. The result is the *Open Systems Interconnection* (OSI) model.

The OSI model does not specify any communication standards or protocols; instead, it simply provides guidelines for dividing up the communication tasks. To simplify matters, the ISO subcommittee took the "divide-and-conquer" approach. By dividing the complex communication process into smaller subtasks, the problem becomes more manageable, and each subtask can be optimized individually.

N O T E It is important to understand that the OSI model is simply a model—a framework—that specifies the functions to be performed. It does not detail how these functions are performed. ISO, however, does certify specific protocols that meet OSI standards for parts of the OSI model. For example, the CCITT X.25 protocol is accepted by ISO as an implementation that provides most of the services of the Network layer of the OSI model.

The OSI model is divided into seven layers as shown in Figure 18.1. Note that Layer 7 is at the top, and Layer 1 is at the bottom. As a result, the OSI model is sometimes referred to as the "upside-down seven-layer cake."

FIGURE 18.1

The OSI seven-layer model and the four-layer DoD model.

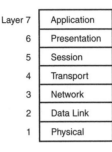

Layer 7	Application	Process/
6	Presentation	Application
5	Session	
4	Transport	Host-to-Host
3	Network	Internet
2	Data Link	Network
1	Physical	Access

OSI Model   DoD Model

> **TIP** One easy way to remember the order of the layers (from the top down) is by making a sentence from the first letters of the layer names: All People Seem To Need Data Processing.

Each layer is assigned a specific set of functions. Each layer uses the services of the layer underneath it and provides services to the layer above it. For example, the Network layer makes use of services from the Data Link layer and provides network-related services to the Transport layer. In other words, Layer *N* uses the services of Layer (*N-1*) and provides services to Layer (*N+1*). Layers communicate by passing parameters called *service primitives* (commands) to each other through predefined addresses called *service access points* (known as "ports" in TCP/IP). Table 18.1 explains the services offered at each of the seven OSI layers.

> **NOTE** The concept of a layer making use of services of and providing services to its adjacent layers is simple. Consider how a company operates: The secretary provides secretarial services to the president (the next layer up) to write a memo. The secretary uses the services of a messenger (the next layer down) to deliver the message. By separating these services, the secretary (application) doesn't have to know how the message is actually carried to its recipient. That way the secretary (application) doesn't have to know everything about how to get a message to the recipient. He merely has to ask the messenger (network) to deliver it. With the addition of a standard messenger service, many secretaries can send memos in this way. ■

Table 18.1 The Functional Networking Responsibility of Each Layer of the OSI Model

Name	Layer	Description
Physical	1	This layer provides the physical connection between a computer system and the network. It specifies connector and pin assignments, voltage levels, and so on.

Name	Layer	Description
Data Link	2	This layer "packages" and "unpackages" data for transmission. It forms the information into frames. A *frame* represents the exact structure of the data physically transmitted across the wire or other medium.
Network	3	Provides routing of data through the network.
Transport	4	Provides sequencing and acknowledgment of transmission.
Session	5	Establishes and terminates communication links.
Presentation	6	Does data conversion and ensures that data is exchanged in a universal format.
Application	7	Provides an interface to the application that a user executes; a "gateway" between user applications and the network communication process.

CAUTION

Do not confuse the Application layer with application programs you execute on the computer. Remember that the Application layer is part of the OSI model that does not specify how the interface between a user and the communication pathway happens; an application program is a specific implementation of this interface. A real application typically performs Application, Session, and Presentation layer services and leaves Transport, Network, Data Link, and Physical layer services to the networking software.

Part

III

Ch

18

Because the OSI model is simply a framework, the layers do not really perform any functions. However, protocol implementations (which are composed mainly of software) perform functions that are associated with an OSI layer. According to the OSI model, layer implementations that correspond with each layer communicate with peer layers in other computers but must do so by sending messages through the lower layers operating in their own *protocol stack*.

N O T E In this context, a *protocol stack* is a hierarchical group of protocols that work together—usually on a single system. ▦

The following section describes layer interactions between different stacks.

How Network Layers Create a Networking Model

According to the OSI model, each layer of a stack communicates with its peer in other computers' stacks. For example, Layer 3 in one system communicates with Layer 3 in another computer system, as illustrated in Figure 18.2.

FIGURE 18.2

Layer 3 of the DOS stack exchanges information with Layer 3 of the UNIX stack.

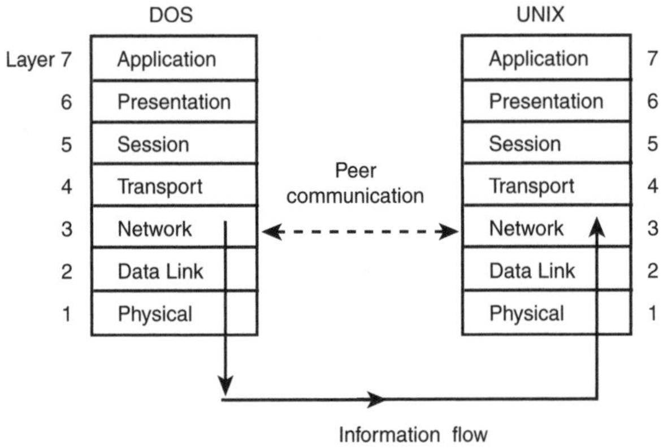

Information flow

When information is passed from one layer down to the next, a *header* is added to the data to indicate where the information is coming from and going to. The header-plus-data block of information from one layer becomes the data for the next. For example, when Layer 4 passes its data to Layer 3, it adds its own header. When Layer 3 passes its information to Layer 2, it considers the header-plus-data from Layer 4 as data and adds its own header before passing that combination down, as illustrated in Figure 18.3.

FIGURE 18.3

Each layer adds its own header before passing the information down to the next layer.

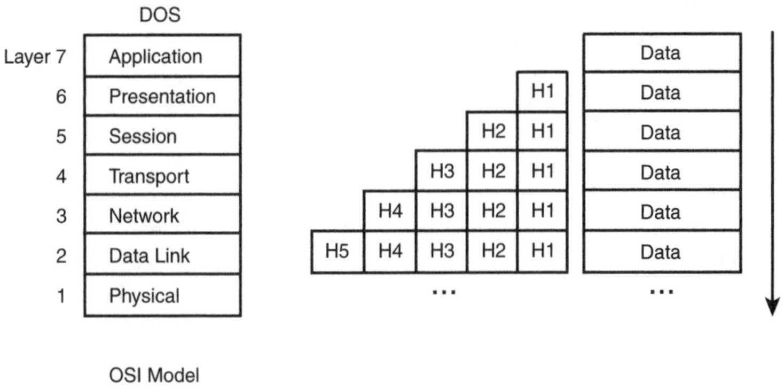

OSI Model

As shown in Table 18.2, for each layer the information units (known as *service data units* within the OSI model) are given different names. Therefore, by knowing the terms used to reference the data, you know which layer of the model is being discussed.

Table 18.2   Terms Used by OSI Layers to Refer to Information Units

OSI Layer	Information Unit Name
Application	Message
Transport	Segment

OSI Layer	Information Unit Name
Network	Datagram
Data Link	Frame (also called packet)
Physical	Bit

N O T E The term *packet* is often used as a generic name for the information units, regardless of the layer. ▧

For instance, suppose that you are using two networked applications based on DOS and UNIX. When the DOS application's Layer 7 needs to accomplish some task, it produces a request. This request (data), along with some Layer 6 parameters (the service primitives or commands), are passed to the DOS application's Layer 6. Layer 6 accepts the request as data and sends a new packet, including Layer 7's data and a header of its own, to the layer below. Eventually, the data packets make their way down to the wire and are transmitted from the DOS application's Layer 1 to the UNIX application's Layer 1.

Each of the UNIX application's layers strips off the corresponding header, performs the requested tasks, and passes what it considers a data packet to the layer above. Finally, the UNIX application's Layer 7 receives the packet from its Layer 6 and interprets the request. As you can see, headers add a lot of overhead (especially when the amount of data to be transmitted is small), but this information is necessary for each application layer to communicate with peer application layers.

It is important to realize that the OSI model is not tangible. The model itself does not cause network communications to occur. Network communications require specific protocols to become tangible processes. Protocols refer to implementation specifications for one or more OSI model layers.

N O T E You can consider the OSI model a library bookcase. You can use a bookcase to organize and categorize books from different authors relating to a variety of subjects. Similarly, computer networking professionals use the OSI model to categorize different protocols according to their functions.

Even though you may consider that a certain book belongs to a particular bookcase shelf ("layer") in your bookcase ("protocol stack"), someone else may prefer to put that book on a different shelf in his bookcase. Likewise, the computer networking industry struggles with the categorization of various protocols and technologies within the OSI model.

Despite the nonstandardization, the OSI model provides a good conceptual framework for discussing the many questions and methods inherent in networking computers. ▧

Part
III

Ch
18

Examining the DoD Model

Although there are several different names for the protocol model associated with TCP/IP, the model is usually referred to as the DoD model because the protocol originated at the U.S. Department of Defense (DoD). The OSI model did not exist when TCP/IP was created. Therefore, TCP/IP followed the four-layer DoD networking model instead of the OSI model. Although TCP/IP can be "forced" to fit the seven-layer OSI model, it is better understood in the context of the original four layers.

The DoD networking model was established in the mid-1960s, much earlier than the OSI model. The DoD model defines a four-layer networking model. Each layer of the model specifies a set of communication protocols. This set of protocols is collectively known as the *TCP/IP protocol suite* or, more correctly, the *Internet protocol suite*. Today, the Internet protocol suite consists of hundreds of protocols. The most common and important of these protocols are discussed later in this chapter.

Although the DoD model predates the OSI model by more than ten years and has only four layers instead of the seven in OSI, some meaningful comparisons can still be drawn between the two models (refer to Figure 18.1):

- The Process/Application layer in the DoD model corresponds to the top three layers of the OSI model. The Process/Application layer provides specific application interfaces between two computer systems.

- The Host-to-Host layer in the DoD model maps to the Transport layer of the OSI model. The Host-to-Host layer is responsible for establishing and maintaining connections.

- The Internet layer in the DoD model maps to the Network layer of the OSI model. The Internet layer is responsible for routing packets between different networks and systems.

- The Network Access layer in the DoD model corresponds to the bottom two layers in the OSI model. The Network Access layer specifies the physical characteristics of the physical connection between networks.

Associated with each layer is one or more protocols that outline how specific networking functions behave. Before looking at some of these protocols, a review of the history of TCP/IP is in order.

Brief History of TCP/IP

In the mid-1970s, the U.S. Department of Defense recognized an electronic communication problem developing within its organization. Communicating the ever-increasing volume of electronic information among DoD staff, research labs, universities, and contractors had hit a major obstacle. The various entities had computer systems from different computer manufacturers, running different operating systems, and using different networking topologies and protocols. How could information be shared?

The Advanced Research Projects Agency (ARPA) was assigned to resolve the problem of dealing with different networking equipment and topologies. ARPA formed an alliance with universities and computer manufacturers to develop communication standards. This alliance specified and built a four-node network that is the foundation of today's Internet. During the 1970s, this network migrated to a new core protocol design that became the basis for TCP/IP.

Some of the initial design goals from the DoD were to build a robust set of common protocols that would allow easy interoperability of different machines and easy configuration of each machine. A robust protocol maintains connectivity between hosts during adverse network conditions, such as broken cables, lost data, and corrupt data. As corporations started to heavily invest in computers and networks, the need to have many different machine architectures interoperate became more evident.

Given that the TCP/IP protocol used by the U.S. Defense Department was already an established protocol that would allow vendors to sell products capable of interoperating with each other, TCP/IP quickly was recognized for its capability to enable communication among a wide variety of different machines in the business environment. The protocol suite is now installed on almost every network-capable host in the world.

N O T E In TCP/IP parlance, a *node* or a *host* can be any intelligent computing device on the network—as long as it is capable of communication and performing local processing. ▪

Part

III

Ch

18

The mention of TCP/IP requires a brief introduction to the Internet because TCP/IP is what the Internet uses. The Internet connects hundreds of thousands of computers. Nodes include universities, many major corporations, and research labs in the United States and abroad. It is a repository for millions of shareware programs, news on any topic, public forums and information exchanges, and email.

Another feature offered by TCP/IP is the remote login capability to any computer system on the network using the TELNET protocol. Because of the number of systems that are interconnected, massive computer resources can be shared, allowing large programs to be executed on remote systems. Furthermore, with the enormous popularity of the World Wide Web (WWW) and the ease with which one may publish information to the Internet, the amount of information available over the Internet is increasing daily.

▶ **See** "Using telnet," **p. 426**

▶ **See** "Understanding Web Servers," **p. 614**

Protocols and RFCs

The TCP/IP protocol suite used in UNIX networking consists of more than 100 protocols. Unlike protocol suites developed by vendors (such as IBM) that are solely specified by the vendor in question, the specification of each protocol in the TCP/IP suite is a joint effort of users from around the world. Indeed, before a protocol within the TCP/IP suite is accepted as a "standard," it must go through a debating stage.

Each protocol is defined by one or more "Requests for Comments" (RFCs). These RFCs are public documents you can obtain from a number of sources. The RFCs describe how a protocol is to be used, as well as how to implement it. They may even list the command sets that must be supported by an application implementing the protocol to be considered compliant.

RFCs can be obtained from the Internet by using the FTP protocol to connect to several different repositories. At the time of this writing, you can retrieve TCP/IP RFCs from the following Internet sites:

```
FTP.CONCERT.NET

FTP.NISC.SRI.COM

NIC.DDN.MIL

NIS.NSF.NET

NISC.JVNC.NET

RS.INTERNIC.NET

SRC.DOC.IC.AC.UK

VENERA.ISI.EDU

WUARCHIVE.WUSTL.EDU
```

N O T E   The host named `RS.INTERNIC.NET` (IP address 198.41.0.9) is the official repository for all RFCs; previously it was `NIC.DDN.MIL` (IP address 192.67.67.20). All other sites are simply "mirror sites" that serve as backups as well as to provide you with a "local" site for better performance. For a list of all available RFCs, retrieve `rfc-index.txt`. ▓

▶ **See** "Using `ftp`," **p. 430**

Table 18.3 lists the pertinent RFCs for establishing a network. Some of these documents go into great detail (more than you ever wanted to know) about how the different protocols function and the underlying specifications and theory. Others are more general and provide key information that can be useful to a network manager. At a minimum, an Internet network manager should know where these documents are located and how to obtain them. They provide information that can help in planning and growing an organization's network.

Table 18.3	RFCs of Interest
RFC Number	**Description**
791	Internet Protocol
	DARPA Internet Program Protocol Specification
792	Internet Control Message Protocol

RFC Number	Description
793	Transmission Control Protocol
	DARPA Internet Program Protocol Specification
950	Internet Standard Subnetting Procedure
1058	Routing Information Protocol
1178	Choosing a Name for Your Computer
1180	A TCP/IP Tutorial
1208	A Glossary of Networking Terms
1219	On the Assignment of Subnet Numbers
1886	DNS Extensions to support IP version 6

Figure 18.4 shows a list of the most common protocols used in UNIX networking. Each of them is discussed in detail in the following sections, starting from the top, the Process/Application Layer.

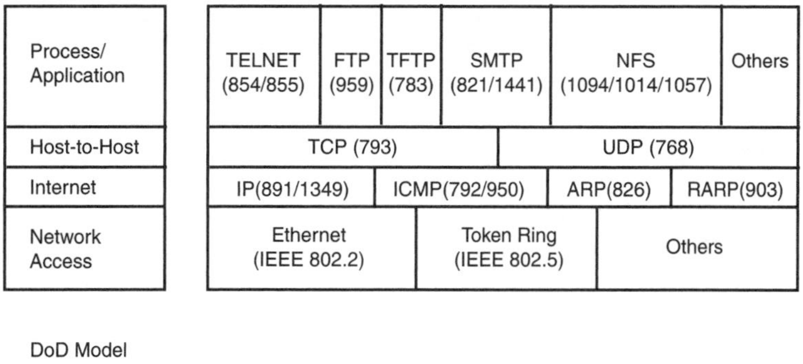

FIGURE 18.4

Common protocols used in UNIX networking, shown with the corresponding RFC or standards numbers.

DoD Model

The Process/Application Layer

At the top layer of the DoD model is the Process/Application layer. Protocols at this layer provide services such as terminal emulation (TELNET), file transfer (FTP), electronic mail (SMTP), file sharing (NFS), and network management (SNMP) to name but a few. Each protocol in this layer is made up of two components: a client program and a server program.

In UNIX terminology, the server program is often referred to as the *daemon program*, or simply the daemon. The daemon runs as a background process on the server. The executable file usually ends with the letter *d* to mark it as a daemon. For example, the daemon program for the TELNET process (discussed later) is called `telnetd`. As illustrated in Figure 18.5, when the client software makes a request to the remote host, the stack sends the packets out across the network; the daemon receives the data and sends the request to the local operating system for processing. The reply is sent back to the daemon, which then sends it back to the client in the reverse direction.

 T I P   The daemons are generally automatically started when the system boots up. If your users are unable to connect to a remote service, such as TELNET, check that the corresponding daemon (such as `telnetd`) is running. You can do that using the `ps` command.

▶ **See** "The `/etc/init.d` Directory," **p. xxx** (Chapter 11)

▶ **See** "Viewing the Process Table," **p. xxx** (Chapter 6)

FIGURE 18.5
The client/server communication path.

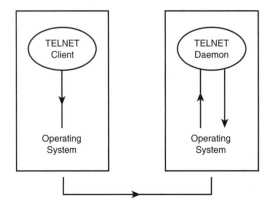

TELNET   The TELNET protocol provides the remote host with a virtual terminal connection to another host, as though there were a direct physical connection. Because UNIX implements devices as drivers, each TELNET session uses a virtual network driver known as *pseudo ttys*. Pseudo ttys are transparent to applications and users. Users appear to be sitting at a terminal directly connected to the remote host, even though the remote host may be thousands of miles away.

▶ **See** "Device Files," **p. 296**

Many client software products implement the TELNET protocol in an executable file also called `telnet`. In most cases, to invoke your terminal emulator, you simply execute this program. However, depending on the developer of the software, this may not always be the case.

 T I P   Many applications require you to use a specific terminal model to take advantage of certain keys or display attributes. Your TELNET software (not the protocol) may not support your existing terminal type. Fortunately, many UNIX applications work with the DEC VT100 terminal type, which almost all TELNET software supports.

The TELNET protocol is defined in RFCs 854 and 855.

▶ **See** "Using `telnet`," **p. 426**

FTP and TFTP   Two file transfer protocols are available: the File Transfer Protocol (FTP, defined in RFC 959) and the Trivial File Transfer Protocol (TFTP, defined in RFC 783).

File transfers using FTP require you to be an authorized user on the remote host; such transfers are subject to the security imposed by the operating system on the user. The user interface program is usually called `ftp`. Using FTP, you can perform a wide range of file and directory related operations, including the following:

- List directories and files
- Send binary or text files
- Retrieve binary or text files

Many sites on the Internet provide a service called *anonymous FTP* that allows users to access remote sites without needing a valid user ID and password. The general login ID is `anonymous`; by convention, the password is `guest` (or no password, should you choose not to use one). If the site doesn't ask you to use `guest` for a password, it is customary to use your Internet email address as the password instead. This gives that site's administrator some idea of where the users are from.

TFTP does not require a user password. You simply must know the name of the host, the location of the file, and the exact filename you want to retrieve. Without this information, you cannot obtain a file using TFTP.

> **CAUTION**
>
> Because of TFTP's lack of security, you should not make important data and programs available via TFTP.

TFTP retransmits the entire file if there is a transmission error. On the other hand, FTP provides a "smart" transfer protocol; if, during transfer, one of the frames is lost or damaged, FTP retransmits the single frame, not the whole file. Because of this extra error correction safeguard, FTP has more overhead than TFTP.

> **N O T E**   It is common for users to use FTP for regular file transfers. TFTP is used mostly by automated procedures, such as a router getting firmware update information or a smart hub getting management information.

▶ **See** "Using `ftp`," **p. 430**

SMTP   One of the most common services provided by networks is electronic mail (email). Email is usually implemented differently from protocols such as TELNET or FTP. The remote site need not be up and running to send email. Email messages are usually stored and then forwarded when the link between the systems is available. Therefore, you use a front-end program (called the *agent*) to compose and read your mail messages. A back-end program (called the *transport engine*) stores and delivers mail.

Part III Ch 18

The Simple Mail Transfer Protocol (SMTP, defined by RFCs 821 and 1441) is used to transport messages between two hosts. The message format is defined by the Standard for the Format of ARPA Internet Text Messages (defined by RFC 822). Fortunately, as the user, you do not have to worry about the specific formatting. Formatting is taken care of by the front-end program.

Each UNIX system comes with a mail front-end; the executable is usually called `mail` or `mailx`. Your site may choose to implement a different front-end (such as `pine` from University of Washington); consult your system administrator. Many different front-ends are available—some free and some commercial software.

▶ **See** "Introduction to the SMTP Protocal," **p. 650**

NFS *Network File System* (NFS) was first developed by Sun Microsystems. NFS is made up of three protocols:

- Network File System (NFS)
- eXternal Data Representation (XDR)
- Remote Procedure Call (RPC)

N O T E   Strictly speaking, NFS is a protocol suite, much like TCP/IP. It is not a single protocol like FTP, for example.

Unlike TELNET and FTP, NFS (defined by RFC 1094) is a "transparent" protocol as far as the end users are concerned. NFS is designed to share file systems between dissimilar machines, such as a PC running DOS and a UNIX host. The NFS server (the machine with the files to be shared) makes its file system appear to be part of the client machine's local computer environment. For example, a PC running TCP/IP and NFS client software may use drive D as the hard drive on a remote UNIX host. To access files from this drive, the PC user gives the standard DOS COPY command. All files appear as local to the user.

N O T E   As part of NFS security, the host system's permission security is enforced through the use of user and group IDs. If the user does not have write permission to a given directory, he or she does not have write permission to that directory with NFS.

To provide transparency between dissimilar systems, the *eXternal Data Representation* protocol (XDR, defined by RFC 1014) allows for the description and encoding of data in a machine-independent format. Continuing with the preceding example, when the PC requests a file from drive D (which is linked to the remote UNIX host), the UNIX system first converts the file contents from UNIX into XDR format before transmitting the file to the PC. After receiving this file, the PC converts it to PC format.

How does the client (the PC in the example) know that it needs to ask the UNIX host for the file? This is where *Remote Procedure Call* (RPC, defined in RFC 1057) comes in. Part of RPC is a "redirector" piece that decides whether the request can be serviced locally or must be processed by the remote host.

RPC is not unique to NFS. There are other RPC implementations but they are not related to NFS. For example, RPCs are used by Remote Registry service of Windows 98 and Windows NT and in printing to remote UNIX printers, but these RPCs are not related to NFS. However, the Remote Procedure Calls defined by RFC 1057 are specific to NFS.

With NFS, users can access files residing on remote host machines transparently, without having to learn any new commands, as they do when using FTP or TELNET.

N O T E   To promote NFS, Sun Microsystems put the NFS, XDR, and RPC specifications into the public domain in the late 1980s. As a result, NFS server and client software is available for a wide range of platforms, ranging from PCs to DEC minis to IBM mainframes. ▪

Two common terms used in NFS are these:

- ▪ Exports   A file system available for sharing to client machines. For example, if you want to make your /usr file system available to remote NFS clients, export /usr.

- ▪ Mountpoints   These identify where on the local file system the remote file system will start. For example, by specifying a mountpoint of /usr/home, the remote file system shows up as subdirectories under /usr/home on your system.

CAUTION

If you have any directories under your mountpoint (/usr/home in the preceding example), you will lose access to them. However, the subdirectories are not deleted, simply hidden. You have access to them again when you dismount the remote file system.

▶ **See** "The NFS Environment," **p. 568**

SNMP   To obtain information from and issue instructions to other devices and systems, the *Simple Network Management Protocol* (SNMP, defined by RFC 1157 and RFCs 1901 through 1910) is used. Just like the other upper-layer protocols discussed in the preceding sections, SNMP uses a client piece (called a *management console*) and a server portion (called an *agent*).

The agent can reside on any TCP/IP device, such as a host, router, or wiring hub. The information you can obtain from the agent's database is known as the *Management Information Base* (MIB). It is up to the management console to query the agent for information. The agent does not automatically report data to the console unless that data is an error condition. Error conditions in SNMP are called *traps*.

Currently, there are two standard management data-related MIBs in use: MIB I (defined by RFC 1356) and MIB II (defined by RFC 1450). MIB I contains about 114 objects (variables), such as device uptime and number of interfaces installed in the device. MIB II contains all MIB I objects plus some extensions for a total of about 172 objects. Originally, the MIBs were designed to manage IP routers. However, MIBs now sometimes contain extensions to include

Part

III

Ch

18

other devices such as smart wiring hubs. Figure 18.6 shows a sample screen of an SNMP manager console (TCPCON.NLM included with all versions of NetWare) looking at an MIB I agent.

FIGURE 18.6

A sample SNMP management console displaying some MIB I information.

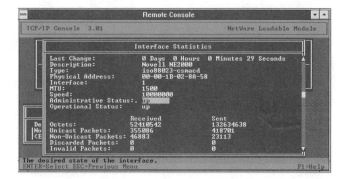

A third standard MIB, called RMON (*Remote MONitoring*, RFC 1757) was ratified by the Internet community. RMON is not an extension to MIB II like MIB II was an extension to MIB I. RMON is designed to provide monitoring information such as average cable utilization, number of frames on the wire, and so on.

N O T E   At the time of this writing, RMON-2 (RFC 2021) is being developed. ▦

Two additional categories of MIBs are experimental MIB and private (or enterprise) MIB. *Experimental MIBs* contain important information about aspects of the network not contained by one of the standard MIBs. When an experimental MIB has been approved by the Internet community, it is then recognized as one of the standard MIBs.

Enterprise MIBs or private MIBs are specific to individual companies for collecting information from their own network devices. For example, Bay Networks sells a private MIB for its manageable hubs. Private MIBs usually provide specific data not available through standard MIBs.

N O T E   A new version of SNMP, called simply SNMP v3 (RFC 2271), is currently under ratification by the Internet standards body. SNMP v3 provides enhanced security, such as secure SET support, among other features. ▦

Associated with each SNMP message or query is a *community* name or password. A community name in SNMP is an ASCII string of up to 32 characters. There are three communities in SNMP:

- ▪ Monitor community   Management console messages containing this name can only read the MIB data.

- ▪ Control community   Management console messages containing this name can read and modify the MIB data.

■ Trap community   Trap messages containing this name are accepted by the management console also set to the same name.

For example, if you want to browse the MIB variable of a TCP/IP device, you must set your monitor community name to that used by the TCP/IP device. If the names do not match, you can't read the MIB.

> **CAUTION**
>
> Community names can contain any characters except for Space, Tab, open square bracket ([), equal sign (=), colon (:), semicolon (;), or the pound sign (#). Like UNIX commands, community names are case sensitive.

In general, community names provide a simple and unsecured method of accessing MIB information. SNMP II will address the security shortcoming.

The Host-to-Host Layer

The Host-to-Host layer is responsible for establishing and maintaining connections. Two protocols are defined in this layer: the *Transmission Control Protocol* (TCP) and the *User Datagram Protocol* (UDP). These protocols are designed to ensure the safe transmission of data between two hosts. A look at how these protocols work provides some insight about why two protocols are defined.

TCP   In network communications, there are basically two types of communication delivery mechanisms between two machines:

■ Connection-oriented, guaranteed delivery

■ Connectionless, non-guaranteed delivery

Connection-oriented delivery means that a logical connection is first established between the two systems before any data is transmitted. At the same time, each transmission is acknowledged to ensure data integrity. *Connectionless* delivery means a "best attempt" delivery. No logical link must first be established, and no acknowledgment of delivery is needed. Connectionless delivery is a faster transmission method because there is less overhead. Because of the lack of checking, the higher-layer protocol must verify that the data is transmitted and received correctly.

> **N O T E**   Consider the difference between making a telephone call and making a radio call. To make a telephone call, you must first dial the desired telephone number and wait for the connection to complete before you can communicate with the other party; usually after you say something at one end, the other party acknowledges by saying "okay." This is connection-oriented, guaranteed delivery.
>
> When you make a radio call (say, using a CB), you simply pick up the microphone and transmit. No prior connection to your calling party is made. And you don't know whether the other party received your call unless they send a reply message back. This is an example of a connectionless, non-guaranteed delivery. ■

The Transmission Control Protocol (TCP, defined by RFC 793) is designed to be a connection-oriented, guaranteed delivery protocol. The following items are included as part of TCP header information:

- Source and destination "ports" to identify which upper-layer protocol the data comes from and goes to. (In the OSI model, these ports are referred to as service access points.)
- Sequence number to ensure that the packets arrive in the correct order.
- Acknowledgment number to acknowledge the total number of packets received.

Each upper-layer protocol is preassigned a unique ("well-known") port number so that TCP knows which protocol stack to hand off the data to. For example, TELNET is assigned a port number of 23 (decimal). Table 18.4 lists some well-known ports.

Table 18.4   Sample Well-Known TCP and UDP Ports

Service Name	Port	Transport type
echo	7	tcp, udp
discard	9	tcp, udp
systat	11	tcp
daytime	13	tcp, udp
netstat	15	tcp
ftp-data	20	tcp
ftp	21	tcp
telnet	23	tcp
smtp	25	tcp
time	37	tcp, udp
name	42	udp
whois	43	tcp
domain	53	tcp, udp
tftp	69	udp
rje	77	tcp
finger	79	tcp
link	87	tcp
supdup	95	tcp
iso-tsap	102	tcp
x400	103	tcp

Service Name	Port	Transport type
x400-snd	104	tcp
csnet-ns	105	tcp
pop-2	109	tcp
hostnames	101	tcp
sunrpc	111	tcp, udp
uucp-path	117	tcp
nntp	119	tcp
ntp	123	tcp
snmp	161	udp
snmp-trap	162	udp
talk	517	udp

N O T E You can find a list of well-known ports used or supported by your UNIX system in the /etc/services file. ▦

N O T E For a complete list of assigned port numbers, refer to RFC 1340. ▦

Part

III

Ch

18

The upper-layer protocol (as specified by the RFCs) decides whether it wants to use the services provided by TCP. For example, TELNET, FTP, and SMTP all use TCP's services. In some cases, such as the ECHO protocol, you can use either TCP or UDP.

N O T E Together, TCP and IP (IP is discussed later in this chapter) are by far the best-known, most-often used protocols in the Internet protocol suite. It is, therefore, common to use the term TCP/IP to refer to the whole protocol suite. ▦

UDP The *User Datagram Protocol* (UDP, defined by RFC 768) is a connectionless, non-guaranteed delivery protocol. It simply accepts and transports the information passed down from the upper-layer protocol. No error checking, correction, or acknowledgment is done by UDP; these tasks are left totally to the upper-layer protocol.

Because there is no established connection in UDP, each packet of information must carry with it its own address information. These types of packets are referred to as *datagrams*. When compared to TCP, UDP's header information is simple. UDP only has four fields (TCP has more than ten fields):

- Source port
- Destination port

- Length
- Checksum

Because it is much faster to use UDP than TCP, many upper-layer protocols use UDP as the transport method of choice. For example, TFTP and NFS use UDP. Because UDP does no error correction, TFTP needs to retransmit the whole file if an error is encountered—TFTP cannot recover by retransmitting the bad frame (because it has no idea which frame was bad). On the other hand, FTP can determine which was the bad frame because FTP uses TCP (with error checking) instead of UDP.

N O T E   NFS traditionally uses UDP, but NFS version 3 (RFC 1813) supports both TCP and UDP.

Segmentation   If a user message or file to be transmitted is larger than a network packet, the communication system must "fragment" a single message into multiple segments before transmitting and then reassemble it after receiving the segments before delivery to the end user. UDP imposes a maximum size of 64KB on the amount of data that can be sent in a single transmission request from the upper-layer protocols. This is because the length field in the UDP header is a 16-bit integer.

On the other hand, although TCP also uses a 16-bit integer for its length field in its header, TCP does not impose a size limit on a transmission. It breaks down the data from the upper-layer protocols into multiple 64KB block "fragments" before handing them to the Internet layer protocol for transmission.

The Internet Layer

The Internet layer of the DoD model is responsible for providing transport, routing packets between different networks and systems, fragmentation and reassembly of datagrams, and device addressing.

A number of protocols function at the Internet layer. Among them are the Internet Protocol (IP), the Internet Control Message Protocol (ICMP), the Address Resolution Protocol (ARP), and the Reverse Address Resolution Protocol (RARP). The function of each of these protocols is discussed in the following sections.

IP   The *Internet Protocol* (IP, defined by RFC 791 and 1349) provides datagram services between TCP/IP hosts. It maps onto the OSI model as part of the Network layer. The Network layer of the OSI model is responsible for moving information around the network.

IP provides the same functionality as the Network layer and helps to get the messages between systems—but it does not guarantee the delivery of these messages. IP may also fragment the messages into chunks and then reassemble them at the destination. For example, in an Ethernet environment when TCP (or UDP) passes down a segment that is 5,000 bytes in size, IP has to break it down into multiple 1,500-byte packets (maximum data size of an Ethernet frame) so that the Ethernet driver can send the information on to the network.

Each of the fragments may take a different network path between systems. If the fragments arrive out of order, IP reassembles the packets into the correct sequence at the destination.

IP provides a connectionless, non-guaranteed delivery of datagrams across the network. This means that data is sent without establishing a prior logical connection, and no acknowledgment is required. Connectionless delivery gives a faster data flow but is not reliable. However, if TCP is used as the Host-to-Host layer protocol, error correction is taken care of. If UDP is used as the Host-to-Host layer protocol, the upper-layer protocols must handle error detection and recovery. There is no need for IP to duplicate the effort.

Because one of IP's functions is to find a route for the datagram to get it to the other host, IP headers contain information such as the source and destination IP addresses. *IP addresses* are software addresses assigned by the network administrator. In the case of the Internet, IP addresses are assigned and regulated by the *Network Information Center*, or simply the *InterNIC*.

N O T E If you are connecting your network to the Internet today, chances are you will be connecting through an Internet service provider (ISP). In this case, your ISP assigns IP addresses instead of you getting them from InterNIC.

N O T E Part of the IP address identifies the IP network (a *software* address). The IP address is divided into two portions: the *network* part and the *host* part. Think of the network part as the street name and the host part as the number on the house.

ICMP The *Internet Control Message Protocol* (ICMP, defined by RFC 792 and 950) is used mainly by routers and hosts to send error messages or control information to other routers or hosts.

For example, if a router finds that, instead of using its own connection to another network, there is a better path (router) for a host to communicate with another host, the router sends an ICMP message to the host to inform the host of the alternative route. Another common use of ICMP messages is for a host to test whether another host is reachable—the equivalent of the `ping` command, which is how a client tests whether a host is reachable.

▶ **See** "Using `ping`," **p. 441**

ARP Each network interface card (NIC, not to be confused with InterNIC, the Internet Network Information Center) has a unique hardware address. If an NIC is to recognize that a frame is addressed to it, the frame must contain the NIC's *hardware address* in its header. So far, all the way from the topmost protocol layer down, only software (IP) addresses have been used. The hardware address information is obtained with the aid of the *Address Resolution Protocol* (ARP, defined by RFC 826).

Each host has an ARP table that contains the IP (software) address to NIC (hardware) address mapping. If the information is not in its table, the host broadcasts an ARP request that asks, for example, "Who is 162.1.4.56?". The host with that particular IP address replies, "Here I am! My NIC address is 08-00-20-11-22-33."

N O T E ARP requests go out as broadcast messages; all TCP/IP devices on the *local* network hear them. Only the device with the appropriate IP address responds to the request. This broadcast/relay process is transparent to the user. ▦

RARP Each TCP/IP host must be assigned a unique IP (software) address. If you have many TCP/IP devices, it is difficult to manage. When you need to change an IP address, you must change that IP address on each individual machine. *Reverse Address Resolution Protocol* (RARP, defined by RFC 903) allows you to manage these IP addresses centrally.

N O T E There are two other protocols you can use to centrally assign IP addresses: *Boot Protocol* (BOOTP) and *Dynamic Host Configuration Protocol* (DHCP). Today, most sites that do central IP address management use DHCP because it is much more flexible than RARP and BOOTP. ▦

ARP looks for a hardware address based on a given IP address. RARP works in the other direction: Given a hardware address, RARP looks for the IP address. You must manually maintain the table of IP-NIC hardware addresses on a system assigned as RARP server.

CAUTION

The drawback of using an RARP server is the need to keep the database that maps IP and hardware addresses up-to-date with any changes in hardware.

IP Addresses One function of IP is moving information around the network. This is accomplished by examining the Internet layer address, and this address determines the systems and the path to send the message. In TCP/IP, this address is called the *IP address*. It is a 32-bit number organized as a series of four octets (8-bit integers), separated by a period. This format is known as the *dotted decimal notation*.

These octets each define a unique address, with part of the address representing a network (and optionally a subnetwork), the *netid*, and part representing a particular node, the *hostid*, on the network.

N O T E Possible IP addresses range from 0.0.0.0 to 255.255.255.255 inclusive. ▦

Several addresses have special meanings on the Internet:

- ▦ An address starting with a zero references the local node within its current network. For example 0.0.0.23 references workstation 23 on the current network. Address 0.0.0.0 references the current workstation.

- ▦ The loopback network address, 127, is important in troubleshooting and network diagnosis. The network address 127.0.0.0 is the local loopback address inside a workstation.

■ The "ALL" address (or broadcast address) is represented by turning on all bits, giving a value of 255. Therefore, 192.18.255.255 sends a message to all nodes on network 192.18; similarly, 255.255.255.255 sends a message to every node on the internet. These addresses are important in use for multicast messages and service announcements.

N O T E Don't confuse internet with the Internet. The lowercase internet is used to describe networks that are interconnected within an organization. The capital Internet refers to the Information Highway. ■

CAUTION

When assigning node numbers to your workstations, don't use 0, 127, or 255.

IP Address Classes

The IP addresses are assigned in ranges referred to as *classes*, depending on the application and the size of an organization. There are five IP network address classes, and the three most common classes are A, B, and C. These three classes represent the number of the most significant bits used to determine the netid and the hostid.

The following summarizes the characteristics of the five IP address classes:

■ **Class A networks**   On a Class A network, the first octet (whose first bit must be 0) identifies the network, and the remaining three octets identify the node. There are 127 possible Class A networks (from 1.0.0.0 to 127.0.0.0), each having up to 16,77,216 nodes. However, network number 127 is reserved, as mentioned earlier and shouldn't be used, leaving a total of 126 assignable Class A network addresses.

■ **Class B networks**   On a Class B network, the first two octets identify the network, and the remaining octets identify the node. The value of the first octet (with the first two bits being 10) is in the range of 128 to 191. There are 16,384 possible Class B networks (ranging from 128.0.0.0 to 191.255.0.0), and each Class B network can have up to 65,534 nodes.

■ **Class C networks**   On a Class C network, the first three octets identify the network, and the remaining octet identifies the node. The value of the first octet (with the first three bits being 110) is in the range of 192 to 223. There are 2,097,152 possible Class C networks (ranging from 192.0.0.0 to 223.255.255.0), and each Class C network can have up to 254 nodes.

■ **Class D addresses**   Class D network addresses (first four bits in the first octet being 1110) are in the range of 224.0.0.0 to 239.255.255.255. These addresses are used for *multicast packets*. Multicast packets are used by many protocols to reach a specific group of devices (such as routers).

■ **Class E addresses**   Class E network addresses (first five bits in the first octet being 11110) are reserved for future use.

> **CAUTION**
>
> Class D and E addresses are not to be assigned to individual hosts on your network.

Class A addresses are used for very large networks or collections of related networks. Many educational institutions are grouped under a single Class A address; companies (such as Xerox) that were part of the founding Internet were each given a Class A address as well. Class A addresses were practically all assigned right from the start.

Class B addresses are used for large networks having more than 254 nodes (but less than 65,534 nodes). Class C addresses are used by most organizations. If you are applying for IP network addresses from InterNIC, you'll be given several Class C addresses because all Class B addresses have been assigned.

N O T E   A joke is that if you want to have a Class B address, you need to purchase a company that has one assigned! ■

N O T E   There aren't sufficient official IP network addresses available for all the organizations that are implementing IP intranets (internal networks that use TCP/IP). A new IP address scheme, called IPng (IP Next Generation), has been proposed to address the shortage. However, with the availability of Network Address Translation (NAT) gateway, the need for IPng is not as urgent as it once was. ■

▶ **See** "Internet Protocol Next Generation (Version 6)," **p. 557**

▶ **See** "Network Address Translator (NAT)," **p. 545**

The following are examples of different class IP addresses:

- 10.12.33.1 is a Class A address. The network number is 10.0.0.0 (netid of 10), and the nodeid is 12.33.1.
- 172.16.67.23 is a Class B address. The network number is 172.16.0.0 (netid of 172.16), and the nodeid is 67.23.
- 192.168.2.77 is a Class C address. The network number is 192.168.2.0 (netid of 192.168.2), and the nodeid is 77.

Subnetworks

Subnetting is the process of dividing a large logical network into smaller physical networks. Reasons for dividing a network may include electrical limitations of the networking technology, a desire to segment for simplicity by putting a separate network on each floor of a building (or in each department or for each application), or a need for remote locations connected with a high-speed line.

The resulting networks are smaller chunks of the whole and are easier to manage. Smaller subnets communicate among one another through gateways and routers. Also, within an organization there may be several subnetworks that are physically on the same network. This may be done to logically divide the network functions into workgroups.

The individual subnets are a division of the whole. Suppose that a Class B network needs to be divided into 64 separate subnets. To accomplish this, the IP network address is viewed in two parts, network and subnetwork, as shown in Figure 18.7. The default assigned number of bits for a Class B network is 16 (the first two octets), and to allow for 64 possible subnets an additional 6 bits ($2^6=64$) are "borrowed" from the host portion, for a total of 22 bits to distinguish the subnetwork. This division results in 64 networks with 1024 nodes in each. The network part can be larger or smaller, depending on the number of networks or the number of nodes per network desired.

FIGURE 18.7

Class B subnetwork masking example.

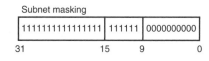

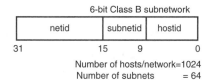

Subnet Masks

Setting a subnet mask is a matter of determining where the network address ends and the host address begins. The subnet mask contains all 1s in the network field and 0s in the host field.

Suppose that a Class C network is composed of the following:

```
N = network
H = Host
NNNNNNNN.NNNNNNNN.NNNNNNNN.HHHHHHHH
```

Each position represents a single bit out of the 32-bit address space. If this Class C network is to be divided into four Class C networks, the pattern would resemble the following:

```
NNNNNNNN.NNNNNNNN.NNNNNNNN.NNHHHHHH
```

The subnet mask would then look like this:

```
11111111.11111111.11111111.11000000
```

Part
III

Ch
18

If this address is written in base-ten dot notation, the subnet mask is 255.255.255.192. This mask is used to communicate among nodes on all subnetworks within this particular network.

If three bits are taken from the host field, eight networks can be formed, and the resulting network mask would be as follows:

```
11111111.11111111.11111111.11100000
```

The subnet mask is 255.255.255.224. Each of the eight networks would have 29 nodes because five address bits are available. (It would be 32 except that all 1s, all 0s, and 127 are not legal addresses.)

This concept can be extended to Class B and Class A networks. The only difference is that the remaining fields are 0 (zero).

Consider a Class B network. The address space is divided as follows:

```
NNNNNNNN.NNNNNNNN.HHHHHHHH.HHHHHHHH
```

If two bits are taken from the host field and added to the network part, the following subnet mask is used:

```
11111111.11111111.11000000.00000000
```

The mask is written as 255.255.192.0.

The bits needed for the subnet mask can be taken from any of the bit positions within the host field—but this leads to complex subnet masks and address exclusions. This should be avoided if at all possible.

Routing   Routing is a method of transferring information between networks. There are several different means by which a router determines how data may be routed—for example, *Routing Information Protocol* (RIP), *Open Shortest Path First* (OSPF), and *Interior Gateway Routing Protocol* (IGRP), to name a few. These protocols are not discussed here because IP routing is the subject of an entire chapter in this book.

▶ **See** "An Overview of Routing Protocols," **p. 513**

The Network Access Layer

The last layer in the DoD model is the Network Access layer. It corresponds to the bottom two layers in the OSI model. The Network Access layer specifies the physical characteristics of the physical connection between networks.

The lowest protocol layer in the TCP/IP suite provides the physical connection for the network. The specifications used in this layer include those of the *Institute of Electrical and Electronics Engineers'* (IEEE) 802 standards and other industry standards:

- IEEE 802.3 for Ethernet: 10BASE-5 (thick coax), 10BASE-2 (thin coax), 10BASE-T (twisted pair), and 100BASE-T (twisted pair).
- IEEE 802.5 for Token Ring: 4 or 16 Mbps over shielded and unshielded twisted pair.

- Fiber Distributed Data Interface (FDDI): 100 Mbps over fiber optics.
- Datapoint ARCnet: 2.5 Mbps over coax cable or twisted pair.

These physical-layer specifications define both the physical wires used for transmission and the electrical impulses sent across the wire. The standards used in the Network Access layer are common across all networking implementations, regardless of whether the network is for UNIX or another networking operating system.

N O T E   The choice of physical layer protocol (that is, hardware) has an impact on the size of the largest payload allowed in the frame (MTU–*maximum transfer unit*). MTU governs whether IP needs to fragment its datagram before transmission. For example, 16 Mbps Token Ring allows for an MTU of 4KB, whereas Ethernet's MTU is only 1500 bytes. ▪

Part of the Network Access layer's header information is the hardware address of the device sending the information (the source address) and the hardware address of the device the information is intended for (the destination address). These hardware addresses are used by certain internetworking devices, such as a bridge. Internetworking devices are discussed in a following section.

N O T E   As an analogy, consider the network as a city block and the hardware address as the street number on a given street.

Often, hardware addresses are referred to as MAC (*Media Access Control*) addresses. ▪

When you must communicate with another TCP/IP device, you will use its IP address (its street name and the house number); ARP looks up the corresponding hardware address (street number) if it is not already in the host's ARP table. With this information, the two devices can communicate with each other.

If your UNIX system is connected to a network, it is most likely one of two types: broadcast or token passing. The topology (the wiring scheme) would be bus, ring, or star. The most commonly used networking hardware today are the following:

- Ethernet
- Token Ring
- FDDI

Ethernet   *Ethernet* is a broadcast system using the bus technology. It allows multiple machines to use and share the same media at a transfer rate of 10 Mbps. The Ethernet hosts may be attached to the same physical coax cable, or each of the machines may be connected into a concentrator (normally referred to as a hub) using UTP (*unshielded twisted pair*) cable. An intelligent central hub may be used to increase reliability. If any individual cable or host becomes deficient, the smart hub disables the port, and all other hosts go unaffected.

Each machine connected to the media has a unique Ethernet MAC address. These addresses are used to send data to and from each card on the media. The Ethernet unit of data, known as a *frame*, has the source and destination addresses in the header of the Ethernet frame.

An Ethernet address is a 48-bit number and is unique to a given Ethernet card in the world, and is preset in the factory. The uniqueness is guaranteed; a vendor owns a prefix, and the vendor serial stamps each new device with a unique identifier in the last half of the address. Typically, MAC addresses are expressed as six two-digit hexadecimal numbers. The following is a MAC address of a Novell NE2000 Ethernet card:

`00-00-1B-02-8A-58`

Here, 00-00-1B is Novell's assigned vendor code, and 02-8A-58 is the "serial number." The vendor prefix assignments were originally performed by Xerox but have been delegated to the IEEE. Table 18.5 lists some typical vendor codes, which are documented in RFC 1700 (Assigned Numbers).

Table 18.5   Examples of Ethernet Vendor Codes

Vender Code	Vendor
00-00-1B	Novell
00-00-4C	NEC Corporation
00-00-E8	Accton Technology Corp.
00-00-F4	Allied Telesis, Inc.
00-AA-00	Intel
00-C0-F0	Kingston Technology Corp.
08-00-09	Hewlett-Packard
10-00-5A	IBM
80-00-2B	DEC

Ethernet is a bus-style network that uses CSMA/CD (*Carrier Sense, Multiple Access, with Collision Detection*) as the protocol for communicating with the physical layer. An Ethernet card that wants to send data first listens (carrier sense) to see whether any other Ethernet cards are transmitting. If the carrier sense finds that no other cards are transmitting, your Ethernet card transmits its data (frame).

The possibility exists for another Ethernet card to transmit at nearly the same time as your Ethernet card. A collision occurs if two Ethernet cards transmit at the same time. When this happens, each card detects the collision through its collision detection circuitry, backs off on the transmission, waits a random amount of time, and then retransmits the frame.

N O T E   The probability of collision goes up as the number of nodes on the same segment increases. This is why people segment Ethernet networks to reduce collisions, thus increasing performance.

Ethernet is the *most* common network in use today. UNIX networking was first implemented on Ethernet networks.

Fast Ethernet   *Fast Ethernet* is capable of 100 Mbps over a half-duplex connection (where one host is sending data while the other is receiving) or 200 Mbps over a full-duplex connection (where a host can send and receive at the same time). Fast Ethernet functions the same as 10 Mbps Ethernet; however, it only runs over UTP cables.

Most 100 Mbps Ethernet cards purchased today generally support both normal and Fast Ethernet.

Token Ring   Token Ring was originally developed by IBM and is commonly used on IBM machines. As the name implies, Token Ring hosts are connected in a logical ring fashion (physically, the network looks like a star), and it uses a token-passing media access method in which a host can transmit data only when it is in possession of a "token" (a special data frame). Because only one token is on a given ring, only one host can transmit at a time, thus eliminating the possibility of collisions as one has on Ethernet networks.

Like 10BASE-T or 100BASE-T Ethernets, Token Ring hosts are connected using hubs. You can use "dumb" hubs, known as multistation access units (MSAUs), or smart hubs where some management functions are built-in. Token Ring is available in two speeds: 4 Mbps and 16 Mbps.

CAUTION

You must not mix Token Ring cards of different speeds on the same ring as that will cause the ring to fail—no device on the ring will be able to transmit or receive any data.

FDDI   *Fiber Distributed Data Interface* (FDDI) offers 100 Mbps datalink technology, similar in performance to Fast Ethernet. Because it uses light as the transmission medium, each FDDI ring is essentially two rings: one for transmitting and one for receiving. Because FDDI uses fiber media, it offers several key benefits:

- Reliability   Optics are immune to electrical interference.
- Low noise   Does not produce any EMI (Electro-magnetic Interference).
- Security   Fiber is almost impossible to tap without you noticing.
- Lightweight   Copper cable, even UTP, is heavy when compared with fiber optics.

The major drawback of FDDI is the cost. Although you can get plastic fiber optics as opposed to glass ones, the associated equipment, such as FDDI cards and hubs, are much more expensive when compared to those used in Ethernet and Token Ring.

Unlike Token Ring, which transmits and receives on the same ring, FDDI is a true full-duplex optical ring capable of 100 Mbps in both directions because the transmit and receive "rings" are separate. FDDI supports both synchronous and asynchronous traffic that can be assigned priorities for reserving bandwidth.

Part
III

Ch
18

Different Types of Internetworking Hardware

Over time, your network will grow and expand. You may need to exchange data with other networks (such as the Internet) or segment your network to reduce the amount of traffic and improve performance. Internetworking devices such as *bridges, routers,* and *gateways* are often used. However, the terms are often used incorrectly or out of context; the following sections clarify these terms with respect to the OSI model and discuss when they should be employed.

What Is a Repeater?

Working at the Physical layer of the OSI model is the *repeater* device. When electrical signals travel across a medium, they attenuate (or fade) as a function of distance traveled. A repeater simply reconditions the signal (bits) and retransmits it. It doesn't care about any addressing information. Repeaters are transparent to protocols.

> **NOTE**   Repeaters cannot be used to connect segments of different topologies, such as Ethernet to Token Ring. However, repeaters can be used to connect segments of the same topology with different media, such as Ethernet UTP to coax Ethernet. ■

Repeaters extend the distance limit of your network segment—and nothing more. Sometimes, repeaters are used as signal splitters (for example, Ethernet multiport repeaters). Because repeaters do not do any filtering, they do not slow down your network.

What Is a Bridge?

A *bridge* operates at the Data Link layer of the OSI model. As Data Link layer devices, bridges have access to hardware (MAC) address information. Using this information, a bridge can filter network traffic based on source and destination hardware addresses.

A bridge keeps track of the hardware addresses for each network segment it is connected to. Suppose that you have two network segments connected via a bridge. Hosts Pluto and Donald are on Segment A, and host Mickey is on Segment B. When the bridge sees a frame from Pluto going to Donald, it knows (from its internal table) that both hosts are on the same segment (both are listed under Interface A), and the bridge ignores the frame. However, if Pluto sends a frame to Mickey, the bridge knows that Mickey is on the other segment (Interface B); therefore the bridge makes a copy of the frame and transmits it to segment B.

TIP   A bridge forwards frames destined for a different segment. Therefore, bridges are often used to cut down, or segment, traffic on a heavy network.

Like repeaters, bridges are transparent to protocols. Bridges can also be used to extend the distance of a segment because bridges also perform the function of a repeater. This type of bridge is usually known as a *transparent bridge* (also known as a *spanning tree* or *learning bridge*). *Source routing bridges*, another type of bridge, are found primarily in IBM Token Ring environments. In TCP/IP-based networks, transparent bridges are most dominant.

Bridges can connect segments of similar topology, such as Ethernet to Ethernet. They also can connect segments of different media, such as coax cable to fiber. Some manufacturers produce *translational bridges* that connect Ethernet with Token Ring (the IBM 8209 bridge, for example).

 TIP If you must connect segments of different topologies, use a router (see the section titled "What is a Router?")

In most cases, users are not aware of the presence of a bridge. However, if users must cross a bridge to get to their destination, they may notice a slight slowdown because the bridge needs to look up the addresses for each frame forwarded. A typical bridge can forward frames at a rate of 10,000 frames/second.

What Is a Switch?

A *switch* operates at the Data Link layer of the OSI model, just like the bridge. However, it is more like a multiport bridge where only one or a few devices are connected to each port. It is generally used to have fast server data in environments where large amounts of data are constantly being transferred between devices.

Suppose that you have two users who do a lot of multimedia work on a UNIX host where megabytes of data are transferred every few seconds. You can connect the UNIX host and each of the two users into a port on a switch (as illustrated in Figure 18.8). That way, it appears to these two users that each has a dedicated link to the server because no one else is on that "segment" to compete for the bandwidth.

Part
III

Ch
18

FIGURE 18.8

A sample switched network configuration.

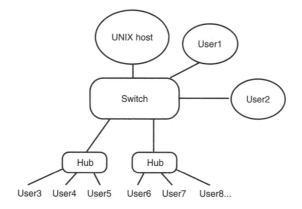

What Is a Router?

A *router* operates at the Network layer of the OSI model. That means it has access to the network (software) address information. Each interface on the router must be assigned a network address. Therefore, routers are *protocol dependent*. Typically, if a router encounters a protocol it doesn't support, it drops the frame.

Suppose that you have TCP/IP, IPX, and AppleTalk on your network, but your router supports only TCP/IP. This means that none of your IPX or AppleTalk devices can communicate with other IPX or AppleTalk devices located on the other side of the router. This arrangement may be useful in isolating traffic by protocol (as compared to using a bridge to isolate traffic by hardware address).

N O T E   Unlike a bridge that sees every frame on the segment, a router only sees the frame if the frame is addressed to the router. Therefore, part of your TCP/IP configuration is to specify the nearest router's IP address if there is a router on the network. ▪

A router is much more intelligent than a bridge in that it can determine the *best* path for a frame to reach its destination. The path may change depending on a number of variables, such as segment utilization (if a link becomes congested, the router picks a different path) and availability of the link (if the more direct path is unavailable because of a downed line, the router reroutes using the next-best path).

Because a router has to do more work than a bridge, the throughput for a router is lower than that for a bridge. A typical router can process about 8,000 frames/second.

Because a router deals with network (software) addresses, it has no idea whether a frame came from Ethernet or Token Ring. Therefore, it is a perfect device for connecting different topologies.

What Is a Brouter?

The preceding section mentioned that routers are protocol dependent. Frames with unknown (unsupported) protocols are dropped. Sometimes, this is not a desirable situation.

In such cases, you may be able to configure your router to route certain protocols and bridge the remaining unsupported protocols. Because a router operates at the Network layer of the OSI model, it has access to the Data Link layer services (where a bridge operates). This type of router is known as a *brouter* (bridging/router).

N O T E   Not all routers can also function as a bridge. Most hardware-based routers are brouters; software-based routers usually don't have the capability to act as a bridge. ▪

What Is a Gateway?

A *gateway* is a device that translates between protocols of different network architectures, such as TCP/IP and SNA. Like routers, gateways are protocol specific. In addition, gateways tend to support only certain upper-layer protocols, such as terminal emulation. For example, if you want to exchange both terminal emulation and electronic mail between two hosts that use different protocols, you may need two separate gateways.

Because a gateway must translate most, if not all, protocol layers, it operates over the entire seven layers of the OSI model. And because of the overhead, it is a much slower device than a router, for example. The forwarding rate varies greatly depending on the protocols being translated.

From Here...

Networks have become an important part of many information systems. The need to share information such as databases and resources such as printers has made networks an integral part of many businesses. This chapter provided you with an in-depth look at the common terms used in computer networking and offered a technical discussion of the most common networking protocols encountered in UNIX. Finally, you learned about the various devices used today in internetworking networks.

- To learn about setting up TCP/IP on your UNIX system, see Chapter 19, "Configuring TCP/IP."

- To find out about IP routing protocols, see Chapter 20, "IP Routing."

- For an overview of advanced networking components and some future technologies, see Chapter 21, "Advanced Networking."

- To learn how to set up and configure network file systems to provide file sharing throughout a network, see Chapter 22, "NFS."

- For information about Internet host naming and domain name configuration, see Chapter 23, "DNS."

Part
III

Ch
18

## CHAPTER 19

Configuring TCP/IP

by Peter Kuo and Jeff Robinson

In this chapter

Overview of TCP/IP Installation

To connect your UNIX system to the network, you'll need either a network card or a modem and a PPP provider. (The provider can be your ISP or anyone who will allow you to connect to his system via a PPP connection.) After this is done, you'll have to reconfigure your UNIX kernel to take advantage of the networking hardware.

▶ **See** "Setting up PPP," **p. 542**

Most BSD-based implementations of UNIX already include TCP/IP networking support as part of the base operating system. Usually, when you first boot a new UNIX installation, a program runs asking whether the machine is to be connected to a network. If you answer yes, the program prompts you for information it needs to configure all the networking features. At times, however, your machine might not initially be installed on a network, or you might need to change the configuration. This chapter describes the configuration files and programs that involve networking your UNIX system.

> **N O T E** Because different UNIX implementations have different ways of installing TCP/IP and other
> software, only general concepts are covered here. However, because the configuration files
> used are universal for all UNIX systems, they are covered in detail.
>
> To simplify discussion, most material presented in this chapter is based on BSD UNIX and Ethernet
> networks. Differences for System V are noted when appropriate. ■

Preinstallation Information

Before you install TCP/IP on your UNIX system, you need to gather some software and hardware information. As you know, every machine on a TCP/IP network must have its own unique IP address. Similarly, although not necessary, each machine should have its own name. This name is used in the hosts file to assist users to access your machine more easily.

▶ **See** "Hostnames and IP Addresses," **p. 423**

You need to obtain a name, valid IP address, subnet mask, and broadcast address information for your machine either from your network administrator, ISP, or a central IP network authority of your organization.

If you are installing the hardware yourself, you must determine what equipment you already have in place and what settings they are using. Depending on your version of UNIX and the hardware platform, you can get the hardware information in several ways. For example:

- On SCO servers (SVR4), the hardware information is displayed during system boot. You can also use the `hwconfig` utility to determine what your system already has in it. The default `hwconfig` display looks similar to this:

```
name=fpu vec=13 dma=- type=80387
name=serial base=0x3F8 offset=0x7 vec=4 dma=- unit=0 type=Standard nports=1
name=floppy base=0x3F2 offset=0x5 vec=6 dma=2 unit=0 type=135ds18
name=console vec=- dma=- unit=vga type=0 12 screens=68k
name=adapter base=0x2000 offset=0xCDC vec=11 dma=- type=eiad ha=0 id=7
```

```
➥fts=std
name=eisarom vec=- dma=- eisa (1.3.0)
name=sme base=0x300 offset=0x1F vec=10 dma=- type=8216 addr=00 00 c0 a2 d5
➥6e
name=tape vec=- dma=- type=S ha=0 id=2 lun=0 bus=0 ht=eiad
name=disk vec=- dma=- type=S ha=0 id=0 lun=0 bus=0 ht=eiad
name=Sdsk vec=- dma=- cyls=496 hds=64 secs=32 fts=sdb
```

This screen tells you what hardware you have, the associated vector (or interrupt), the I/O base address, DMA, and some other hardware specific information.

TIP On some systems, you can also use /etc/conf/bin/idcheck or /etc/conf/cf.d/ vectorsinuse to determine what equipment your system currently holds.

- On AIX and many BSD systems, you can use the lsdev command to get a list of installed devices:

```
# lsdev -C -F "class subclass type description" ¦ sort
adapter          mca          ppr        POWER Gt3i Graphics Adapter
adapter          mca          sio_1      Standard I/O Planar
adapter          sio          fda        Standard I/O Diskette Adapter
adapter          sio          hscsi      Standard SCSI I/O Controller
adapter          sio          ient_1     Standard Ethernet Adapter
adapter          sio          keyboard   Keyboard Adapter
adapter          sio          mouse      Mouse Adapter
adapter          sio          ppa        Standard I/O Parallel Port Adapt
adapter          sio          s1a_1      Standard I/O Serial Port 1
adapter          sio          s2a_1      Standard I/O Serial Port 2
adapter          sio          tablet     Tablet Adapter
bus              sys          mca        Microchannel Bus
disk             scsi         1000mb     1.0 GB SCSI Disk Drive
diskette         siofd        fd         Diskette Drive
fpa              sys          fpa1       Floating Point Processor
hft              node         hft        High Function Terminal Subsystem
if               EN           en         Standard Ethernet Network Inter
if               EN           ie3        IEEE 802.3 Ethernet Network Inter
if               LO           lo         Loopback Network Interface
ioplanar         sys          ioplanar_1 I/O Planar
keyboard         sio.kb       kb101      United States keyboard
logical_volume   lvsubclass   lvtype     Logical volume
logical_volume   vgsubclass   vgtype     Volume group
lvm              lvm          lvdd       N/A
memory           sys          memory     64 MB Memory Card
mouse            sio.ms       mse_3b     3 button mouse
planar           sys          sysplanar1 CPU Planar
pty              pty          pty        Asynchronous Pseudo-Terminal
sys              node         aio        Asynchronous I/O
sys              node         sys        System Object
sysunit          sys          sysunit    System Unit
tape             scsi         8mm5gb     5.0 GB 8mm Tape Drive
tcpip            TCPIP        inet       Internet Network Extension
```

Part
III

Ch
19

■ On some BSD systems, you can also look in one of the subdirectories under /usr/sys or
/sys/i386 for the configuration file used to build the current kernel. This file lists the
devices and their settings known to the kernel. The following are two (partial) sample
listings of such a configuration file. The first is from a PC-based BSD system:

```
machine                 "i386"
cpu             "I586_CPU"
ident           abcd
maxusers        64
options                 "MAXMEM=131072"
options                 "NMBCLUSTERS=4096"

options                 "CHILD_MAX=400"
options                 "OPEN_MAX=800"
#options                MATH_EMULATE            #Support for x87 emulation
options                 INET                    #InterNETworking
options                 FFS                     #Berkeley Fast Filesystem
options                 NFS                     #Network Filesystem
#options                MSDOSFS                 #MSDOS Filesystem
#options                "CD9660"                #ISO 9660 Filesystem
options                 PROCFS                  #Process filesystem
options                 "COMPAT_43"             #Compatible with BSD 4.3
options                 "SCSI_DELAY=15"         #Be pessimistic about Joe
➥SCSI device
options                 BOUNCE_BUFFERS          #include support for DMA
➥bounce buffers
options                 UCONSOLE                #Allow users to grab the
➥console
options                 KTRACE
  [...]
controller      isa0
controller      pci0

controller      fdc0    at isa? port "IO_FD1" bio irq 6 drq 2 vector fdintr
disk            fd0     at fdc0 drive 0

controller      wdc0    at isa? port "IO_WD1" bio irq 14 vector wdintr
disk            wd0     at wdc0 drive 0

controller      wdc1    at isa? port "IO_WD2" bio irq 15 vector wdintr
disk            wd2     at wdc1 drive 0

device                  wt0     at isa? port 0x300 bio irq 5 drq 1 vector
➥wtintr
device                  mcd0    at isa? port 0x300 bio irq 10 vector mcdintr
device                  mcd1    at isa? port 0x340 bio irq 11 vector mcdintr
device pca0 at isa? port IO_TIMER1 tty

pseudo-device   loop
pseudo-device   ether
pseudo-device   log
pseudo-device   sl      1
pseudo-device   tun     1
pseudo-device   pty     256
```

```
pseudo-device   gzip                  # Exec gzipped a.out's
pseudo-device   snp     3
pseudo-device   bpfilter        4         #Berkeley packet filter
```

The second example is from a MIPS machine:

```
ident           "DONALD"
machine         mips
cpu             "DS5000"
maxusers        160
processors      1
maxuprc         50
physmem         128
timezone        5 dst 1
maxdsiz         64
smmax           1024

options         QUOTA
options         INET
options         NFS
options         RPC
options         DLI
options         UFS
options         NETMAN
options         LAT
options         CDFS
options         PACKETFILTER
options         AUDIT
options         SYS_TPATH
options         DECNET

makeoptions     ENDIAN="-EL"

config          vmunix  root on rz1a  swap on rz1b and rz0b and rz2b
➥dumps on rz1b

adapter         ibus0       at nexus?
adapter         ibus1       at nexus?
adapter         ibus2       at nexus?
adapter         ibus5       at nexus?
adapter         ibus6       at nexus?
adapter         ibus7       at nexus?
controller      asc0        at ibus?        vector ascintr
disk            rz0         at asc0         drive 0
disk            rz1         at asc0         drive 1
tape            tz0         at asc0         drive 0
device          ln0         at ibus?        vector lnintr
device          dc0         at ibus?        vector dcintr

scs_sysid       1

pseudo-device   nfs
pseudo-device   rpc
  [...]
pseudo-device   decnet
pseudo-device   tc
```

Part
III

Ch

19

With the hardware configuration information in hand, you can then cross reference the hardware options that your new Ethernet supports and determine what addressing to select.

After you have all the information available, you can proceed to the next step: installing the Ethernet card.

Installing the Hardware

Unless your machine comes preinstalled with an Ethernet card, you need to install one. Depending on the hardware and warranty coverage, you might be able to install the card yourself, or you might need to call in your hardware vendor's field service engineer to install it for you.

> **CAUTION**
>
> Before you purchase a network card for your UNIX system, make sure that the vendor has a UNIX driver for it. For PC-based UNIX systems, such as SCO, sticking with known-brand Ethernet cards is a safe choice—for example, Intel, 3COM, and Novell/Microdyne.

 When installing Ethernet cards, it is important that you set the card to use the correct media type—thin coax, thick coax, or twisted pair. Depending on the card, this may be selected via either hardware jumper settings or software configuration utility.

 On some systems, such as IBM RS/6000, you'll need to restart the machine with a cold boot (that is, turn the power off and then on) for a change in Ethernet port selection (say, from thin coax to thick coax) to take effect; a warm boot isn't sufficient.

If on rebooting your system the kernel recognizes your card, then you're ready to continue on to configure TCP/IP. Otherwise, you'll need to build a new kernel to add support for your particular network card.

Making a New Kernel

The UNIX kernel needs to know about every installed device and how to use it. Fortunately, many types of hardware, such as hard drives and tape drives, conform to a standard already supported by the kernel, but sometimes this is not the case. If you were to add a new device to a DOS PC, all you would need to do is run the supplied program or include the new device driver in the system's CONFIG.SYS file. Not so with UNIX systems. If you want to add a new device to a UNIX machine not already supported by the kernel, you have to create a new kernel.

N O T E It may sound complicated that you need to create a "new kernel," but it is not as bad as it sounds. As a matter of fact, you routinely need to create a new kernel when adding a new device, and the documentation supplied with the new device generally includes all the steps necessary to install it. ▓

▶ **See** "Device Files," **p. 296**

The steps for creating a new kernel depend on whether your version of UNIX is based on BSD or System V. Typically, BSD versions already include TCP/IP networking, and most System V versions (such as SCO) install the TCP/IP software as part of the initial bootup installation program.

The exact steps for new kernel creation vary between UNIX versions and implementations, but they all involve updating some configuration files and compiling some C programs. BSD versions of UNIX include a program called /etc/config that makes the changes to configuration files for you. Some vendors include a menu-driven program to ease the task. For example, SCO has the *system administrator shell* (SAS, sysadmsh), AIX comes with SMIT, and HP/UX has SAM. Consult your system manual for the exact procedures necessary to modify your UNIX kernel.

N O T E The hardware information you collect during the preinstallation phase is used when you update the kernel with the new hardware information. The IP address and the other software information is used in the next step. ▨

N O T E You'll need to reboot the machine for the new kernel to take effect. ▨

Configuring the Network Card

Even though the necessary device drivers needed for networking are loaded when the new UNIX kernel is booted, the network interface still needs to be configured. The ifconfig (interface configuration) utility provides this function. You should be logged in as root before using the ifconfig command to make changes to the interface settings.

N O T E Generally, ifconfig is found in the /etc directory, but on some systems it is in the /sbin directory. ▨

N O T E For some versions of UNIX, such as SCO, the network card configuration step is performed at the time when you re-create a new kernel. However, you can still use ifconfig to make changes later. ▨

With ifconfig, you can turn the interface on or off, assign an IP address to the interface, or define the subnet mask and broadcast address. The common usage for ifconfig is:

```
ifconfig interface-name ip-address netmask mask broadcast address
```

where *interface-name* is the name of the device driver defined in the kernel. If you have multiple NICs in the machine, each card must be separately configured using ifconfig. To apply a setting to all NICs in the machine, you can replace the *interface-name* with the -a flag instead.

N O T E   On some SVR4 systems, such as SCO, the `ifconfig` command syntax is of the form:

`ifconfig` *interface-name* `netmask` *mask ip-address* ▪

For instance, to configure the `ln0` Ethernet interface, the command is as follows:

`# ifconfig ln0 192.168.12.200 netmask 255.255.255.0 broadcasts 192.75.168.255`

This assigns the Class C IP address of 192.168.12.200 to the interface, with the default netmask, and a broadcast address of 192.168.12.255. To see what the current setting of an interface is, the command is as follows:

```
# ifconfig ln0
ln0: 192.75.12.200 netmask ffffff00
flags=0x463<DYNPROTO,RUNNING,NOTRAILERS,BROADCAST,UP> broadcast: 192.75.12.255
#
```

N O T E   Some implementations of `ifconfig` also return the MAC address of the interface queried. ▪

The interface is automatically set to up (enabled) when you give it a new IP address. Should the need arise, you can use the `ifconfig` utility to enable or disable the interface:

```
ifconfig interface-name up
ifconfig interface-name down
```

If your network is subnetworked using routers, you'll also need to use the `route` command to get the routing setup.

▶ **See** "UNIX Routing Protocol Daemons," **p. 530**

Testing Your TCP/IP Connection

At this point, your TCP/IP network should be up and running. You can verify that its working by `ping`ing other hosts on your network or have other hosts `ping` it.

▶ **See** "Using ping," **p. 441**

If every other line of your `ping` message states that the network is unreachable, chances are that your netmask was set incorrectly.

If you're unable to `ping` other hosts, try `ping`ing yourself at 127.0.0.1, the loopback address. If you can `ping` the loopback but not the network, then chances are good that your NIC is either defective or misconfigured. Make sure that the IRQ and I/O address settings of the hardware match the software settings you provided to the kernel.

If `ping` gives you one line that looks normal and then your screen stops, and you know the remote host that you're `ping`ing is online, there is a good chance that your NIC isn't configured correctly. A common error is an IRQ or I/O address conflict, or the hardware setting doesn't match the software setting you provided to the kernel.

If your settings are accurate, verify that you are physically connected to the network using the proper port on your Ethernet card. For example, if you are connected through the AUI port (thick cable Ethernet), make sure that the kernel is configured to address the AUI port. If the kernel is set to use the wrong port, you'll need to make the change, rebuild the kernel, and reboot the system.

 TIP You might need to cold boot the machine for a change in Ethernet port selection (say, from thin coax to thick coax) to take effect.

After you have verified your TCP/IP connectivity, you can start enjoying all the different services it offers. However, to make life easier, there are some configuration files that you should create and update.

TCP/IP Network Configuration

Several configuration files provide TCP/IP-related networking information. Three have already been discussed, /etc/hosts, /etc/hosts.equiv, and /etc/services. Others include /etc/networks, /etc/netmasks, and so on. These files are discussed in the following sections.

NOTE On some non-BSD UNIX systems, such as Solaris, the TCP/IP configuration files are located in the /etc/inet directory. For compatibility with BSD-based operating systems, many of the TCP/IP-related files in /etc/inet are symbolically linked to /etc. ▇

▶ **See** "Hostnames and IP Addresses," **p. 423**

▶ **See** "The r-Utilities," **p. 436**

The *hosts* File

The /etc/hosts file has been discussed previously in some detail. Therefore, only the highlights and additional information that pertain to the operating of TCP/IP networks are reviewed and discussed here. The hosts file contains a list of host to IP address mappings. Applications look up hostnames to obtain the IP address to connect to a host. As you know, it is easier to remember a hostname such as sco1 than the IP address 10.1.123.45.

The /etc/hosts file is also used during the boot process to set the IP address of your machine. On some UNIX systems, altering your IP address in the /etc/hosts file and then rebooting permanently changes your IP address. Therefore, the first thing you should do is make sure that there are at least two entries in your hosts file: one for the loopback address and one for the host itself. A hosts file is simply an ASCII text file that contains a list of hostnames and their corresponding IP numbers. The following is a sample hosts file:

```
# This is a sample hosts file from sco1.dreamlan.com.
# Updated by Peter, Aug 12, 1998 @ 12:30pm
10.1.123.45     sco1
```

```
10.1.123.46      sco2    peter    testbox #sco-database-server
10.2.11.45       linux1
10.2.11.46       vms      database
10.3.83.14       router
127.0.0.1        localhost         loghost loopback
```

The syntax used by the hosts file is straightforward. As with all UNIX script files, any text after the hash symbol (#) is treated as comment and is ignored. The IP address and its corresponding hostname are listed one set per line: starting with the IP address (which is four sets of numbers, separated by a period), followed by a tab or one or more spaces, followed by the hostname. For example, in the preceding sample hosts file:

```
10.1.123.45      SCO1
```

10.1.123.45 is the IP address and SCO1 is the hostname. You can list more than one hostname per IP address. The first one listed is known as the official hostname, and the rest are referred to as aliases. For example:

```
10.1.123.46      sco2    peter    testbox #sco-database-server
10.2.11.46       vms      database
```

both have multiple hostnames per IP address listed. You can use either vms or database to access the host whose IP address is 10.2.11.46. Similarly, you can use SCO2, peter, or testbox to access the host whose IP address is 10.1.123.46. However, you *cannot* use sco-database-server to access the IP address 10.1.123.46 because this name is placed behind the # symbol, which causes the name to be treated as a comment.

Because the hosts file is located in the /etc directory where normal users generally have no write-access, it is the system administrator's responsibility to keep this file accurate and up-to-date.

The localhost entry in the file should *never* be altered or deleted. The localhost interface using IP address 127.0.0.1 is a "loopback" network interface that is configured on your machine. This loopback interface allows client/server applications running on your host to communicate with each other.

There should always be an entry for a host called loghost; it can be an alias, but the name needs to be defined. This entry is required by your system's syslogd daemon. The syslogd daemon logs messages from applications and the operating system. syslogd sends all the messages to the host declared as loghost. Given the previous sample hosts file, this host records the messages in the file /var/adm/messages.

CAUTION

After you have the /etc/hosts file up-to-date, you can create your /etc/hosts.equiv file if needed. However, because of the potential security risk posed by using the /etc/hosts.equiv file, you should consider not using this feature or at least consider using the .rhosts file instead.

▶ **See** "The /etc/hosts.equiv File," **p. 437**

▶ **See** "The $HOME/.rhosts File," **p. 438**

The *netmasks* File

The /etc/netmasks file defines the subnetwork mask(s) that will be configured on your hosts' network interfaces. The file has only two columns. The first column specifies the network number. The second column defines the netmask to be set on each network interface attached to the specified network.

▶ **See** "Subnetworks," **p. 470**

The network number in the first column must always be defined by using the network number as a Class A, B, or C; do not use the adjusted network number that is a result of subnetting. Sample entries located in the /etc/netmasks follow:

```
# The /etc/netmaks file on the host sco1
#
# Class A address split into Class C networks
10.0.0.0          255.255.255.0
# Class B address split into network of 1022 hosts networks
172.16.0.0        255.255.240.0
# Class C network split into 30 host networks
199.71.122.0      255.255.255.224
```

In the preceding example, any network interface in the network 199.71.122.0 is given a subnet mask of 255.255.255.224.

N O T E Not all versions of UNIX uses the /etc/netmasks file. When the file is not used, netmasks are specified via the ifconfig utility. ▓

The *networks* File

For simplicity, the /etc/hosts file allows hostnames to be used instead of IP addresses. The same idea can be extended to networks. Each of your IP (sub)networks can be given a name defined in the file /etc/networks. Utilities such as netstat (discussed later in this chapter) display the network name instead of the network number, if an entry exists in the /etc/networks file. A sample /etc/networks file follows:

```
#
#       Network numbers
#
loopback        127             # fictitious internal loopback network
novellnet       130.57 # Novell's network number

#
# Internet networks
#
arpanet         10      arpa    # historical network
milnet          26              # not so historical military net
```

Notice that the file format is just about the reverse of the hosts file: The network name comes first, followed by the network number, and then followed by any aliases.

Part
III

Ch

19

The *services* File

Because of the client/server relationship used by UNIX network services (a client and a dae-mon), the client software informs the server which service it wants to access by including a port number within the packet requesting the service. Such a port is referred to as a "well-known port" because it is predefined to be associated with a particular service. Your server host must have a list of the well-known ports for services that you want to connect to. The /etc/services file contains a list of service names, port numbers, and the transport layer protocol to be used to connect to the server.

> **N O T E** It is assumed that the client and the host use the same port number for a given service. In some cases, for security reasons, a UNIX administrator may move a service, such as TELNET, from the well-known port of 23 to something else. If you're going to telnet to this host, you must know which port the TELNET service is now on or you'll not be able to connect. ▣

The /etc/services file contains many lines because many service ports exist for you to connect to. Following is a truncated version of a /etc/services file. This file includes the process name along with the port and protocol associated with it:

```
#
#        Network service mappings.  Maps service names to transport
#        protocol and transport protocol ports.
#
echo        7/udp
echo        7/tcp
discard     9/udp      sink null
discard     9/tcp      sink null
systat      11/tcp
daytime     13/udp
daytime     13/tcp
netstat     15/tcp
ftp-data    20/tcp
ftp         21/tcp
telnet      23/tcp
smtp        25/tcp     mail
time        37/tcp     timserver
time        37/udp     timserver
name        42/udp     nameserver
whois       43/tcp     nicname      # usually to sri-nic
domain      53/udp
domain      53/tcp
hostnames   101/tcp    hostname     # usually to sri-nic
sunrpc      111/udp
sunrpc      111/tcp
# File truncated.
```

You might notice that some process names have several entries. This is because in some cases, different protocols can be used to request the same service.

If new services are required on the machine, an entry in the /etc/services file needs to be created. Many network-oriented software products that you install automatically create an entry in the file.

> **N O T E** Sometimes ports are also referred to as sockets even though sockets typically include the
> IP address in addition to the port number. ▨

The *resolve.conf* File

When you are using DNS for name resolution instead of the /etc/hosts file, you'll need to set up a DNS lookup file called resolve.conf. This file is located in the /etc directory, along with the other TCP/IP-related configuration files. The setup is simple and takes only a few lines:

```
domain dreamlan.com
nameserver   10.75.12.110
nameserver   10.75.12.200
nameserver   10.75.12.103
```

The first line identifies the domain your host is in, or the "default domain." In the preceding example, the default is dreamlan.com. Any hostnames that are not fully qualified will have dreamlan.com appended to the end. For example, if a user executes the command:

```
telnet vms
```

DNS tries to resolve vms.dreamlan.com for a result. You can list multiple nameservers for redundancy or in case one nameserver doesn't have the name but another one does. They are queried in the order listed.

> **N O T E** The resolve.conf file lists only three nameserver addresses. However, some implemen-
> tations support up to nine entries. ▨

If you are connecting to the Internet via an ISP, the nameserver addresses will most likely be given to you by your ISP, unless you maintain your own DNS nameservers in-house.

▶ **See** "Configuring DNS Servers," **p. 606**

Part
III

Ch
19

RPC Services

As previously mentioned, many services in the UNIX network environment have well-known ports. Because it is possible to run out of well-known ports, Sun Microsystems created RPCs as part of its NFS work. RPC is an acronym for *Remote Procedure Call*. The server-side daemon does not listen on a well-known port, but instead listens on an arbitrary port. The client does not know the port number to connect to, unless it first asks the server what port the specific service is offered on.

When the server-side daemon starts, it registers itself with a process named rpcbind or portmap (or portmapper, on some systems) and picks an arbitrary port number it listens on. The rpcbind or portmap process remembers the now-available services and their arbitrary port number registrations. When a client wants one of these services, well-known port 111 is used by the client to send RPC queries to rpcbind or portmap to obtain the corresponding port number for the service.

For instance, your host tries to make a connection to the server for service "abc." Your host first sends a query to port 111 on the server. The query asks what port the particular service ("abc") is offered on. The server replies with a port number if the service is registered through either the rpcbind or the portmap process. After the port number is known by your host, a regular network connection to the new port is established to access the service.

When your host makes a query to the server for a port number, it does so using an RPC number. These RPC numbers are listed in the /etc/rpc file. Many applications add their RPC numbers to this file during installation. Rarely does the system administrator need to manually add entries to this file, unless the file is accidentally altered, overwritten, or corrupted. Following is a sample /etc/rpc file:

```
% cat /etc/rpc
portmapper      100000  portmap sunrpc
rstatd          100001  rstat rup perfmeter
rusersd         100002  rusers
nfs             100003  nfsprog
ypserv          100004  ypprog
mountd          100005  mount showmount
ypbind          100007
walld           100008  rwall shutdown
yppasswdd       100009  yppasswd
etherstatd      100010  etherstat
rquotad         100011  rquotaprog quota rquota
sprayd          100012  spray
3270_mapper     100013
rje_mapper      100014
selection_svc   100015  selnsvc
database_svc    100016
rexd            100017  rex
alis            100018
sched           100019
llockmgr        100020
nlockmgr        100021
x25.inr         100022
statmon         100023
status          100024
bootparam       100026
ypupdated       100028  ypupdate
keyserv         100029  keyserver
sunlink_mapper  100033
tfsd            100037
nsed            100038
nsemntd         100039
showfhd         100043  showfh
ypxfrd          100069  ypxfr
pcnfsd          150001
prestoctl_svc   390100  presto
%
```

For example, if you want to access the ypbind service on the remote host, your host sends a request with RPC number 100007 as part of the request data to port 111 on the remote host.

The */etc/inetd.conf* File

A UNIX system may offer many services that are only used occasionally. Recall that a daemon process must be listening on the well-known port for that service. This could lead to many daemon processes listening but not actually receiving a connection for a long time. These idle daemons would take up a lot of system resources.

Instead, a "super daemon" named `inetd` is used. It is capable of listening on many well-known ports at the same time yet takes up few system resources. When a connection is being made to a port that `inetd` is listening on, `inetd` starts the appropriate daemon to manage the service on that port.

The file `/etc/inetd.conf` is the configuration file for `inetd`. This file essentially tells `inetd` what ports to monitor and what daemons to start for each port should a connection be desired. Each new service that is not to run as a standalone daemon needs to be entered in the `inetd.conf` file.

Depending on the implementation, the `/etc/inetd.conf` file has either six or seven fields as follows:

```
service-name    socket-type    proto    wait-status    [user]    server-pathname
args
```

These fields are explained in Table 19.1. A sample `/etc/inetd.conf` file follows:

```
% cat /etc/inetd.conf
# Internet server configuration database
#
#echo      stream  tcp  nowait  /etc/miscd              echod
#echo      dgram   udp  wait    /etc/miscd              echod
#discard   stream  tcp  nowait  /etc/miscd              sinkd
#discard   dgram   udp  wait    /etc/miscd              sinkd
systat     stream  tcp  nowait  /etc/miscd              systatd
daytime    stream  tcp  nowait  /etc/miscd              daytimed
quote      stream  tcp  nowait  /etc/miscd              quoted
finger     stream  tcp  nowait  /etc/tcpd               usr/local/etc/phfingerd
telnet     stream  tcp  nowait  /etc/tcpd               telnetd
time       dgram   udp  wait    /etc/miscd              timed
tftp       dgram   udp  wait    /usr/etc/tftpd          tftpd -r /tftpboot
exec       stream  tcp  nowait  /etc/rexecd             rexecd
login      stream  tcp  nowait  /etc/tcpd               rlogind
shell      stream  tcp  nowait  /etc/tcpd               rshd
comsat     dgram   udp  wait    /etc/comsat             comsat
talk       dgram   udp  wait    /etc/tcpd               talkd
ntalk      dgram   udp  wait    /etc/tcpd               ntalkd
bootp      dgram   udp  wait    /usr/etc/bootpd         bootpd -i -d
ident      stream  tcp  nowait  /usr/local/etc/in.identd  in.identd

# CSO Nameserver.  CPU limit based on cpu speed & database size.
# 30 sec good for 1 MIP cpu/80,000 entry db.
# 5 sec good for 5 MIP cpu/1,000 entry db.
# If no qi owner (qiserv) run as root.
# was
# csnet-ns  stream   tcp  nowait  /usr/local/qi/qi  qi -d -t30
```

Part

III

Ch

19

```
# and for 2.1
# ns          stream   tcp   nowait   /cwis/cso/bin/qi   qi -d -t45

# Mail transfer
pop            stream   tcp   nowait   /etc/tcpd                    /usr/local/etc/ipop2d
pop3           stream   tcp   nowait   /etc/tcpd                    /usr/local/etc/ipop3d
imap           stream   tcp   nowait   /usr/local/etc/imapd         imapd
# netlogger    stream   tcp   nowait   /usr/local/bin/netlogger     netlogger

# Sendmail
smtp           stream   tcp      nowait   /etc/tcpd            /usr/lib/sendmail -bs

# wuarchive ftpd
ftp            stream   tcp      nowait   /usr/local/etc/ftpd      ftpd -aL
%
```

Table 19.1   Fields in the /etc/inetd.conf File

Field	Description
service-name	The name of the service listed in /etc/services.
socket-type	The type of socket the service uses. Valid entries include stream, dgram (datagram), raw, and rdm (reliably delivered message).
proto	The transport layer protocol used for communication.
wait-status	nowait allows multiple inbound connections. wait only allows a single connection at a time.
user	The name of user (usually root) who owns the server process when it runs. The effective permissions of the server are those assigned to that user. This field is not used on some systems.
server-pathname	The name of the daemon (including path) that is started when a connection is established on the service port mentioned in service-name.
args	Any command-line arguments needed to process the request correctly. As a minimum, the command name is entered in this field.

Unless you add a new service or disable a currently active one (putting a '#' at the beginning of the entry in the services file), you shouldn't need to edit inetd.conf. If you do, you need to restart inetd to activate your changes.

Different Types of Network Interfaces

Many different UNIX platforms have many different types and models of network interfaces that may be attached. Configuring these network interfaces (either using ifconfig or one of the menu-driven utilities) requires you to know the name of the interface. Following is a list of some of the network interface names on common flavors of UNIX:

SUN

le	Lance Ethernet Card
qe	Quad Port Ethernet Card
hem	1 Hundred Megabit Ethernet Card
qfe	Quad Port Ethernet Card
tr	Token Ring Card
elx	3COM Etherlink III Ethernet card
nei	NE2000 Ethernet Card

HP

lan	Local Area Ethernet Interface

IRIX

ec	Ethernet Card

AIX

en	Ethernet Card

Digital UNIX

ln	Ethernet Card
tu	Ethernet Card

Each of the interface names is followed by a number, which represents the interface number in the machine. For instance, the first interface on a SUN machine is named le0, the second is named le1, the third le2, and so on. This is the same naming convention used by other devices, such as tape drives and terminals.

Part
III

Ch

19

Working with Network Interfaces

Monitoring, viewing parameters, and configuring network interfaces is accomplished using the ifconfig utility. The ifconfig utility only provides sessional configuration changes. That is, if the machine is rebooted, the settings are cleared, and the settings from the /etc/hosts and /etc/netmasks files are used. Permanent alteration requires editing the hosts and netmasks files. The following sections discuss the use of ifconfig utility.

Viewing Your Interfaces

The ifconfig command uses the -a option for viewing all the interfaces present on your machine. The ifconfig command accepts a single interface name instead of the -a option to display the parameter for only one interface. Following is the output from the `ifconfig -a` command executed on a Solaris system:

```
lo0: flags=849<UP,LOOPBACK,RUNNING,MULTICAST> mtu 8232
        inet 127.0.0.1 netmask ff000000
le0: flags=863<UP,BROADCAST,NOTRAILERS,RUNNING,MULTICAST> mtu 1500
        inet 199.71.122.50 netmask ffffffe0 broadcast 199.71.122.63
        ether 8:0:20:72:fe:4f
```

You can see that the machine has an `lo0` interface, which is the machine's "loopback" interface. You can also see that the host has an `le0` interface. This is an Ethernet card that has been installed on the host.

The flags between the angle braces <> on the `le0` interface are UP, BROADCAST, NOTRAILERS, RUNNING, and MULTICAST. Each of these flags has a special meaning that is listed in Table 19.2.

Table 19.2   Meaning of Interface Flags as Reported by *ifconfig*

Flag	Description
UP	The interface is online.
BROADCAST	This interface is sending and receiving broadcasts.
NOTRAILERS	Disable the use of a "trailer" link level encapsulation.
RUNNING	The network card driver and streams module are running.
MULTICAST	The interface supports multicast subscription.

The `inet` directive is followed by the IP address of the interface. The netmask and broadcast directives are followed by the netmask and broadcast address, respectively, as configured on the interface. You will notice the netmask is expressed in hexadecimal even though you may have entered it using the dotted decimal notation. The `mtu` is the *maximum transmission unit* of the interface in bytes. For many types of network cards, the `mtu` has an upper limit, for example, 1500 for Ethernet. The last piece of information shown after the `ether` directive is the Ethernet address for the interface, also in hexadecimal.

Changing Your Network Interface Parameters

Permanent changes to the interfaces should be made in the `/etc/hosts` and `/etc/netmasks` files. However, you may have to change some of the interface parameters without rebooting your host. Remember that although the `ifconfig` command allows you to change any and all of the interface parameters, the changes are only sessional and are forgotten after the machine is rebooted. Table 19.3 shows the available options to change interface parameters with `ifconfig`. The syntax for the command is `ifconfig interface_name specifications`.

Table 19.3 *ifconfig* **Options**

Options	Description
up/down	Bring the interface online or offline.
mtu	Specify the maximum transfer unit, in bytes, for the network interface.
metric	Specify the metric or cost value for routing.
inet	Specify the IP address for the interface.
netmask	Specify the netmask for the interface. The netmask may be entered using either the dotted decimal notation or in dotted hex notation starting with 0x.
broadcast	Specify the broadcast address for the interface. Most often the + symbol may be used to have the broadcast address calculated from the IP address and the netmask.

The `ifconfig` command accepts a single or multiple specifications on a single command line. Here are several examples of using the `ifconfig` command:

■ Bring the interface named `le0` offline and then back online:

```
ifconfig le0 down
ifconfig le0 up
```

■ Set the IP address of the `le0` network interface to `199.71.122.50`, and set a netmask of `255.255.255.0`:

```
ifconfig le0 inet 199.71.122.50 netmask 255.255.255.0
```

■ Calculate the broadcast address for the `le0` network interface from the assigned netmask and IP address:

```
ifconfig le0 broadcast +
```

N O T E Any changes made with `ifconfig` take effect immediately. ■

CAUTION

If you are connected over the network to the host on which you are performing remote configuration administration, you may lose your connection as soon as you reconfigure the interface.

The *netstat* Command

After you know that your TCP/IP configuration is working, you need to know how well it is communicating. The `netstat` utility can be used to gather information and statistics about your

Part

III

Ch

19

network interfaces, established network connections, routing table information, and protocol usage information. The amount of information displayed depends on what command-line options are included. Table 19.4 lists the available options for the netstat program.

Table 19.4 *Netstat* Options

Option	Definition
-a	Display the state of all sockets.
-r	Display the kernel routing table.
-i	Display interface statistics.
-p	Display the ARP table.
-s	Display protocol information.
-n	Display numbers instead of hostnames and service names.

A closer look at the outputs from the -a, -r, and -i options is presented in the following sections.

Interpreting the Output of *netstat -a*

The netstat -a command shows the state of all network connections. The output is broken into two main sections, one for UDP connections and one for TCP connections.

The UDP connections are shown in the following example. Only two fields exist in the output, the Local Address and the State. The Local Address is the IP address or hostname of the machine that is connected followed by the port number or service name that is in use. If the Local Address is a * this means that a daemon is listening on the port, but no connection has been established. The State of the connection is either idle or unbound. The following is a sample output:

```
UDP
Local Address        State
-------------------- ------
*.sunrpc             Idle
*.*                  Unbound
localhost.domain     Idle
toronto.domain       Idle
corp.domain          Idle
testing.domain       Idle
research.domain      Idle
*.tftp               Idle
*.lockd              Idle
*.time               Idle
*.echo               Idle
*.discard            Idle
*.daytime            Idle
*.chargen            Idle
```

```
*.bootps          Idle
*.syslog          Idle
*.32786           Idle
*.32787           Idle
*.nfsd            Idle
*.32795           Idle
*.32796           Idle
```

The TCP connections are shown in the following example. The Local Address is the IP address or hostname followed by the port number or service name that is in use on your host. The Remote Address is the IP address or hostname followed by the port number or name. A * represents that the IP address of port is unknown.

```
TCP
    Local Address        Remote Address     Swind Send-Q Rwind Recv-Q State
------------------- -------------------- ---- ------ ---- ------ ------
    *.*                  *.*                 0     0     0     0 IDLE
    *.sunrpc             *.*                 0     0     0     0 LISTEN
    *.37500              *.*                 0     0     0     0 IDLE
    *.767                *.*                 0     0     0     0 BOUND
    *.32771              *.*                 0     0     0     0 LISTEN
    *.32772              *.*                 0     0     0     0 LISTEN
    *.32773              *.*                 0     0     0     0 LISTEN
    *.domain             *.*                 0     0     0     0 LISTEN
    *.ftp                *.*                 0     0     0     0 LISTEN
    *.telnet             *.*                 0     0     0     0 LISTEN
    *.time               *.*                 0     0     0     0 LISTEN
    *.echo               *.*                 0     0     0     0 LISTEN
donald3.telnet       tester.1314          8115     0  8760     0 ESTABLISHED
donald2.telnet       john_laptop.1032     8015     0  8760     0 ESTABLISHED
```

The State filed describes the state of the connection. The TCP connection can be in many different states. Table 19.5 describes the possible states of a connection.

Table 19.5   TCP Connection States

State	Description
CLOSED	The socket is not being used.
LISTEN	Listening for incoming connections.
SYN_SENT	Actively trying to establish a connection.
SYN_RECEIVED	Initial Synchronization on the connection is under way.
ESTABLISHED	Connection is established.
CLOSE_WAIT	Remote connection closed and waiting to shut down socket.
FIN_WAIT_1	Socket closed and the connection is being shut down.
LAST_ACK	Waiting for last acknowledgment.
FIN_WAIT_2	Socket closed and waiting for remote machine to shut down.

Part

III

Ch

19

Interpreting the Output of *netstat –r*

The netstat -r command displays the kernel routing table. The kernel routing table is used by your host to decide where it will send an IP datagram. The destination can be a host, a network number, or a wildcard ("default" route). The Gateway specifies the machine your host forwards the datagram to if direct delivery cannot be made. If the Gateway is your host's IP address, then your host performs the final delivery of the datagram.

▶ **See** "Types of Routes," **p. xxx** (Chapter 20)

The Flags field can contain four different letters. The letter U shows the route is up and available. The letter H specifies the route is a host type route. The G flag means that the route uses an intermediate gateway to perform delivery of an IP datagram using this route. The D flag means that the route was added to the table as a result of an ICMP redirect. An ICMP redirect is a packet usually sent from a router that informs your host of a shorter path to the final destination. The following is a sample output from a netstat -r command:

```
% netstat -r
Routing tables
Destination            Gateway              Flags      Refcnt Use         Interface
aeolus                 192.75.12.252        UGHD       0      811         ln0
204.225.13.9           192.75.12.252        UGHD       0      27          ln0
localhost              localhost            UH         12     13138       lo0
csncd2                 192.75.12.252        UGHD       1      5448        ln0
csncd1                 192.75.12.252        UGHD       1      7914        ln0
204.225.13.63          192.75.12.252        UGHD       0      1239        ln0
default                sco1.dreamlan.com    UG         7      72559       ln0
204.225.8              192.75.12.252        UG         0      102         ln0
192.197.152            192.75.12.119        UG         0      87          ln0
204.225.9              192.75.12.252        UG         0      0           ln0
204.225.10             192.75.12.252        UG         0      1376        ln0
192.197.154            192.75.12.140        UG         0      6296        ln0
204.225.11             192.75.12.5          UG         0      540         ln0
204.225.12             192.75.12.5          UG         0      299         ln0
ethernet               blaze                U          53     3193736     ln0
204.225.13             192.75.12.252        UG         0      8805        ln0
204.225.14             192.75.12.252        UG         0      3348        ln0
192.197.151            192.75.12.252        UG         0      2679        ln0
```

Interpreting the Output of *netstat –i*

The netstat -i command displays statistics pertaining to each installed interface on your host. The command horizontally displays the statistics for each interface name in the Name column. The MTU is the maximum transmission unit size for the datalink interface. The Network is the network name or number to which the interface is attached. If a network name appears, it is being looked up in the file /etc/networks.

The Ipkts is the number of packets the interface has processed. The Ierrs is the number of input errors that have been received on the interface. If you have a larger percentage of input errors when compared against the number of input packets, this could be an indication that your host has an IP address conflict. The Opkts and Oerrs specify the number of output packets and output errors, respectively. If a high number of output errors exists, a bad network card or transceiver could be at fault.

The Collis field is the number of Ethernet collisions your interface has been involved in. This does not measure the overall number of collisions on the Ethernet segment. If the ratio of Collis to Opkts is consistently more than 5 percent, your Ethernet is probably flooded with too much traffic.

If Queue is a non-zero number, then there are packets that can't be transmitted out. This is symptomatic of a network cabling problem.

The following is a sample output from a netstat -i command:

```
% netstat -i
Name  Mtu   Network    Address    Ipkts    Ierrs  Opkts    Oerrs  Coll  Queue
ln0   1500  LAT        none       3450415  0      4323499  2      7065  0
ln0   1500  DECnet     BLAZE      3450415  0      4323499  2      7065  0
ln0   1500  ethernet   sco1       3450415  0      4323499  2      7065  0
lo0   1536  loop       localhost  579603   0      579603   0      0     0
```

The loopback interface (lo0) doesn't provide any real useful information because no network traffic travels through it.

Protocol Statistics

On occasion, you may want to have detailed statistics on your host's network communication, broken down by protocol. This can be provided by using the netstat -s command:

```
% netstat -s
ip:
        2395092 total packets received
        0 bad header checksums
        0 with size smaller than minimum
        0 with data size < data length
        0 with header length < data size
        0 with data length < header length
        1095 fragments received
        0 fragments dropped (dup or out of space)
        0 fragments dropped after timeout
        0 packets forwarded
        7 packets not forwardable
        0 redirects sent
icmp:
        2300 calls to icmp_error
        0 errors not generated 'cuz old message was icmp
        Output histogram:
                echo reply: 235
                destination unreachable: 2300
        241 messages with bad code fields
        0 messages < minimum length
        0 bad checksums
        0 messages with bad length
```

Part

III

Ch

19

```
         Input histogram:
                 echo reply: 560
                 destination unreachable: 6734
                 source quench: 34
                 routing redirect: 13
                 echo: 235
                 #10: 277
                 time exceeded: 110
         235 message responses generated
tcp:
         2901413 packets sent
                 4601638 data packets (2003712173 bytes)
                 8054 data packets (1682071 bytes) retransmitted
                 349781 ack-only packets (279146 delayed)
                 25 URG only packets
                 68 window probe packets
                 555526 window update packets
                 49948 control packets
         4232438 packets received
                 1940508 acks (for 2003242165 bytes)
                 35830 duplicate acks
                 0 acks for unsent data
                 2705991 packets (1916503735 bytes) received in-sequence
                 7564 completely duplicate packets (2584377 bytes)
                 694 packets with some dup. data (34682 bytes duped)
                 42675 out-of-order packets (14850492 bytes)
                 732 packets (174 bytes) of data after window
                 8216 window probes
                 2892 window update packets
                 961 packets received after close
                 936 discarded for bad checksums
                 0 discarded for bad header offset fields
                 0 discarded because packet too short
         22983 connection requests
         9429 connection accepts
         29710 connections established (including accepts)
         32964 connections closed (including 1512 drops)
         2780 embryonic connections dropped
         1923462 segments updated rtt (of 1954942 attempts)
         9524 retransmit timeouts
                 3 connections dropped by rexmit timeout
         26 persist timeouts
         38968 keepalive timeouts
                 1376 keepalive probes sent
                 161 connections dropped by keepalive
udp:
         1495422 total udp requests
         0 incomplete headers
         10 bad data length fields
         1 bad checksum
         25380 application port unused
         25390 total input dropped
    %
```

From Here...

This chapter provided information on installing and configuring TCP/IP networking on your UNIX host. You learned about the various TCP/IP-related configuration files, such as /etc/hosts and /etc/services. You now have the knowledge to use ipconfig to make changes to your system's interfaces and use netstat to gather statistics about the interfaces.

■ To find out about IP routing protocols, see Chapter 20, "IP Routing."

■ For an overview of advanced networking components and some future technologies, see Chapter 21, "Advanced Networking."

■ To learn how to set up and configure network file systems to provide file sharing throughout a network, see Chapter 22, "NFS."

■ For information about Internet host naming and domain name configuration, see Chapter 23, "DNS."

Part
III

Ch
19

IP Routing

by Peter Kuo and Jeff Robinson

Overview

A large network is generally divided into segments for a variety of reasons. Some reasons are related to the underlying technologies; others are related to geographical locations. Some of the best reasons to isolate network segments are based on network usage. If a lot of traffic in a network is between a few nodes, it is best to isolate those devices from the rest of the network. The isolation keeps traffic local between the power users and provides a more responsive network to the rest of the network users. Routers are generally used in such situations. The routers act as a "traffic barrier" by forwarding only information that must be exchanged from one network to the other.

N O T E   Generally, a router is a dedicated hardware device whose function is routing. However, if your UNIX host has more than one network interface, it also can function as a router. ▨

An essential part of the IP protocol is its capability to route packets to and from many different networks. All hosts on an IP network today perform a routing algorithm each time an IP datagram is to be delivered over their network to another host. *IP routing* is the process by which a host decides where an IP packet is to be sent. Your host may be capable of performing the final delivery of a datagram (that is, the packet is for a host that is local to yours), or an intermediate host, known as a router, may be required to route the datagram from your network to another.

N O T E   Because most of the TCP/IP protocols were developed before the introduction of the OSI model, terminologies used by the TCP/IP protocols do not always follow that of the OSI model. The most notable difference is TCP/IP's use of the term *gateway*. In the context of TCP/IP routing, gateway refers to a router and not a gateway (which translates protocols, in the way it is understood and used today). Therefore, you'll see constant references to gateways in UNIX documentation, but what they really mean are routers. ▨

In either case, your host consults a table that contains a list of destination networks, known as the *routing table*, that your host can reach either directly or indirectly through a router. If your host does not have a correctly configured routing table, you will most likely not be able to communicate with all the hosts located on different segments throughout your network.

On larger networks, the routing table on routers and many hosts might possibly change often, due to additional network segments being added or removed, or changes in the network topology. A routing protocol may be used to automate the updating of a host's or router's routing table. When properly implemented, routing protocols can be highly effective. Otherwise, one incorrectly configured router on a network can potentially disrupt the whole network.

How Are IP Datagrams Delivered?

The following example can help you better appreciate what happens to an IP packet when it is sent from one host to another as it crosses routers. The sample network shown in Figure 20.1 consists of four network segments, all using a netmask of 255.255.0.0, connected via two routers:

■ 100 Mbps Ethernet, IP network 10.1.0.0

■ 10 Mbps Ethernet, IP network 10.2.0.0

■ 100 Mbps FDDI Ring, IP network 10.3.0.0

■ 1.544 Mbps T1 WAN link, IP network 10.4.0.0

FIGURE 20.1

A sample network that consists of four IP segments connected by three routers.

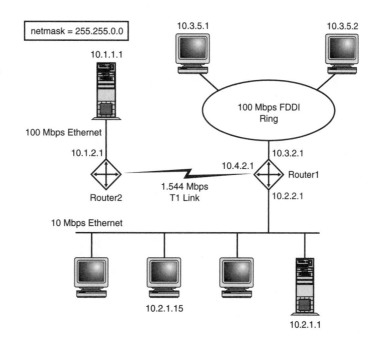

Before discussing how an IP packet is routed, you need to first know a little about the format of an IP data frame.

IP Packet Format

Because this is not a book about protocols, the gory details of an IP packet's headers are not covered. Instead, high-level coverage that gives you a good understanding about routing is presented.

An Ethernet IP frame can be divided into six fields, as illustrated in Figure 20.2:

■ Destination MAC address   It contains the 6-byte MAC address of the device to which the packet is destined.

■ Source MAC address   It contains the 6-byte MAC address of the device that transmitted the frame.

■ Ether type   It identifies the type of protocol being carried by the frame.

■ Destination IP address   It contains the 4-byte IP address of the device to which the packet is destined.

Part
III

Ch
20

- Source IP address   It contains the 4-byte IP address of the device that transmitted the frame.

- Data   Information (for example, a request or a reply).

FIGURE 20.2

An IP frame can be viewed as being made up of six fields.

Dest. MAC	Src. MAC	Ether Type	Dest. IP	Src. IP	Data
08-00-20-00-12-A4	08-00-20-13-A5-4F	IP	10.2.1.1	10.2.15.1	Data

The network interface of an IP host (the device driver, rather) is interested in the MAC addresses, whereas the routers (the routing algorithms, actually) are interested in the IP address information carried within the frame.

N O T E   The concepts about IP packet format presented here and the following examples are applicable to other frame types, such as Token Ring, and any other routable protocols, such as IPX and AppleTalk.

Local Segment

In Figure 20.1, the workstation 10.2.1.15 wants to communicate with the UNIX server 10.2.1.1. The TCP/IP software in the workstation determines from its routing table that the destination host is on the same network because the network portion of the IP addresses (10.2) is the same for both hosts; therefore, sending data between hosts on the same IP network does not need to involve a router.

N O T E   Regardless of whether a router is on the network, each IP host maintains a routing table. The minimal routing table maintained by an IP host consists of one entry: the IP network to which the host is connected.

To compose the frame for transmission, the TCP/IP software needs the hardware address, or the *Media Access Control* (MAC) address, of the UNIX server. If it's not already known, the TCP/IP stack finds the MAC address using the *Address Resolution Protocol* (ARP). The workstation's TCP/IP stack inserts that MAC address in the Destination MAC Address field of the frame and its own MAC address (determined from the NIC installed) in the Source MAC Address field of the frame; the workstation also inserts the IP address of the UNIX server in the Destination IP Address field and its own IP address in the Source IP Address field. The frame is then transmitted onto the wire.

▶ **See** "ARP," **p. 467**

When the workstation transmits the IP packet onto the wire, all devices on that segment "see" this frame. The UNIX server sees its own MAC address in the Destination MAC Address field of the frame, takes the frame, and processes it. The UNIX server uses the MAC address in the Source MAC Address field as the destination MAC address in its reply messages. In this manner, two devices learn about each other's MAC addresses.

The other devices, including the router, ignore the frame because it is not addressed to them.

Single Routed Segment

If a frame needs to cross routers, the data frame addressing is a little more complicated. Let's say that in this instance, the workstation 10.3.5.2 wants to communicate with the UNIX server 10.2.1.1. The TCP/IP software in the workstation determines from its routing table that the destination host is not on the same network because the network portion of the destination IP address is 10.2 and the workstation itself is on network 10.3; therefore, it needs to use a router. However, which router should it use if there are more than one router on its FDDI ring?

When you install the TCP/IP software, you are generally asked to specify a *default router* (gateway). This entry is not used when you are communicating locally. When you need to communicate outside your network, however, all frames are addressed to this default router.

To compose the frame for transmission in this scenario, the TCP/IP software needs the MAC address of the router. If it's not already known, the TCP/IP stack finds it using ARP. The workstation's TCP/IP stack inserts that MAC address in the Destination MAC Address field of the frame and its own MAC address in the Source MAC Address field of the frame; the workstation also inserts the IP address of the UNIX server in the Destination IP Address field and its own IP address in the Source IP Address field. The frame is then transmitted onto the wire.

N O T E If you compare the address fields of an IP packet destined for a local host with that of an IP packet destined for a remote host, the only difference is in the contents of the destination MAC address. ▪

After the router (Router1 in the example) receives the frame, it "unpacks" the frame by stripping off the MAC information. The router then looks at the IP information (destination IP address) and checks with its routing table to see where the next stop is. If the destination is on a network directly connected to this router (as is the case in this example), the router uses ARP to determine the MAC address of the UNIX server and creates a *new frame* using that information and its own MAC address—only the MAC addresses are changed; none of the higher level protocol information, including IP addresses, are altered.

The UNIX server knows that the frame came from a router because the source IP address's network number (10.3) found within the frame is different from its own network (10.2). The replies from the UNIX server back to the workstation follow the reverse path.

Multiple Routed Segments

If, however, the first router is not directly connected to the destination (as would be the case if workstation 10.3.5.2 wanted to communicate with the UNIX host 10.1.1.1), the router looks in its routing table to find where the next hop (router) is, uses ARP to determine that router's MAC address, and sends a new frame with the new information. This process continues until the frame reaches a router directly connected to the destination network.

Part
III

Ch
20

In other words, when multiple routers are involved, each time the information is passed on by a router, new source and destination MAC addresses are used on the frame, but the remaining data (including the source and destination IP addresses) is untouched.

If there are multiple paths to the same destination network, the path with the lowest "cost" is determined by the routing selection protocol being used by the routers. Some routing protocols are more efficient when links of different transmission speeds are involved because they use the link speed as one of the metrics in calculating the cost of a path, whereas others simply use the number of hops (distance) as the metric. (A *metric* is "some" unit of measurement.)

> **CAUTION**
>
> You can easily see why it is important to have the routing tables of all your routers up-to-date and consistent with each other. Any old routing information along the path of the frame can result in lost data, causing retransmissions in the best case (that is, poor performance) and application crashes and inability to communicate throughout your internet in the worst case.

Now that you understand how IP routing operates, a look at the various IP routing protocols gives you the knowledge to select and implement a routing protocol suitable for your particular environment.

Why Use Routing Protocols?

Initially, a router only knows about the networks or subnets to which it is directly connected. It learns about other networks by two means: static routes and routing protocols.

A *static route* is a path in a router's routing table that is manually configured by a network administrator. For each network or host destination, the network administrator configures the next hop router and the cost associated with the route. This information is never changed (unless manually changed by the system administrator), even if a portion of the path becomes unavailable. For example, in Figure 20.3, a static route is configured for Router1 so that to reach Network B, it must go through Router2.

Should the path between Router1 and Router2 or between Router2 and Router3 go down, Router1 cannot reach Router3 through an alternative path until it is manually reconfigured.

This is not a problem if the connectivity between the two networks is not critical because it can take some time before Router1 can be reconfigured. However, this option is not viable if the link is mission-critical or automated path reconfiguration is desired. In such a case, a *routing protocol* is required so that routers can exchange path information automatically and update any route changes dynamically.

FIGURE 20.3

A static route example.

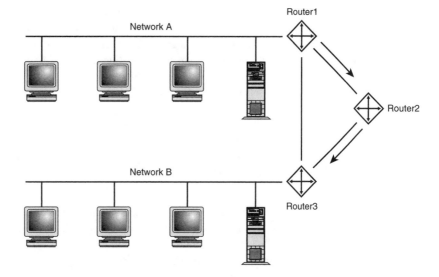

An Overview of Routing Protocols

Many different TCP/IP routing protocols are used in the TCP/IP world. They are not compatible with each other, though. Therefore, to resolve IP routing problems, it is essential that you understand the different routing protocols.

The four routing protocols discussed in some detail in later sections are as follows:

- Routing Information Protocol (RIP)
- Open Shortest Path First (OSPF)
- Interior Gateway Routing Protocol (IGRP)
- Router Discovery Protocol (RDISC)

This chapter does not try to explain all the details of these protocols because you can easily refer to the various RFCs for such information. The information presented here, however, gives you a good working understanding of each of the protocols.

Before learning about the individual routing protocols, however, you must understand the classification of routing protocols used today.

Part

III

Ch

20

Classification of Routing Protocols

To intelligently talk about routing protocols (regardless of the actual implementation), you need to learn some more buzzwords. First, you need to know that routing protocols are divided into two different "classes":

- Interior routing protocols
- Exterior routing protocols

Interior routing protocols, sometimes known as *interior gateway protocols* (IGPs), are generally used within an autonomous system to dynamically determine the best route to each network or subnet. An *autonomous system* (AS) is a group of routers (portions of a network, usually within the control of one organization) that share information through the *same* routing protocol. Each autonomous system is assigned a unique identification number. The AS number is used by some routing protocols to control the exchange of routing information.

N O T E On the Internet, the AS concept is standardized by the registration of autonomous systems. A group of networks on the Internet under a common administration is considered an autonomous system and must be registered as such with the InterNIC Registration Services. Registration provides an autonomous system number to your autonomous system. ▪

N O T E The term *autonomous system* within the IP context is synonymous with the term *routing domain* within the International Standards Organization's (ISO) terminology. ▪

Exterior routing protocols (EGPs), also known as *interdomain routing protocols*, are used to exchange routing information between different autonomous systems. There is also a specific routing protocol called EGP, as specified by RFC 827.

Depending on the algorithm used to determine routes, costs of paths, and so on, routing protocols are further classified:

- Distance-vector routing protocols
- Link-state routing protocols

In *distance-vector routing protocols*, each router keeps a routing table of its perspective of the network. For example, as shown in Figure 20.4, `Router1` sees that Networks A and B are directly connected to it (one hop away), whereas Network C is two hops away. However, `Router2` sees Networks B and C as one hop away, and Network A as two hops away. The two routers "see" the network differently.

FIGURE 20.4

A sample network consisting of two routers and three network segments and its routing tables.

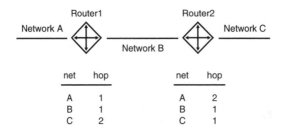

net	hop		net	hop
A	1		A	2
B	1		B	1
C	2		C	1

N O T E Distance-vector routing is sometimes known in the literature by other names. The two most popular alternative names are Ford-Fulkerson routing algorithm, after the people who invented the algorithm (L.R. Ford, Jr., and D.R. Fulkerson, Flows in Networks, Princeton University Press, 1962) and the Bellman-Ford algorithm because it was based on the Bellman Equation (R.E. Bellman, Dynamic Programming, Princeton University Press, 1957). ▪

Each router takes the routing information passed to it, adds one hop to the route (to account for its own presence), and passes the updated information to the next router in line. In essence, distance-vector routing protocols use "secondhand" information from their neighbors.

> **CAUTION**
>
> Because a router that uses distance-vector routing protocols has no way to validate the information a neighbor sends it, any erroneous routing information eventually is propagated to all routers within the network. Therefore, it is important that all routing tables be accurate.

Distance-vector routing protocols select the "best route" based on a metric. The metric used is different based on the actual protocol. One drawback of distance-vector routing protocols is that when routers send updates, they send entire routing tables. To keep the information up-to-date, the updates are *broadcast* at regular, fixed intervals.

Link-state routing protocols work just the opposite of how distance-vector routing protocols work. With a link-state routing protocol, each router calculates a "tree" of the entire network with itself as the root (as illustrated in Figure 20.5).

FIGURE 20.5

Network layout as "seen" by Router3 using link-state routing protocols.

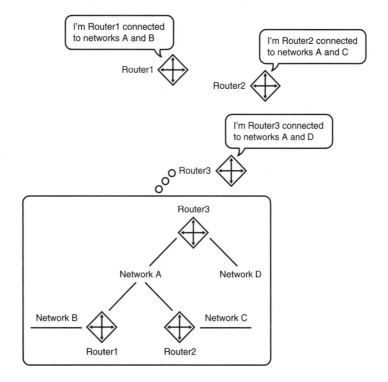

Part
III

Ch
20

In this example, Router3 constructs a network layout based on the routing information received *directly* from Router1 and Router2. Under link-state, each router distributes information about its directly connected networks and their associated metrics only; it does not redistribute information learned from other routers. Therefore, contrary to distance-vector routing protocols, link-state routing protocols use only "firsthand" information.

The routers only include the best path derived by the metric to other nodes (routers). When a router detects changes in the state of its direct link (for example, a link comes up or goes down), the router distributes (via multicasts) the change to all routers through a process called *flooding*. Flooding updates contain only state change information (hence, the term link-state protocols).

N O T E   In general, these flooding packets are small and are sent infrequently. They contribute little to the overall network traffic unless routes change often. ▨

Comparison of Distance-Vector and Link-State Routing

There is a continuing debate as to which of the routing protocol "types" is better. To make an informed decision, you need to know the limitations of each routing protocol type.

Routing Information Convergence Time   The biggest disadvantage of distance-vector protocols is the time it takes for information to spread to all routers after a change has occurred in the network topology. This period is known as the *convergence time*. For a large network, the convergence time can indeed be long; and during this time, data frames have a much greater chance of getting misrouted and lost because of the *count-to-infinity* problem (discussed in the following section).

On small LANs, it is acceptable in many cases to choose a distance-vector protocol. However, as your network starts to grow with many routers and hosts being added along with a variety of real-time services such as voice and video, a fast link-state routing protocol is much more effective because it has a much faster convergence time and doesn't have the count-to-infinity problem.

Count-to-Infinity Problem   Distance-vector routing protocols can take a long time to converge after a topological change. The reason for this is easily illustrated using the sample network shown in Figure 20.6.

FIGURE 20.6

A simple count-to-infinity problem.

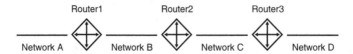

Router1 Router2 Router3

Network A   Network B   Network C   Network D

Using the distance-vector algorithm, the distances between Network D and the various routers are as follows:

- ▨ One hop from Router3 (directly connected)
- ▨ Two hops from Router2 (through Router3)
- ▨ Three hops from Router1 (through Router2 and Router3)

If the link between Router2 and Router3 is down or Router3 fails, Router2 (after having waited for 180 seconds) removes Network D's route from its routing table by setting the metric for Network D to 16 (unreachable). However, Router1 sends a RIP update to Router2 indicating that it can reach Network D at a lower cost (two hops). Router2 then adds one hop count to this route and updates its routing table with this "new" route (reach Network D through Router1).

Router1 thinks it can reach Network D through Router2 (in two hops), and Router2 thinks it can reach Network D through Router1 (in three hops). You now have a routing loop! In this case, any data destined for Network D is routed back and forth between Router1 and Router2 until it dies of old age (the "time-to-live" timer in the IP packet expires).

However, over time as the routers continue to update among themselves, the hop count to Network D continually increases and eventually reaches 16 hops ("infinity," unreachable), and the entry is removed from all routers. But as you can see, it can take a while, especially if you have a large network of routers.

Some distance-vector routing protocols, such as RIP, use a technique called *split horizon* to prevent such routing loops. Under split horizon, no routing information is passed back in the direction from which it was received. For instance, Router1 informs Router2 that it is one hop away from Network A. Router2 takes that information, adds one to the hop count for Network A, and passes that to Router3 on Network C, but not back to Router1 because that is the router from which it received the information.

Unfortunately, split horizon doesn't solve all cases of count-to-infinity problems. It helps in a linear network, as illustrated in the preceding simple example. More networks, however, contain redundant routes for fault-tolerant purposes, which reduces the effectiveness of split horizon. Figure 20.7 shows a network with multiple paths.

FIGURE 20.7

A complex count-to-infinity problem involving multiple paths.

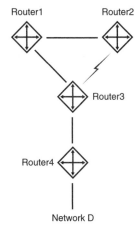

Router1   Router2

Router3

Router4

Network D

Part
III

Ch
20

Router3 informs Router1 and Router2 that Network D is two hops away from it, thus the routing tables in Router1 and Router2 list Network D as three hops away. If Router4 fails or the link between Router3 and Router4 goes down, Router3 knows that Network D is no longer reachable and informs Router1 and Router2 of the fact. Due to split horizon, Router1 and Router2 cannot tell Router3 about their knowledge of Network D. However, between Router1 and Router2, a "valid" path still exists.

Router1 learns from Router2 that it is two hops away from Network D. Router1 adds one hop to that route and passes the information (three hops to Network D) to Router3, but not to Router2 because of split horizon. Router1 can send information about Network D to Router3 because Router3 no longer advertises a route to Network D. Router3 now thinks it is four hops away from Network D through Router1. It passes that information to Router2. Router2 now thinks it is five hops away from Network D through Router3. Router2 propagates this to Router1. Router1 turns this into six hops and passes this information onto Router3. Eventually, a hop count of 16 is reached, and split horizon didn't help much!

What can you do? You can use two more tricks: *poisoned reverse* and *triggered updates*.

With split horizon, routes are not advertised back onto the interface they were learned from. With poisoned reverse enabled, such routes are advertised back out the same interface from which they are learned but with a metric of 16. This immediately breaks the routing loop between any two routers. It helps to speed up the convergence time in the count-to-infinity problem but does not necessarily eliminate it entirely.

FIGURE 20.8

A simple IP network in which Router2 has poisoned reverse enabled.

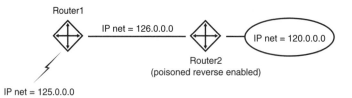

Following are two packet captures. This sample IP network has two routers as shown in Figure 20.8. Following is the RIP update from Router1:

```
rip: ================== Routing Information Protocol ==================
        Command: Response
        Version: 1
        Family ID: IP
            IP Address: 125.0.0.0
            Distance: 1
```

The RIP update from Router2 when poisoned reverse is used is as follows:

```
rip: ================== Routing Information Protocol ==================
        Command: Response
        Version: 1
        Family ID: IP
            IP Address: 120.0.0.0
            Distance: 1
        Family ID: IP
            IP Address: 125.0.0.0
            Distance: Not Reachable
```

```
Family ID: IP
     IP Address: 126.0.0.0
     Distance: Not Reachable
```

As you see in the first of the two packet traces, Router1 advertises to Network 126.0.0.0 a route to Network 125.0.0.0 with a hop count of one as expected. In the second packet trace, Router2 advertises a route to Network 120.0.0.0 with a hop count of one, also as expected. Because it has poisoned reverse enabled, however, Router2 also advertises network 125.0.0.0 (its local network) and network 126.0.0.0 (learned from Router1) as not reachable.

From a quick comparison of the two RIP packets, you can see that poisoned reverse generates more update traffic (larger update messages). On a large network, especially on a backbone, this added traffic could cause network congestion problems.

Consider the case of a building backbone connecting many different floors. On each floor, a router connects the backbone to a local network. Using split horizon, only the local network information is broadcast onto the backbone. But with poisoned reverse, the router's update message includes all the routes it learned from the backbone (with a metric of 16), as well as its own local network. For a large network, almost all the entries in the routing update message indicate unreachable networks.

 TIP

In many cases, you may opt to use split horizon without poisoned reverse to conserve bandwidth and accept the slower convergence time.

Often, routers enable split horizon automatically, and poisoned reverse needs manual configuration.

If your router supports triggered updates, coupling it with poisoned reverse can greatly minimize the convergence time. *Triggered updates* cause the router to send a RIP update when a route's metric is changed, even if it is not yet time for a regular update message.

CAUTION

Be careful with the use of triggered updates because it can cause much broadcast traffic, similar to a broadcast storm.

 TIP

The count-to-infinity problem in using distance-vector protocols can be avoided by designing your network without router loops.

If you must have multiple paths for redundancy, consider using a link-state protocol, such as OSPF. Or simply keep in mind how distance-vector routing protocols work, fix your downed link as soon as you can, or reset the routers to force a new routing table to be built.

Part

III

Ch

20

Security A potential security risk exists when routing protocols are used to exchange routing information with other routers on the network. Many routing protocols exchange the routing information without any authentication or verification. Your host or router may receive a route advertisement, but what is to indicate the information is credible? Some routing protocols, such as OSFP and RIP II, support password authentication. If you are attempting to provide a secure network environment, consider using a routing protocol that offers security, or no routing protocol at all (and use static routes).

Distance-Vector or Link-State? After reading through the preceding considerations, you'll probably want to use link-state protocols because they offer so many advantages. But before you jump in with both feet, consider the following items in addition to those discussed previously:

- Memory   Generally, given the same network, a router using a distance-vector routing protocol requires less memory than when a link-state routing protocol is used.

- Bandwidth usage   It is difficult to compare the bandwidth consumed by the two algorithms. Proponents of either type of protocol can demonstrate a topology in which their favorite uses far less bandwidth than the other. Although detailed studies need to be conducted, it is generally felt that the bandwidth used in either algorithm is modest and should therefore not be the criterion by which one algorithm or the other is chosen.

- CPU load   Similar to bandwidth usage, it is difficult to say with certainty what the CPU load posted by the two algorithms is. However, general experience shows that distance-vector protocols require less CPU power than the link-state protocols.

- Functionality   Link-state protocols most certainly offer more functionality than distance-vector. For instance, it is easier to troubleshoot and to discover the topology of the network when link-state protocols are used. By querying any one router in a network that uses a link-state routing protocol, you can obtain the full knowledge of the network topology because each router builds a complete "tree" of the entire network with itself as the root.

   Troubleshooting a network is easier in link-state routing because a single router can be queried, and from its LSP (link-state protocol) database, all the broken links can be discovered (assuming that the original topology is known).

If you have a small- to medium-size network that has few WAN links, distance-vector routing will work just fine. If you have a fairly large network that has many subnets or many WAN links, link-state routing would be a good choice.

Routing Information Protocol (RIP)

One of the most widely used interior gateway protocols is the *Routing Information Protocol* (RIP; RFC 1058/1723). RIP is a distance-vector routing protocol as discussed earlier. The original version, RIP I, was first introduced in 1988. The current version of RIP is version 2 (referred to as RIP II).

Because distance-vector routing protocols have regular, fixed update intervals, RIP's update is sent every 30 seconds. If a route is learned through RIP update messages and then a subsequent update message does not refresh this route within 180 seconds (six update cycles), the route is assumed to be unreachable and is removed from the routing table.

N O T E RIP classifies routers as active and passive (silent). *Active routers* advertise their routes (reachability information) to others; *passive routers* listen and update their routes based on advertisements but do not advertise. Typically, routers run RIP in active mode, whereas hosts use passive mode.

CAUTION

Those who are familiar with Novell's protocols should not confuse this RIP with the RIP used by NetWare. Although they bear the same name and perform a similar function, NetWare RIPs are sent once every 60 seconds.

For RIP, hop counts are used as the route selection metric. In Figure 20.4, Router1 "sees" that Network C is farther away than Network A or B because Network C has a metric (hop count) of two, whereas the others have a metric of one. If Router1 learns (from another router not shown in the figure) of another path to Network B with, say, two hops, it discards that new route because it has a higher metric.

N O T E A RIP metric of 16 (hops) means that the destination is not reachable.

RIP is probably the most common routing protocol used today because it is easy to implement. RIP has some serious limitations, however. For example, RIP I data carry no subnet mask information, which limits RIP to advertise only network information (no subnet information), or requires RIP routers to make assumptions about the subnet mask. The latter makes it vendor–implementation–specific and often causes interoperability problems. Also, RIP I doesn't use any authentication; therefore, it is possible for a rogue router to advertise false route information and give rise to network routing issues.

  If you are experiencing routing problems, check the routing tables of the routers involved and see whether RIP is enabled and if so, which version of RIP. Some network administrators who want to cut down on the amount of broadcast traffic on their networks disable RIP on the routers and use static routes instead.

Some routers enable you to adjust the RIP update timer to reduce broadcasts. If you do this, check that all other RIP routers are configured similarly. Otherwise, you might see routes "come and go" on certain routers, resulting in intermittent routing problems.

Part

III

Ch

20

RIP version 2 (RFC 1723; more commonly known as RIP II) adds capabilities to RIP. Some of these capabilities are compatible with RIP I, and some are not. To avoid supplying information to RIP I routes that could be misinterpreted, RIP II can only use noncompatible features when its packets are multicast. On interfaces that are not capable of IP multicast, RIP I compatible packets are used that don't contain potentially confusing information.

Some of the most notable RIP II enhancements are as follows:

- Next hop   The primary ones are the capability to advertise a next hop to use other than the router supplying the routing update. This is useful when advertising a static route to a "dumb" router that does not run RIP because it avoids having packets destined through the dumb router from having to cross a network twice.

    RIP I routers ignore next hop information in RIP II packets. This may result in packets crossing a network twice, which is exactly what happens with RIP I. So this information is provided in RIP I compatible RIP II packets.

- Network mask   RIP I assumes that all subnetworks of a given network have the same network mask. It uses this assumption to calculate the network masks for all routes received. This assumption prevents subnets with different netmasks from being included in RIP packets. RIP II adds the capability to explicitly specify the network mask with each network in a packet.

    Although RIP I routers ignore the network mask in RIP II packets, their calculation of the network mask will quite possibly be wrong. For this reason, RIP I compatible RIP II packets must not contain networks that would be misinterpreted. These networks must only be provided in native RIP II packets that are multicast.

- Authentication   RIP II packets may also contain an authentication string that can be used to verify the validity of the supplied routing data. The simple password method used provides little security in the presence of network monitoring software. Authentication can be used in RIP I compatible RIP II packets, but be aware that RIP I routers will ignore it.

CAUTION

Not all routers support RIP II. Make sure that your routers use the same routing protocol.

N O T E   Some routers can support RIP I and RIP II simultaneously.

Open Shortest Path First (OSPF)

Open Shortest Path First (OSPF) is a link-state routing protocol and was first introduced in 1989 (RFC 1131/1247/1583). More IP sites are converting to OSPF from RIP because it completely eliminates the count-to-infinity problem.

N O T E   *Open* in OSPF implies that the protocol is not proprietary.

Using "cost" as the metric, OSPF can support a much larger internet than RIP. Remember, in a RIP-based internet, you can't have more than 15 routers between any two networks (because 16 hops means unreachable). This sometimes results in having to implement more links for large networks.

N O T E   Using cost, an OSPF metric can be as large as 65,535. ▨

Similar to RIP II, OSPF supports variable length subnetting. This permits the network administrator to use a different subnet mask for each segment of the network. This greatly increases the flexibility and number of subnets and hosts that are possible for a single network address. OSPF also supports authentication on update messages.

Other than exchanging routing information within an autonomous system, OSPF can also exchange routing information with other routing protocols, such as RIP and *Exterior Gateway Protocol* (EGP). This can be done using an *autonomous system border router* (ASBR).

> **CAUTION**
>
> If you are using multivendor routers in a mixed RIP and OSPF environment, make very sure that routes are redistributed between routing protocols in a consistent manner.
>
> It is possible to create routing loops because a router does not increment the hop count when going from RIP to OSPF and back to RIP.

It is beyond the scope of this chapter to go into the details of OSPF concepts, OSPF areas, and other OSPF protocols (such as the OSPF Hello Protocol). Refer to RFC 2328 for the latest definition of OSPF Version 2.

Interior Gateway Routing Protocol (IGRP)

For a long time on the Internet, routers used the *Interior Gateway Routing Protocol* (IGRP) to exchange routing information. Although IGRP is also a distance-vector routing protocol, it uses a number of variables to determine the metric for route selection:

- Bandwidth of the link
- Delay due to the link
- Load on the link
- Reliability of the link

By considering these variables, IGRP has a much better, and real-time, handle on the link status between routers. IGRP is much more flexible than RIP which is based solely on hop count. IGRP can better reflect the type of link and choose a more appropriate path than RIP can.

Consider the sample network shown in Figure 20.9. The links between Router1 and Router2 and between Router2 and Router3 are T1 links (1.544 Mbps), whereas the link between Router1 and Router4 is a 56 Kbps line. RIP doesn't know the difference in line speed between the paths and sends traffic from the workstations to the host over the slower 56 Kbps line rather than the T1 lines simply because the 56 Kbps "path" has a lower hop count. IGRP uses the more efficient T1 lines.

The update interval for IGRP is every 90 seconds, as compared to every 30 seconds for RIP.

Part

III

Ch

20

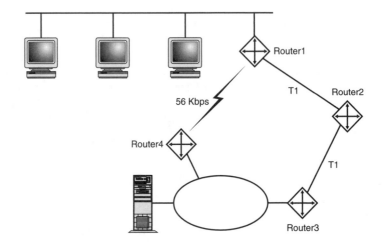

FIGURE 20.9

RIP chooses the slower 56 Kbps link, whereas IGRP uses the high-speed T1 lines.

However, like RIP, when an update is sent, the whole routing table is sent.

> **N O T E**   IGRP was originally developed by Cisco Systems, Inc., and used extensively by the Internet. That's why for a long time when you acquired a link to the Internet, you were required to use a Cisco router. Now IGRP is supported by many other router vendors. ▪

Router Discovery Protocol (RDISC)

Sometimes even if you have not configured dynamic routing on an IP router, routes may be automatically added to your routing table by the *Internet Control Message Protocol* (ICMP).

ICMP was first introduced in 1980 (RFC 792/1256). Its function is to provide a dynamic means to ensure that your system has an up-to-date routing table. ICMP is part of any TCP/IP implementation and is enabled automatically. No configuration is necessary. ICMP messages provide many functions, including route redirection and connectivity testing (the `ping` utility).

▶ **See** "Using `ping`," **p. xxx** (Chapter 17)

For example, if your workstation forwards a packet to a router, and that router is aware of a shorter or faster path to your destination, the router will send your workstation a "redirection" message informing it of the shorter or faster route.

In the newer implementation of ICMP (RFC 1256), there is a router discovery feature. Strictly speaking, the *Router Discovery Protocol* (RDISC) is not a routing protocol but a way to inform hosts of the existence of routers. The protocol is split into two portions: the server portion, which runs on routers, and the client portion, which runs on hosts.

> **N O T E**   RDISC is best used in a small network within an autonomous system. ▪

The *router discovery server* runs on routers and announces their existence to hosts. It does this by periodically multicasting or broadcasting a *router advertisement* to each interface on which it is enabled. These router advertisements contain a list of all the router addresses on a given interface and their preference for use as a default router.

Initially, these router advertisements occur every few seconds and then fall back to every few minutes (default is every 10 minutes). In addition, a host may send a *router solicitation* to which the router responds with a unicast router advertisement (unless a multicast or broadcast advertisement is due momentarily).

Each router advertisement contains an *advertisement lifetime* field indicating for how long the advertised addresses are valid. This lifetime is configured such that another router advertisement will be sent before the lifetime has expired. A lifetime of zero is used to indicate that one or more addresses are no longer valid.

On systems supporting IP multicasting, the router advertisements are by default sent to the all-hosts multicast address 224.0.0.1. However, the use of broadcast may be specified. When router advertisements are being sent to the all-hosts multicast address or an interface is configured for the limited-broadcast address 255.255.255.255, all IP addresses configured on the physical interface are included in the router advertisement. When the router advertisements are being sent to a net or subnet broadcast, only the address associated with that net or subnet is included.

A host listens for router advertisements via the all-hosts multicast address (224.0.0.2), if IP multicasting is available and enabled, or on the interface's broadcast address. When starting up, or when reconfigured, a host may send a few router solicitations to the all-routers multicast address, 224.0.0.2, or the interface's broadcast address.

When a router advertisement with non-zero lifetime is received, the host installs a default route to each of the advertised addresses. If the preference is ineligible, or the address is not on an attached interface, the route is marked unusable but retained. If the preference is usable, the metric is set as a function of the preference such that the route with the best preference is used. If more than one address with the same preference is received, the one with the lowest IP address is used. These default routes are not exportable to other protocols.

When a router advertisement with a zero lifetime is received, the host deletes all routes with next-hop addresses learned from that router. In addition, any routers learned from ICMP redirects pointing to these addresses are deleted. The same happens when a router advertisement is not received to refresh these routes before the lifetime expires.

N O T E RDISC is a rather new implementation for some routers; therefore, not all routers support this router discovery feature. ■

Other Routing Protocols

The preceding sections discussed *interior gateway protocols* (IGPs), which are by far the routing protocols encountered most often in the field. However, at times you may encounter some exterior routing protocols. *Exterior routing protocols* are used to connect two or more autonomous systems (see Figure 20.10). Two exterior routing protocols—*Exterior Gateway Protocol*

Part
III

Ch
20

(EGP; RFC 827/904) and *Border Gateway Protocol* (BGP; RFC 1105/1163/1267)—are briefly discussed here so that you can be familiar with them.

FIGURE 20.10

Linking two autonomous systems using an exterior routing protocol.

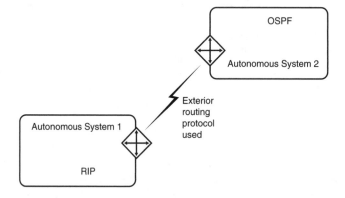

Introduced in 1982, EGP is the earliest exterior routing protocol. Routers using EGP are called *exterior routers*. Exterior routers share only reachability information with their neighboring exterior routers. EGP provides no routing information—an EGP router simply advertises a route to a network; therefore, no load balancing is possible on an EGP network.

In 1989, BGP was introduced. BGP uses TCP as the transport layer connection to exchange messages. Full path information is exchanged between BGP routers, thus the best route is used between autonomous systems.

N O T E As of this writing, the latest version of BGP is BGP v4 (BGP-4) as described by RFC 1771. ■

Maintaining the Kernel Routing Table

Each UNIX operating system contains a *kernel routing table*, sometimes known as the *kernel forwarding table*. The routing table, stored in RAM, is a list of destinations and gateways required to perform IP datagram delivery.

The kernel routing table can be viewed using the netstat command:

```
% netstat -r
Routing tables
Destination          Gateway           Flags    Refcnt  Use     Interface
127.0.0.1            127.0.0.1         UH       0       16796   lo0
10.10.1.0            10.10.1.5         UG       0       0
10.10.2.0            10.10.1.5         UG       0       43809
10.10.3.0            10.10.1.5         UG       0       31713
10.10.56.0           10.10.1.5         UG       0       1202
205.150.233.12       199.71.122.193    UH       0       0       ppp0
199.45.92.32         199.71.122.37     UG       0       4282
199.45.92.192        199.71.122.51     UG       0       5283
```

▶ **See** "Interpreting the Output of netstat -r," **p. 502**

The Destination field contains a host IP address and network number or the word "default" to represent a default route. The Gateway field (some implementation shows this, correctly, as router) is the IP address of the host that datagram will be forwarded to. If the Gateway address is the IP address of your host, then your host performs final delivery of the datagram. The IP address located in the Gateway field must be adjacent, meaning that the gateway must be on the same network segment.

The Flags field identifies the type of route and possibly how the route was added to the table. The possible flags are listed in Table 20.1.

Table 20.1   Routing Table Flags

Flag	Description
D	This route is a result of an ICMP redirect.
G	The route is to a gateway/router.
H	The route is to a host. If this flag is not set, the route is to a network or subnetwork.
M	The route has been changed by an ICMP redirect.
U	The route is up and available.
<null>	If this flag is not set, then the destination can be reached directly.

The Refcnt field (some implementation shows this as Ref) shows the number of routes that are using the same data link address. The Use field shows the number of packets that have been delivered using this route. The Interface column displays the interface that performs final delivery. The Interface field is blank if an intermediate gateway is used for datagram delivery.

The routing table can include three types of routes:

- Host routes
- Network routes
- Default routes

Host Routes

Host routes are routing table entries that represent a route to a single IP address or host. A host route can be identified by having an H in the Flags field. The following example shows a host route that would allow your host to reach the host with an IP address 199.71.122.51 through a gateway having IP address 10.10.1.10:

```
Destination          Gateway              Flags  Ref   Use     Interface
-------------------  -------------------  ----   ----  ------- --------
199.71.122.51        10.10.1.10           UH     0     4282
```

> **N O T E**   A host route, if known, *always* is chosen first from the routing table, before a network, or
> default route is chosen. ▪

Network Routes

A *network route* is the most common type of route in the routing table. Network routes are used in the routing table to represent a whole network as a destination that your host is capable of reaching. Network routes are identified in the routing table when the Destination field is *not* the word "default," and the Flags field contains a G.

Following is an example of a network route in the routing table. This network route specifies that this host will forward IP datagrams destined to the network 204.212.181.0 to the router with an IP address of 10.10.1.5:

```
Destination          Gateway              Flags  Ref   Use     Interface
-------------------- -------------------- ----   ----  ------- --------
204.212.181.0        10.10.1.5            UG     22    9836
```

Default Routes

A *default route* is the route of last resort. If your host searches for a host or network route to match the destination IP address, and neither route exists in the routing table, your host uses the default route to forward the datagrams for delivery.

The following routing table entry shows a default route that has datagrams forwarded to a router with an IP address of 10.10.1.100:

```
Destination          Gateway              Flags  Ref   Use     Interface
-------------------- -------------------- ----   ----  ------- --------
default              10.10.1.100          UG     106   2369
```

Maintaining the Routing Table

Maintaining the routing table on hosts and routers is an important job. This can also be a time-consuming task. There are primarily two methods of maintaining the kernel routing table on hosts and routers. First, you could manually enter each route on every host under your administration on the network (that is, using static routes). This provides a secure environment but potentially could be time consuming as your network grows or changes.

Second, you might choose to implement a routing protocol to automatically update the routing tables on your hosts and routers. This method is less time consuming for host and router routing table configuration, but many can have some security concerns (as discussed earlier in this chapter).

Static Routes

Static routes are fixed entries in the routing table. These routes are added to the routing table when an interface on your local host becomes available, or the system administrator uses the route command to manually add a route.

Static routes are best for simple networks, for networks whose configuration changes relatively infrequently, or when security (as related to routing) is a concern.

Dynamic Routes

Dynamic routes are most commonly added to the routing table through the use of a routing protocol. Dynamic routing table entries may also appear as a result of an ICMP redirect.

An ICMP redirect occurs if your host forwards a datagram to a router and that router knows of a better router you should forward the datagram to. ICMP redirects often occur when a host uses a single default route when multiple routers are available for routing. An ICMP redirect always results in a host route being added to your kernel routing table; such a route is identified with a D in the Flags field.

The *route* Command

The route command can be used to add static routes to the kernel routing table. The route command can add all three types of routes—host, network, and default. The route command does not, however, add the routes permanently to any startup or configuration files. If you add routes manually, the routes will be lost after the host reboots. The route command entries can be added to applicable startup scripts to ensure that the routes are added each time the host starts up.

▶ **See** "Start and Kill Scripts," **p. 282**

The syntax for manually adding a route follows:

```
route add  [ host ¦ net ] destination  gateway  metric
```

For example, the following command adds a host route to an IP host (199.71.122.51) using the gateway whose IP address is 10.10.1.5 and a metric of 1:

```
$ route add host 199.71.122.51 10.10.1.5  1
```

The following example shows the command used to add a network route so that your host uses the gateway whose IP address is 10.10.1.102 to reach a remote office whose network number is 192.168.37.0; this route has a cost metric of 1:

```
$ route add net 192.168.37.0 10.10.1.102 1
```

The following command adds a default route entry to the kernel routing table. The host uses the router with IP address 10.10.1.55 as the default router; this route also uses a metric of 1:

```
$ route add default 10.10.1.55 1
```

A route can be deleted from your routing table using the route delete command. The following three commands will remove the three routes that were added in the preceding examples:

```
$ route delete 199.71.122.51 10.10.1.5
$ route delete 192.168.37.0 10.10.1.102
$ route delete default 10.10.1.55
```

Part

III

Ch

20

The routing table can be flushed so that a new one is built from scratch. The `route flush` command flushes all the static and dynamic routes from the kernel routing table, except those routes added due to a direct interface in the host.

 The `route` command also accepts hostnames and network names defined in the `/etc/hosts` and `/etc/networks` files.

▶ **See** "TCP/IP Network Configuration," **p. 489**

Two `route` command options can help you troubleshoot routing problems:

■ `route get`   Looks up and displays the route for a destination.

■ `route monitor`   Continuously reports any changes to the routing information base, routing lookup misses, or suspected network partitionings.

 When using the `route` command, the `-n` option can be used to bypass attempts to print host and network names symbolically when reporting actions. The process of translating between symbolic names and numerical equivalents can be time consuming, and may require correct operation of the network; thus, it may be expedient to forgo this, especially when attempting to troubleshoot networking operations.

UNIX Routing Protocol Daemons

Most UNIX machines serve as good IP routers. For a UNIX host to be a router, you should have at least two network interfaces properly installed in the host—they can be two NICs or one NIC and one modem. The host will have each interface connected to the network that you want to route between. Each interface needs to be properly configured with an IP address, netmask, and broadcast address for the network to which it is attached.

UNIX has many routing protocol daemons that you can use to configure your host as a router. The following outlines the general steps you need to take to configure a system for IP routing:

1. Determine whether the machine being configured serves as a router or nonrouter. For a router, you need to configure the host to allow the capability to forward datagrams from one network interface to another. This is generally referred to as *IP forwarding*.

   Depending on the platform, the procedure is different. Table 20.2 shows how to enable IP forwarding on several different platforms.

2. Determine the routing protocols to be used to communicate with other machines. For a nonrouting host, typically use RDISC and/or the RIP protocol. For a router, typically use the RDISC protocol and at least one internal routing protocol (RIP or OSPF). For an exterior router of an autonomous system, also choose an exterior routing protocol (BGP or EGP).

3. Select the routing daemon that implements the protocols selected in the preceding step. Use of the RDISC protocol requires use of the RDISC daemon (`in.rdisc`). Either the

routed or gated daemon can be used for the RIP protocol. If you also need to use any of the following protocols in conjunction with RIP (OSPF, EGP, or BGP), you must use gated to implement RIP. It is recommended that routed be used only for simple networks. Remember that routed and gated cannot both be used; they are mutually exclusive.

4. Configure the system for the routing daemons selected.

N O T E On some systems, such as Solaris, routed is known as in.routed. The name routed is used here.

On some systems, such as SCO, in.rdisc is known as irdd (*Internet Router Discovery* daemon). The name in.rdisc is used here. ▪

N O T E The gated daemon is a publicly available routing daemon capable of supporting many different routing protocols. It is sometimes included with the version of UNIX that you have.

If you don't have gated, you can get it from the following site using anonymous FTP:

ftp://ftp.merit.edu:/net-research/gated/ ▪

▶ **See** "Using ftp," **p. 430**

Table 20.2   Enabling IP Forwarding on Different Platforms

Platform	Description
SCO UnixWare	Use the /etc/inet/menu command to enable a menu that allows you to configure the machine as a gateway.
Solaris	IP forwarding is automatically enabled if you have two or more network interfaces installed. You can manually change the kernel variable using the ndd command. The following command would manually enable IP forwarding: ndd -set /dev/ip ip_forwarding 1
HP	Use the SAM utility. Type sam at the command line. The graphical interface allows you to convert the host to a router.
Linux	Enable the ip_forwarding kernel variable and recompile the kernel.
Digital UNIX	Automatically enabled.
SCO System V	Automatically enabled.

Part
III

Ch
20

CAUTION

If you want to run routed, make sure that the file /etc/gated.conf does not exist. If it does, you must remove it, move it to another directory, or rename it. Otherwise, the gated daemon executes instead of routed the next time your host reboots.

The *gated* Configuration File

The gated configuration file is /etc/gated.conf by default. The file consists of a sequence of statements terminated by a semicolon (;). Statements are composed of "tokens" separated by white space that can be any combination of blanks, tabs, and new line characters.

This structure simplifies identification of the parts of the configuration. Comments may be specified in either of two forms. One form begins with a pound sign (#) and runs to the end of the line. The other form, C style, starts with a "/*" and continues until it reaches "*/".

The *routed* Configuration File

The routed daemon uses the /etc/gateways file to initialize static routes to distant networks. When routed starts, it reads the /etc/gateways file (if it exists) and installs the routes defined there into its routing table. Each line in the /etc/gateways file has the following syntax:

net *net-name*[/*net-mask*] gateway *router-address* [metric *cost*] [active¦passive]

or

host *host-name* gateway *router-address* [metric *cost*] [active¦passive]

The entries for networks begin with the keyword net, and entries for specific hosts begin with the keyword host. Table 20.3 summarizes the parameters used in the file.

Table 20.3   The */etc/gateways* File Parameter

Parameter	Description
net *net-name*	*net-name* refers to the IP address of the network or name of network in the /etc/networks file. It is the final destination to which to route the packet.
host *host-name*	*host-name* refers to the IP address or name of host in the /etc/hosts file. It is the final destination to which to route the packet.
gateway *router-address*	*router-address* refers to the IP address of the router to which to forward packets.
metric *cost*	*cost* refers to the cost of the route. The value ranges from 1 to 16 (unreachable). If not specified, the default is 1.
active¦passive	Routes can be active or passive. *Active* routes expire automatically after a certain period of time, if new information on that route is not received. *Passive* routes remain permanently in RAM and do not expire. If not specified, routes default to passive routes.

In the following example, a packet to the host 134.33.43.2 can be sent to the router at 144.79.4.3. This entry is marked as permanent in the routing table; the cost of this route defaults to 1:

```
host 134.33.43.2 gateway 144.79.4.3 passive
```

In the following example, a packet to the network 233.230.225.0 can be sent to the router at 129.24.10.11. This entry is marked active. It is assumed that router 129.24.10.11 can participate in routing message exchanges. If no router updates are heard from the router 129.24.10.11 about the route to 233.230.225.0, the specified router entry will be timed-out and removed from the router table; the cost of this route is set to 4:

```
net 233.230.225.0 gateway 129.24.10.11 metric 4 active
```

Implementing RIP I Using *routed*

UNIX hosts that are not routers will run in quiet or passive mode. Usually, the daemon `routed` is started with the `-q` option. The `routed` daemon starts automatically on most platforms; however, a startup script may need to be created on some UNIX platforms.

UNIX routers that need to support the RIP protocol in "shout" mode must run the `routed` daemon with the `-s` option. The `routed -s` command starts the RIP protocol broadcasting on all network interfaces configured on the router.

> **CAUTION**
>
> After the `routed` daemon has been started on a host or router, manually adding or deleting routes should be avoided. Otherwise, the routing table may freeze (that is, no updates are accepted) after it has been altered manually, making `routed` ineffective. The only way to fix this is to stop and restart the `routed` daemon.
>
> Use the `/etc/gateways` file to make route changes.

> **CAUTION**
>
> Any routes placed in the routing table prior to starting the `routed -s` daemon on routers will result in the router advertising these routes automatically.

Implementing RIP I Using *gated*

The `gated` daemon uses a file named `/etc/gated.conf` instead of a command-line argument to obtain its configuration information.

The `gated` daemon is flexible and configurable. The `gated` distribution contains many sample configuration files that you can use as a starting point. Sample configuration files for RIP I follow:

```
#
# enable rip i
#
rip yes {
    interface all ripin ripout ;
} ;
```

```
static {
          default gateway 10.10.1.102 retain ;
} ;
```

The preceding configuration file enables RIP and adds a static default route to the routing table when the gated daemon starts.

> **N O T E**   The interface statement allows you to be specific as to which interfaces support RIP and which one does not. Also, you can be even more specific by using the directives ripin/ noripin and ripout/noripout. ◾

The following configuration runs RIP in quiet mode; it only listens to packets, no matter how many interfaces are configured:

```
#
rip yes ;
{
     nobroadcast ;
} ;
#
```

This configuration should work for any system that runs RIP I and has only one network interface:

```
#
# don't time-out the network interface
#
interface 136.66.12.2 passive ;
#
# enable rip
#
rip yes ;
#
```

Implementing RIP II Using *gated*

Because routed supports only RIP I, you need to use the gated daemon to implement RIP II and other routing protocols (such as OSPF). The /etc/gated.conf file to support RIP II is similar to the preceding file to support RIP I. The following /etc/gated.conf file performs the same function as the RIP I example previously shown, except that the RIP II protocol is used:

```
#
# enable rip ii
#
rip yes {
     interface all version 2 ripin ripout ;
} ;
static {
     default gateway 10.10.1.102 retain ;
} ;
```

> **N O T E**   The key here is the use of the directive "version 2." ◾

Implementing OSPF Using *gated*

The OSPF routing protocol is implemented using the gated daemon. The following sample /etc/gated.conf file implements a simple single, nonauthenticated area for routers to e xchange routing information:

```
#
# using ospf, no rip
#
rip no ;
# The remainder of the routing information is exchanged using OSPF
# we have only a single area - backbone
ospf yes ;
backbone {
     #any ospf packets are considered valid
     authtype none ;
     interface all {priority 5} ;
};
```

The next example uses a simple, eight-character, plain text password to authenticate the information exchange:

```
# no rip, use ospf
rip no;
ospf yes {
     backbone {
          authtype simple ;
          interface all
          {
               priority 5;
               enable;
               authkey "Password" # 8 char max
          };
     };
};
```

Implementing RDISC Using *in.rdisc* and *irdd*

To implement the RDISC protocol on your routers and hosts, the in.rdisc daemon is usually used; on some systems, it is called irdd. The in.rdisc daemon has five options, as listed in Table 20.4.

Part
III
Ch
20

Table 20.4   Options for the *in.rdisc* Daemon

Option	Description
-s	The daemon starts in client mode. Three solicits for routers occur. If an answer is received from a router within three solicits, the daemon continues to run; otherwise, the daemon stops.
-f	The daemon sends three solicits and runs the daemon even if no responses from routers are received.

continues

Table 20.4 Continued

Option	Description
-r	The daemon acts in router mode. The daemon sends a multicast message to all the hosts every 10 minutes by default.
-p	If the daemon is using the -r option, a preference value can be included to have the default routers on the clients ordered in their routing table. A higher preference value indicates a more preferable router.
-T	Used in conjunction with the -r options. The option specifies the time interval between router advertisements in seconds, instead of using the default 10 minutes.

The irdd daemon found in SCO offers a few more configuration options. It uses a /etc/ irdd.conf file that controls the behavior of irdd. The syntax for this control file is simple: Lines starting with the pound-sign (#) character are ignored, and keywords that take a value are specified as *keyword=value*. Values may be specified in base 8, 10, or 16. The following keywords are recognized:

- broadcast   Specifies that messages should be sent to the broadcast address, rather than being multicast.

- defadvertise   Specifies that the default behavior is to advertise all interfaces. This can be overridden on a per-interface basis. If this keyword is not specified, the default behavior is to not advertise interfaces. If the system is configured as a host, this keyword is ignored.

- defadvmin   Specifies the default minimum interval for advertisements, specified in seconds. This is used only when the system is configured as a router. If this keyword is not specified, the value defaults to 75 percent of the maximum advertisement interval. The smallest legal value is 3.

- defadvmax   Specifies the default maximum interval for advertisements, specified in seconds. This is used only when the system is configured as a router. If this keyword is not specified, the value defaults to 600. The smallest legal value is 4.

- defdiscover   Specifies that the default behavior is to discover routers on networks attached to all interfaces. This can be overridden on a per-interface basis. If this keyword is not specified, the default behavior is to not perform router discovery on interfaces. If the system is configured as a router, this keyword is ignored.

- deflifetime   Specifies the default lifetime value for advertisements. If this keyword is not specified, the default lifetime is three times the maximum advertisement interval. If the system is configured as a host, this keyword is ignored.

- defpreference   Specifies the default preference value for advertisements. If this keyword is not specified, the default preference is 0. A preference value of 0x80000000 means that hosts should ignore this system. If the system is configured as a host, this keyword is ignored.

- **interface** This keyword identifies configuration information for a particular interface. Interfaces are specified by name—for example, ln0. The following per-interface keywords are recognized: advertise, advmax, advmin, broadcast, discover, lifetime, and preference. These per-interface keywords allow the default values to be overridden on a per-interface basis. Per-interface keywords not specified cause those values to be initialized to the default or to the value specified using one of the default keywords.

- **static** This command is only used by systems configured as hosts (that is, this command is ignored if the system is configured as a router). It causes the relationship with a specified router to be statically configured. The static keyword takes one argument, which is the hostname or IP address of the router.

  Two per-static keywords affect the behavior of the static command. The first is preference, which assigns the specified preference to the specified router. This is useful for configuring multiple static routers with different priorities.

  The second per-static keyword is noupdate, which causes router discovery messages received from the specified router to be ignored. This is useful for testing or in the event that it is desirable to assign a different preference to the router than it is advertising, possibly to work around a configuration problem.

Following are two sample /etc/irrd.conf files. The first example is typical for a system configured as a router:

```
# sample router discovery configuration
defadvertise                    # advertise all interfaces
defadvmax=1200                  # twenty minutes
deflifetime=2700                # forty-five minutes
defpreference=4000
interface e3B0 broadcast        # no multicast on this lan
interface wdn0 preference=0     # override preference
```

The preceding sample configuration causes irdd to function as follows:

- Multicast on all interfaces except e3B0.

- Advertisements are generated with a preference of 4000, except on interface wdn0, which is advertised at a preference of 0. Advertisements are sent at random intervals between 15 and 20 minutes. Advertisements are valid for up to 45 minutes.

The second example is typical for a system not configured as a router:

```
# sample router discovery configuration
#
# perform discovery on all interfaces in addition
# to static router below
#
defdiscover
#
# our routers can't hear multicasts yet
#
broadcast
#
# add 75.1 as our preferred router even though it doesn't advertise
```

Part
III

Ch
20

```
#
static 128.212.75.1 preference 100000
#
# ignore anything we hear from 75.67 and never use it
#
static 128.212.75.67 noupdate preference=0x80000000
```

From Here...

In this chapter, you gained an in-depth understanding of the different IP routing algorithms and the various routing protocols, such as RIP and OSPF. You also read about how to configure your UNIX host to function as a router and learned to use different daemons, such as gated and routed, to implement the various routing protocols.

- For an overview of advanced networking components and some future technologies, see Chapter 21, "Advanced Networking."

- To learn how to set up and configure network file systems to provide file sharing throughout a network, see Chapter 22, "NFS."

- For information about Internet host naming and domain name configuration, see Chapter 23, "DNS."

- To learn more about network and general security issues, see Chapter 26, "Security."

## CHAPTER 21

Advanced Networking

by Chris Negus

In this chapter

What Is Advanced Networking?

Whether on workstations, mainframes, or microcomputers, the UNIX operating system has always led the field in computer networking advances. With Dial-Up Networking features (using protocols such as PPP), UNIX can support both client and server connections. To protect a company's computer resources, UNIX systems provide the tools for setting up private networks, firewalls, and proxy servers.

UNIX systems are among the first software products to provide support for a variety of emerging networking standards. In particular, the Internet Protocol Next Generation (IPng) Version 6 recommendation is setting the future direction to improve such things as Internet routing capabilities, privacy, and authentication standards. For handling multicast content on the Web, UNIX systems contain utilities that support the MBONE topology for prototyping multicast routing and delivery of live content (such as audio and video) to end users.

This chapter describes the following topics:

- Point-to-Point Protocol (PPP)   This section describes PPP, as well as how to set up on both client and server computers for PPP on a UNIX system.

- Private networks, firewalls, and proxy servers   This section describes how to use these UNIX network security features. It tells about how to manage private network addressing, protect your network from the outside world using firewalls, configure proxy servers to control access to applications, and use network address translation (NAT).

- MBONE   This section describes how the MBONE topology works and what UNIX features are available to MBONE routing and content delivery.

- Internet Protocol Next Generation (IPng)   This section describes the IPng Version 6 (IPv6) standard and its impact on UNIX system network administration.

Implementing Point-to-Point Protocol (PPP)

Point-to-Point Protocol (PPP) provides a method of establishing links between points on a network and then allowing a variety of network layer protocols to negotiate and communicate over those links. Though multiple protocols are supported, today PPP is most often used in some of the following ways:

- By client computers (such as a home PC) to reach server computers (such as a UNIX server at an Internet service provider) using standard telephone lines.

- By a UNIX system acting as a router for a small group of computers (such as a small business or home LAN) to an ISP using telephone or leased lines. (This is a low-cost method of providing Internet access to a group of computers.)

- By a UNIX system routing traffic for a large business, routing traffic over an ISDN connection.

To connect to the Internet, only a few pieces of information need to be provided by the client for PPP, such as the server's telephone number, the user's login and password, and some DNS addresses. However, as an administrator, there are ways to tune PPP to control transmission rates, encryption techniques, and other features.

What Is PPP?

PPP was designed to allow an easy way to exchange packets between two network points that may be connecting different types of computers, routers on the same type of network, or bridges to different types of networks. Though PPP allows complex protocols and negotiations to be used within its structure, it is intended to provide a simple interface for the end users and administrators that actually use PPP.

Three major components that make up the PPP standard: encapsulation, Link Control Protocol (LCP), and Network Control Protocols (NCPs). Encapsulation defines the structure of how multiprotocol datagrams are created and stored. The LCP defines how the data link connection between two points is established and managed. The NCP defines the structure in which different network layer protocols can be used.

The PPP standard is defined in a set of documents that make up the Official Internet Protocol Standards referred to as Requests for Comments (RFCs). The main Point-to-Point Protocol RFC is RFC-1661. Other RFCs that describe different aspects of PPP are listed in the note below.

▶ For information on RFCs, **see p. 723**

Most of the PPP RFCs describe topics of interest to companies that develop their own PPP products or protocols. As a UNIX administrator or end user, you don't need to know most of the details of the PPP standard. (Just as you don't need to know how an engine works to be able to drive a car.) Instead, the rest of this section focuses on how to set up and use PPP from a UNIX system.

> **N O T E** Different RFCs were created to define or propose changes to particular aspects of PPP. Different network protocols and encryption schemes that can be incorporated into PPP are among the features detailed in different RFCs. You can find RFCs at several Web locations, including the RFC Editor home page (http://www.rfc-editor.org).

> **RFC 2284 - PPP Extensible Authentication Protocol (EAP)**
>
> **RFC 2153 - PPP Vendor Extensions**
>
> **RFC 2023 - IP Version 6 over PPP**
>
> **RFC 1994 - PPP Challenge Handshake Authentication Protocol (CHAP)**
>
> **RFC 1990 - The PPP Multilink Protocol (MP)**
>
> **RFC 1989 - PPP Link Quality Monitoring**
>
> **RFC 1968 - The PPP Encryption Control Protocol (ECP)**
>
> **RFC 1762 - The PPP DECnet Phase IV Control Protocol (DNCP)**

Part

III

Ch

21

continues

continued

RFC 1662 - PPP in HDLC-like Framing

RFC 1661 - The Point-to-Point Protocol (PPP)

RFC 1638 - PPP Bridging Control Protocol (BCP)

RFC 1570 – PPP LCP Extensions

RFC 1552 – PPP Internetwork Packet Exchange Control Protocol (IPXCP)

RFC 1332 – PPP Internet Protocol Control Protocol (IPCP) ▨

PPP in UNIX

Every major version of the UNIX system contains some level of support for PPP. Most provide some friendly interface (a form or menu-driven command) to set up PPP. Underneath that interface, however, are standard UNIX configuration files used by a variety of features.

Setting up PPP on a UNIX system can be very tricky—especially if you are not used to working with UNIX system files. Though your UNIX system probably has a simplified method for configuring PPP, chances are the result will be entries in configuration files that you may eventually need to edit manually.

Configuration files that are modified by PPP are associated with several different UNIX components. For example, you might need to modify UUCP files (such as devices and systems files) to configure the modem and dial-up chat script used by PPP. IP information needs to go into basic TCP/IP files (such as the /etc/hosts file) to identify such things as the locations of the DNS servers.

Some believe that UNIX systems have lost market share as both Internet clients and servers because PPP is much simpler to configure on MS Windows systems. Although that may be true, UNIX still tends to include more in-depth PPP features and offer greater flexibility.

N O T E Some UNIX administrators are unhappy with the versions of PPP that are delivered with some UNIX systems. For that reason, they may use third-party or free PPP software products available today. Check out the following Stokely Consulting PPP/SLIP page for links to PPP UNIX products that you can obtain:
http://www.stokely.com/unix.serial.port.resources/ppp.slip.html. ▨

The text that follows describes the general steps for configuring PPP (clients and servers).

Setting Up PPP

The descriptions in this section tell you how to set up PPP from a client computer (such as a PC running UNIX from home) to a server computer (such as the Internet server at your place of business). In many cases, you will want to use UNIX as the server and use Windows 95 computers as clients. Refer to Windows 95 documentation for information on setting up PPP on Windows 95 clients.

CAUTION

Because UNIX versions of PPP and network devices differ significantly, consult the documentation that comes with your UNIX system for specific PPP instructions. Use this text as a general guide in setting up PPP.

Different procedures are needed for client and server PPP connections. The following descriptions assume that the client is calling the server (although the server can call the client, it's not as common).

The Dial-Out PPP Client   Here is the general setup required for a client (outgoing) PPP connection:

■ Configure a modem that can dial out to the PPP server. (This is usually done with entries in the /etc/uucp/Devices and /etc/uucp/Dialers files.)

■ Add a Systems entry to configure the chat that happens when the client calls the server. This defines such things as the modem to use, the telephone number of the server's modem, and the login/password used for your PPP connection.

■ Add the domain name and the name server addresses to your computer, so that the host computers you try to contact can resolve the names into IP addresses.

■ Configure the PPP interface options. (These options may include what types of compression to use, how long the connection should be idle before disconnecting, and transmission speeds.)

When a request is made that requires communication to the PPP server (someone requests an URL or a telnet to do remote login), the client tries to dial out to the server and establish an IP connection.

The Dial In PPP Server   To configure a server to allow clients to connect using PPP, follow these general guidelines:

■ Add a user login for the PPP connection. (Typically, the client logs in to the UNIX system using a username that starts up a PPP connection instead of just opening a standard UNIX shell.)

■ Identify the IP addresses of the client computers and DNS servers.

■ Configure the PPP interface options.

Testing PPP

The most obvious way to test your PPP connection is to try to start up the connection from the client and send data across that connection. The general steps that occur when a client tries to connect to a PPP server are as follows:

1. A client process, such as an Internet browser, requests a connection to an Internet server.

2. The client computer tries to establish a network connection to the server (often by dialing a modem at an ISP).

Part

III

Ch

21

3. The client establishes a link with the server.

4. An authentication process occurs, where the client identifies itself with a username and password.

5. A network layer connection is established between the client and the server.

Usually a simple `ping` command to the server causes a connection to start up to the server.

When the client requests a PPP connection, UNIX reads the Systems entry for the PPP connection and dials the remote computer (the PPP server). When the remote computer's modem picks up the call, the client logs in, and the two sides negotiate connection parameters and start up the connection. If the connection is successful, `ping` should give you a message that the connection to the requested host is alive.

Private Networks, Firewalls, and NAT

Because of the great success of the Internet, TCP/IP protocols and utilities have become the predominant tools for creating networks. Many companies that don't even need to connect to the Internet are using TCP/IP with their private networks. Those who do want Internet connectivity are using firewalls and proxy servers to protect the boundary between their networks and the outside world.

When a company designs its own computer network, many policy issues have an impact on how the network is set up. This section describes TCP/IP security and addressing issues including: private networks, firewalls, proxy servers, and network address translation.

Private Networks

Some organizations will set up a network using TCP/IP without intending for that network to be connected to the Internet. This type of network is referred to as a private network. There are several reasons why an organization might want to set up a private network:

- Company computers have no need for outside connectivity. (For example, a network might connect computers that manage a manufacturing facility that never needs to communicate outside of the factory.)

- For security reasons, Internet connectivity can present a danger. (For example, a nuclear power plant or a military network might want to completely prevent any outside access.)

- Only email is needed. Limited Internet connectivity may be available by setting up a single gateway machine that simply allows such things as email and netnews. In this case, host computers don't have to be uniquely addressable from the Internet and, therefore, can remain private.

With a private network, a network administrator can avoid many of the security concerns that Internet connectivity brings. Security issues can be more focused on internal, rather than external computer security. Also, the administrator doesn't need to beg for unique IP addresses for the network. Instead, special IP addresses can be used that will be unique within the company.

What IP Addresses Do I Use? A set of IP addresses have been set aside by the Internet Assigned Numbers Authority (IANA) specifically for use by private networks. Because these addresses are not intended to be accessible by the general Internet, they can be reused by private networks. If your network is connected to the Internet, packets to these addresses should never cross your router to or from the Internet.

▶ **See** the section in Chapter 19, "TCP/IP Network Configuration," for information on IP addresses.

Class A, B, and C IP addresses are reserved for private networks. The single Class A address would be most appropriate for a private network that requires millions of addresses on a single subnetwork (very rare). You could use any of the Class B addresses for a private network with nodes in the thousands. A Class C network would be appropriate for a network with a couple hundred nodes or less.

The following chart shows the IP network numbers that have been set aside for private networks:

Network Class	Network number	Addresses Per Network Number
A	10.0.0.0	16,777,216
B	172.16.0.0 through 172.31.00	65,536
C	192.168.0.0 through 192.168.255.255	256

You can have a mixture of private and public IP addresses on your network. The key is that you only use private numbers for those hosts that don't need IP connectivity outside the private network (or set up something like NAT, described later). With the private numbers, however, the host can communicate freely with hosts using public or private numbers that are on the private network.

N O T E Before you make a decision to use private IP numbers, you should be fairly sure that the hosts won't need to become public IP hosts in the near future. Updating a large private network with new IP addresses could take a lot of time to redo. If it is in question, you might want to use public addresses and set up a firewall to restrict access to hosts you want to keep private. ▪

A Request for Comments (RFC) that looks into addressing for private IP networks is "Address Allocation for Private Internets," (RFC-1918). This RFC steps you through the pros and cons of setting up a private IP network. It also details the private IP address space.

Network Address Translator (NAT) If you want your network to use a limited number of IP addresses but still connect to the Internet, network address translator (NAT) is one way of using fewer IP addresses while still maintaining a level of Internet connectivity. Until the next generation of the Internet takes effect, NAT is becoming an accepted method for slowing the rate of IP address consumption. (See the description of IPng later in this chapter for information about future addressing standards.)

Part
III

Ch

21

NAT is a technique that allows IP addresses to be reused by more than one domain connected to the Internet. NAT works by implementing a NAT translation table at the router that connects the domain to the general Internet. This router is referred to as a *stub border router*.

The trick is that each stub border router must have a globally unique IP address (or set of addresses). Addresses within the stub domain, however, are not globally unique and may be reused by other stub domains. (The routers running the NAT tables do not advertise the addresses used within the stub domain to the worldwide Internet.)

When a host with a non-unique address (within the stub domain) sends a packet to a host on the Internet, the stub router changes the non-unique address to a unique address. This is done by either taking an address from a pool of addresses or by reusing a single IP address and assigning a unique port number to it. The latter technique uses fewer IP addresses because each address can have many ports. When packets are returned from the Internet, the stub router translates the unique address to the non-unique one.

Firewalls

If you don't want your company completely cut off from the Internet, but you want to limit who can access your local network and what they can access, a firewall is a good place to start. A firewall creates a boundary between two computer networks by allowing one network to control access between it and the other network.

Firewalls are usually set up by a company that has a computer network used primarily by employees to do their work. Connections to the Internet from that network are restricted to a limited number of routers and host systems. Traffic from the Internet can be restricted by denying access to most host computers on the local network or by limiting what services can be requested.

A firewall protects your company's network in many of the same ways a guarded front gate protects a person's property. You can monitor those who try to come in, you can restrict where they can go, and you can limit what they can view. For your firewall, that entry point is represented by a single machine (or at least a very few machines), through which all traffic from the Internet must pass.

Even many networks consisting primarily of PCs running MS Windows use UNIX systems for their firewalls. UNIX systems are generally more stable and contain more firewall features than any Microsoft systems available today.

One of the most common firewall configurations is the Dual Homed Firewall topology (see Figure 21.1).

As you can see from Figure 21.1, the firewall separates the private secure network from the public insecure network. Here, the company's Web server and router connection to the Internet is outside the firewall. The client computers, used by company employees, lie behind the firewall. The firewall resides on a *bastion host*, which most likely is a UNIX system with firewall software installed.

FIGURE 21.1
A dual homed firewall monitors traffic that crosses to or from outside networks.

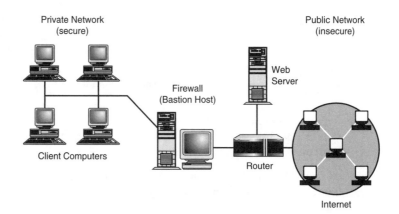

What a Firewall Can and Can't Do   As any computer security expert will tell you, a firewall should be part of a total security policy for your company. It should not be expected to prevent every potential security breach. To get an idea of how firewalls should fit into your security policy, the following information describes what a firewall can and can't do.

Following are some of the things a firewall can do for your organization's network:

- Provide a single point of protection from an outside network. If all traffic goes through the firewall, you can focus logging, monitoring, and auditing procedures on that machine.

- Block unauthorized access from the outside network. This can be done at the network level by the router blocking requests for access to unauthorized IP addresses or ports on the local network.

- Selectively allow or deny access to particular services on your network from an outside network. For example, you may allow email and netnews to enter your network from the outside network but deny remote login requests. This is typically done from a proxy server. (See the "Proxy Servers" section later in this chapter.)

- Hide details of your network from the general Internet. By doing such things as network address translation and IP forwarding, the firewall can keep information about your network private, such as the names and IP addresses of hosts on your network.

Most firewall features can be implemented completely on a UNIX system. Network level firewalls, however, are often implemented on dedicated router machines.

Firewalls should not, as mentioned earlier, be expected to prevent every potential security breach that could occur with your computer networks. Here are some security problems that a firewall can't stop:

- Backdoors into the network. Modems that are connected to the hosts in your network can circumvent a firewall because incoming calls will bypass the firewall completely.

Part

III

Ch

21

■ Unauthorized people with passwords. If you allow access to restricted services with a login and password, if a user gives away that information, the unauthorized person becomes the authorized person (as far as the network is concerned). Likewise, when employees leave (especially those who don't leave happily), you should immediately clear their login accounts, or the firewall will continue to extend them the courtesy of your network.

■ Tapes, floppies, and other backup media. If unauthorized people gets their hands on your data that has been copied onto a backup medium, they might have information that you want protected. Backup data needs to be protected as much as your network does.

The bottom line is that, for a firewall to protect your network computing resources, employees that have access to those resources need to use good judgment when it comes to protecting the authority they are given.

How a Firewall Works   Although there are different levels of security and different types of services that can be implemented on a firewall, you can expect to find some features in most firewall products. Some services include IP packet filtering, IP packet forwarding, logging and auditing, mail forwarding, and proxy server features. (Proxy servers are described later.)

IP Packet Filtering   Using a set of rules created by the network administrator, the firewall can permit or deny access to services requested by IP packets. A packet that requests a service that is not acceptable by the rules that are set on the firewall is denied access. Packets can be filtered based on IP address (source or destination), protocol requested (TCP, UDP), port number (source or destination), or direction of request (inbound or outbound).

IP Packet Forwarding   Some applications, such as Real Audio, require that IP connections be established directly between the client and the server. This could mean allowing an Internet client to connect to a server behind your firewall or a client on your secure network connecting to a server on the Internet. In this case, the firewall uses IP forwarding to allow a connection between the two parties that the firewall cannot break.

IP forwarding should be allowed selectively, because it allows users to bypass some security features of the firewall. For example, the firewall can't closely monitor the connection or protect the IP address of the computer behind the firewall.

Logging and Auditing   Because all communications between the outside network and your network must pass through the firewall, you can gather a great deal of information about what passes that boundary. Logging features can let you have records kept of service requests that are denied. You can keep records of URLs that are accessed by your users.

The level of logging and auditing you do is up to you. Typically, you will at least log denial of services because they may reflect someone trying to get into your network. With a higher level of logging turned on, however, you can keep track of all traffic that goes through the firewall.

Mail Forwarding   Even at some risk of compromising the security of the network, most private networks will at least allow email to be forwarded to users from the Internet. Typically, the firewall uses a mail protocol, such as SMTP, to deliver incoming email from the Internet to a mail server on the local network.

Working with the local mail server, the firewall prevents hostnames or addresses associated with the local network from being sent to the outside by changing any local information used to information that can appear to the outside world. (For example, instead of the email bearing the user's hostname, the firewall may change the email address to reflect the company domain name, such as `billg@thebigcompany.com`.)

▶ **See** "The `sendmail` Configuration File," **p. 658**

Proxy Servers

It might not suit your needs to make your firewall a brick wall. There are some network applications you want to allow your people to use to reach the Internet (such as a Web browser or file transfer). Likewise, you might want to allow some clients from the Internet, with proper authentication, to access some applications on your network (such as a remote login program such as telnet). To safely manage the running of applications that cross the boundary between your network and the Internet, you can use a proxy server.

In configuring your proxy server, you need to decide whether your basic approach is to only disable a few network applications (allowing the rest) or disallow most applications (specifically allowing a few). The most secure method is the latter.

When you consider what network applications to allow the people on your local network to use to communicate with the Internet, consider the following network applications available with most UNIX systems:

- HTTP (Web Server)
- HTTPS (Secure Web Server)
- FTP (File Transfer Protocol)
- Telnet (remote login)
- IRC (Internet Relay Chat)
- Gopher (document search tool)

By setting up these and other applications on a proxy server, you can protect the anonymity of your user's host computers. The route back to the user goes through the firewall, so there is no direct IP connection between the user's computer and the Internet host.

One of the most popular proxy servers is the Socks Version 5 (Socks5) proxy server.

The Socks5 Proxy Server

A Socks5 proxy server can be used to provide some advanced firewall and proxy features from a variety of UNIX systems. A Socks5 server authenticates clients requesting connections, authorizes or denies those requests, sets up proxy connections, and forwards the data.

Because application data is passed through the Socks5 server, Socks5 provides many features for managing the network applications. For example, Socks5 can collect network data, screen it, filter it, and audit the data flow. From the client's perspective, the client can negotiate with Socks5 to ensure integrity and privacy of the client session.

Part
III

Ch
21

> **N O T E** Socks5 features that were not in Socks version 4 include support for authentication and support for UDP proxies. ▨

Socks5 is based on a variety of standards. RFCs that help define Socks5 include RFC-1928 (covers the Socks5 protocol), RFC-1929 (describes Socks5 username/password authentication), and RFC-1961 (details Socks5 GSS-API authentication).

Obtaining Socks5   A reference implementation of Socks5 is available from NEC USA. You can download any of several different UNIX versions of Socks5-related software packages from the Socks Version 5 page from NEC (`http://www.socks.nec.com/socks5.html`) or from the NEC Socks5 FTP site (`ftp://ftp.nec.com/pub/socks`). Scroll down to Socks5 resources and click on Download socks5.

From these sites, Socks5 is available on the following systems:

- Solaris 2.5 (Sparc)
- Solaris 2.5 (Intel)
- SunOS 4.1
- AIX 4.1
- OSF1 4.0
- IRIX 6.2
- HP/UX 10.20
- Linux 2.0
- Linux 1.3
- FreeBSD 2.2
- BSDi 3.0

The Socks5 package is made up of the Socks5 server, client libraries (static and shared), and some client applications. Related Socks5 tools include: SocksCap (software to allow WinSock applications to cross Socks5 servers), Socks5Watcher (graphical tool for viewing Socks5 server activity), Socks5WatchAG (tool for delivering real-time data to Socks5Watcher), and Sock5Tools (two perl scripts, including one that summarizes Socks5 log messages and one that converts Socks version 4 server data to version 5).

Administering Socks5   Utilities in the Socks5 package let you prepare applications for use by Socks5 and configure how the Socks5 protocol behaves. Here are descriptions of some of those utilities.

The `runsocks` Script   The `runsocks` utility is a shell script that prepares an application to be used by Socks5, without recompiling the application. The `libsocks5.conf` file is used to set environment variables that will be accessed by `runsocks` to prepare the Socks5 applications.

The `socks5` Daemon   Most of the work of Socks5 is done by the `socks5` daemon. When client processes request an application be started, the `socks5` daemon authenticates the client making the request and processes the request.

Authentication is done by the socks5 daemon in one of two ways: using a username and password or using Kerberos 5. To use Kerberos 5 authentication, socks5 had to be built with Kerberos libraries.

The socks5 *Configuration File* The behavior of the socks5 daemon can be configured using the socks5 configuration file (/etc/socks5.conf). With this configuration file, you can add the following types of entries:

- ban   Indicates a host from which socks5 will not accept connections.

- auth   Identifies the different types of authentication socks5 can use.

- route   Associates certain addresses with certain interfaces. In this way, different interfaces can be assigned to hosts outside and inside the local network.

- set   Used to set a variety of variables to appropriate values. Examples of variables include SOCKS5_CONFFILE (for defining additional configuration files) and SOCKS5BINDINTFC (for specifying the host and port number socks5 runs on). The socks5(1) manual page contains a complete listing of these variables.

- proxy-type   Identifies the type of proxy server as Socksv5, Socksv4, or noproxy (to make a direct connection).

- permit   Sets the rule for when socks5 permits a connection to a particular application.

- deny   Sets the rule for when socks5 denies a connection to a particular application.

Other types of entries allow you to set patterns to identify hosts, ports, authentication methods, commands, users, and servers.

The Mbone

The Mbone is an experimental network created to deliver and test live, multicast audio and video over the Internet. In effect, the Mbone acts as a virtual network overlaid on the Internet because the existing Internet wasn't designed to handle multicast data. The Mbone's mission is to act as a prototype for developing the infrastructure to support worldwide live broadcasts and conferencing on the Internet.

Mbone began from efforts by the Internet Engineering Task Force (http://www.ietf.org), which accepted the IP Multicast Protocol RFC-1112 as the basis for multicasting on the Internet. In fact, the first use of the worldwide Mbone was to carry multicasts of live IETF meetings. Today, much of the use of the Mbone is to serve those who support the Internet, both in the type of information it carries and in serving as a means for testing multicast tools and protocols. Its direction is guided by the IETF Mbone Deployment Working Group (http://www.ietf.org/html.charters/mboned-charter.html).

The network resources that make up the Mbone are provided by network providers and private companies on a voluntary basis. Many of the contributors are companies with vested interest in the Internet, such as computer and networking equipment vendors.

Part
III

Ch
21

TIP You can find Mbone topology visualizations at `http://www.nlanr.net/PlanetMulticast` or `http://www.caida.org/Tools/Manta/summary.html`. By selecting a VRML view, you can see a 3D view. In that view, click on Mbone end points to see text describing the location of the end point.

Most of the tools and protocols used with Mbone run on UNIX systems. The Mbone routing daemons, administrative commands, and end user programs that are available for UNIX systems are described later in this chapter. Other sections also describe how to join the Mbone and how to find out what content is "playing" on Mbone.

How Does the Mbone Work?

Routers used in today's Internet (based on Internet Protocol version 4) don't support features needed to effectively route multicast packets. To transmit multicast data over Internet routers that don't support multicasting, Mbone routers use a method known as *tunneling*.

Tunneling is how Mbone routers pass multicast packets across non-Mbone routed networks without those packets being interpreted. Today's routers don't support different levels of quality of service. Therefore, a packet that needs to arrive in a timely basis to be effective (such as live broadcast data) is treated no differently from any other packet (such as those carrying email).

To get around the quality of service problem, Mbone routers treat networks using intervening, non-Mbone routers as tunnels. At each end point of a tunnel are routers that support multicasting. When a multicast packet arrives at a tunnel entry router, it is encapsulated and transmitted as normal unicast data until it reaches the end point of the tunnel. There the encapsulation is stripped off, and the packet is again treated like multicast data.

The first and most popular protocol for routing on the Mbone is DVMRP (Distance Vector Multicast Routing Protocol). This protocol is implemented with the `mrouted` routing utility (described later). An alternative to DVMRP is PIM (Protocol Independent Multicast). PIM operates in either dense mode (for local area networks) or sparse mode (for wide area networks). The two protocols are designed to interoperate, although currently, interoperability is prone to errors.

What Content Is Available on Mbone?

As noted earlier, the most popular use of the Mbone today is to broadcast live content that is of interest to the Internet community. Although the Mbone has some routes linking sites all over the world, most Mbone traffic does not cross continents. Besides multicasting IETF meetings, Mbone traffic that does go around the world includes multicasts by scientific organizations (such as CERN), universities (such as Columbia University), and companies (such as Netscape Communications) to multicast meetings and seminars.

To see a schedule of Mbone sessions, open the Mbone Session Agenda Web page (`http://www.cilea.it/MBone/agenda.html`). Click on Browse the Mbone Session Agenda, and you can select the Mbone multicast schedule for the year and the month you choose. To schedule your own Mbone session on the Global Agenda, click on Book a time slot and then enter information about your broadcast.

To interactively view what sessions are available on the Mbone, use the sdr command (Session Directory Tool). Using sdr, you can view which sessions are offered on the Mbone, advertise sessions you want to make available, and place calls to individuals over the Mbone. If you see a session that interests you, click on the session name. Information about the session will be displayed in the pane. Double-click on the session name, and the appropriate tool (audio, video, white board, or text) starts up for you to join the session. (See the description of Mbone tools for a further description of sdr.)

How to Join Mbone

The general process of joining Mbone is to first get some background information about Mbone, find a connection to the Mbone, get the equipment you need to connect, and install and run the necessary software tools to use the Mbone. The following sections describe these steps.

Getting Mbone Information   Before you join Mbone, you should read some of the materials available that describe the Mbone. Here are several documents available on the Web that can give you a good start:

- Frequently Asked Questions (FAQ) on the Multicast Backbone (MBONE) by Steve Casner (http://www.mediadesign.co.at/newmedia/more/mbone-faq.html)   This FAQ describes what the Mbone is, how it works, what you need to participate, and what documentation is available.

- MBONE, the Multicast BackbONE by Mike Macedonia and Don Brutzman (http://www-mice.cs.ucl.ac.uk/mice/mbone_review.html)   Gives a good description of the Mbone, its protocols, its topology, and its tools. Though some of the information is outdated, it is still a good reference.

> **CAUTION**
>
> Much of the information available on the Internet about Mbone is either several years old or missing. Most notably, the mbone.com site seems to be unavailable, making the many references to it from other pages useless. For up-to-date information, speak to the person handling Mbone technical support from your ISP or post a message to the Mbone mailing list.

Because the Mbone and its supporting tools are in such a constant state of change, to keep up with the latest information, you should join the Mbone mailing list. Chances are, many of the problems you encounter have already been discussed at length in this group. A good way to start is to download the archive of the Mbone mailing list. It is located at:

ftp://venera.isi.edu/mbone/mbone.mail

Part
III

Ch
21

The archive currently holds messages back to January 1996. If searching this archive doesn't answer your questions, you can join the mailing list and post questions yourself. To join the Mbone mailing list, send an email message to the following address:

```
majordomo@zephyr.isi.edu
```

Add the following line to the text (not to the Subject line):

```
    subscribe mbone-na
```

This subscribes you to the Mbone Mailing list.

Getting a Connection to the Mbone   If you are using a network from a small business, school, or other organization that is not a network provider, you should begin by contacting your ISP. Most major ISPs will already have a connection to the Mbone that you can tap into. Technical support can probably give you the IP addresses and other information you need to connect.

If your ISP doesn't have an Mbone connection, there is probably a business or college in your area that will let you hook into the Mbone through them. A popular method of finding someone who will let you connect to his or her Mbone router is to post a message to the Mbone mailing list. In the message, tell the person who you are and why you want the connection. Chances are you will find someone to help.

If you are a network provider, you should directly contact the Mbone mailing list for the country or region you are in. The following is a list of addresses from the Mbone FAQ that you can use to post a request for a connection to top-level connections to the Mbone:

- Australia   `mbone-oz-request@internode.com.au`
- Austria   `mbone-at-request@noc.aco.net`
- Canada   `canet-mbone-request@canet.ca`
- Denmark   `mbone-request@daimi.aau.dk`
- France   `mbone-fr-request@inria.fr`
- Germany   `mbone-de-request@informatik.uni-erlangen.de`
- Italy   `mbone-it-request@nis.garr.it`
- Japan   `mbone-jp-request@wide.ad.jp`
- Korea   `mbone-korea-request@cosmos.kaist.ac.kr`
- Netherlands   `mbone-nl-request@nic.surfnet.nl`
- New Zealand   `mbone-nz-request@waikato.ac.nz`
- Singapore   `mbone-sg-request@technet.sg`
- UK   `mbone-uk-request@cs.ucl.ac.uk`
- Europe   `mbone-eu-request@sics.se`
- N. America   `mbone-na-request@isi.edu`
- Other   `mbone-request@isi.edu`

The information you receive from the Mbone request will help you coordinate your connection to an Mbone tunnel.

Setting Up the Mbone Connection   The one piece of equipment you must have to connect to the Mbone is a machine to do routing. For computers using UNIX, Mbone routing can be done by the `mrouted` utility. The following UNIX (or UNIX-like) platforms can be used to provide Mbone routing:

- AIX
- DEC Alpha/OSF1
- HP/UX
- i386 BSDI
- FreeBSD
- Linux
- NetBSD
- SGI/Irix
- Solaris (SPARC)
- Solaris (x86)
- SunOS 4.1.x

Some of these operating systems have multicast support built in (such as NetBSD and BSDI). Other UNIX systems may require kernel updates and additional utilities to do multicast routing.

Using Mbone Utilities with UNIX

Although the Mbone protocols might someday provide the foundation for broadcasting entertainment on the Internet (much as cable television does today), most of the tools available now are most suitable for business and education. There are utilities for doing videoconferencing, audio communications, and white boards. There are also, of course, many tools for monitoring and managing the Mbone.

The most extensive archive of Mbone software available can be found at the Mbone Software Archive from Merit Network (`http://nis.nsf.net/~mbone/index/titles.html`). If you are working with a particular operating system, click on Index of Binaries by Platform and then select the platform you are using.

The following text describes some of the most popular multicast utilities available for UNIX today.

Multicast Routing Utilities   A variety of tools are available for setting up multicast routing, monitoring traffic, and debugging problems. Here are descriptions of some of those utilities:

- `mrouted`   Manages routing for multicast networks (such as the Mbone). The routing protocol it implements is Distance-Vector Multicast Routing Protocol (DVMRP). It works in cooperation with other `mrouted` routers, supporting tunnels when necessary to

Part

III

Ch

21

transmit packets across unicast routers. Multicast interfaces can be defined in the /etc/mrouted.conf file (indicated by the IFF_MULTICAST flag being set).

■ mrinfo   Displays configuration information about a multicast router. If available, the following information is displayed: router's version number, addresses of neighboring multicast routers, routing metrics, thresholds, and flags.

■ mtrace   Displays information about the path from a multicast source to a multicast receiver. This utility can be used to debug connection problems by showing each hop along the transmission, each hop's address, packets transmitted, and any errors encountered.

■ map-mbone   Displays multicast routers that can be reached from the selected router (by default, the local host is the starting point). Like mrinfo, map-mbone shows multicast router version numbers, neighboring multicast router addresses, and metrics, thresholds, and flags (if that information is available).

Multicast Announcement Utilities   Interactive tools for viewing and starting multicast sessions on the Mbone are the best way to find and connect to sessions. The most popular tool is sdr (Session Directory), which obsoletes the sd command. The following are descriptions of sdr, as well as other utilities for working with multicast announcements:

> **CAUTION**
>
> Bandwidth on the Mbone is precious. Don't jam up the worldwide Mbone with frivolous content. Besides not being a nice thing to do, you will probably be bombarded with unhappy email.

■ sdr   Lets you view what Mbone sessions are available, advertise your own session to the Mbone, or make a call to an individual over Mbone. For each session, you can see the type of media the session will use (audio, video, white board, text, and so on), when the session will take place, and the area it reaches. The area can be as small as your local network or as large as the worldwide Mbone.

■ ssd   Provides conference announcements and entry control, while working in tandem with various conference utilities (such as audio, video, and white board utilities). This tool can be integrated with Web browsers.

■ teleport   Provides information about activities of other members of a workgroup. Using this information, you can determine whether members are available for collaboration using multicast collaboration tools (such as vic, vat, and wb).

Multicast Audio Utilities   Tools that can be used for audioconferencing on the Mbone are as follows:

■ fphone   Allows audioconferencing that can support multiple unicast and multicast conversations. This tool was developed by members of the High-Speed Networking group at INRIA. It is compatible with the vat and rat commands.

■ nevot   The Network Voice Terminal supports audioconferencing over the Mbone. It is supported on several different platforms, including HP/UX, SGI Irix, Solaris, and SunOS.

- `vat` Allows multihost audioconferencing over the Mbone. It is compatible with a variety of utilities, including `fphone`. It runs on most UNIX systems, and there is even a port that works on Windows 95.

Multicast Video Utilities   Multicasting is needed to turn a one-way video stream into a multiperson conference. Several tools can be used to do multicast video over the Mbone:

- `ivs` The INRIA Videoconferencing System (`ivs`) lets you use UNIX workstations to send multicast audio and video over the Mbone. Most of the compression techniques used (called codecs) are done by the software, so very little extra hardware is needed. Versions of `ivs` run on SGI Irix, Solaris, and SunOS.

- `nv` With `nv`, you can send and receive slow frame rate video. The `nv` utility operates over UDP/IP protocols, but you can also multicast the transmission. Most `nv` features can be handled better by `vic`. However, `nv` uses X Window technology that allows `nv` to send video of a user's screen.

- `vic` The `vic` utility is probably the most flexible video utility available for multicasting from UNIX systems. It can be configured to run effectively on low-bandwidth as well as high-bandwidth networks. To provide real-time support, `vic` incorporates the Real-time Transport Protocol (RTP), version 2.

Multicast Text and White Board Utilities   The most basic type of multicast communications allows users to type words to be transmitted to a group of users. White board utilities let users transmit pictures and drawings (just as they would on a white board in a conference room). The following are descriptions of utilities that can be used to transmit text and drawings over the Mbone:

- `mumble` Allows text-based conversations to take place over the Mbone. It runs on the following UNIX versions: Linux, SGI Irix, Solaris, and SunOS.

- `nt` Lets multiple users share a text editor over the Mbone.

- `wb` Allows users on the Mbone to share a white board surface to draw words and pictures. Within `wb`, you can also export, view, and change PostScript files.

Internet Protocol Next Generation (Version 6)

Along with the huge growth of the Internet have come some problems that were not foreseen by its architects. TCP/IP was originally designed to provide addresses for a limited number of subnetworks and large computers, not the millions of PCs and, eventually, mobile and handheld devices that are competing for addresses. Likewise, demands on IP routing and increased security concerns have also increased with the Internet's growth.

To deal with the issues of the evolving Internet, the Internet Engineering Task Force (IETF) began the Internet Protocol Next Generation (IPng) effort. The most recent version of this effort is referred to as Internet Protocol Version 6 (Ipv6).

Part

III

Ch

21

What Is IPng?

The IPng is the effort undertaken by the architects of the Internet to make improvements for the Internet of tomorrow, without interrupting the flow of today's Internet. The task is like what a growing city must do to upgrade its highway system, while making sure that everyone can still get to work in the morning.

In evaluating how to create new versions of the Internet, the IETF takes into account not only what problems need to be fixed with the Internet today but also where it is going tomorrow. The changes would take the current Internet version (IPv4) and evolve it (rather than totally overhaul it) into the new version (IPv6).

By far, the most important issue needing to be addressed in IPv6 is Internet growth. Not only will more IP addresses be needed to meet demands, but those items needing addresses will become more mobile and potentially much more numerous than computers (such as pagers and cellular phones). To meet those demands, Internet protocols to handle those devices would need to be simpler and be prepared to deal with mobile clients.

The Main Features of IPv6

The direction of IPv6 sets the Internet on a course to become more like a massive, information infrastructure than just a computer network. The protocols that make up the core of IPv6 became public on September 18, 1995, with the IETF Proposed Standard. The IPv6 features were specified in RFC-1883 "Internet Protocol, Version 6 (IPv6) Specification."

Other RFCs define different aspects of IPv6. RFC 2373 covers "IP Version 6 Addressing Architecture." Methods for transitioning to the new routing methods are covered in RFC 2185, "Routing Aspects Of IPv6 Transition," and RFC 1933, "Transition Mechanisms for IPv6 Hosts and Routers."

Some of the major feature changes between IPv6 and IPv4 are as follows:

- Expanded addressing   IP addresses are now larger and represent a more complex and flexible hierarchy of addresses.

- Quality of service   New flow labeling allows the sender to ask for special handling of packets or to let packets belong to a selected traffic flow. This allows improvements in quality of service.

- Authentication and privacy features   New extensions were added to improve the integrity and confidentiality of data.

The following sections describe some of the new IPv6 features in detail.

Expanded Addressing   The existing IPv4 IP addresses are represented by 32 bits; the new IPv6 addresses use 128 bits. This new address size is expected to create an address space that would allow thousands of unique addresses for every person in the world. Not only does this structure allow for more addresses, but it also allows for different types of addresses.

Instead of identifying a node on a network, the new 32-bit addresses point to an interface, associated with a particular node. There are three types of addresses, each representing a different type of interface:

- Unicast   An address of this type point to a single interface on a particular network node.
- Anycast   This type of address identifies a set of interfaces. With an Anycast address, the packet may be sent to one of many different nodes that falls into that set of interfaces. In this way, a packet can go to the node nearest the sender that can fulfill the requirement.
- Multicast   This address type also identifies a set of interfaces. However, in this case, the packet is delivered to all interfaces associated with the address. This type of address would be used for such things as live audio or video broadcasts that require a single flow of data be directed to many clients.

N O T E   No broadcast addresses are set aside in the new address scheme. Therefore, it is legal for a field to contain all zeros or all ones. An address of all zeros or all ones on a subnetwork was previously reserved as a broadcast address.

You can represent the new 128-bit addresses as eight 16-bit numbers, separated by colons. For example, a new address might look like the following:

```
1080:0:0:0:1080:800:100C:319A
```

There are other ways in which this new 128-bit address can be expressed. One method is to show one or more zeros in address fields by simply showing two colons together. For example, the address 0:0:0:0:1080:800:100C:319A could be expressed as follows:

```
::1080:800:100C:319A
```

The high-order octet distinguishes between the different address types. A multicast address begins with the value FF (11111111). Any other address can be either unicast or anycast (no distinction is made between unicast and anycast types of addresses).

Of the available address space, only 15 percent is currently defined. The other 85 percent is reserved for future use. With this address structure in place, new address types can be added easily in the future, and practically an unlimited number of devices can come online.

Quality of Service   Each IPv6 header contains a 24-bit flow label field. Using this field, the packet can include a request that the packet be assigned to a specific flow of data by the IPv6 router. By requesting a specific data flow, a transmission can get a higher quality of service than the average transmission might receive.

A 4-bit priority field lets the source of the flow identify a traffic class for the flow. Priorities 0 through 7 identify traffic priority that can wait in cases of congestion. Priority values of 8 through 15 are used for flows that require a constant rate of delivery.

Delivery of content such as email or netnews would fall into the first category, whereas audio and video traffic would fall into the second category. In this way, traffic that requires delivery without interruption to be effective (such as audio) can be assured of a higher priority in reaching its destination.

Part
III

Ch
21

▶ For information on how routing is currently done on the Internet **see** "An Overview of Routing Protocols," **p. 513**

Authentication and Privacy As online commerce continues to grow on the Internet, security measures to make commercial transactions safe have received high priority. Two security features from IPv4 for authenticating packets and ensuring confidentiality of the information they hold have been made mandatory in IPv6. Those features are the authentication header and encapsulated security payload, respectively.

The *authentication header* is used to provide security between two points on a network (such as two hosts, two gateways, or a host and a gateway). Data in the authentication header can be used to ensure that the network node you are communicating with is who it says it is. This method is quite flexible allowing, for example, an organization to employ authentication from its gateway to outside, untrusted hosts, while not requiring authentication among the trusted hosts on its own local network. Both host and gateway, in this arrangement, must support authentication for communication to occur.

The way the authentication head works is that before sending an IP packet, the sender computes the authentication contents using a secret authentication key. The receiver verifies the authentication data when it receives the packet. By default, MD5 encryption algorithm is used to encrypt the authentication data. (Other algorithms can also be used.)

Although the authentication header can verify the identity of two communicating peers, it does not ensure the integrity or confidentiality of the data being communicated. Those features are implemented using the *encapsulating security payload* (ESP).

To protect the integrity of data being sent across the network, ESP does what its name implies: It encapsulates the data. Encapsulation can be done on just the upper layer protocol (referred to as Transport Mode) or of the whole IP datagram (referred to as Tunnel Mode). The contents of the datagram are encrypted and a cleartext header is added to the new datagram.

Impact of IPv6 on UNIX Systems

Despite being several years in development, the IPv6 standard is still far from worldwide implementation. Though it is designed to be implemented in stages (that is, without the entire Internet changing simultaneously to IPv6), it is still only in the prototype arena. There are several reasons why IPv6 may take awhile to catch on.

IPv4 IP addresses have not run out yet. Some believe they will not run out for several years (especially with stop-gap methods to conserve numbers), whereas others believe the coming onslaught of Internet-ready devices will cause addresses to run out much sooner. In the meantime, however, no authority is assigning IPv6 addresses, so they couldn't be used yet in a production environment.

Networks that can achieve the greatest benefit from IPv6 implementation are those that need the expanded address capability and/or support for special quality of service features. If a network doesn't require those features, you might not want to incur the overhead that comes with authenticating hosts, encrypting data, and using other IPv6 features.

If your company or organization can benefit from those features, there are several UNIX implementations of IPv6 you can try out today. You might even feel better knowing that you are not alone. If you want, you can connect up to an experimental IPv6 network that is in use today called the 6Bone. (See the note below for further details.)

> **N O T E** The 6Bone is an IPv6 backbone, created independently of the IETF IPv6 standards effort. This backbone is supported by a number of organizations (ISPs, networking products vendors, and so on) in North America, Europe, and Asia that needed a way to develop and test IPv6 products, as well as a means of developing operational procedures for managing IPv6 networks.
>
> According to the 6Bone workgroup charter (available at `http://www.6bone.net/6bone_IETF_charter.html`), the 6Bone is a global Internet "testbed" of IPv6 transport and routing to help do the following:
>
> - Create "practice and experience" informational RFC documents from those creating and using IPv6 technologies.
> - Provide feedback to help IETF IPv6-related activities.
> - Develop procedures to help transition to native IPv6.
> - Develop ways to share information to aid in operation of global IPv6 routing.
>
> If you want to join 6Bone, the 6Bone workgroup recommends you first subscribe to the 6Bone mailer. (Place the words `subscribe 6bone` in an email message to `majordomo@isi.edu`.) The workgroup suggests you have at least one host and router dedicated to using IPv6. Information for choosing equipment and setting up your hosts and routers is available from the 6Bone site (`http://www.6bone.net`).

IPv6 for Solaris   A prototype release of the IPv6 for Solaris product is available for "evaluation and experimentation" purposes. To run it, you need either Solaris 2.5 or 2.5.1.

Protocol changes to the IP layer for IPv6 for Solaris are pervasive. They include support for unicast and multicast addresses, IPv6 address resolution, TCP/IP and UDP over IPv6, IPv6 fragmentation and reassembly, and IPv6 packet forwarding. It also supports IPv6 over IPv4 automatic and configured tunneling, to provide a means of transition between the two protocols.

At the user and administration levels, most TCP/IP commands and procedures have been changed to accommodate IPv6. New address and protocol changes have resulted in updated `finger`, `getent`, `inetd`, `telnet`, `ftp`, `tftp`, `rlogin`, `rsh`, `rcp`, `rdist`, and `sendmail` commands and daemons. DNS services and lookup procedures have also been updated.

You can read about and download IPv6 for Solaris from the IPv6 for Solaris Web page (`http://playground.sun.com/pub/solaris2-ipv6/html/solaris2-ipv6.html`). Versions are available for Sparc and x86 systems.

IPv6 APIs Support in SCO UnixWare   UnixWare 7 has created a set of IPv6 application programming interfaces (APIs) to allow developers to write applications that work in IPv4 and

Part
III

Ch
21

IPv6 environments. According to SCO, applications developed using these APIs can be used in both IPv4 and IPv6 environments without requiring any changes. The IPv6 APIs include new data structures and functions that the developer must use when writing network applications.

N O T E The first set of IPv6 APIs that come with UnixWare is not accompanied by an IPv6 protocol stack.

IPv6 in AIX 4.3   Support for IPv6 in AIX version 4.3 focuses on providing a smooth migration for network applications to IPv6, while still allowing existing IPv4 applications to run without problems. In the first IPv6-compatible release, basic TCP/IP applications such as telnet, ftp, rlogin, mail, and others will all be upgraded for IPv6.

Special attention has been paid to IPv6 security, with support for IPsec implemented in AIX version 4.3. Authentication headers and encapsulated security payloads are supported to provide security services to ensure the authentication of hosts and to improve security of data.

AIX 4.3 also supports secure IP tunneling between two systems. Supported tunnel modes include IPv6 over IPv4 and automatic tunneling to IPv4 compatible addresses. IPsec security procedures support includes the following: Message Digest 5 (MD5), Hashed Message Authentication Coded (HMAC), Data Encryption Standard (DES), and Commercial Data Masking Facility (CDMF).

AIX 4.3 does not include IP forwarding. It also does not yet support some advanced TCP/IP services including the following: NFS, routeD, DFS, DHCP, NTP, and others.

To find out more about IPv6 features in AIX 4.3, see the new features section of the AIX 4.3 Migration Guide (http://www.developer.ibm.com/library/aix4.3/43.html).

Digital UNIX AlphaServer with IPv6   The Digital UNIX IPv6 AlphaServer contains a full range of IPv6 services. This product runs on the 64-bit Digital UNIX (version 4). Besides supporting many of the host features of IPv6, Digital UNIX IPv6 also supports routing features (such as packet forwarding and RIPv6).

With this product, you can run IPv6 versions of many of the TCP/IP features you would expect to find in UNIX. Currently, it supports X Windows, FTP, Telnet, DNS (server and resolver), and many Web server and browser features. AltaVista search engine has also been upgraded to IPv6, along with a variety of networking testing utilities that have been made IPv6-compatible.

Along with the Digital UNIX IPv6 AlphaServer, Digital offers a free connection to the 6Bone. Digital also offers the support you need to get the 6Bone connection up and running.

For more information on Digital's IPv6 efforts, visit the Digital IPv6 InfoCenter at http://www.digital.com/info/ipv6. There you can find IPv6 information on Digital products, white papers, technical articles, and training support. There are also links to sites with information about 6Bone, IETF, and IPng.

Dedicated IPv6 Routers   For more advanced IPv6 routing features than are available today in UNIX systems, you will probably want to get a dedicated router that supports IPv6. Following is a list of companies that have router implementations of IPv6 and some Web sites where you can get more information:

- 3Com Corporation (`http://www.3com.com/nsc/ipv6.html`)
- Bay Networks (`http://www.baynetworks.com/products/Routers/Protocols/2789.html`)
- Cisco Systems (`http://www.cisco.com/warp/public/732/ipv6/index.html`)
- Nokia (`http://www.iprg.nokia.com/ipv6/`)

From Here...

UNIX systems continue to be the platform of choice for advances in computer networking that drive the future of the Internet. Full implementations of TCP/IP standards allow such things as point-to-point communications (with the PPP protocol) and tools such as firewalls and proxy servers for configuring secure networks.

A full set of UNIX utilities is available to use with the experimental Mbone network as it is being employed to develop multicast audio and video tools and protocols. Most UNIX systems offer platforms that can be integrated with the 6Bone experimental network as well, as that network is being used to develop the next generation of Internet protocols and procedures.

- Chapter 17, "Networking Essentials," provides a general description of UNIX networking features.
- Chapter 19, "Configuring TCP/IP," provides information on how addressing is done today on the Internet.
- Chapter 20, "IP Routing," includes information on how messages are currently routed on the Internet.
- Chapter 23, "DNS," contains descriptions of the Domain Name System, along with procedures for setting up DNS on a UNIX system.

Network Services

## CHAPTER 22

NFS

by Terry W. Ogiltree

In this chapter

Introduction to Distributed File Systems

Perhaps the most useful feature of a networked computer system from a user's point of view is the capability to access data that resides on a computer other than the one the user is logged in to. Distributed computing has many advantages over the old centralized model that was in use for so long. When your entire user base is situated on a single computer with all the data and programs your business needs to operate, you have a single point of failure. If the system goes down, no work gets done. By dividing up your users and data and grouping them on computers by function, you can minimize the possibility of putting many people out of work in the event of a single system failure.

Still, it can be difficult to draw a line between user functions. Some users do not fit neatly into a particular category and need to access files on another computer. Early in the development of the TCP/IP protocol suite and the various utilities closely related to it, this capability was provided by using FTP, File Transfer Protocol. FTP allows a user to copy a file from a remote computer to his own so that manipulation of the data can be done locally.

Although FTP may appear at first to solve the problem of remote data access, it has a few drawbacks. If more than one user regularly accesses the same file or files to make changes, coordinating these changes can become unwieldy as the number of users increases. For example, if the user forgets to copy the file back to its original location after making changes, then the next user who makes a copy of the file finds herself working on a file that does not contain these changes. In a busy environment, the possibility of this happening is high. If the file is large, the time spent uploading and downloading the file can become a limiting factor when many users need to modify the same file.

Other TCP/IP utilities can also be used for remote file access. For example, a user can use telnet to establish a remote login and then issue commands to the remote computer to manipulate the data. However, this relegates the user's desktop workstation, usually a powerful machine, to the role of dumb terminal. Applications that are used to access or change data in files on the remote computer must also reside on the remote computer.

Sun Microsystems developed NFS, the Network File System, to address these problems. Instead of copying a file to the local computer or workstation, NFS allows a user to access a remote file system while making it appear to be a local file system to the user. Ideally, the access time should be around 80 percent that of accessing a local file system. Compared to the time spent copying files back and forth, this is an acceptable limitation. By making the remote file system function like a local file system, no application program changes are needed.

▶ **See** "Files, Directories, and Permissions," **p. 111**

The NFS Environment

Although NFS is usually thought of as an application, it consists of several different protocols that perform specific functions. Sun Microsystems has published the specifications for NFS so that other vendors can easily implement these protocols to allow for remote mounting of file systems independent of the operating system of the computers. The most widely used version of NFS (version 2) is based on RFC 1094. Version 3 of NFS, as documented in RFC 1813, adds better support for wide area networking. At this time, Sun is working on Public NFS, with a goal of making NFS easier to use in an Internet environment. Most of this chapter deals with version 2 because it is the most widely used.

ON THE WEB

You can get more details about NFS and the Public NFS project at Sun's Web site:

`http://www.sun.com/solaris/networking/pubnfs.html`

ON THE WEB

Requests for Comments (RFCs) are a method used to disseminate information about technologies related to networking and the Internet. Reading RFCs can give you much more detail about a specific protocol or technology than can be covered in the scope of this book. A good Web site you can visit to obtain copies of many important RFCs and pointers to other Web sites that deal with RFC related material is:

`http://www.cisco.com/warp/public/459/3.html`

Other buzzwords you hear in relation to NFS are RPC (Remote Procedure Call) and XDR (eXternal Data Representation). NFS is implemented by using routines made up of remote procedure calls. XDR is used as the data format so that data from different systems can be represented in a common format for interchange.

In addition, the Mount protocol is used to make the initial connection to a remote file system.

The Remote Procedure Call (RPC) Protocol

The RPC protocol describes a client/server technology. In its simplest form, a *client* (such as an application on a workstation) formats a request and then transfers control to the *server* to take an action based on that data. The server does the necessary processing and returns the data, and control of the procedure, to the client. RPC was developed by Sun for use in NFS, but it has since been used for many other client/server based products.

The daemon responsible for RPC is called rpcbind, and it runs on both the client and the server side of the process.

RPC procedures can be grouped together into programs, which can be grouped together to form a *service*. A service is identified by a unique number, so that more than one service can operate at any given time. When an application needs to make use of a service, it can use the different programs that make up the service to perform specific actions. For example, when designing an NFS service, one program may be responsible for determining a file's attributes, whereas another program can be responsible for the actual transfer of data between the client and server computers.

As just stated, a unique service number is used to identify different network services that run on a particular system. The file /etc/rpc is usually used to define the number-to-service mapping. You don't just make up numbers in this file—if you did, your computer would not be compatible with other computers when using services. Instead, the RFC for RPC defines the numbers used for many common services, as shown in Table 22.1.

Table 22.1   Numbers Used to Identify RPC Services

Unique Service Number	Name of Service
100000	portmapper
100001	rstat_svc
100002	rusersd
100003	nfs
100004	ypserv
100005	mountd
100007	ypbind
100008	walld
100009	yppasswdd
100010	etherstatd
100011	rquotad
100012	sprayd
100013	3270_mapper
100014	rje_mapper
100015	selection_svc
100016	database_svc
100017	rexd
100018	alis
100019	sched
100020	llockmgr
100021	nlockmgr
100022	x25.inr
100023	statmon
100024	status

Unique Service Number	Name of Service
100026	bootparam
100028	ypupdated
100029	keyserv
100069	ypxfrd
150001	pcnfsd

One of the more important services shown in Table 22.1 is the portmapper service. When a client and server communicate, a *port* number is used to identify the connection. You might think that the connection could be defined by the network addresses the client and server are using. That would be fine, if only one connection were necessary. However, in most practical uses, two computers communicating across a network are not using a single simple connection. Instead, many different functions are being performed by different services, hence the need for port numbers to identify each connection uniquely. The portmapper service (which uses port 111 for UDP and TCP) manages these services and port number assignments so that each service can communicate with its client computer without confusing itself with messages destined for another service.

N O T E   Don't get confused with port numbers and the numbers assigned to services. Service numbers are used to identify a particular RPC service. Port numbers identify connections between two computers that use a service. ■

UDP or TCP?

Many critics mistakenly believe that NFS relies solely on UDP for communications, therefore making it unreliable and a little more difficult to implement in code. If UDP won't check to find out whether a packet it sent to a server was ever received, then it is up to the application to make such a check. UDP just provides the transport.

TROUBLESHOOTING

You have a client and server on different networks, and the client cannot mount any of the file systems being exported by the NFS server. Check to see whether you have used the UDP or the TCP protocol for the NFS server by examining the inetd.conf file. Remember that if you are using UDP, then you might need to configure your router to be sure that it is correctly passing the UDP traffic between networks.

TCP, however, can be used for a more reliable connection, in which case the TCP layer takes care of acknowledging packets sent or received, relieving the application of this burden. TCP is a connection-based protocol that guarantees delivery of packets of data. TCP uses a system of acknowledgments that confirm the arrival of a data packet sent to a remote machine. Lost packets are retransmitted when an acknowledgment fails to arrive on time. It does get a little more complicated than that, because a one-to-one acknowledgment scheme would use a lot of network bandwidth. TCP can use a technique that acknowledges multiple packets with a single acknowledgment to speed up things.

N O T E   Using TCP as a transport for NFS is gaining in popularity. One of the main reasons for this is that you can use it to allow for file sharing between different operating system platforms. When choosing a network protocol to connect dissimilar computer platforms, TCP/IP seems to be the common protocol suite that is offered by most vendors.

▶ **See** "Networking Essentials," **p. 421**

Using XDR to Exchange Data

To exchange data between two computer systems running different operating systems, you must have a common format to represent the data. You might think that just using the ASCII character set and 8-bit bytes would be all that is required. However, even among machines that use an 8-bit format, you will find that some use a format referred to as little-endian, with the least significant bit in the byte being the first bit. Others use a big-endian format, which is just the opposite. It gets even more complicated when you consider the format used to represent numeric data. When using a multiple-byte value to represent a floating point number, for example, you need to know which bits are used for the exponent and which are used for the mantissa.

The External Data Representation (XDR) standard is used by NFS. You can find the details of this standard by reading RFC 1014. XDR is a C-like notation for representing data. XDR isn't a programming language itself but only a method of describing the format used to store data. Any particular item, character or numeric value, is usually represented in XDR by using four bytes (32-bits), and XDR considers the lower bytes to be the most significant.

Signed integers are stored using two's complement notation and range in value from –2147483648 to +2147483647. Unsigned integers can range from zero to 4294967295. Hyper integers and unsigned hyper integers are 8 bytes (64 bits) in size and can be used to represent larger integers. Floating point formats are also defined, as are the enum type (familiar to C programmers) and a boolean type. Structures, arrays, constants and many other data types are also defined.

When you consider that NFS and RPC are designed to be implemented on almost any kind of computer hardware or software architecture, using an extensible data description format such as XDR makes the process much easier.

The NFS Protocol and the Mount Protocol

The NFS protocol is not a protocol like TCP or UDP. It doesn't define how two computers handshake when establishing a communications session. Instead, NFS is a defined set of procedures (called *primitives*) that are executed via RPC to allow an action to be performed on a remote computer. It is also a *stateless* protocol. This means that the server does not have to maintain information about the state of each client. If the server fails (or the network fails), the client needs only to repeat the operation. The server doesn't have to rebuild any data tables or other structures to recover the "state" of a client after a failure. By constructing NFS to operate in a stateless manner, the protocol is greatly simplified.

It is important to note that certain operations, such as file or record locking, do require a *stateful* protocol of some sort. Implementations of NFS accomplish this by using another protocol to handle the specific function. NFS itself is composed of a set of procedures that deal with file access.

When traversing a directory tree, NFS bores down through the hierarchy one level at a time. This is because the representation of pathnames varies widely among different operating systems. For example, a UNIX file system begins with a root directory (\) and uses the slash character to separate each directory component from another. Digital's OpenVMS concatenates directories by using a period as a separator and encloses the entire path in square brackets ([]). One solution to this problem would be to define a standard pathname convention, similar to using XDR to represent data, but this would require translating the pathname at both ends of the connection, adding more complexity to the protocol.

The RPC procedures that make up the NFS protocol are as follows:

- Null   This is the "do nothing" routine. It is provided in all RPC services and allows the server to perform testing and timing operations.
- Get File Attributes   Used to get the file attributes of a file on a remote system.
- Set File Attributes   Used to set the file attributes of a file on the remote server.
- Get File System Root   This procedure is no longer used. Instead, the mount protocol performs this function.
- Look Up a Filename   This procedure returns the file handle for a file.
- Read from Symbolic Link   This returns information about symbolic links to a file on the remote server.
- Read from File   Use this procedure to read data from a file on a remote system.
- Write to Cache   This procedure is not used in version 2. It will be used in version 3.
- Write to File   This procedure is used to write data to a file on a remote server.
- Create File   Use this to create a file on the remote server.
- Remove File   This procedure is used to delete a file on the remote server.
- Rename File   This procedure renames a file on the remote server.
- Create Link to File   Creates a hard link (in the same file system) to a file.
- Create Symbolic Link   This procedure creates a symbolic link (can be used to link a file across file systems). A symbolic link is a pointer to a file.
- Create Directory   Use this procedure to create a directory on the remote server.

- Remove Directory   Deletes a directory (which should contain no files) on the remote server.
- Read from Directory   This procedure gets a list of files from a directory on the server.
- Get File System Attributes   This procedure returns information about the file system on the remote server, such as the total size and available free space.

One thing you will quickly notice is that there is no provision in these procedures to open or close a file. Because NFS is a stateless protocol, it doesn't handle file opens or closes. Instead, the Mount protocol performs this function and returns a file handle to NFS. The mountd daemon runs on both the client and server computer and maintains a list of current connections. When a client unexpectedly crashes, this could cause a problem when it reboots. Most implementations of NFS take care of this by having the client send a message to the NFS server when it boots telling it to unmount all its connections with this client, allowing it to start again from scratch.

The Mount protocol consists of only a few procedures compared to the NFS protocol:

- Null   This is the "do nothing" procedure just like the one listed under the NFS protocol.
- MNT   This procedure mounts a file system and returns to the client a file handle and the name of the remote file system.
- UNMT   This is the opposite of the MNT procedure. It unmounts a file system and removes from its table the reference to it.
- UMNTALL   Similar to the UNMT procedure, but this one unmounts all remote file systems being used by the NFS client.
- EXPORT   Returns a listing of exported file systems.
- DUMP   Returns a list of file systems on a server that are currently mounted by a client.

▶ **See** "RFCs," **p. 725**

What Is *automount*?   NFS only uses the Mount protocol when it initially makes a connection from a client to an NFS server. After that, the mountd daemon keeps track of client/server connections. You will find that some newer versions of NFS allow for a daemon called automount to run. automount can be useful in that it doesn't keep a connection open for an extended period of time. Instead, a remote file system is only "mounted" when it needs to be accessed by a client. An automount map is used to keep track of directories serviced by the daemon.

Using the automount daemon can also help prevent problems that can arise when using remote file systems. For example, if a client has made a "hard" mount to a remote file system and it becomes unavailable, the client process can freeze up. If the automount daemon is used instead, this does not happen.

NFS Clients

For a client computer to access a remote file system using NFS, the client must have RPC server daemon running. Depending on the particular NFS you are using, UDP and TCP also are required.

The `biod` daemon is used on the client system to communicate with the remote NFS server and process the data transferred between the two.

Users can mount a file system offered by an NFS server, provided they are not prevented from mounting the file system by the server, by using the `mount` command.

Client Daemons

On the client side of the NFS process three daemon processes are used. The first is called `biod`, which stands for block input/output daemon. This process is responsible for performing the input/output with the NFS server on behalf of the user accessing the remote file system.

If you are going to make more than moderate use of NFS on your client computer, you might want to start up more than one `biod` process. The syntax used to start a `biod` daemon is as follows:

```
/etc/biod [number of daemon processes]
```

You will normally find that the daemon is started in the `/etc/rc.local` startup file. Modify this file if you want to change the number of daemons running on your system.

N O T E   Don't simply decide to start a lot of `biod` daemons at boot time thinking you are going to improve performance. The daemon process, like any other process running on the system, uses up system resources, especially memory. Start out with one or two daemons if you are using a workstation dedicated to one user. If you are on a computer that has multiple users who access NFS as a client, test your performance by increasing the number of daemons until NFS performance is satisfactory, without sacrificing overall system performance.

By starting more than one daemon, your system can process multiple NFS requests in parallel. However, note that many times the network is a bottleneck when accessing files remotely, and increasing the number of `biod` daemons does nothing to improve the performance of the network.

The `biod` daemon is a client process. You should not run it on an NFS server unless that server is also a client of another NFS server. ▨

In addition to the `biod` daemon, the `lockd` and `statd` daemons also run on the client. For more information on these, see Server Daemons, elsewhere in this chapter.

Mounting Remote File Systems

You can use the `mount` command to mount a local file system, and you can also use the command to mount a remote NFS file system. The syntax for using `mount` to mount a file system being exported by an NFS server follows:

```
mount -F nfs -o options machine:filesystem mountpoint
```

TIP In some versions of UNIX, the syntax for mounting a remote NFS file system is a little different. For example, in SCO UNIX, you use a lowercase "f" and an uppercase NFS:

```
mount -f NFS -o options machine:filesystem mountpoint
```

In BSD UNIX, you even find a command called `mountnfs`, which uses the system call `mount` to perform most of its functions. This version of the `mount` command comes with many additional parameters, including the capability to specify on the `mount` command line whether to use UPD or TCP as the underlying transport mechanism.

Be sure to check the man page for the `mount` command on your system to get the correct syntax.

In the string you supply for *machine:filesystem*, substitute the hostname of the remote server that is exporting the file system you want to mount for *machine*. Substitute the name of the file system for *filesystem*. For example:

```
mount -F nfs -o ro zeta:usr/public/docs /usr/docs
```

causes the remote file system on host zeta, called `/usr/public/docs`, to be made accessible in the local file system hierarchy at the `/usr/docs` directory. This is just like you mount other local file systems into the local hierarchy. Underneath the `/usr/docs` directory, you can access any other subdirectories that exist on host zeta under the `/usr/public/docs` directory.

You can use the `-o` parameter to specify options for the `mount` command. In the preceding example, the `ro` option was used to make the remote file system read-only when accessed by users on the local computer. Some of the more useful options are as follows:

- `rw` This mounts the file system for local read-write access, which is the default.
- `ro` This mounts the file system for local read-only access.
- `suid` Allows `setuid` execution.
- `nosuid` Disallows `setuid` execution.
- `timeo=x` Use this option to supply a timeout value (specified in tenths of a second). The mount command fails if it cannot mount the remote file system within this time frame.
- `retry=x` The `mount` command attempts to mount the remote file system *x* number of times (each attempt lasting for the length of time specified by the `timeo` parameter).
- `soft` This parameter causes an error to be returned if the mount is unsuccessful. This is the opposite of the `hard` option.
- `hard` This parameter causes the mount attempt to continue until it succeeds. This is the opposite of the `soft` option.

For more command-line parameters and options, see the man page for the `mount` command for your particular system.

Part

IV

Ch

22

> **CAUTION**
>
> Although a computer can be either an NFS server or an NFS client, or perhaps both a server and a client, it should be obvious that you should not try to mount an exported file system on the same server that is exporting it. This would lead to a looping condition that could cause unpredictable problems.

In the `mount` command, *mountpoint* is the path to the location in the local file system where the remote NFS file system appears. The directory specified by *mountpoint* must exist before you can issue the `mount` command. If any files exist in the *mountpoint* directory, users will no longer have access to them after a remote filesystem is attached to the directory with the `mount` command. The files are not lost, however. When the remote file system is unmounted, you will again be able to see the files that exist in the *mountpoint* directory.

> **N O T E** If you attempt to mount a remote file system on a mountpoint that is itself a symbolic link, the actual mountpoint becomes the actual directory pointed to by the symbolic link. ▪

Using the *fstab* File

If you want a client computer to mount a remote file system each time it boots and relieve the user of this chore, you can make an entry for each remote file system in the file `/etc/fstab`. This file lists all file systems that are to be mounted by the computer, including local ones. Each entry in this file should be in the following format:

```
filesystem directoryname type options freqency pass
```

TROUBLESHOOTING

After you edit the file `/etc/fstab`, you find out that clients can no longer mount the file systems being exported by the server. Most of the time this is due to mistakes made in the `fstab` file. Always keep a backup copy of any important system configuration file when you are making changes so that you can recover quickly in case of errors. Common errors include listing directory paths for export that do not exist or, on the client side, listing a mountpoint that does not exist. Check to be sure that any options you provide in the `fstab` file are correct for the type of directory you are offering for export.

For a remote file system, such as NFS, the syntax for the first field is `hostname:path`. Hostname is the name of the remote computer host that is exporting the file system, and `path` is the directory path of the exported file system.

The `directoryname` field is used to indicate the path for the mountpoint on the local system where the remote file system will be mounted.

The third field is used to indicate the type of file system. Because the fstab file is used to describe both local and remote file systems to be mounted, and not just NFS systems, it can be one of any of the following values:

- ▓ ufs   This is a typical local UNIX File System.
- ▓ mfs   Memory File System.
- ▓ nfs   Network File System.
- ▓ swap   Indicates a disk partition used for swapping by the virtual memory system.
- ▓ msdos   An MS-DOS compatible file system.
- ▓ cd9660   A CD-ROM file system as defined by ISO 9660.
- ▓ procfs   A file system used to access data about processes.
- ▓ kernfs   A file system used to access kernel parameters.

The fourth field is a comma-delimited list of mounting options for the file system. See the previous section, titled "Mounting Remote File Systems" for options you can use here.

The fifth field is used by the dump command to determine which file systems are to be dumped for backup purposes. Because the client will be importing a file system from a remote server using NFS, this is typically set to zero on the client that is importing the file system. It is assumed that the exporting server will be responsible for backing up its local file systems.

The sixth field, pass, like the frequency field, is usually set to zero. It is used to indicate on which pass the fsck utility is to check the file system. Again, because the client is importing a file system from a remote server, it is assumed that the remote server that exports the file system is responsible for consistency checking for its own local file systems.

> **CAUTION**
>
> The order in which you place entries into /etc/fstab is important. Utilities that use this file process the entries in the order they appear. For example, if you are going to mount a file system at a mountpoint that is on another file system, you must mount the parent file system before you attempt to mount the child file system, or the mountpoint for attaching the child file system will not yet exist when the system attempts to mount it.

Permissions and Options

In Chapter 5, "Files, Directories, and Permissions," you learned about how files and directories can be secured so that only users who need access to the data will be granted it. When accessing a directory across the network using NFS, this can be confusing. Because the administrator on any particular computer can assign UIDs and GIDs as he sees fit, it is important to coordinate these IDs when allowing users to access files from another system. To allow users authenticated access, you should place an entry in the password file on the remote machine for the user who will mount the file system remotely. The user does not have to actually go through the logon process, but the entry must exist in the password file, with an appropriate UID and GID to allow access to files and directories.

▶ **See** "Administering User Accounts and Groups," **p. 233**

Unmounting Remote File Systems

You can remove access to a remote file system from your local file system hierarchy by using the unmount command or by using the unmountall command to unmount all remote file systems that are currently mounted. When using the unmount command, you should specify as a command-line parameter the mountpoint where you mounted the remote file system, not the name of the file system. For example, if you used this command to mount an NFS file system:

```
mount -F nfs -o ro zeta:usr/public/docs /usr/docs
```

then to unmount this file system, you would enter:

```
umount /usr/docs
```

After you have unmounted a remote file system, the directory on which it was mounted reverts to normal use. That is, any files or subdirectories contained in that directory once again are available for use by users.

NFS Servers

A computer can be an NFS server or an NFS client, or it can be used to perform both functions. Because you are actually setting up a file server in the client/server sense, you should choose a computer to use as an NFS server that has the hardware capabilities needed to support your network clients. For example, if you are going to use the NFS server to allow clients to view documentation that gets used only occasionally, then you would not need to use a computer with a fast CPU or SCSI disks subsystems. Conversely, if you are going to export a directory or list of directories that you expect to be heavily accessed by many users, plan your hardware accordingly. In addition to CPU and disk drive capabilities, don't overlook the network interface card (NIC) used to attach the server to the network.

Setting up an NFS server is relatively easy. The administrator notes which directories are to be exported and places entries in the /etc/exports file on the server. The exportfs program, which usually is started at boot time, obtains its information from this file and uses this data to make available your exported directories to other computers (NFS clients).

Server Side Daemons

On the NFS server, the nfsd daemon process handles requests from NFS clients. The nfsd daemon interprets the request and passes it off to the appropriate I/O system to perform the actual functions required. The daemon communicates with the biod daemon (see "Client Daemons" earlier in this chapter), processing its requests and returning data to the requester.

Part
IV

Ch
22

A typical NFS server is set up to serve multiple clients. Just as you should start up multiple biod daemons on the client so that requests can be processed in parallel fashion, you should also set up multiple copies of the nfsd process so that the server can handle client requests in a timely manner.

Starting nfsd daemons is usually done at boot time. The syntax for the command is as follows:

```
/etc/nfsd [number of nfs daemons to start]
```

For example, if you want to start up five copies of the nsfd daemon at boot time, modify your startup scripts to include the command:

```
/etc/nfsd 5
```

> **N O T E** As UNIX systems are implemented using threads, you will find that you might not have to start up multiple copies of the nfsd or biod daemons. Instead, a multithreaded process can handle numerous requests at the same time, by using a separate thread for each operation. Digital UNIX 4.0 is an example of a multithreaded operating system, based on the Mach kernel. If you are running Digital UNIX, you do not need to start multiple copies of the nfsd daemon to improve performance.

In addition to the nfsd daemon, the NFS server also runs the lockd daemon to handle file locking and the statd daemon, which helps coordinate the status of current file locks.

Sharing and Unsharing File Systems

When the system is booted, the exportfs program reads the information in the /etc/exports configuration file (see "Configuration Files" later in this chapter). The exportfs program is usually started by the /sbin/init.d/nfs.server script file, but this may vary, depending on the particular implementation of UNIX you are using. You can also execute the exportfs command after the system has booted to export one or more directories. Indeed, if you make changes to the /etc/exports file while the system is up and running, then you will have to use the exportfs command (with the -a parameter) to make the changes take effect. If you are not sure which directories are currently being exported, you can execute the command with no options, and it will show you a list of directories currently being exported. Use the -a parameter to cause the information in /etc/exports to be reloaded after you make changes.

The syntax for this command varies depending on what actions you want to perform:

```
/usr/sbin/exportfs [-auv]
/usr/sbin/exportfs [-uv] [dir ...]
/usr/sbin/exportfs -i [-o options] [-v] [dir ...]
```

Command-line parameters and options you can use with this command are as follows:

▪ a   As described previously, this causes exportfs to read the /etc/exports file and export all directories it finds entries for in this file. However, if used with the -u parameter it causes all directories to be unexported.

- ■ i You can specify certain options in the /etc/exports file to be associated with each directory to be exported. This parameter tells exportfs to ignore the options you place in this file.

- ■ u This parameter is used to stop exporting a directory (or all directories if used with the -a option).

- ■ v This tells exportfs to operate in "verbose" mode, giving you additional feedback in response to your commands.

The options you can specify after the -o qualifier are the same you use in the /etc/exports file (see "Configuration Files" later in the chapter).

The first form of the syntax allows you to export (-a) or unexport (-u) all directories listed in /etc/exports. This is probably the most often used form because you can specify the other options you need on a per-directory basis in the /etc/exports file. For example:

```
exportfs -a
```

causes all directories listed in /etc/exports to be available for use by remote clients.

```
exportfs -au
```

causes your NFS server to stop sharing all the directories listed for export in the /etc/exports file.

The second form can be used to export or unexport (stop exporting) a particular directory (or directories) instead of all directories. You specify the director(ies) on the command line. You can use this form if you want to stop sharing a particular directory because of system problems or maintenance, for example. Using this syntax:

```
exportfs -u /etc/users/purch
```

causes the NFS server to stop sharing the /etc/user/purch directory with remote users.

The third form can be used to ignore the options you specify in the /etc/exports file so that you can specify them (using the -o parameter) on the command line. You will use this only in special cases, because you can just as easily change the options in the /etc/exports file if the change were a permanent one. If, for example, you want to make an exported directory read-only that is currently set to be read-write, you could use the following command:

```
exportfs -o ro /etc/users/purch
```

CAUTION

It is never a good idea to make changes "on-the-fly" by using the exportfs command online if you intend for the changes to be permanent. Instead, change the configuration file /etc/exports and use the exportfs -a command to make the changes. If you just make the changes online, the odds are that you will forget to place the changes in the file, putting it off until later, and when the system reboots, your changes will be lost. Use the online command to make temporary changes only.

Configuration Files

To make a file system, or a portion of a file system, available for export to other computers on a regular basis, you should add the directories to the `/etc/exports` file. The format for an entry in this file is as follows:

```
directory [-option, …]
```

Of course, *directory* is a pathname for the directory you want to share with (or export to) other systems. The options that you can include are as follows:

- `ro`   The directory is made available to remote users in a read-only mode. If you do not specify this option, the default is read-write, and remote users will be able to change data in files on your system.

- `rw=hostnames`   You can use this option to specify a host or hosts that you want to have read-write access. Any host not included in *hostnames* will have only read access to the file system.

- `anon=uid`   If a request is made to access the exported file system by an unknown client, you can use this parameter to set the UID used for anonymous users.

- `root=hostnames`   Users who have root access on a system listed in *hostnames* can gain root access on the exported file system.

- `access=client`   A client (either hostname or net group name) can have mount access to this file system.

For example:

```
/etc/users/purch -access=acct
/etc/users/docs -ro
/etc/users/preliminary/docs -rw=yoko
```

In this file, the first directory, `/etc/user/purch`, which stores purchase order files, is shared with a group called acct—the accounting department. The `/docs` directory can be accessed by anyone in read-only mode. The `/preliminary/docs` directory can be accessed in read-only mode by most users, but users on the computer whose hostname is yoko have read-write access.

CAUTION

Although NFS is a great technology for sharing data among hosts on a network, give considerable thought to the matter before using NFS to export sensitive or critical data. Using the `root=hostnames` parameter, for instance, gives users root access to the files you export, opening up all sorts of security holes if you do not carefully monitor your system and the files that are exported.

N O T E   Only some of the most used parameters in the `/etc/exports` file have been discussed in this chapter. See the man page for `exportfs` for your system to get a complete listing.

Using the *share* Command

Some versions of UNIX, such as System V or newer versions of SunOS, use the `share` command instead of the `exportfs` command to make directories available for exporting. Because both commands do essentially the same thing, the syntax of the `share` command is similar to the `exportfs` command:

```
share [-F nfs] [-o options] [ -d description] path
```

In this format, `-F nfs` is used to indicate the type of remote file system being used. Some UNIX systems allow for not just NFS, but also other types of distributed file systems, such as RFS (Remote File System). You can use the `-d` parameter to provide a description of the directory path you are exporting, and you can provide, as options, parameters of the same type that you use with `exportfs` (for example, `ro`, `rw`, `anon`, and so on). The part of the command is `path`, which is the directory path to export.

The `share` command uses the file `/etc/dfs/dfstab`, rather than the `/etc/exportfs` file. You can use any text editor to edit `dfstab` and include in the file a line for each directory path you want to export. When the system is being booted, the `shareall` command is executed, which reads the `dfstab` file to determine the directories that will be made available to remote clients.

 TIP If you execute the `share` command without using the `-F` parameter to specify the type of remote file system, then the first entry in the file `/etc/dfs/fstypes` is used as a default.

You can also execute the `shareall` command online if you want, and this is the standard way to begin sharing new directory paths you have just added to the `dfstab` file. The syntax for the `shareall` command is as follows:

```
shareall [-F FSType] [- ¦ filename]
```

Here the `-F` parameter is again used to list the file system types (just like the `share` command). If you end the command with the hyphen character (-), then `shareall` accepts input from standard input. If you specify a filename, that file is used to determine the directories to share. If you do not specify a filename, then, of course, the default file `dfstab` is used.

Finally, you can use the `unshare` and `unshareall` commands to stop sharing specific directories. Both commands use the `-F` parameter to specify the file system type just like the `share` command does. Additionally, the `unshare` command allows you to specify options specific to the file system type by using the `-o` command-line parameter. You can use this if you want to change the way in which a directory path is being shared (for example, `unshare -F nfs -o options`).

Monitoring and Troubleshooting NFS File Systems

Because NFS is a network service, you will find many of the TCP/IP utilities to be handy when trying to troubleshoot NFS problems or performance. Should a remote file system become suddenly unavailable, you might first try to determine whether the remote server itself is still online or whether it has dropped off the network. You can use the `ping` command to determine simple availability. `ping` uses ICMP packets that are echoed back from the remote system. If no echo comes back, the system is either off the network (that is, it's crashed), or you may have a network problem that prevents the communications from getting through.

The `tracert` utility can be used when `ping` fails to determine how far along the network route the packet is getting on its trip to the remote system. Use this when trying to isolate the particular point of failure in the network.

▶ **See** "Networking Essentials," **p. 421**

Another useful command is specific to NFS: `nfsstat`. This command shows you statistics about NFS and RPC. The syntax for `nfsstat` follows:

```
nfsstat [-cnrsz] [vmunix.n] [core.n]
```

You can use the following options:

- ■ c   Shows only client-side information.
- ■ s   Shows only server-side information.
- ■ n   Shows only statistics for NFS, both client and server side.
- ■ r   Shows only statistics for RPC, both client and server side.
- ■ z   This option is used to zero out the statistics. You can combine it with other options to zero out statistics referred to by those options (for example, `-zc` to zero client-side information). Write access to `/dev/mem` is required to zero statistics.
- ■ `core.n`   The name of the system's core image.
- ■ `vmunix.n`   The name of kernel image.

If you do not supply any options with the `nfsstat` command, all statistics are shown. The statistical data displayed depends on the options you choose. For an example, see the man page for `nfsstat` for your particular system.

By making it a regular practice to examine the output from the `nfsstat` command, you can become a better judge of how your system is operating. For example, you can plot data about NFS calls to determine when it is necessary to increase the number of client- or server-side daemons responsible for NFS on your systems.

N O T E   Many third-party and user-written tools are available on the Internet that you can use to assist you in monitoring or troubleshooting NFS. For example, at the ftp site:

ftp.fc.net

you will find, under the directory /pub/security, the NFS watch utility. It can be used to monitor NFS requests on your local network. Log in to this ftp site using the username anonymous. Give your email address as a password as a courtesy to the providers of this site.

You will also find many other good tools at this site. ■

The `showmount` command can be helpful when you want to know which remote hosts have file systems mounted from a particular host computer. You can use this when troubleshooting connection problems. For example, you may think that a client has a remote file system mounted, but by using this command, you can see that the server host does not list the client. You can also use the command to show a list of directory paths currently being exported by a particular host.

This command has the following syntax:

`showmount [-ade3] [hostname]`

The command-line parameters you can use are as follows:

- a   Lists all mountpoints using the format of *hostname:path*, where *hostname* is the name of a client that has mounted the exported directory.
- d   Displays a list of directories that are remotely mounted by clients.
- e   Displays a list of exported directory paths for host.
- 3   Causes the command to use version 3 of the Mount protocol.

The command gets its information from the `mount` daemon. Note, however, that because NFS is a stateless protocol, the information is not guaranteed to be correct. For example, if a client has mounted a remote file system and then the client crashes, the information still shows up when you use the `showmount` command. If the client uses a `umount` command, then the `mount` daemon will be aware that it has unmounted the file system, and the information will be accurate.

The Automount File System

Earlier in this chapter, you learned that the Mount protocol takes care of the details of making a connection for the NFS client to the NFS server. To access a remote file system on an NFS server, it is necessary to use the `mount` command to make the remote file system available at a mountpoint in the local file system.

A newer development in NFS technology is the `automountd` daemon. This process listens for NFS requests and mounts the remote file system on an as-needed basis. In most typical implementations, the temporary mount remains in effect for about 5 minutes and then times out.

The `automountd` daemon is usually started at boot time in the `/etc/rc.local` file, but you can also enter it as a command after the system is up and running. When a user on the client computer tries to access a file that is referenced in an automount map, the `automountd` daemon checks to see whether the file system for that directory is currently mounted. If it is not, the daemon temporarily mounts the file system so that the user's request can be fulfilled.

An `automount` map is a file that tells the daemon where the file system to be mounted is located (the remote host) and where it should be mounted in the local file system (the mountpoint). The map can also include options for the mount process, such as if it is to be mounted read-only. When `automount` actually mounts a file system, it doesn't really mount it at the mountpoint, however. Instead, it usually uses a mountpoint of /tmp_mnt. It then creates a symbolic link at the mountpoint to point to this directory.

The *automount* Command

The automount command is usually executed during startup (in the /etc/rc.local file) but you can execute it online if needed. The automount command starts the automountd daemon, which is responsible for processing NFS mount requests as they are defined in special files called map files.

The syntax for this command is as follows:

```
automount     [-mnTv] [-D name=value] [-f master-file]
[-M mount-directory] [-tl duration] [-tm interval]
[-tw interval][directory mapname [- mount-options]]
```

The options you can use include the following:

- m   This tells automount to ignore directory-mapname pairs listed in the master map file.
- n   This causes dynamic mounts to be disabled. If a directory is already mounted, then the user's request succeeds, but no further file systems are mounted.
- T   This sets up the daemon to provide trace information about each request, which is sent to standard output.
- v   Verbose. This causes the daemon to send status messages to the console.
- D *name=value*   Use this to define automount environment variables. The text associated with *value* is assigned to the variable name.
- f *master map file name*   Use this to provide the name of the master map file to the automount daemon.
- M *mountpoint directory*   Use this option to specify a directory to use for the temporary mountpoint (default is /tmp_mnt).
- tl *time value*   This option specifies how long a file system should stay mounted after the last user request before automount automatically dismounts it. The default is usually 5 minutes.
- tm *time value*   This option specifies the amount of time (in seconds) that should elapse between attempts to mount a file system. The default is usually 30 seconds.
- tw *time value*   Similar to the tm option, this option specifies the amount of time (in seconds) between attempts to unmount a file system that has exceeded its cached time. The default is usually 1 minute.
- *mount_options*   Options specified here are applied to all the directories listed in the map file. However, if options are listed in a map file, they override those listed here on the command line.

Master Maps

The master map is used to supply the `automount` daemon with a list of maps. It also contains `mount-options` for those maps. The master map file is usually named `/etc/auto.master`. The syntax for the entries in a master map file is as follows:

```
mount-point    map    [mount-options]
```

The `mount-point` is the pathname of the local directory for an indirect map specified in the map column. If the map specified in the map column is a direct map, then the `mount-point` is usually `/-`. The data listed under the map column is used to find the map that contains the actual mountpoints and the locations of the remote file systems.

Any data you supply under `mount-options` is used when mounting directories in the map file associated with it.

Following is an example of a master map file. Note that lines beginning with the pound-sign (#) are comments.

```
#mount-point        map                 options
/etc/users              /etc/auto.usr         -ro
/-                      /etc/auto.direct    -rw
```

In this example, when the `automountd` daemon determines that access is needed for files found in the `/etc/users` directory, it looks for another map file, named `auto.usr`, to get the reset of the information. Because the `-ro` options are specified for this entry, they are applied to the file system designated in the `auto.usr` map file.

The dummy argument `/-` indicates that the map file it points to (`auto.direct`) is a direct map file. A direct map file contains the mountpoints and the remote file system information needed to complete the mounts.

Direct Maps

A direct map indicates which remote file systems can be mounted into the local file system and what the mountpoint should be. This kind of map doesn't point to any other map file. It's pretty straightforward (and direct). You can specify mount options in the file, as the syntax for each entry shows:

```
key    [mount-options]    location
```

In this syntax, the `key` is actually the mountpoint for this entry. `Mount-options` are the typical `mountd` daemon options discussed elsewhere in this chapter. `location` is a string in the format of *machine:pathname*, where *machine* is the hostname of the remote system that the file system actually resides on, and *pathname* is the path to the directory on that file system. To provide for redundancy, you can specify more than one location. If you do, the `automount` daemon queries all locations and takes the first one to respond to its requests.

Indirect Maps

An indirect map is almost the same as a direct map, with the exception that the first field (key) is not a full pathname. Instead, it is just a pointer to an entry in the master map file. Directories listed in an indirect map file are mounted under the mountpoint specified by the master map (or specified on the command line if different). You can list multiple directories in an indirect map file, and each of these remote file system directories is mounted under the mountpoint designated in the master map file, which contains a reference to the indirect map.

Check the man pages on your system to be sure of the syntax for options used in map files because they may vary just like options do for the mount command among different UNIX systems.

Setting Up NFS Servers and Clients

Before you actually sit down at the computer console and start setting up an NFS server, create a worksheet that contains all the information you will need. This makes your job easier during the initial setup and serves to document the process. On this worksheet, specify the number of server daemons you want to start and the protocol (TCP or UDP) to use on the server. Unless you expect the server to handle a large volume of transactions, you might want to initially accept the default number of daemons. Next, create a list of directory paths you want to export. For each directory path, list the host clients that you will allow to access each directory path and the type of access (read-write or read-only).

For example:

```
Server Name:  BCATL1          Number of nfsd daemons: 15      Protocol:  UPD
Directory Path                Hosts Allowed Access            Type of Access
/usr                          bcatl2 bcatl3                   read/write
/etc/purch                    bcatl3 yoko                     read only
/etc/payables                 bcatl2                          read/write
/etc/invoices                 bcatl3 yoko                     read only
/dist                         bcatl2 bcatl3 yoko              read only
```

You might have to edit several startup configuration files to start up NFS. Some of these, such as /etc/services, /etc/hosts, and /etc/protocols can be replaced by using a name service. For more information about these files and the syntax used by each, see Chapter 19, "Configuring TCP/IP." For more information about network naming services, see Chapter 23, "DNS."

Some of the startup configuration files that you might have to edit include the following:

- ▓ /etc/inetd.conf This file is used to start network server daemons. You will find the basic TCP/IP services, such as ftp and telnet here, along with services that use RPC, such as NFS daemons. Each line in this file starts with a service name (which must be listed in the /etc/services file), along with the type of socket to use (for example, stream or datagram), the protocol used by the service, and other information needed to start the daemon.

■ /etc/netgroups You can use this file to create network-wide groupings of hostnames. By grouping hosts under netgroup names, you can simplify the process of exporting file systems later by referring to the group name instead of having to list each hostname.

■ /etc/exports This is the file you edit to list the directory paths that you want to make available for exporting. When the system is booted, a script file named rc.local is responsible for executing the exportfs command, which reads this file.

You can test your edits by rebooting the system. Of course, this might not be practical in a production environment where you need to schedule downtime in advance. You can, however, execute the necessary commands online to start the NFS server daemons and then execute the exportfs command to allow clients to mount your exported directories. To start the NFS server daemon and start exporting directories, use the following commands:

```
/usr/etc/nfsd [number of daemons]
/usr/etc/exportfs -a
```

Remember that the -a command-line parameter for exportfs tells the daemon to export all directory paths listed in the /etc/exports file.

After you have set up the server, you will then have to configure a client so that you can mount each exported directory path to test that it is available and accessible in the mode you have specified. First, make sure that the client daemon biod is running. You can check this by using the ps command. This daemon is also usually started in the rc.local file, so you might have to edit this file if you do not see the daemon running.

TROUBLESHOOTING

Where should you begin investigating when a client computer hangs or if a program stalls when mounting or accessing a remote file system using NFS? Check the command-line options you used for the mount command. Remember, if you use the option hard (that is, mount -o hard…), then if the server that offers the exported directory fails for some reason, the client may hang as it continually tries to mount the file system that is no longer available. If you regularly experience this type of problem, change the option to -o soft, instead. Using the soft mount option causes the client to generate an error if it cannot mount the remote file system.

If you find that a client or application has hung, and the server that offers the directory path for export is still up and functioning normally, it might be that the NFS server daemon or the client biod daemon has encountered problems. You can use the kill command to delete the server daemon(s) and then restart them manually to determine whether this is the problem.

To test mounting a remote file system, you can simply execute the mount command with the appropriate syntax. You can also configure the client by editing the /etc/fstab file and making entries for the remote file systems you want mounted at boot time. (See "Using the fstab File" earlier in this chapter.)

Using NFS With Non-UNIX Clients

Although the Network File System was originally developed by Sun for use with UNIX systems, its popularity has motivated developers for other computer platforms to adopt it as a file sharing solution. In a typical office network, you may have many large UNIX servers doing the heavy-duty processing, but rely on Intel-based PCs running operating systems from MS-DOS up to Windows 98 or Windows NT. If this is the case in your business, you can still take advantage of NFS capabilities by installing an NFS client application on your PC.

Many manufacturers provide UNIX-compatible utilities for PCs, some as a package containing many utilities, and some as individual products. It would be impossible to list all the products in this book, but you might find that "The PC-Mac TCP/IP & NFS FAQ list" is a good starting point. This FAQ has a lot of information about the different products available and feature comparisons, along with tips for installing and configuring different products and troubleshooting tips. You can access the FAQ at the following address:

```
http://www.eden.com/html/faq.html
```

From Here...

Using NFS in your network can help solve the headaches associated with trying to make multiple copies of files or directories available to users on different computers. If you distribute documentation for your applications this way, for example, you only have to update the documentation at one place instead of having to do so on multiple machines. A single copy is always much easier to maintain in a busy environment than multiple copies of information. This is even more true for data that changes regularly.

NFS is closely related to several other topics covered in this book:

■ Chapter 17, "Networking Essentials," introduces you to networking in general and covers some basic troubleshooting tools you will need to use.

■ Chapter 18, "Internetworking," continues the discussion of networking but delves into the complexities of the underlying protocols and data structures used in the TCP/IP suite and other network protocols used by most UNIX systems.

■ Chapter 19, "Configuring TCP/IP," is a must-read before you begin to think about setting up NFS. This chapter covers the basics of setting up hostnames and addresses in the configuration files, among other topics.

■ Chapter 26, "Security," can point you to the tools you will use to ensure that access to your computers and their data is kept secure and protected from harm by those who do not need access to it.

## CHAPTER 23

DNS

by Sriranga Veeraraghavan and Jeff Robinson

In this chapter

A Brief History of the Internet

To understand the Domain Name System (DNS), it is important to know a little about the history of the Internet and its precursor, ARPAnet.

The Internet began in the late 1960s as an experimental wide area computer network funded by the Department of Defense's Advanced Research Projects Agency (ARPA). This network, called ARPAnet, was intended to allow government scientists and engineers to share expensive computing resources. During this period, only government users and a handful of computers were ever connected to ARPAnet. It remained that way until the early 1980s.

In the early 1980s, two main developments led to the popularization of ARPAnet: The development of the Transmission Control Protocol and the Internet Protocol (TCP/IP), which standardized connectivity to the ARPAnet for all computers, and U.C. Berkeley's version of UNIX, known as BSD. BSD was the first UNIX distribution to include TCP/IP as a networking layer. Because BSD was available to other universities at a negligible cost, the number of computers that could connect to ARPAnet soared.

All of a sudden, thousands of computers were connected to a network that had been designed to handle a few computers. In many cases, these new computers were simultaneously connected to a university network and ARPAnet. At this point, it was decided that the original ARPAnet would become the backbone of the entire network, which was being called the Internet.

In 1988, the Defense Department decided that the ARPAnet project had continued long enough and stopped funding the project. At this point, the National Science Foundation (NSF) took over and supported the Internet until 1995, when private companies such as BBNPlanet, MCI, and Sprint took over the backbone.

Now millions of computer users are on the Internet daily, and the numbers keep rising.

▶ **See** "Examining the DoD Model," **p. 454**

HOSTS.TXT File

In the early days when only a few hundred computers were connected to the ARPAnet, every computer had a file called HOSTS.TXT. UNIX modified the name to /etc/hosts. This file contained all the information about every host on the network, including the name to address mapping. Because there were so few computers, the file was small and could be maintained easily.

▶ **See** "TCP/IP Network Configuration," **p. 489**

The maintenance of the HOSTS.TXT file was the responsibility of SRI-NIC located at the Stanford Research Institute in Menlo Park, California.

When administrators to change this file, they emailed the request to SRI-NIC, which would incorporate the requests once or twice a week. This meant that administrators also had to periodically compare their HOSTS.TXT files against the SRI-NIC HOSTS.TXT file, and if the files were different, the administrator had to FTP a new copy of the file.

As the Internet started to grow, the idea of centrally administering hostnames as well as deploying the HOSTS.TXT file became a major issue. Every time a new host was added, a change had to be made to the central version, and every other host on ARPAnet had to get the new version of this file. In addition to this problem, several other issues with a single file were encountered. Table 23.1 shows major problems.

Table 23.1   Problems with *HOSTS.TXT*

Problem	Reason
Name uniqueness	The single flat file could not handle duplicate names, which meant that machine names would eventually run out.
Server and network load	The maintenance of an updated HOSTS.TXT file required administrators to constantly download new copies of the file. This caused unnecessary traffic on the network and an unbearable load on the SRI machine responsible for handling the download requests.
Maintenance issues	Every request for a hostname addition, deletion, or update required someone at SRI-NIC to update the HOST.TXT file. As the number of hosts increased, it was not possible to perform updates in a reasonable time frame.
Consistency	Every computer on ARPAnet need to have the latest version of HOSTS.TXT, but there was no automatic way of distributing update versions. If two computers had different versions, the entire network would often get confused.

Overview of the Domain Name Service

In the early 1980s, the SRI-NIC called for the design of a distributed database to replace the HOSTS.TXT file. The new system was known as the Domain Name System (DNS). ARPAnet switched to DNS in September 1984. It has been the standard method for publishing and retrieving hostname information on the Internet ever since.

DNS is a distributed database built on a hierarchical domain structure that solves the inefficiencies inherent in a large monolithic file like HOSTS.TXT. Under DNS, every computer that connects to the Internet connects from an Internet domain. Each Internet domain has a name server that maintains a database of the hosts in its domain and handles requests for hostnames. When a domain becomes too large for a single point of management, subdomains may be delegated to reduce the administrative burden.

Domain Structure

Domains in the DNS system create a hierarchical structure similar to the structure of the UNIX file system.

▶ **See** "The UNIX File and Directory Structure," **p. 112**

DNS has a root domain, ".", at the top of its tree much like the UNIX File Systems has a root directory, /. Subdomains in DNS are equivalent to subdirectories in the file system.

If a particular directory contains too many files, you usually create a subdirectory and move many of the related files into this new directory. This helps to keep directories and files organized. The same principle applies to DNS. When a domain has too many hosts, a subdomain is usually created for hosts that are related in some manner. Usually, this relation is something such as a physical location, department, or organization.

Subdomains can be created at any time without consulting any higher authority within the tree. A newly created subdomain is then free to create other subdomains. The relationship between a domain and its subdomain can be thought of as a parent and child relationship. The parent domain must know which machine handles the subdomain database information so that it will be able to inform other name servers of who holds the information for the subdomain. When a parent creates a subdomain, it is known as *delegation*. The parent domain delegates authority for the child subdomain to the subdomain's name server.

Root Domain   The root domain is the starting point in DNS name space. All domains and hosts are located underneath the root domain. The root level domain currently has 13 name servers maintained by the NIC that can answer queries. Their names are `a.root-servers.net.`, `b.rootservers.net.`, `c.rootservers.net.`, and so on. Under the root domain are several "top level" domains.

Top Level Domains   Top level domains are located directly under the root domain. The two types of top level domains are as follows:

- Organizational
- Geographical

The organizational top level domains identify machines belonging to a particular type of organization within the United States. The geographical domains identify machines located within a particular country. Table 23.2 gives the names of the top level organizational domains.

A complete list of the geographical domains can be found at the following Web site:

`www.iana.org/domain-names.html`

In general, each of the geographical domains has subdomains with the names listed in Table 23.2 to make it easy for users to identify specific types of organizations within that country.

Table 23.2   Organizational Top Level Domains

Domain	Description
com	Commercial organizations
edu	Educational organizations
gov	Government (US) organizations
mil	Military (US) organizations

Domain	Description
net	Network organizations and ISPs
org	Nonprofit organizations
arpa	Used for inverse address lookups

Fully Qualified Domain Names

Each domain has a Fully Qualified Domain Name (FQDN) within the DNS tree. This means that each domain has its own unique place in the name space and is represented by an FQDN, which is similar to a pathname in the file system. To identify the FQDN for a particular domain, you start by first getting the name of the current domain, then adding the name of the parent domain, and then adding the name of the grandparent's domain, and so on until you reach the root of the tree. This method is the reverse of the method used to construct directory names in the UNIX file system.

▶ **See** "The UNIX File and Directory Structure," **p. 112**

An example of a Fully Qualified Domain Name follows:

`arc.nasa.gov.`

This particular domain name corresponds to NASA's Ames Research Center. From this name, you can tell that arc is a subdomain of the nasa domain, which is itself a subdomain of the gov top level domain. In this representation, the strings between the dot character, (.), are called labels. The last . represents the root domain and indicates that this is an FQDN.

> **CAUTION**
>
> All Fully Qualified Domain Names must have a dot at the end or the local or current domain name will be appended to the name. Most client applications, called resolvers, are forgiving and fix this for you; however, DNS servers are not as forgiving. Forgetting the trailing dot in DNS database files accounts for more than 80 percent of the mistakes made in DNS databases. Don't forget the dots!

DNS Naming Rules   Several restrictions are imposed on DNS domain names and hostnames to make the system robust and scalable. By definition, DNS names can contain only alphanumeric characters in the set [A–Z,a–z,0–9] and the dash character "-". The effective set of characters is even smaller because DNS names are not case sensitive. This allows DNS to function properly on many different platforms, such as Windows and DOS, but it limits all hostnames to the lowercase letters [a–z].

In addition to the naming restrictions, the following restrictions are also present:

- The maximum number of characters a domain name or label can have is 63 characters.
- The maximum number of subdomains is 127.
- The maximum number of characters in an FQDN is 255.

These restrictions keep the DNS tree manageable by limiting its depth to five or six levels.

Domains and Zones

So far, we have described DNS in terms of domains and subdomains. In addition to this, there is another classification known as a *zone*.

In terms of the DNS naming tree, a domain corresponds to a particular node or point in the tree and all the nodes underneath it. A zone is a piece of the naming tree that is under the administrative control of a particular machine.

When a domain becomes too large a subdomain is created to clean up the naming tree. At some point, it will be necessary to delegate responsibility for the subdomain to another administration and its name server. The subdomain becomes a separate zone because it has a different name server. This process is known as delegation.

Whenever a portion of the tree is served by a new administration, then a new zone is created. Therefore a domain may be comprised of several zones. Figure 23.1 shows that the learnix.ca domain is comprised of two zones. One administration serves learnix.ca. and ott.learnix.ca., whereas another administration serves tor.learnix.ca.. The saws show where the tree has been cut, and a new zone has been created.

A name server is required for the learnix.ca. zone, and a different name server is required to serve the information for tor.learnix.ca zone.

FIGURE 23.1

Domains and zones.

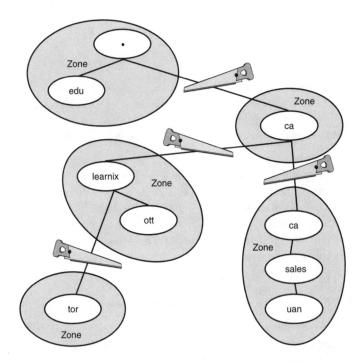

DNS Name Servers

Special programs that store information about the domain name tree are called *DNS resolvers* or *name servers*. These programs usually have the complete information about some part of the domain name tree. The main types of name servers are as follows:

- Primary name servers
- Secondary name servers
- Caching only name servers

Collectively, these name servers are called *full service resolvers* because they are capable of receiving queries from clients and other name servers. A full service resolver always maintains a cache of items that it has already looked up. It also performs recursive queries to other name servers, if it does not have a cached answer for a query that it receives.

Another type of name server is called a *stub resolver*. The stub resolver is a C library function that allows programs to directly query the name server for host name information.

Primary Name Server

Each DNS domain has a primary server that contains the authoritative zone database file. This file contains all the hostnames and their corresponding IP addresses for the domain along with several other pieces of information about the zone. This information is stored in the form of resource records, which are explained in the next section.

Primary name servers answer queries with authoritative answers for the zone in which they are located. To service client requests, primary name servers normally query other name servers to obtain the required information. They also maintain a memory cache to remember information returned by other name servers. The primary name server's database is also used to delegate responsibility for subdomains to other name servers.

To change the information for a domain, the zone database file on the primary name server must be changed. The zone database contains a serial number that must be incremented each time the database is altered; this ensures that secondary name servers recognize the changes.

Secondary Name Server

Each domain should have at least one secondary server for redundancy purposes. The secondary obtains a copy of the zone database, usually from the primary name server. The secondary serves authoritative information for the zone just as the primary does.

Secondary name servers normally query other name servers to obtain information from other name servers to answer client requests. Similar to primary name servers, secondary name servers have a memory cache that remembers information returned by other name servers.

Zone Transfers   Periodically, the secondary contacts the primary and checks whether any changes have occurred to the zone database. This is accomplished by comparing the serial numbers located in the zone database file.

If the serial number on the primary is larger than the serial number on the secondary, the secondary performs a zone transfer. A zone transfer is simply the secondary name server contacting the primary to obtain a new copy of the zone database.

N O T E If the serial number for one of your zones becomes very large and you want to reset it to a smaller number, you will need to purge the current serial number from all your secondary name servers.

First, you must change the primary name server to use the new serial number. Then you have to log in to every secondary name server and shut down the name server. After the secondary name servers are shut down, you need to remove their name database files. When you restart the secondary name servers, they get new copies of the database files and thus they use the new reset serial number. ▮

Caching Only Name Server

Caching only name servers do not serve authoritative information for any zones. Clients query this name server, and it forwards the query to other name servers until an answer for the query is found. When an answer is found the cache only name server remembers the answer for a period of time. If the same client, or other clients make the same query again, this name server gives the answer stored in cache, instead of forwarding the query to another name server. Cache only name servers are generally used to reduce DNS traffic over slow or expensive network connections.

DNS Query Example

Figure 23.2 illustrates how a DNS query is handled. This section steps through the entire resolve process to make sure that you understand.

FIGURE 23.2
A DNS query.

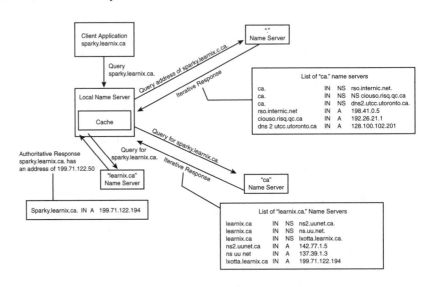

The steps in the process are as follows:

1. The stub resolver on the client system sends a query to the local name server asking for the IP address of sparky.learnix.ca.

2. The local name server looks in its cache to see whether it has a cached entry for sparky.learnix.ca., learnix.ca., or ca.. In this case, it does not have these entries, so proceed to the next step.

3. The local name server sends the query to one of the root name servers.

4. The root name server definitely does not know the IP address of sparky.learnix.ca., but it does know the IP address of the name servers for the ca. domain because it is the parent of that domain. The root name server returns the address of a name server to query. This type of answer from the root server is known as an iterative response as it just forwarded you to another name server.

5. The local name server caches the list of the ca. name servers and their IP addresses.

6. The local name server then queries one of these name servers to see whether it knows the IP address of sparky.learnix.ca..

7. The top level ca. domain does not know the address of sparky.learnix.ca., thus it also gives an iterative response by returning a list of the learnix.ca. name servers. The ca. name server has a list of the learnix.ca. name servers in its zone because it has delegated the domain learnix.ca. to them.

8. The local name server caches the list of name servers for the learnix.ca. domain.

9. The local name server now queries one of the learnix.ca. name servers for the IP address of sparky.learnix.ca.. This name server holds the domain information for the learnix.ca. domain, and therefore it can return an authoritative response to the query for the IP address of sparky.learnix.ca. The learnix.ca. name servers return all the address records that are associated to sparky.learnix.ca. in its database.

10. The local name server caches the IP address record of sparky.learnix.ca., and then responds to the client machine with the IP address of sparky.learnix.ca., which is 199.71.122.50.

Non-Authoritative Responses   If the client machine were to query the local name server a short time later for the IP address of sparky.learnix.ca. The local name server would have the IP address record cached. The local name server would answer the query with the data located in its cache. This data returned did not come directly from the authoritative domain, so the response is classified as non-authoritative.

Resource Records

DNS resource records are entries stored in the DNS database. The DNS database is a set of ASCII text files that contain information about the machines in a domain. This information is stored in a specific format examined in this section.

Information is added to a domain by adding resource records to the database located on a primary name server. When a query is made to a name server, the server returns one or more resource records containing either the exact answer to the query or information pointing to another name server in the name space to look for the answer.

The resource records on a primary name server are stored in a zone database, which is made up of at least three files:

- db.*network* (for example, db.10.8.11)
- db.*domain* (for example, db.learnix)
- db.127.0.0

The first file contains the mapping of IP addresses to hostnames for a given network. The second file contains the reverse mapping of hostnames to IP addresses. The third file contains a mapping for the localhost. Examples of each of these files are given latter in this section.

Each database file has three main sections:

- The Start of Authority section (SOA)
- The name server section(NS)
- The database section

Each of these sections has one or more DNS resource records. The syntax of a DNS resource record can be in one of the following forms:

- [*TTL*][*class*] *type data*
- [*class*][*TTL*] *type data*

The first two fields, *TTL* and *class*, are optional fields which correspond to the "time-to-live" and the class of the record.

The TTL is a decimal number that indicates to the name server how often this particular record needs to be updated. Usual values range from a few minutes to a few days. If this field is blank, it is assumed to be 3 hours.

The *class* field indicates which class of data the record belongs to. The only class that is used is the IN class, corresponding to Internet data.

The type field is a required field and describes the type of data in the record. Table 23.3 gives a complete list of the available types and their descriptions.

Table 23.3　Types of Resource Records

Type of Record	Description of Data
A	Host IP Address
AAAA	IPv6 Host Address
NS	Name Server Identification

Type of Record	Description of Data
PTR	Associates an IP Address with a Hostname
SOA	Start of Authority
WKS	Well-Known Service
HINFO	Host Info
MX	Mail Exchanger
TXT	General Purpose Text Records
CNAME	Canonical Name or Alias

Start of Authority (SOA) Section

The Start of Authority resource record is located at the top of each file in the zone database. The SOA includes many pieces of information primarily used by the secondary name server. An example SOA record follows with a full explanation of its components.

```
learnix.ca.    IN SOA lxotta.learnix.ca.       hostmaster.learnix.ca. (
               309                 ;serial number
               21600               ;refresh (3hrs)
               3600                ;retry (1hr)
               432000              ;expire (5 days)
               3600 )              ;minimum (1hour)
```

The first field contains the name of the domain for which this database is authoritative. In this case, this database file is authoritative for the domain learnix.ca.. You could also use an "@" symbol here as it represents the ORIGIN, which is automatically set to the authoritative domain as specified is the /etc/named.boot file. The ORIGIN is best thought of as the current domain. Anytime you use the "@" symbol it stands for the ORIGIN. The ORIGIN is also appended to any names that are not fully qualified (names that do not have a trailing dot).

The IN specifies the class Internet.

The SOA declares the resource record to be of type Start of Authority.

Next, you need to specify the fully qualified name of the primary server for the domain. In this case, the primary is lxotta.learnix.ca..

After the primary server, you specify the email address of the person responsible for the domain. The actual email address is hostmaster@learnix.ca., but the "@" has been replaced with a dot "." because the "@" symbol represents the ORIGIN.

An open parenthesis is used to specify the next five pieces of information.

Inside the parentheses you specify the serial number, refresh interval, retry interval, expire, and minimum TTL values.

- Serial number   The serial number indicates the revision of the database file. The number should be incremented each time a change is made to the database file.

- Refresh   The refresh rate indicates in seconds how often the secondary names should return to compare the serial number of the zone database.

- Retry   The retry value indicates in seconds how often the secondary should attempt to reach the primary if the refresh attempt failed.

- Expire   The expire is the period of time the secondary continues to retry before the secondary name server ceases to serve the data for the zone.

- Minimum TTL   The minimum TTL is a value in seconds that specifies how long querying name servers will be allowed to cache responses that originate from this zone. This value can be overridden on an individual basis using the TTL field on the resource record, mentioned in the preceding section "Resource Records."

CAUTION

Remember to increment the serial number after every alteration to the database file. If you forget, your secondary name servers will not zone transfer and synchronize. Your secondary name servers will not see the changes that you have made on the primary.

Name Server (NS) Section

The name server section is the second section in each of the files in the zone database. It contains a name server resource record, NS, for each of the primary and secondary name servers for the zone that the database serves. The following example shows the name server section for the learnix.ca. zone. The address records, explained in the next section, have to exist for each of the name servers specified if they are in the current zone.

```
; This is the name server section of the zone database file

learnix.ca.    IN    NS    lxotta.learnix.ca.
learnix.ca.    IN    NS    ns.uunet.net.

; Include the address record for any name servers that
; cannot be looked-up somewhere else in DNS

lxotta.learnix.ca.    IN    A    199.71.122.50
```

Database Section

The database portion of the zone file contains all the resource records that contain the data for the hosts in the zone. Three main types of records are encountered in this section. In the db.*network* file, you will encounter PTR records. In the db.*domain* file, you will encounter A and CNAME records.

First let's look at an excerpt from a domain file, db.learnix, which contains both A and CNAME records:

```
jazz      IN   A    199.71.122.34
rock      IN   A    199.71.122.35
donald    IN   A    199.71.122.36
```

```
; Martin is a router with two network interfaces
martin      IN    A     199.71.122.37
            IN    A     192.168.1.1
; Specify the web server as martin using a CNAME record
www         IN    CNAME   martin.learnix.ca.
; Specify the ftp server as donald using a CNAME record
ftp         IN    CNAME   donald
```

A Record   An A record is an address record used for providing translations for hostnames to IP addresses. The following record:

```
donald      IN    A     199.71.122.36
```

indicates that the IP address of the hostname donald is 199.71.122.36. Because there is no period after the name donald, the domain of the current SOA record will be used to for the host.

The database section should contain an A record for every hostname in the domain.

CNAME Record   The Canonical Name (CNAME for short) record makes it possible to alias hostnames. This is useful for giving common names to large servers. For example, it is nice to have the server that handles both Web traffic and ftp traffic for a domain respond to the names www and ftp. This can be achieved by using the CNAME record. From the preceding example, the line:

```
ftp         IN    CNAME   donald
```

causes the name server to respond with the IP address of the host with the name donald each time a request is made for the hostname ftp. To use a CNAME record, you must have an A record for the host.

PTR Record   The pointer or PTR records are typically seen in the db.*network* or the db.127.0.0 files. They are used for reverse address resolution, which is used by the name server to turn an IP address into a hostname. An example of a PTR record follows:

```
2.11.8.10.in-addr.arpa. IN PTR         kanchi.bosland.us.
```

This example allows for the IP address 10.8.11.2 to be reverse resolved as kanchi.bosland.us. For IP address to hostname resolution to work properly, the IP address needs to be in reverse order.

The reason has to do with the structure of DNS. Because DNS is a distributed database, information is obtained by querying for a key in the database. When you want to use an IP address to look up a hostname, the IP address must act as the key in the database.

To look up a hostname from an IP address, the NIC creates a special domain known as IN-ADDR.ARPA. This domain stands for inverse address. It is a name space in the form of a tree containing all the class A, B, and C IP addresses being used.

Each of these inverse domains is delegated to a name server operated by the company that owns the Class A, B, or C address.

Learnix, Inc., owns the Class C IP address 199.71.122.0. The NIC has delegated authority of the 122.71.199.in-addr.arpa. domain to the ns.learnix.ca. name server. The ns.learnix.ca. name server must hold authoritative information for the domain 122.71.199.in-addr.arpa. The ns.learnix.ca. name server is most likely primary for the domain 122.71.199.in-addr.arpa. The learnix name server will be required to have a zone database containing all its IP addresses within the 199.71.122.0 address space and the hostname that belongs to that IP address.

N O T E Make sure to enter all the hostnames in the reverse address zone. Many Internet servers attempt to look up a hostname from your incoming IP address. If the hostname cannot be found, the server may deny you access. ▪

Complete Zone Files

This section contains the three files that make up the zone database for the learnix.ca domain. These illustrate the format of the zone database files and can be used as reference when setting up your own domain.

db.learnix Database File This file is the db.domain file for the learnix domain. It contains the SOA record for that domain along with listing the name servers and the hosts in the domain.

```
learnix.ca.      IN SOA lxotta.learnix.ca.      hostmaster.learnix.ca. (
                 309               ;serial number
                 21600             ;refresh (3hrs)
                 3600              ;retry (1hr)
                 432000            ;expire (5 days)
                 3600 )            ;minimum (1hour)

; This is the name server section of the zone database file

learnix.ca.    IN    NS    lxotta.learnix.ca.
learnix.ca.    IN    NS    ns.uunet.net.

; Include the address record for any name servers that
; cannot be looked-up somewhere else in DNS

lxotta.learnix.ca.    IN    A    199.71.122.50

jazz       IN    A    199.71.122.34
rock       IN    A    199.71.122.35
donald     IN    A    199.71.122.36
; Martin is a router with two network interfaces
martin     IN    A    199.71.122.37
           IN    A    192.168.1.1

; Specify the web server as martin using a CNAME record
www        IN    CNAME    martin.learnix.ca.
; Specify the ftp server as donald using a CNAME record
ftp        IN    CNAME    donald
```

db.199.71.122 Database File The db.199.71.122 database contains the SOA, name server section, and PTR resource records necessary to perform reverse name lookups on the hosts in this domain. One thing to note in this file is that the defined origin for the IP addresses 34 to 37 is used.

```
122.71.199.in-addr.arpa.    IN SOA lxotta.learnix.ca.
```

```
hostmaster.learnix.ca. (
                309             ;serial number
                21600           ;refresh (3hrs)
                3600            ;retry (1hr)
                432000          ;expire (5 days)
                3600 )          ;minimum (1hour)

; This is the name server section of the zone database file

@    IN    NS    lxotta.learnix.ca.
@    IN    NS    ns.uunet.net.

34         IN    PTR    jazz.learnix.ca.
35         IN    PTR    rock.learnix.ca.
36         IN    PTR    donald.learnix.ca.
37         IN    PTR    martin.learnix.ca.
```

***db.127.0.0* Database File**   The db.127.0.0 file is used to resolve the IP address 127.0.0.1 to the hostname localhost.

```
127.in-addr.arpa.    IN SOA lxotta.learnix.ca.        hostmaster.learnix.ca. (
                309             ;serial number
                21600           ;refresh (3hrs)
                3600            ;retry (1hr)
                432000          ;expire (5 days)
                3600 )          ;minimum (1hour)

; This is the name server section of the zone database file

@    IN    NS    lxotta.learnix.ca.

1.0.0.127.in-addr.arpa.    IN    PTR    localhost.
```

Configuring DNS Clients

UNIX machines get their name server configuration information from the file /etc/ resolv.conf. To configure a machine as a DNS client, you need to edit this file and specify the correct domain and name server.

Three main commands or directives can be placed in this file. They are given in Table 23.4.

Table 23.4   Resolver Directives

Directive	Description
domain	This directive is appended to partially qualified domain names that are looked up in DNS.
search	This directive allows multiple domain names to be attempted for partially qualified domain names.
nameserver	This directive tells the resolver which machines to send DNS queries. This directive may be specified up to three times to provide redundancy. Identify name servers using IP addresses. If no name servers are specified, the resolver will look to 127.0.0.1.

N O T E   To add a comment in the `resolv.conf` file, start a line with the semicolon (;) character. If a semicolon is encountered on any line, all the characters after it are ignored. ▪

An example of a `/etc/resolv.conf` file is as follows:

```
; This is an example of the /etc/resolv.conf file on a DNS client
domain learnix.ca

; You can specify up to 3 name servers

nameserver 199.71.122.50
nameserver 199.45.110.50
nameserver 205.139.91.50
```

The search directive, not shown in the preceding example is used as follows:

```
search domain1 domain2 …
```

If you had the line:

```
search bosland.us berkeley.edu
```

The name server would search for hosts in the domains `bosland.us` and `berkeley.edu`. This allows for users to enter just the hostnames for any hosts in the given domains. If two hosts have the same name in the different domains, the order of the domains given to the search directive dictates which host is contacted.

N O T E   Most UNIX systems do not come with DNS enabled. One of the first things that a system administrator needs to do when setting up a new machine is configure it to use the proper name resolution.

To enable DNS on Solaris 2.x, HP/UX 10.x, and Linux, modify the file `/etc/nsswitch.conf` to have a line similar to the following:

```
hosts: files dns
```

To enable DNS on Digital UNIX, edit the `/etc/svc.conf` file to include a line similar to the following:

```
hosts:local,bind
```

To enable DNS on FreeBSD, edit the file `/etc/hosts.conf` to include a line with the word `bind`. ▪

Configuring DNS Servers

Before setting up DNS and configuring your name servers, you should have applied for your domain name and have your own set of IP addresses.

Applying for a domain name can be done in several different ways. The best way is to obtain a registration form from `http://rs.internic.net`.

The NIC can be contacted directly at the following address:

> Network Solutions
> Attn: InterNIC Registration Services
> 505 Huntmar Park Drive
> Herndon , VA, 20170

The NIC application for a domain name requires that you have at least two DNS servers working and functional. This can sometimes be tricky if it is your first domain setup.

If you are a subdomain that is not located directly under the top level domains, then make sure that the administrator of the domain above you has properly delegated your domain. He or she needs to know the names and IP addresses of your name servers.

Perform an inventory of all the machines that will be included in your DNS setup. Decide whether you need just a single domain, or if subdomains are required due to large numbers of hosts or physical location of hosts. If subdomains are required, decide which hosts will be in which domains.

Berkeley Internet Name Domain (BIND)

The Berkeley Internet Name Domain (BIND) is the most frequently used implementation of DNS. BIND on UNIX is implemented through the `in.named` daemon.

Almost all vendors bundle an `in.named` daemon that supports the BIND protocol; however, for security reasons, consider downloading and compiling the latest version of BIND. The latest version may be obtained from Internet Software Consortium located at:

`http://www.isc.org.`

This section looks at configuring and running BIND.

Boot File The `/etc/named.boot` file provides the `in.named` configuration information, so each time that name server starts, it knows what to serve.

The boot file uses several key directives listed in Table 23.5.

Table 23.5 /etc/named.boot File Directives

Directive	Description
Directory	The directory that contains the zone database files.
Cache	Used to load initial entries into the name server cache (usually the root servers).
Primary	Declares that this name server will be a primary server for a particular zone. The zone and the database must be specified with this directive.
Secondary	Declares that this name server will be secondary for a particular zone. The zone, IP address of the primary name server, and the database file must be specified with this directive.

An example of a `/etc/named.boot` file follows:

```
Directory                                   /var/named
Cache           .                           db.cache
Primary         learnix.ca                  db.learnix
Primary         122.71.199.in-addr.arpa.    db.199.71.122
Primary         127.in-addr.arpa.           db.127
```

The Directory directive in the preceding example tells in.named to expect the database files to be located in the /var/named directory.

The Cache directive forces in.named to initially load a list of the root servers from the file db.cache, which is to be located in the /var/named directory.

The Primary statements tell in.named that it is the primary, authoritative name server for three domains: learnix.ca, 122.71.199.in-addra.arpa., and 127.in-addr.arpa., and to load the zone information into the cache from the specified database file.

Cache File   The cache file contains a list of resource records for the root name servers and their IP addresses. These resource records are loaded into the cache as soon as the name server is started. The latest list of the root servers can be obtained from:

ftp://rs.internic.net/netinfo/root-servers.txt

Following is an abstract from the db.cache file that shows four root level name servers and their IP addresses:

```
.                      3600000  IN  NS   A.ROOT-SERVERS.NET.
A.ROOT-SERVERS.NET.    3600000      A    198.41.0.4

.                      3600000      NS   B.ROOT-SERVERS.NET.
B.ROOT-SERVERS.NET.    3600000      A    128.9.0.107

.                      3600000      NS   C.ROOT-SERVERS.NET.
C.ROOT-SERVERS.NET.    3600000      A    192.33.4.12

.                      3600000      NS   D.ROOT-SERVERS.NET.
D.ROOT-SERVERS.NET.    3600000      A    128.8.10.90
```

Starting BIND

Now that you have all the database files configured and ready to go, all you need to do is start the in.named daemon. As the Superuser, just type the following:

```
# in.named
```

at the command prompt to start the name server process. On most systems, you need to be root to make sure that the process starts correctly.

The next time the UNIX server reboots, the in.named automatically starts simply because you created the /etc/named.boot file.

Testing Your Name Server

Testing your name server is essential to ensure that the name server is functioning properly. Several tools are available for testing and querying a name server. The nslookup command is the most common tool for testing your name server.

The nslookup command is an interactive tool that allows you to query name servers. Simply type nslookup at the command prompt, and the nslookup command prompts you with a > character.

```
$ nslookup
Default Server:  lxotta.learnix.ca
Address:  199.71.122.50

>
```

The Control D sequence exits nslookup. Following are many examples of performing DNS lookups with nslookup.

The nslookup command looks for (A) records in DNS. You can look up a hostname by simply typing the host and domain name of a machine.

```
> www.netscape.com
Server:  lxotta.learnix.ca
Address:  199.71.122.50

Name:     www-me1.netscape.com
Address:  204.152.167.20
Aliases:  www.netscape.com

>
```

Part
IV
Ch
23

You can query other types of resource records by changing the query type in nslookup. The following example changes the query type to SOA records. We show querying the SOA record for the learnix.ca domain.

```
> set q=soa
> learnix.ca
Server:  lxotta.learnix.ca
Address:  199.71.122.50

learnix.ca
        origin = lxotta.learnix.ca
        mail addr = hostmaster.learnix.ca
        serial = 1997120309
        refresh = 21600 (6 hours)
        retry   = 3600 (1 hour)
        expire  = 432000 (5 days)
        minimum ttl = 3600 (1 hour)
learnix.ca       nameserver = ns.uunet.ca
learnix.ca       nameserver = ns2.uunet.ca
learnix.ca       nameserver = ns.uu.net
learnix.ca       nameserver = lxotta.learnix.ca
ns.uunet.ca      internet address = 142.77.1.1
ns2.uunet.ca     internet address = 142.77.1.5
ns.uu.net        internet address = 137.39.1.3
lxotta.learnix.ca        internet address = 199.45.92.97
lxotta.learnix.ca        internet address = 199.71.122.194
lxotta.learnix.ca        internet address = 199.71.122.50
>
```

To query a PTR record, set the query type to "PTR" and type the IP address.

```
> set q=ptr
> 192.9.9.100
Server:  lxotta.learnix.ca
Address:  199.71.122.50

100.9.9.192.in-addr.arpa       name = www.Sun.COM
```

Queries made by nslookup are made to the name servers listed in the /etc/resolv.conf file. If you want to query an alternative server, the server command can be used when in nslookup interactive mode.

```
> server 205.139.91.50
Default Server:  learnix.learnix.com
Address:  205.139.91.50
```

Configuring a Secondary Name Server

Configuring a secondary name server requires a similar setup as the primary. The following /etc/named.boot file would be used to configure a secondary name server:

```
Directory                                       /var/named
Cache           .                               db.cache
Primary         127.in-addr.arpa.               db.127
Secondary       learnix.ca            199.71.122.50    db.learnix
Secondary       122.71.199.in-addr.arpa.   199.71.122.50    db.199.71.122
```

The two secondary directives inform in.named that your server is to be a secondary name server for the domains learnix.ca and 122.71.199.in-addr.arpa.

The secondary directive specifies the zone, IP address of the primary server, and local file used to store the zone information.

The secondary name server must also be added to the list of name servers for the zone on the primary server.

The alterations to the name server section of the db.learnix file, on the primary, is as follows:

```
; This is the name server section of the zone database file
; The db.learnix file

learnix.ca.    IN    NS    lxotta.learnix.ca.    ; primary
learnix.ca.    IN    NS    ns.uunet.net.         ; secondary
; Our newly added secondary
learnix.ca.    IN    NS    squeaky.learnix.ca.
; Add an address record for squeaky below
squeaky.learnix.ca.    IN    A    199.71.122.55    ; new secondary

; Include the address record for any name servers that
; cannot be looked-up somewhere else in DNS

lxotta.learnix.ca.    IN    A    199.71.122.50
```

The adjusted name server section of the db.199.71.122. file is as follows:

```
@    IN    NS    lxotta.learnix.ca.        ; primary
@    IN    NS    ns.uunet.net.             ; secondary

; The new secondary name server is added below
@    IN    NS    squeaky.learnix.ca        ; new secondary
```

Delegating a Subdomain

Creating a subdomain is accomplished by adding NS records into the name database file.

Creating a subdomain named `darkwing` in the `learnix.ca.` domain would result in the following additions to the name server section of the `db.learnix` zone file:

```
; This is the name server section of the zone database file

learnix.ca.      IN    NS    lxotta.learnix.ca.
learnix.ca.      IN    NS    ns.uunet.net.

; Include the address record for any name servers that
; cannot be looked-up somewhere else in DNS

lxotta.learnix.ca.    IN    A    199.71.122.50

; Delegating the darkwing.learnix.ca. sub-domain

darkwing.learnix.ca.    IN    NS    duckula.darkwing.learnix.ca.

; We need a "glue" record for duckula.darkwing.learnix.ca
; A glue record is an ( A ) record for the host in the domain below learnix.ca.

duckula.darkwing.learnix.ca.    IN    A    205.212.181.151
```

An NS record is used to delegate authority of the `darkwing.learnix.ca.` domain. A "glue" record, in the form of an (A) record is used to specify the IP address of the name server, `duckula.darkwing.learnix.ca.`, for the domain `darkwing.learnix.ca`. A "glue" record is only required, if the name server for the new domain is in a zone located below the domain that is delegating the domain.

Setting Up Mail Exchangers

Mail exchangers are hosts capable of receiving Internet mail for an entire domain. MX records allow users to send mail to *user@domain* instead of *user@host.domain*.

Usually a domain has more than one mail exchanger. The MX resource record in DNS specifies the mail exchanger for your domain. In the following example, we make `jazz` and `donald` the two mail exchangers for the domain `learnix.ca.`. We then need to add the following two MX records to the `db.learnix` file:

```
learnix.ca.      IN    MX    10    jazz
learnix.ca.      IN    MX    20    donald
```

The MX records specify a preference value and the mail exchanger host. `jazz` has a preference value of 10 and is preferable to `donald`, who has a preference of 20. The Internet host will try delivering mail to `jazz` before `donald`, when trying to deliver mail to the `learnix.ca.` domain.

Troubleshooting and Debugging DNS

One of the main debug tools you have with `in.named` is having the daemon dump its cached database to a text file. To have `in.named` dump its cache, you must send the daemon an INT signal. The file `/etc/named.pid` contains the process ID of `in.named`. The following command sends the INT signal to `in.named`:

```
kill -INT `cat /etc/named.pid`
```

The file `/var/tmp/named_dump.db` contains the cache information that was dumped. The cache file looks identical to a zone database file.

The `in.named` daemon also supports debug logging. To start the daemon logging, send the daemon a USR1 signal as follows:

```
kill -USR1 `cat /etc/named.pid`
```

The logging information is logged in the `/var/tmp/named.run` file. If the USR1 signal is sent to the daemon, the verbosity of the logging information increases. To reset the debug level to "0," send the daemon a USR2 signal.

The HUP signal may be sent to the named daemon each time a zone database is changed. The HUP signal rereads the databases without having to kill and restart the `in.named` daemon. The following example sends the HUP signal to `in.named`:

```
kill -HUP `cat /etc/named.pid`
```

▶ **See** "Dealing with Signals," **p. 189**

CAUTION

If alterations are made to the `/etc/named.boot` file, the `in.named` daemon must be stopped and restarted to see the changes.

From Here...

This chapter covered the historical motivations for the creation of DNS. The chapter looked at the different types of name servers and demonstrated a sample DNS query. It also examined the creation and maintenance of the DNS database files. Finally, the chapter examined the configuration and troubleshooting of BIND. With the material covered in this chapter, you should have a good idea as to how name resolution works on the Internet. From here, you can go to one of the following topics:

- Chapter 24, "Apache Web Server," covers one of the most commonly used Web servers on UNIX. Web servers rely heavily on DNS to function properly.

- Chapter 25, "Sendmail and POP," covers the configuration of mail services on UNIX. Mail delivery also depends heavily on DNS.

- Chapter 27, "Performance Tuning," gives you helpful advice on configuring networking on UNIX systems so that your users (including DNS clients) always have optimal performance.

Apache Web Server

by Nalneesh Guar

Understanding Web Servers

The rapid expansion of the World Wide Web (WWW) far exceeds the expectation of its creators. The Web or the Internet is more than just a means of information dissemination. Today, the Web provides application, database, and multimedia functionality to millions of surfers all over the world.

There are three primary components to the Web, namely the Web server, the network, and the Web client. As of this writing, the Apache Web server constitutes approximately 53 percent of the deployed servers. Teams of volunteer software developers spread all over the world write the Apache Web server. The source code and binary executables (most OS) of the Apache Web server are freely available from Apache's Web site (http://www.apache.org). The Apache server presents a modular architecture with many configuration options.

This chapter assumes that you are familiar with the Internet and the basic terminology associated with it. We will focus on the installation and configuration of the Apache server. Because Apache provides several configuration options, it is not possible to demonstrate the combined effect of every configuration option available in Apache. Instead, the approach presented here suggests basic concepts, ideas, and examples to elucidate the Apache Web server.

The Web server enables you to publish information on the Internet. The Hypertext Transport Protocol (HTTP) is the access medium used by Web browsers to view the information provided by a Web server. Typically, Web servers provide access to a single Web site such as www.mcp.com. However, it is not uncommon for a Web server on a single computer to serve Web sites of different Internet domains. The role of the Web server is to serve content in response to client uniform resource locator (URL) requests. The Web content can be static or dynamically generated. Although static Web pages are created using the Hypertext Markup language (HTML), the Common Gateway Interface (CGI) provides dynamic Web content on the Web server. For example, confirmation numbers generated at the end of a transaction are dynamic. The following section provides an overview of HTTP, CGI, and URL.

HTTP

The Hypertext Transfer Protocol is an application level protocol for distributed, collaborative, and hypermedia information systems. The HTTP version 1.0 (HTTP/1.0) specified in RFC 1945 is widely deployed over the Web. HTTP/1.0 uses request/response semantics to transfer data in mime-like messages. The WWW Consortium or the W3C (http://www.w3.org) develops the HTTP standards. The latest release of the protocol is HTTP/1.1, which is still an Internet draft standard. HTTP/1.1 overcomes many limitations of its precursor HTTP/1.0. Specifically, the protocol allows for a single TCP connection for subsequent HTTP requests, facilitates caching, and allows for multiple sites to be served off a single IP address. The Apache Web server version 1.2 and above implements the HTTP/1.1 draft standard.

All HTTP traffic on the Internet takes place over TCP. By default, port 80 on the server is used to fulfill HTTP requests. A client such as a Web browser always initiates requests. The HTTP message consists of requests from clients to the server and the response of the server to the clients. A Web browser initiates the request using the GET method. The GET method specifies requests to the Web server for a unified resource identifier (URI). The URI may point to a static Web page or a CGI script. The Web server responds with a POST method to the requested URI. If the Web server is successful in identifying the resource referenced by the URI, then a "text/html" response is sent to the Web browser. The request-response sequence can be simulated using the telnet program. Listing 24.1 displays the request-response sequence to the www Web server operating on port 80. The response is generated after you type in GET /index.html HTTP/1.0 return return.

Listing 24.1   Typical HTTP *GET* Request

```
# telnet www 80
Trying 10.10.10.13...
Connected to www.mcp.com.
Escape character is '^]'.
GET /index.html HTTP/1.0 return return

HTTP/1.1 200 OK
Date: Thu, 25 Jun 1998 16:07:04 GMT
Server: Apache/1.2.0
Last-Modified: Fri, 01 May 1998 21:18:33 GMT
ETag: "3743-1e6-354a3c29"
Content-Length: 486
Accept-Ranges: bytes
Connection: close
Content-Type: text/html

<html>
<head><title>Welcome to the Web</title>

</head>
</html>

Connection closed by foreign host.
```

Browsers that understand HTTP/1.1 will generate a GET HTTP/1.1 request. The response returned by the Web server is interpreted by the Web browser and displayed in the browser window. Let us examine the key (highlighted) elements in the Web server response in Listing 24.1.

■ HTTP/1.1 200 OK   This entry describes that the Web server meets the HTTP/1.1 standards. The status code and its meaning 200 OK follow. The browser uses the server status codes to interpret the response results. Almost every Web user is familiar with the 404 Not Found message. This message results if the Web server is unable to find a match for the requested URI. The HTTP/1.0 specification defines other messages that are sent back to the Web browser.

■ Server: Apache/1.2.0   This entry describes the server vendor string and the server version.

- ■ Content-Length: 486 This entry describes the length of the response in bytes. The server returns a 400 Bad Request error code if it cannot determine the length of the request message's content.
- ■ Content-Type: text/html This entry describes the mime type being returned.

The Web server response is the result of an URL query. So, what is an URL?

URLs

The uniform resource locator (URL) is used to locate the network resources via the referenced protocol. The syntax for the URL is as follows:

```
"protocol:" "//" host[ ":" port ] [unique identifier]
```

where *protocol* is the name of the application level protocol. Web page requests use the http protocol. Other protocols are ftp and nntp. The specified hostname is any host for which an IP address can be obtained. The Web client requests the IP address information via a DNS server or host file depending on the client system configuration. The port specifies the TCP port on which the server is accepting requests. If the protocol is HTTP and the port value is not specified, then the port 80 is assumed.

The unique identifier for the accessed resource is the path relative to the document root. The document root parameter is defined during server configuration. The document root is a location on the server where Web content resides. For example, the Web server might refer to the document root as /usr/local/web, but the Web client will refer to the directory as /. All documents are accessed relative to document root location. The Web server does not permit any Web client to traverse the directory tree above document root.

Often the acronym URL is used interchangeably with URI. To avoid any confusion, we will use URL to refer to the complete Web address of a resource. The following is an example of an URL and its components.

```
http://www.mcp.com/NewBooks/computers.html
Protocol://host(port 80 assumed)unique identifier
```

CGI

The Common Gateway Interface (CGI) is a standard that provides an interface to external applications from Web servers. A CGI program is executed in real-time and is used most of the time to present dynamic information to the users of a Web site. It is important to understand that the CGI program is processed on the Web server. Web servers that serve CGI programs are easily overloaded due to the load placed by the programs. Accessing databases to present information to users is a simple application of CGI.

Most Web servers require that the CGI programs be installed in a special directory on the server. In addition, the Apache Web server can be configured to recognize CGI files by their extension such as .cgi (see the following Caution). CGI programs can be written in any high-level programming language such as C/C++, FORTRAN, and BASIC and in an interpreted language such as PERL, TCL, or a UNIX shell. All CGI programs must have their executable bit turned on.

▶ **See** "Choosing a Shell," **p. 47**

CAUTION

Permitting CGI scripts in an explicitly named directory is also referred to has script-aliased CGI. This is a commonly used approach for a security conscious site. Additionally, script-aliased CGI in contrast to the extension-based or non-script-aliased CGI provides management advantages. On a server that provides individual user Web sites, the script-aliased CGI is the more secure option.

A client requesting a CGI program in its URL will cause the server to execute the program in real-time. The output of the program, if any, is sent directly to the requesting client. Two methods, GET and POST are available to CGI programmers to pass variables to the program. The GET method utilizes the QUERY_STRING environmental variable to pass the arguments to the CGI program. The QUERY_STRING is the string immediately followed by the first ? in the URL. The variables and the values are separated by an =, and each pair is separated by the &. Search engines often use the GET method. For example:

```
http://www.mcp.com/catalog/catalog.htm?type=computer&books=software
```

The POST method uses the standard input to provide data to the CGI program. CGI programs that use the POST method utilize the CONTENT_LENGTH variable to determine the amount of data to be read from the standard input.

Although CGI programs deliver dynamic content to the Web browsers, they also pose significant security risks. The very fact that CGI programs are run by users unknown to the server should caution a Web administrator. Intruders have been able to break into systems by using commonly known flaws in CGI programs. Several CGI libraries are freely available on the Internet which provide functions for safe CGI programming.

ON THE WEB

`http://www.csclub.uwaterloo.ca/u/mlvanbie/cgisec` Provides programming techniques that focus on writing safe CGI programs

`http://www.sunworld.com/swol-08-1998/swol-08-security.html?0817i` Provides general secure UNIX programming techniques

Apache Server Installation

The Apache server was originally based on the NCSA httpd server version 1.3. It was feared that the NCSA Web server contained many security holes. This prompted a group of programmers to apply patches to the NCSA Web server. The resulting Web server was a patchy server and hence the name Apache server. Since then, the server has been rewritten from scratch.

This section describes the planning and installation of the Apache Web server.

Part
IV

Ch
24

Preparing to Install Your Server

The preparation for the installation of the Web server depends on whether the Web server will serve as an Internet or an intranet Web server. Careful planning during the initial stages of a Web server deployment pays rich dividends in the long run. The following aspects should be considered:

- Type of content being provided
- Identifying the anticipated hits on the Web server
- Obtaining a valid IP address for the server
- Adding the server to the name server database
- Procuring the hardware for the Web server
- Administration and maintenance of the Web server
- Backup of the Web server
- Securing the Web server

Web servers can be used to provide static HTML pages, applications, audio, video clips, and other multimedia content. The default choice for high-end Web servers utilized by many organizations and ISPs is UNIX servers. The truly high-volume Web sites benefit by using servers with multiple CPUs. Any hardware that provides scalability leaves room for expanding hardware instead of migrating to a more powerful system. To begin with, select server hardware that provides the capability to expand CPUs, memory, and disk space. Adding components to the server can accommodate an increase in the volume of traffic. Servers that perform significant server side processing greatly benefit by adding more CPU and memory.

Bug fixes, hot fixes, updates, and patches to the OS enhance the server performance. Additionally, many patches are being applied to plug security holes in the OS. Keeping current with the changes presents a proactive approach in terms of server maintenance.

The SPECweb96 can be consulted with regard to the performance of the different Web server hardware. However, the SPECWeb96 should not be the sole deciding factor in favor of a particular server.

ON THE WEB

`http://www.specbench.org/osg/web96`   Provides benchmarks on the performance of Web servers on different platforms

Faster hard disks on Web servers can provide significant improvements in the performance of the server. Because most of the data is read-only on Web servers, implementing RAID on the Web server improves read access and provides for redundancy in the event of a disk failure. Many servers implement RAID (Redundant Array of Inexpensive Disks) level 5 as an inexpensive solution to provide for improved access and fault tolerance. Using Caching controllers (available with most storage arrays) and making in-memory cache as large as possible alleviate problems associated with slow disk access.

▶ **See** "Adding Hard Disk Devices," **p. 303**

▶ **See** "Creating File Systems," **p. 330**

Most high-performance Web servers are connected via a full T1, a fractional/full T3, or a better connection. However, the speed of the link itself should not be the only deciding factor. The pipe of the Internet service provider to the backbone can influence the effectiveness of a network link. The bandwidth offered by a connection can determine maximum number of hits that a connection can sustain. A full T3 line yields only about 5MB/sec or about 400 operations/second (with 100 percent utilization). Therefore, a server with a SPECweb96 rating of 1500 ops/sec may be underutilized when connected with a full T3 connection to the Internet backbone. Using mirrored servers assists in meeting higher sustained demands.

TIP The proximity of the Internet service providers to the Commercial Internet Exchange, MAE East or MAE West, provides better connectivity. The choice of an Internet service provider should also be based on the ISP having multiple, diverse connections to the Internet. This provides for redundancy in the event that if one of the connections were to drop, the other connections continue to provide connectivity.

Part
IV

Ch
24

Any client browser accessing a Web site goes through multiple hops before reaching the Web site. Each hop adds on to the latency due to the routers involved. Most organizations solve the latency issues by locating mirrored servers at different geographic locations. The location of the server is decided based on the anticipated community of users. For example, a retail chain with a nationwide presence across the United States might want to set up mirrored servers in San Francisco, Denver, Dallas, Atlanta, Washington DC, and New York. Using products such as the Distributed Director from Cisco Systems (http://www.cisco.com) facilitates this solution. Additionally, the DNS system can be set up to provide load balancing.

Obtaining Apache Server Software

The Apache Web server is available from Apache's Web site at http://www.apache.org. The Apache Web server software can be downloaded from its Web site free of charge. The software is available in compressed tape archive (tar) format and binaries. You may also download the software from ftp://ftp.apache.org. The Apache Web site provides many mirror sites all over the world. A listing of the mirror sites can be found at http://www.apache.org/mirrors. As of this writing, the latest release of Apache is a maintenance release version 1.3. All downloadable files are PGP signed for security purposes.

The uncompressed Apache source occupies less than 5MB on the hard disk. Make sure that you have sufficient space prior to uncompressing and extracting the files from tape archive. Additionally, you need space for the compiled binaries and object files. Use the following to prepare the Apache files for compilation:

```
# gunzip -c Apache-1.3.0.tar.gz | tar xvf -
```

The command creates the Apache distribution directory structure that contains the build configuration file, Apache source tree, support utilities, and documentation. You may use the UNIX zcat instead of the gunzip command for downloaded file that ends with the .z extension.

> **N O T E**   The gunzip is part of the gzip package from the GNU free software foundation. The
> software can be downloaded from ftp://prep.ai.mit.edu. For more information on
> GNU software, visit http://www.gnu.org. ■

Apache binaries are available for a few platforms only. If you want to use the binaries, skip over to the section "Basic Apache Configuration" later in this chapter. Before you compile the Apache server, you should explore the standard Apache modules.

Apache Modules

Apache uses directives for the server configuration. Directives are like commands that define the functionality of the Apache server. Directives are module specific. In other words, the Apache server recognizes a directive only when the required module is compiled at build time. Certain modules are compiled by default to provide the basic server functionality. You can disable module compilation by commenting out the module names in the Apache build configuration file. Fewer modules will result in a smaller binary. In addition to the standard modules, Apache provides contributed modules with its distribution. Table 24.1 provides a list of standard modules supported by the Apache development group. The contributed modules are not listed here. A list of the contributed modules can be found in the Apache documentation.

Table 24.1   Standard Apache Modules

Module	Description	Default
Core	Core Apache features.	Yes
mod_access	Host based access control.	Yes
mod_actions	Apache 1.1 and later. Filetype/method-based script execution.	Yes
mod_alias	Aliases and redirects.	Yes
mod_asis	The .asis file handler.	Yes
mod_auth	User authentication using text files.	Yes
mod_auth_anon	Anonymous user authentication, FTP style.	No
mod_auth_db	User authentication using Berkeley DB files.	No
mod_auth_dbm	User authentication using DBM files.	No
mod_autoindex	Automatic directory listings.	Yes
mod_browser, Obsolete	Apache 1.2 and above only. Set environment variables based on User-Agent strings. Replaced by mod_setenvif in Apache 1.3 and up.	Yes
mod_cern_meta	Support for HTTP header metafiles.	No
mod_cgi	Invoking CGI scripts.	Yes

Module	Description	Default
mod_cookies, Obsolete	Support for Netscape-like cookies. Replaced in Apache 1.2 by mod_usertrack.	No
mod_digest	MD5 authentication.	No
mod_dir	Basic directory handling.	Yes
mod_dld, Obsolete	Apache 1.2.* and earlier. Start-time linking with the GNU libdld. Replaced in Apache 1.3 by mod_so.	No
mod_dll	Apache 1.3b1 to 1.3b5 only. Replaced in 1.3b6 by mod_so. Compiled by default in Windows only.	UNIX No
mod_env	Passing of environments to CGI scripts.	No
mod_example	Apache 1.2 and up. Demonstrates Apache API.	No
mod_expires	Apache 1.2 and up. Apply Expires: headers to resources.	No
mod_headers	Apache 1.2 and up. Add arbitrary HTTP headers to resources.	No
mod_imap	The imagemap file handler.	Yes
mod_include	Server-parsed documents.	Yes
mod_info	Server configuration information.	No
mod_isapi	Windows ISAPI Extension support. Compiled by default in Windows only.	UNIX No
mod_log_agent	Logging of User Agents.	No
mod_log_common	Up to Apache 1.1.1 Standard logging in the Common Log file Format. Replaced by the mod_log_config module_log_config.	Yes
mod_log_config	In Apache 1.2 and up. User-configurable logging replacement for mod_log_common.	Yes
mod_log_referer	Logging of document references.	Yes
mod_mime	Determining document types using file extensions.	Yes
mod_mime_magic	Determining document types using "magic numbers."	No
mod_mmap_static	Mapping files into memory for faster serving.	No
mod_negotiation	Content negotiation.	Yes
mod_proxy	Caching proxy capabilities.	No
mod_rewrite	Apache 1.2 and up. Powerful URI-to-filename mapping using regular expressions.	No

Part

IV

Ch

24

continues

Table 24.1 Continued

Module	Description	Default
mod_setenvif	Apache 1.3 and up. Set environment variables based on client information.	Yes
mod_so	Apache 1.3 and up. Experimental support for loading modules (DLLs on Windows) at runtime. Compiled by default on Windows only.	UNIX No
mod_speling	Apache 1.3 and up. Automatically correct minor typos in URLs.	No
mod_status	Server status display.	
mod_userdir	User home directories.	Yes
mod_unique_id	Apache 1.3 and up. Generate unique request identifier for every request.	
mod_usertrack	Apache 1.2 and up. User tracking using Cookies replacement for mod_cookies.c.	

Compiling and Installing Your Server

Compiling Apache involves three steps:

1. Select Apache modules to be included. This step involves modifying the build configuration file in the src directory of the Apache distribution. You will notice that by default many modules are automatically included. In fact, these modules are included with the binary distribution. If the binary for your platform is available and all you need is the default modules, then you may save yourself the need to compile Apache. Other Apache modules are commented in the configuration file. Uncomment the modules you need in preparation for generating the platform specific configuration file.

2. Generate server-specific configuration files. Examine the build configuration file for the EXTRA_CFLAGS, LIBS, LDFLAGS, and INCLUDES. See Table 24.2 for a description of these options.

Table 24.2 Configuration File Options

Build Flags	Description
EXTRA_CFLAGS	Used to specify options for the C Compiler on your platform
LIBS	Specifies path to required libraries
LDFLAGS	Specifies the flags for linking the various compiled objects
INCLUDES	Specifies the location of the include files

After you are satisfied with the options in the configuration file, run:

```
# ./configure
```

The configure script examines your server platform and displays messages during the process. At the end of the process, the script generates a `Makefile`. The `Makefile` contains all the information necessary for compiling the Apache Web server.

3. Compile the Web server daemon. Start the compilation by running:

```
# make
```

A successful compilation results in the creation of the Apache `httpd` executable in the `src` directory.

Apache is designed to run from the directory in which it was compiled. If you want to use a different directory to run Apache, then copy the Apache `httpd` executable and the `conf`, `logs`, and `icons` directories to that location.

```
# cp -R httpd conf logs icons <destination directory>
```

The following sections discuss the Apache server configuration files and directives.

Part

IV

Ch

24

Basic Apache Configuration

Prior to running the Apache server, you must configure the server configuration files. The configuration files themselves are a collection of directives. A description of the Apache configuration files and the directives follows.

N O T E   The server configuration files should not be confused with the Apache build configuration file as discussed under the section on "Apache Server Installation." Although the Apache server configuration files are required for the Apache server daemon, the Apache build configuration file is used only for Apache rebuilds.

Apache Configuration Files

The Apache configuration consists of directives in three files, namely `httpd.conf`, `access.conf`, and `srm.conf` in the `conf` directory. Directives in the files are module-specific. The Apache distribution provides default configuration files namely `httpd-dist.conf`, `access-dist.conf`, and `srm-dist.conf`. You may copy the distribution files to files without the `-dist` extension and then edit them to suit your needs. In addition to the three configuration files, Apache reads the `mime.types` file at startup. This section focuses on the Apache configuration files and its implications on the server.

The *httpd.conf* File   The `httpd.conf` file or the server configuration file contains general attributes of the server, such as the `http` port, server type, server name, location of log data, proxy configuration, virtual host configuration, and much more. The `httpd.conf` file is parsed when the Apache Web server is started. All lines beginning with a # are comments and are ignored by the server. Although, the `httpd.conf` file with the Apache distribution is interlaced with comments, making inappropriate changes to this file can cause the Apache Web server to not work. Listing 24.2 displays a simple `httpd.conf` file adapted from the `httpd-dist.conf` file.

Listing 24.2 *httpd.conf* The Server Configuration

```
# ServerType is either inetd, or standalone.
ServerType standalone

# Port: The port the standalone listens to. For
# ports < 1023, you will
# need httpd to be run as root initially.

Port 80

# ServerName allows you to set a host name which is
# sent back to clients for your server if it's
# different than the one the program would get
# (i.e. use "www" instead of the host's real name).
# Note: You cannot just invent host names and hope
# they work. The name you define here must be a
# valid DNS name for your host. If you don't
# understand this, ask your network administrator.

ServerName www.mcp.com

# If you wish httpd to run as a different user
# or group, you must run
# httpd as root initially and it will switch.
# User/Group: The name (or #number)
# of the user/group to run httpd as.
# On SCO (ODT 3) use User nouser and Group nogroup
# On HPUX you may not be able to use shared memory
# as nobody, and the suggested workaround is to
# create a user www and use that user.

User web
Group web

# ServerAdmin: Your address, where problems with
# the server should be emailed.

ServerAdmin webmaster@mcp.com

# ServerRoot: The directory of the server's config,
# error, and log files are kept in

ServerRoot /usr/local/httpd

# ErrorLog: The location of the error log file.
# If this does not start
# with /, ServerRoot is prepended to it.

ErrorLog logs/error_log
```

```
# TransferLog: The location of the transfer log
# file. This file lists all clients/browsers
# accessing the web server. If this does not start
# with /, ServerRoot is # prepended to it.

TransferLog logs/access_log

# PidFile: The file the server should log its pid to
PidFile logs/httpd.pid

# ScoreBoardFile: File used to store internal server
# process information. Not all architectures require
# this.  But if yours does (you'll know because
# this file is created when you run Apache) then you
# *must* ensure that no two invocations of Apache
# share the same scoreboard file.
ScoreBoardFile logs/apache_status

# HostnameLookups: Log the names of clients or just
# their IP numbers
#   e.g.   www.apache.org (on) or
#          204.62.129.132 (off)
# The default is off because it'd be overall better
# for the net if people had to knowingly turn this
# feature on. Reduces DNS lookup overhead and
# improves server performance.

HostnameLookups off

# Timeout: The number of seconds before receives
# and sends time out

Timeout 300

# KeepAlive: Whether or not to allow persistent
# connections (more than one request per
# connection). Set to "Off" to deactivate.

KeepAlive On

# MaxKeepAliveRequests: The maximum number of
# requests to allow during a persistent connection.
# Set to 0 to allow an unlimited amount. We
# recommend you leave this number high, for maximum
# performance.

MaxKeepAliveRequests 100

# KeepAliveTimeout: Number of seconds to wait
# for the next request

KeepAliveTimeout 15

# Number of servers to start --- should be a
# reasonable ballpark figure.
```

Part

IV

Ch

24

continues

Listing 24.2   Continued

```
StartServers 5

# Limit on total number of servers running, i.e.,
# limit on the number of clients who can
# simultaneously connect --- if this limit is ever
# reached, clients will be LOCKED OUT, so it should
# NOT BE SET TOO LOW. It is intended mainly as a
# brake to keep a runaway server from taking
# UNIX with it as it spirals down...

MaxClients 150
```

The configuration file in Listing 24.2 informs the Apache Web server on startup that this is a standalone server (ServerType standalone) serving requests on port 80 (Port 80). The server will be known as www.mcp.com (ServerName www.mcp.com) and has a corresponding entry in the primary DNS of the mcp.com domain.

All Web server-related problems should be reported to webmaster@mcp.com (ServerAdmin webmaster@mcp.com). The Web server will be run as the user Web and group Web (User web, Group web). The Web user and the Web group are already created on the server. For security purposes, run the Apache sever as any user other than root.

▶ **See** "Creating User Acounts," **p. 242**

All server configuration files are located in /usr/local/httpd (ServerRoot /usr/local/ httpd). The error logs and transfer logs will be stored in the /usr/local/httpd/logs directory (ErrorLog logs/error_log, TransferLog logs/access_log).

Apache supports the single TCP or persistent connection for subsequent HTTP requests by implementing the KeepAlive directive. The KeepAlive feature improves the performance of the Web server by reducing the overhead caused by opening and closing a socket for each HTTP request. Our httpd.conf file uses this feature (KeepAlive on). Additionally, the configuration file specifies that the server waits for up to 15 seconds (KeepAliveTimeout 15) between subsequent requests from each client to maintain a persistent TCP connection. Any requests after this timeout period are established as a new TCP connection. Furthermore, a client is allowed up to 100 HTTP requests (MaxKeepAliveRequests 100) under a persistent connection. This number should be increased if you anticipate a higher number of client requests. The server can limit the number of clients connecting simultaneously. This might be necessary to prevent overloading the server. In our configuration file, the limit is set to 150 (MaxClients 150). All clients after this limit are locked out.

The httpd.conf file provides other directives for configuring the Apache Web server as a proxy server and as a virtual host. These directives are discussed in later sections.

The *srm.conf* File   The srm.conf or the resource configuration file provides directives such as the location of the document root, server settings, and formatting of results. Additionally, the configuration file includes directives that allow you to modify the default behavior of the

Apache Web server. Listing 24.3 displays a sample srm.conf file adapted from the srm-dist.conf file.

 TIP Basic Apache installation may not require modifications to the resource configuration (srm.conf) file. You may simply copy the srm-dist.conf file to srm.conf.

Listing 24.3   *srm.conf* The Resource Configuration File

```
# DocumentRoot: The directory out of which you will
# serve your documents. By default, all requests are
# taken from this directory, but symbolic links and
# aliases may be used to point to other locations.

DocumentRoot /web

# DirectoryIndex: Name of the file or files to use
# as a pre-written HTML directory index.  Separate
# multiple entries with spaces.

DirectoryIndex index.html default.html greetings.cgi

# FancyIndexing is whether you want fancy
# directory indexing or standard

FancyIndexing on

# AddIcon tells the server which icon to show
# for different files or filename extensions

AddIconByType (TXT,/icons/text.gif) text/*
AddIconByType (IMG,/icons/image2.gif) image/*
AddIconByType (SND,/icons/sound2.gif) audio/*
AddIconByType (VID,/icons/movie.gif) video/*

AddIcon /icons/binary.gif .bin .exe
AddIcon /icons/binhex.gif .hqx
AddIcon /icons/tar.gif .tar
AddIcon /icons/world2.gif .wrl .wrl.gz .vrml .vrm .iv
AddIcon /icons/compressed.gif .Z .z .tgz .gz .zip
AddIcon /icons/a.gif .ps .ai .eps
AddIcon /icons/layout.gif .html .shtml .htm .pdf
AddIcon /icons/text.gif .txt
AddIcon /icons/c.gif .c
AddIcon /icons/p.gif .pl .py
AddIcon /icons/f.gif .for
AddIcon /icons/dvi.gif .dvi
AddIcon /icons/uuencoded.gif .uu
AddIcon /icons/script.gif .conf .sh .shar .csh .ksh .tcl
AddIcon /icons/tex.gif .tex
AddIcon /icons/bomb.gif core

AddIcon /icons/back.gif ..
```

Part
IV

Ch
24

continues

Listing 24.3   Continued

```
AddIcon /icons/hand.right.gif README
AddIcon ("DIR",/icons/folder.gif) ^^DIRECTORY^^
AddIcon /icons/blank.gif ^^BLANKICON^^

# DefaultIcon is which icon to show for files
# which do not have an icon explicitly set.

DefaultIcon /icons/unknown.gif

# AddDescription allows you to place a short
# description after a file in server-generated
# indexes.
# Format: AddDescription "description" filename

# ReadmeName is the name of the README file
# the server will look for by
# default. Format: ReadmeName name
#
# The server will first look for name.html,
# include it if found, and it will
# then look for name and include it as plaintext
# if found.
#
# HeaderName is the name of a file which should
# be prepended to directory indexes.

ReadmeName README
HeaderName HEADER

# IndexIgnore is a set of filenames which directory
# indexing should ignore
# Format: IndexIgnore name1 name2...

IndexIgnore *.gif *.jpg .??* *~ *# HEADER* README* RCS

# AccessFileName: The name of the file to look
# for in each directory for access control
# information.

AccessFileName .htaccess

# DefaultType is the default MIME type for
# documents which the server cannot find the type
# of from filename extensions.

DefaultType text/plain

# Redirect allows you to tell clients about
# documents which used to exist in your server's
# namespace, but do not anymore. This allows you to
# tell the clients where to look for the relocated
# document.
# Format: Redirect fakename url
Redirect /subscriptions http://subscriptions.mcp.com
```

```
# Aliases: Add here as many aliases as you need
# (with no limit). The format is
# Alias fakename realname
# Note that if you include a trailing / on fakename
# then the server will require it to be present in
# the URL.  So "/icons" isn't aliased in this
# example.

Alias /icons /opt/web/icons
Alias /applets /opt/web/applets
# ScriptAlias: This controls which directories
# contain server scripts.
# Format: ScriptAlias fakename realname

ScriptAlias /cgi-bin /opt/web/cgi-bin

# If you want to use server side includes, or CGI
# outside ScriptAliased directories, uncomment the
# following lines.

# AddType allows you to tweak mime.types without
# actually editing it, or to
# make certain files to be certain types.
# Format: AddType type/subtype ext1

# AddHandler allows you to map certain
# file extensions to "handlers", actions unrelated
# to filetype. These can be either built into the
# server or added with the Action command (see
# below)
# Format: AddHandler action-name ext1

# To use CGI scripts:
AddHandler cgi-script cgi

# Customizable error response (Apache style)
#   these come in three flavors
#     1) local redirects
ErrorDocument 404 /cgi-bin/missing_handler.pl
#   n.b. can redirect to a script or a document
# using server-side-includes.
#
#     2) external redirects
ErrorDocument 402 http://subscription.mcp.com/subscription_info.html
```

Part
IV

Ch
24

The first directive in the configuration file is the DocumentRoot directive. This directive specifies the location where Apache will look for the requested URLs. The DirectoryIndex directive is used to specify a list of possible index files to be used in order. In our configuration, the Web server attempts to run the index.html file. If this file fails, then the default.html file is run, and finally greetings.cgi is run. Specifying more than one file for the DirectoryIndex directive is particularly important in environments where multiple individuals use different filenames for index files.

Sometimes it is desirable to provide a more customized view of the directory listing especially for downloading files. These may include fancy icons, brief description, and selectively displaying files by their extensions. A combination of directives is used to achieve the customized view of the directory listing. Let's examine the directives one by one:

- ▓ `FancyIndexing` This directive can be set to on or off. Once set to on, it allows fancy display of directory.

- ▓ `AddIcon` This directive specifies the image to be used when displaying a file with a given extension, directory, or blank lines.

  `AddIcon icons/compress.gif .gz .Z .z`

  It is always better to provide a text alternative alongside the icon URL for browsers that cannot display images. This is achieved by using:

  `AddIcon ("DIR", icons/burst.gif) ^^DIRECTORY^^`

- ▓ `AddIconByType` This directive specifies icons based on mime types. Apache looks in the file `mime.types` to determine the matching icon:

  `AddIconByType (TXT,icons/txt.gif) text/plain`

- ▓ `AddDescription` This directive provides a brief description for the file name or extension.

  `AddDescription "White Paper for Technology Summit" white_paper.html`

- ▓ `IndexIgnore` This directive causes matched wildcard and full filenames to not display.

  `IndexIgnore *.gif *.jpg`

Most Web servers use many file systems to store the content served by them. This might also be necessary depending on the topology of the Web site. The `Alias` directive is useful in addressing the requirements of such servers. Any URL referred with the alias location causes the Web server to retrieve the document from the location pointed by the alias. Even though `DocumentRoot` points to `/web`, the URL `http://www.mcp.com/images/txt.gif` causes the Web server to retrieve the file from `/opt/web/images` location.

Unlike `Alias`, the `Redirect` directive is used to redirect the browser/client to an alternate server on the Internet. This is common when servers are relocated or the Web content is reorganized on different servers. In our configuration file, all content meant for `http://www.mcp.com/subscriptions` is redirected to `http://subscriptions.mcp.com`.

Most Web administrators prefer to specify a file extension and a location for CGI scripts. This is achieved by using the `ScriptAlias` and the `AddHandler` directives. In our configuration file, specify that only the CGI scripts located in `/opt/web/cgi-bin` be run by the Web server. Additionally, specify that the Web server recognizes the scripts that have a `.cgi` extension as valid CGI scripts. Apache contains the built-in handler `cgi-script` needed to execute the CGI script.

The `Actions` directive can be used to specify new actions for a given extension. The idea is to write a CGI script to process a file based on its extension before the file is served. The following directives demonstrate the use of `unzip.sh` as the action to handle `gnu` compressed files and serve the files uncompressed to the requesting client. We have invented the my-gnu-compressed MIME for our example.

```
AddHandler my-gnu-compressed gz
Action my-gnu-compressed /cgi-bin/unzip.sh
```

```
Where unzip.sh is
#!/bin/sh
echo "Content-type: text/html"
echo
/usr/local/bin/gzip -d -c $PATH_TRANSLATED
```

The c flag tells gzip to uncompress the files and output the result to the standard output. The PATH_TRANSLATED variable specifies the full path of the compressed file with the .gz extension.

Getting back to our configuration file, Apache provides directives to handle the error messages returned by the server in an elegant manner. We are handling all missing document error messages by a PERL CGI script. This script can be automatically configured to send out messages to the Webmaster or the development group about the missing document error. Additionally, we are directing all error messages relating to the error message 402 to the URL http://subscription.mcp.com/subscription_info.html.

You have seen that the srm.conf file provides a means to customize the default behavior of the Apache Web server. The following section describes access control for Web server content.

The *Access.conf* File   The access.conf or the access configuration file specifies server settings for the types of services allowed and the circumstances under which access is allowed. Access control for specific directories is specified on a per-directory basis (see Listing 24.4).

Part IV

Ch 24

Listing 24.4   *access.conf* The Access Configuration File

```
# Set up access for our DocumentRoot

<Directory /web>

# This may also be "None", "All", or any
# combination of "Indexes",
# "Includes", "FollowSymLinks", "ExecCGI", or
# "MultiViews".

# Note that "MultiViews" must be named *explicitly* # --- "Options All"
# doesn't give it to you (or at least, not yet).

Options Indexes FollowSymLinks

# This controls which options the .htaccess files in
# directories can override. Can also be "All", or
# any combination of "Options", "FileInfo",
# "AuthConfig", and "Limit"

AllowOverride None

# Controls who can get stuff from this server.
```

continues

Listing 24.4   Continued

```
order allow,deny
allow from all

</Directory>

# CGI directory exists, if you have that configured.

<Directory /opt/web/cgi-bin>
    AllowOverride None
    Options None
</Directory>

# Allow server status reports, with the URL of
# http://www.mcp.com/server-status
<Location /server-status>
    SetHandler server-status
    order deny,allow
    deny from all
    allow from .mcp.com
</Location>

# There have been reports of people trying to abuse
# an old bug from pre-1.1 days.  This bug involved a
# CGI script distributed as a part of Apache.
# By uncommenting these lines you can redirect these
# attacks to a logging script on phf.apache.org.
# Or, you can record them yourself, using the script
# support/phf_abuse_log.cgi.

<Location /cgi-bin/phf*>
    deny from all
    ErrorDocument 403      http://phf.apache.org/phf_abuse_log.cgi
</Location>
```

The first directive in the access.conf configuration file specifies the access setting for the DocumentRoot directory. The <Directory /web> and the </Directory> tags are used to specify block settings for DocumentRoot. The Directory directive is a block directive, meaning that the directives specified apply only to the /web directory. Similarly there exist the <FILES files> </FILES> and the <LOCATION URL> </LOCATION> directives for files and URL, respectively.

Apache allows you to define the terms under which to allow access from or deny access to specific IP addresses, hostnames, or groups of addresses and hostnames. The allow from and the deny from directives are used to specify these. You can use the order directive to specify the order in which to process the directives. Let's examine the order directive.

Order allow, deny

This means that a client requesting access to a server resource is permitted only if the client matches the criteria as defined by allow from. If the client's name appears in the allow from list, then the client is allowed. If the client's name appears in the deny from list or does not appear in the allow from list, access is denied. This directive is usually specified when most clients are permitted. The reverse Order deny, allow is used when most clients are to be denied access. For example, you might want to restrict the administration of your Web server using CGI scripts to your domain. The allow from and the deny from directives can specify the partial IP address (209.204), complete IP addresses (209.204.137.2), fully qualified host names (www.mcp.com), and domain names (mcp.com).

TROUBLESHOOTING

The host based access control is not working. Often you will try to allow or restrict access by hostname. The most common causes for the problem are:

- Incorrect hostname   Check the spelling for the hostname.

- Server restart   You have not restarted the server after specifying host-based access in the configuration files.

- Aliases   The hostname you have specified is actually an alias for another hostname. Apache gets the real name instead of the alias causing the host-based access rule to fail.

- Improper reverse domain lookup   You can build Apache to perform a reverse name lookup by specifying the DMAXIMUM_DNS under EXTRA_CFLAGS in the Apache build configuration file.

    EXTRA_CFLAGS=-DMAXIMUM_DNS

This causes the Apache server to ensure that a particular host address is really assigned to the name it claims to be, at the expense of the server performance. The host-based access fails if the reverse name lookup is improperly configured for the domain.

The *Mime.types* File   The mime.types file defines the mime types to be sent to the client for a given file extension. The client uses the mime type information sent by the server to handle the content appropriately. Extra types are often added to the mime.types file or by using the AddType directive in the resource configuration file. Listing 24.5 displays a partial mime.types file.

Listing 24.5   *mime.types* The Mime Type Definition File

```
#Mime Type                   Extension
application/octet-stream     bin dms lha lzh exe class
application/oda              oda
application/pdf              pdf
application/postscript       ai eps ps
application/powerpoint       ppt
application/rtf              rtf
application/x-bcpio          bcpio
application/x-cdlink         vcd
```

Single Configuration File

The Apache distribution installs with the three configuration files namely `httpd.conf`, `srm.conf`, and `access.conf`. On startup, the Apache server parses one file at a time and in the order specified. Apache can be configured to use only one configuration file. This requires that the following lines be included in the `httpd.conf` file.

```
AccessConfig /dev/null
ResourceConfig /dev/null
```

Now the Apache server relies only on a single server configuration file. All the directives of the `srm.conf` and the `access.conf` file can be placed in the `httpd.conf` file. You can also call the `httpd.conf` file anything you want, but this requires that you tell the Apache server using the `f` flag the name of the configuration file that you want to use.

Advanced Apache Configuration

In the previous section, the Apache server configuration files and directives were introduced. By now, you are wondering about implementing user-based access control and running multiple Web servers from a single machine. Look no farther. This section talks about the advanced Apache features including setting up user authentication, setting up individual Web servers, virtual hosts, and proxy servers.

User Access Control

Apache can be used to restrict access to Web content based on user authentication, permitting only authorized users. Apache allows for different types of authorization control. These include basic and Digest (MD5 digest and shared secret). As of this writing, no browser supports the Digest method. The `AuthType` directive can be used to specify the type of authorization. Users wanting to use the services offered by the Web server are required to provide a password to authenticate themselves. The `AuthUserFile` directive specifies the username and password information. This is a file that contains the usernames and their encrypted passwords separated by a colon. The user's file is generated on the server by compiling and running the `htpasswd` program. The `htpasswd` is not compiled by default. The `htpasswd` source code is available in the support directory of the Apache distribution. This utility can be used to create a new user file and add to the user's file. To create a new user file, use the following command:

```
# htpasswd -c /usr/local/httpd/conf/userfile Ann
```

The command prompts for Ann's password. Additional users can be added to the user file without using the `c` flag.

> **CAUTION**
>
> Do not manually edit the user file. Additionally, never place the user file under `DocumentRoot`. This makes the file available for browsing.

Apache defines realms for access to the Web content. A realm is a collection of Web content that can be accessed with the same realm/user password. Different realms on a server can require different passwords by providing different user files. Realms are defined by using the AuthName directive. Apache provides the AuthGroupFile directive to group users by authorization groups. The AuthGroupFile is a plain text file that contains group names and their members. Finally, the Require directive is used to specify the users or groups (must exist in the password/group file) who are required to provide a password to access the server. The keyword valid-user is used to specify any user listed in the user file.

Listing 24.6 specifies the user-based authentication for the /web/secret and /web/pricing location. It requires that the admin group has access to the /web/secret location and that the sales group be allowed to access the /web/pricing location after providing a valid password. It is important to note here that searching a large text file is inefficient. Apache provides other database-based modules (mod_auth_db and mod_auth_dbm) which provide better performance for authenticating against a database of many users.

Listing 24.6   User-Based Authentication

```
##
#     User Authentication
##
<Directory /web/secret>
    AuthName      Administrators Only
    AuthType      Basic
    AuthGroupFile      /usr/local/httpd/conf/groupfile
    AuthUserFile      /usr/local/httpd/conf/userfile
    Require      group admin
</Directory>

<Directory /web/pricing>
    AuthName      Authorized Sales Team
    AuthType      Basic
    AuthGroupFile      /usr/local/httpd/conf/groupfile
AuthUserFile      /usr/local/httpd/conf/userfile
    Require      group sales
</Directory>
```

Part

IV

Ch

24

User authentication can be implemented at the configuration file and at a directory level. The configuration file implementation involves adding the authentication directives to the configuration files, typically httpd.conf or the access.conf files. If you add the directives in both files, then the directives in the access.conf override the directives in the httpd.conf file. Any changes to the configuration file directives require restarting the Apache server.

The authentication scheme can be implemented at the directory level. This implementation requires the .htaccess file which contains the authentication directives. Listing 24.7 displays the .htaccess file for the /web/pricing directory.

Listing 24.7   User Authentication via the *.htaccess* File

```
AuthType      Basic
AuthGroupFile    /usr/local/httpd/conf/groupfile
AuthUserFile    /usr/local/httpd/conf/userfile
Require       group sales
```

The advantage of the .htaccess file is that any changes made to the file are immediately effective. This means that the Apache Web server reads the file every time an object is accessed in the directory. This method is not very effective but saves the trouble of having to restart the Web server.

The server checks the username and password and, if they are valid, returns the page. If the username is not listed in the user file or not permitted, or if an invalid password is supplied, then the user is not allowed access. The Web server returns the 410 Unauthorized status. The browser may ask the user to retry the username and password.

Whenever Apache handles a request, the server always checks for the .htaccess file in the directory in which the requested file resides and all its parent directories. This includes parent directories above the DocumentRoot. This can adversely affect the performance of the server. The behavior of the server can be modified by specifying the AllowOverride None directive for DocumentRoot and setting the override option to All for the directory that requires the special access permissions. Listing 24.8 displays these settings.

Listing 24.8   Directory Specific *.htaccess*

```
<Directory />
    AllowOverride None
</Directory>

<Directory /web/pricing>
    AllowOverride All
</Directory>

<Directory /web/secret>
    AllowOverride All
</Directory>
```

TROUBLESHOOTING

User Authentication does not work. You may experience that the user authentication is not working as expected. The following will assist you in pointing the root of the problem:

> ■ Authentication Module   By default mod_auth is the authoritative module for user authentication. If you are using other authentication modules, then make sure that you have indeed compiled the modules in the Apache server. You may check whether the module was compiled by running the Apache server daemon with the -1 flag.

■ AuthUser and AuthGroup files   If you are using the mod_auth modules, then check the availability and the permissions on the specified user and group files.

■ Default authoritative module   It is possible to configure the Apache server so that some users are authenticated by the mod_auth module, whereas some are authenticated by other authentication modules. This kind of fall-through user authentication is enabled by using the Auth?Authoritative off directive. The ? refers to the module name. For example, the mod_auth_db defines the AuthDBAuthoritative directive. The default (on) setting prevents the fall-through authentication to the next module. This causes the Apache to pass the user from one authentication module to another when the user ID is not found in the respective database. The server returns an OK if the user is found and Denied otherwise. The default setting for this directive is on.

Users' Individual Web Servers

Users in an organization often like to serve personal Web content such as technical documents, pictures, applications, and so on. It is impractical to provide every user with the permissions to add to the DocumentRoot directory of the Web server. Apache provides the UserDir directive to address this particular situation. The UserDir directive is part of the mod_user module compiled in by default. The UserDir directive specifies the name of a parent directory that contains a single folder for each user on the system. Apache also defines the keyword public_html to specify a folder by that name in every user's home directory as the repository for the user Web content. The URL for a user joe's individual Web content document profile.html is written as http://www.mcp.com/~joe/profile.html. Table 24.3 shows the actual directory accessed based on UserDir directive specified.

Table 24.3   Translated *UserDir* Directives

UserDir Directive	Translated System Directory
UserDir public_html	{joe home dir}/public_html/profile.html
UserDir /web/users	/web/users/joe/profile.html
UserDir http://www.mcp.com/usr	http://www.mcp.com/usr/joe/profile.html

Sometimes it is desired that only a few users be permitted to provide Web content. Adding the keyword enable followed by a space-delimited list of users does this. Similarly, users can be denied the privilege by using the keyword disable. Not supplying a list of users after the disable keyword disables all users except those specified after the enable keyword. Thus the following sets of directives deny Web-hosting privilege to all users except Ann, Bob, and Chuck.

```
UserDir disable
UserDir enable Ann Bob Chuck
```

On most systems, the home directory for the root user is specified as /. For security purposes, it is always a good idea to specify the directive UserDir disable root.

N O T E Experienced Web administrators should monitor the error log files. This file provides information on failed access to individual users' Web directories. You may see an error message as follows:

```
[Sat June 29 01:30:29 1998] access to /home/bob/public_html/funscript.cgi failed
for badhost@intruders.com, reason: File does not exist.
```

Occasionally, intruders will attempt to run CGI scripts via a user's home page. If security is improperly configured, the intruder may be able to gain access to the system. For this reason, many administrators prefer to specify a directory for CGI scripts rather than a file extension. ■

Virtual Hosts

Most ISPs and large organizations serve many Web sites from a single server. This provides for greater savings in hardware, software, and administrative costs. To a client/browser the single server appears as multiple Web sites. This process of hosting multiple Web sites on a single hardware platform is referred to as *virtual hosting*. Apache provides block directives that facilitate virtual hosting. Previously, HTTP/1.0 required that a separate IP address be used for each virtual host, thus wasting IP address space. HTTP/1.1 allows for multiple servers to be hosted while being bound to the same IP address. However, this requires that the DNS entry for both hostnames point to the same IP address. Adding the sets of directives in Listing 24.9 to the server configuration file in Listing Listing 24.2 allows hosting of the Web site for www.macmillan.com from the same server that hosts www.mcp.com.

N O T E Virtual hosting is the practical approach to hosting multiple Web sites from a single server platform. This results in ease of server administration and reduced hardware and management costs. However, virtual hosting might not be effective if some of the Web sites hosted by the server are extremely busy. The busy site might adversely impact the performance of the other sites hosted by the Web server. ■

Listing 24.9   Using Virtual Host Directives

```
<VirtualHost www.macmillan.com>
    ServerAdmin     webmaster@macmillan.com
    DocumentRoot    /web2
    ServerName       www.macmillan.com
    ErrorLog        logs/MacMillan/error_log
    TransferLog     logs/MacMillan/access_log
</VirtualHost>
```

If the Apache Web server cannot resolve the server name specified by the ServerName directive, then the following error messages are logged, and Apache stops.

```
Cannot determine local host name
Use ServerName to set it manually
```

The `VirtualHost` block directive can be inserted in the server configuration file to be loaded at server startup. The maximum number of file descriptors that can be opened by a process limits the number of virtual hosts hosted by a Web server. Each virtual host consumes at least two file descriptors in opening the transfer and error log files. This situation is confirmed by the `Unable to fork()` messages in the error logs. Using a single log file solves this problem.

Proxy Server

The Apache Web server can be configured to provide Web proxy services. This means that Apache behaves like a client to retrieve and cache content from other servers and then forward it to a client on the local area network. It is important to mention here that the Web browser software has to be configured to point to the proxy server to fulfill all remote HTTP requests. Apache requires that the `mod_proxy` module be compiled before it can provide the proxy functionality. The directives defined for the proxy module will not be effective if the `mod_proxy` module is not compiled with the Apache server. Listing Listing 24.10 displays the directives required for Apache to function as a proxy server.

Part IV
Ch 24

Listing 24.10 Using Proxy Server Directives

```
# Proxy Server directives.

ProxyRequests On

# Block access to the sites that contain these words

ProxyBlock *.uk www.sex
# Cache Parameters

# Fetch directly for these servers
NoProxy www.mcp.com www.mcmillan.com

# Store Cache files here
CacheRoot /usr/local2/proxy
# CacheSize in Kilo Bytes

CacheSize 20000
# Hours after which the server will remove data exceeding
# the max specified by CacheSize

CacheGcInterval 4
# Hours after which the cache will expire even after the
# server specifies a date in the future

CacheMaxExpire 24

# If documents are fetched and no expiration times are
# specified then expire after 1 hour
```

continues

> **Listing 24.10   Continued**
>
> ```
> CacheDefaultExpire 1
>
> # Do not cache access to these servers
>
> NoCache www.changesoften.com www.weatherreport.org latestscores.com
> ```

The first directive `ProxyRequests On` enables the server to act as a proxy server. The `ProxyBlock` directive causes the proxy server to block access to the specified sites. The `NoProxy` directive specifies that the listed hosts should always be served directly without forwarding the request to any remote proxy servers. The directive is generally used within intranets. The `CacheRoot` specifies the `/usr/local2/proxy` directory to store the cache files of the proxy server. The file system that contains the `CacheRoot` must be at least as large as the value specified by the `CacheSize` directive. In our proxy configuration directives, we specify 20MB as the `CacheSize`. Busy proxy servers should use higher values. The `CacheGcInterval` directive specifies the time in hours after which the server removes data larger than the value specified by `CacheSize`. A busy proxy server should set a low value to prevent the file system from being filled up. The `CacheMaxExpire` directive specifies the time in hours for which the cached documents are retained in the cache. The `NoCache` directive specifies a list of hosts from which the content will not be cached.

Starting/Stopping the Apache Server

After you have configured the Apache server, you can start the `httpd` server by using the following command line:

```
# httpd -d /usr/local/httpd
```

The server expects the `httpd.conf` file to be available in `/usr/local/httpd`. You may specify an alternate server configuration file using the `f` flag. `httpd` accepts the following flags obtained by typing `httpd -?`.

```
# httpd -?
Usage: httpd [-d directory] [-f file] [-v] [-h] [-l]
-d directory : specify an alternate initial ServerRoot
-f file : specify an alternate ServerConfig File
-v : show version number
-h : list directives
-l : list modules
```

On startup, the server spawns a number of child HTTP processes specified by the `StartServers` directive in the `ServerConfig` file. The `httpd` process will exit if the configuration file is found to have errors. The server also creates a file specified by the `PidFile` directive that stores the process ID of the parent server. Sending the `TERM` signal to the parent `httpd` process causes it to immediately kill all its children and then itself:

```
# kill -TERM `cat /usr/local/httpd/logs/httpd.pid`
```

The HUP signal, on the other hand, kills all the child processes but does not kill the parent process. Instead, the parent rereads the ServerConfig file, reopens log files, and begins accepting new HTTP requests. All currently processed requests to the server are immediately terminated by the HUP signal. The USR1 signal should be used to provide a truly graceful server restart. The USR1 signal causes the parent process to instruct the child process to exit after processing the current request. The parent rereads the configuration files and reopens the log files. The parent process then replaces its child with a new process to begin processing any new requests.

▶ **See** "UNIX Processes," **p. 81**

TROUBLESHOOTING

The server will not start. This is definitely a cause of concern. After all, you have gone through the trouble of compiling and configuring the server. To troubleshoot a server start failure check the following:

- ▓ Configuration files   Make sure that the server configuration file is in the location where the server expects to find it. Check the file permissions. Use the -f and -d flags to tell the Apache server about an alternative location for the Apache configuration file.

- ▓ Check error logs   The error log file is specified by the ErrorLog directive. The error log provides details on the reason for the server start failure.

Part
IV

Ch
24

From Here...

The Apache server provides many powerful features to meet the organizational Web server needs. The features are implemented via directives contained in the Apache modules. Apache provides the capability to configure virtual hosts and a proxy server on a Web server. Where security is paramount, Apache can be configured to provide host-based security and user authentication.

The Apache distribution includes server documentation that lists and describes the directives used in configuring Apache. In addition to the standard set of modules, there are many contributed modules. The contributed modules define additional directives to enhance the functionality of the Apache server. This chapter has defined many useful directives required in configuring the Apache Web server. The reader is directed to the Apache documentation when detailed information is desired.

The following Web resources provide valuable information on the Apache Web server and the Web in general.

- ▓ The Apache Group, http://www.apache.org   This site provides up-to-date information about the latest Apache releases, bugs, FAQs, and other sought-after information on the Apache server.

■ Apache Week, `http://www.apacheweek.com` This site provides interesting articles on the Apache server.

■ The World Wide Web Consortium, `http://www.w3.org` You can learn a great deal about the ongoing development of the Web at this site.

The following chapters provide more related information.

■ Chapter 19, "Configuring TCP/IP," provides details on configuring the IP addresses for your Web servers.

■ Chapter 23, "DNS," shows you how to configure the DNS for your Internet domain. This is useful in adding your Web server to your domain.

sendmail and POP

by Chris Negus and Jeff Robinson

Overview of Electronic Mail

Electronic mail (email) was one of the first uses of the Internet and remains one of the most popular. Over the years it has progressed from plain text messages forwarded over telephone lines to messages that can include text or HTML, along with a variety of attachments, that can be transparently forwarded anywhere in the world on the Internet.

For email users, email begins and ends with the Mail User Agent (MUA). The MUA is a program that lets the user gather, read, manage, and send email messages. Whereas some MUAs are simple text-based programs (such as the `mailx` command), others contain more graphical, friendly interfaces (such as Eudora).

Despite the differences in email programs, standards in how email messages are formed and delivered make it possible for people using different email tools to communicate. Standards such as Simple Mail Transfer Protocol (SMTP) and Multipurpose Internet Mail Extensions (MIME) define how email messages are formatted and delivered.

The tools that actually distribute email messages to their destinations across the network are referred to as Mail Transfer Agents (MTA). Although several MTAs are available for UNIX, the most popular one is called `sendmail`. The `sendmail` utility runs on the mail server, receiving and storing messages for its users and delivering queued messages to the mail servers that hold the recipients' messages.

To gather and read their email, users (typically working from a PC) request that the mail server download their messages so that the messages can be accessed from the user's computer. A common protocol that lets users download messages from a mail server is called Post Office Protocol (POP).

Figure 25.1 shows the basic components that make email possible on the Internet.

FIGURE 25.1

sendmail and POP manage delivery of email messages.

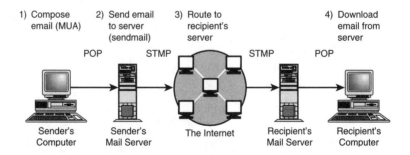

As illustrated in Figure 25.1, following are the basic steps that occur when a user sends email to another user over the Internet:

1. Using an MUA (such as `mailx` or Eudora), a user composes a message and queues it for delivery.

2. From the user's computer, the email is forwarded to the user's mail server using POP (or a similar protocol).

3. The mail server, using an MTA (such as `sendmail`), transfers the mail message over the network to the recipient's mail server.

4. The recipient contacts the mail server (often by clicking on Receive from the recipient's PC), and the recipient's messages are downloaded from the mail server (using POP or similar protocol).

N O T E If a user is working on a mainframe computer, the mail server may actually be on the same computer the user is logged on to. In this case, the POP protocol is not needed to gather mail because the user can simply run the mail program locally.

This chapter describes how email is used on a typical UNIX system. Besides describing different MUAs, it describes the different standards that make email possible. In particular, however, the chapter focuses on how to set up email on a UNIX system using `sendmail` and POP features.

▶ **See** "Overview of Networking," **p. 422**

Using Email (MUAs)

As an email user, most things such as protocols and transfer agents are invisible to you. Your view of email is through the program you use to compose, send, read, and manage messages. Although this program is known as a Mail User Agent (MUA), you probably know it better by a name such as `mailx`, Netscape Messenger Mailbox, or Microsoft Outlook Express.

The first MUAs used with UNIX were completely text-based. You type the name of the program (such as `mail` or `mailx`), and you see a list of messages received in your mailbox. By typing letters and numbers, you can select messages to read, save them in file directories, respond to them, or remove them. You can also compose and send your own text-based messages (using your favorite text editor).

Today, both the interfaces and content of email have become more sophisticated. Email programs have become more tightly integrated with the Internet. Web browsers, such as Netscape Communicator and MS Internet Explorer, now come with integrated email programs that can contain Web content (such as HTML) and can be launched from the browser or from within a Web page.

The following list shows some of the most popular email programs available today. The URL shows where you can download a copy of each program.

 T I P If you are looking for an email program, be sure to try before you buy. Every email program today is either free or offered on a trial basis (for a limited time) or with limited features. Go to the email URLs in the following list to find out how to download a free copy.

■ `mailx` This utility comes free with most UNIX systems (although it is simply called `mail` on some systems). It is text-based and runs in a UNIX shell. (The `mailx` utility is described later in this chapter.)

▨ Netscape Communicator (http://www.netscape.com)   This popular browser comes with its own MUA called Netscape Messenger. It is graphical and runs in many platforms. (The Messenger Mailbox is described later in this chapter.)

▨ Eudora (http://www.eudora.com)   This is a commercial, GUI-based MUA that runs primarily on MS-Windows systems. A free version of Eudora is available (Eudora Lite). The company also offers extensions to UNIX mail servers (such as the Qpopper POP server).

▨ Microsoft Outlook (http://www.microsoft.com/ie)   Outlook Express is offered free with Internet Explorer. Although it is a reduced version of Outlook 98, it offers a GUI-based mail interface that contains enough mail features to suit most needs. Although it runs on the PC, UNIX versions of Outlook Express are available that run on HP/UX and Sun Solaris UNIX systems.

▨ Elm (http://www.myxa.com/elm/elm.ftp.html)   Elm is a free MUA developed by a cooperative group of volunteers called the Elm Development Group. It is a text-based mail program that runs on many UNIX systems. (The last major release was Elm 2.4. Development of 2.5 is inactive.)

▨ Pine (http://www.washington.edu/pine)   This is a simple UNIX mail interface, originally based on Elm, which has since taken its own course. It was created at the University of Washington at Seattle. There is still development work going on with it today.

To illustrate the features commonly available in MUAs, the next sections describe one program that represents text-based email (the mailx utility) and one that shows what a graphical interface can do (Netscape Communicator Messenger Mailbox).

Using a Text-Based MUA (*mailx*)

Those who use UNIX primarily from the UNIX shell often use mailx to read and send mail. The mailx command is text-based. You won't see any fancy graphics, but you can select and work with mail messages without your fingers leaving the keyboard.

Reading Email with *mailx*   To read and manage incoming mail messages, simply type:

```
$ mailx
```

Headings for each of the mail messages that are stored in your incoming mailbox appear. Your mailbox is stored in a file, the location of which depends on your UNIX system and your username. (Typical locations are /var/mail/user or /usr/mail/user.) Here is an example of the output from mailx showing four new mail messages:

```
mailx version 4.2  Type ? for help.
"/var/mail/chrisn": 4 messages 4 unread
>U  1 mikeb@snowbird    Mon Aug 17 17:26    13/318
 U  2 rambo@alta        Thu Aug 20 00:10    15/379
 U  3 ibin@brighton     Thu Aug 20 00:12    14/327
 U  4 root@canyons      Thu Apr 18 00:31    15/366
?
```

The output from `mailx` shows you whether the message has been read (U means it is unread), the message number, the email address of the sender, the date and time the mail arrived, and the number of lines and characters in the message (lines/characters).

After the ? prompt appears, here are some of the things you can do with `mailx`.

- Press Enter to display the next unread message.
- Type a number (in this case, from 1 to 4) to display the message associated with that number.
- Type e to open the current message in your text editor.
- Type d to delete the current message.
- Type r to respond to all the recipients of the current message.
- Type R to respond to just the author of the current message.
- Type s *file* to save the current message to a file (replacing *file* with the name you want).
- Type ? to see the list of all `mailx` commands.

You can combine the letters and numbers to act on one or more messages. For example, R3 would respond to the author of message 3. The command d2-4 deletes messages 2 through 4.

Besides these basic commands, other commands let you use `mailx` with other UNIX utilities. For example, type ! to escape to a shell and run a command before returning to `mailx`. Type Pipe *n cmd* to pipe one or more of the messages to a shell command (replacing *n* with one or more message numbers and *cmd* with the command to use).

When you are finished with `mailx`, you can exit from it using one of two commands:

- Type x to exit from `mailx`, without making any changes. (The next time you start `mailx`, the mailbox will be exactly the same as when you began the current session.)
- Type q to exit from `mailx`, making any changes that occurred during the session. (For example, deleted messages will be removed and messages you viewed will no longer appear as unread.)

Composing Email with *mailx*   To send an email message using `mailx`, you can either compose a message within `mailx` or send an existing message (one you have in a file) with `mailx`. For example, if you want to compose a message to bob@parkcity, you could type the following from a UNIX shell:

```
$ mailx bob@parkcity
```

At this point, `mailx` may ask you to enter other information, such as the subject of the message. After that is done, just begin typing in the message. When you are finished, press a Ctrl+D on a line by itself, and the email is queued for distribution.

While you are composing the email message, there are several commands you can use. Here are some examples:

Part

IV

Ch

25

- ~e   Open the current message in your text editor (probably ed, emacs, or vi).

- ~v   Open the current message in your visual editor (probably emacs or vi).

- ~r *file*   Read a file into the current message (replacing *file* with the name of the file you want).

- ~m *n*   Insert a mail message you received into the current message. (Replace *n* with a message number or range of numbers to include.)

Although mailx is not the easiest or most intuitive mail program to use, it is still used today. For example, a UNIX system administrator might telnet or rlogin to his base computers to check his email with mailx. It's much quicker and easier than starting up a GUI mail program.

Using a GUI-based MUA (Netscape Messenger)

The most popular Internet browsers come with their own mail programs. Microsoft Internet Explorer comes with Outlook Express (a reduced function version of Outlook 98). Netscape Communicator has a program called Netscape Messenger. Both present a graphical user interface (GUI) to the user.

If you are using the Netscape Communicator browser, you can open the Netscape Messenger by clicking on Communicator—>Messenger Mailbox. A Netscape Messenger Mailbox appears, as shown in Figure 25.2.

FIGURE 25.2

Manage email graphically with Netscape Messenger.

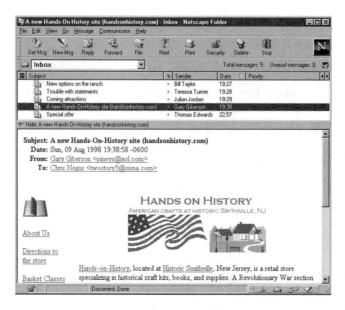

Although the layout of the Messenger Mailbox can be changed, Figure 25.2 shows the default display. Select functions from the menu bar and toolbar at the top. In the middle, the header for each message appears. At the bottom, the selected message is displayed.

Messages sent and received by Netscape Messenger can be in either plain text or HTML format. This example shows an HTML message. Not only does the HTML appear in the message, but it also can be used like HTML by the recipient (for example, animated GIFs move, you can click on links to other sites, and fonts appear as they would on a Web page).

Here are some highlights of how you can manage your email with Netscape Messenger:

- Double-click on a message header to display the message in a separate window.
- Click on any heading over the message listing to sort by that heading (for example, Subject, Sender, Date, or Priority).
- Click on Get Msg to download new messages from the mail server.
- By default, incoming mail goes into your Inbox folder. With a message selected, click on File, then click on another folder name to move the message to that folder.
- Click on Next to go to the next mail message.
- If the message includes an attachment (a document, sound clip, graphic, or other type of file), a paper clip appears on the message. The attachment's name appears in a box in the message. Click on the name to save the attachment to hard disk or to display it.

To send your own email message to someone else, click on New Msg from the Messenger Mailbox window. A window, similar to the one shown in Figure 25.3, appears that is ready for you to compose your message.

Part
IV

Ch
25

FIGURE 25.3

Compose Netscape email in HTML or text.

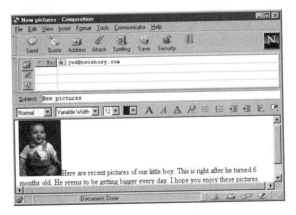

In this example, the message being created is in HTML format. Basic tools let you change font types, colors, and sizes. Text can also be put in bold, italic, or underscore. Paragraphs can be adjusted and indented. Graphics can be inserted into the body of the text.

> **NOTE** Not all MUAs can read HTML text. To a text-based mail program, an HTML message will appear as text (showing all the HTML codes in the message). ■

Icons in the header let you select addresses for the email from an address book, add attachments, or set special mail options. The mail options let you choose to have the message encrypted, signed, or encoded using Uuencode rather than MIME. You can change the message format to text instead of HTML.

To send the mail message, click on Send. Your message is sent to your mail server (either locally or using POP), where it will be forwarded to the proper recipients.

Understanding Email Protocols

Without standards in how email is transferred, messages are formatted, headers are used, and recipients are addressed, mail programs wouldn't be able to interoperate on the Internet. Fortunately, there is a rich set of email standards that clarify how all the different parts of email can work together.

Simple Mail Transfer Protocol (SMTP) is the standard used to send email from one mail server to another over the Internet. (The sendmail program implements SMTP, as do other MTAs.) Because SMTP is so simple and was designed when email was just English and plain text, other standards have been added to enhance SMTP. Multipurpose Internet Mail Extensions (MIME) and SMTP service extensions are two such standards.

Introduction to the SMTP Protocol

The Simple Mail Transfer Protocol (SMTP) is designed to standardize the way mail messages are delivered across computer networks. Although SMTP was intended to be used on any reliable network transport, the Internet (and other TCP/IP networks) is where SMTP is most commonly used.

SMTP is defined in several RFCs, in particular "Simple Mail Transfer Protocol" (RFC 821) and "Requirements for Internet Hosts—Application and Support" (RFC 1123). RFC 821 is the basic standard for SMTP. RFC 1123 contains a more detailed walk-through and suggestions for SMTP implementations.

▶ **See** "RFCs," **p. 725**

Because, as the name implies, SMTP is simple, extensions have been added to handle various needed enhancements. These include:

- ■ SMTP Service Extensions (RFC 1651)   Defines the framework in which SMTP senders and receivers can request special services for mail transfer.
- ■ MIME (Multipurpose Internet Mail Extensions) Part One (RFC 1651) and Part Two (RFC 1652)   Define a method for including a variety of data types in a mail message. This allows you to include images and audio files in a mail message.

SMTP provides end-to-end transport, meaning that SMTP manages the mail transmission from the mail client (sender's SMTP) to the mail server (receiver's SMTP). Addressing is most commonly done using domain style addressing (that is, user@domain). The specific path a message takes is managed by Internet routers.

▶ **See** "Configuring DNS Clients," **p. 605**

Compare domain style addressing to, for example, the old source routing method of sending email where the address can include each hop a message takes to its destination. Because each host is only responsible for getting the message to the neighboring host, you might not know for a few days that your email didn't make it.

N O T E UUCP (UNIX-to-UNIX copy) originally used source route addressing, but it is less common today. For example, the email address snowbird!tiger!brighton!chris indicates a message sent to the user chris on the host named brighton. Your computer would queue the message to snowbird and then forward it to tiger, which would then send it to brighton. Your computer would lose track of the message after it was sent to snowbird.

An SMTP Transaction

SMTP carries out mail transmissions by establishing a communications channel and sending data (the mail message) across that channel. During transmission, the SMTP protocol sends the header and body of the message, wrapped in what is called an envelope (containing the source and destination address).

The following general steps occur during an SMTP transmission:

1. The MUA (user email program) queues a message to the SMTP sender. (The MUA either places it in the server's mail queue or has it sent there via a POP server.) The envelope surrounding the message is populated with the addresses supplied by the user (or through expanding a requested mailing list).

2. The SMTP sender creates a connection to the SMTP server. The server that responds to the service is either available or not available.

3. The sender sends either a HELO or EHLO message. (HELO requests service without extensions; EHLO means the sender needs to use one or more extensions to send the mail.) To HELO, the server responds with the server's domain name. To EHLO, it responds in one of the following ways:

   • If the server doesn't support extensions, it returns a command unrecognized message. The sender can either try again and send the message without extensions or, if it needs the extensions, it can quit the transmission.

   • If the server does support extensions, it returns a 250 OK message, which includes a list of extensions it supports.

4. If the sender is happy with the service available, it sends a MAIL command to the server. With that command is the *reverse-path* to the sender (for example, MAIL FROM <user@domain>). The server responds with a 250 OK message.

5. The sender sends a RCPT TO: forward-path command to the server (one for each user to receive the message). The server responds with a 250 OK message for each valid user.

6. The sender sends a DATA command, alerting the server that the message is coming. The server responds that it is ready to receive mail input and tells the sender what character sequence to send when data is finished being sent.

7. The sender sends the message, ending with the data termination sequence. The server replies with `250 OK` if it receives the data without error.

8. With the transmission complete, the sender can elect to: `QUIT`, request if there are messages to receive from the server, or send another message.

9. On the server side, the message is held by the server until the user for which the message is intended requests to read the message (or rather, to download it to the user's computer using POP).

During this transmission, SMTP can also send a variety of other commands. Some of these commands include: `TURN` (to change the direction of transmission between the sender and receiver), `RSET` (to abort the current mail transaction), `VRFY` (to confirm that the argument identifies a user), `EXPN` (to confirm that the argument identifies a mailing list), and `NOOP` (to have the receiver send an OK reply).

Mail Header Syntax

The header of each mail message contains information that describes how the message should be handled. The header tells where the message came from, where it is going, when it arrived, and sometimes indicates the type of content in the message.

Although some of the header information can be entered by the user who sends the mail (such as the recipient's To: address), other headers are added along the way (for example, the Date: is added when the message is received). The following section describes some of the headers in mail messages.

N O T E   Whereas text-based mail programs show you some header information, GUI-based mail programs typically hide the details of the mail headers. To see mail headers, most GUI-based mail programs have an option that lets you View Source of the message. This shows you the complete ASCII text of the message. ▪

In a mail message, all header lines are together at the beginning of the message. Each header line is ended with a carriage return. The body of the message begins with first blank (null) line. Headers fields are in the form:

`fieldname: fieldbody`

Following are some of the fields you will commonly see in the mail message headers, along with descriptions of each one:

▪ Return-Path: Shows the address back to the user who sent the message. The last transport node adds this information.

▪ Received: Shows the addresses of each transport service that transferred the message, along with other information such as the date and time it was received by each node. You could use this information to trace back the path of the transfer.

▪ Date: Shows the date and time the mail message was received by the SMTP server.

▪ From: Shows the address of the user who sent the message.

- Subject: Shows the subject of the message that was entered by the user.
- Sender: Indicates the person who sent the message. Can be different from the From: value if the author of the message is not the person who sent it.
- To: Lists the user, or users, to whom the message is addressed.
- Cc: Lists the user, or users, who are not the primary recipients but are still receiving copies of the message.
- Errors-to: Shows the address of the user who will receive errors that occur during the transmission.
- Message-ID Shows an identifier that uniquely identifies a particular version of a particular mail message. The ID is generated by the client that sends the message.

For a more complete listing of mail header fields, refer to "Standard for the Format of ARPA Internet Text Messages" (RFC 822). The following is an example of a mail message header:

```
Return-path: <webguy@twostory.com>
Received: from cs2 [111.111.176.28] by mail.twostory.com
  (SMTPD32-4.03) id A8094830132; Fri, 29 May 1998 17:43:05 MDT
Date: Fri, 29 May 1998 17:45:32 -0600
From: "Webguy" <webguy@twostory.com>
Subject: Hello to Everyone!
To: <chris@handsonhistory.com>
Errors-to: errors@twostory.com
Reply-To: <webguy@twostory.com>
Message-ID: <001e01bd8b5b$dec26ad0$1cb0d2d1@cs2.twostorycorp>
```

After a blank line, the body of the message begins.

Mail Addressing and Routing with DNS

By far the most popular, and recommended, addressing style for email is DNS (domain name system) style of addressing. DNS addressing assumes that every user in every domain on the network can be uniquely addressed. The most common ways to express DNS addressing are as follows:

```
user@domain
UserName <user@domain>
```

So, here are some examples of domain-style addresses:

```
chris@handsonhistory.com
Christopher Jones <chris@handsonhistory.com>
```

Notice that, in the second example, you can precede the address of the recipient (user/domain) with the person's real name. On most mail programs, the real name is displayed instead of the address if both are present.

As noted earlier in this chapter, source route style addressing (where the exact hops the message takes to the destination are specified) should be discouraged. In most cases, routing should be left to the Internet routers to find the best path. Issues that relate to the routing of mail messages are described in "Mail Routing and the Domain System" (RFC 974).

▶ **See** "An Overview of Routing Protocols," **p. 513**

Part

IV

Ch

25

One case in which source routing might be needed has to do with mail gateways. If an email message must leave the Internet and find its way across a mail gateway to a host computer on another type of network, the specific route the message must take after it leaves the Internet may need to be entered. For example, for the address:

```
comp1!comp2!comp3!tom@outmail.com
```

the address `outmail.com` might represent an email gateway to another network. That network might require hops from `comp1` to `comp2`, before it reaches the user `tom` on `comp3`.

SMTP Service Extensions

To include content in mail messages that is more than plain text in English, service extensions were added to SMTP. These extensions allowed an SMTP sender to request special services, such as 8-Bit MIME or different message sizes.

Because not all SMTP servers support the service extensions, a new SMTP command was added so that an SMTP client could ask the server what service extensions (if any) it supports. Instead of sending the `HELO` command during SMTP conversations, a client sends `EHLO`. If the server supports service extensions, it returns a list of which extensions it supports that looks like the following:

```
250-twostory.com says hello
250-8BITMIME
```

This example shows that the server supports 8-bit MIME extensions. For descriptions of how this feature is implemented, see "SMTP Service Extensions" (RFC 1651). Specific SMTP service extensions are described in "SMTP Service Extension for 8bit-MIMEtransport" (RFC 1652) and "SMTP Service Extension for Message Size Declaration" (RFC 1653).

Multipurpose Internet Mail Extensions (MIME)

For mail messages to contain different types of data in the message bodies, a new feature was added called Multipurpose Internet Mail Extensions (MIME). This was implemented by adding a new header field called:

```
Content-Type:
```

The Content-Type header (first defined in "A Content-type Header Field for Internet Messages" RFC-1049), defines data contained in the body of a mail message by its type and subtype. Details of the MIME standard are contained in two other RFCs:

- RFC 1521—MIME (Multipurpose Internet Mail Extensions) Part One: Mechanisms for Specifying and Describing the Format of Internet Message Bodies.

- RFC 1522—MIME (Multipurpose Internet Mail Extensions) Part Two: Message Header Extensions for Non-ASCII Text

The value of the Content-Type header is divided into content-type and subtype pairs. The following are some of the valid Content-Type values:

- ■ `text`   Identifies the mail message content as being textual information. Different subtypes identify the text as belonging to a particular character set or kind of formatted text.

- ■ `image`   Identifies the message content as being an image file. For example, image/bmp represents a bitmap image and image/GIF represents a GIF image.

- ■ `multipart`   Identifies the message as containing several different types of data.

- ■ `message`   Identifies the contents of the message as another encapsulated mail message.

To most users, the content (and even the existence of) the Content-Type header should be invisible. Instead, when a user views the mail message from a GUI-based mail program, the different types of content may appear as an attachment or simply display as a special type of text (such as HTML).

Introduction to *sendmail*

`sendmail` by far is the most flexible, configurable, and popular MTA within the Internet community today. Versions of `sendmail` can be installed and configured on every major type of UNIX system. However, along with flexibility comes complexity.

Over the years, `sendmail` has developed a reputation of being cryptic. To deal with that issue, however, newer tools such as the M4 macro processor make configuration much easier than in the past. The M4 macro processor is discussed later in this chapter.

Because `sendmail` is not delivered with every UNIX system, you might need to download a copy from the Internet. You might also want to download `sendmail` if your UNIX system has an older version of `sendmail`. `sendmail` is freely distributed.

To download `sendmail`, go to the `sendmail` site (`http://www.sendmail.org`). This site offers links to the latest versions of `sendmail`, along with documentation you will need to install and set up `sendmail`. (The current release of sendmail is 8.9.)

> **CAUTION**
>
> `sendmail` is run with Superuser privileges and, therefore, is subject to security risks. Because `sendmail` security flaws have been exploited so often, you should keep up with the latest patches and fixes constantly being offered with `sendmail`.

As noted earlier, `sendmail` transmits email messages on the Internet using SMTP. This section describes how to configure `sendmail`, while describing how `sendmail` implements different aspects of SMTP.

Compiling *sendmail*

The recommended way to compile `sendmail` is to use the `Build` script that comes with the distribution. Simply type the following:

```
sh BUILD
```

and the `Build` script gathers the information it needs to properly compile `sendmail` for your UNIX system. The operating system you are using will have a major impact on the amount of tweaking you need to do to get `sendmail` compiled properly.

You can find specific details for compiling `sendmail` for your UNIX system at the `sendmail` site (`http://www.sendmail.org/compiling.html`). We strongly recommend that you refer to that site for the latest details and workarounds for compiling `sendmail`.

The Role of DNS in *sendmail*

The role of DNS in `sendmail` is to look up all mail exchangers for a particular domain and resolve their names to an IP address, allowing for a connection to an appropriate foreign mail server. A mail exchanger is a host willing to accept mail for a domain.

First, `sendmail` must parse the recipient's email address and then determine which part is the username and which part is the domain name. (This is discussed later in the chapter.)

After the domain name is isolated, `sendmail` takes the domain name and attempts to look up a mail exchanger for the destination domain. If a mail exchanger does not exist for the domain, `sendmail` attempts to deliver it directly to the domain IP address, if it exists. The domain would have an IP address if the administrator used an "A" resource record in DNS.

Mail exchangers are much preferred because they allow other domains to try several machines for mail delivery to your domain. It is best to have redundancy in any network setup, and `sendmail` is no exception.

The following example shows how the `nslookup` command can be used to display information about mail exchangers on your network.

```
Type:           nslookup
You will see:   Default Server: lxotta.learnix.ca
                Address:  199.71.122.50
                >
Type:           set querytype=mx
You will see:   >
Type:           sun.com
You will see:   Server:  lxotta.learnix.ca
                Address:  199.71.122.50

        sun.com preference = 10, mail exchanger = mercury.Sun.COM
        sun.com preference = 20, mail exchanger = venus.Sun.COM
        sun.com preference = 30, mail exchanger = Sun.COM
        sun.com preference = 40, mail exchanger = mars.sun.com
        mercury.Sun.COM internet address = 192.9.25.1
        venus.Sun.COM   internet address = 192.9.25.5
        Sun.COM internet address = 192.9.9.1
        mars.sun.com    internet address = 192.9.22.1
```

The first four lines of the final output, show you that SUN has four mail exchangers. You also see a preference value for each MX record returned. A lower preference value indicates a more preferable mail server.

When `sendmail` attempts to send mail to the `sun.com domain`, it always attempts to send mail to the host `mercury.Sun.COM first`. If that fails, `sendmail` then attempts delivery to the host `venus.Sun.COM` and so on.

If mail cannot be delivered to any of the mail exchangers at the current time, `sendmail` queues the mail for later delivery. Usually `sendmail` queues the mail and retries delivery every hour. The retry delivery time may be changed.

The last four lines show the IP addresses of the mail exchangers that were found in the preceding example.

T I P To incorporate MX (Mail Exchanger) records in DNS, use an MX resource record in your DNS zone database file, similar to the following:

```
.ca.          IN    MX    10    lxotta.learnix.ca.
learnix.ca    IN    MX    20    lxhhp2.learnix.ca
learnix.ca    IN    MX    30    lxsfhhp2.learnix.com
```

---

sendmail Aliases

`sendmail` uses aliases to convert a recipient's address to another format. `sendmail` aliases are normally located in a file named `/etc/mail/aliases`.

Two mandatory aliases are as follows:

```
postmaster:     root
Mailer-Daemon:  postmaster
```

N O T E The `newaliases` command rebuilds the random access database for the mail aliases file `/etc/aliases`. It is run automatically by `sendmail` (in the default configuration) whenever `/etc/mail/aliases` is newer than `/etc/mail/aliases.pag`. If, however, after editing the `/etc/mail/aliases` file `sendmail` does not recognize the new aliases, you might need to run the `newaliases` command to rebuild the alias table. ▨

Following are some examples:

Suppose Jeff has an email address of `jeff@learnix.ca`. One day Jeff moves to the US office and receives a new email address. The administrator of the `learnix.ca` mail server could add an alias to the file `/etc/mail/aliases` similar to the following:

```
jeff:       Jeff.Robinson@learnix.COM
```

All mail being delivered to the mail server for Andy should be forwarded to the host on his desk. The aliases file on the mail server would contain the following:

```
andy:       andy@martin.darkwing.learnix.ca
```

Learnix administration requires a way to send an email message to all instructors. Several possibilities are available here, depending on how many Sun instructors there are.

You could use a comma-separated list in the aliases file.

Part
IV

Ch

25

```
instructors@learnix.ca:     andy,jeff,anita,anuja,tyler
```

You could also specify a file that contains the all the instructors' mail addresses.

```
suninst@learnix.ca:     :include: /etc/all_sun_instructor_mail_addresses
```

To have email diverted directly to a file rather than a user's mailbox, use the following syntax.

```
nobody:          /dev/null
evals@learnix.com:     /var/spool/evals
```

To have email forward directly to a program as standard input, use the following syntax:

```
alert@learnix.ca:     ¦ /opt/bin/page_alert
```

> **CAUTION**
>
> sendmail aliases are recursively resolved. This means that sendmail, after finding an alias for a username, will once again try to look up the new name, to see whether it too has an alias.
>
> Consider the following:
>
> ```
> jeff@learnix.ca:   /dev/null
>
> postmaster:        root
>
> root:              jeff@learnix.ca
> ```

To investigate how an address is being locally resolved, you can use the sendmail command with the -bv options.

```
/usr/lib/sendmail -bv username
```

The *sendmail* Configuration File

The sendmail configuration file, generally named sendmail.cf, contains several classes of information that determine the behavior of sendmail on your host. Following is a list of the items found in the sendmail.cf file:

- Options determine the values of numerous sendmail parameters. For instance, file and directory paths, operational control switches, and timeout values.

- Macro and class definitions provide names for strings and sets of strings. For instance, domain name of your host, set of alternative names, and information used in header definitions and rewriting rules.

- Header definitions are templates used to specify required and optional message headers and their formats. The header appears at the top of each mail message your mail server processes.

- Mailer definitions specify the programs used to deliver various kinds of mail (for instance, local mailbox delivery or delivery to a file or program) as well as specifying details of sendmail's interaction with them.

- Rewriting rule sets are used to parse and transform addresses. In addition to controlling the appearance of addresses and directing special handling of certain classes of addresses, rewriting rules are used by sendmail to determine, for each message recipient, the final delivery address, the mailer to use, and the host system where the message should be delivered (or relayed).

***sendmail* Options**   sendmail options are set in its configuration file with the single-letter command: a capital O. In versions before 8.7, all options had single-letter names. For example, the option A held the pathname of the alias file. Beginning with version 8.7, all options can be referred to by full names. For instance, the pathname of the alias file is now specified by option AliasFile. The old single-letter option names are still recognized for backward compatibility.

To avoid any ambiguity between the older single-letter form and the new full-name form, a space (which might not appear between the O command and the single-letter option being defined) must appear between the O command and the full name.

For example, to set the name of the alias file in the old style, use the following:

```
OA/usr/lib/aliases
```

whereas with the new style, employ:

```
O AliasFile=/usr/lib/aliases
```

Here are some examples of new style sendmail options:

```
O AliasFile=/etc/mail/aliases
O QueueDirectory=/var/spool/mqueue
O DeliveryMode=background
O TempFileMode=0600
O HelpFile=/etc/mail/sendmail.hf
O SmtpGreetingMessage=$j Sendmail $v/$Z; $b
O StatusFile=/etc/mail/sendmail.st
```

Macro Definitions   Macro definitions are equivalent to a variable in most programming languages. A macro can hold a single string with no spaces. A macro variable is defined by the letter "D." The letter following the "D" is the name of the macro, and everything else is the value placed in the macro variable.

To assign a macro variable, use the following syntax:

```
DMlearnix.com
```

sendmail references the macro using the following syntax:

```
$M
```

Macros may be used to assign new macros. For example, consider the following:

```
Dj$w.$m
```

sendmail includes many built-in macro variables. These variables are predefined each time sendmail starts. A short list of built-in variables is as follows:

$w	Hostname
$m	Internet domain name

$v   Current version of sendmail

$b   Date in RFC822 format

Several macro variables required to be defined in the sendmail.cf file are as follows:

$j   Official domain name for the local machine

$n   Identity of the error message sender

$o   Characters that separate address components

Class Macros   Class macros are similar to an array, in that they can store several elements, however, they are referenced in a peculiar way. To define a class macro, use the following syntax:

```
CWlearnix.com   ott.learnix.ca   van.learnix.ca
```

Referencing a class macro requires a special syntax. $=x matches any phrase in class x. For example, if you have an email address of jeff@learnix.com and you define:

```
Cwsun.com  learnix.com
```

You could conclude the following:

jeff@$=W   True

jeff@sparky.$=w   False

sendmail Header Definition   Following is an example of a sendmail header definition. The definition includes many sendmail macros that are resolved each time the header is placed at the top of an email.

```
H?P?Return-Path: <$g>
HReceived: $?sfrom $s $.by $j ($v/$V) id $i; $b
H?D?Resent-Date: $a
H?D?Date: $a
H?F?Resent-From: $q
H?F?From: $q
H?x?Full-Name: $x
HSubject:
H?M?Resent-Message-Id: <$t.$i@$j>
H?M?Message-Id: <$t.$i@$j>
HErrors-To:
```

Mailer Definition   The following example shows three mail delivery agents. Each agent delivers mail in a different way:

```
Mlocal,        P=/bin/mail, F=lsDFMAw5:/|@SnE, S=10/30, R=20/40,
               T=DNS/RFC822/X-Unix,
               A=mail -f $g -d $u
Mprog,         P=/bin/sh, F=lsDFMoeu, S=10/30, R=20/40, D=$z:/,
               T=X-Unix,
               A=sh -c $u
Mrelay,        P=[IPC], F=mDFMuXa8, S=11/31, R=61, E=\r\n, L=2040,
               T=DNS/RFC822/SMTP,
               A=IPC $h
```

The `P=` defines the program the mailer uses to deliver the mail. The `S=` and `R=` define the rule sets applied to the sender and receiver address, if this mailer is chosen.

Rule Sets Address rewriting rules are the essence of `sendmail`'s power and complexity. They can be seen as a simple, specialized, text-oriented programming language.

Two critical tasks that `sendmail` performs (rather than being hard-coded in the `sendmail` program itself) are expressed in the language of rewriting rules, making it relatively easy to configure `sendmail`'s behavior flexibly, without modifying its internal code. In these tasks, `sendmail` does the following:

1. Examines each recipient's address to determine which of several mail delivery agents should be used to send the message to, or closer to, the recipient. This is accomplished by rule set number 0.

2. May transform addresses in both the envelope and the message header to facilitate delivery or reply.

When `sendmail` is presented with a message, it examines the addresses in the envelope and the header fields (From:, To:, Sender:, and so forth). Each address is placed in an area called the *workspace*, and depending on whether the address is for a sender or a recipient and whether it came from the envelope or a message header field, certain rule sets are applied to the address in a prescribed order. Also, after the appropriate mail delivery agent is determined for a particular message, an associated rule set is applied.

How Rule Sets Are Organized Rewriting rules are organized into rule sets. A *rule set* is a small program consisting of an ordered sequence of rules. The program acts on the address in the workspace, applying each rewriting rule as long as its matching clause matches the address in the workspace. When it does not, the next rule in sequence is tried. Viewed this way, a rule set is a function acting on an address, which returns a modified address.

Rule sets are identified by number; each new rule set begins with an S followed by its identifying number. Each rule in the set follows. Rules always begin with the letter R. A rule set ends when another rule set or command beginning with an "R" is used. For example:

```
S17
R$* @$=W    $1@sparkylearnix.com        this is a rule
```

Rewriting rules appear cryptic, but they are actually conceptually simple. A rule contains a left-hand side (LHS), a right-hand side (RHS), and, optionally, a comment, separated from each other by one or more tabs. Note that space characters (which can be used to separate tokens for readability) are not valid rule-part separators.

When a rule is applied to the address in the workspace, the left-hand side is compared to the address as a pattern. If the pattern matches, the address in the workspace is replaced by the rule's right-hand side.

The pattern matching proceeds simply. Ordinary words are matched literally. Operators, which begin with a dollar sign ($), have the following meanings on the left-hand side:

Part

IV

Ch

25

```
$*    Match zero or more tokens
   $+    Match one or more tokens
   $-    Match exactly one token
   $=x   Match any phrase in class x
```

If an operator matches part of the address in the workspace, then the matched token(s) is assigned to the positional operator $n, where n is 1 for the first match, 2 for the second such match, and so forth. For example, applying the left-hand side `$- @ $*` to `jeff@ottawa.learnix.ca`, you have a match that assigns `jeff"` to $1 and `ottawa.learnix.ca` to $2.

When a left-hand side pattern match succeeds, the workspace is replaced with the contents of the rule's right-hand side. Analogous to matching, the replacement process copies literal tokens from the left-hand side to the workspace and gives a special interpretation to operators. Some of the recognized right-hand side operators include the following:

```
$n                    Substitute the nth matched  token from the lhs
   $>n                    Call rule set n
   $#mailer               Specify delivery agent, mailer
   $@host                 Specify host
   $:user                 Specify user
```

Continuing with our example, if the workspace address is `jeff@ottawa.learnix.ca` and the current rule is:

```
R$-@$*        andy@$2
```

then the workspace will be rewritten as `andy@ottawa.learnix.ca`.

The `$>n` symbol tells `sendmail` to go to rule set n after the current rewrite rule has been processed. This mechanism acts like a subroutine facility. For example, it is sometimes necessary to make sure that an address is in the standard form `sendmail` expects when applying rewriting rules. This operation of *canonicalization* is done by rule set 3. A rule to invoke rule set 3 looks like the following:

```
$*     $:$>3
```

The `$:` at the beginning of the right-hand side in this example is the "one-time only" prefix. It stops `sendmail` from applying the rule repeatedly, which it would do if not restrained. The left-hand side (`$*`) means "match anything."

Rules for Resolving Envelope-Recipient Addresses   The mailer, host, and user specification symbols are used to resolve envelope-recipient addresses. These constructs appear only in rule set 0, which uses rewrite rules to parse and resolve recipient addresses. For example, after some involved application of rule set 0, `sendmail` will at last decide that an address is local and resolve the host (this one), the user (the addressee), and the mailer (whatever local mailer has been configured) with this rule:

```
R$+    $#local $: $1
```

In this example, the address in the workspace, which consists of one or more tokens (`$+`), is the name of a local user (`$: $1`) and should be delivered by the local mail delivery agent (`$#local`).

Normally, a rule works as an `if,` `then` `else` statement. The left-hand side is the `if` statement used for pattern matching. If the left-hand side matches the address, then the right-hand side action will be performed. When the rewriting rule on the left-hand side is complete, the left-hand side of the same rule is once again applied. This allows for built-in recursion and can also lead to loops.

`sendmail` provides two operators that have special meaning when they appear as the first token on the right-hand side. The `$:` operator instructs `sendmail` to apply this rule only once, even if it matches, to prevent infinite looping. Ordinarily, a rule is applied repeatedly, until it fails to match.

The `$@` operator instructs `sendmail` to exit from the rule set immediately, returning the remainder of the right-hand side as the rule set's result.

Using the M4 Macro Processor

The M4 macro processor allows you to create a custom `sendmail.cf` file from a small list of elements that you want to have configured. The `sendmail` source distribution includes all the required macro files. You only need to create a few small files.

All versions of `sendmail.8.7.x` or higher software distribution include all M4 macro files necessary to generate a custom `sendmail.cf` file automatically.

I normally extract the `sendmail` distribution into my `/opt/src` directory. Assume that you have done the same for the following example. First, you must create a macro file. The following example shows a `mail-hub.mc` file that creates a `sendmail.cf` file for the `learnix.ca.` domain.

```
vi   /opt/src/sendmail.8.8.6/cf/cf/mail-hub.mc
# VERSIONID is a macro that stuffs the version information into the
# sendmail.cf file

VERSIONID('@(#)Learnix Sendmail May 3, 1998')

# You must specify an OSTYPE to properly configure things such as the
# pathname of the help and status files, the flags needed for the local
# mailer, and other important things.

OSTYPE(solaris2)dnl

# This example is specific to the Learnix.ca domain.
DOMAIN(learnix.ca)dnl

# These describe the mailer that will be supported by the Learnix domain
MAILER(local)dnl
MAILER(smtp)dnl
```

You might want to include some specifics for the `learnix.ca` domain. This is put in the file `learnix.ca.m4` located in the subdirectory `cf/domain` under the `sendmail` distribution.

```
vi   /opt/src/sendmail.8.8.6/cf/domain/learnix.ca.m4
divert(0)
# Set the Version ID for the learnix sendmail.cf file
VERSIONID('@(#) Learnix Sendmail May 3, 1998')
```

```
# The will tell sendmail to accept mail for the domain "learnix.ca"
# You can include many domain names separated by spaces
Cwlearnix.ca

# This mail host will translate all domain names to "learnix.ca"  before mail
➥leaves
MASQUERADE_AS(learnix.ca)

# Do not include UUCP mail support
FEATURE(nouucp)
```

 TIP   A list of all the "features" and directives are located in the README file in the `cf` subdirectory of the sendmail distribution.

To generate a `sendmail.cf` file, use the `m4` command. The `m4` command requires two arguments: the `m4` template file, and the `m4` macro file. M4 generates STDOUT, which needs to be redirected to a file named `sendmail.cf`. The following example assumes that the `m4` command is located in the `/usr/ccs/bin` directory. Alter the pathname as necessary for your host. In the following line, you create the `sendmail.cf` file.

```
/usr/ccs/bin/m4  ../m4/cf.m4  mail-hub.mc  >  sendmail.cf
```

Finally, you need to move the `sendmail.cf` file into the `/etc/mail` directory. Stop and restart the `sendmail` daemon.

NOTE   Following are a few things to note about M4:

- The entry dnl stands for delete through newline in the `mail-hub.mc` file. Because M4 is streams-based and does not understand the concept of "lines," this is done to avoid a lot of whitespace in the output.

- M4 macros are expanded even when they are commented out.

- define is an M4 keyword and should be contained within quotes if used in a comment. ■

Running *sendmail*

`sendmail` has many command-line arguments, which alter the way `sendmail` behaves. Table 25.1 illustrates each command-line argument.

Table 25.1   *sendmail* Options

Option	Description	Other Names
sendmail -v	Verbose mode	
sendmail -bd	Run in daemon mode	smtpd
sendmail -bi	Initialize the alias database	newalias
sendmail -bm	Be a mail sender	

Option	Description	Other Names
sendmail -bp	Print the mail queue	mailq
sendmail -bs	Send SMTP to standard output	
sendmail -bt	Address test mode	
sendmail -q 1h	Retry the mail queue every 1 hour	
sendmail -d	Debug mode	

Troubleshooting *sendmail*

One of the best tools to help troubleshoot sendmail is the debugging option. The debug options can be given two numbers separated by a decimal.

The first number defines the category of debugging information, and the second number defines the amount of information given by sendmail. A larger value for the second number means more debugging information will be generated. Table 25.2 lists the most commonly used debugging categories.

Table 25.2 Debugging Options for *sendmail*

Debug Option	Description
-d 0	General debugging
-d 1	Show sender info
-d 3	Print load average
-d 4	Enough disk space
-d 5	Show events
-d 6	Show failed mail
-d 7	Queue filename
-d 8	DNS name resolution
-d 9	Trace RFC 1413 queries
-d 10	Show recipient delivery
-d 11	Show selected delivery agents
-d 12	Show mapping of relative host
-d 13	Show delivery
-d 14	Show header field commas

continues

Part

IV

Ch

25

Table 25.2 Continued	
Debug Option	**Description**
`-d 15`	Show network get request activity
`-d 16`	Outgoing connections
`-d 17`	List MX hosts
`-d 18`	Show SMTP replies
`-d 19`	Show ESMTP parameters
`-d 20`	Show resolving delivery agent
`-d 21`	Trace rewriting rules
`-d 22`	Trace tokenizing of address
`-d 27`	Trace aliasing
`-d 41`	Show reason queue failed

The Post Office Protocol

Post Office Protocol (POP) is a client-side initiated protocol. This simply means that it works opposite to SMTP. Whereas SMTP is used to forward mail from one machine to another, the Post Office Protocol retrieves any new mail.

POP is much like going to see whether you have mail in the mailbox everyday, and if so, you take it home. The only difference is that you probably want to check for new email more frequently than once a day. A value of every 15 minutes would be realistic.

Periodically, a client machine asks the mail server whether it has any new mail. If new mail is present on the server, the client machine downloads it to the local machine. A copy of the mail message might not be retained on the server, depending on the configuration of POP.

After all incoming messages have been received, any out-going mail that the client machine has queued is passed to the mail server for delivery. The MTA (hopefully `sendmail`) on the server is responsible for delivery of the mail beyond this point.

POP on the Server

On the POP server, a special process must be available. This process is called `popd`, which stands for *POP daemon*. A *daemon* is a server process that is not attached to a controlling terminal and usually handles client connections.

When `popd` gets an incoming request for mail service, it checks the user account name and password associated with the requested mail account. If that information is correct, the mail messages are downloaded to the client and, at the client's option, deleted from the server's mailbox for the user.

POP on the Client

POP features are integrated with most MUAs available today. If you are using Netscape Communicator Messenger, click on Get Msg. From Microsoft Outlook Express, click on Send and Receive. In both cases, your mail server is queried for messages that have been received for you by the mail server.

When your POP client is first set up, it needs at least the following information:

- The location of the mail server
- Your user account name
- The password for your user account

When you request to download your mail, this information is automatically passed to the mail server.

From Here...

Electronic mail is one of the most popular uses of the Internet. Most email users create, send, and receive email with a Mail User Agent (MUA). The MUA is either represented by a GUI-based mail reader (such as Eudora) or a text-based mail reader (such as `mailx`).

The infrastructure that supports email on the Internet centers on a protocol called SMTP. This protocol, as well as related standards, defines how mail messages are transferred and formatted, and what types of data they can include.

On the mail servers, many of which are UNIX systems, Mail Transfer Agents (MTAs) such as `sendmail` are implemented to transfer mail messages. Daemons such as `popd` listen for queries from users who want to download their mail messages. These utilities work together to make sending and receiving email simple for end users.

- Chapter 17, "Networking Essentials," includes a general description of UNIX networking features.
- Chapter 23, "DNS," has information about domain names used by email.
- Chapter 26, "Security," contains security considerations associated with UNIX and the Internet.

Part
IV

Ch
25

Security

by Terry W. Ogiltree

In this chapter

Physical Security and Security Policies

Although a UNIX system administrator in a busy environment will find that everyday user management tasks take up a lot of time, the most important task that must be done on a daily basis is making sure that the system (or network) is secure. The term "secure," though, can mean several different things. It can refer to providing sufficient mechanisms to ensure that only those who need to access the system and the data files it holds are able to do so. It can mean that the data is put to a backup tape on a daily basis so that in the event of a catastrophe the data can be restored, possibly to a different system, and users can continue to work. It can mean physical security, such as when you institute a locked-door policy for the computer room to prevent someone from rebooting the computer or damaging it.

The types of security discussed in this chapter can be summarized in three general categories:

- Physical security
- Operating system security
- Application security

Security should be a high priority issue from the beginning. When you first plan to install a computer system or network, you should consider security issues in all stages of planning. This includes creating a safe physical environment to house the computer hardware. A safe physical environment means that you should be sure that only those employees who need to have physical access to any particular computer system will have access. In many companies, this is done by using a locked-door computer room. A locked-door on the computer room protects the systems inside from possible tampering. Also consider environmental protection systems, such as an uninterruptible power supply (UPS) and some sort of fire-extinguishing system (such as Halon gas).

Although you might not consider a UPS to be a safety device, it really is. When the system abruptly halts due to a power failure, data can be left in an inconsistent state, and if you do not have an adequate backup policy, you can lose data. A UPS system can buy you the time needed to perform a normal shutdown of the computer when the power fails, thus preventing unnecessary data loss.

Just as important is a security policy—a written security policy, that is. Any person who uses the computer or network in any way should have to read and understand your company's computer security policy. You should have a form that the user signs to demonstrate that she has indeed read and understands the policy, and will abide by it. The Human Resources department is probably the best group to manage this with your users. The reason for a policy that is written down and acknowledged by the user is so that, in the case of a violation, the user can be held responsible. This can mean a simple reprimand or, in the case of a major security breach, legal proceedings. Without a written, signed policy, you will find it much more difficult to proceed against a malicious user.

What Should the Security Policy Cover?

Although specific items that relate directly to your business or organization should be included, the following items should definitely be covered in your written security policy:

- **Definitions** Define what constitutes the computer system or network resources covered by the policy. This can include computer servers, workstations, the network, peripherals, data, software programs, and so on.

- **Responsibility and accountability** Each user is responsible for any use or access made via any logon account assigned to him. Include precautions about sharing accounts or allowing access to your account inadvertently—by writing down your password, for example. Also cover information that is extracted from the network, such as the proper disposal of computer printouts.

- **Incident reporting policy and hierarchy** State what specific actions need to be taken and list supervisors who are to be contacted in the case of any security problem.

- **Acceptable usage** The policy should state that the network and computer systems attached to it are to be used for business purposes only. Also state that actions such as "probing" (trying to access data or information that you are not entitled to, such as another user's directory or email) are not acceptable use.

- **Software and copyright infringement** All applications that run on any computer system in the network are to be provided by or approved by the company. No user may install, run, store, or otherwise use any computer program that is not provided for or approved by the company. No computer system may be used to store or retrieve copyrighted information without the explicit consent of the copyright owner. Removing floppy disk drives (or disabling them) and monitoring remote access accounts help to enforce this policy.

- **Privacy and confidentiality** Just as it would be improper for an employee to discuss or disseminate confidential information outside the workplace, make it clear that privacy rights and confidentiality are to be respected with regards to the computer system or network, and any information stored or retrieved by it.

- **Reporting security incidents** All users should be required by the policy to report to the appropriate supervisor any known misuse of the computer system or network, or any other security breach. If you use virus detection software, you should state what actions a user should take to report and clean up such an attack.

- **Unlawful actions** The computer system or network should not be used to perform any unlawful action. This can include harassing or making threats to other individuals and downloading unacceptable content from the Internet (such as pirated software or pornography). It should also include using the computer system or network to compromise any other computer system or network, such as that of a vendor or competitor.

- **Penalties** State clearly actions that will be taken against anyone who knowingly violates anything covered in the security policy.

Part

IV

Ch

26

■ Physical security—State that no computer hardware is to be attached to, or used to access, the computer system or the network that is not approved by the appropriate supervisor. This might include a user bringing in a laptop computer from home, for example, and attaching it to the network. With the proliferation of external storage devices (such as floppy disk drives, Iomega Zip drives, or Superdisk drives), you might want to explicitly include them also.

After you create a draft of a security policy that you think is sufficient, have it reviewed by other department heads in your organization for suggestions. There might be legal requirements based on your business type or locality that dictate changes to be made. Others who have been at your business for many years might be able to offer suggestions based on incidents that have happened in the past that you are not aware of.

> **CAUTION**
>
> Although a good security policy for your employees will go far in helping you protect your data and MIS resources, do not overlook outside vendors or contractors. When shopping around for an outside resource, don't just review the technical capabilities of the vendor. Ask about and question the vendor's own internal security policies and procedures. Check with your legal department to be sure that any contracts entered into with third parties include the same guarantees that you require of your employees.
>
> If you allow network connections with outside vendors, do you adequately monitor their use or limit the connections to only the required resources? If you allow dial-in remote access to your network, do you routinely change the account password or disable the account afterwards? Do you reuse the same password when you reactivate an account used by an outside source?

Operating System Security

The computer hardware is useless without an operating system (that is, UNIX). The operating system authenticates users who want to use the system and enforces the rules you set up for accessing data stored on the computer's storage devices. The operating system is also responsible for *auditing* accesses made, but you need to understand auditing and be sure that you correctly set up user accounts to be able to obtain the fine detail of information you will need to determine whether the system security has been violated. So, when considering operating system security, remember that it is a two-pronged approach: Lock things up tightly and then carefully check to see that your locking mechanisms are working (auditing).

The operating system uses a login process to authenticate users and establish access capabilities. Each terminal line that does not currently have a user logged in to it is monitored by the getty program. This program presents the user with the login: prompt. After you enter a username, the getty program launches the login program, which is responsible for prompting you to enter a password. The login program then checks the passwd file (and possibly the shadow password file) to authenticate the user trying to log in to the system.

But that is not all that the `login` program does. It can also, depending on how the system administrator has configured the system, perform other functions:

- Determines whether the login is permitted. The user may be denied access to the specific terminal due to login class restrictions, or by an entry in the `/etc/login.access` file, which denies access based on hostname/username.
- Checks to see whether the user's password has expired, and if so, prompts the user to enter a new password.
- Changes protection or ownership of certain devices if specified in the file `/etc/fbtab`.
- Performs other authentication actions specific to the system, such as S/Key authentication.
- Sets up the user's environment: search path, default working directory, terminal type, command shell, and so on.
- Prints a "message of the day."
- Updates accounting files, if enabled.

Login Security

The login program is the first line of defense for keeping unwanted users out of your computer. Under UNIX, this is controlled by the `login` program, which uses the `etc/passwd` file to determine whether to allow someone in, and to some extent, to tell the operating system what the user is allowed to do. The `passwd` file is basically just an ASCII text file that contains information about each user, including an encrypted password. The fields that are stored in this file are as follows:

- User's login name
- Encrypted password
- UID number
- Default GID number
- GCOS field (full name, phone number, and so on)
- User's home directory
- Default login shell

▶ **See** "Understanding the Login Process," **p. 34**

▶ **See** "Understanding Users and Groups," **p. 234**

Don't Use Generic User Accounts   When adding a new user to your system, be sure that you tie that user to the account name that is used to log in. One of the worst things you can do from a security standpoint is to create "generic" accounts—that is, an account used by more than one person. If you have a particular department that rarely uses the computer but needs to login occasionally, and there are several employees in that department, it can be tempting to simply create a single account (such as "maintenance") and allow everyone in that department to use the account when needed.

But this method, though it makes your job easier by giving you fewer user accounts to manage, provides no accountability. Should someone who uses that account cause damage to your system or its data, there would be little you could do to prove which person used the account when the damage occurred. Always remember that good security practices involve both setting up the system correctly and having the capability to audit actions performed on the system after the fact. If you find suspicious activity in a log file, it does you no good to have a username to blame if you cannot determine who used the username.

Use Good Passwords!

This may seem obvious, but what is a good password? Well, it's one that is hard to guess! Never allow users to use common names or words that can be found in a dictionary as their passwords. As bad as it may seem, curse words are frequently used as passwords and are very easily guessed by an experienced hacker. Enforce a policy that makes each user choose a password that is at least eight characters long. If you demand a password longer than eight characters, then the odds are that the user will write it down somewhere and then it becomes only a matter of time before it falls into someone else's hands.

Some ideas to use when instructing your users on choosing a good password are as follows:

- Combine more than one word to make a single password. Don't use words that naturally go together, however. For example, AppleZonk might be a good choice, but RecordPlayer would not.
- Use nonalphabetic characters somewhere in the password. This includes both numeric characters and punctuation marks.
- Passwords in UNIX are case-sensitive. Use a password that has both upper- and lower-case characters in it.

The most straightforward method of guessing a password, after you have a user's account name, is to just guess by using a program that uses a dictionary of common words and often used passwords. Such a program just keeps encrypting possible passwords and comparing them to the encrypted values found in the password file. If the password is a common word or name, or a password that has been found by the intruder to be in widespread use (such as the local football team name), then it will be guessed by this method pretty quickly.

CAUTION

Don't force your users to use passwords that are difficult for them to remember. Although you do not want the password to be too easy to guess, having one that is overly long or so cryptic that it is difficult to remember will result in users writing them down. One idea is to use passwords that are phonetically easy to say, yet are spelled differently than what you would find in a dictionary. Because the English language is full of strange spelling variations, this should be an easy task.

ON THE WEB

`ftp://info.cert.org/pub/tools/crack` You can protect yourself against easy to guess passwords by using the same tools a hacker would. You can get a program called Crack from this ftp site.

You can access this ftp site anonymously to get the Crack utility. Run this program regularly against your `passwd` file to see whether it can "crack" any of your accounts. If so, change the password for that account immediately and have a short talk with the user who set the password about the importance of keeping his username and password secure.

The `passwd` command comes with a feature that can help you decide on a new password. Use the `-a` command-line option, and the `passwd` command supplies a list of passwords that it generates:

`passwd -a username`

The `passwd` program then lists several choices that the user can choose from and then prompts the user to enter the new password of her choosing.

Protect the */etc/passwd* File

The `passwd` file is readable by all users on the system. Even though the actual password that is stored in the file is encrypted, an intruder can still use the information found here to attempt to compromise your system. Many hacker programs found on the Internet can be used to "crack" an encrypted password.

One solution is to use a separate file to store user passwords. This is called a "shadow" file. Check the documentation that comes with your brand of UNIX to see whether there is a facility for encrypting passwords and storing them in a separate file. Unlike the `passwd` file, the shadow password file is not world-readable.

▶ **See** "The Shadow File," **p. 237**

Passwords are not the only important information that can be obtained from the `passwd` file. Just having a user's username can help an intruder. After the intruder has an account name, a brute-force attack method can be used to try to guess the password for the account. Of course, if the intruder has your entire `passwd` file to look at, then his chances of cracking at least one account password are increased greatly.

Many times an administrator will find it helpful to make a printed copy of the `passwd` file so that he can review it when adding or removing users from the system. If you must print out important information such as this, then dispose of it in a secure manner. A paper shredder can be purchased for under $100 at any good office supply store. If you don't have one, get one, and then use it!

One of the easiest methods used to gain access to the `passwd` file is through anonymous FTP. If you are careless when you set up the area that anonymous FTP users can access, you may find that you are literally giving away your data. Indeed, if you can find no specific use for allowing anonymous logins via FTP, then you should disable this feature altogether.

Part

IV

Ch

26

Fake Logon: The Password Thief!

Always make sure that when you sit down at a terminal and log in to your system that you are indeed going through the normal logon procedures. A common technique for stealing passwords is to write a program that mimics the logon sequence, including soliciting the username and password. Such a program then stores the data it gathers in a place that the password thief can get it and usually exits by giving you an error message. After the program exits, you log on again using the regular logon program.

Few users would be suspicious at getting a failed logon and would simply log on again. That is why this type of program is so easy to implement. Of course, the password thief must find some way to run the program in the first place. The easiest method is to find a terminal that is already logged in and just run the program. A good rule to put into your security policy is that no user should leave a terminal session unattended. This includes terminal windows opened from a PC terminal emulator program as well as actual CRTs.

Unnecessary System Services

Ask any novice administrator what each network service is used for, and you'll probably get many different answers. Many times during a security audit, you will find services or applications running on the system that no one has any idea of what they are used for. A good rule of thumb is that if you don't know what it does, and you can't find out who uses it, then get rid of it. You shouldn't just remove applications or services from your system abruptly if you're not sure what they're for. You can do this in an orderly manner. If you have good documentation policies at your site, you will probably find the information you need there. If not, you can experiment.

First, make sure that you can restore the program or service if you find out that you are wrong. Make sure that you have a good backup. You may delete a particular service, thinking that it is not being used, only to find out later that the service is rarely used, or is being used by another service or another program. Again, there is no good substitute for good documentation, so if you have to experiment by removing something from the system, be sure you know how to put it back. A pretty safe method for doing this is to delete the program and its files right after a full backup, but while users are off the system. This can be done overnight or on weekends, unless you are running a 24/7 shop. If taking the system away from users is not practical, then you can use another "test" system instead. Use your backup tapes to create a test system that is identical to the production system and use it when you experiment with removing programs and data files.

The TCP/IP suite of protocols and services contains many components that are not needed at all sites. Table 26.1 shows a list of some of these that you might not want to keep on your system. Keeping unnecessary (or unused) services running on your computer is similar to having a house that has doors you never use. You might never use them, but someone else can.

Table 26.1 TCP/IP Services to Remove from Your System

Service name	Description
uucp	UNIX-to-UNIX Copy
finger	Provides information about users
tftp	Trivial File Transfer Protocol
talk	Provides text communications between users
bootp	Provides network info to clients
systat	Gives out current system info
netstat	Gives out current network info, such as current connections
rusersd	Shows users logged on
walld	Allows sending a message to all users
rexd	Remote execution utility

To remove any particular service, you should comment out or delete them in the /etc/ inetd.conf file and then reboot the system. Also, review this file (along with all other important system configuration files) regularly to be sure that no one has made changes that you are not aware of.

▶ **See** "The /etc/inetd.conf File," **p. 495**

Dial-In/Dial-Out Security

Protecting your computer network from malicious use or sabotage is much easier when you have some control over the users and the physical environment in which they work. However, this is often not the situation. Most computers or networks in use today in the business environment require some type of remote access so that users who are "on the road" or who work from home (telecommute) can share the same data and application resources as users who are physically present at the workplace. For this reason, you might need to take additional precautions beyond those you normally use to secure your systems.

Never attach dial-in modems (or other devices of a similar nature, such as ISDN TAs) directly to a computer system on your network. Instead, use a router or some type of dedicated remote access server for this purpose. If at all possible, never allow full access to the network for users who use dial-in. Limit this type of access to specific functions. For example, if a salesperson needs to dial-in from remote locations to access sales information or download orders, write script files that provide only these functions and prevent any other type of program from running.

You might even consider using a standalone workstation for users who need to dial-in and leave data for later processing. Using this method, you can use other programs to examine the data.

You can then use removable-storage (floppy disks, for example) to move the data to a production machine and use batch processing techniques to update data files. By using a standalone workstation, you can limit any potential damage to just the one machine. You can be proactive and have on-hand written instructions and source files needed to completely rebuild this standalone workstation should it be compromised. It's much easier to rebuild a single workstation to put it back to a known state than it is to spend time tracking down problems on the network.

Although you might think that if you concentrate on dial-in access and set up elaborate mechanisms to close any security loopholes that this might entail, do not forget the often overlooked dial-out modem. If you have a digital phone system at your workplace, you will probably have users who request an analog phone line so that they can attach a modem to their PCs or UNIX workstations. Users should not use their workstation to dial-out to their personal ISPs to check email or access the Internet during business hours. Remind them that their workstations are connected to the company network, and this opens up the entire network to virus attack or other security breaches. If dial-out access is required for a business purpose, use a dedicated modem bank and audit the phone numbers that are dialed to be sure that the modems are being used for their intended purpose.

Auditing and System Log Files

In several other chapters, you read about various programs and how to use their log files to get information about their use. Table 26.2 presents a list of the more common log files used on a typical UNIX system and the type of information that you can get from them.

Table 26.2   System Log Files

Log File Name	Description
/usr/adm/wtmp	Keeps track of all logins, showing the username, terminal, and connect time. System shutdowns (not crashes!) are also listed in this file. Use the last command or the ac command to view information in this file.
/etc/utmp	Similar to the wtmp file, but this file usually contains only information about users currently logged on.
/var/adm/sulog	This file records usage of the su (switch user) command.
/var/adm/aculog	Records use of dial-out utilities, such as tip or cu.
/var/log/cron	Records usage of the cron utility.
/var/adm/lpd-errs	Records printer problems.
/var/adm/acct	Process accounting log file. Use the sa command or the lastcomm command to view this log file.

Using the *syslog* Logging Facility

In addition to the log files just mentioned, the `syslog` utility can be used to set up logging for many components of the UNIX system. This facility makes it easy for an administrator to configure, in one place, where messages will be sent by various programs. To use this message logging feature, you need to edit a configuration file and tell it what kinds of messages (originating program and message severity) you want to track. You can also designate in this file the name of the log file (or the system console device) that you want any particular messages to be directed to.

The `syslog` daemon (`syslogd`) is started at system boot time, and the configuration file is usually `/etc/syslog.conf`, but you can specify an alternative file using the `syslog` command. The syntax for the `syslog` command is as follows:

```
/etc/syslog [-mN] [-ffilename] [-d]
```

The options you can use are as follows:

- m   Set the mark interval. The default is 20 minutes.
- f *filename*   Specify a file other than `/etc/syslog.conf` as the configuration file.
- d   Turn on debugging.

Configuring the *syslogd* Daemon Using the *syslog.conf* File   The administrator can use the `syslogd` configuration file to specify the source of messages to be logged, the type of messages to log (severity), and the actual destination of the logged messages.

Use any text editor you are familiar with to edit or make new entries in this file. Each entry is one line long and consists of a *selector* followed by a tab character and then an *action* to be performed:

```
selector        action
```

The `selector` field is composed of two parts and consists of a system facility (where did the message originate?) together with a level of severity. The format for the `selector` field follows:

```
facility.severity
```

You can place more than one selector on a line by using the semicolon character as a separator:

```
Facility.severity;facility.severity …
```

Table 26.3 lists the keywords you can use for the facility when editing the `syslogd` configuration file.

Table 26.3   Facility Names Used *syslog* Configuration File

Facility Name	Description
user	Generated by user applications
kern	Kernel messages

continues

Part

IV

Ch

26

Table 26.3   Continued

Facility Name	Description
mail	Mail system messages
daemon	System daemons
auth	The authorization system (for example, login)
lpr	Line printer spooler system
news	USENET
uucp	UUCP (not currently implemented)
cron	cron and at
local0-7	Reserved for local use
mark	Timestamp messages
*	All of the above except for mark

TIP   If for some reason you want to stop the syslogd daemon, you will need to kill it. For that, you need the process ID (PID) of the daemon. This is usually found in the file /etc/syslog.pid.

You combine the facility with the particular severity level of messages you want to capture. The severity levels you can use are listed in Table 26.4.

Table 26.4   Severity Levels Used in *syslog.conf*

Severity Level	Description
emerg	Panic condition. Something usually broadcast to all users.
alert	A condition that needs immediate attention.
crit	Warnings about critical situations.
err	Other errors not warranting emerg, alert, or crit.
warning	Warning messages.
notice	Situations that require attention, but not as important as a warning or other error. Not necessarily an error condition.
info	Informational messages.
debug	Messages generated by programs run in a debug mode.
none	Suppresses messages for this entry.

Finally, after you combine a particular facility with the level of severity of message you want reported, you need to tell the `syslogd` daemon where to send the message. The contents of the *action* field can be any of the following:

- A file   The filename must begin with the slash character. Messages sent to the file by the `syslogd` daemon are appended to the end of the file.
- Another computer   Use the @ at-sign character, followed by a computer hostname. The `syslogd` daemon sends messages to the corresponding `syslogd` daemon on that system.
- One or more usernames   Messages are sent to the terminal that the user(s) are logged in to. If you specify more than one username, separate them by commas.
- The asterisk character (*)   If you use this in the selector field, the `syslogd` daemon sends the message to all users logged in to the system when the message is generated.

For example, to indicate that the daemon should send all messages generated by the kernel to the system console, you would use the following syntax:

```
kern.*/dev/console
```

Or, if you wanted all error messages of any importance generated by the mail system to be sent to the user responsible for the mail system, you could create an entry such as:

```
mail.*johnson
```

where Johnson is the username of the employee responsible for the mail system.

It is often a good idea to send important messages to another host for security purposes. After a knowledgeable hacker breaks into your system, the last thing he will try to do is cover his tracks. If you direct important messages to another computer, you can make this process more difficult. The following line entered into the `syslog.conf` file sends important authorization and kernel messages to another host named Yoko on the network:

```
Kern.*;auth.*@yoko.com
```

You probably won't use the asterisk character for every entry. Sometimes there are messages you do not need to examine on a regular basis (such as non-error informational messages). Instead, use another severity level to specify the types of messages:

```
Mail.crit;lpr.debug            /var/adm/messages
```

NOTE   By default, the `syslogd` daemon also sends certain message types, such as all critical messages, to a default file in addition to the location you specify in the `syslog.conf` file. Check your man pages for the default files for your particular UNIX implementation. ■

Network Security

About the only way you can guarantee that a computer is totally safe from intruders is to lock it away in a room by itself, disconnected from any network or dial-up lines, and never allow users to log on to the system. In reality, most computers today exist in a network of some sort, so you must also be sure to take care of potential security problems that arise from this environment.

Earlier in this chapter in the section "Unnecessary System Services," the importance of disabling unnecessary TCP/IP services was discussed. Because any network can open up your system to potentially many different sources of attack, you should spend the time required to become familiar with possible sources of these types of problems.

Some of the more common problems you will encounter on the network include spoofing, sniffing, and denial of service attacks. You may find that the source of these problems is an internal user, but more likely you will encounter these types of problems when you connect your network to the Internet. If you do connect to the Internet, then you should be sure to install a firewall between your network and the Internet. A firewall is a collection of tools that can be used to control which network packets are allowed to pass between the two systems. Firewalls exist as host-based products or can be situated on a network router.

Network Sniffers

What started out as a diagnostic tool is now a favorite of the hacker community. Network analyzers, sometimes referred to as network sniffers, allow you to capture network traffic and examine the contents. A network sniffer can be a dedicated hardware device, or it can be a program running on a computer on your network. As you probably already know, each packet sent out onto an Ethernet network contains both source and destination addresses. However, each host connected to the network needs to be able to read the headers of all packets that come its way before it can determine whether the packet is destined for it. When the interface finds a packet addressed to its host, it interrupts the CPU and sends the data up the network protocol stack to be handled as needed by the host.

Setting a network interface to *promiscuous* mode allows it to capture all packets that come its way. Although sniffers come in many different types, most allow you to filter out certain types of packets by source and destination addresses, as well as protocol type and other factors. An unauthorized network sniffer on your network can literally read the name and password you send to a remote host, and this information can then be used to compromise your system.

CAUTION

Try to avoid using any protocol or utility on your network that allows the transmission of usernames and passwords. The `rlogin` protocol family relies on a mutual trust mechanism (using an `.rhosts` file, for example), to avoid sending this authentication data across the network. If you do decide to use utilities such as `rlogin` or `rcp`, be sure to secure the `.rhosts` files (and the `/etc/hosts.equiv` file) so that they cannot fall into the wrong hands.

See Chapter 17, "Networking Essentials," for more information about using `rlogin`, `rsh`, and `rcp`, and for how to configure (and make safe) the files used by these utilities.

Names and passwords are not the only thing that can be compromised, however. Confidential information, such as credit card numbers or other information of a personal sort can fall into the wrong hands. Think of a network sniffer just as you do a telephone line wire tap. Anything that goes out through the wire can fall into unwanted hands.

Protecting yourself against this kind of problem requires constant vigilance. The first thing to do is to be sure that the network is physically secure. Although the important servers on your network may be locked safely away in a computer room, how secure are the network cables themselves? Do you have hubs or mini-hubs distributed about the building in different offices? Can anyone just walk up and plug in another cable?

TIP Network sniffers can be of a hardware or a software type, and this problem is not unique to UNIX systems. If you have Windows NT Servers on your network, for example, it is possible for a user to install the network monitor utility that comes with Microsoft's System Management Services (SMS). Although a limited version of the network monitor comes with Windows NT Server and allows the user to view packets destined for just that particular computer, the SMS version allows the user to intercept all network traffic.

In addition to physical security, you can try to limit the damage caused by this sort of thing by segmenting your network. When you use a simple network hub to connect your computers together, you are essentially setting up one large network segment, with all traffic flowing through each connection. Instead, become familiar with bridges or routers and use them to limit network traffic to local segments only. If you allow your network to be connected to the Internet, be sure you use a firewall and understand how it works and what functions it actually performs. For more information about bridges and routers see Chapter 18, "Internetworking." To read about firewalls and laying out your network, see Chapter 21, "Advanced Networking."

Part
IV

Ch
26

Spoofing

As the old saying goes, nothing is ever what it seems to be. From fake email to computers impersonating known hosts, many problems are associated with correctly identifying users and computers on the network. Spoofing on the network can be as simple as disconnecting a computer from the network and attaching one that the hacker controls, using the same hostname and address, to more complex schemes such as ARP spoofing, which relies on tinkering at a low level in the protocol stack and fooling a computer into using the wrong physical address for an IP address.

What is ARP and how can it be spoofed? The Address Resolution Protocol is a common method used by computers on the network to determine what a remote host's physical address is. The IP address of a computer is a logical address. The actual hardware address, which is burned into the network interface when it is manufactured, is needed before actual communications can take place. To obtain a remote computer's hardware address, a computer sends out a broadcast message asking "what is the hardware address for this IP address?" The host that recognizes its IP address responds with a network packet that contains the actual hardware address. Each computer then stores these hardware addresses in an ARP table and can consult it for further connections.

However, entries in ARP tables time out quickly. Although many methods are used in ARP spoofing, the simplest is to just power down (or remove from the network) a host and, after giving the ARP tables on other hosts time to release the entry from their ARP tables, bring online another that uses the same IP address.

You can prevent this type of spoofing by putting permanent entries into the ARP table for hardware-IP address combinations. Permanent entries are not removed after a timeout period, so it is much more difficult to impersonate a host using this method.

Denial of Service Attacks

A computer hacker is not always out to gain access to your system to discover your secrets or steal your confidential data. Some simply want to make your life miserable and can do this by preventing you from using the system. This can be something as simple as causing a server daemon to function improperly, making the entire system inaccessible to your users.

One easy method is to use an anonymous FTP site that allows write access. The hacker simply fills up the disk with useless data, therefore preventing it from being used for its legitimate purpose. This can occur on any file system on your host if an unauthorized user gains access to your computer. Another potential source that can fill up a disk quickly is unwanted email attacks.

Using a separate disk and file system for your ftp site or your email files can help limit the damage caused by these simple attacks. Obviously, you would not want to put your financial programs and data on a file system that could be compromised in this manner.

Other more complex methods that can be used to impede functionality of your system are being discovered all the time. Malicious users who are knowledgeable about networking protocols and your operating system can take advantage of little-known bugs that almost always creep up after a software release. For this reason, be sure to always review any patches, especially those related to security matters, that your vendor issues. Also keep the source material for these patches handy at all times. You might be forced to reinstall the operating system after a catastrophic system invasion, and you would need to restore any additional patches also.

Packet Filtering Can Be the First Line of Defense

Packet filtering involves examining each network packet that passes through a router and, depending on a set of rules that the system administrator can configure, accepting or rejecting the packet. The rules that can be created to decide which packets get through are usually based on the packet's source or destination address or the source or destination TCP or UDP port number. For example, you could set up a rule that allows incoming packets only from a list of hosts you select or denies incoming packets based on a list of hosts that have caused you problems. To be more specific, you could set up a rule that prevents `telnet` connections by filtering port 23. You could use a combination of address and port number to allow or deny access to certain services based on the host address.

Although packet filtering can provide some security from outside attacks, it does have its shortcomings. First, remember that source addresses can be faked, and in that case packet filtering might fail to keep out unwanted traffic. Second, if you rely solely on packet filtering, you will end up with a complex set of rules. If you decide to disallow a specific service by disabling packets by port number, you will usually find that there need to be one or more exceptions to the rule. That means you have to put in additional rules to allow the exceptions. As the network and users change, you need to keep track of which rules need to be changed, and it can become unmanageable.

Another shortcoming of packet filtering is that not all products allow for a logging capability. Because you will have a hard time testing a complex set of filtering rules, you need to be able to have a log file that you can review periodically to determine whether you have correctly coded what you intended.

Finally, packet filtering looks only at the data stream on the packet level. No context is kept to determine whether one packet is related to any other packet. Each packet is accepted or rejected based only on how it fits the rule base you configure. For example, a DNS service relies on a request/response mechanism. A packet filter has no way of knowing that an incoming DNS response packet is being sent in response to a previous outgoing DNS request.

Despite its shortcomings, packet filtering can be adequate for small networks and when the amount and type of traffic passing through the router is not complex. For larger networks, it can be used as the first line of defense, along with other firewall technologies to further enhance security.

What Are Application Gateways?

Part
IV

Ch
26

Application gateways are more complex than basic packet filters. They maintain state information about each connection and can require the user or application to provide authentication before access is granted. When you decide to let specific application traffic pass through the router's packet filtering mechanism, you can use an application gateway (sometimes referred to as a *proxy server*) to further control which packets are allowed through.

Incoming connections to a particular service, such as FTP or Telnet, make connections based on the address of the application gateway. After any authentication, if required by the gateway, then a connection is made from the gateway to the actual host where the service resides. This allows you to hide from the outside world the addresses and other information about your internal network. Most application gateways also provide logging capabilities so that you can check to be sure they are performing as you expect.

Securing Remote Administration Using *ssh*

As discussed earlier in this chapter, the r login utilities (`rlogin` and `rsh`) are not good utilities to use when security is important because they transmit passwords across the network as clear text. The Secure Shell (or, `ssh`), is meant to be used as a replacement for these utilities and provides the following additional capabilities:

- Passwords are not sent across the network as clear text.
- `ssh` can provide for encryption of the data transfer, even X11 connections.
- `ssh` can help prevent DNS/IP spoofing.

`rsh` and `rlogin` rely on sending a password across the network or on using files on the remote system to list the hostnames and usernames that are allowed to log in to the system without using a password. These files, `/etc/hosts.equiv` and `.rhosts` (in the user's directory), can be "hijacked" by a knowledgeable hacker and then used to compromise your system. If you list a hostname in `/etc/hosts.equiv`, then you effectively have to trust every host that each of those hosts trusts. Instead, you should use the Secure Shell client (`ssh`).

Although `ssh` uses the same host equivalence files, it is usually configured to use additional authentication methods that are more secure, such as RSA-based host authentication, whereby the remote system is able to verify the client host's key before login is permitted. In addition to using RSA-based authentication to verify the host, you can also use public/private key pairs for individual users to further enforce secure logins.

 If you want to use `ssh`, but do not want to have the `/etc/hosts.equiv` or `.rhosts` files on your system, which would also allow `rsh` and `rlogin` to be used, you can use the files `/etc/shosts.equiv` and `.srhosts` instead. The Secure Shell utility uses these files just as it does the regular host equivalence files, but the `rsh` and `rlogin` utilities do not.

After authentication has succeeded, then data transfer is encrypted. The user can also forward X11 connections and arbitrary TCP/IP ports over the secure channel.

Cops

Cops (written by Dan Farmer, of Satan fame) stands for Computer Oracle and Password System. It is a collection of more than a dozen utilities that can be used to improve security on UNIX systems. The utilities are used to ferret out security problems so that the user or administrator knows where to concentrate on trying to make the system less vulnerable. Cops does not fix security problems, but only finds them so that you can take action. Although Cops does not provide nearly the functionality that a program such as Satan does, it is much easier to use (just type cops), and therefore is more likely to see actual use by a busy administrator.

Some things that Cops utilities look for include the following:

- File and directory permissions—device modes and permissions.
- Bad passwords and security of password files.
- Finds root SUID files and determines whether they are writable or whether they are shell scripts. Checks for write access to startup files.

- Performs CRC (cyclic redundancy check) checks on key system files to detect tampering.
- Security of anonymous FTP setup.

Depending on the version you install, other capabilities may be present. You can download Cops from the Computer Emergency Response Team (CERT) Web site using the following URL:

```
http://www.cert.org/ftp/tools/cops/
```

Satan

Who would be the best person to ask about securing your house from a burglar? Why, the burglar, of course. This is the approach taken by a program that gained a lot of notice in the news media and on the Internet a few years back: Satan. With a name like that, it is no wonder that the media paid such close attention to the program. The function of the program, however, pretty much merits the name. The Satan program is an extensible utility that can be used to probe your network and computer hosts, trying to take advantage of known security holes, to break in. The authors of the program (Farmer & Venema) wrote a paper (which you can find on the Internet) titled "Improving the Security of Your Site by Breaking Into It." This is how Satan works.

> **N O T E** Although there are stories about how the authors chose the name Satan for their tool, they say that Satan stands for "Security Analysis Tool for Auditing Networks." ■

Satan is also easy to use. If you were to try to compromise your own system to test your security, you would have to spend many hours going through a manual process, using the correct tools to discover each bug or security hole. Satan uses an Internet browser interface (just point and click) and can be used to automate the process.

> **T I P** You can get Satan from a variety of sources on the Internet. There is no charge for the program.
>
> ```
> ftp.mcs.anl.gov/pub/security/satan-1.1.1.tar.Z
> ftp.nenet.dk/pub/security/tools/satan/satan-1.1.1.tar.Z
> ftp.acsu.buffalo.edu/pub/security/satan-1.1.1.tar.Z
> ```
>
> The preceding URLs are just a few of the places you can access using anonymous FTP to download Satan. After you download the compressed file, you need to expand it and then follow the directions for compiling the components written in C.

Part IV
Ch
26

What does Satan actually do? Depending on the type of scan you select (from a light scan to a heavy scan), Satan performs a variety of checks to see what is running on the target system(s). It can check ports for TCP, gopher, http, FTP, and so on. Satan looks for vulnerabilities involving FTP, NFS, NIS files, Trivial FTP access, Remote Shell Access and sendmail, and other network services. The actual probes that Satan makes depend on the type of scan you select and a set of inference rules. After you download the Satan distribution file and uncompress it, you will end up with several subdirectories under a directory called /rules. These directories, and the type of rules stored therein, are as follows:

- /facts These rules are used to deduce new facts based on the data Satan gathers.

- /hosttype These rules are used to help Satan determine the type of host by examining "banners" displayed by the operating system or utilities, such as FTP or sendmail.

- /services These rules are used by Satan to determine what kind of host it is probing based on the services it finds—that is, server or client.

- /todo These rules are used to decide what Satan will do next, based on scans already run against specific hosts.

- /trust Satan decides what type of hosts this system trusts.

- /drop These are rules that Satan uses to decide what facts to ignore. Currently, this includes only a rule that tells Satan to ignore NFS exported CD-ROM directories.

Other directories include PERL routines, binary executables, HTML files, and documentation, among others. Satan creates many directories with many files. It is not a utility program that you can put on a floppy disk and carry from site to site!

TIP Does the name of this security analysis tool offend you? On the opening HTML screen (called the Satan Control Panel) is an option titled "Couldn't you call it something other than 'SATAN'?" You can tell Satan to change his name to Santa! You can also access Satan's documentation from this first page.

Remember that performing a security scan using Satan should not be something you do just one time and then assume you are safe. You can use this tool regularly to detect changes in your system that may lead to vulnerabilities. You can also add your own rules to extend the types of checks that Satan makes, based on your experience and the types of problems that are important to monitor at your site.

Pretty Good Privacy (PGP)

Because intercepting traffic flowing on the Internet is not really a difficult thing to do, you might want to investigate some sort of encryption scheme to use to protect your data. The Pretty Good Privacy (PGP) program, created by Phillip Zimmerman, is about the most popular utility used on the Internet today—partly because it works well and partly because you can obtain a free copy.

Many different types of encryption and authentication schemes are available today, such as DES or Kerberos. Some are based on a using a single key to encrypt data, whereas others use a two-key method called Public Key Encryption.

> **CAUTION**
>
> Be sure to check with your legal department to assess the current state of local laws and import/export laws that relate to encryption software before you use PGP to send or receive information. In some countries, encrypting data is against the law—period. In others, you must register the software or keys used. In the U.S., it is against the law to export encryption software that uses a large key size.

Understanding Public and Private Key Encryption

Single-key systems use the key for encrypting the data and for decrypting it. To effectively use this type of system to encrypt your data, you must devise a method of giving the key to those you want to be able to read your data. You must keep this single key private. If it falls into the wrong hands, then anyone can use it to decrypt the data. Worse, they can use it to encrypt fake data or messages to fool others into thinking you had safely done so.

Public key encryption uses a two-key method. You encrypt the data with one key and use another key to decrypt the data. The keys are related by a mathematical function. One key is termed the *public key*, and the other is called the *private key*. Only one key, the public key, needs to be distributed to others, and it is used to encrypt a message that is to be sent to you. Because only you have a copy of the other half of the key pair, your secret key, then only you can decrypt the message and read it. To make your secret key more secure, PGP uses a pass phrase, like a password, to unlock the secret key.

It should be obvious at once that you can freely distribute the public key half of your key pair. Anyone who possesses your public key can send messages to you safely encrypted and theoretically readable only by you. But how about the reverse situation? When you receive an encrypted message, how can you verify that the message actually comes from the person it says it is from? Just because an email message, for example, is signed "Sincerely, John Doe," can you be sure it was really created and sent to you by John Doe? Anyone who has a copy of your public key could easily create a bogus message, sign someone else's name, encrypt the message, and then send it to you.

PGP allows for the application of a digital signature to an encrypted file to help solve this problem. The person using your public key to send you an encrypted message can use her own *secret key* to sign the message. You can then use that person's public key to verify that the message probably did indeed originate from that person. In both cases, it is necessary that only the secret keys be protected. You never really have to worry about who possesses a copy of your public key, so long as the messages you decrypt are digitally signed by their sender and you possess a copy of their public key to confirm it.

N O T E   PGP is a public key encryption system based on patented technology called RSA public key encryption. The name RSA is taken from the initials of the developers of the technology: Rivest, Shamir, and Adelmen.

Part
IV

Ch
26

How to Obtain, Compile, and Configure PGP

You can get a copy of PGP for many different computer platforms via the Internet. Although binary versions are available for some systems, such as DOS or Macintosh, if you want to use PGP on a UNIX system, you have to compile it from the source.

One Web site that has sources for a freeware version of PGP and instructions for compiling it is maintained by the Massachusetts Institute of Technology (MIT):

```
http://web.mit.edu/network/pgp.html
```

Here you'll find binary distributions for PGP 5.0 for Linux, Windows 95, Windows NT, and Macintosh, along with the source distribution for UNIX systems. They also have available the earlier version 2.6.2 distributions if you prefer. Because this is freeware, remember that is for noncommercial use only.

If you need to use PGP at work, you can purchase it from Network Associates at its Web site:

```
http://www.nai.com/default_pgp.asp
```

Compiling PGP on Your System   If you download PGP from the MIT Web site, you can choose to download either a .zip file or .tar file. If you use the .zip file version, be sure to unpack the compressed file using unzip -a. This is because the .zip file uses the MS-DOS carriage-return/linefeed format for text files. One of the files you will find after you unpack the .zip or .tar file is called setup.doc, which contains information about compiling the source code on different systems. The GNU CC compiler is assumed when you use the make command to perform the build but is not required. Read the setup.doc file carefully to determine whether you have any problems with the compilation.

Configuring PGP   You need to create a directory to use for PGP and, to make matters simple, set the environment variable PGPPATH to point to this directory. For example:

```
# mkdir .pgp
# setenv PGPPATH /usr/ogletree/.pgp
```

Next, generate a public/private key pair. When using the PGP program, the -k command-line parameter is used to refer to options that involve key management functions. To generate a new key pair, -kg is used:

```
# pgp -kg
```

After you enter this command, PGP asks you for the following information:

- Key Size   The larger a key is the harder it will be to break. Larger keys, though, also operate slower during the encryption/decryption process. You can enter:
  1   512 bits.
  2   768 bits.
  3   1024 bits.
  Or you can enter a number other than 1–3 to designate a specific key size.

- Key User ID Enter a name that will be used to refer to the key. The common method of naming keys is to use your name followed by your email address enclosed in angle brackets. For example, `Terry W. Ogletree <ogletree@bellsouth.net>`. You don't need to spend a lot of time deciding on the key name when you first generate a key pair because you can later attach other names to a single key. This is useful when, for example, you have more than one email address and want the key to be referred to by more than one name.

- Pass Phrase When you log on to your system, you use a password to authenticate yourself to the operating system. PGP uses a *pass phrase*, instead, to provide increased security. When prompted, you should enter a string of characters, which can be a series of words, characters, or punctuation marks, for this value. Remember that this phrase will be used to access your own secret key, so it should be a phrase you can easily remember, but one that is difficult for others to guess. Because the phrase is not echoed as you enter it, you are asked to reenter it to confirm that you have indeed entered the phrase you think you have. Do not write down this phrase, of course, but also do not forget it. If you forget your pass phrase, you can no longer use your secret key.

- Random typing To generate a sequence of truly random numbers, PGP next asks you to simply start typing—anything you want because it ignores the text you enter. Instead, the program uses the timing of your keystrokes to generate the series of random numbers. PGP issues a "beep" sound when it has finished timing your keystrokes, and you can then stop typing.

After you have answered these prompts, PGP generates the key pair. This process may take some time, depending on the length of the key you selected. So that you will not think the program has become hung or has stopped responding, a series of dots are printed on the screen while it is generating the key pair.

Managing Keys and "Key Rings" Just as you can use a key ring to store the keys to your house and auto, PGP uses key rings to store your private secret keys and to store the public keys that you obtain from others.

The secret key ring stores your secret keys along with information needed to access them, such as the pass phrase. You should protect the file that holds your secret keys, though. If a malicious user were to gain access to your secret key ring, he would not be able to use it right away to decrypt messages sent to you because he would not know what pass phrases you had used to protect your secret keys. However, like any form of encryption, having the secret key ring makes it much easier for a malicious user to try to get at your secret keys by hacking away at the data until a secret key is discovered.

 TIP Although it is simple to create a `.pgp` subdirectory on your computer's hard drive and use that directory to store your PGP files, if you are using a workstation, you might want to consider putting PGP on a floppy disk instead. The advantage is that you can lock away the floppy disk and almost guarantee that your key rings and other data do not fall into untrustworthy hands. On a multiuser system such as UNIX, you must always be on guard against someone gaining access to your files. If the data is locked away in a desk drawer or safe, it will be much harder to get at.

Part
IV

Ch
26

The public key ring (*filename*=keys.asc) is used to store the public keys you receive from others, along with other data such as *trust parameters*. Although you need to have another's public key before you can send the person an encrypted message, you might find that it is not practical to store all the public keys that you will need. Indeed, unless you exchange data or email with another person regularly, it might be just too time consuming to bother with managing keys for one-time communications.

PGP public key servers are used to help solve this problem. A network of key servers exists on the Internet that are used to store public keys of those who want them to be available to the general public. To have your key available via the public key servers, you need to "publish" it, which is simply a matter of extracting it to a file and sending it to the key server network by using the ADD command.

When you publish your public key on one key server, you do not have to worry about sending it to other key servers because they communicate amongst themselves and replicate the information. When you want to locate the public key of another person, you simply send an email to this same address and use the GET *userid* command.

ON THE WEB

Pgp-public-keys@keys.pgp.net   For more information on PGP Public Key Servers and the commands you use to access them, send an email with the text "help" in the subject line.

Using PGP

After you have installed PGP and created a key-pair, you can distribute your public key and begin to use PGP to encrypt messages or files. The first step, then, is to extract your public key from your key ring into a file that you can give to someone else. The following command is used to extract the public key:

```
PGP -kx userid keyfile [key ring]
```

Userid is the name that you gave the key when you first built it. You do not have to enter the entire name of the user ID, but just enough text to uniquely identify it. For example, if the user ID you chose was Terry William Ogletree <ogletree@bellsouth.net>, you could use the following:

```
PGP -kx ogletree keyfile
```

The value you specify for *keyfile* is used as the output ASCII text file that contains your public key. This is the file you give to others whom you want to be able to decrypt your messages. You can send this file to a public key server, or you can personally give the file to another person.

When you receive a public key file, you need to add it to your key ring before you can use it. The syntax for doing this follows:

```
PGP -ka filename
```

If you are not sure which keys are in the key ring file, you can view the contents by using the PGP -kvv command. Over time, you will find that you have public keys that are no longer valid. To remove a key from your key ring, use the PGP -kr command.

Encrypted Messages   You use your private key to encrypt a message you want to send to someone who possesses your public key. First, create the message you want to send. This can be a simple ASCII text file, or possibly a word processor document or a graphics file. Use the -e parameter to encrypt a file:

```
PGP -e message_file userid
```

Where message_file is the file you want to encrypt, and userid is the user ID for the public key of the recipient of the message. The output file from the encryption command will be a binary file. However, many email programs or other mechanisms of transferring files perform better when you use a simple ASCII text file. PGP has the capability to output an encrypted file in ASCII format, typically called *ASCII Armor*. You use the -a command-line parameter to specify that the output file should be ASCII text:

```
PGP -ea message_file userid
```

Digital Signatures   You can also sign the message, using your secret key, so that the recipient can confirm that the message indeed was sent by you. To sign an encrypted message using your secret key, use the -a option on the command line:

```
PGP -sea message_file userid
```

When you use this option to sign the message, PGP prompts you to enter your pass phrase so that it can unlock your secret key. If your secret key was not protected by a pass phrase, then anyone who was able to obtain a copy of your secret key would be able to sign messages so that they appeared to come from you. Remember to protect your pass phrase. Do not write it down and never give it to another person.

Decrypting PGP Messages

When you receive a file that has been encrypted, you can use PGP to decipher the message:

```
PGP filename
```

Because the message was signed using your public key, PGP needs to use your secret key to decrypt it. For this reason, PGP asks you to enter your pass phrase to continue. After you enter the pass phrase for your secret key, PGP attempts to decrypt the message. If it was signed by the sender, PGP also tries, using the user's public key found on your key ring, to verify the signature.

CERT—The Computer Emergency Response Team, and Other Internet Resources

The Computer Emergency Response Team (CERT), located at Carnegie Mellon University, was created by the Department of Defense in 1989 to assist in protecting the Internet. CERT

Part
IV

Ch
26

responds to security concerns discovered by users on the Internet and issues bulletins about these issues. Their Web site contains a wealth of information about not only specific problems but also general guides for installing a new system or performing a security audit of an existing system. There is also a collection of tools you can use. For example, you can download Crack, Cops, and Satan from this site. You can access CERT's Web page at:

`www.cert.org`

You can access CERT's ftp site at:

`ftp://info.cert.org`

CERT also regularly issues messages via an email mailing list. To subscribe, send an email request to:

`Cert-advisory-request@cert.org`

Many other resources on the Internet are helpful with security in general, and many are specific to the UNIX operating system. Some of the more useful ones are listed here:

- CIAC   After the famous (or infamous) Internet work was able to penetrate many computers on the Internet, the U.S. Department of Energy created the Computer Incident Advisory Capability group (CIAC), which is located at Lawrence Livermore National Laboratory. You can access its Web site at `http://ciac.llnl.gov`.

- BUGTRAQ   This is an email mailing list that you can subscribe to. Its messages involve not just UNIX but also other operating systems and networking security problems. To subscribe, send an email message to `listserv@netspace.org`.

- Oxford University Libraries Automation Service   This Web site contains links to many different Frequently Asked Questions (FAQs) related to computer security. You can get to this site by using the URL:
  `http://www.lib.ox.ac.uk/internet/news/faq/comp.security.unix.html`.

- RSA   This Web site, for the RSA Data Security company, is a good source for information about industry standards for encryption technology:
  `http://www.rsa.com/standards`.

- NIST   The National Institute of Standards and Technology is dedicated to applying technology and promoting standards. Here you will find more information about standards for encryption technology: `http://www.nist.gov`.

Also be sure to read the article that eventually led to the Satan security product: "Improving the Security of Your Site by Breaking Into it," by Dan Farmer and Wietse Venema. You can find a copy of this article at
`http://www.alw.nih.gov/Security/Docs/admin-guide-to-cracking.101.html`.

In addition, many newsgroups on the Internet enable you to interact with others on an ongoing basis to discover or resolve security issues. Some of these include the following:

- `comp.security.unix`
- `comp.security.misc`
- `alt.security`

Finally, one of the best places you can obtain information about security issues pertaining to your particular version of UNIX is your vendor. You might be required to have a support contract with your vendor to receive updates from them, so be sure to check on that. For example, if you are running a Linux system, you would do better to run a commercial version that has the backing of a vendor, such as Red Hat Linux, rather than one that is supported only by users on the Internet. Remember that you get what you pay for. Or, to paraphrase a famous saying, anything you get for free is worth what you paid for it.

From Here...

Security encompasses everything involved with your computer or network, from the actual physical location to the users, hardware, and software. For this reason, the administrator in charge of security issues for a site must wear a number of hats and possess a wide range of knowledge. Other chapters in this book that will be helpful include the following:

- Chapter 2, "Logging In," is a good place to start reading to help you understand user accounts and the importance of good password security.

- Chapter 5, "Files, Directories, and Permissions," shows you the techniques for protecting files and directories so that they are accessed only by authorized persons.

- Chapter 21, "Advanced Networking," helps you become familiar with some of the concepts behind TCP/IP networking that can better enable you to recognize security breaches in your network configuration.

Part
IV

Ch
26

## CHAPTER 27

Performance Tuning

by Terry W. Ogiltree

In this chapter

The Performance Tuning Process

One of the most important tasks a system administrator has to deal with on a continuing basis is performance monitoring and tuning the system or network. The skills involved in this type of job include hardware, operating system, and application skills. In addition, a good knowledge of networking principles may be required if your computer is part of a network, which is almost always the case in today's business world.

System monitoring and performance tuning are closely intertwined. You must monitor the system and be aware of your configuration before you can successfully attempt to make tuning decisions on a regular basis.

In Figure 27.1 you can see that the relationship is a circular one.

FIGURE 27.1

The monitoring-tuning cycle.

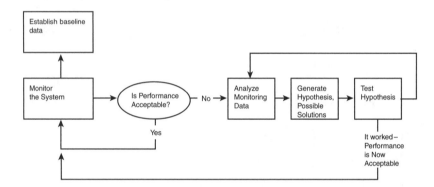

Monitoring is an ongoing process. When a performance problem is noticed, you can use the monitoring data to confirm it. It's one thing to say that "the system is running slow," and quite another to say "program x took 50 percent longer to run this time." By being knowledgeable about your system workload, you will be able to more accurately detect when things are not going so well.

When a problem arises, you can use the data you gather and, by comparing it to your baseline data, create hypotheses about where the actual bottleneck exists. From these hypotheses, you can devise possible solutions. You test each solution by implementing it and evaluating any change on system performance that results, using your monitoring data as a baseline. With this approach, you can systematically eliminate areas that are not affecting performance and quickly focus your attention and work on areas that can improve performance.

After you tune the system and fix problems, you go back to your day-to-day monitoring procedures.

Defining Performance

Usually, you do not have to go looking for performance problems—users will readily make them apparent to you. However, by establishing a baseline of acceptable performance, you will be able to empirically define actual performance degradations by using measurable system performance statistics. The types of data that you decide to monitor will depend on the configuration of your system. This means that you need to be keenly aware of the components that make up your computer system and how they interact.

Understanding Your System Configuration   For example, you should know how your disk or disk subsystems are set up. Are you using RAID? If so, what type of RAID are you using? Do you have more than one disk controller? Do you have a single or multiple CPU setup? Are you connected to the network using 10MB or 100MB Ethernet? FDDI? What type of hardware bus is connecting this all together?

> **N O T E**   Although this book is about the UNIX operating system, it is important for a good administrator to be highly knowledgeable about the hardware components on which UNIX is running. Chapter 12, "Device Management," covers the techniques you will use when configuring hardware components on your system. But if you do not understand how these components do their job, you may find yourself stymied when trying to improve their performance. Indeed, if you do not know the capabilities of your hardware, you won't know whether you can improve performance. For more information about RAID technologies, see "Use RAID Disk Systems for Maximum Performance" elsewhere in this chapter.
>
> If you want to pursue this further, another excellent source of information about RAID technology can be found on the Web site run by the RAID Advisory Board:
>
>   `http://www.raid-advisory.com/`
>
> Information about specific parts of your computer hardware, such as the bus, CPU, and so on, can usually be obtained from an obvious source—your vendor. ▪

Each component of the system that can be considered *consumable* by users who access the system is a resource that you need to monitor. A physical hard disk has a finite capacity for storing data. Users store programs and data on disks. Therefore, a disk is a resource you need to monitor. The same can be said for system memory, as in a multiuser system such as UNIX, because many users' processes are competing to use as much of it as they can get from the operating system to run efficiently. Other resources include software components, such as kernel configuration parameters or application configurations.

> **N O T E**   Don't forget that system performance changes dramatically over time. In a business environment, you know this happens at least once a month—when doing accounting close-outs. However, over longer periods of time, new users are gradually added to the system, or an application begins to get more use or a wider user audience. Other nodes are added to the network. It is important to remember that establishing a baseline of acceptable performance is not a one-time thing. You should continually reevaluate the system on an ongoing basis. ▪

If you are lucky enough to be the one who ordered everything and were present when it was installed, you can use the order processing documents and other hardware and software documentation that came with the system to begin keeping a record of your configuration. If not, you might find that a vendor hardware or software contract is a good place to start. If neither of these is the situation, then you will need to take a physical inventory. Document each component of your system as best you can, including peripherals and application software.

Part
IV

Ch

27

Examine the Interaction of the Pieces   After you have an inventory of the components of your system, you can start to analyze how they work together. A good place to begin is to investigate which software applications are being used regularly. By using the many tools provided with the UNIX operating system to gather performance statistics, you should learn how different applications you run affect system resource usage.

You may find that a performance bottleneck is being caused because too many users are accessing a particular program at the same time of day, forcing a bottleneck on a memory or disk resource. This can be an easy problem to solve if you can spread out the use of the program over a period of time. One of the most common solutions to performance problems is to spread the workload over a longer period of time. In many situations, computers remain idle much of the time, such as at night or on weekends. Scheduling low-priority jobs to run in a detached manner can be a much more cost-effective solution than purchasing additional computing power. When looking at hardware, consider how it is being used in normal operations. If you have adequate disk storage but are experiencing long access times even when the disk is not heavily loaded with users, you may find the problem is one of disk fragmentation. You can solve this kind of problem by using a disk analysis and defragmentation utility as needed. You may indeed have adequate resources but may not be managing them efficiently.

Analyzing Data

When you begin to attack a performance problem, you should already be armed for battle. That is, you should not wait until you need to use the tools described in this chapter to learn how to use them and how to interpret the data they reveal. You must have a good understanding of what the statistical data means in relation to the components that make up the system.

 Analyzing the data you gather can be a complex task. However, UNIX has many tools to help you with the process of taking a mountain of data and reducing it to a more manageable chunk. This chapter describes the tools you gather data with. Tools such as grep and awk, along with the sort utility can help you reduce and organize the data and are described in detail in Chapter 3, "UNIX Shells and System Commands." If you become proficient in using the built-in tools and utilities, you will save yourself a lot of time and manual labor.

You need to know not only that virtual memory involves swapping pages of data in and out of memory with a backing store on disk, but also what an acceptable swapping rate is for your system and its workload. When you detect a slowdown, you can begin by examining data for the virtual memory system by using vmstat (see "Using vmstat to Monitor CPU and Memory," later in this chapter), for example, to get information about memory and disk performance. If you are not familiar with the data that this utility can return, you will have a hard time deciding which component of the system to focus on next. Is it a memory shortage or is the swap file too small? Are more than one disk used for swapping or is it all on a busy disk?

Viewing raw data may not give you a hint as to a solution. When analysis of a more complex nature is required, you can always use the output from the commands used to gather statistical data as data to import into a spreadsheet or other analysis program. A quick scan of the trade magazines will provide you with a wealth of third-party tools that can be used for this purpose.

N O T E Understanding how processes are created and how the UNIX operating system schedules each one to run is a prerequisite to interpreting the data you can gather using the tools described in this chapter. In Chapter 6, "UNIX Processes," you will find an in-depth discussion of the life cycle of a process, as well as the concept of process classes and priorities. ▪

Creating a Hypothesis

After you gather data about the running system and analyze it, you then create a hypothesis about the probable cause of system degradation. A hypothesis is nothing more than a good, educated guess. It provides a starting point so that you can begin to test making changes to the system to improve performance. Because the purpose is to create a situation that can be tested, your hypothesis needs to be realistic and testable. A hypothesis of "The users are just stupid," for example, would be difficult to test and is not likely to lead to a solution that you can implement.

"The swap file is on a disk that also contains a database, and the high I/O rate on this disk is the reason the system is running slow" is a much better hypothesis. In this example, you can move the database to another disk or possibly dedicate a disk to the swap file. You can then measure the performance to see whether it has improved.

Testing and Verifying

After you formulate a hypothesis about system performance degradation, you should decide which component of the system to change to test the hypothesis. This can be something simple such as changing a kernel variable or something time consuming such as rearranging the disk subsystem.

When you conduct the test, you should try to do so under the same conditions as when the performance slowdown occurs. If this is not practical, try to simulate the same conditions. Don't depend on users' responses to determine whether the test is successful, either. Instead, gather data and compare them to your baseline and to the data gathered during performance slowdown. If the numbers don't change, it's time to rethink the process (analyze data) and try again (another hypothesis).

If you work in a large computing environment where time is a precious commodity, you may find that investing in a standalone system to use for performance simulation purposes may be worth its cost. In companies that are racing to solve year-2000 problems, this is almost a must. For solving performance problems, having a separate system which you can use without having to worry about user complaints is also a good idea.

Another use for a separate system like this could be for capacity planning purposes—the proactive side of performance monitoring and tuning. Suppose that you are trying to implement a RAID solution and don't know whether a striped or mirrored solution would be best for your workload. Trying to simulate both on a production system would be very time consuming, resulting in a lot of downtime for your users. Making a copy of the data onto the test system and performing the tests there would probably be safer and more cost effective.

Part
IV

Ch
27

Implementing Solutions

Implementing a solution can involve many different things. If your testing shows that you have a hardware deficiency, you can implement the solution by purchasing and configuring additional hardware. If the operating system needs to be tuned, you may find yourself modifying kernel variables or rebuilding the kernel. Implementing a performance solution for an end-user application can be something like moving it to a different disk or maybe even by realizing that the application itself lacks the horsepower required, so you replace or upgrade it.

Sometimes the solution is a procedural one where you have to inform users or possibly restrict access. This can involve your person-to-person skills. However, you will usually find that users are more likely to change if you can show them (remember the numbers?) that the end result will help them get their work done faster.

Performance Strategies

In addition to vigilant monitoring of your system, there are other things you can do to ensure your system is running at peak performance. Choosing the right hardware for the job is an obvious strategy if you happen to be the one who is purchasing the hardware. By using the tools provided with UNIX to manage your users and resources, you can also become proactive about performance management.

Capacity Planning

Closely related to performance management and tuning is the concept of capacity planning. When setting up a system, or when deciding to add resources to an existing system, you should not just wildly guess at what you think you will need. Instead, use forecasting techniques and review documentation provided by hardware and software vendors to plan ahead of time for what your needs will be. It is much easier to buy the right system up front than it is to justify the additional costs later to make upgrades.

Using load simulators and exerciser programs (usually provided by the hardware or operating system vendor) you can make intelligent guesses about required capacity. Performance data for the current system can also be used to forecast trends when you are planning for future capacity.

Use RAID Disk Systems for Maximum Performance

RAID is an acronym for Redundant Array of Inexpensive Disks. You might see it called Redundant Array of Independent Disks in some literature, which is probably more accurate when you look at the cost of a good disk subsystem. RAID actually refers to more than one technique of using a group of disks together as a unit to provide for enhanced performance or fault tolerance.

The four basic types of RAID you will find in popular use today are as follows:

- RAID Level 0   The data stream is divided into blocks, and the blocks are written not to a single disk but across several disks. By using multiple controllers and disks, you can increase I/O throughput. This RAID technique is referred to as *disk striping*.

- RAID Level 1   In this technique, data is written in its entirety to a disk and also to one or more other disks in the array. This technique is referred to as *disk mirroring*. Mirroring can provide for fault tolerance because disk failure can go unnoticed to users so long as at least one member of the mirror set is still online. Although this technique may increase read I/Os a little, writes will take longer, so this level of RAID is not considered a solution to performance problems.

- RAID Level 3   This RAID level provides for increased I/O throughput by using disk striping techniques like level 0, and it also provides for a level of fault tolerance by calculating a parity stripe and writing this data to a separate disk. If a disk in the stripe set fails, the data on the parity disk can be used to regenerate the data. Because I/O is spread across several disks (and usually several controllers), I/O performance is increased.

- RAID Level 5   Similar to RAID Level 3, using this technique the parity stripe is also written across the multiple disks in the array rather than being restricted to a separate disk. Because the data is striped, I/O performance is generally increased.

These RAID techniques can be implemented in software or hardware. However, for performance reasons, a separate disk subsystem that performs the RAID functions can be a better choice. Disk subsystems can be purchased from a variety of vendors and provide many features, such as hot-swapping disks and online backup of data. It is common to combine more than one RAID technique in a disk subsystem. For example, you might set up the disk array to use both mirroring (level 1) and striping (level 0).

Using Quotas

No matter how much disk real estate you purchase, your users will always fill it up in record time. One common problem is *orphan files*—those left around from long ago but no one remembers exactly what they are for or what they do. Picking through disk directories trying to determine what every file is used for can be time consuming. A full disk is not necessarily a happy disk. Disks function more efficiently when they are not close to being full. Fragmentation begins to occur more rapidly on a disk that has little free space available.

▶ **See** "Monitoring File Systems," **p. 341**

In most instances, keeping directories cleaned up is best left to the individual users because they are presumably the ones who know what they need to do their jobs. However, using disk quotas motivates users to pay closer attention to the disk space they consume and, hopefully, to put it to better use.

Because disks are the slowest part of the system anyway, taking precautions before performance suffers just makes sense.

Part
IV

Ch
27

Use Accounting to Track Usage

Using the accounting functions provided by UNIX can allow you to isolate resource usage to particular users or programs retroactively. Accounting data can also be a great help when trying to forecast capacity for new hardware purchases. Using accounting data for charge-back purposes can also be a technique for controlling resource usage in a system where performance is at a premium.

Two basic types of accounting you can use are login/logout accounting and process accounting. Login/logout accounting will help you determine which users are accessing the system over a period of time. Process accounting is more detailed and will show you statistics on a per-command, per-user basis.

You must first set up the log file on your system to start collecting login/logout accounting data. The file /usr/adm/wtmp can be used to track user login and logouts, including connect time. You must create this file—if it does not exist, the statistics are not collected. The login process and the init process both write information to this file. You can use the ac command to produce a readable summary of the data you collect.

The syntax for the ac command is as follows:

```
ac [-w wtmp] [-p][-d] [usernames] ...
```

and the options you can use with it are as follows:

- ▓ w Use this to specify a file other than /wtmp as the accounting log file.
- ▓ p Use this switch if you want the output report to show totals by individual, rather than just the grand total.
- ▓ d This switch produces a report that runs from midnight to midnight. If you specify any *usernames* on the command line, the report will be produced only for those usernames.

> **CAUTION**
>
> If you decide to enable login/logout accounting by creating the /usr/adm/wtmp file, don't forget to check it often to monitor its size. This file keeps growing, collecting data, until you truncate it. Don't let the accounting log file become a source of performance problems itself.

Using the data you can get from the accounting file enables you to track system performance problems and relate them to the users who are accessing the system. This information can also be useful when you are trying to reschedule user access to spread out the workload when you are not able to add resources to your system.

The ac command is not the only command you can use to access information in the /wtmp accounting file. For example, the last command uses the data in this file to display the last login of a particular user or terminal.

To access process accounting information you can use the sa command to summarize information collected in the /usr/adm/acct file. However, you must first turn on process accounting to start collecting the information. The accton command starts the collection process. You can use accton *filename* to specify an alternative data file. The sa command is used to summarize the information because the accounting file can become large over a short period of time.

The syntax for the sa command varies between different UNIX variants, but some of the more general options you can use with it are as follows:

```
/etc/sa [-options] [file]
```

- *file*   you can specify an alternate file to use. The default is /usr/adm/acct. Use the accton *file* command to create the file.

- a   This option causes all commands to be listed in the report. By default, commands that are executed only once or that have unprintable characters in them are not categorized and are listed under "other."

- b   This sorts the data by the sum of system and user time divided by the number of calls. The default sort is by the sum of user and system time but ignores the number of calls made.

- c   This adds the percentage over total time to the output.

- d   Causes a sort by the average number of disk I/O operations.

- l   Causes system and user time to be separated; they are usually reported together.

- m   Shows the number of processes and CPU minutes by user.

- r   Reverses the sort order.

As you can see, you can get a lot of information about how your system is used, specifically the commands used and the users who execute them, from process accounting.

CAUTION

When free disk space drops below 2 percent, process accounting will stop. It will start up again when free space rises above 4 percent. Of course, if your disk space gets this low, then disk space itself becomes the problem, and process accounting will be the least of your worries.

Check the documentation for your particular system to get more information about system accounting processes and the tools you can use to access the information. For example, Digital UNIX 4.0 supplies the administrator with a wealth of script files that can be used to analyze data found in accounting files so that you do not have to spend time constructing your own tools.

Common Performance Bottlenecks

Some of the most common performance problems encountered today have to do with growth. New releases of software and adding new applications to the system are common. The resulting need to increase hardware resources soon becomes apparent. Still other performance

Part
IV

Ch
27

problems creep up because of programs that were coded inefficiently or from applications that have not been updated to take advantage of newer hardware components.

As the system grows and changes, you need also to be aware that you may have to make changes to the kernel configuration to take advantage of new software or hardware. Changes to the size of buffer and cache structures may be needed.

The network is another major bottleneck in today's business world. If you are on an intranet or the Internet, you know that distributed processing and remote processing techniques make network speed a vital factor in achieving acceptable performance.

Although judging performance on any particular computer depends on factors unique to the hardware, software, and usage patterns, it is still possible to generalize about common resource bottlenecks. The slowest part of any computer system is usually the disk I/O portion. Disks are slower than memory access by a great deal. In general:

- Disk space and fragmentation   A full disk is like a full person. That is, both work a lot slower. When disk space on any disk becomes more than 75 percent full, consider adding storage or rearranging files to move the load to a different disk. Several products (such as Executive Software's Diskeeper) are available to check for disk fragmentation.

- Disk accesses   A disk that is heavily accessed will present slow response times to users as their I/O requests pile up in a queue. Consider rearranging files to move some to another disk. If you have more than one disk on the same controller, consider the controller the bottleneck and move the heavily accessed disk to use a controller by itself.

- Paging rate   Monitor your system during times of a normal workload and get an idea of what an acceptable rate of paging is. What is acceptable depends on the response your users expect. When paging becomes excessive, you can either add memory or, possibly, spread out the paging file across several disk drives, with each drive being on a different controller. You can use the `vmstat` command to get information about paging rates.

- Page file size   When a paging file becomes more than 80 percent used its response time begins to slow. Increase the page file size.

- Memory   Paging is a good indicator of how adequate the memory is on your system. Remember that memory is much faster than disk access, and the more you add, in general, the faster the system runs.

System Hardware and Peripherals

Of the hardware components in your system, perhaps the slowest part is the disk drives. They are also some of the components quickest to use up its capacity. Whereas the virtual memory system can enable you to configure and tune physical memory to increase performance and capacity, when a disk resource becomes full or slow, you almost always have to add capacity unless you can solve the problem by archiving data not needed at this time to offline storage.

The problems you can encounter with disks include buses and controllers as well. Adding another disk to the system in hopes of spreading out files to increase I/O throughput makes a lot more sense if you place the disks on separate controllers. So when you start to look for bottlenecks in disk resources, don't overlook the components that make up the disk subsystem.

How you manage the data on disk storage can also be a cause of a bottleneck. If applications are spending most of their time reading data from disks and doing very little updating, then you may be able to solve a disk I/O related bottleneck by using a RAID striping technique. The point is that buying additional hardware is not always the solution to resource depletion. The way you configure and manage a resource is important also.

The CPU can be a potential bottleneck in systems with large databases and a large user population. In higher-end UNIX systems, you can find solutions to CPU performance in clustering and symmetrical-multiprocessing (SMP) techniques. Clustering allows two or more computers to share selected resources, such as disks, and presents them to the user as though they were the same. SMP takes this further by placing more than one CPU in a single computer. Techniques for shared access to memory locations and other resources are used, and processes can be scheduled to run on one or more processors (depending on the implementation).

With bottlenecks involving memory, you might be inclined to purchase more if your tuning attempts do not result in a significant gain. Memory is dramatically cheaper than it was several years ago, and it is not uncommon to find high-end production systems running a database engine with gigabytes of physical memory. "Buy more memory" is a performance solution that has been around for a long time. And it usually works.

Applications

No matter what the hardware configuration, when tuning the system doesn't produce the required results, you have to ultimately get down to looking at individual programs to see how they utilize system resources. Making changes at this level is a complex task. It presumes that the applications are coded locally and that programmers are available to make the appropriate changes.

Depending on the UNIX variant, you will find debugging tools that can be used to establish detailed statistics on the way a particular program functions.

Kernel

When you make changes to the hardware on your system, you cannot ignore the fact that you may have to adjust certain kernel variables or add components to the kernel and perform a rebuild. Even workload changes on a system can prompt for the need to make kernel changes. For example, the size of buffers or queues in some data structures can be adjusted to provide for increased performance as the system workload changes.

Another important factor in keeping your system running efficiently is to be sure to keep up to date with patches or bug-fixes issued by the vendor. In addition to fixing problems with the system, these minor updates often include enhanced code or support for new devices.

When making changes to the kernel, always be sure that you can test your changes and then back out of them should they not work as expected. Always keep a copy of the existing kernel as a backup when you are recompiling a new version to test.

Part
IV
Ch
27

Network

Bottlenecks in network performance can be much more difficult to track down and resolve because a network involves more than one computer system and usually involves more than one person who is in charge of managing the systems. Network bandwidth can be quickly consumed by applications making large data transfers across the network. Excessive use of broadcast packets for name resolution wastes bandwidth when more efficient methods (DNS) are available.

Examine your network topology closely to be sure that you are locating resources in the right place. A common error from a performance viewpoint is to place a resource on one side of a router while the majority of the users are on the other side. This can result from a business reorganization where people move but resources don't. Keep users that work together on the same network segment so that they can communicate in a local network rather than across a routed connection.

Become familiar with the operating system(s) installed on any routers that you are responsible for. Incorrect configuration of router parameters can dramatically affect network performance. Often the out-of-the-box default configuration is not adequate when superior performance is required.

Gathering Statistics: Tools to Use

There are several tools that you can use to get basic, detailed statistical information about the system's performance. Some are used to show information relating to the operating system and how resources are being used. Other tools can be used to look at individual applications to analyze their usage of these resources to provide feedback to programmers wanting to make their programs run more efficiently. Still other tools can be used to examine network resources and topology to help solve network performance problems.

Basic utilities you can use to gather information about the operating system, current users, and running processes are as follows:

- `ps` Use this to display data about executing processes.
- `vmstat` Shows information about virtual memory, including paging, disk, memory and CPU statistics.
- `iostat` Shows statistics involved in disk or terminal I/O.
- `ipcs` Shows statistics related to interprocess communications (IPC).
- `uptime` Shows how much time has passed since the system was booted, with information about the average number of jobs running in the past 1, 5, and 15 minute periods.

Tools to use when examining network performance include the following:

- `netstat` Shows statistics from data structures related to network activity.
- `snoop` Use this to capture and display network packets for diagnosing network problems.
- `tpcdump` Use this utility to gather information about packets on the network. This utility allows you to select packets using boolean expressions.

- ping   Helpful when diagnosing network connectivity and congestion problems.

- w   This short command shows statistics about "who is on the system." This includes CPU usage, logon time, and how long a user's process has been idle.

- nfsstat   Shows statistics related to the Network File System (NFS).

- traceroute   Shows the hosts a packet is routed through to reach its destination. Use to diagnose network congestion.

Finally, you will find a list of tools to use when analyzing application programs to determine whether you can recode them to run more efficiently:

- dbx   Source level debugger.

- prof   Analyzes data from profile files (produced by programs linked with the -p switch of many compilers) and shows parts of code that consume time and resources.

- gprof   Another utility to analyze program functioning, this one uses data files (produced by programs linked with the -xpg or -pg switch of some compilers) and shows which code segments are called the most often.

TIP The man pages for these tools can get you started using them right away. You can also find resources on the Web to help you with these tools along with many others. For example, the dbx User's Guide is available online at many university sites such as:

http://squish.ucs.indiana.edu/ebt-bin/nph-dweb/dynaweb/SGI_Developer/dbx/
@Generic__BookTocView/9074;cd=4;td=10

Using *ps* and *uptime* for General System Information

For a quick overview of how the system is running, use the ps command. You will see a quick snapshot of the system, showing all the running processes and the amount of CPU time each is consuming. Although you can use other commands to gather much of the same information you see with this command, this snapshot approach gives you a good overall idea of current system usage and provides a good place to start looking for bottlenecks or troubled applications.

In Listing 27.1, you can see typical output from the ps command, using the -aux command-line switches. For the complete syntax of the ps command, see Chapter 3, "UNIX Shells and System Commands."

Part
IV
Ch
27

Listing 27.1   Output from the *ps* Command

USER	PID	%CPU	%MEM	VSZ	RSS	TT	STAT	STARTED	TIME	COMMAND
root	0	3.3	0.0	282	16	P3	I	09Aug98	00:02:00	(swapper)
root	1	1.2	0.0	244	116	??	I	09Aug98	13:02:11	init
james	232	0.0	0.0	122	1120	??	I	09Aug98	00:12:00	irc
garret	247	0.0	0.0	232	122	p4	S	09Aug98	04:13:02	mxxez
togle	249	0.0	0.0	320	224	p4	R	09Aug98	00:00:04	ps -uax

Listing 27.1 is sorted in order of decreasing usage of CPU time, making it easy to quickly see which process is consuming the most of that resource. You can also see the percentage of physical memory used by each process (%MEM), as well as the amount of virtual memory used (VSZ), along with the command currently executing. The RSS column shows the actual amount of physical memory used by the process. This can be misleading, however, because it can include shared memory used by more than one process.

The process state column (stat) shows the state of each process. This is indicated by a single letter, usually one of the following:

- R   The process is runnable.
- U   Sleeping, uninterruptible.
- S   Sleeping.
- I   Idle.
- T   Stopped.
- H   Halted.
- W   Swapped out to disk.
- >   The process has exceeded the soft limit on memory requirements.
- +   This is a process group leader with a controlling terminal.
- N   This process is running at a reduced priority.
- <   This process is running with a raised priority.

N O T E   Because this command produces a snapshot of the actual running system, you will note that even the ps command itself is shown in the display as it gathers and displays the information for you. ▪

If you note a large number of processes swapped out, you should focus your tuning efforts on physical and virtual memory. Review the processes you see listed to determine whether some can run at another time. Finding a single process consuming a large percentage of CPU power can be fixed temporarily by lowering the process's priority (by us of the nice or renice command). It takes the process longer to complete, but other processes can complete quicker. If you notice a particular program or user that should not be on the system at all, you can obtain the process ID by using the ps command and then use the kill command to terminate the process.

Often, after using the ps command to get a quick idea of the current system load, you use the information you gather to point you to other tools that can further isolate the bottleneck.

The *uptime* and *w* Commands   The uptime command is a quick way to find out how long your system has been running. You can also get an idea of the load being placed on the system during the past 15 minutes. The load averages displayed indicate the number of jobs that were in the run queue during the time period covered. In Listing 27.2, you can see a sample of the display, showing the current time, system uptime, and the average loads for the last 1, 5, and 15 minute intervals.

Listing 27.2   Output from the *uptime* Command

```
# uptime
9:56AM up 3 days,  17:25, 3 users, load averages: 6.33, 18.42, 19.01
```

N O T E   Again, depending on the UNIX variant you are using, your mileage may vary. For example, in Digital UNIX, the load averages are for the last 5, 30, and 60 seconds. Under HP/UX, though, they are, like BSD versions, averages for the last 1, 5, and 15 minutes. ■

The w command ("who is on the system?") is similar to the uptime command. The first line output by the w command shows the same basic information about system uptime and load averages. After that, you will see displayed information about each user, including the login terminal, login time, and the command the user is executing.

Using *vmstat* to Monitor CPU and Memory

The virtual memory system allows users to run programs with a larger "virtual" address space than current physical memory constraints allow. Program segments and data not currently needed by a running process may get swapped out to a backing store on disk, known as a paging file or swap file. Although the capability to offer a larger address space to applications allows for the creation of larger and more complex programs, the downside is that when pushed to the limit, system response time can slow down dramatically when pages of memory are constantly being flushed out to disk so that competing processes can run.

You can use the vmstat command to check on the state of your system's virtual memory components. You can obtain statistics about virtual memory that include disk, CPU, and memory statistics. Although the syntax varies depending on the particular implementation of UNIX you are using, the command usually allows you to specify a count and an interval. The following example uses the BSD syntax for the command:

```
vmstat -c 4 -w 2
```

This command generates a line of data every 2 seconds (-w 2) and terminates after displaying four lines (-c 4) of data. The complete syntax for the command is as follows:

```
vmstat [-ims] [-c count] [-M core] [-N system] [-w wait] [disks]
```

You should be able to guess from the previous example what the –c and –w switches are used for. The other parameters you can use are as follows:

- ■ i   Shows the number of interrupts taken by each device since the system was booted.

- ■ M core   Causes a list of values associated with a name list to be extracted from *core* (the default is /dev/kmem).

- ■ N system   Extracts the name list from *system* rather than the default /bsd.

- ■ m   Displays statistics on kernel memory usage.

- ■ s   Displays statistics about paging related activity.

In Listing 27.3, you can see the single-line output of the vmstat command when used with no command-line switches. The headings for each column may seem cryptic at first, but the size of the display prevents longer names.

Listing 27.3   Output of the *vmstat* Command

```
Procs      memory        page                 disk     faults      cpu
r b w    avm  fre    re at pi po fr de   sr  r0 r1   in   sy cs us sy id
2 0 0   2148 564     1  2  1  0  0 68    0   6  0    2   68  7 12  3 66
1 0 0   2148 540     0  0  0  0  0 68    0   0  2    6   42 40  0  2 98
1 0 0   1244 600     0  0  0  0  0 68    0   8  0    3  122 32  0  0 42
```

The first line of headers in this display groups the columns below by categories: process states, memory usage, paging activity, faults, and CPU usage. When you execute the vmstat command with the -c switch, the first line displayed shows statistics since the system was booted. Subsequent lines of the display show data for the period since the last line displayed. You can use this iterative feature of the command to gather data over a period of time when you are trying to diagnose memory resource problems.

Under the heading procs, you will see displayed the number of processes in the r (run queue), b (blocked, waiting for a resource), and w (runnable but swapped out) states. If you consistently see a number of processes in the w column, you should investigate further to find out which processes are waiting. You should then determine whether there is an actual lack of a resource or if some process is consuming a resource at a rate greater than necessary. You can look quickly to the end of the display line to see whether the CPU is potentially the resource that is lacking. If you see a large percentage under the id column (idle), then you may assume that a resource bottleneck is not occurring because of CPU usage. You can examine the statistics under the us (user time) and sy (system time) columns to see whether it is the operating system or user applications that are consuming the CPU resource.

Under the memory category, you can see the number of 1024-byte pages of memory currently active (avm) and the number of pages available on the free list (fre). If the number of pages on the free list remains consistently low and you notice a lot of paging activity, then you are possibly running out of actual physical memory. Consider adding more memory or spreading out the system load over a longer time period.

To check on paging and swapping, look at the data under the page category. The date you will find here is the per-second, average over a 5-second period. The individual headings are as follows:

- re   Number of pages that have been reclaimed from the inactive list
- pi   Number of pages paged in
- po   Number of pages paged out
- fr   Number of pages freed
- sr   Number of pages considered for pageout

If you notice a large number of pages being swapped in or out, compared to your normal baseline usage, investigate paging activity further. You can use the `iostat` command to determine whether a particular disk is being heavily used for swapping. If this is so, rearrange the swap space across several disks, preferably on separate controllers to see whether this remedies the situation.

After the `sr` column, you see information about disk activity, specifically the number of operations per second. In the example in Listing 27.3, the `w0` and `w1` columns show two disks on this system. The columns are created by using the first letter of the disk name and the unit number of the disk.

N O T E The columns used to display data for disk operations may be different on your system. Also, if you have more than four disks on the system, only the first four are displayed by default. You can specify individual disks on the command line (`[disks]`) to get information about other disks on the system. ▨

Using *iostat* to Monitor Disks

Just about the slowest thing you will find on a computer (excluding the user, of course) is the disk system. Whether you have a few single disks on a small system or are connected to a disk subsystem that provides controller-based RAID and other functions, you will still find that sending data to and getting data from the disk system is a tedious, time-consuming procedure. A process may wait many CPU cycles after submitting an I/O request before it receives back the requested data. Retrieving the same data from another memory location would be much faster.

In memory, caches and buffers help to relieve this problem by holding data to be written in memory for a short period of time instead of performing direct I/O to the disk for each request from a process. Frequently accessed data can then be quickly read from the cache buffer, thus saving a time-consuming physical disk I/O. Still, a disk can be overwhelmed, and you can use the `iostat` command to help isolate problems with disk activity.

Disk I/O statistics are not the only data reported by this command. The `iostat` command shows I/O statistics for terminals and the CPU as well. The syntax for the `iostat` command for Digital UNIX is as follows:

```
iostat [drive ...] [interval] [count]
```

A similar syntax for BSD variants follows:

```
iostat [-c count] [-M core] [-N system] [-w wait] [drives]
```

Both versions allow you to specify an interval and count (similar to the `vmstat` command syntax) and to list specific disk drives. A single line of output is produced for each interval, first showing statistics since boot time, thereafter each line showing statistics since the previous interval. Listing 27.4 shows sample output from the `iostat` command.

Part
IV

Ch

27

Listing 27.4   Output from the *iostat* Command

```
     tty    rz1      rz2        cpu
 tin tout bps tps  bps tps  us ni sy id
    1    2   2   0    0   0  16  2 10  0   4  86
    0   45   0   0    0   0  43  2  2  0   6  92
   22   59   0   0    0   0   0  0  8  0   7  85
```

For terminals, you can see the total number of characters in/out (`tin`, `tout` columns) per second. For disks, the bytes transferred per second (`bps`) are expressed in kilobytes. The number of actual transfers per second is shown in the `tps` column. If the disk supports it, you may see a column labeled `msps`, which shows the average seek times for each disk. Finally, in the CPU category, you can see the percentage of time the CPU spends in user mode, user mode running at a low priority (`nice`), system time, and CPU idle time.

N O T E   The name `iostat` would lead one to believe that the statistics output by this command would be related to input/output operations. Yet, you can also get statistics showing the percentage of time the CPU spends in different modes, such as user, system, or idle time. If you wonder what this data has to do with input/output statistics, don't worry; there is a good reason. Knowing what the system is doing during heavy I/O loads can help diagnose the problem. If, for example, you note that the CPU is spending a large percentage of its time in idle mode, yet disk I/O statistics are heavy, then you can make a good assumption that reducing the disk bottleneck probably makes the system run a lot faster.

It is also important to remember that you can get this CPU information using this command, because the name of the command won't give you a hint when you're looking for the appropriate utility. ▪

Use this command to determine when disks on your system are being overloaded and to make decisions of whether to add capacity or redistribute the workload across different disk devices. You can also use the data here to determine whether applications are not behaving correctly. If an application that is making extensive use of a disk is performing repeated small data transfers, you will see a higher rate in the `tps` column—transfers per second—in relation to a smaller data size in the `bps` column.

Using *netstat* to Monitor Network Interfaces

This command can be used to gather extensive statistical information about the operation of your network. The syntax for this command varies considerably between different implementations, so you should consult the man pages for your system to get the complete syntax. Some of the more useful command-line switches for use with the `netstat` command are as follows:

- ▪ a   Shows statistics about the state of sockets of the Internet protocol.
- ▪ i   Shows statistics about network interfaces.
- ▪ n   By default, `netstat` trys to resolve addresses to hostnames. Use this switch to suppress this and display addresses instead.

- r   Shows the host's routing table. If used with the -s switch, it will show routing statistics instead.

- s   Shows statistics on a per-protocol basis, such as total packets received and sent, errors, and so on.

You can use the data obtained from the netstat command to diagnose performance problems on the network. You can isolate network devices that are experiencing a high rate of output errors (netstat -i or netstat -I). You can display the host's routing table to try to determine whether an intermediary host along a route is causing problems for the network.

Memory is also an important resource when trying to provide for adequate network functioning. Buffers for network transfers are allocated in memory, and other data structures must be present. Using the -m command you can get information about memory structures, including denied or delayed memory requests.

In Chapter 19, "Configuring TCP/IP," the netstat command is covered more fully, showing examples of some of the more common uses.

Using *nfstat* to Monitor NFS

Network file systems (NFS) allows file systems to be mounted remotely so that access to files appears to users as if they were local. Because all data access is done via the network, you might need to monitor NFS activity to determine whether it is the cause for degraded network performance.

The nfsstat command displays both client and server NFS statistics. The display can often fill more than one page, so you might want to use the more command to paginate the output. The output depends on the UNIX variant you are using, but you will be able to see timeout, retransmission, and wait errors along with information about cache hits and misses.

▶ **See** "Monitoring and Toubleshooting NFS File Systems," **p. 583**

Using *tcpdump* or *snoop* to Monitor the Network

The TCP/IP protocol suite is the standard network protocol for UNIX systems. It is also used by many other operating systems that connect to the Internet. Monitoring network performance starts with monitoring the network adapter devices and their functions. You should continue by checking information pertaining to the TCP/IP protocol suite when trying to track down network performance problems.

The tcpdump utility can provide you with extensive information about TCP/IP and related protocols. With this utility, you can display or capture packet headers based on boolean expressions. The command-line switches and syntax for this command can get complicated, and a provision is made (via the -F switch) to get input for the filter from a file.

The complete syntax (BSD) for the tcpdump command is as follows:

```
tcpdump [ -deflnNOpqStvxX ] [ -c count ] [ -F file ] [ -i interface ] [ -r file ]
[ -s snaplen ] [ -w file ] expression
```

The obvious switches are -c to have the command stop after capturing the specified *count* number of packets, and -I to specify the network device interface. The *expression* parameter is used to specify the filter. Filter expressions are made up of components called *primitives*, which consist of an ID and a qualifier. The three main types of qualifiers you can use are as follows:

- **type** Type qualifiers are used to indicate the kind of thing the ID is. For example, an ID can be a port number (*port* type), network ID (*net* type), or a computer hostname (*host* type).
- **dir** Directional qualifiers are used to indicate the direction of a data transfer, to or from a host, for example. The qualifiers you can use for directional purposes are: src (source), dst (destination), src or dst, and src and dst. If you do not provide a directional qualifier, then src or dst will be used by default.
- **proto** Protocol qualifiers are used to filter out packets for particular protocols. The qualifiers you can use may depend on the implementation but should include ether, fddi, ip, arp, rarp, tcp, and udp.

For example, the command:

```
tcpdump host unix1
```

would display information from packets arriving at and departing from the host named unix1. There are also a few other keywords you can use in addition to those just listed. These include gateway, broadcast, less, and greater. You can also use the and, or, and not keywords to combine primitives into more complex expressions. In the following example, the filter expression selects packets for the ip protocol arriving to or departing from unix1 and any other host *except* for the host unix99.

```
tcpdump ip host unix1 and not unix99
```

Some of the switches you can use with the tcpdump command include:

- **d** Dump the compiled packet-matching code to standard output and stop.
- **e** Prints the link-level header on each dump line.
- **f** Prints foreign host addresses instead of translating to hostnames.
- **F** *file* Causes the filter expression information to be read in from the file named *file*. Any other filter information you specify on the command line is ignored, and the file is used instead.
- **i** *interface* Specifies the interface on which tcpdump is to listen for network packets.
- **l** Makes stdout line buffered. This is useful when using redirection to view the data as it is captured.
- **n** Suppresses name conversion. For example, addresses will be printed instead of hostnames or port names.
- **N** Suppresses printing of domain name qualification information. Using this switch causes tcpdump to print unix1 instead of unix1.atl.biznesnet.com, for example.

- q Prints less protocol information—"quick" display.
- w and r Use -w to cause the packet stream to be written to a file (-w *filename*). Use -r to read the data back in later for analysis (-r *filename*).

For examples of the type of data that will be displayed on output, see the man page for this command on your system. Each protocol contains data that is specific to it so that the display format can vary dramatically.

The *top* Command

The top command is used to show the top 15 processes consuming the most CPU resources. The display is formatted to fit the screen and is updated continuously. You can use this tool to get a quick snapshot of system performance just as you do with the ps command. Listing 27.5 shows a truncated form of this output. This output was produced using the top command by itself, with no command-line switches.

Listing 27.5 Truncated Listing from the *top* Command

```
Last pid:  1433;  load averages: 1.33, 1.15, .75              14:59:01
20 processes:  1 running, 18 sleeping, 1 stopped
CPU states:  5.7% user,  0.0% nice, 3.4% system, 0.8% interrupt, 90.1% idle
Mem:   11M Active, 2788K Inact, 6420K Wired, 3517K Buf, 9888K Free
Swap:  74M Total, 64K Used, 74M Free
PID  USERNAME    PRI NICE SIZE    RES STATE    TIME   WCPU     CPU COMMAND
111  clayton      2    0  176K   544K RUN      0:03   5.35%   5.35% yx113
108  root        18    0  332K   544K pause    0:01   2.10%   2.30% cron
149  root        18    0  456K   308K pause    0:00   0.00%   0.00% csh
```

In the display, the first few lines show summary information about the system as a whole: process states, CPU states, memory, and swapping data. Underneath this section follows a more detailed display showing the "top" processes that are using the most CPU resources. The number of processes displayed is usually from 10-15—just enough to fill a screen—but you can change this with a command-line switch. The columns in this display are as follows:

- PID The process ID.
- USERNAME The username associated with the process.
- PRI The priority at which the process is now running.
- NICE The nice amount, if any, for this process (ranges from –2 to 20).
- SIZE The total size (in kilobytes) of the process.
- RES The total size (in kilobytes) of resident memory for the process at this time.
- STATE The state of the process, which can be sleep, WAIT, run, idl (idle), zomb, or stop.
- TIME The total number of CPU seconds used by the process.
- WCPU Weighted average of CPU usage.
- CPU Raw CPU usage.

Part
IV

Ch
27

The values in the CPU column (raw CPU usage) are used to sort the output on the display, showing the processes at the top that are consuming the most CPU time. If your performance problem is CPU-related, a quick review of the system with top should help you zero in on the misbehaving process or processes.

The syntax for the top command (BSD) is as follows:

```
top [ -SbiInqu ] [ -dcount ] [ -stime ] [ -ofield ] [ -Uusername ] [ number ]
```

The command-line switches are as follows:

- S   Include system processes (such as the swapper process), which are not shown by default.
- b   Run in batch mode. This is the default when using a dumb terminal (one that doesn't support cursor addressing) or when sending the output to a file. In this mode, keyboard commands are ignored, with the exception of ^C and ^\.
- n   Run in noninteractive mode. This is the same as batch mode (-b).
- i   Run in interactive mode. This is the default when using an intelligent terminal that can use cursor addressing. Certain commands (see "Using Interactive Commands with top" later in this chapter) can be entered at the keyboard to update or alter the display.
- I   This switch suppresses the display of idle processes, which are displayed by default.
- q   Use renice to run at –20. When the system is extremely slow, you may need to use this to effectively run the top command.
- u   This switch suppresses translating UID numbers to usernames. It may possibly make the top command run faster.
- d count   The display is updated count number of times and then the top command exits. On an intelligent terminal, the default for count is infinite—that is, it runs until you stop it, continually updating the screen. For unintelligent terminals, the default is 1 display.
- s time   This sets the number of seconds between screen updates. The default for time is 5 seconds.
- U username   This limits the display of processes to those owned by a particular user, username.

TIP You can use the environment variable TOP to set defaults for the top command. Note, however, that when you set some switches in the TOP variable, such as –S, unexpected results may occur. This is because switches that toggle a feature on or off (-S, -I, -u), can be toggled again if they are repeated on the command line more than once. For example, if you set up the TOP variable with –S, then system processes will be shown in the display if you execute the top command. However, if you execute the top command and use –I on the command line as a switch, then it will negate the –I in the TOP variable, and system processes will not be displayed!

In some systems, you may find another switch, -o field, which can be used to change the default sort order used by the top command. You substitute a column name as shown in the output display (for example, PID, PRI, CPU) for *field* in the command, and the display is sorted by the data in that column.

Using *top* Usually, you can use the top command without any switches to get a good idea of system performance. If you normally do not want to see things such as idle processes, you should set up the TOP environment variable to suppress these so that you do not have to use the -I switch each time you use the command.

On a busy system, you might find that the process running top is not getting enough CPU time to perform its job. If the screen is hanging every few seconds when you are trying to use top to troubleshoot the system, you might try increasing the priority for the command with the -q switch to renice the process to –20:

```
# top -q
```

If you are already in the display, you can try entering the interactive command r to renice your own process (see "Using Interactive Commands with top" later in this chapter).

You can also use the top command to collect data that you can analyze later. By using redirection, you can send the output of the command to a file:

```
# top -d 50 -s 60 > watch.dat
```

In this case, the file watch.dat would act as a sink for the data produced by the top command. The -d switch sets the command to output 50 screen updates at 60 second intervals (-s 60).

Note that the default top command can output a lot of text data over a short period of time if you set the interval to a small number. When collecting data in this manner, you would do best to first do a little examining of the problem and use this logging to a text file method when you are ready to monitor selected processes or users to narrow your search. For example, if your analysis has so far determined that the user clayton is the probable culprit in recent performance problems, then log only his or her processes:

```
# top -d 50 -s 120 -U clayton > clayton.txt
```

After collecting the data, you can either scan it visually to locate irregularities or edit the file to massage it for input into another program such as a spreadsheet.

When you isolate specific users or applications whose resource consumption is out of proportion to what you expect, you should try to reorganize the user's working habits or study the application to see whether it can be improved. If you have a user, for example, who always runs a large number of reports during a busy time of the day, talk to the user and try to schedule the reporting applications to run in the background preferably at off-peak hours.

If you have an application that seems to make wasteful use of resources, such as frequent small data transfers, work with the programmer to see whether the program can be restructured in such a way as to allow batching I/O or finding some other way to lower resource usage. With the many tools and application programming interfaces used today, many programmers spend their time trying to get programs to function without spending much time on analysis beforehand.

Part
IV

Ch
27

If you consider the costs an application incurs during its lifetime, making smart decisions beforehand or good modifications afterwards that save a little time per run can result in a huge savings for many years to come if the program is run frequently.

Using Interactive Commands with *top*   When you are running top in interactive mode, the screen is updated every 5 seconds. You can use Ctrl+L (^L) if you want the screen updated at once. To exit the program, use the letter q (for quit). If you need help with commands, enter the letter h or the question mark (?) character. Otherwise, when watching the display, you can also use the following commands to provide input to the running program:

- d   Use this to change the number of displays. For example, if you used top -d 60 to start the display and decide later you want to use a different number, enter d, and the display prompts you for a new number.
- n   Use this to change the number of processes that are displayed. You are prompted to enter a new number.
- #   Identical to the n command to change the number of processes displayed.
- s   This is used for the same thing as in the command-line switch -s. Use it to change the number of seconds between screen updates. After you enter the s command, you are prompted to enter a new number.
- k   You can kill any process in the display by entering the letter k. You are prompted for a PID, and the process is killed.
- r   Use this to change the priority (nice) of a process or processes. After you enter the r command, you are prompted with "renice". Enter a nice value and a process PID, separated by a space.
- u   In this case, the lowercase letter u is used for the command to change the processes displayed by selecting a username. In the command-line version of this switch, the uppercase letter U is used. After you enter the u command, you are prompted to enter a username or usernames. If you enter the plus sign (+), all processes for all usernames are displayed.
- e   This command shows a list of system errors that have occurred since the last kill or renice command.
- i or I   Use either the upper- or lowercase letter i to toggle the whether idle processes are shown in the display.

When running in interactive mode, you can watch active processes and narrow your search. When you find a process that is causing a bottleneck, you can reduce its priority (r command for renice) or, if it's possible, kill the offending process and run it later. You can check for error messages that result from your actions (e command).

Other Performance Tools

In addition to the standard utilities that come with UNIX, you will find many other tools available, both from the operating system vendors and from third parties, to help you diagnose performance problems.

Digital UNIX Performance Manager 4.0D

Digital UNIX provides a product called Performance Manager, which is an SNMP (Simple Network Management Protocol) based system that allows you to evaluate the performance parameters remotely for different network nodes. A Management Workstation is used as the monitoring node and can be used to gather information about remote nodes concerning CPU, memory, and file and disk performance among other things. For example, Performance Manager can be used to gather statistics on Digital UNIX's Advanced File System (AFS), or on statistics related to Digital UNIX's clustering technology. Support is also provided for monitoring and configuring Oracle 7 by using Performance Manager.

Performance Manager (currently version 4.0D) allows you to set up alert situations so that you can be notified (by message window, email, pager, and so on) when abnormal situations occur. In addition, you can collect and archive data over time and analyze it later. Performance Manager also allows you management capabilities so that you can perform management activities on remote nodes to take corrective action. This is not a trivial product but instead a comprehensive application suite that can provide a lot of assistance in a busy site. For more information on Digital's Performance Manager, see your system documentation.

 TIP For more information about Digital UNIX or the Performance Manager product, go to the Web site at: `http://www.unix.digital.com/`

Sun's SE Toolkit and Virtual Adrian

You can visit Sun's Web site to get information about performance for its hardware and operating systems. You can find links here to get the SE Toolkit, an unsupported kit that gives you the SymbEL interpretive language that can be used to create performance monitoring utilities. One of the more popular of these rule-based script programs is called Virtual Adrian, written by Adrian Cockcroft, of Sun Microsystems.

 TIP You can get the most recent version of SE Toolkit at the URL: `http://www.sun.com/sun-on-net/performance/se3/`
This new version provides support for Solaris 2.5, 2.5.1, and 2.6 support for SPARC and x86.

In addition to the Virtual Adrian program, you can check Sun publications and Web sites for other script files you can use with the SE Toolkit for specific performance problems.

From Here...

Monitoring the system and keeping its performance up to expectations is a large part of the system administrator's job. The tools provided by UNIX give you the capability to gather the data necessary to make decisions about resource configuration and usage. Vigilant monitoring of the system is the best way to detect performance problems before they become unwieldly.

Part
IV

Ch
27

■ See Chapter 3, "UNIX Shells and System Commands," for more information about system commands, such as ps.

■ By reading Chapter 5, "Files, Directories, and Permissions," you will become more familiar with how a process is run, how it makes use of system resources, and how the renice command can be used to change the priority of a process.

■ Chapter 7, "Essential Shell Scripting," and Chapter 8, "Advanced Shell Scripting," can guide you toward creating script files that use the tools discussed in this chapter, and thus automate many of your system management performance tasks.

■ Chapter 18, "Internetworking," gives you a lot of insight into the workings of the network as well as its components, such as bridges and routers.

Appendixes

RFCs

by Chris Negus

Requests for Comments (RFCs) began as a way of creating informal working notes for network development and have evolved into the major method of creating and distributing information to the people who build the Internet. Today, more than 2,300 RFCs specify information about how the Internet works.

The Internet Architecture Board (IAB) maintains the list of RFCs. Anyone in the Internet community, however, can submit documents for acceptance as an RFC. Besides needing to be of some use to the Internet community and being presented in the proper format, there are few restrictions on the range of information an RFC can cover.

RFCs are submitted on nearly any subject relating to computer communications. Many RFCs represent key Internet standards, such as Transmission Control Protocol (RFC 793). Others are informational, such as "Answers to Commonly Asked New Internet User Questions" (RFC 1177). Some RFCs are highly specialized, such as "Definitions of Managed Objects for Drip-Type Heated Beverage Hardware Devices Using SMIv2" (RFC 2325), which describes a way to interface your coffee machine to the Internet.

Many new RFCs today are setting a course for the next generation of the Internet. For example, "IPv6 Multicast Address Assignments" (RFC 2375) discusses how IP addresses will be assigned for multicasting in the new address scheme. Likewise, "An IPv6 Aggregatable Global Unicast Address Format" (RFC 2374) describes how new unicast addresses will work. This appendix describes the different types of RFCs available and where you can get copies of RFCs. It also lists RFCs that may be of general interest to UNIX users, developers, and administrators, as well as RFCs that define particular topics of interest (such as PPP, `mail`, or Next Generation Internet Protocol).

N O T E   RFCs are, by far, most useful to those who develop software and hardware products for the Internet. Many contain far more details than are needed by someone who is just using the protocol. If you are creating an Internet application or routing product, RFCs are a must. For the average UNIX user, however, RFCs listed as FYIs probably offer you the most useful information. ▨

Information About RFCs

To understand how to use RFCs, it helps to know how they are organized, how they can become standards, and how you can tell which ones are most current. The following are a few tips about RFCs:

▨ Once published, an RFCs is never revised or republished under the same number. If a protocol needs to be updated, a new RFC is created, and the old one is listed as Obsolete.

▨ Simply publishing an RFC on a protocol doesn't make it a standard. The RFC must go through a set of steps for acceptance as a standard. (See the section, "The Internet Standards Process," for further information.)

▨ An RFC that is on track to become a standard is assigned both a state and a status. The state identifies where it is in the standards process, and the status describes whether it is required (or optional) that the protocol be implemented by a vendor who wants to make a compliant Internet product.

■ Not all RFCs will, or are intended to, become standards. However, to become an Internet standard, a protocol must be published as an RFC.

When you search for an RFC (as described in the following section, "Finding RFCs"), the information returned by the search tells you not only the name and number of the RFC you are searching for but other information as well. For example, it will be noted whether the RFC is made obsolete by a later RFC (or whether an RFC obsoletes earlier ones), and the status of the RFC in the standards process is also noted.

Finding RFCs

After the RFC is accepted by the Internet Engineering Steering Group (IESG), RFCs are distributed to the world without restriction. One of the best ways to access RFCs is through RFC databases available on the Internet. Certain FTP sites let you download RFCs by their number. However, if you are not sure of the RFC number, search tools are available that let you find RFCs based on search strings you enter.

The USC Information Sciences Institute offers a searchable database of RFCs that you can access on the Internet. You can locate an RFC by entering a search string that identifies the RFC's number, title, or author. The address of the search page follows:

`http://info.internet.isi.edu/7c/in-notes/rfc`

Figure A.1 shows the results of a search for RFCs that include the word *encryption* in them. You can click on the name at the beginning of each bulleted item to display the RFC it represents.

FIGURE A.1
Search for RFCs from the USC Information Sciences Institute site.

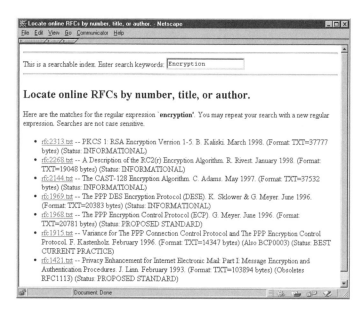

RFCs are usually just available in plain text format, giving them maximum flexibility for delivery and use. However, some RFCs also have HTML versions available. (All RFCs at the USC site are available in plain text, though some also are available in PostScript and HTML format.)

The Internet Standards Process

As the Internet has grown, the importance of standardizing the protocols and applications that make the Internet work has also grown. If different companies are to create routers to exchange data, mail applications to share messages, and FTP servers to download documents, they need to agree on the specifics of how those functions interoperate.

As noted earlier, Internet standards are represented by RFCs (though not all RFCs become standards). For a protocol to become a standard, it goes through a series of enhancement states. It begins as a proposed standard, then becomes a draft standard, and finally becomes a standard. At each level, the protocol goes through more refinement and testing. You should understand a few things about the relationship between standards and RFCs:

- An RFC that represents a standard is noted with a standard number. When the RFC is referenced, the standard it represents also is usually noted (for example, RFC 2300 is usually referenced with the words: Also STD0001).

- A standard number for a particular protocol does not change. However, if a protocol is revised in the future, a new RFC is created, and the standard is assigned to that RFC instead.

- A standard can be represented by several RFCs. For example, the SMTP standard [STD 10] is represented by three RFCs: 821, 1870, and 1869.

Types of Internet Standards   There are two types of Internet standards. One type of standard represents protocols that apply to the entire Internet (see Table A.1), and the other type applies to specific types of networks (see Table A.2). Each standard is represented by one or more RFCs.

The following tables of Internet Standards are reprinted from Internet Official Protocol Standards (RFC 2300). Each table shows the standard protocol identifier, the protocol name, the status, the RFC number, and the standard number. Note that RFC 2300 itself represents a standard; one that is updated every 100 RFC numbers.

Table A.1 shows standards that apply to the entire Internet. Table A.2 shows standards that apply to specific network types that need to implement IP standards. (Note that all standards in Table A.2 are elective.)

Table A.1 Standard Protocols

Protocol	Name	Status	RFC	STD	*
———	Internet Official Protocol Standards	Req	2300	1	
———	Assigned Numbers	Req	1700	2	
———	Host Requirements – Communications	Req	1122	3	
———	Host Requirements – Applications	Req	1123	3	
IP	Internet Protocol	Req	791	5	
as amended by:					
———	IP Subnet Extension	Req	950	5	
———	IP Broadcast Datagrams	Req	919	5	
———	IP Broadcast Datagrams with Subnets	Req	922	5	
ICMP	Internet Control Message Protocol	Req	792	5	
IGMP	Internet Group Multicast Protocol	Rec	1112	5	
UDP	User Datagram Protocol	Rec	768	6	
TCP	Transmission Control Protocol	Rec	793	7	
TELNET	Telnet Protocol	Rec	854, 855	8	
FTP	File Transfer Protocol	Rec	959	9	
SMTP	Simple Mail Transfer Protocol	Rec	821	10	
SMTP-SIZE	SMTP Service Ext for Message Size	Rec	1870	10	
SMTP-EXT	SMTP Service Extensions	Rec	1869	10	
MAIL	Format of Electronic Mail Messages	Rec	822	11	
CONTENT	Content Type Header Field	Rec	1049	11	
NTPV2	Network Time Protocol (Version 2)	Rec	1119	12	
DOMAIN	Domain Name System	Rec	1034, 1035	13	
DNS-MX	Mail Routing and the Domain System	Rec	974	14	
SNMP	Simple Network Management Protocol	Rec	1157	15	
SMI	Structure of Management Information	Rec	1155	16	
Concise-MIB	Concise MIB Definitions	Rec	1212	16	
MIB-II	Management Information Base-II	Rec	1213	17	
NETBIOS	NetBIOS Service Protocols	Ele	1001, 1002	19	

Part
V

App
A

continues

Table A.1   Continued

Protocol	Name	Status	RFC	STD	*
ECHO	Echo Protocol	Rec	862	20	
DISCARD	Discard Protocol	Ele	863	21	
CHARGEN	Character Generator Protocol	Ele	864	22	
QUOTE	Quote of the Day Protocol	Ele	865	23	
USERS	Active Users Protocol	Ele	866	24	
DAYTIME	Daytime Protocol	Ele	867	25	
TIME	Time Server Protocol	Ele	868	26	
TFTP	Trivial File Transfer Protocol	Ele	1350	33	
TP-TCP	ISO Transport Service on top of the TCP	Ele	1006	35	
ETHER-MIB	Ethernet MIB	Ele	1643	50	
PPP	Point-to-Point Protocol (PPP)	Ele	1661	51	
PPP-HDLC	PPP in HDLC Framing	Ele	1662	51	
IP-SMDS	IP Datagrams over the SMDS Service	Ele	1209	52	
POP3	Post Office Protocol, Version 3	Ele	1939	53	
OSPF2	Open Shortest Path First Routing V2	Ele	2328	54	*

Table A.2   Network-Specific Standard Protocols

Protocol	Name	State	RFC	STD	*
IP-ATM	Classical IP and ARP over ATM	Prop	2225		*
IP-FR	Multiprotocol over Frame Relay	Draft	1490		
ATM-ENCAP	Multiprotocol Encapsulation over ATM	Prop	1483		
IP-TR-MC	IP Multicast over Token-Ring LANs	Prop	1469		
IP-FDDI	Transmission of IP and ARP over FDDI	Net Std	1390	36	
IP-X.25	X.25 and ISDN in the Packet Mode	Draft	1356		
ARP	Address Resolution Protocol	Std	826	37	
RARP	A Reverse Address Resolution Protocol	Std	903	38	
IP-ARPA	Internet Protocol on ARPANET	Std	BBN1822	39	
IP-WB	Internet Protocol on Wideband Network	Std	907	40	

Protocol	Name	State	RFC	STD	*
IP-E	Internet Protocol on Ethernet Networks	Std	894	41	
IP-EE	Internet Protocol on Exp. Ethernet Nets	Std	895	42	
IP-IEEE	Internet Protocol on IEEE 802	Std	1042	43	
IP-DC	Internet Protocol on DC Networks	Std	891	44	
IP-HC	Internet Protocol on Hyperchannel	Std	1044	45	
IP-ARC	Transmitting IP Traffic over ARCNET Nets	Std	1201	46	
IP-SLIP	Transmission of IP over Serial Lines	Std	1055	47	
IP-NETBIOS	Transmission of IP over NETBIOS	Std	1088	48	
IP-IPX	Transmission of 802.2 over IPX Networks	Std	1132	49	
IP-HIPPI	IP over HIPPI	Draft	2067		

[Note: an asterisk at the end of a line indicates a change from the previous edition of this document.]

Becoming an Internet Standard   For a protocol to become a standard, it must pass through a series of steps referred to as *states*. When the RFC is published, its state is noted on the RFC itself. Noted along with the state is the RFC's requirement level. Following is a list of states an RFC can be assigned.

- Standard   Indicates that the RFC is an official Internet standard that has been approved by the Internet Engineering Steering Group (IESG). At this point, it is assigned an official standard number.

- Draft Standard   Indicates that the RFC is being seriously considered for standard approval. During this period, the IESG encourages active testing and comments before the RFC becomes a standard.

- Proposed Standard   Indicates that the RFC may be considered for standardization in the future. It is likely, however, that the RFC will go through significant changes before becoming a standard.

- Experimental   Indicates an RFC for a protocol that is probably being used for research purposes. The protocol should not be implemented, unless the person expects to participate in the research.

- Informational   Usually indicates an RFC originally published by an independent vendor that is not on track to become a standard. It is published in an RFC as a service to the Internet community.

- Historic   Indicates an RFC that represents a protocol that is either outdated, superseded by another RFC, or is of no particular interest to the Internet community.

Along with the state of an RFC is the requirement level (or status) of the RFC. Valid requirement levels include the following:

- Required   Indicates that to be compliant, a networking product must implement the protocol described in the RFC.

- Recommended   Indicates that a networking product should implement the protocol described in the RFC. Though it is not required, by not implementing it, the vendor might not be fully compatible with similar products.

- Elective   Indicates that it is not required that you implement the protocol in this RFC at all. However, if you do implement the protocol, it is suggested that you do it the way described in the RFC.

- Limited Use   Indicates that the protocol should only be implemented in limited circumstances. This may be because the protocol is either highly specialized or experimental.

- Not Recommended   Indicates that the RFC is not recommended for general use. The RFC may be outdated or limited in scope.

For Your Information (FYI) RFCs

If you want information about the Internet that focuses more on general topics and questions than on technical details, FYIs are a good place to start. Different levels of information are available in FYIs. For example, there are FYIs that answer questions appropriate to beginning Internet users and those that answer common questions that may be asked by a more technical audience.

You can search for FYIs from USC Information Sciences Institute at the following address:

`http://info.internet.isi.edu/1/in-notes/fyi`

Many of the FYIs at this site are available in HTML format (so you can follow links in the documents to find related information). The following is a list of FYI RFCs available.

- FYI 1   FYI on FYI: Introduction to the FYI Notes. G.S. Malkin, J.K. Reynolds. Mar-01-1990. (Updates FYI0001) (Updated by FYI0001) (Also RFC1150)

- FYI 2   FYI on a network management tool catalog: Tools for monitoring and debugging TCP/IP internets and interconnected devices. R. Enger & J. Reynolds. June 1993. (Updates RFC1147) (Also RFC1470)

- FYI 3   FYI on where to start: A bibliography of internetworking information. K.L. Bowers, T.L. LaQuey, J.K. Reynolds, K. Roubicek, M.K. Stahl, A. Yuan. Aug-01-1991. (Updates FYI0003) (Updated by FYI0003) (Also RFC1175)

- FYI 4   FYI on Questions and Answers—Answers to commonly asked "New Internet User" Questions. A. Marine, J. Reynolds, & G. Malkin. March 1994. (Obsoletes RFC1177, RFC1206, RFC1325) (Also RFC1594)

- FYI 5   Choosing a name for your computer. D. Libes. Aug-01-1991. (Updates FYI0005) (Updated by FYI0005) (Also RFC1178)

- FYI 6   FYI on the X Window System. R.W. Scheifler. Jan-01-1991. (Also RFC1198)

- FYI 7   FYI on Questions and Answers: Answers to commonly asked "experienced Internet user" questions. G.S. Malkin, A.N. Marine, J.K. Reynolds. Feb-01-1991 (Also RFC1207)

- FYI 8   Site Security Handbook. B. Fraser. September 1997. (Obsoletes RFC1244) (Also RFC2196)

- FYI 9   Who's Who in the Internet: Biographies of IAB, IESG, and IRSG Members. G. Malkin. May 1992. (Obsoletes RFC1251) (Also RFC1336)

- FYI 10   There's Gold in Them Thar Networks! or Searching for Treasure in all the Wrong Places. J. Martin. January 1993. (Obsoletes RFC1290) (Also RFC1402)

- FYI 11   X.500 Implementations Catalog-96. C. Apple, K. Rossen. April 1997. (Obsoletes RFC1632, RFC1292) (Also RFC2116)

- FYI 12   Building a Network Information Services Infrastructure. D. Sitzler, P. Smith, A Marine. February 1992. (Also RFC1302)

- FYI 13   Executive Introduction to Directory Services Using the X.500 Protocol. C. Weider, J. Reynolds. March 1992. (Also RFC1308)

- FYI 14   Technical Overview of Directory Services Using the X.500 Protocol. C. Weider, J. Reynolds, S. Heker. March 1992. (Also RFC1309)

- FYI 15   Privacy and Accuracy Issues in Network Information Center Databases. J. Curran, A. Marine. August 1992. (Also RFC1355)

- FYI 16   Connecting to the Internet—What Connecting Institutions Should Anticipate. ACM SIGUCCS. August 1992. (Also RFC1359)

- FYI 17   The Tao of IETF—A Guide for New Attendees of the Internet Engineering Task Force. The IETF Secretariat & G. Malkin. November 1994. (Obsoletes RFC1539, RFC1391) (Also RFC1718)

- FYI 18   Internet Users' Glossary. G. Malkin. August 1996. (Obsoletes RFC1392) (Also RFC1983)

- FYI 19   FYI on Introducing the Internet—A Short Bibliography of Introductory Internetworking Readings. E. Hoffman & L. Jackson. May 1993. (Also RFC1463)

- FYI 20   FYI on "What is the E. Krol & E. Hoffman." May 1993. (Also RFC1462)

- FYI 21   A Survey of Advanced Usages of X.500. C. Weider & R. Wright. July 1993. (Also RFC1491)

- FYI 22   Frequently Asked Questions for Schools. J. Sellers & J. Robichaux. May 1996. (Obsoletes RFC1578) (Also RFC1941)

- FYI 23   Guide to Network Resource Tool. EARN Staff. March 1994. (Also RFC1580)

- FYI 24   How to Use Anonymous FTP. P. Deutsch, A. Emtage, & A. Marine. May 1994. (Also RFC1635)

- FYI 25   A Status Report on Networked Information Retrieval: Tools and Groups. J. Foster. August 1994. (Also RFC1689, RTR0013)

- FYI 26   K-12 Internetworking Guidelines. J. Gargano, D. Wasley. November 1994. (Also RFC1709)

- FYI 27   Tools for DNS debugging. A. Romao. November 1994. (Also RFC1713)

- FYI 28   Netiquette Guidelines. S. Hambridge. October 1995. (Also RFC1855)

- FYI 29   Catalogue of Network Training Materials. J. Foster, M. Isaacs, & M. Prior. October 1996. (Also RFC2007)

- FYI 30   A Primer on Internet and TCP/IP Tools and Utilities. G. Kessler, S. Shepard. June 1997. (Obsoletes RFC1739) (Also RFC2151)

- FYI 31   Humanities and Arts: Sharing Center Stage on the Internet. J. Max, W. Stickle. October 1997. (Also RFC2150)

- FYI 32   Hobbes' Internet Timeline. R. Zakon. November 1997. (Also RFC2235)

Categories of RFCs

RFCs are numbered sequentially as they are created. So, to find the most current RFCs on the subject you are interested in, you need to do some research. To make that task a bit easier, we've noted categories of RFCs that may be of interest to UNIX users and listed the RFCs that apply to each category.

RFCs About RFCs

To understand the scope, organization, and standards bodies associated with the RFC process, you could check out the following RFCs:

- RFC 2360   Guide for Internet Standards Writers. G. Scott. June 1998. (Also BCP0022) (Status: BEST CURRENT PRACTICE)

  Provides tips to standards writers on how to create their RFC to be clear and precise.

- RFC 2300   Internet Official Protocol Standards. J. Postel. May 1998. (Obsoletes RFC2200, RFC2000, RFC1920, RFC1880, RFC1800, RFC1780, RFC1720, RFC1610, RFC1600, RFC1540, RFC1500, RFC1410, RFC1360, RFC1280, RFC1250, RFC1200, RFC1140, RFC1130, RFC1100, RFC1083) (Also STD0001) (Status: STANDARDS TRACK)

  This is the standard RFC that describes how RFCs are organized and standardized. Each RFC is listed in groups by requirement level. This RFC represents Standard 1 and is replaced with an updated RFC about every 100 RFCs.

- RFC 2119   Key words for Use in RFCs to Indicate Requirement Levels. S. Bradner. March 1997. (Also BCP0014) (Status: BEST CURRENT PRACTICE)

  Covers how to interpret wording used to describe requirements in RFCs.

- RFC 1818   Best Current Practices. J. Postel, T. Li & Y. Rekhter. August 1995. (Also BCP0001) (Status: BEST CURRENT PRACTICE)

  Describes the subcategory of RFCs that contain technical information endorsed by the IAB but are not official standards.

- RFC 1311   Introduction to the STD Notes. J. Postel. March 1992. (Status: INFORMA-TIONAL)

  Describes the standard subseries of RFCs. It lists the latest standards and their related RFCs. It also describes the process of numbering and creating standards.

- RFC 1601   Charter of the Internet Architecture Board (IAB). C. Huitema. March 1994. (Obsoletes RFC1358) (Status: INFORMATIONAL)

  Contains the Internet Architecture Board (IAB) charter. It also describes the roles and duties of its various members.

- RFC 1543   Instructions to RFC Authors. J. Postel. October 1993. (Obsoletes RFC1111, RFC0825) (Obsoleted by RFC2223) (Status: INFORMATIONAL)

  Describes how to create RFCs and the policies that go into getting an RFC published.

- RFC 1160   Internet Activities Board. V. Cerf. May-01-1990. (Obsoletes RFC1120) (Status: INFORMATIONAL)

  Provides a history of the Internet Activities Board.

General Internet RFCs

The following RFCs answer common questions about the Internet and describe some of the most general standards associated with the Internet.

- RFC 1594   FYI on Questions and Answers—Answers to Commonly Asked "New Internet User" Questions. A. Marine, J. Reynolds, & G. Malkin. March 1994. (Obsoletes RFC1325) (Also FYI0004) (Status: INFORMATIONAL)

- RFC 1207   FYI on Questions and Answers: Answers to Commonly Asked "Experienced Internet User" Questions. G.S. Malkin, A.N. Marine, J.K. Reynolds. Feb-01-1991. (Also FYI0007) (Status: INFORMATIONAL)

- RFC 1700   ASSIGNED NUMBERS. J. Reynolds,J. Postel. October 1994. (Obsoletes RFC1340) (Also STD0002) (Status: STANDARD)

  Lists and describes various numbers and keywords associated with various Internet protocols. This RFC is also Standard 2.

- RFC 1812   Requirements for IP Version 4 Routers. F. Baker. June 1995. (Obsoletes RFC1716, RFC1009) (Status: PROPOSED STANDARD)

  Describes requirements for network layer protocols. In particular, this RFC describes protocols needed to create and interface with IP routers.

- RFC 1122   Requirements for Internet hosts—communication layers. R.T. Braden. Oct-01-1989. (Status: STANDARD)

  Describes requirements associated with being a host on the Internet. In particular, lower-level network protocols are discussed, such as the link layer, IP layer, and transport layer.

- RFC 1123   Requirements for Internet hosts—application and support. R.T. Braden. Oct-01-1989 (Updates RFC0822) (Updated by RFC2181) (Status: STANDARD)

Companion RFC to 1122. Describes the upper-layer network protocols that need to be supported by an Internet host. This RFC is updated, though not obsoleted by "Clarifications to the DNS Specification." (RFC 2181)

File Transfer Protocol (FTP) RFCs

The following RFCs relate to File Transfer Protocol (FTP):

- RFC 2228   FTP Security Extensions. M. Horowitz, S. Lunt. October 1997. (Updates RFC0959) (Status: PROPOSED STANDARD)
- RFC 1635   How to Use Anonymous FTP. P. Deutsch, A. Emtage, & A. Marine. May 1994. (Also FYI0024) (Status: INFORMATIONAL)
- RFC 959   File Transfer Protocol. J. Postel, J.K. Reynolds. Oct-01-1985. (Obsoletes RFC0765) (Updated by RFC2228) (Status: STANDARD)

Finger RFCs

The following RFCs relate to the Finger protocol:

- RFC 1288   The Finger User Information Protocol. D. Zimmerman. December 1991. (Obsoletes RFC1196, RFC1194, RFC0742) (Status: DRAFT STANDARD)
- RFC 1196   Finger User Information Protocol. D. P. Zimmerman. Dec-01-1990. (Obsoletes RFC1194, 742) (Obsoleted by RFC1288) (Status: DRAFT STANDARD)

Firewall RFCs

The following RFCs relate to Internet firewalls:

- RFC 2356   Sun's SKIP Firewall Traversal for Mobile IP. G. Montenegro, V. Gupta. June 1998. (Status: INFORMATIONAL)
- RFC 1579   Firewall-Friendly FTP. S. Bellovin. February 1994. (Status: INFORMATIONAL)

Internet Protocol Version 6 RFCs

The following RFCs relate to the IP Next Generation Protocol (IPv6):

- RFC 2375   IPv6 Multicast Address Assignments. R. Hinden, S. Deering. July 1998. (Status: INFORMATIONAL)
- RFC 2374   An IPv6 Aggregatable Global Unicast Address Format. R. Hinden, M. O'Dell, S. Deering. July 1998. (Obsoletes RFC2073)
- RFC 2292   Advanced Sockets API for IPv6. W. Stevens, M. Thomas. February 1998. (Status: INFORMATIONAL)
- RFC 2185   Routing Aspects of IPv6 Transition. R. Callon, D. Haskin. September 1997. (Status: INFORMATIONAL)
- RFC 2133   Basic Socket Interface Extensions for IPv6. R. Gilligan, S. Thomson, J. Bound, W. Stevens. April 1997. (Status: INFORMATIONAL)

- RFC 2030   Simple Network Time Protocol (SNTP) Version 4 for IPv4, IPv6 and OSI. D. Mills. October 1996. (Obsoletes RFC1769) (Status: INFORMATIONAL)
- RFC 1970   Neighbor Discovery for IP Version 6 (IPv6). T. Narten, E. Nordmark & W. Simpson. August 1996. (Status: PROPOSED STANDARD)
- RFC 1933   Transition Mechanisms for IPv6 Hosts and Routers. R. Gilligan & E. Nordmark. April 1996. (Status: PROPOSED STANDARD)
- RFC 1924   A Compact Representation of IPv6 Addresses. R. Elz. April 1996. (Status: INFORMATIONAL)
- RFC 1887   An Architecture for IPv6 Unicast Address Allocation. Y. Rekhter & T. Li, Editors. December 1995. (Status: INFORMATIONAL)
- RFC 1885   Internet Control Message Protocol (ICMPv6) for the Internet Protocol Version 6 (IPv6). A. Conta, S. Deering. December 1995. (Status: PROPOSED STANDARD)
- RFC 1883   Internet Protocol, Version 6 (IPv6) Specification. S. Deering & R. Hinden. December 1995. (Status: PROPOSED STANDARD)
- RFC 1881   IPv6 Address Allocation Management. IAB & IESG. December 1995. (Status: INFORMATIONAL)
- RFC 1752   The Recommendation for the IP Next Generation Protocol. S. Bradner & A. Mankin. January 1995. (Status: PROPOSED STANDARD)
- RFC 1726   Technical Criteria for Choosing IP The Next Generation (IPng). C. Partridge & F. Kastenholz. December 1994. (Status: INFORMATIONAL)
- RFC 1550   IP: Next Generation (IPng) White Paper Solicitation. S. Bradner & A. Mankin. December 1993. (Status: INFORMATIONAL)

Mail RFCs

The following RFCs are related to electronic mail on the Internet:

- RFC 2368   The mailto URL scheme. P. Hoffman, L. Masinter, J. Zawinski. July 1998. (Updates RFC1738, RFC1808) (Status: PROPOSED STANDARD)
- RFC 2162   MaXIM-11 - Mapping between X.400 / Internet mail and Mail-11 mail. C. Allocchio. January 1998. (Obsoletes RFC1405) (Status: EXPERIMENTAL)
- RFC 2142   Mailbox Names for Common Services, Roles and Functions. D. Crocker. May 1997. (Status: PROPOSED STANDARD)
- RFC 2110   MIME Email Encapsulation of Aggregate Documents, such as HTML (MHTML). J. Palme, A. Hopmann. March 1997 (Status: PROPOSED STANDARD)
- RFC 2077   The Model Primary Content Type for Multipurpose Internet Mail Extensions. S. Nelson, C. Parks, Mitra. January 1997. (Status: PROPOSED STANDARD)
- RFC 2049   Multipurpose Internet Mail Extensions (MIME) Part Five: Conformance Criteria and Examples. N. Freed & N. Borenstein. November 1996. (Obsoletes RFC1521, RFC1522, RFC1590) (Status: DRAFT STANDARD)

■ RFC 2048   Multipurpose Internet Mail Extensions (MIME) Part Four: Registration Procedures. N. Freed, J. Klensin, & J. Postel. November 1996. (Obsoletes RFC1521, RFC1522, RFC1590) (Also BCP0013) (Status: BEST CURRENT PRACTICE)

■ RFC 2047   MIME (Multipurpose Internet Mail Extensions) Part Three: Message Header Extensions for Non-ASCII Text. K. Moore. November 1996. (Obsoletes RFC1521, RFC1522, RFC1590) (Updated by RFC2184, RFC2231) (Status: DRAFT STANDARD)

■ RFC 2046   Multipurpose Internet Mail Extensions (MIME) Part Two: Media Types. N. Freed & N. Borenstein. November 1996 (Obsoletes RFC1521, RFC1522, RFC1590) (Status: DRAFT STANDARD)

■ RFC 2045   Multipurpose Internet Mail Extensions (MIME) Part One: Format of Internet Message Bodies. N. Freed & N. Borenstein. November 1996. (Obsoletes RFC1521, RFC1522, RFC1590) (Updated by RFC2184, RFC2231) (Status: DRAFT STANDARD)

■ RFC 2033   Local Mail Transfer Protocol. J. Myers. October 1996. (Status: INFORMATIONAL)

■ RFC1985   SMTP Service Extension for Remote Message Queue Starting. J. De Winter. August 1996. (Status: PROPOSED STANDARD)

■ RFC 1957   Some Observations on Implementations of the Post Office Protocol (POP3). R. Nelson. June 1996. (Updates RFC1939) (Status: INFORMATIONAL)

■ RFC 1939   Post Office Protocol - Version 3. J. Myers & M. Rose. May 1996. (Obsoletes RFC1725) (Updated by RFC1957) (Also STD0053) (Status: STANDARD)

■ RFC 1893   Enhanced Mail System Status Codes. G. Vaudreuil. January 1996. (Status: PROPOSED STANDARD)

■ RFC 1869   SMTP Service Extensions. J. Klensin, N. Freed, M. Rose, E. Stefferud, & D. Crocker. November 1995. (Obsoletes RFC1651) (Also STD0010) (Status: STANDARD)

■ RFC 1844   Multimedia Email (MIME) User Agent Checklist. E. Huizer. August 1995. (Obsoletes RFC1820) (Status: INFORMATIONAL)

■ RFC 1424   Privacy Enhancement for Internet Electronic Mail: Part IV: Key Certification and Related Services. B. Kaliski. February 1993. (Status: PROPOSED STANDARD)

■ RFC 1423   Privacy Enhancement for Internet Electronic Mail: Part III: Algorithms, Modes, and Identifiers. D. Balenson. February 1993. (Obsoletes RFC1115) (Status:PROPOSED STANDARD)

■ RFC 1422   Privacy Enhancement for Internet Electronic Mail: Part II: Certificate-Based Key Management. S. Kent. February 1993. (Obsoletes RFC1114) (Status: PROPOSED STANDARD)

■ RFC 1421   Privacy Enhancement for Internet Electronic Mail: Part I: Message Encryption and Authentication Procedures. J. Linn. February 1993. (Obsoletes RFC1113) (Status: PROPOSED STANDARD)

■ RFC 1344   Implications of MIME for Internet Mail Gateways. N. Borenstein. June 1992. (Status: INFORMATIONAL)

- RFC 1343   A User Agent Configuration Mechanism for Multimedia Mail Format Information. N. Borenstein. June 1992. (Status: INFORMATIONAL)
- RFC 1339   Remote Mail Checking Protocol. S. Dorner, P. Resnick. June 1992. (Status: EXPERIMENTAL)
- RFC 976   UUCP mail interchange format standard. M.R. Horton. Feb-01-1986. (Updated by RFC1137) (Status: UNKNOWN)
- RFC 974   Mail routing and the domain system. C. Partridge. Jan-01-1986. (Status: STANDARD)
- RFC 821   Simple Mail Transfer Protocol. J. Postel. Aug-01-1982. (Obsoletes RFC0788) (Also STD0010) (Status: STANDARD)

Network File System (NFS) RFCs

The following RFCs relate to NFS:

- RFC 2339   An Agreement Between the Internet Society, the IETF, and Sun Microsystems, Inc. in the Matter of NFS V.4 Protocols. The Internet Society, Sun Microsystems. May 1998. (Status: INFORMATIONAL)
- RFC 2224   NFS URL Scheme. B. Callaghan. October 1997. (Status: INFORMATIONAL)
- RFC 2055   WebNFS Server Specification. B. Callaghan. October 1996. (Status: INFORMATIONAL)
- RFC 2054   WebNFS Client Specification. B. Callaghan. October 1996. (Status: INFORMATIONAL)
- RFC 1813   NFS Version 3 Protocol Specification. B. Callaghan, B. Pawlowski, & P. Staubach. June 1995. (Also RFC1094) (Status: INFORMATIONAL)
- RFC 1094   NFS: Network File System Protocol specification. Sun Microsystems Inc. Mar-01-1989. (Also RFC1813) (Status: INFORMATIONAL)

Point-to-Point Protocol (PPP) RFCs

The following RFCs relate to Point-to-Point Protocol:

- RFC 2284   PPP Extensible Authentication Protocol (EAP). L. Blunk, J. Vollbrecht. March 1998. (Status: PROPOSED STANDARD)
- RFC 2153   PPP Vendor Extensions. W. Simpson. May 1997 (Updates RFC1661, RFC1962) (Status: INFORMATIONAL)
- RFC 1994   PPP Challenge Handshake Authentication Protocol (CHAP). W. Simpson. August 1996. (Obsoletes RFC1334) (Status: DRAFT STANDARD)
- RFC 1968   The PPP Encryption Control Protocol (ECP). G. Meyer. June 1996. (Status: PROPOSED STANDARD)
- RFC 1962   The PPP Compression Control Protocol (CCP). D. Rand. June 1996. (Updated by RFC2153) (Status: PROPOSED STANDARD)

- RFC 1661   The Point-to-Point Protocol (PPP). W. Simpson, Editor. July 1994. (Obsoletes RFC1548) (Updated by RFC2153) (Also STD0051) (Status: STANDARD)

Telnet RFCs

The following RFCs relate to the telnet protocol:

- RFC 856   Telnet Binary Transmission. J. Postel, J.K. Reynolds. May-01-1983. (Obsoletes NIC 15389) (Status: UNKNOWN)
- RFC 855   Telnet Option Specifications. J. Postel, J.K. Reynolds. May-01-1983. (Obsoletes NIC 18640) (Status: STANDARD)
- RFC 854   Telnet Protocol Specification. J. Postel, J.K. Reynolds. May-01-1983. (Obsoletes RFC0764, NIC 18639) (Status: STANDARD)

World Wide Web RFCs

The following RFCs relate to the World Wide Web:

- RFC 2276   Architectural Principles of Uniform Resource Name Resolution. K. Sollins. January 1998. (Status: INFORMATIONAL)
- RFC 2368   The mailto URL scheme. P. Hoffman, L. Masinter, J. Zawinski. July 1998. (Updates RFC1738, RFC1808) (Status: PROPOSED STANDARD)
- RFC 2070   Internationalization of the Hypertext Markup Language. F. Yergeau, G. Nicol, G. Adams, M. Duerst. January 1997. (Status: PROPOSED STANDARD)
- RFC 2068   Hypertext Transfer Protocol—HTTP/1.1. R. Fielding, J. Gettys, J. Mogul, H. Frystyk, T. Berners-Lee. January 1997. (Status: PROPOSED STANDARD)
- RFC 1945   Hypertext Transfer Protocol—HTTP/1.0. T. Berners-Lee, R. Fielding & H. Frystyk. May 1996. (Status: INFORMATIONAL)
- RFC 1866   Hypertext Markup Language— 2.0. T. Berners-Lee & D. Connolly. November 1995. (Status: PROPOSED STANDARD)
- RFC 1738   Uniform Resource Locators (URL). T. Berners-Lee, L. Masinter, & M. McCahill. December 1994. (Obsoletes RFC2396) (Updated by RFC2368) (Status: PROPOSED STANDARD)
- RFC 1630   Universal Resource Identifiers in WWW: A Unifying Syntax for the Expression of Names and Addresses of Objects on the Network as Used in the World-Wide Web. T. Berners-Lee. June 1994. (Status: INFORMATIONAL)

TCP-UDP Common Ports

by Sriranga Veeraraghavan

In this chapter

Introduction

This appendix is adapted from material covered in RFC 1700.

The Internet Assigned Numbers Authority (IANA) is the central coordinator for the assignment of unique parameter values for Internet protocols. The IANA is located at and operated by the Information Sciences Institute (ISI) of the University of Southern California (USC). The IANA is chartered by the Internet Society (ISOC) and the Federal Network Council (FNC) to act as the clearinghouse to assign and coordinate the use of numerous Internet protocol parameters.

The Internet protocol suite, as defined by the Internet Engineering Task Force (IETF) and its steering group (the IESG), contains numerous parameters, such as Internet addresses, domain names, autonomous system numbers (used in some routing protocols), protocol numbers, port numbers, management information base object identifiers, including private enterprise numbers, and many others.

The common use of the Internet protocols by the Internet community requires that the particular values used in these parameter fields be assigned uniquely. It is the task of the IANA to make those unique assignments as requested and to maintain a registry of the currently assigned values.

Most of the protocols are documented in the RFC series of notes. Some of the items listed are undocumented. Further information on protocols can be found in the memo, "Internet Official Protocol Standards" (STD 1).

N O T E   If you are developing a protocol or application that requires the use of a link, socket, port, protocol, and so on, contact the IANA to receive a number assignment.

```
Joyce K. Reynolds
Internet Assigned Numbers Authority
USC - Information Sciences Institute
4676 Admiralty Way
Marina del Rey, California  90292-6695

Electronic mail: IANA@ISI.EDU
Phone: +1 310-822-1511
```

Requests for parameter assignments (protocols, ports, and so on) should be sent to <iana@isi.edu>.

Requests for SNMP network management private enterprise number assignments should be sent to <iana-mib@isi.edu>. ▓

Well-Known Port Numbers

The Well-Known Ports are controlled and assigned by the IANA and on most systems can only be used by system (or root) processes or by programs executed by privileged users.

Ports are used in the TCP [RFC 793] to name the ends of logical connections that carry long-term conversations. For the purpose of providing services to unknown callers, a service contact port is defined. This list specifies the port used by the server process as its contact port. The contact port is sometimes called the "well-known port."

To the extent possible, these same port assignments are used with the UDP [RFC 768].

The assigned ports use a small portion of the possible port numbers. For many years, the assigned ports were in the range 0–255. Recently, the range for assigned ports managed by the IANA has been expanded to the range 0–1023.

Table B.1 lists some of the most commonly used ports assigned by the IANA.

Part

V

App

B

Table B.1   IANA Controlled Port Assignments

Keyword	Decimal	Description
	0/tcp	Reserved
	0/udp	Reserved
tcpmux	1/tcp	TCP Port Service Multiplexer
tcpmux	1/udp	TCP Port Service Multiplexer
echo	7/tcp	Echo
echo	7/udp	Echo
discard	9/tcp	Discard
discard	9/udp	Discard
systat	11/tcp	Active Users
systat	11/udp	Active Users
daytime	13/tcp	Daytime
daytime	13/udp	Daytime
qotd	17/tcp	Quote of the Day
qotd	17/udp	Quote of the Day
chargen	19/tcp	Character Generator
chargen	19/udp	Character Generator
ftp-data	20/tcp	File Transfer [Default Data]
ftp-data	20/udp	File Transfer [Default Data]
ftp	21/tcp	File Transfer [Control]
ftp	21/udp	File Transfer [Control]

continues

Table B.1   Continued

Keyword	Decimal	Description
telnet	23/tcp	Telnet
telnet	23/udp	Telnet
smtp	25/tcp	Simple Mail Transfer
smtp	25/udp	Simple Mail Transfer
time	37/tcp	Time
time	37/udp	Time
rap	38/tcp	Route Access Protocol
rap	38/udp	Route Access Protocol
nameserver	42/tcp	Host Name Server
nameserver	42/udp	Host Name Server
nicname	43/tcp	Who Is
nicname	43/udp	Who Is
login	49/tcp	Login Host Protocol
login	49/udp	Login Host Protocol
domain	53/tcp	Domain Name Server
domain	53/udp	Domain Name Server
bootps	67/tcp	Bootstrap Protocol Server
bootps	67/udp	Bootstrap Protocol Server
bootpc	68/tcp	Bootstrap Protocol Client
bootpc	68/udp	Bootstrap Protocol Client
tftp	69/tcp	Trivial File Transfer
tftp	69/udp	Trivial File Transfer
gopher	70/tcp	Gopher
gopher	70/udp	Gopher
finger	79/tcp	Finger
finger	79/udp	Finger
www-http	80/tcp	World Wide Web HTTP
www-http	80/udp	World Wide Web HTTP
hostname	101/tcp	NIC Host Name Server

Keyword	Decimal	Description
hostname	101/udp	NIC Host Name Server
pop2	109/tcp	Post Office Protocol - Version 2
pop2	109/udp	Post Office Protocol - Version 2
pop3	110/tcp	Post Office Protocol - Version 3
pop3	110/udp	Post Office Protocol - Version 3
sunrpc	111/tcp	SUN Remote Procedure Call
sunrpc	111/udp	SUN Remote Procedure Call
uucp-path	117/tcp	UUCP Path Service
uucp-path	117/udp	UUCP Path Service
nntp	119/tcp	Network News Transfer Protocol
nntp	119/udp	Network News Transfer Protocol
ntp	123/tcp	Network Time Protocol
ntp	123/udp	Network Time Protocol
netbios-ns	137/tcp	NetBIOS Name Service
netbios-ns	137/udp	NetBIOS Name Service
netbios-dgm	138/tcp	NetBIOS Datagram Service
netbios-dgm	138/udp	NetBIOS Datagram Service
netbios-ssn	139/tcp	NetBIOS Session Service
netbios-ssn	139/udp	NetBIOS Session Service
imap2	143/tcp	Interim Mail Access Protocol v2
imap2	143/udp	Interim Mail Access Protocol v2
snmp	161/tcp	SNMP
snmp	161/udp	SNMP
snmptrap	162/tcp	SNMPTRAP
snmptrap	162/udp	SNMPTRAP
xdmcp	177/tcp	X Display Manager Control Protocol
xdmcp	177/udp	X Display Manager Control Protocol
irc	194/tcp	Internet Relay Chat Protocol
irc	194/udp	Internet Relay Chat Protocol

Part

V

App

B

continues

Table B.1   Continued

Keyword	Decimal	Description
ipx	213/tcp	IPX
ipx	213/udp	IPX
imap3	220/tcp	Interactive Mail Access Protocol v3
imap3	220/udp	Interactive Mail Access Protocol v3
netware-ip	396/tcp	Novell NetWare over IP
netware-ip	396/udp	Novell NetWare over IP
https	443/tcp	https MCom
https	443/udp	https MCom
exec	512/tcp	remote process execution
login	513/tcp	remote login a la telnet
syslog	514/udp	
printer	515/tcp	spooler
printer	515/udp	spooler
talk	517/tcp	
talk	517/udp	
ntalk	518/tcp	
ntalk	518/udp	
utime	519/tcp	unixtime
utime	519/udp	unixtime
router	520/udp	local routing process (on site);
timed	525/tcp	timeserver
timed	525/udp	timeserver
courier	530/tcp	rpc
courier	530/udp	rpc
netnews	532/tcp	readnews
netnews	532/udp	readnews
netwall	533/tcp	for emergency broadcasts
netwall	533/udp	for emergency broadcasts
uucp	540/tcp	uucpd

Keyword	Decimal	Description
uucp	540/udp	uucpd
uucp-rlogin	541/tcp	uucp-rlogin
uucp-rlogin	541/udp	uucp-rlogin
klogin	543/tcp	kerberos rlogin
klogin	543/udp	kerberos rlogin
kshell	544/tcp	krcmd
kshell	544/udp	krcmd
ipcserver	600/tcp	Sun IPC server
ipcserver	600/udp	Sun IPC server
doom	666/tcp	doom Id Software
doom	666/tcp	doom Id Software
kerberos-adm	749/tcp	kerberos administration
kerberos-adm	749/udp	kerberos administration
	1023/tcp	IANA Reserved
	1024/udp	IANA Reserved

Part
V

App
B

Registered Port Numbers

The registered ports are not controlled by the IANA and on most systems can be used by ordinary user processes or programs executed by ordinary users.

Ports are used in the TCP [RFC 793] to name the ends of logical connections that carry long-term conversations. For the purpose of providing services to unknown callers, a service contact port is defined. This list specifies the port used by the server process as its contact port. Although the IANA cannot control uses of these ports, it does register or list uses of these ports as a convenience to the community.

To the extent possible, these same port assignments are used with the UDP [RFC 768].

A list of registered ports in the range 1024–65535 can be found at:

```
ftp://ftp.isi.edu/in-notes/iana/assignments/port-numbers
```

Protocol and Service Names

Table B.2 lists some of the Official Protocol Names as they appear in the Domain Name System WKS records and the NIC Host Table. Their use is described in [RFC 952].

A protocol or service may be up to 40 characters taken from the set of uppercase letters, digits, and the punctuation character hyphen. It must start with a letter and end with a letter or digit.

Table B.1   Protocol Names and Descriptions

Keyword	Description
ARP	Address Resolution Protocol
AUTH	Authentication Service
BOOTP	Bootstrap Protocol
BOOTPC	Bootstrap Protocol Client
BOOTPS	Bootstrap Protocol Server
CHAOS	CHAOS Protocol
CHARGEN	Character Generator Protocol
CLOCK	DCNET Time Server Protocol
COOKIE-JAR	Authentication Scheme
DAYTIME	Daytime Protocol
DISCARD	Discard Protocol
DOMAIN	Domain Name System
ECHO	Echo Protocol
FINGER	Finger Protocol
FTP	File Transfer Protocol
FTP-DATA	File Transfer Protocol Data
HOSTNAME	Hostname Protocol
ICMP	Internet Control Message Protocol
IGMP	Internet Group Management Protocol
IGP	Interior Gateway Protocol
IMAP2	Interim Mail Access Protocol version 2
IP	Internet Protocol
IPCU	Internet Packet Core Utility
IPPC	Internet Pluribus Packet Core
LOGIN	Login Host Protocol
MAIL	Electronic Mail Messages
MUX	Multiplexing Protocol

Keyword	Description
NAMESERVER	Host Name Server
NETBIOS-DGM	NETBIOS Datagram Service
NETBIOS-NS	NETBIOS Name Service
NETBIOS-SSN	NETBIOS Session Service
NICNAME	Who Is Protocol
NNTP	Network News Transfer Protocol
NTP	Network Time Protocol
OSPF	Open Shortest Path First Interior GW Protocol
POP2	Post Office Protocol - Version 2
POP3	Post Office Protocol - Version 3
PPP	Point-to-Point Protocol
QUOTE	Quote of the Day Protocol
RARP	A Reverse Address Resolution Protocol
SNMP	Simple Network Management Protocol
SMTP	Simple Mail Transfer Protocol
SUN-RPC	SUN Remote Procedure Call
TCP	Transmission Control Protocol
TELNET	Telnet Protocol
TFTP	Trivial File Transfer Protocol
TIME	Time Server Protocol
UDP	User Datagram Protocol
NNTP	Network News Transfer Protocol
UUCP-PATH	UUCP Path Service

Part

V

App

B

Glossary

by Chris Negus

abort   To immediately cancel a process without finishing the current processing.

AIX   An IBM version of UNIX System V (with some BSD enhancements).

application   A computer program that carries out tasks for the end user.

ASCII (American Standard Code for Information Interchange)   Definition of codes that represent the numbers, letters, punctuation, and control codes used to represent text in most computer systems.

awk   Program that performs procedures based on searches for pattern matches.

background job   A program, usually begun from a user shell, that continues to run while the shell is released to start other programs. A background process can be started by adding an ampersand (&) to the end of a shell command.

back up   The act of copying data from its original storage location (usually a hard disk) to another medium (such as a tape, removable disk, or network file server) for safe keeping.

batch   Command used for queuing one or more commands for execution at a later time (usually when the system is less busy).

baud rate   The speed of transmission over modems or terminal lines.

Berkeley Software Distribution (see BSD)   Implementation of UNIX developed by the University of California at Berkeley.

bin directory   UNIX system directory that contains many user level commands and utilities.

bin login   UNIX system login that has limited administrative rights to add and remove commands and utilities.

block device   A device that stores information in blocks of characters (such as a disk drive).

boot   To start up a standalone program (most often the computer operating system).

Bourne shell (see shell and sh)   UNIX command processor created by Steve Bourne at AT&T Bell Laboratories.

C language   Programming language created by Dennis Ritchie of AT&T Bell Laboratories used to write application and system programs. (Much of the UNIX system was written in C.)

cc (C compiler)   Program that compiles C language programs.

cd   UNIX shell command used to change to a different current directory.

character device   A device that interprets input and output one character at a time (such as a terminal device).

chgrp   Command used to change the group assigned to a particular file to a different group.

chmod   Command used to change the read, write, and execute permissions assigned to the owner, group, and other bits on a file or directory.

chown   Command used to change a file's owner assignment.

client   A process that requests a service from another process (typically a server).

col   Command that filters the output from a troff or nroff command so that control characters are removed (usually used so that output could be seen on a terminal screen).

command line   The place where a user types commands to be interpreted by the shell.

command prompt   The character (or characters) output by the shell, indicating that it is ready to accept input. By default, the user prompt is a dollar sign ($), and the root user prompt is a pound sign (#).

compiler   Program that interprets source code and converts it into lower level code (such as an executable file). See cc.

cp   Command used to copy a file from one location to another in the UNIX file system.

cpio   Command used to copy and convert a group of files into a single archive or, conversely, to expand an archive of files into the original set of files. Often used for doing backups.

cron   Daemon used to run preconfigured commands at specific times.

cu   Command used to call other UNIX systems for remote login. This is a UUCP utility.

current directory   The directory that the shell uses to interpret relative paths.

cursor   Marker on the screen that indicates where input is active.

daemon   Process that runs in the background of a UNIX system, waiting for an action to occur. For example, some UNIX daemons listen for requests from a network and then allow a user to log in, copy files, or view a Web page.

date   Command that displays or changes the current system date and time.

debugger   Command used by programmers to check for problems (or bugs) in their code.

dev directory   UNIX system directory that contains device files that provide access to devices (such as terminals, printers, and tape drives).

device driver   UNIX system component providing access to hardware (or sometimes software) devices on a particular UNIX system.

Devices file   File used to assign ports and devices used for communication by UUCP commands.

df   Command used to display space available on UNIX file systems.

Dialers   File used to assign different types of devices available to be used by UUCP commands.

diff   Command used to determine the differences between the contents of two UNIX text files.

Part

V

App

C

directory   Location in a UNIX file system tree that contains files and other directories (subdirectories).

domain   A structure used to organize and identify computers on a network.

Domain Name System (DNS)   Domain structure used to organize the host computers in the Internet. Levels in the domain are separated by dots (for example, `host1.abc.com`).

dot   The period character (.) used to identify the current directory to the shell or to separate parts of a domain name.

dot dot   Two period characters (..) used to identify the directory that is one level above the current directory.

download   Process of copying data or an application program to a client computer from a server computer.

du   Command used to display available disk storage space.

echo   Command used to output characters to the display terminal.

ed   Simple command used to edit text file.

env   Command used to list current shell environment variables.

environment variable   Character string interpreted by the shell to represent a value. For example, on some UNIX systems, `$HOME=/home/chris` identifies the current home directory as `/home/chris`. Others require variables be set using the `setenv` command.

executable   A file that has the execute bit set so that it can be run as a program.

exit   Command used to exit from the current shell.

fdisk   Command used to change disk partitions or set the active partition for booting.

file system   An organization of files and directories, representing all or part of one or more hard disks.

find   Command used to scan the contents of a UNIX file system and output lists of file and directory names based on user criteria.

finger   Command used to determine information about a UNIX user, such as username and when the user last logged in.

firewalls   One or more computers set up as a buffer between a private network and a public network, providing a focal point to manage network traffic in and out of the private network.

ftp   Command (and associated protocol) used to manage the copying and listing of files to and from a host system over a network. Stands for File Transfer Protocol.

group   Set of one or more users that can be given access to particular files and directories. A group is represented by a name and a group ID.

group ID   The number assigned to a particular group.

hosts   Locations representing nodes on a computer network.

HP/UX   Hewlett-Packard version of the UNIX system.

Hypertext Markup Language (HTML)   Document markup language used as the basis for creating Web pages. HTML documents allow inclusion of different data types and links to other Web locations.

`init` state (see system state).

`init`   Command used to change the current state of the computer. This could mean shutting down (`init 0`), multiuser mode (`init 2 or 3`), or reboot (`init 6`).

installation   The process of adding software to a computer.

Internet   Worldwide computer network providing access to millions of computers via the interconnection of public and private networks under a common naming and address hierarchy.

Internet Protocol (see IP).

Internet Protocol Next Generation (IPng) Version 6   A set of specifications created to provide a migration path from the current Internet protocols (IPv4) to the future Internet protocols (IPv6).

Internet service provider (ISP)   Organization that allows Internet access to individuals or companies on a subscription basis.

IP (Internet Protocol)   An internetworking protocol used to provide datagram services to higher level protocols (such as TCP and UDP).

IP address   Name or number identifying the location of a node in an IP network (such as the Internet).

IP packet forwarding   Method of allowing data to bypass a network firewall to provide a service between a node on the private network and a node on the public network.

IPv6 (see Internet Protocol Next Generation).

IRIX   Silicon Graphics version of the UNIX system.

kernel   The heart of the UNIX system, providing interfaces between user processes and computer hardware.

`kill`   Command used to end a user process while it is still running.

Korn shell (see shell and `ksh`)   Shell command interpreter created by David Korn at AT&T Bell Laboratories.

`ksh`   Command used to start the Korn shell command interpreter.

link   Feature used to connect a file or directory to another file or directory.

Linux   Popular UNIX-like operating system that is distributed freely.

Part
V
App
C

login   Process whereby a username and password are entered into a UNIX system to provide access to that system.

lp   Command used to send a file to a UNIX printer.

lpq   Command used to display the content of a printer queue.

ls   Command used to list the contents of a directory and, optionally, details about file sizes and permissions associated with each file and directory.

Mail Transfer Agent (MTA)   Program that implements the protocols that transfer electronic mail across the network between mail servers. (See sendmail.)

Mail User Agent (MUA)   Program that provides user access to electronic mail services. Examples are mailx and Eudora.

mailx   Command that lets a user compose, send, receive, read, and manage mail messages.

man   Command used to print UNIX manual (man) pages.

man pages   Documents that describe the features and options for individual UNIX components (commands, files, devices, and so on).

Mbone   Experimental network used to test Internet multicasting protocols and applications.

mkdir   Command used to create a directory in a UNIX file system.

mknod   Command used to create a special device file.

mnttab   File that contains mounted file system information.

more   Command used to control the output of text to a terminal.

mount   Command used to connect a device or remote file system to the local file system tree.

mountpoint   The location in the local file system where a device or remote file system is mounted.

multicast   Method of simultaneously delivering a stream of data to numerous nodes on a network.

multiplexing   Process of transmitting two or more communications streams over a single communications line.

multiprocessing   Act of managing multiple processes on the same operating system simultaneously.

multiprocessor   A computer that incorporates more than one central processing unit (CPU) so that they can be managed at the same time by the operating system.

Multipurpose Internet Mail Extensions (MIME)   Internet standard that allows multiple data types to be identified and incorporated in a mail message.

mv   Command used to move a file or directory to another location in the UNIX file system.

`netmask`   Method of masking an IP address so that different parts of the address can be used to designate the host and network identifiers.

Network Address Translation (NAT)   Method for allowing private networks to reuse IP addresses without conflict.

Network File System (NFS)   UNIX facility that allows file systems to be shared among UNIX systems over a network.

NFS (see Network File System).

node name   Name used to identify a host computer to a UUCP network.

`nroff`   Command used to format text intended for printing on a line printer or character terminal.

nuucp login   Administrative login used to manage UUCP facilities.

OSI (Open Systems Interconnection)   International standard used to separate networking functions into a set of seven layers and accompanying interfaces between the layers.

packet   Unit of data that is transmitted over a network.

parent directory   The directory that is directly above the current directory in the file system tree.

`passwd`   Command used to add or change a user password. Also the name of the UNIX file that contains the usernames and password information.

password   A string of letters and numbers associated with a user login that, if protected properly, keeps other users from accessing a user's computer resources.

PATH   The hierarchy of directories that leads to a particular file or directory. Also, the shell environment variable that indicates the location of executable files for the user.

permissions   The rules that define what access a user, group, and all others have to a file, directory, device, or other node in a file system.

`pg`   Command used to manage the output of a text file on a terminal screen. (Similar to the `more` command.)

`ping`   Command used to contact a computer on a TCP/IP network to determine whether it is currently running and accessible to the network.

pipe   Shell feature used to direct the output of one command to the input of another (using the | symbol).

Point-to-Point Protocol (PPP)   Protocol used to allow serial communications between network nodes (used on TCP/IP networks).

POSIX (Portable Operating System Interface for UNIX)   IEEE standard for defining interfaces between application programs and the operating system.

Post Office Protocol (POP)   Protocol used to allow mail user agents to retrieve (and optionally remove) email message from a server for a particular user.

PostScript   Document format created by Adobe Systems to describe the content and layout of a page. Postscript output can be interpreted by PostScript-compatible printers.

private networks   A network that is managed by an individual organization and is often protected from access by the outside world.

process   A running instance of a program.

protocol   A set of rules that govern communications between two peer processes.

proxy server   A computer that manages service requests for a network.

ps   Command used to display a list of running processes.

pwd   Command used to list the name of the working directory for the current shell.

reboot   Process of restarting a running or hung operating system.

Request for Comments (RFC)   Documents used to contain information that is useful to the Internet community. RFCs can be informational or can represent required standards for Internet protocols.

root directory   Top of the UNIX file system tree. Represented by a slash (/).

root user   Special administrative user that, typically, has complete control of a UNIX system.

routing   Networking function that manages how data are transmitted between nodes on a network.

sar (System Activity Reporter)   Command that produces information about a computer's processing and resource usage.

SCO UnixWare   UNIX operating system produced by Santa Cruz Operation that is directly descended from UNIX System V.

sendmail   Daemon process that manages the transfer of email between network mail servers on UNIX systems.

server   A computer that offers some service to users on a network. For example, there are Web servers, file servers, and print servers.

sh   Command that implements the Bourne shell command interpreter.

shell   Interface that provides a method for allowing users to enter commands and access the file system.

shell scripts   Set of UNIX commands gathered together in a file so that they can be run as a program.

Simple Mail Transfer Protocol (SMTP)   Protocol used to define how email is transferred between mail servers.

Solaris   Version of the UNIX System V operating system maintained by Sun Microsystems to run on personal computers.

spell   Command used to check the spelling in a text document.

sticky bit   Method for setting a bit on a program (usually one that is run often) so that it remains in memory.

Streams   Input/output system for creating modular device drivers.

su   Command used to access super user (root) privileges.

subdirectory   Directory directly below the current directory in the file system.

sync   Command used to write the contents of the system buffers to the hard disk.

system state   Method of setting the level of access currently available for the UNIX system.

TCP (Transmission Control Protocol)   Protocol that provides reliable transmission of data between end systems. TCP relies on IP for the actual transmission of data.

telnet   Command providing remote login functions on TCP/IP networks.

troff   Text formatting command that formats pages for typesetting printers.

ulimit   Feature that limits the size of files on a UNIX system.

umask   Command that sets the default permission for files and directories a user creates.

umount   Command used to unmount a mounted UNIX file system.

UNIX system   A multiuser, multitasking operating system that runs on a variety of hardware platforms. It is the most popular operating system used for network servers and workstations.

UNIX System V   Descendent of the original UNIX operating system created by AT&T Bell Laboratories.

UNIX-to-UNIX copy (See UUCP).

UUCP   Command for copying files between UNIX systems. Also represents commands used for other networking features, such as remote login (cu) and remote execution (uux).

vi   Visual editor used with UNIX. Provides full-screen, character-based editing functions for plain text files.

Web server   Computer that hosts Web pages to the Internet or other TCP/IP networks.

who   Command used to list the users currently logged on to a UNIX system.

World Wide Web (WWW)   Framework for identifying and interconnecting hypertext (HTML) and other content on the Internet.

xterm   Program that opens a shell window in an X Window System session.

X Window System   Graphical network interface for launching and displaying applications.

Part

V

App

C

What's on the CD-ROM

This appendix briefly describes the contents of the CD-ROM. In addition to the file descriptions included here, please be sure to read the README file for further information and instructions.

Please note that the file names listed here are the original UNIX names. If you mount this CD-ROM as a vanilla ISO9660 system, the names might be mangled somewhat to fit those conventions. The names are roughly mnemonic, but, if all else fails, you can look in the YMTRANS.TBL table.

Top-level files on the CD-ROM

The following top-level files are included:

- cdlndir: Script to install packages from the CD-ROM. A description of how to use this program is in the top-level README file.
- COPYING: The GNU General Public License (GPL) version 2.
- COPYING.LIB: The GNU Library General Public License (LGPL) v2.
- DISTRIB: Free Software Foundation order form.
- MANIFEST: This appendix.
- README: General notes and installation instructions.
- SERVICE: The GNU service directory.

Software Included on the CD-ROM

Here is a list of the included software:

automake-1.3/

This is Automake, a Makefile generator. It was inspired by the 4.4BSD make and include files, but aims to be portable and to conform to the GNU standards for Makefile variables and targets.

Automake is a Perl script. The input files are called Makefile.am. The output files are called Makefile.in; they are intended for use with Autoconf. Automake requires that certain things be done in your configure.in.

autoconf-2.12/

Autoconf is an extensible package of m4 macros that creates a non-interactive configuration script for a package from a template file. The template file lists the operating system features that the package can use, in the form of m4 macro calls, and can also contain arbitrary shell commands. Autoconf requires GNU m4.

Autoconf-generated configure scripts are currently being used by many GNU packages, and will be used by more in the future.

bash-2.02.1/

BASH (the Bourne Again SHell) is a Posix-compatable shell with full Bourne shell (sh) syntax and some C-shell commands. BASH supports emacs-style command-line editing, job control, functions, and on-line help. Instructions for compiling BASH may be found in the README file.

bc-1.05/

An arbitrary precision arithmetic language. It is much more useful than expr in shell scripts.

binutils-2.7/

This is a beta release of a completely rewritten binutils distribution. These programs have been tested on various architectures. Most recently tested are Sun3 and Sun4s running SunOS4, as well as Sony News running NewsOS3. However, because this is a beta release taken directly from an evolving source tree, there might be some problems. In particular, the programs have not been ported to as many machines as the old binutils. There are also features of the old versions that are missing on the new programs. We would appreciate patches to make things run on other machines; especially welcome are fixes for what used to work on the old programs!

This release contains the following programs: ar, demangle, ld (the linker), nm, objcopy, objdump, ranlib, size, strip, and gprof.

The BFD (the Binary File Descripter) library is in the subdirectory bfd and is built along with GDB (which uses bfd).

See the README file for further instructions on where to look for building the various utilities.

Part

V

App

D

bison-1.25/

Bison is an upwardly compatible replacement for the parser generator yacc—with more features. The README file gives instructions for compiling Bison; the files bison.1 (a man page) and bison.texinfo (a GNU Texinfo file) give instructions for using it.

calc-2.02f/

Calc is an extensible, advanced desk calculator and mathematical tool that runs as part of GNU Emacs. It comes with source for the Calc Manual, which serves as a tutorial and reference. If you wish, you can use Calc as a simple four-function calculator only, but it provides additional features including choice of algebraic or RPN (stack-based) entry, logarithmic functions, trigonometric and financial functions, arbitrary precision, complex numbers, vectors, matrices, dates, times, infinities, sets, algebraic simplification, differentiation, and integration. Instructions for installing Calc for emacs are in the README file.

Cortex_d/

Video frame grabber device driver for the Cortex I.

cperf-2.1a/

This is a program to generate minimally perfect hash functions for sets of keywords. GCC was optimized by using this program. Other programs that must recognize a set of keywords may also benefit from using this program. Instructions for compiling cperf can be found in the README file. Note that a C++ version of cperf (called gperf) is included in the libg++ distribution. This version is for those who do not want to install C++ in order to compile a single program.

cvs-1.10/

CVS is a collection of programs that provide software release and revision control functions. CVS is designed to work on top of RCS version 4. It will parse older RCS formats, but cannot use any of its fancier features without RCS branch support. The README file contains more information about CVS.

cxdrv-0.86/

The device driver for the cx100 frame grabber is designed as a dynamically loadable module for the Linux kernel. The distribution encloses the device proper, a library of useful functions and a few sample programs using the grabber.

diffutils-2.7/

diff compares files showing line-by-line changes in several flexible formats. GNU diff is much faster than the traditional UNIX versions. This distribution includes diff, diff3, sdiff, and cmp. Instructions for compiling these are in the README file.

dld-3.3/

dld is a library package of C functions that performs dynamic link editing. Programs that use dld can add compiled object code to or remove such code from a process anytime during its execution. Loading modules, searching libraries, resolving external references, and allocating storage for global and static data structures are all performed at run time.

dld works on VAX, Sun 3, SPARCstation, Sequent Symmetry, and Atari ST machines.

doschk-1.1/

This program is intended as a utility to help software developers ensure that their source file names are distinguishable on MS-DOS and 14-character SYSV platforms.

emacs-20.3/

GNU Emacs is an extensible, customizable full screen editor. Read the README and INSTALL files for a full description of the parts of GNU Emacs, and the steps needed to install it. This distribution includes the complete GNU Emacs Manual.

enscript-1.6.1/

The GNU ascii to PostScript converter.

fileutils-3.16/

These are the GNU file-manipulation utilities. Instructions for compiling these utilities are in the README file. The fileutils package contains the following programs: `chgrp`; `chmod`; `chown`; `cp`; `dd`; `df`; `dir`; `du`; `ginstall`; `ln`; `ls`; `mkdir`; `mkfifo`; `mknod`; `mv`; `rm`; `rmdir`; `touch`; `vdir`.

findutils-4.1/

This package contains the GNU find, xargs, and locate programs. find and xargs comply with POSIX 1003.2 (as far as I know). They also support some additional options, some borrowed from UNIX and some unique to GNU.

gas-2.3/

GAS is the GNU assembler. Version 2 has many changes over previous GAS releases. Most notable among the changes are the separation of host system, target CPU, and target file format (making cross-assembling much easier). Many CPU types and object file formats are now supported.

Read the gas-2.3/gas/README file for instructions on building and using GAS.

Part
V

App
D

gawk-3.13/

GNU version of awk.

gcc-2.8.1/

The GNU C Compiler. In addition to supporting ANSI C, GCC includes support for the C++ and Objective C languages.

gcc-vms-1.42/

The GNU C Compiler for VMS. In addition to supporting ANSI C, GCC includes support for the C++ and Objective C languages.

gcl-2.2/

GNU Common Lisp (GCL) has a compiler and interpreter for Common Lisp. It is very portable and extremely efficient on a wide class of applications. It compares favorably in performance with commercial Lisps on several large theorem prover and symbolic algebra systems.

It supports the CLtL1 specification but is moving toward the proposed ANSI definition. It is based on AKCL and KCL. KCL was written by Taiichi Yuasa and Masami Hagiya in 1984, and AKCL has been developed by William Schelter since 1987.

GCL compiles to C and then uses the native optimizing C compilers (GCC). A function with a fixed number of args and one value turns into a C function of the same number of args and returns 1 value, so it cannot really be any more efficient on such calls. It has a conservative GC that allows great freedom for the C compiler to put Lisp values in arbitrary registers. It has a source level Lisp debugger for interpreted code, with display of source code in the other Emacs window. It has profiling tools based on the C profiling tools, which count function calls and percentage of time.

CLX works with GCL. There is an Xlib interface via C.

gdb-4.17/

This is the GNU source-level debugger. A list of the machines supported as targets or hosts, as well as a list of new features, appears in the gdb-4.12/gdb/NEWS file.

Instructions for compiling GDB are in the gdb-4.12/gdb/README file.

The BFD (the Binary File Descripter) library is in the subdirectory bfd and is built along with GDB (which uses it).

gdbm-1.7.3/

GNU dbm is a set of database routines that use extendible hashing, and works similar to the standard UNIX dbm routines. This is release 1.7.3 of GNU dbm.

ghost-2.6.1/

This program is an interpreter for a language that is intended to be (and very nearly is) compatible with the PostScript language. It runs under X on UNIX and VMS systems, and also runs on MS-DOS machines. It will drive either displays or low- to medium-resolution printers.

Instructions for compiling Ghostscript are in the README file.

Fonts for Ghostscript are in the directory ghost-2.6.1/fonts.

ghostview-1.5/

Ghostview allows you to view PostScript(TM) files on X11 displays. Ghostview handles the user interface details and calls the ghostscript interpreter to render the image. Instructions for compiling ghostview are in the README file.

glibc-1.09.1/

This directory contains a beta release of the GNU C Library.

The library is ANSI C-1989 and POSIX 1003.1-1990 compliant and has most of the functions specified in POSIX 1003.2. It is upward compatible with the 4.4 BSD C library and includes many System V functions, plus GNU extensions.

Version 1.09.1 adds support for Sun RPC, mmap and friends, and compatibility with several more traditional UNIX functions. It runs on Sun-3 (SunOS 4.1), Sun-4 (SunOS 4.1 or Solaris 2), HP 9000/300 (4.3BSD), SONY News 800 (NewsOS 3 or 4), MIPS DECstation (Ultrix 4), DEC Alpha (OSF/1), i386/i486 (System V, SVR4, BSD, SCO 3.2 & SCO ODT 2.0), Sequent Symmetry i386 (Dynix 3) & SGI (Irix 4).

Texinfo source for the GNU C Library Reference Manual is included; the manual still needs to be updated.

GNU studio lets you define new kinds of streams, just by writing a few C functions. The fmemopen function uses this to open a stream on a string, which can grow as necessary. You can define your own printf formats to use a C function you have written. Also, you can safely use format strings from user input to implement a printf-like function for another programming language, for example.

Extended getopt functions are already used to parse options, including long options, in many GNU utilities.

Porting the library is not hard. If you are interested in doing a port, please get on the mailing list by sending electronic mail to `bug-glibc-request@prep.ai.mit.edu`.

See the file INSTALL for instructions on building the library.

gnats-3.2/

GNATS (GNats: A Tracking System) is a bug-tracking system. It is based on the paradigm of a central site or organization that receives problem reports and negotiates their resolution by electronic mail. Although it's been used primarily as a software bug-tracking system so far, it is sufficiently generalized so that it could be used for handling system administration issues, project management, or any number of other applications.

grep-2.2/

This package contains version 2.0 of grep, egrep, and fgrep. They are similar to their UNIX counterparts, but are usually faster. Instructions for compiling them are in the README file.

groff-1.11a/

Groff is a document formatting system, which includes drivers for Postscript, TeX dvi format, and typewriter-like devices, as well as implementations of eqn, nroff, pic, refer, tbl, troff, and the man, ms, and mm macros. Groff's mm macro package is almost compatible with the DWB mm macros and has several extensions. Also included is a modified version of the Berkeley me macros and an enhanced version of the X11 xditview previewer. Written in C++, these programs can be compiled with GNU C++ Version 2.5 or later.

gzip-1.2.4/

This is a new compression program free of known patents that the GNU Project is using instead of the traditional compress program (which has patent problems). Gzip can uncompress LZW-compressed files but uses a different algorithm for compression that generally yields smaller compressed files. This will be the standard compression program in the GNU system.

hp2xx-3.1.4/

GNU hp2xx reads HP-GL files, decomposes all drawing commands into elementary vectors, and converts them into a variety of vector and raster output formats. It is also a HP-GL previewer. Currently supported are

Vector formats:

- Encapsulated PostScript
- Uniplex RGIP
- Metafont, and various special TeX-related formats
- Simplified HP-GL (line drawing only), for imports

Raster formats:

- IMG, PBM, PCX, HP-PCL (including Deskjet & DJ5xxC support)

Previewers:

- UNIX: X11
- OS/2: PM & Full-screen
- DOS: (S)VGA & HGC
- ATARI
- AMIGA
- VAX: UIS

indent-1.9.1/

This is the GNU modified version of the freely-distributable indent program from BSD. The file indent.texinfo contains instructions on using indent.

ispell-3.1.20/

ispell is an interactive spell checker that finds unrecognized words and suggests "near misses" as replacements. Both system and user-maintained dictionaries can be used. Both a standalone and GNU Emacs interface are available.

Some people may notice that the ispell 4.0 distribution has been replaced with ispell 3.1. The version numbering for this program has been screwy—it doesn't mean that we're using an older version of ispell. Ispell 3 and 4 were maintained in parallel, but version 3 is actually much more advanced. We decided to switch to it.

Eventually ispell 3 will support a GNU-style configuration script to make it a little easier to build.

Jacal/

JACAL is a symbolic mathematics system for the simplification and manipulation of equations and single and multiple valued algebraic expressions constructed of numbers, variables, radicals, and algebraic functions, differential, and holonomic functions. In addition, vectors and matrices of the above objects are included.

JACAL is written in Scheme. A version of Scheme (IEEE P1178 and R4RS compliant) written in C is available with JACAL.

SCM runs on Amiga, Atari-ST, MacOS, MS-DOS, OS/2, NOS/VE, Unicos, VMS, UNIX and similar systems.

libg++-2.8.1.1a/

The GNU C++ library is an extensive collection of C++ forest classes, a new IOStream library for input/output routines, and support tools for use with G++. Among the classes supported are Obstacks, multiple-precision Integers and Rationals, Complex numbers, arbitrary length Strings, BitSets, and BitStrings. There is also a set of pseudo-generic prototype files available for generating common container classes.

Instructions are in the libg++-2.7.2/libg++/README file.

libobjects-0.1.19/

This is a library of general-purpose, non-graphical Objective C objects designed in the Smalltalk tradition. It includes collection objects for maintaining groups of objects and C types, streams for I/O to various destinations, coders for formatting objects and C types to streams, ports for network packet transmission, distributed objects (remote object messaging), pseudo-random number generators, character string classes, and time handling facilities.

libstdc++-2.8.1.1a/

If you are receiving this as part of a GDB release, see the file gdb/README. If with a binutils release, see binutils/README; if with a libg++ release, see libg++/README, and so on. That'll give you information about this package—supported targets, how to use it, how to report bugs, and so on.

libtool-1.1/

This is GNU libtool, a generic library support script. libtool hides the complexity of using shared libraries behind a consistent interface.

lynx-2.8/

A text-based Web browser.

m4-4.1.4/

GNU m4 is an implementation of the traditional UNIX macro processor. It is mostly SVR4 compatible, although it has some extensions (for example, handling more than 9 positional parameters to macros). m4 also has built-in functions for including files, running shell commands, doing arithmetic, and so on. Autoconf needs GNU m4 for generating configure scripts, but not for running them.

make-3.71/

This is GNU Make. GNU Make supports many more options and features than the UNIX make. Instructions for using GNU Make are in the file make.texinfo. See the file README for installation instructions.

mcalc/

This is an improved version of Jeff Schmidt's (www.pschmidt@gwis.com) lcalc loan calculator program. Jeff's original program produced lightning-fast loan amortization tables, but it had virtually no options or features and was awkward to use. The original program forms the core of this update, as is explicitly permitted under terms of the GPL.

metahtml-5.08/

Meta-HTML Server.

mh-e-5.0.2.1/

The mh mode for emacs.

mtools-3.5/

Mtools is a public domain collection of programs to allow UNIX systems to read, write, and manipulate files on an MS-DOS file system (typically a diskette).

mule-1.1.4/

Mule is a MULtilingual Enhancement to GNU Emacs 18. It can handle not only ASCII characters (7 bits) and ISO Latin-1 (8 bits), but also Japanese, Chinese, Korean (16 bits) coded in the ISO2022 standard and its variants (EUC, Compound Text). For Chinese there is support for both GB and Big5. In addition, Thai (based on TIS620) and Vietnamese (based on VISCII and VSCII) are also supported. A text buffer in Mule can contain a mixture of characters from these languages. To input any of these characters, you can use various input methods provided by Mule itself. In addition, if you use Mule under some terminal emulator (kterm, cxterm, or exterm), you can use any input methods supported by the emulator.

mv1000drv/

This is the device driver for the Mutech MV-1000 PCI-framegrabber. The functions are similar to the Mutech driver/library.

This driver is not supported by Mutech. The driver is part of a larger project called XGRAS.

mysql-3.20.13/

SQL database server.

nethack-3.2.2/

NetHack 3.2 is a new enhancement to the dungeon exploration game NetHack. It is a distant descendent of Rogue and Hack, and a direct descendent of NetHack 3.1 and 3.0.

NetHack 3.2 is the product of two years of very intensive effort by the NetHack Development Team and its porting sub-teams. Many parts of 3.1 were rewritten for NetHack 3.2, and many new features were added.

nmh-0.27/

The new and improved version of mh. Fixes many security bugs of mh.

octave-2.09/

GNU Octave is a high-level language, primarily intended for numerical computations. It provides a convenient command line interface for solving linear and nonlinear problems numerically.

oleo-1.6/

Oleo is a spreadsheet program (better for you than the more expensive spreadsheet). It supports X Window and character-based terminals, and can generate embedded PostScript renditions of spreadsheets.

Keybindings should be familiar to Emacs users and are configurable by users.

There is relatively little documentation for Oleo yet. The fileUSING contains what there is.

perl-5.004_04/

This is version 5.004_04 of Larry Wall's perl programming language. Perl is intended as a faster replacement for sed, awk, and similar languages. The file README contains instructions for compiling perl.

Part

V

App

D

plotutils-2.5.1/

This is release 2.1.5 of the GNU plotutils (plotting utilities) package, including release 1.5 of GNU libplot: a function library for two-dimensional device-independent vector graphics, including vector graphics animations under the X Window System. The package has its own Web page: `http://www.gnu.org/software/plotutils/plotutils.html`.

In the top-level source directory, the file INSTALL contains generic instructions dealing with installation of a GNU package, and the file INSTALL.pkg contains package-specific installation instructions. Please read them in full, as well as this file, before attempting to install the package.

qcam-0.7c/

xfqcam uses an xforms-based control panel to allow real-time changing of the QuickCam settings: contrast, brightness, white balance, bpp and image size. In addition, you can click a button called "take picture" and a pgm file "snapshot" will be created. It basically works like QuickPic under Windows.

rcs-5.7/

RCS, the Revision Control System, manages multiple revisions of files. RCS can store, retrieve, log, identify, and merge revisions. It is useful for files that are revised frequently, such as programs, documentation, graphics, and papers.

sed-2.05/

This is a newer version of GNU sed, with many bug fixes. It also uses a beta test version of the rx library, instead of the older and slower regex library. (Because that library is still in beta test, sed version 1 is also included on this CD-ROM.)

Instructions for building GNU sed are in the README file.

sh-utils-1.16/

These are the GNU shell utilities, comprising small commands that are frequently run on the command line or in shell scripts. Instructions for compiling these utilities are in the README file README. The sh-utils package contains the following programs: `basename`; `date`; `dirname`; `echo`; `env`; `expr`; `false`; `groups`; `hostname`; `id`; `logname`; `nice`; `nohup`; `pathchk`; `printenv`; `printf`; `pwd`; `sleep`; `stty`; `su`; `tee`; `test`; `true`; `tty`; `uname`; `users`; `who`; `whoami`; `yes`.

siag-2.80/

siag is an office package for UNIX, including word processor, spreadsheet, and presentation graphics.

smalltalk-1.1.5/

This is the GNU implementation of Smalltalk, an object-oriented programming language. Instructions for compiling it are in the README file.

speaker-1.0.1/

Speakerphone application for US Robotics and Rockwell voice modems.

superopt-2.5/

The superoptimizer is a function sequence generator that uses a exhaustive generate-and-test approach to find the shortest instruction sequence for a given function.

The GNU superoptimizer and its application in GCC is described in the ACM SIGPLAN PLDI'92 proceedings.

tar-1.11.2/

Tar is a program used for archiving many files in a single file, which makes them easier to transport.

GNU tar includes multivolume support, the ability to archive sparse files, automatic archive compression/decompression, remote archives, and special features to allow tar to be used for incremental and full backups. Unfortunately, GNU tar implements an early draft of the POSIX 1003.1 ustar standard that is different from the final standard.

Adding support for the new changes in a backward-compatible fashion is not trivial.

Instructions for compiling GNU tar can be found in the README file.

Part

V

App

D

termcap-1.2/

This is a standalone release of the GNU Termcap library, which has been part of the GNU Emacs distribution for years but is now available separately to make it easier to install as libtermcap.a. The GNU Termcap library does not place an arbitrary limit on the size of termcap entries, unlike most other termcap libraries. Included is extensive documentation in Texinfo format. Unfortunately, this release does not have a termcap database included. Instructions for building the termcap library are in the README file.

Termutils-2.0/

GNU terminal control utilities tput and tabs. tput is a program to enable shell scripts to portably use special terminal capabilities. Although its interface is similar to that of terminfo-based tput programs, it actually uses termcap. tabs is a program to set hardware terminal tab settings.

See the file INSTALL for compilation and installation instructions.

texinfo-3.9/

This package contains a set of utilities related to Texinfo, which is used to generate printed manuals and online hypertext-style manuals (called info). Programs and interfaces for writing, reading, and formatting texinfo files are available both as standalone programs and as GNU Emacs interfaces. See the README file for directions on how to use the various parts of this package.

textutils-1.22/

These are the GNU text utilities, commands that are used to operate on textual data. Instructions for compiling these utilities are in the README file. The textutils package contains the following programs: `cat`; `cksum`; `comm`; `csplit`; `cut`; `expand`; `fold`; `head`; `join`; `nl`; `od`; `paste`; `pr`; `sort`; `split`; `sum`; `tac`; `tail`; `tr`; `unexpand`; `uniq`; `wc`.

uucp-1.06/

This version of UUCP was written by Ian Lance Taylor. It will be the standard UUCP system for GNU. It currently supports the f, g (in all window and packet sizes), G, t and e protocols, as well a Zmodem protocol and two new bidirectional protocols. If you have a Berkeley sockets library, it can make TCP connections. If you have TLI libraries, it can make TLI connections. Other important notes about this version of UUCP, and instructions for building it, are in the README file.

uuencode-1.0/

Uuencode and uudecode are used to transmit binary files over transmission mediums that do not support other than simple ASCII data.

Please read the Uuencode.rea file for installation instructions.

VideoteX-.06/

With this program and the included driver it's possible to receive, display, store and print videotext pages from a videotext-interface.

There's a command-line version that can be used mainly for batch-operation, and an interactive version using the X Window System and the XView toolkit. You also can use VideoteXt to display pages from INtv's videotext-service in the WWW.

vim-5.3/

`vi` improved.

wdiff-0.05/

wdiff compares two files, finding which words have been deleted or added to the first for getting the second.

We hope eventually to integrate wdiff, as well as some ideas from a similar program called spiff, into some future release of GNU diff.

wget-1.5.3/

GNU Wget is a free network utility to retrieve files from the World Wide Web using HTTP and FTP, the two most widely used Internet protocols. It works non-interactively, thus enabling work in the background, after you've logged off.

XcallerID-1.1/

XCallerID is a caller ID program for Linux. It consists of two separate entities: the xcid daemon, which stores incoming calls in a database, and the XCallerID client, which allows updating of the database.

xlogmaster-1.4.4/

This is the Xlogmaster version 1.4.4. The Xlogmaster is a program that allows easy and flexible monitoring of all logfiles and devices that allow being read via cat (like the /proc devices). It allows you to set a lot of events based on certain activities in the monitored logfiles/devices and should prove very helpful for almost anyone.

For additional information and tutorial see the ./doc directory.

Part

V

App

D

Index

GNU GENERAL PUBLIC LICENSE

Version 2, June 1991

Copyright © 1989, 1991 Free Software Foundation, Inc.

675 Mass Ave, Cambridge, MA 02139, USA

Everyone is permitted to copy and distribute verbatim copies of this license document, but changing it is not allowed.

Preamble

The licenses for most software are designed to take away your freedom to share and change it. By contrast, the GNU, General Public License, is intended to guarantee your freedom to share and change free software—to make sure the software is free for all its users. This General Public License applies to most of the Free Software Foundation's software and to any other program whose authors commit to using it. (Some other Free Software Foundation software is covered by the GNU Library General Public License instead.) You can apply it to your programs, too.

When we speak of free software, we are referring to freedom, not price. Our General Public Licenses are designed to make sure that you have the freedom to distribute copies of free software (and charge for this service if you wish)., You can also receive source code or can get it if you want it, and change the software or use pieces of it in new free programs. Our General Public Licenses also make sure that you know you can do these things.

To protect your rights, we need to make restrictions that forbid anyone to deny you these rights or to ask you to surrender the rights. These restrictions translate to certain responsibilities for you if you distribute copies of the software, or if you modify it.

For example, if you distribute copies of such a program, whether gratis or for a fee, you must give the recipients all the rights that you have. You must make sure that they, too, receive or can get the source code. And you must show them these terms so they know their rights.

We protect your rights with two steps: (1) copyright the software, and (2) offer you this license which gives you legal permission to copy, distribute and/or modify the software.

Also, for each author's protection and ours, we want to make certain that everyone understands that there is no warranty for this free software. If the software is modified by someone else and passed on, we want its recipients to know that what they have is not the original, so that any problems introduced by others will not reflect on the original authors' reputations.

Finally, any free program is threatened constantly by software patents. We wish to avoid the danger that redistributors of a free program will individually obtain patent licenses, in effect, making the program proprietary. To prevent this we have made it clear that any patent must be licensed for everyone's free use or not licensed at all.

The precise terms and conditions for copying, distribution, and modification follow.

GNU GENERAL PUBLIC LICENSE

TERMS AND CONDITIONS FOR COPYING, DISTRIBUTION, AND MODIFICATION

0. This License applies to any program or other work which contains a notice placed by the copyright holder saying it may be distributed under the terms of this General Public License. The "Program" below, refers to any such program or work, and a "work based on the Program" means either the Program or any derivative work under copyright law: that is to say, a work containing the Program or a portion of it, either verbatim or with modifications and/or translated into another language. (Hereinafter, translation is included without limitation in the term "modification".) Each licensee is addressed as "you".

Activities other than copying, distribution, and modification are not covered by this License; they are outside its scope. The act of running the Program is not restricted, and the output from the Program is covered only if its contents constitute a work based on the Program (independent of having been made by running the Program). Whether that is true depends on what the Program does.

1. You may copy and distribute verbatim copies of the Program's source code as you receive it in any medium, provided that you conspicuously and appropriately publish on each copy an appropriate copyright notice and disclaimer of warranty; keep intact all the notices that refer to this License and to the absence of any warranty; and give any other recipients of the Program a copy of this License along with the Program.

    You may charge a fee for the physical act of transferring a copy, and you may offer warranty protection in exchange for a fee.

2. You may modify your copy or copies of the Program or any portion of it, thus forming a work based on the Program, and copy and distribute such modifications or work under the terms of Section 1 above, provided that you also meet all of these conditions:

    a) You must cause the modified files to carry prominent notices stating that you changed the files and the date of any change.

    b) You must cause any work that you distribute or publish, that in whole or in part contains or is derived from the Program or any part thereof, to be licensed as a whole at no charge to all third parties under the terms of this License.

    c) If the modified program normally reads commands interactively when run, you must cause it, when started running for such interactive use in the most ordinary way, to print or display an announcement including an appropriate copyright notice and a notice that there is no warranty (or else, saying that you provide a warranty) and that users may redistribute the program under these conditions, and telling the user how to view a copy of this License. (Exception: if the Program itself is interactive but does not normally print such an announcement, your work based on the Program is not required to print an announcement.)

    These requirements apply to the modified work as a whole. If identifiable sections of that work are not derived from the Program, and can be reasonably considered independent and separate works in themselves, then this License, and its terms, do not apply to those sections when you distribute them as separate works. But when you distribute the same sections as part of a whole which is a work based on the Program, the distribution of the whole must be on the terms of this License, whose permissions for other licensees extend to the entire whole, and thus to each and every part regardless of who wrote it.

    Thus, it is not the intent of this section to claim rights or contest your rights to work written entirely by you; rather, the intent is to exercise the right to control the distribution of derivative or collective works based on the Program.

    In addition, mere aggregation of another work not based on the Program with the Program (or with a work based on the Program) on a volume of a storage or distribution medium does not bring the other work under the scope of this License.

3. You may copy and distribute the Program (or a work based on it, under Section 2) in object code or executable form under the terms of Sections 1 and 2 above provided that you also do one of the following:

    a) Accompany it with the complete corresponding machine-readable source code, which must be distributed under the terms of Sections 1 and 2 above on a medium customarily used for software interchange; or,

    b) Accompany it with a written offer, valid for at least three years, to give any third party, for a charge no more than your cost of physically performing source distribution, a complete machine-readable copy of the corresponding source code, to be distributed under the terms of Sections 1 and 2 above on a medium customarily used for software interchange; or,

c) Accompany it with the information you received as to the offer to distribute corresponding source code. (This alternative is allowed only for noncommercial distribution and only if you received the program in object code or executable form with such an offer, in accord with Subsection b above.)

The source code for a work means the preferred form of the work for making modifications to it. For an executable work, complete source code means all the source code for all modules it contains, plus any associated interface definition files, plus the scripts used to control compilation and installation of the executable. However, as a special exception, the source code distributed need not include anything that is normally distributed (in either source or binary form) with the major components (compiler, kernel, and so on) of the operating system on which the executable runs, unless that component itself accompanies the executable.

If distribution of executable or object code is made by offering access to copy from a designated place, then offering equivalent access to copy the source code from the same place counts as distribution of the source code, even though third parties are not compelled to copy the source along with the object code.

4. You may not copy, modify, sublicense, or distribute the Program except as expressly provided under this License. Any attempt otherwise to copy, modify, sublicense or distribute the Program is void, and will automatically terminate your rights under this License. However, parties who have received copies, or rights, from you under this License will not have their licenses terminated so long as such parties remain in full compliance.

5. You are not required to accept this License, since you have not signed it. However, nothing else grants you permission to modify or distribute the Program or its derivative works. These actions are prohibited by law if you do not accept this License. Therefore, by modifying or distributing the Program (or any work based on the Program), you indicate your acceptance of this License to do so, and all its terms and conditions for copying, distributing or modifying the Program or works based on it.

6. Each time you redistribute the Program (or any work based on the Program), the recipient automatically receives a license from the original licensor to copy, distribute or modify the Program subject to these terms and conditions. You may not impose any further restrictions on the recipients' exercise of the rights granted herein. You are not responsible for enforcing compliance by third parties to this License.

7. If, as a consequence of a court judgment or allegation of patent infringement or for any other reason (not limited to patent issues), conditions are imposed on you (whether by court order, agreement, or otherwise) that contradict the conditions of this License, they do not excuse you from the conditions of this License. If you cannot distribute so as to satisfy simultaneously your obligations under this License and any other pertinent obligations, then as a consequence you may not distribute the Program at all. For example, if a patent license would not permit royalty-free redistribution of the Program by all those who receive copies directly or indirectly through you, then the only way you could satisfy both it and this License would be to refrain entirely from distribution of the Program.

If any portion of this section is held invalid or unenforceable under any particular circumstance, the balance of the section is intended to apply and the section as a whole is intended to apply in other circumstances.

It is not the purpose of this section to induce you to infringe any patents or other property right claims or to contest validity of any such claims; this section has the sole purpose of protecting the integrity of the free software distribution system, which is implemented by public license practices. Many people have made generous contributions to the wide range of software distributed through that system in reliance on consistent application of that system; it is up to the author/donor to decide if he or she is willing to distribute software through any other system and a licensee cannot impose that choice.

This section is intended to make thoroughly clear what is believed to be a consequence of the rest of this License.

8. If the distribution and/or use of the Program is restricted in certain countries either by patents or by copyrighted interfaces, the original copyright holder who places the Program under this License may add an explicit geographical distribution limitation excluding those countries, so that distribution is permitted only in or among countries not thus excluded. In such case, this License incorporates the limitation as if written in the body of this License.

9. The Free Software Foundation may publish revised and/or new versions of the General Public License from time to time. Such new versions will be similar in spirit to the present version, but may differ in detail to address new problems or concerns.

   Each version is given a distinguishing version number. If the Program specifies a version number of this License which applies to it and "any later version", you have the option of following the terms and conditions either of that version or of any later version published by the Free Software Foundation. If the Program does not specify a version number of this License, you may choose any version ever published by the Free Software Foundation.

10. If you wish to incorporate parts of the Program into other free programs whose distribution conditions are different, write to the author to ask for permission. For software which is copyrighted by the Free Software Foundation, write to the Free Software Foundation; we sometimes make exceptions for this. Our decision will be guided by the two goals of preserving the free status of all derivatives of our free software and of promoting the sharing and reuse of software generally.

    NO WARRANTY

11. BECAUSE THE PROGRAM IS LICENSED FREE OF CHARGE, THERE IS NO WARRANTY FOR THE PROGRAM, TO THE EXTENT PERMITTED BY APPLICABLE LAW. EXCEPT WHEN OTHERWISE STATED IN WRITING THE COPYRIGHT HOLDERS AND/OR OTHER PARTIES PROVIDE THE PROGRAM "AS IS" WITHOUT WARRANTY OF ANY KIND, EITHER EXPRESSED OR IMPLIED, INCLUDING, BUT NOT LIMITED TO, THE IMPLIED WARRANTIES OF MERCHANTABILITY AND FITNESS FOR A PARTICULAR PURPOSE. THE ENTIRE RISK AS TO THE QUALITY AND PERFORMANCE OF THE PROGRAM IS WITH YOU. SHOULD THE PROGRAM PROVE DEFECTIVE, YOU ASSUME THE COST OF ALL NECESSARY SERVICING, REPAIR OR CORRECTION.

12. IN NO EVENT, UNLESS REQUIRED BY APPLICABLE LAW OR AGREED TO IN WRITING, WILL ANY COPYRIGHT HOLDER, OR ANY OTHER PARTY WHO MAY MODIFY AND/OR REDISTRIBUTE THE PROGRAM AS PERMITTED ABOVE, BE LIABLE TO YOU FOR DAMAGES, INCLUDING ANY GENERAL, SPECIAL, INCIDENTAL OR CONSEQUENTIAL DAMAGES ARISING OUT OF THE USE OR INABILITY TO USE THE PROGRAM (INCLUDING BUT NOT LIMITED TO LOSS OF DATA OR DATA BEING RENDERED INACCURATE OR LOSSES SUSTAINED BY YOU OR THIRD PARTIES OR A FAILURE OF THE PROGRAM TO OPERATE WITH ANY OTHER PROGRAMS), EVEN IF SUCH HOLDER OR OTHER PARTY HAS BEEN ADVISED OF THE POSSIBILITY OF SUCH DAMAGES.

    END OF TERMS AND CONDITIONS

Linux and the GNU system

The GNU project started 12 years ago with the goal of developing a complete free UNIX-like operating system. "Free" refers to freedom, not price; it means you are free to run, copy, distribute, study, change, and improve the software.

A UNIX-like system consists of many different programs. We found some components already available as free software—for example, X Window and TeX. We obtained other components by helping to convince their developers to make them free—for example, the Berkeley network utilities. Other components we wrote specifically for GNU—for example, GNU Emacs, the GNU C compiler, the GNU C library, Bash, and Ghostscript. The components in this last category are "GNU software". The GNU system consists of all three categories together.

The GNU project is not just about developing and distributing free software. The heart of the GNU project is an idea: that software should be free, and that the users' freedom is worth defending. For if people have freedom but do not value it, they will not keep it for long. In order to make freedom last, we have to teach people to value it.

The GNU project's method is that free software and the idea of users' freedom support each other. We develop GNU software, and as people encounter GNU programs or the GNU system and start to use them, they also think about the GNU idea. The software shows that the idea can work in practice. People who come to agree with the idea are likely to write additional free software. Thus, the software embodies the idea, spreads the idea, and grows from the idea.

This method was working well—until someone combined the Linux kernel with the GNU system (which still lacked a kernel), and called the combination a "Linux system."

The Linux kernel is a free UNIX-compatible kernel written by Linus Torvalds. It was not written specifically for the GNU project, but the Linux kernel and the GNU system work together well. In fact, adding Linux to the GNU system brought the system to completion: it made a free Unix-compatible operating system available for use.

But ironically, the practice of calling it a "Linux system" undermines our method of communicating the GNU idea. At first impression, a "Linux system" sounds like something completely distinct from the "GNU system." And that is what most users think it is.

Most introductions to the "Linux system" acknowledge the role played by the GNU software components. But they don't say that the system as a whole is more or less the same GNU system that the GNU project has been compiling for a decade. They don't say that the idea of a free UNIX-like system originates from the GNU project. So most users don't know these things.

This leads many of those users to identify themselves as a separate community of "Linux users", distinct from the GNU user community. They use all of the GNU software; in fact, they use almost all of the GNU system; but they don't think of themselves as GNU users, and they may not think about the GNU idea.

It leads to other problems as well—even hampering cooperation on software maintenance. Normally when users change a GNU program to make it work better on a particular system, they send the change to the maintainer of that program; then they work with the maintainer, explaining the change, arguing for it and sometimes rewriting it, to get it installed.

But people who think of themselves as "Linux users" are more likely to release a forked "Linux-only" version of the GNU program, and consider the job done. We want each and every GNU program to work "out of the box" on Linux-based systems; but if the users do not help, that goal becomes much harder to achieve.

So how should the GNU project respond? What should we do now to spread the idea that freedom for computer users is important?

We should continue to talk about the freedom to share and change software—and to teach other users to value these freedoms. If we enjoy having a free operating system, it makes sense for us to think about preserving those freedoms for the long term. If we enjoy having a variety of free software, it makes sense for to think about encouraging others to write additional free software, instead of additional proprietary software.

We should not accept the splitting of the community in two. Instead we should spread the word that "Linux systems" are variant GNU systems—that users of these systems are GNU users, and that they ought to consider the GNU philosophy which brought these systems into existence.

This article is one way of doing that. Another way is to use the terms "Linux-based GNU system" (or "GNU/Linux system" or "Linux" for short) to refer to the combination of the Linux kernel and the GNU system.

The FreeBSD Copyright

SE Using UNIX, 3rd Edition

Sams Publishing

This CD-ROM distribution contains software produced by various authors, including those affiliated with the Free Software Foundation. See the CD-ROM information in the book, or read the file MANIFEST for a list of software on the disc.

The following information is from the Free Software Foundation. There are no precompiled programs on this CD-ROM. You will need a C compiler to build most of this software (programs which need another type of interpreter or compiler normally provide the C source for a bootstrapping program).

This CD-ROM is in vanilla ISO-9660 format. Vanilla ISO-9660 format places some limitations on length and acceptable characters in file and directory names. Since the CD-ROM is read-only, you must have disk space for installed executables, documentation, and object files (the last only during compilation). The amount of space you'll actually need for building programs varies. For example, to go through the normal stages of building GCC 2.8, you'll need approximately 60 to 80 megabytes of space. Other programs hardly need any space at all. However, you do not necessarily need to copy the source files themselves off the CD-ROM.

If your system supports symbolic links, you can make a tree of symbolic links somewhere on your hard disk and build the software as if the files have been copied (some programs haven't been converted to use GNU configure yet and you have to edit the files yourself before compilation, requiring you to copy them first. You can minimize the amount of copying that must be done by building a symlink tree, then for just those files you need to edit, delete the symlink, and copy the corresponding file from the CD-ROM. The disadvantage of all this is that it is more tedious because it isn't automated). Unfortunately, if your system does not support symbolic links you will have to copy all the sources for any packages you want to build onto a disk as well.

As an example, to build GCC you might simply do the following:

```
$ mkdir /scratch/build-gcc
$ cd /scratch/build-gcc
$ sh /cdrom/gcc-2.8/configure sparc-sun-sunos4.1
$ make
```

This won't be quite so easy because all the file names on the CD-ROM are mangled. Instead, you will have to build a symlink tree on another disk where the names can be unmangled, and do your builds from that. The program for installing symlink trees is called "cdlndir" (which may appear to you as "CDLNDIR.", "CDLNDIR.;1", "cdlndir.", or "cdlndir.;1" because of the aforementioned differences in CD-ROM drivers).

The sequence of commands to type might be as follows:

```
$ sh /cdrom/cdlndir --verbose /cdrom/gcc_28 /scratch/build-gcc
$ cd /scratch/build-gcc
$ sh ./configure sparc-sun-sunos4.1
$ make
```

Note that if your CD-ROM driver leaves versions numbers visible on the files on the CDROM, you will have to put quotes around their names to keep your shell from interpreting the semi-colon as the end of one command and the start of another:

```
$ sh '/cdrom/cdlndir;1' --verbose /cdrom/gcc_258 /scratch/build-gcc
```

(The driver should never put version numbers on directories, but if you experience this, put quotes around the directory name also). This command will create the directory /scratch/ build-gcc if it does not already exist, then symlink all the files from /cdrom/gcc_258 on the CD-ROM into that directory, with appropriate demangling so the symlink names represent the original UNIX file names.

The "—verbose" option isn't required, but it makes the program tell you what it's doing as it goes along. If you're planning to install large amounts of the software from the CD-ROM, the script will take a long time to run and it is helpful to know what it is doing. If you want to save this output into a file so you can search through it later, redirect it to a file (this command and the following use redirection operators extant in any bourne shell):

```
$ sh /cdrom/cdlndir -v /cdrom/gcc_258 /scratch/build-gcc > log 2>&1
```

Or you can save to a log and see the output on your terminal at the same time:

```
$ sh /cdrom/cdlndir -v /cdrom/gcc_28 /scratch/build-gcc 2>&1 ¦ tee log
```

You can link/copy as much of the CD-ROM source tree as you want. The script works recur-sively, so if you do

```
$ sh /cdrom/cdlndir --verbose /cdrom /scratch/build
```

It will make /scratch/build a shadow of the entire CD-ROM (don't be surprised if it takes a while for the script to complete in this case). Detection of what format the CD-ROM is in (Rock Ridge or vanilla ISO-9660) is automatic. If it fails for some inexplicable reason, the "—iso9660" option may make cdlndir behave better.

If your system does not support symbolic links you will have to run cdlndir with the "—copy" option, which will actually copy over the files instead. Note that you will need disk space for both the sources and the object files in this case.

The ISO-9660 standard requires that file names without any extension end with a ".", but some drivers strip this (as well as version numbers) from file names. cdlndir should automatically detect if this is happening, but if it fails to do so you can give it a clue with the "no-trailing-dot" option.

Lastly, the "help" option to cdlndir will print out a summary of its options. A list of the top-level files of interest and a brief description of all the software packages in this distribution are in the file MANIFEST (which may appear on the CD-ROM as "manifest." or another analogous names to the ones mentioned when mangling occurs).

We sincerely hope everything works correctly but it's difficult to foresee every possible problem. If a program has a bug, you should send a bug report to the address indicated for that program. Usually the README or INSTALL file for that package says what this address is).

N O T E Some programs on this CD-ROM will have to be uncompressed and/or untarred. To do this, simply follow the instructions below.

1. Insert CD-ROM in drive.
2. Mount CD-ROM, in general, by typing

   `mount -tiso9660 /dev/cdrom <mountpoint>`

CAUTION

Mountpoint must exist before using this command.

3. Locate package you want to extract.
4. Extract package by typing

   `zcat <mountpoint><location><software_package> ¦ tar xvf -`

5. Follow the installation instructions in the software packages you extract.

By opening this package, you are agreeing to be bound by the following agreement:

Some of the programs included with this product are governed by the GNU General Public License, which allows redistribution; see the license information for each product for more information. Other programs are included on the CD-ROM by special permission from their authors.

You may not copy or redistribute the entire CD-ROM as a whole. Copying and redistribution of individual software programs on the CD-ROM is governed by terms set by individual copyright holders. The installer and code from the author(s) is copyrighted by the publisher and the author. Individual programs and other items on the CD-ROM are copyrighted by their various authors or other copyright holders. This software is sold as-is without warranty of any kind, either expressed or implied, including but not limited to the implied warranties of merchantability and fitness for a particular purpose. Neither the publisher nor its dealers or distributors assumes any liability for any alleged or actual damages arising from the use of this program. (Some states do not allow for the exclusion of implied warranties, so the exclusion may not apply to you.)

This CD-ROM uses long and mixed-case filenames requiring the use of a protected-mode CD-ROM Driver.